Attitudes towards Sexuality in Judaism and Christianity in the Hellenistic Greco-Roman Era

Enoch, Levi, and Jubilees on Sexuality

The Dead Sea Scrolls on Sexuality

THE DEAD SEA SCROLLS *on* SEXUALITY

Attitudes towards Sexuality in Sectarian and Related Literature at Qumran

William Loader

William B. Eerdmans Publishing Company
Grand Rapids, Michigan / Cambridge, U.K.

Published 2009 by
Wm. B. Eerdmans Publishing Co.
2140 Oak Industrial Drive N.E., Grand Rapids, Michigan 49505 /
P.O. Box 163, Cambridge CB3 9PU U.K.

Printed in the United States of America

14 13 12 11 10 09   7 6 5 4 3 2 1

ISBN 978-0-8028-6391-1

www.eerdmans.com

Contents

CHAPTER FOUR

CHAPTER FIVE

Acknowledgments

This book reflects the fruit of the second year of my ongoing research on attitudes towards sexuality in Judaism and Christianity of the Hellenistic era, part of a five year project funded through an Australian Professorial Fellowship from the Australian Research Council, which I commenced mid 2005.

Murdoch University has provided invaluable infrastructure support, not least through the electronic inter-library loan scheme which has found obscure literature for me from all over the world. I have also benefited greatly from my annual pilgrimage to the Theologicum library in Tübingen University, where I have always received a warm welcome and support from the Institut für antikes Judentum und hellenistische Religionsgeschichte under the leadership of Professor Hermann Lichtenberger.

I am especially grateful to those who read and commented on earlier drafts of the main sections of book: Annette Steudel on chapters 1 – 3; Kelley Coblentz Bautch on chapters 4 – 8; James VanderKam on chapters 5 – 8, and Esther Eshel on *Genesis Apocryphon.* I am grateful to Mary J. Marshall who carefully read the whole and helped me see what authors' eyes seldom see. I also express my appreciation to William B. Eerdmans Jr for his support and encouragement, and for his willingness to publish the results of this research.

The first drafts of this work began to appear not long after the birth of our first grandson, Philip, July, 2006. The delight of observing the miracle of infant growth, even though mostly from afar, has accompanied my ongoing encounter with these obscure texts of our common humanity. Fittingly, publication now comes barely a month after birth of his new sister, Sofia.

Introduction

This investigation forms part of a larger project focussed on understanding attitudes towards sexuality in Judaism and Christianity in the Hellenistic Greco-Roman era. By sexuality I mean all matters pertaining to sexuality, rather than the narrower sense of sexual theory and gender formation, on the one hand, and acts of sexual intercourse, on the other.

In this volume I give attention to the Dead Sea Scrolls. This term also has the potential to be misleading. It refers, strictly speaking, to the literature recovered mostly from eleven caves near the shores of the Dead Sea in close proximity to the site known as Qumran. These caves included many documents already known to us, not least the writings we now find in the canon of the Hebrew scriptures, and some, such as Tobit and Ben Sira, which form part of what Christians have called the apocrypha. The latter will receive attention in a future volume of this research. Three major works also found, at least in part, in the Qumran literature, were the focus of the previous volume, *Enoch, Levi, and Jubilees on Sexuality*:[1] the collection now known as *1 Enoch* (all but 37 – 71), the *Aramaic Levi Document*, and the *Book of Jubilees*. That volume also included brief discussion of the *Book of Giants*.

These works are important in their own right, but also as background for understanding the documents to be considered in this volume. The myth of the Watchers, for instance, which finds its fullest expression in the *Book of the Watchers*, *1 Enoch* 6 – 11 and 12 – 16, and thence in *Jubilees*, plays a significant role in many of them. This includes the elaboration of the story in early parts of the *Genesis Apocryphon*, which, in parallel to *1 Enoch* 106 – 107, tells of

[1] William Loader, *Enoch, Levi, and Jubilees on Sexuality: Attitudes Towards Sexuality in the Early Enoch Literature, the Aramaic Levi Document, and the Book of Jubilees* (Grand Rapids: Eerdmans, 2007)

Lamech's fear that Noah is an offspring of their sexual adventures. It is also reflected both in accounts of the Watchers fearfully awaiting their judgement and in the identification of evil spirits as their bastard offspring, who now plague humanity. Despite the gross act of sexual immorality which brought chaos to the world, neither their offspring, the giants, nor their surviving spirits, the bastards, are depicted as perpetuating sexual wrongdoing, as one might have expected.

The theme of intermarriage to Gentiles, both by priests and by ordinary people, a significant element in the priestly instruction of *Aramaic Levi Document*, similarly finds it echo in many documents which we consider here, including in the closely related works of priestly wisdom, the *Testament of Qahat* and the *Visions of Amram*. All three, in addition, display an acceptance of marriage to nieces. By contrast, *Jubilees* clearly assumes this is forbidden, as does the *Temple Scroll*, an issue made central to the accusations of the *Damascus Document* (D) against its opponents.

Jubilees also makes prohibition of intermarriage a major theme, but this concern is surprisingly absent in the *Temple Scroll*, and in D, which otherwise treats *Jubilees* as an authoritative text. This is not the only surprise that emerges from consideration of the texts below. Another is the extent to which what began as highly contentious, namely interpretation of laws pertaining to sexuality, all but vanishes from discourses of conflict, especially in most sectarian documents. Thus the earlier works raise expectations and provide an important context for the investigation which follows.

The present work considers the remaining documents of the Dead Sea Scrolls. Some are widely recognised as belonging to a particular Jewish sect, which appears to have much in common with what Josephus and Philo reports of the Essenes, prompting many to see them as literature of that sect. From such sources expectations arose early that we should find allusions to the famed Essene celibacy among the documents. These will be revisited in what follows. Others works appear to be writings collected and valued by those who placed the scrolls in the caves, but not necessarily having a direct connection with the sect, some because they are earlier (not least, the biblical material) and others because they were composed elsewhere and belonged among literature which we might imagine other groups using at the time. This will account also for the degree of diversity among the documents, for instance, in relation to marrying nieces, mentioned above, and the wider variety of scribal hands and styles evident among the documents.

In dealing with this complex array of material I shall seek to take into account what is and is not sectarian inasmuch as this is possible and is broadly recognised. This means that the concluding assessment cannot simply collate the findings as though all the documents belong to a unified system or a unified community, but needs to identify tendencies, trends, and common values, while respecting the integrity of each writing. The fragmentary state of much of the material is a further difficulty, both for reconstruction of what survives and for assessing the significance of what is absent: was an idea deliberately omitted or was it present, but among the material which has not survived? This is not an arena for people obsessed with the power to know and have answers and therefore to make such answers up by fanciful constructions when they are not there.

Fortunately, some documents have survived almost in their entirety or at least with extensive consecutive material. This is the case with the *Temple Scroll*. The situation is more complex with *4QMMT* and D, but these three preserve sufficient material, including material relevant to matters of sexuality, to make it worthwhile to give each a separate chapter. D has by far the most material pertinent to the theme. The following four chapters deal with the other documents under four main headings. Inevitably the categories are not absolute. Among the works gathered in the first, "Legal Texts" is the *Community Rule*, that concludes with a hymn, which belongs closely with the material of the next chapter, "Liturgical and Related Material". In the same way some liturgical material contains segments related not only to law, but also to "Biblical Exposition", the theme of chapter six, a title which, in turn, could also serve to describe much legal material. The same overlaps occur with the material in chapter seven, "Wisdom Texts". On the whole, however, the groupings make it possible to consider such texts together. The aim is not, however, to reach conclusions about each group, but within each chapter to give individual attention to distinct works and their significance. The final chapter, "Concluding Assessment", then correlates the findings of the investigation of each individual writing within the four groups as well as those of the first three chapters.

While comments on very short or fragmentary texts and on those with little pertaining to sexuality are necessarily brief, there are a number of other documents which warrant more extensive treatment. These include the *Community Rule*, the *Rule of the Congregation*, the *Thanksgiving Hymns*, the *Genesis Apocryphon*, *1/4Q Instruction*, the *Visions of Amram*, and the *Wiles of the Wicked Woman*.

The Hebrew and Aramaic texts are available in a number of editions. The series, *Discoveries in the Judaean Desert* (*DJD*),[2] is a foundational resource and unless otherwise indicated forms the basis for discussion. I also make reference to *The Dead Sea Scrolls Study Edition* (*DSSSE*),[3] the *Princeton Theological Seminary Dead Sea Scrolls Project* (*PTSDSSP*),[4] and the *Dead Sea Scrolls*

[2] *Discoveries in the Judaean Desert* (Oxford: Clarendon, 1955-).

[3] Florentino García Martínez, and Eibert J. C. Tigchelaar, ed. *The Dead Sea Scrolls Study Edition* (2 vols; Leiden: Brill, 1997, 1998).

[4] James H. Charlesworth et al., ed. *The Dead Sea Scrolls: Hebrew, Aramaic, and Greek Texts with English Translations. Vol. 1-* (The Princeton Theological Seminary Dead Sea Scrolls Project; Tübingen: Mohr Siebeck; Louisville: Westminster John Knox Press, 1994-).

Electronic Library (*DSSEL*).[5] In reproducing the Hebrew or Aramaic texts I have not reproduced the more subtle indications of readability and decipherment, but have used smaller font to reproduce letters which are conjectured through reconstruction, in order to make clearer the difference between what can be read and what is reconstructed. Where I provide my own translation I indicate this with an asterisk. Otherwise I make use of the translations in the above as well as that of Vermes (V)[6] and Wise, Abegg, and Cook (WAC).[7] Translations of biblical material are from NRSV, unless otherwise indicated. I have sought to designate particular documents with full titles in the initial reference (e.g., *Temple Scroll*), thereafter using both the shortened title and the document number, each preceded by the standard convention of using cave number and the letter, Q, for Qumran (e.g., 11QT[a]/11Q19).

[5] Emanuel Tov, ed. *The Dead Sea Scrolls Electronic Library* (rev. ed. 2006; Provo: Brigham Young University; Leiden: Brill, 2006). This incorporates earlier material found in *The Dead Sea Scrolls Reader* (6 vols; ed. Donald W. Parry and Emanuel Tov; Leiden: Brill, 2004).

[6] Geza Vermes, *The Complete Dead Sea Scrolls in English* (London: Penguin, 1997).

[7] Michael Wise, Martin Abegg Jr., and Edward Cook, *The Dead Sea Scrolls: A New Translation* (rev. ed.; San Francisco: HarperSanFrancisco, 2005).

CHAPTER ONE

Attitudes towards Sexuality in the *Temple Scroll*

The longest scroll to be recovered from the site at Qumran, $11QT^a$/11Q19,[1] bears the name, the *Temple Scroll*, because of the dominance of the temple as a theme. Portions of two further copies of the work have been preserved from Cave 11, $11QT^b$/11Q20, preserving 16 columns, and $11QT^c$/11Q21, three small fragments, but this is uncertain. In addition, parts of the work may be preserved in $4QT^b$/4Q524.[2] A substantial portion of the *Temple Scroll*, 3 – 13.8 and 30.3 – 47.18, deals with the structure of the temple. Within that discourse on the structure we also find instruction about the calendar of feasts, 13.9 – 30.2, and, appended to the section on the temple structure, a discussion of purity laws, 48:1 – 51:10, also

[1] The Hebrew text and English translation which form the basis of the discussion in this section follow *DSSSE* unless otherwise indicated.

[2] For an overview of the extant material see Sidnie White Crawford, *The Temple Scroll and Related Texts* (Companion to the Qumran Scrolls 2; Sheffield: Sheffield Academic Press, 2000) 12-16. She also discusses $4QT^a$?/4Q365a, but concludes: "It is unlikely that this fragmentary material represents another copy of the Temple Scroll; it is more likely to be part of the source material that was used in the redaction of the Temple Scroll" (15). See also her earlier discussion where she raised the question in Sidnie White, *DJD* 13, 319-33, and the response of Florentino García Martínez, "New Perspectives on the Study of the Dead Sea Scrolls," in *Perspectives on the Study of the Old Testament and Early Judaism* (ed. F. García Martínez and E. Noort; VTSup 73; Leiden: Brill, 1998) 230-48, and Florentino García Martínez, "The Temple Scroll and the New Jerusalem," in *The Dead Sea Scrolls after Fifty Years: A Comprehensive Assessment* (ed. Peter W. Flint and James C. VanderKam; Leiden: Brill, 1999) 2.431-60, who argues that "4Q365a is part and parcel of 4Q365 and thus belongs to a copy of the Reworked Pentateuch" (435).

informed by an understanding of the temple. The final section, 51:11 – 66:17, sometimes designated, the Deuteronomic paraphrase (although it also includes material from Numbers), goes beyond the focus on the temple to deal with wider concerns, not least in 57 – 59 which contain laws concerning the king.[3]

The beginning and ending have been lost, although it is possible that we can identify some of the content of col. 67 containing material now preserved by a few letters in 4QT^b/4Q524,[4] and col. 2 will have formed part of the redactional introduction. The work draws heavily on older sources. This is particularly apparent in the Deuteronomic paraphrase, but also to be supposed for the material concerning the temple structure, the calendar, and the royal law.[5] The scroll presents instruction as given directly by Yahweh to Moses on Mt Sinai (51.6-7; cf. also 44.5), assuming the setting of Exodus 34.[6] In that sense it matches the setting claimed by *Jubilees*, but here the revelation is direct, and not mediated by an angel.

The dating of 4QT^b/4Q524 to 150-125 B.C.E. would rule out the composition of the *Temple Scroll* in the time of Hyrcanus or Janneus, as many had earlier proposed, who noted Hyrcanus' innovation of a wheeled mechanism in relation to the slaughter house, matching the instructions in 34.4-9.[7] It would also rule out the possibility that the work is a product of the community that settled at Qumran.[8] However, we cannot be certain that 4QT^b/4Q524 belongs to the *Temple Scroll* and not to a precursor. It is, nevertheless, likely that the *Temple Scroll* itself was composed some time in the first half of the second century, although it is difficult

---

[3] On the structure and sources see the overview in White Crawford, *Temple Scroll*, 22-24.

[4] Emile Puech, *DJD* 25, 85-114, reconstructs col. 67 on the basis of fragments from 4QT^b/4Q524 with French translation (103-108). A German translation is offered in Annette Steudel, ed. *Die Texte aus Qumran II: Mit Masoretischer Punktation, Übersetzung, Einführung und Anmerkungen* (Darmstadt: Wissenschaftliche Buchgesellschaft, 2001) 1-157, 155-57, and an English translation, in *DSSEL*.

[5] On the biblical sources see Dwight D. Swanson, *The Temple Scroll and the Bible: The Methodology of 11QT* (STDJ 14; Leiden: Brill, 1995).

[6] On this see White Crawford, *Temple Scroll*, 18.

[7] For the review of research see White Crawford, *Temple Scroll*, 24-25, and on 30.4-9 and its significance, 36-37.

[8] On the unlikelihood of authorship at Qumran on grounds of differences in legal interpretation, especially in vows, oaths and calendar, see Lawrence H. Schiffman, "The Temple Scroll and the Systems of Jewish Law of the Second Temple Period," in *Temple Scroll Studies: Papers Presented at the International Symposium on the Temple Scroll, Manchester, December 1987* (ed. George J. Brooke; JSPSup 7; Sheffield: JSOT Press, 1989) 241-55, 242-52.

to be more precise.[9] It shares some elements in common with the *Book of Jubilees* and the *Aramaic Levi Document*, including use of the solar calendar, the positive focus on the Levites,[10] and an overall stance that is not polemical, although it also differs from these.[11] It is also interesting that no extant document from Qumran quotes it as authoritative.[12]

---

[9] García Martínez, "Temple Scroll and the New Jerusalem," concludes that elements in the "Kings Law" suggest discussion before the investiture of Simon reflected indirectly in 1 Macc 1:48, and so suggests that "a date towards the mid-second century BCE seems assured" (444). See also Florentino García Martínez, "Temple Scroll," in *EncDSS*, 927-33, 931-32. Johann Maier, *The Temple Scroll: An Introduction, Translation and Commentary* (JSOTSup 34; Sheffield: Sheffield Academic Press, 1985), notes a lack of Greek influence in the vocabulary, arguing against a date much after 175 B.C.E., with which White Crawford, *Temple Scroll*, concurs (and misreads García Martínez above in support), but she notes that a dependence on *Jubilees*, as the observations of Gershon Brin, "Regarding the Connection Between the Temple Scroll and the Book of Jubilees," *JBL* 112 (1993) 108-109, may indicate, would favour a date closer to the middle of the century (25-26). Brin, however, speaks of connection, not dependence, as William John Lyons, notes in "'An Unauthorized Version': The *Temple Scroll* in Narratological Perspective," in *New Directions in Qumran Studies: Proceedings of the Bristol Colloquium on the Dead Sea Scrolls, 8-10 September 2003* (ed. Jonathan G. Campbell, William John Lyons and Lloyd K. Pietersen; London: T&T Clark, 2005) 126-48, 146 n. 57.

[10] On the heightened significance of the Levites in the *Temple Scroll* see Jacob Milgrom, "Studies in the Temple Scroll," *JBL* 97 (1978) 501-23, 501-504; see also Hans-Aage Mink, "The Use of Scripture in the Temple Scroll and the Status of the Scrolls as Law," *SJOT* 1 (1987) 20-50, 26-28; White Crawford, *Temple Scroll*, 56-57. On the common Levitical interest shared also with *Jubilees* and D see George J. Brooke, "The Temple Scroll: A Law unto Itself?" in *Law and Religion: Essays on the Place of the Law in Israel and Early Christianity* (ed. Barnabas Lindars; Cambridge: James Clarke, 1998) 34-43, 164-66, especially 36-40.

[11] On the similarities and differences between the *Temple Scroll* and *Jubilees*, see James C. VanderKam, "The Temple Scroll and the Book of Jubilees," in *Temple Scroll Studies: Papers Presented at the International Symposium on the Temple Scroll, Manchester, December 1987* (ed. George J. Brooke; JSPSup 7; Sheffield: JSOT Press, 1989) 211-36, who concludes that "the scroll and *Jubilees*, while not in perfect harmony, are extremely close to one another, as long as one recognizes that their authors were responding directly and primarily to different parts of the pentateuch" (231). *Jubilees* looks to an eschatological temple in 1:17, 27, 29, not to one to be built prior to the eschaton, as in the *Temple Scroll* (232). Here VanderKam is responding critically to the suggestion of Ben Zion Wacholder, "The Relationship between 11QTorah (The Temple Scroll) and the Book of Jubilees: One Single or Two Independent Compositions," *SBLSP* (1985) 205-16. See also Michael Owen Wise, *A Critical Study of the Temple Scroll from Qumran Cave 11* (Studies in Ancient Oriental Civilization 49; Chicago: Oriental Institute, 1990) 87-98; Martha Himmelfarb, "Sexual Relations and Purity in the Temple Scroll and the Book of Jubilees," *DSD* 6 (1999) 11-36; Lawrence H. Schiffman, "Pre-Maccabean Halakhah in the

Within its extensive material, matters pertaining broadly to sexuality play a secondary role, although at some points they raise significant issues of interpretation and make distinctive claims. This is particularly so in the apparent forbidding of sexual intercourse within "the city of the temple" and in the laws concerning the king. Our discussion will examine each reference in turn, within its context.

1 Warnings about Idols (2.1-15)

The first decipherable remains of 11QT[a] /11Q19 bring a citation of Exod 34:10-16 (2.1-7a, 11b-15) into which the author has introduced after Exod 34:13 an extrapolation in 2.7b-11a, which warns the people to burn the idols and not to retrieve from them their gold or silver and bring it home into their houses. The extrapolation would make sense in a time of conquest (as originally in its narrative setting in the entry into Canaan) and might reflect disapproval of pillaging during recent or current wars of conquest which entailed destruction of temples and shrines. The issue could have arisen in the time of Judas Maccabeus or his successors, including the conquests of Hyrcanus.[13]

Dead Sea Scrolls and the Biblical Tradition," *DSD* 13 (2006) 348-61, who writes: "Because of many agreements between this scroll and MMT, it seems that the sources of the Temple Scroll, which in no way reflect the sectarian posture of the full-fledged sect of the Hasmonean period, represent the pre-Maccabean heritage of the Sadducean/Zadokite trend, or of some subgroup within it" (355).

[12] On this see Hartmut Stegemann, "The Literary Composition of the Temple Scroll and its Status at Qumran," in *Temple Scroll Studies: Papers Presented at the International Symposium on the Temple Scroll, Manchester, December 1987* (ed. George J. Brooke; JSPSup 7; Sheffield: JSOT Press, 1989) 123-48, 127-28, 143-45; Sidnie White Crawford, "The Rewritten Bible at Qumran," in *The Bible and the Dead Sea Scrolls: Volume 1: Scripture and the Scrolls* (ed. James H. Charlesworth; Waco: Baylor University Press, 2006) 131-47, 138.

[13] Other material relating to idolatry in the *Temple Scroll* occurs in its paraphrase of Deuteronomy. In 51.19 – 52.3 it cites Deut 16:21-22. In 54.8-18 it paraphrases Deut 13:2-6, and continues in 54.19 – 55.1 with Deut 13:7-12. In 55.15 – 21 the author brings Deut 17:2-5. In these the variations are minor. In 55.2-14, however, based on Deut 13:13-19, there is a more significant difference. It limits the destruction of cities to those where all inhabitants, not just some, have practiced idolatry (55.3). Lawrence H. Schiffman, "Non-Jews in the Dead Sea Scrolls," in *The Quest for Context and Meaning: Studies in Biblical Intertextuality in Honor of James A. Sanders* (ed. Craig A. Evans and Shemaryahu Talmon; BIS 28. Leiden: Brill, 1997) 153-71, suggests that this may reflect the Hasmonean situation, "which led at times to the destruction, without the necessary investigation and trial, of entire

Beyond the insertion, it is difficult to evaluate the significance of the citation, itself, for reflecting the author's attitudes towards sexuality. Exodus brings the warning against making a covenant with the inhabitants of the land first in 34:12, "Take care, not to make a covenant", השמר לך פן תכרת ברית, and then in 34:15, simply as, "not to make a covenant", פן תכרת ברית. The *Temple Scroll* repeats השמר the second time (2.12; cf. 2.4). It then reproduces the warning, which focuses on enticement to idolatrous practices which might include sharing sacrificial meals and taking foreign daughters as wives, who would, in turn, entice their husbands to idolatry.

> [14](השמר) פן תכרת ברית ליושב הארץ וזנו אחרי אלהיהם וזבחו לאלהיהם וקרא לך ואכלת מזבחו
> 16 ולקחת מבנתיו לבניך וזנו בנתיו אחרי אלהיהן והזנו את בניך אחרי אלהיהן
>
> (Take care) not to make a covenant with the inhabitants of the land, for when they prostitute themselves to their gods and sacrifice to their gods, someone among them will invite you, and you will eat of the sacrifice. 16 And you will take wives from among their daughters for your sons, and their daughters who prostitute themselves to their gods will make your sons also prostitute themselves to their gods. (Exod 34:15-16: NRSV adapted; 11QT^a/11Q19 2.12-15)

We may assume that, since the author cited this passage, it will have had some importance, but beyond that, we have no way of knowing whether it has particular relevance to his context. Had he added an extrapolation concerning it, as he did on Exod 34:13, we would be on surer ground. The text does not assume the war and pillaging reflected in that extrapolation, but, as in Exodus, the opposite, namely positive relations, including participation in sacrificial meals, which might pose a different kind of danger. In the light of the blanket ban on the king's marrying

---

cities. Our author may have wanted to clarify that Hellenistic Jews, no matter how extreme, could not be destroyed in this manner if, as he argued, the entire city had not participated in idolatrous worship" (157). In Lawrence H Schiffman, "The Septuagint and the Temple Scroll: Shared Halakic Variants," in *The Septuagint, Scrolls and Cognate Writings: Papers Presented to the International Symposium on the Septuagint and Its Relations to the Dead Sea Scrolls and Other Writings* (ed. George W. Brooke and Barnabas Lindars; Atlanta: Scholars, 1992) 277-97, he also notes that this halakhic variant, adding "all", is also reflected in the Septuagint text of Deuteronomy (283-84). The expansion of the laws about the captive wife also suggests it might have been an issue of current relevance for the author. On this see our discussion on pp. 30-31 below.

[14] 11QT^a /11Q19 begins with השמר "Take care", which it has added to the Exodus text, and breaks off in 2.15 before the last word, אלהיהן "their gods". It also uses the fuller consonantal vowel forms throughout, whereas the text cited follows the MT script.

foreign women, it is likely that here the concern, as in 1 Kings 11:1-2; Ezra 9:1-2; and Neh 10:31 (Eng. 10:30), is wider than the Canaanite nations mentioned in the biblical text.[15] Sexual language appears here also metaphorically to depict the lure of idolatry. The foreign peoples "whore" זנה after their gods; and their daughters, taken as wives, might lead Israel's sons to do the same. Taking daughters as wives assumes a degree of peaceful relations. Its danger, also expressed in sexual language, is that they might entice their husbands to idolatry. Idolatry is the primary concern in forbidding such intermarriage. But this all remains within the citation.

Apart from here, where we cannot determine its weighting, and in the royal law, where the concern is with the king, nothing elsewhere suggests that the author sees intermarriage as a major problem, as apparently in *4QMMT*, nor that he extends it, as does the author of *Jubilees*, to include all kinds of intermarriage and the dangers not only of idolatry, but also of the evils of sexual wrongdoing to which the partner is exposed and which bring defilement on the people and the temple. Nor is there any indication of concern about women as bearers of illicit knowledge such as sorcery, as in the *Book of the Watchers*, nor about priests choosing inappropriate partners, as perhaps there, but especially in the *Aramaic Levi Document*.

2 Sexuality and the Temple

The focus of the sections on the temple structure lies elsewhere than on issues of sexuality.[16] This is also true of the tradition about the calendar of feasts which the author has interpolated into the account of the temple. In the account of its structure, however, we see a first indication of a more restrictive attitude towards women. They are not permitted to eat the Passover meal, which is preserved for

---

[15] So Schiffman, "Non-Jews," 158.

[16] On the temple structure and its relation to previous outlines of the temple and to the Herodian temple, see Johann Maier, "The Architectural History of the Temple in Jerusalem in the Light of the Temple Scroll," in *Temple Scroll Studies: Papers Presented at the International Symposium on the Temple Scroll, Manchester, December 1987* (ed. George J. Brooke; JSPSup 7; Sheffield: JSOT Press, 1989) 23-62; and Mathias Delcor, "Is the Temple Scroll a Source of the Herodian Temple," in *Temple Scroll Studies: Papers Presented at the International Symposium on the Temple Scroll, Manchester, December 1987* (ed. George J. Brooke; JSPSup 7; Sheffield: JSOT Press, 1989) 67-89. While noting the similarity of structure, Maier speaks of "two entirely opposite tendencies: that underlying the Temple Scroll is an exclusive one, expanding the area that is off-limits to certain groups (lay Israelites, women, Gentiles); the Herodian tendency on the contrary restricts the cultic areas to a smaller area and expands the areas that have non-cultic purposes" (51).

males twenty years of age and above (17.8-9).[17] This matches the delineation between the court of the male Israelite over 20 years of age and that of the women, children, and proselytes (after the third generation; 39.5; 40:6-7) in the new outer court.[18] Foreigners are forbidden entry absolutely. The innovative outer court reflects an attitude towards degrees of holiness which ranks men and women differently. The texts are fragmentary, but clear. In referring to the court of the males, the work declares:

> No woman shall enter it nor any boy until the day 8 on which . . . [. . .] to YHWH give half a shekel 9 as a memorial in their villages. (39.7-9)[19]

Similarly, it describes the outer court:

> 5 [. . .] And you shall make a th[i]rd courtyard [. . .] 6 [. . .] for their daughters and for foreigners, who were bor[n . . .]. (40.5-6)

The structure assumes a progression of degrees of holiness, beginning with the Holy of Holies, moving to the Holy Place, then the court of the priests, the court of the male Israelites, and then the court of women, children and proselytes. As Maier notes, this represents "an extreme solution, demarcating the Men's Court as a square court on its own, shifting the limits for ordinary Israelite men and women to a third court and entirely excluding non-Jews from the sanctuary".[20] This pattern will be reflected later in Herod's temple, though not in the gigantic proportions given in the *Temple Scroll.*[21]

Such a hierarchy of degrees of holiness raises questions about the role of gender which reach far beyond our consideration of the *Temple Scroll* and have complex anthropological roots. They include such notions as the appropriateness of nakedness in holy places, the particular status of women and issues of purity, and the place of sexual relations. The *Temple Scroll* includes an attempt to institutionalise such differences in a structured way which symbolises an underlying attitude towards gender and sexuality. As such it is elaborating and

---

[17] Hannah K. Harrington, *The Purity Texts* (London: T&T Clark, 2004) 101.

[18] On the courts, see White Crawford, *Temple Scroll*, 37-40.

[19] On this see Lawrence H. Schiffman, "Exclusion from the Sanctuary and the City of the Sanctuary," *HAR* 9 (1985) 306-18, 305-306.

[20] Johann Maier, "Purity at Qumran: Cultic and Domestic," in *Judaism in Late Antiquity, Part V: Section One: Theory of Israel* (ed. Alan J. Avery-Peck, Jacob Neusner, and Bruce D. Chilton; Leiden: Brill, 2001) 91-124, 101.

[21] On the agreement between the *Temple Scroll*, tannaitic sources, Josephus, and second temple practice, see Lawrence H. Schiffman, "Laws Pertaining to Women in the Temple Scroll," in *The Dead Sea Scrolls: Forty Years of Research* (ed. D. Dimant and U. Rappaport; Jerusalem: Magnes Press, 1992) 210-28.

extending distinctions already deeply rooted in Israelite tradition reflected in the Pentateuch.

These issues are addressed further by the author of the *Temple Scroll*, partly by again citing biblical sources, but also by elaboration and additional restrictions. Of particular note in this regard are the instructions concerning the priests, as they begin and end their shifts.

ולוא תהיה שמה 7 תערובת *vacat* וא[יש] כי יהיה לו מקרה לילה
לוא יבוא אל 8 כול המקדש עד אשר [יש]לים שלושת ימים
וכבס בגדיו ורחץ 9 ביום הראישון וביום הש[ל]ישי יכבס בגדיו ורחץ
ובאה השמש אחר 10 יבוא אל המקדש
ולוא יבואו בנדת טמאתמה אל מקדשי וטמאו
11 *vacat* ואיש כיא ישכב עם אשתו שכבת זרע
לוא יבוא אל כול עיר 12 המקדש
אשר אשכין שמי בה שלושת ימים

and there shall be no 7 mingling there. *Blank* And the m[an] who has had a nocturnal emission shall not enter 8 the whole temple until three days have [pa]ssed. He shall wash his clothes and shall bathe 9 on the first day and on the th[i]rd day he shall wash his clothes /and bathe/; and after the sun has set 10 he shall enter the temple. But they shall not enter my temple with their soiled impurity and defile it. 11 *Blank* And a man who lies with his wife and has an ejaculation, for three days shall not enter the whole city of 12 the temple in which I shall cause my name to dwell. (45.6-12)

There is to be no "mingling" תערובת in the change of shifts (as already in 45.4). This is probably as simple as forbidding priests from dallying in chatter among themselves within their court. It has no sexual reference here, unlike the use of the word in *4QMMT* (B 48; C 8; possibly B 80).[22] In 45.7 we find reference to nocturnal emissions. These receive attention in Lev 15:16-18.

16 If a man has an emission of semen, he shall bathe his whole body in water, and be unclean until the evening. 17 Everything made of cloth or of skin on which the semen falls shall be washed with water, and be unclean until the evening. 18 If a man lies with a woman and has an emission of semen, both of them shall bathe in water, and be unclean until the evening.

Leviticus makes clear that the concern is with the purity of the temple:

[22] The case against seeing a reference to sexual relations here is partly the use of the same verb in 45.4 in a different sense and the implied prohibition of sexual relations producing seminal emission in the city. On the other hand, it is striking that the issues of seminal emission immediately follow here, so that ולוא תהיה שמה תערובת "and there shall be no mingling there" might be seen to function as a kind of summary for what follows.

> 31 Thus you shall keep the people of Israel separate from their uncleanness, so that they do not die in their uncleanness by defiling my tabernacle that is in their midst. 32 This is the ritual for those who have a discharge: for him who has an emission of semen, becoming unclean thereby, 33 for her who is in the infirmity of her period, for anyone, male or female, who has a discharge, and for the man who lies with a woman who is unclean. (15:31-33)

In Leviticus 22 this is applied, in particular, to priests.

> No one of Aaron's offspring who has a leprous disease or suffers a discharge may eat of the sacred donations until he is clean. Whoever touches anything made unclean by a corpse or a man who has had an emission of semen, 5 and whoever touches any swarming thing by which he may be made unclean or any human being by whom he may be made unclean – whatever his uncleanness may be – 6 the person who touches any such shall be unclean until evening and shall not eat of the sacred donations unless he has washed his body in water. 7 When the sun sets he shall be clean; and afterward he may eat of the sacred donations, for they are his food. (22:4-7)

Deuteronomy has a similar provision, related to men preparing for war.

> When you are encamped against your enemies you shall guard against any impropriety. 10 If one of you becomes unclean because of a nocturnal emission, then he shall go outside the camp; he must not come within the camp. 11 When evening comes, he shall wash himself with water, and when the sun has set, he may come back into the camp. 12 You shall have a designated area outside the camp to which you shall go. (Deut 23:9-12)

In all these instances, the rule is that the man remains unclean until the evening; he must wash his body, and then becomes clean after sunset. Lev 15:17 indicates that the washing includes also his clothes: "Everything made of cloth or of skin on which the semen falls shall be washed with water". The *Temple Scroll* goes beyond these requirements. While addressing the matter of priests in 45.6-10, it is clear from 46.16-18, which banishes all who have had nocturnal emissions to a quarantine outside the city, that this is to be applied to all men, as in Lev 15:16-18.[23] They are not to enter the temple for three days, must wash their clothes (without qualification) and bathe on the first day and do the same again on the third day, bathing at sunset.[24] The extension to three days appears to reflect a

[23] Yigael Yadin, *The Temple Scroll* (3 vols; Jerusalem: Israel Exploration Society, 1977-83) 1. 288, 281; White Crawford, *Temple Scroll*, 45-46.

[24] The insistence that people remain totally impure until sunset contrasts with the later rabbinic idea of טבול יום ("immersed on that day") which understood a person to have partial purity after immersion. So Yadin, *Temple Scroll*, 1. 332-34; Joseph M. Baumgarten, "Sadducean Elements in Qumran Law," in *The Community of the Renewed Covenant: The*

homogenising of the requirements in Lev 15:16-18, cited above, with those of Exod 19:10-15. There we read:

> the LORD said to Moses: "Go to the people and consecrate them today and tomorrow. Have them wash their clothes and prepare for the third day, because on the third day the LORD will come down upon Mount Sinai in the sight of all the people." (19:10-11)

The result is a twofold ablution and a twofold laundering.[25] As Milgrom explains, "The impure male who wishes to enter the Temple-city must make two transitions – from impure (*tame'*) to common (*ḥol*), and from common to holy (*qadoš*)".[26] Accordingly, re-entry into the city and re-entry into the temple reflect two stages. This also makes sense of the apparent discrepancy which Yadin noted, namely that while those with nocturnal emissions are banished from the city of the temple according to 46.16-18, the author speaks of their re-entry in relation not to the whole city, but to "any part of the temple" 45.7-8.[27] That is the end of the process and in the context, focuses on priests. The concern is with the temple:

Notre Dame Symposium on the Dead Sea Scrolls (ed. E. Ulrich and J. C. VanderKam; Notre Dame: University of Notre Dame Press, 1994) 27-36, 29; Lawrence H. Schiffman, "The Impurity of the Dead in the Temple Scroll," in *Archaeology and History in the Dead Sea Scrolls: The New York University Conference in Memory of Yigael Yadin* (ed. L. H. Schiffman; JSPSup 8; Sheffield: JSOT Press, 1990) 135-56, 148.

[25] Cf. 4QD^{g}/4Q272 1 ii.3-7, which applies the strict provisions of the *zab* to the man with seminal emissions.

[26] See Jacob Milgrom, "Deviations from Scripture in the Purity Laws of the Temple Scroll," in *Jewish Civilization in the Hellenistic-Roman Period in Jerusalem* (ed. Shemaryahu Talmon; JSPSup 10; Sheffield: JSOT Press, 1991) 159-67, 162. Rather than being an innovation he suggests that evidence from Philo (*Leg.* 3.63) indicates the author may be "following an ancient tradition" (162). See also his discussion of layers of impurity in Jacob Milgrom, "First Day Ablutions in Qumran," in *The Madrid Qumran Congress: Proceedings of the International Congress on the Dead Sea Scrolls, Madrid 18-21 March, 1991* (ed. J. T Barrera and L. V. Montaner; Leiden: Brill, 1991) 2. 561-70, 562-64, and earlier, Milgrom, "Studies," 513-17. On the author's equation of the encampment with the Temple-city, see Yadin, *Temple Scroll*, 1. 287-89. See also Florentino García Martínez, "The Problem of Purity: The Qumran Solution," in Florentino García Martínez and Julio Trebolle Barrera, *The People of the Dead Sea Scrolls: Their Writings, Beliefs and Practices* (Leiden: Brill, 1995) 139-57, 141-47, who notes the extension of the level of purity required in the temple to the whole city and of what applies to priests to the whole people.

[27] Yadin, *Temple Scroll*, notes the anomaly that, while those with nocturnal emissions are banished from the city of the temple according to 46.16-18, the author speaks of their re-entry in terms of entering "any part of the temple" (45.7-8), but explains the latter as resulting from the focus on the procedure of purification, which will have envisaged a two

ולוא יבואו בנדת טמאתמה אל מקדשי וטמאו

they shall not enter my temple with their soiled impurity and defile it. (45.10)

The ejaculation of semen becomes of much greater importance than in Leviticus, although the same assumptions prevail, namely, that it renders a man unclean. This has, of course, nothing to do with sin, but belongs to part of everyday life, in this instance, to involuntary emission of semen during sleep.[28] The author employs the word נדה, here, to describe seminal emission, a word preserved in P for menstrual impurity, though H uses it of incest in Lev 20:21.[29] Its use with the broader meaning is to be assumed here as also in 66.13, rather than making reference also to women, here.[30]

The purification requirements are assumed to be the same in the case where the ejaculation is deliberate in the act of sexual intercourse and the same restriction applies. Both Lev 15:16, 32 and 22:4 assume that the provision applies to any emission of semen. Like Lev 15:18, the *Temple Scroll* makes separate reference to ejaculation during sexual intercourse.

And a man who lies with his wife and has an ejaculation, for three days shall not enter the whole city of the temple in which I shall cause my name to dwell. (45.11-12)

---

stage process of re-entry into the city and then entry into the temple (1. 286-87). See also 2. 192.

[28] As Himmelfarb, "Sexual Relations," observes: "While it is not wrong to be impure, it is wrong to delay purification" (15).

[29] On this see Himmelfarb, "Sexual Relations," 15. She also notes that in Lev 18:24-30 H uses the verb טמא to speak of defilement of the land through incest (15). The *Temple Scroll* reflects the stance of H. This is evident also in its use of Num 5:2 for instruction about confinement, rather than the P material in Leviticus 13; 15; and Numbers 19, which require no such separation (16-17).

[30] Mayer I. Gruber, "Purity and Impurity in Halakic Sources and Qumran Law," in *Wholly Woman, Holy Blood: A Feminist Critique of Purity and Impurity* (ed. Kristin de Troyer, Judith A. Herbert, Judith Ann Johnson and Anne-Marie Korte; Harrisburg: Trinity Press International, 2003) 65-76, derives from this text the view that it assumes "that notwithstanding Lev 18:19 and 20:18 Jews might engage in menstrual intercourse". Accordingly she translates: "They [i.e., man and woman] should not go to My Temple in her menstrual impurity and [thereby] defile [it]" (73). This is possible only if one understands that the author is already referring to men and women in 45.10, as in 45.11, and does not see her menstrual impurity as a cause for the impurity, which, as she notes, would be very rare, but seminal emission. But 45.10 is better taken with what precedes to refer to men and נדה to refer to their nocturnal seminal emissions. This broader use of נדה in the *Temple Scroll* is evident also in 66.13 (based on Lev 20:21). Only in 45.11, then, do we move to men and women.

While this relates to sexual intercourse outside "the city of the temple" and when it is permissible to enter the city, by implication it also assumes prohibition of sexual intercourse within the city,[31] and this applies not only to priests, but also to all men. Such a prohibition is found in CD 12.1-2, "No-one should sleep with a woman in the city of the temple, defiling the city of the temple with their impurity".[32] Here in the *Temple Scroll*, however, (as in the Samaritan Pentateuch), it is expressed not simply as sexual intercourse "with a woman", but, with what Brin calls greater "nicety", as sexual intercourse "with his wife".[33] As Yadin noted,[34] prohibition of sexual intercourse (in order to avoid emission of semen) in relation to sacred place and time again reflects Exod 19:14-15, where it belongs to the heightened state of purity in which the people are to prepare themselves for the encounter with Yahweh:

> So Moses went down from the mountain to the people. He consecrated the people, and they washed their clothes. 15 And he said to the people, "Prepare for the third day; do not go near a woman." (Exod 19:14-15)

As Milgrom observes, "Thus not only the mountain but also the camp, situated in its proximity, is endowed with a sacred status. Once the tabernacle is built it virtually becomes a portable Sinai, endowing the wilderness camp with Sinaitic sanctity".[35] Yadin points also to 1QSa/1Q28a 1.25-26, which speaks of members of the council or assembly sanctifying themselves for three days.[36] Similar assumptions are reflected in 1 Sam 21:4, where the priest, Ahimelech, insists that David's companions must not have had sexual intercourse, if they are to receive the holy loaves: "The priest answered David, 'I have no ordinary bread at hand, only holy bread – provided that the young men have kept themselves from women'."[37] Japhet[38] points also to 2 Chron 8:11, which reports the quarantining of Pharaoh's daughter by Solomon:

---

[31] So Yadin, *Temple Scroll*, 1. 288

[32] See our discussion on pp. 166-67 below.

[33] Gershon Brin, *Studies in Biblical Law: From the Hebrew Bible to the Dead Sea Scrolls* (Sheffield: Sheffield Academic Press, 1994) 115.

[34] Yadin, *Temple Scroll*, 1. 287-88.

[35] Milgrom, "First Day Ablutions," 562.

[36] Yadin, *Temple Scroll*, 1. 289. Cf. D, which assumes that although a person who has completed purifications that day (*tebul yom*) could not enter the temple until after sunset, they could still enter the city the same day. See Cecilia Wassen, *Women in the Damascus Document* (SBL Academia Biblica 21; Atlanta: SBL, 2005) 102, similarly 104 and my discussion on pp. 166-67 below.

[37] See Sara Japhet, "The Prohibition of the Habitation of Women: The Temple Scroll's Attitude Toward Sexual Impurity and Its Biblical Precedents," *JANES(CU)* 22 (1993) 69-87, who argues that this accounts for the different treatment in the *Temple Scroll* between

> Solomon brought Pharaoh's daughter from the city of David to the house that he had built for her, for he said, "My wife shall not live in the house of King David of Israel, for the places to which the ark of the LORD has come are holy."

The precise application of this restriction in the *Temple Scroll* is not altogether clear because of a certain ambiguity occasioned by the reference to עיר המקדש "the city of the temple", also present in the parallel restriction in the *Damascus Document* (D) (12.1). If it refers to the entire city, in which the temple complex is located, then the restriction implies that couples living in the city are not to engage in sexual intercourse and, therefore, to do so only outside the city. Yadin argued that it implies also that women were not even to be permanent residents in the city and this he sees as a source for the notion of celibacy among the Essenes, at least those resident in the city, and points to similar provisions in 1QM/1Q33 7.3-4 concerning the camp.[39] Levine, taking up a suggestion of Ginzberg in his discussion of D,[40] challenged the practicality of this suggestion in relation to both intercourse and to the distance of toilets if we assume temple city means the city as a whole, suggesting instead that the temple city refers in these instances not to the city as a whole but to the temple precincts.[41] This changes the meaning significantly.

According to this view, in 45.11b-12a כול עיר המקדש "the whole city of the temple" refers to "the broad but well-defined Temple compound, including the buildings, courts, and walls ... a sanctified compound with the Temple in its center".[42] It receives some support from the enormous extent of the outer court which would have been large enough to encompass the whole city,[43] but, on this

---

the enhanced strictness in relation to women during menstruation and after childbirth which applies to all cities, and the primary focus of concern with the relation of seminal emission to the holy city (78-79).

[38] Japhet, "Prohibition," 79-86. Referring to the attitude reflected here in Chronicles and in the *Temple Scroll*, the *War Scroll* and D, she writes: "Common to all of these texts is that they attribute greater force and severity to sexual impurity, particularly in its regular manifestations, opposing this aspect of human existence as to the realm of the sacred" (86).

[39] Yadin, *Temple Scroll*, 1. 288-89.

[40] Louis Ginzberg, *An Unknown Jewish Sect* (New York: Jewish Theological Seminary Press, 1976) 74.

[41] Baruch Levine, "The Temple Scroll: Aspects of its Historical Provenance and Literary Character," *BASOR* 232 (1978) 5-23, 14-17.

[42] Japhet, "Prohibition," 86.

[43] So Magen Broshi, "The Gigantic Dimensions of the Visionary Temple in the Temple Scroll," in *Understanding the Dead Sea Scrolls: A Reader from the Biblical Archaeology Review* (ed. H. Shanks; New York; Vintage, 1993) 113-15, who notes that its dimensions are four times the size of Herod's temple and match the extent of the entire city

view, the two are not to be equated. Schiffman, mediating the positions of Yadin and Levine, suggested that the author envisaged the temple complex, the city of the temple, as being large enough to encompass all but the upper city of the city of the author's day, but that כול עיר המקדש "the whole city of the temple" designated the temple complex extending to its outer courts, and not Jerusalem as a whole.[44] The temple complex, including the outer court, is within the city and is separated from the rest of the city by a moat or mound, though the *Temple Scroll* says nothing specific about the space beyond the divide:[45]

> You shall make a trench around the temple, one hundred cubits wide, which will separate the holy temple from the city, and they will not enter suddenly my temple and will not defile it. (46.9-11)[46]

---

in the second century B.C.E. (115). See also Schiffman, "Exclusion," 317; Eyal Regev, "Reconstructing Qumranic and Rabbinic Worldviews: Dynamic Holiness vs. Static Holiness," in *Rabbinic Perspectives: Rabbinic Literature and the Dead Sea Scrolls: Proceedings of the Eighth International Symposium of the Orion Center for the Study of the Dead Sea Scrolls and Associated Literature, 7-9 January, 2003* (ed. Steven D. Fraade, Aharon Shemesh, and Ruth A. Clements; STDJ 62; Leiden: Brill, 2006) 87-112, 95; Carla Sulzbach, "Of Temples on Earth, in Heaven, and In-Between," in *The Changing Face of Judaism, Christianity, and Other Greco-Roman Religions in Antiquity: Presented to James H. Charlesworth on the Occasion of his 65th Birthday* (ed. Ian H. Henderson and Gerbern S. Oegema with the assistance of Sara Parks Richter; SJSHRZ 2; Gütersloh: Gütersloher Verlagshaus, 2006) 166-85, 180-81.

[44] Schiffman, "Exclusion", 317-18; "The city of the sanctuary would occupy much of the Jerusalem of his day, but the citizenry would still be living outside the *temenos*" (317). See also Schiffman, "Laws Pertaining to Women," 211; Lawrence H. Schiffman, "The Theology of the Temple Scroll," *JQR* 85 (1994) 109-23, 119.

[45] On this see White Crawford, *Temple Scroll*, who notes absence of reference to dwellings around the temple as in Ezek 45:3-4 and the *New Jerusalem Scroll* and historical temples. She also notes that the *Temple Scroll* "makes no provision for the realities of every day life for Jerusalem" including quarantine areas for women, but also a cemetery (49). The rationale for a barrier assumes, however, that there are people outside it whose rushed entry is to be prevented (see 46.9-11, which follows) so probably referring to residents rather than visitors who would enter through the gates.

[46] Jorunn Økland, "The Language of Gates and Entering: On Sacred Space in the *Temple Scroll*," in *New Directions in Qumran Studies: Proceedings of the Bristol Colloquium on the Dead Sea Scrolls, 8-10 September 2003* (ed. Jonathan G. Campbell, William John Lyons and Lloyd K. Pietersen; London: T&T Clark, 2005) 149-65, comments that "If the whole city were holy there would be no need of the trench" (161). Yet this need not be the case, if one sees different levels of sanctity, here marked by the trench. He concludes, however, that "the extended Temple not only consumes all of the *area* formerly occupied by city space, it simultaneously seems to have consumed the whole *concept* of the

According to Gruber, then, men and women would be resident in the rest of the actual city where sexual intercourse was not forbidden, but if they espoused the teaching of the *Temple Scroll*, they would need to ponder the options if they discovered that their bedroom fell within the area prescribed by the blueprint of the *Temple Scroll*: they could relocate, abstain, or join another sect![47]

If we are to understand "city of the temple" to refer only to the temple complex, then the issue is not about whether people living in the city as a whole beyond the temple precincts engaged in sexual intercourse or had sexual emissions, but only that those who did have sexual emissions, nocturnal or through engagement in sexual intercourse, in the rest of the city or anywhere else, were not to enter the temple complex until they had undergone the required purification. In the case of the former, where it is assumed they are within the city of the temple, that is, the temple, they are to leave it and remain in one of the three places east of the city (46.16-18). The prohibition of sexual intercourse within the temple complex, expressed in D, would be an implication also in the *Temple Scroll*. In addition, the absence of provision of a location for women in menstruation or after childbirth would reflect the fact they would not be assumed to be resident in the temple complex, into whose outer court they could come on a temporary basis as worshippers.[48]

We noted early the anomaly to which Yadin drew attention, that those with nocturnal emissions were banished from the city of the temple and then elsewhere the author speaks of their re-entry as re-entry into the temple. If the city of the temple is just another way of referring to the total temple complex, then the apparent anomaly disappears, as Schiffman argues.[49]

The identification of "the city of the temple" with the temple complex creates, however, its own problems. If that is supposed to be its meaning in D, then why would it be necessary to state that sexual intercourse is forbidden in the temple precincts? Would not all have assumed this to be so, anyway?[50] There is also the problem that the places of quarantine for those with nocturnal emissions (and the toilets) are not just outside the temple precincts, but clearly outside the city, itself, as Schiffman acknowledges.[51] This assumes, that, though it is not stated, re-entry

---

Holy City! This observation fits well with the fact that in several other Qumran texts, Jerusalem is simply referred to as 'the city of the sanctuary' (עיר המקדש)" (161).

[47] Gruber, "Purity and Impurity," 73-74.

[48] So Schiffman, "Exclusion," 313.

[49] So Schiffman, "Exclusion," 307.

[50] Wassen, *Women*, notes that it would be "entirely redundant" (99).

[51] Schiffman, "Exclusion," who writes that Yadin "is no doubt correct that these areas must have been outside the entire city of Jerusalem" (313), referring to Yadin, *Temple Scroll*, 1. 307-308.

into the city of those who had a nocturnal emission must have been an issue and that the same issue would also apply to those men who had an emission during sexual intercourse. That implies, then, indeed, that, matching the banishment from the city of those with accidental emissions, those with intentional emissions should not be there and should not enter there.

According to Milgrom, normally one would not read the construct phrase עיר המקדש "city of the temple" as referring to something less than the city as a whole.[52] Therefore many continue to affirm Yadin's view that the whole city is meant.[53] In addition, as White Crawford notes in her review of research, "4QMMT equates the מקדש with the Temple and the camp, מחנה, with Jerusalem".[54] She observes that, given the many common features which *4QMMT* and the *Temple Scroll* share, "it can be argued that the Temple Scroll understands the meaning of עיר in the same way that 4QMMT understands the meaning of מחנה and that their use of המקדש is the same."[55] She continues, however, with the caution: "since the language is different, and 4QMMT specifically mentions Jerusalem while the Temple Scroll does not, the evidence of 4QMMT is merely suggestive and not conclusive."[56] One might also point to the assumptions of Jerusalem's special holiness reflected in the right to have its purity protected, preserved already in the decree of Antiochus III, who forbad bringing impure animals or their hides into the city (Josephus *A.J.* 12.145-146).[57]

If the whole city and not just the temple complex is intended, as seems likely, this need not, however, entail the assumption, that women were not resident in the

---

[52] So Jacob Milgrom, "The City of the Temple," *JQR* 83 (1994) 125-28, 126.

[53] So Yadin, *Temple Scroll*, 1. 288-89; Milgrom, "Studies," 517-18; Maier, "Purity at Qumran," 102-104; Harrington, *Purity Texts*, 14; Økland, "Language of Gates," 161; Gabriele Boccaccini, "Qumran and the Enoch Groups: Revisiting the Enochic-Essene Hypothesis," in *The Bible and the Dead Sea Scrolls: The Princeton Symposium on the Dead Sea Scrolls: Volume 1: Scripture and the Scrolls* (ed. James H. Charlesworth; Waco: Baylor University Press, 2006) 37-66, 47; Ben Zion Wacholder, *The New Damascus Document: The Midrash on the Eschatological Torah of the Dead Sea Scrolls: Reconstruction, Translation and Commentary* (STDJ 56; Leiden: Brill, 2007), who points to the use of עיר המקדש "city of holiness" to refer Jerusalem in 4Q248 1 6-7 (341).

[54] Sidnie White Crawford, "The Meaning of the Phrase עיר המקדש in the Temple Scroll," *DSD* 8 (2001) 242-54, 248.

[55] See *4QMMT* B 29-31; 60-62 and on this see Silvia Castelli, "Josephan 'Halakha' and the 'Temple Scroll': Questions of Sources and Exegetic Traditions in the Laws on Purity," *Henoch* 24 (2002) 331-41, who points out that the notion of the entire city being identified as "the camp" and forbidden for lepers and those suffering from gonorrhea is also assumed in Josephus *B.J.* 5.227 and in Rev 20:9 (335).

[56] White Crawford, "Meaning of the Phrase עיר המקדש," 248.

[57] Yadin, *Temple Scroll*, 1. 240. See also Harrington, *Purity Texts*, 15.

city, as Yadin supposed,[58] but only that sexual intercourse was forbidden. As Japhet points out, the issue is not women as such, but men and their seminal emission during intercourse, and, in any case, not all women may be assumed to be engaging in sexual intercourse. One cannot, therefore, argue from the implication of prohibited sexual relations in the city to absence of women there or to their presence only on a temporary basis.[59] Thus one need not see here a precursor of the alleged celibacy of the Qumran sect, as Yadin supposed, because, as more recent research has made probable, not all were celibate in any case, though some were.[60] It is not impossible that the author may have envisaged holy Jerusalem with residents consisting primarily of celibates, perhaps celibate men, in a manner that prefigures the later demarcations of the sect.

White Crawford seeks to avoid the impracticality of forbidding sexual intercourse in the city, by proposing that all residents in the city as a whole are to be understood as temporary. Then the stricture applies to all residents, all of whom are temporary. She has also revived a suggestion first put forward in relation to D by Rabin,[61] namely that the limitation equates to those imposed in Islam in relation to pilgrim cities. She writes:

> If the Temple City has a special status over against other cities, and a particular role as a pilgrimage city, then special regulations can be ordained for it, including the ban on sexual intercourse within the city. Those couples on pilgrimage to the holy city would be expected to refrain from sexual intercourse while there and for three days beforehand, while priests would likewise refrain during their period of service.[62]

On this basis she argues that the reference is to the entire city, but that

---

[58] Yadin, *Temple Scroll*, 1. 288-89. So also Milgrom, "Studies," 513, 517.

[59] Japhet, "Prohibition," 72. White Crawford, *Temple Scroll*, argues a solution which assumes the city has no permanent residents (47), but that makes little sense of the provision for the other three categories of people to be quarantined.

[60] See the discussion in Annette Steudel, "Ehelosigkeit bei den Essenern," in *Qumran Kontrovers: Beiträge zu den Textfunden vom Toten Meer* (ed. Jörg Frey and Hartmut Stegemann with the collaboration of Michael Becker and Alexander Maurer; Einblicke 6; Paderborn: Bonifatius, 2003) 115-24 and my discussion on pp. 369-76 below.

[61] C. Rabin, *The Zadokite Documents* (Oxford: Clarendon Press, 1958) 59.

[62] White Crawford, "Meaning of the Phrase עיר המקדש," 249. "Abstinence from sexual intercourse was called for at the shrine of Oropos in Pergamon, although both men and women were allowed in" (251). In Islam "a pilgrim wears a special garment, and sexual intercourse is prohibited for the duration of the *hajj*. Access to the pilgrimage sites of Mecca and Medina are limited to Muslims; non-Muslims risk death for violating the prohibition. Hinduism likewise calls for asceticism while on pilgrimage; these practices (called *niyamas*) include special food laws and abstinence from sexual intercourse" (252).

> sexual intercourse would be banned during the period of temporary residence. However, those who discovered a skin disease, gonorrhea or had a nocturnal emission during their temporary residence would have to be put outside in the quarantine areas. Thus Yadin is partially correct; women were banned from permanent residence in the city. But so was everyone else.[63]

That somewhat compounds the problem, especially if we want to assume some degree of realism in what the author imagines. She notes there are no comments or provisions relating to housing outside the barrier surrounding the temple, not even of the residence of the king, concluding that the *Temple Scroll* probably does not envisage permanent residences around the compound and so also makes no provision for a cemetery, nor for purification requirements after death.[64] The absence of provisions for women in menstruation or after childbirth similarly indicates no permanent residents. She also points to the restriction of vessels to only those made of skin from animals properly slaughtered in the temple. But these are largely arguments from silence, of which perhaps the most significant is the absence of reference to a place of confinement for women, to which we shall return below.

The issue of practicalities may not lie with our interpretation but with the text itself which is not beyond making other unrealistic demands, such as the implication that people not excrete on the sabbath (because toilets are located beyond the acceptable limits of movement on the sabbath; 46.13-16).[65] Clearly the city has a more holy status than all other cities. This, then, implies for the city a degree of holiness which would be profaned through sexual intercourse.[66] This restriction has something in common with the prohibition in *Jubilees* of sexual intercourse on the sabbath. There the concern is sacred time. Here, the concern is with sacred space.[67] *Jubilees* also assumes sexual intercourse is forbidden in

---

[63] So White Crawford, *Temple Scroll*, 49. See also White Crawford, "Meaning of the Phrase עיר המקדש," 251.

[64] White Crawford, "Meaning of the Phrase עיר המקדש," 249-50.

[65] See Lutz Doering, "Purity Regulations concerning the Sabbath in the Dead Sea Scrolls and Related Literature," in *The Dead Sea Scrolls: Fifty Years after Their Discovery: Proceedings of the Jerusalem Congress, July 20-25, 1997* (ed. Lawrence H. Schiffman, Emanuel Tov, and James C. VanderKam; Jerusalem: Israel Exploration Society in cooperation with the Shrine of the Book, Israel Museum, 2000) 600-609, 608.

[66] Cf. Wacholder, *New Damascus Document*, who proposes on the basis of parallel concerns in 47.3-6a and 48.14b-17a that the *Temple Scroll* forbids it in all cities (202). It is hard to see how these parallels justify that conclusion, since in the latter men with seminal emissions are not included among those to be quarantined.

[67] On the difference in understanding of holy space between P and H, see Himmelfarb, "Sexual Relations," 14-16, where she notes that P locates God's dwelling as in the temple and interprets purity law accordingly, whereas H sees the land as holy. "While P worries

sacred space, but applies that to the garden of Eden, which it designates as a temple, the Holiest Place on earth. It does not give any indication which would suggest a wider prohibition, although the underlying assumptions are the same. None of this requires absence of any permanent residents. I consider it more likely that the author envisaged celibate ones as well as temporary visitors who would also be expected to abstain from intercourse while in the holy city.

It is important to recognise what lies at the heart of the concern in this prohibition in 45.11-12. Its focus is not sexual relations as such, nor any notion that women are polluting and might pollute a man through sexual intercourse,[68] but ejaculation of semen.[69] Some light is thrown on the context of these concerns also through what immediately follows. There we read about others who are either forbidden entry into the city or who must undergo purification. The terms, עיר "the city" and עיר המקדש "the city of the temple" are used in parallel to one another and clearly refer to the city, not just the temple.

> *Blank* No blind person 13 shall enter it all their days; and they shall not defile the city (עיר) in whose midst I dwell 14 because I, YHWH, dwell in the midst of the children of Israel for ever and always. 15 Every man who purifies himself from his discharge shall count for himself seven days for his purification. He shall wash on the seventh day 16 his clothes and bathe his body completely in living water. Afterwards he shall

---

that the impurity caused by genital flow will defile the sanctuary, H suggests that forbidden sexual relations will defile the land, which H understands as holy and thus, like the sanctuary itself, susceptible to defilement" (15-16). Accordingly H can apply purity language to issues not directly related to the temple, such as incest, where in Leviticus 18 and 20 it employs purity language which is found in P in contexts of concern with defilement of the sanctuary. See also Aharon Shemesh, "The Holiness According to the Temple Scroll," *RevQ* 19/75 (2000) 369-82, who notes the *Temple Scroll's* affinity with H and closeness to D in not confining Yahweh's presence to the temple. Observing the author's regular revision of statements that speak of defiling the sanctuary, into statements concerned with God's holiness dwelling among the people, he argues that from the twofold structure of the camp and the sanctuary in the wilderness the *Temple Scroll* has developed a threefold form, where the camp now equates to the holy city, which is of a higher level of purity than the other cities, which also have their level of holiness (380-81). "The redactor of the Temple Scroll rejects the priestly idea that uncleanness can defile the temple 'at a distance', which stems from the perception that God's presence resides exclusively in the temple precincts. Instead, he attributes the obligation to remain pure to the [sic] God's presence everywhere within the people of Israel" (374).

[68] On this misconstrual see Gruber, "Purity and Impurity," who writes of Lev 15:18 that it "declares unequivocally that it is the male who by emission of semen defiles himself and his sexual partner and that her becoming defiled is solely the result of physical contact with her partner's ejaculate" (67), an assumption also shared by the *Temple Scroll* (71-73).

[69] So rightly White Crawford, *Temple Scroll*, 45.

> enter the city 17 of the temple (עיר המקדש). And anyone who is impure through contact with a cor/p/se shall not enter it until they have purified themselves. *Blank* And no leper 18 nor infected person shall enter it until they have purified themselves, and when he has purified himself then he shall offer the … (45.12b-18)

The prohibition of blind people from entering the city reflects an extension of a restriction on priests to all the people and may reflect the extension of the prohibition of entry of physically impaired priests to the general population (cf. Lev 21:16-23),[70] although, as Olyan argues, the language better reflects 2 Sam 5:8 ("The blind and the lame shall not come into the house").[71] The blind, here, are representative of all with physical impairment.[72] This is more likely than that it reflects concern that blind people will not be able to see to avoid impurity, although this rationale is offered in *4QMMT* B 49-54.[73] The words, "they shall not defile the city (עיר) in whose midst I dwell," reflect Num 5:3b ("they must not defile their camp, where I dwell among them"), where it applies to other polluting people. The expansion of this prohibition from the sanctuary to the whole city is reflected already in Isa 52:1 ("Awake, awake, put on your strength, O Zion! Put on your beautiful garments, O Jerusalem, the holy city; for the uncircumcised and the unclean shall enter you no more").[74]

In 45.13 the author addresses the issue of genital discharge, probably gonorrhea. The requirements match Lev 15:13. There is no heightening, as in the case of emission of semen. The beginning of the next column preserves the word, "trader" (רוכל), in the context of comments about entering the temple, perhaps an echo of Zech 14:21, but using a different noun. The focus on the temple's sanctity continues in 46 with the provision for keeping unclean birds away and the instruction about the trench or mound to separate the city from the temple.

We then find another passage which insists on extreme measures to preserve the city's sacredness. It requires that latrines be located outside the city 3000 cubits to the north-west and to be constructed in a manner in which excrement is not seen (46.13-16).[75] As Magness notes, the concern with privacy was quite

---

[70] Yadin, *Temple Scroll*, 1. 289-91; Harrington, *Purity Texts*, 14.

[71] Saul M. Olyan, "The Exegetical Dimensions of Restrictions on the Blind and the Lame in Texts from Qumran," *DSD* 8 (2001) 38-50, 40.

[72] So Yadin, *Temple Scroll*, 1. 289-91; Schiffman, "Exclusion," 309-10. Cf. 1QM/1Q33 7.4 and 1QSa/1Q28a 2.6 and their discussion on pp. 209-209, 211-12 below.

[73] So Olyan, "Exegetical Dimensions," who notes that the *Temple Scroll*'s placement of the exclusion of the blind here among other pollutants indicates that this is the primary concern (40).

[74] So Olyan, "Exegetical Dimensions," 41.

[75] On the identification of a latrine at Qumran matching the specifications of the *Temple Scroll*, see Jodi Magness, "Two Notes on the Archaeology of Qumran," *BASOR* 312 (1998) 37-44, 37-40, and Jodi Magness, *The Archaeology of Qumran and the Dead Sea*

unusual at the time, though it has become a norm in modern western society.[76] Deut 23:13 lays down a requirement for discharging one's excrement outside the camp: "With your utensils you shall have a trowel; when you relieve yourself outside, you shall dig a hole with it and then cover up your excrement", but the *Temple Scroll* goes far beyond this. A similar requirement is found in the *War Scroll* which requires a distance of 2000 cubits from the camp (1QM/1Q33 7.6b-7). Significantly, these distances have implications, probably deliberate, in relation to the sabbath, because they exceed the limits of how far one could walk on the sabbath,[77] and imply that defecation on the sabbath was prohibited, a notion which Josephus reports as characteristic of the Essenes (*B.J.* 2.147-149).[78] Magness observes: "The sectarians differed from contemporary Jews and non-Jews in regarding defecation as a polluting activity associated with impurity", and in the requirement of privacy for defecation, reflecting also the sect's concern with exposure of genitals.[79] The *Temple Scroll* also reflects these values.[80] This, therefore, continues the focus on the city, and coheres with the strictness reflected in the prohibition on sexual intercourse in the city.

Scrolls (Grand Rapids: Eerdmans, 2002) 105-13. She notes, however, that the location of the toilet at Qumran does not indicate that the issue of distance applied to the camp in the *War Scroll* and to the temple city in the *Temple Scroll* is relevant (110). See, however, Stephanie Harter, Françoise Bouchet, Kosta Y. Mumcuoglu, and Joe E. Zias, "Toilet Practices Among Members of the Dead Sea Scrolls Sect at Qumran (100 BCE-68CE)," *RevQ* 21/4 (2004) 579-84, who suggest it may have served as an emergency toilet for those not able to make the distance to the proper toilet. They also note the inadequate hygienic conditions with immersion pools without change of water and land with only thin layers of soil for burying faeces, and suggest the discrepancy in ages of death between Qumran and Jericho probably reflects these inadequate conditions.

[76] Magness, *Archaeology of Qumran*, 105-107.

[77] As Magness, *Archaeology of Qumran*, notes, in rabbinic Judaism it was 2000 cubits, but in CD 10.21 (cf. also 11.5), only 1000 cubits (109-10). 4Q265 7.4b-5a, however, allows a distance of 2000 cubits.

[78] So Magness, *Archaeology of Qumran*, 108-10, where she rejects the argument of Albert Baumgarten, "The Temple Scroll, Toilet Practices, and the Essenes," *Jewish History* 10 (1996) 9-20, who denies a connection. See also Harrington, *Purity Texts*, 106.

[79] Magness, *Archaeology of Qumran*, 110. She notes that "this concern for toilet privacy explains the placement of the toilet in L51 at the extreme western end of the room. Not only was this toilet located in a 'roofed house,' but it would not have been visible to passersby" (111).

[80] It is interesting to read Mark 7:15 in this light, as though it reflects a debate about what is a more serious cause of uncleanness, food or excretion, but such seems far from what Mark would have envisaged, and, from what we know of Jesus, also from his concerns.

Equally significant is the instruction which follows, to which we have already made reference, based on Num 5:2,

> You shall make three places, to the East of the city, separate from each other, to which shall 18 come the lepers and those afflicted with a discharge (הזבים) and the men who have an emission of semen. (46.17-18)

> Command the Israelites to put out of the camp everyone who is leprous, or has a discharge, and everyone who is unclean through contact with a corpse; 3 you shall put out both male and female, putting them outside the camp; they must not defile their camp, where I dwell among them. (Num 5:2-3)

Of the three categories the author replaces those who are unclean through touching a corpse with those who have had a seminal emission. This need not indicate a lowered concern with corpse impurity, as Japhet suggests,[81] since elsewhere the author expands the rituals for its purification, including additional washing and laundering and a more rigorous cleansing of the house and its utensils.[82] The omission might be partly explained by the fact that the three categories occur together in Leviticus 13 – 15, whereas corpse impurity is dealt with in Numbers 19. They all reflect occurrences which are likely to be unforeseen.[83] It does, however, reflect a heightened concern with seminal emissions. As Himmelfarb notes, the *Temple Scroll's* adaptation of Num 5:2 "shows a more severe attitude toward the impurity of genital flow than do the laws of Leviticus 12 and 15 and even Num. 5:2".[84] This can be qualified still further: the severe attitude is with seminal emission, not genital flow as such, which includes discharges. According to the P tradition in Leviticus 12 and 15 these people still remain within the community. In 48.14-17 the author uses Num 5:2 again to detail confinement of people also from ordinary cities.

> In every city you shall make places for those contaminated 15 with leprosy, and with sores and with scabies so that they do not enter your cities and defile them; and also for those who have a flux 16 and for women when they are in their menstrual impurity and after giving birth, so that they do not defile in their midst 17 with their menstrual impurity. (48.14-17)

---

[81] Japhet, "Prohibition," 77.

[82] So Himmelfarb, "Sexual Relations," 19-20.

[83] So Himmelfarb, "Sexual Relations," 17, 21.

[84] Himmelfarb, "Sexual Relations," 17.

It matches the provision to be made for the holy city except that now the third category consists of women during menstruation or after childbirth, and men unclean through seminal emission are not included.[85]

It is interesting that no such provision is made for women in relation to the holy city, at least in the parts of the columns which have survived.[86] If one assumes that these people leave the holy city as soon as these conditions arise, then the silence, if there really is one, might imply there are to be no women in the city.[87] This could be related to the implied prohibition of sexual intercourse in the city, although women is a much broader category than married women who engage in sexual intercourse, and the temple structure assumes women will visit the outer court. As we have seen, the absence of reference to women's confinement has been taken to imply that all residents of the city are temporary: women would live away from the city and not approach it if in a state of impurity. But then it is hard to see why the same might not be said of those for whom provision is made. The author may assume that woman were to live elsewhere and would be likely to know of their menstrual impurity (and certainly, impurity after childbirth) and so would not find themselves temporarily in the city with an unexpected onset of menstruation.[88] This all assumes the missing portions contained no such reference. Even in 46.17-18, however, it is quite possible that זבים includes reference to women. Cohen notes in relation to Num 5:1-4, which the *Temple Scroll* cites here, "The category *zāb* certainly includes the first and fourth categories of Leviticus 15 (the male and female 'oozers'); it probably includes also the third category (the menstruant) and perhaps even the second (the ejaculant)" (cf. Lev 22:4).[89]

The concern with impurity is reflected also in the extension of corpse impurity (already in 49.5-19) to include contact with bones (50.5-9), with lizards (50.20-21; 51.1-4) and also women who have been pregnant, but where the foetus has died

---

[85] Schiffman, "Laws Pertaining to Women," draws attention to Josephus' view in *A.J.* 2.261 that the biblical laws physically excluded women and notes that this view is preserved in one version of *m. Nid.* 7.4 and matches the practices of the Samaritans, Falashas and Karaites (212).

[86] Maier, "Purity at Qumran," however, comments: "It is clear that the Temple Scroll similarly excluded from the City of the Sanctuary women during their period of impurity; the pertinent regulations probably were in the lost passages of the columns 45-46 and 46-47" (104). See also Japhet, "Prohibition," who assumes the author would have subsumed Jerusalem under the same requirements as other cities in this regard (77 n. 19).

[87] So Yadin, *Temple Scroll*, 1. 289, 304; 2. 200; Harrington, *Purity Texts*, 104.

[88] Similarly Himmelfarb, "Sexual Relations," 21.

[89] Shaye J. D. Cohen, "Menstruants and the Sacred in Judaism and Christianity," in *Women's History and Ancient History* (ed. Sarah B. Pomeroy; Chapel Hill: University of North Carolina Press, 1991) 271-99, 275.

(50.10-19). For the time that the foetus "is dead within her she shall be impure like a grave" (50.11).[90]

Overall, one could say that the emphasis on the degrees of holiness of the temple and city has produced a heightened strictness in relation to the emission of semen, including the emission of semen in sexual intercourse, so that the author does, indeed, imply that sexual intercourse is forbidden in the holy city. But these are not concerns directly with sexuality, although they impinge on how sexual relations are viewed. Biblical requirements relating to seminal emissions are made much stricter, compared with those for discharges of gonorrhea. As Japhet notes, "the Scroll intensified the severity of the impurity derived from sexual organs".[91] The displacement of sexual intercourse from the holy city seems extreme, but appears to be matched by extreme requirements about toilets. Japhet concludes:

> The Pentateuch made the impurity of a discharge equal to that of leprosy, but it did not take such a severe view of the menstrual flow, postpartum bleeding, and the impurity of a seminal emission. The Scroll, by contrast, intensifies significantly the conception of the impurity of regular bodily functions, and this is expressed with respect to menstruation, childbirth, and seminal emission.[92]

What we are seeing in the *Temple Scroll* is the effect of a heightened sense of the sacred in terms of space. The implications are uneven. They have strong impact on areas broadly pertaining to sexuality, including nakedness (distant location of toilets), nocturnal emission (enhanced purification requirements), sexual intercourse (excluded from the temple city), women in menstruation and after childbirth (confinement in quarantine), and women generally (put further from the centre in the court structure of the temple).

3 The Deuteronomic Paraphrase

In the next section we shall give separate consideration to the "Law of the King", which contains extensive material appended to its citation of Deut 17:14-18 (and probably also 19-20) in 56.12-21. It is the major expansion within what is otherwise largely a re-presentation of Deuteronomy with little change apart from putting all instruction in the mouth of Yahweh.[93] The use of the sources is similar

---

[90] On this see Schiffman, "Impurity of the Dead," 150-51; White Crawford, *Temple Scroll*, 44-45; Harrington, *Purity Texts*, 74-75.

[91] Japhet, "Prohibition," 77.

[92] Japhet, "Prohibition," 78.

[93] On the contrast between this clearly defined use of Deuteronomy and the loose selective use of Leviticus and Numbers in the first two thirds of the *Temple Scroll*, see

to the author's use of Exodus 34 in 2.1-15. Here, the material derives from within Deuteronomy 12; 13; 16 – 23, as well as Numbers 30.[94] This part of Deuteronomy includes some significant material pertaining to sexuality. In what follows, the aim will be to focus on such material, whether the author uses it or bypasses it, and then how he uses it. Again, we face the problem identified in considering the citation of Exodus, namely, to what extent a citation really tells us anything specific about the author's priorities and attitudes.

The opening section, 51.11 – 52.4, which cites Deut 16:18 – 17:1, includes a brief addition in 51.14, warning against defiling "the House" by perverting justice and taking bribes, reflecting the author's concern with the temple. In 51.16b-18 it adds a comment about what to do with the person convicted of taking bribes, and follows it in 51.19-21 with a warning about behaving as the nations behave, concerned with idolatry. Sexual depravity of the nations is not in view. The next passage remotely related to sexuality concerns a woman's oath (53.16 – 54.5), where the author uses Num 30:1-9, remaining close to the text. That passage includes reference to the vows of widows and divorcees (54.4; Num 30:10 MT),

---

Heinz-Josef Fabry, "Das Buch Levitikus in den Qumrantexten," in *Levitikus als Buch* (ed. Heinz-Josef Fabry and Hans-Winfried Jüngling, BBB 119; Berlin: Philo, 1999) 309-41, 332. As Sidnie White Crawford, "Reading Deuteronomy in the Second Temple Period," in *Reading the Present in the Qumran Library: The Perception of the Contemporary by Means of Scriptural Interpretations* (ed. Kristin de Troyer and Armin Lange; SBLSymS 30; Atlanta: SBL, 2005) 127-40, puts it, "If Deuteronomy functions as a 'second law' in the Torah, both a recap of Exodus, Leviticus, and numbers and an enlargement of their codes to emphasize life in the land, then the *Temple Scroll* is a kind of 'third law' meant to recap and expand Deuteronomy by the exegetical techniques and legal interpretation of the priestly circles in which the *Temple Scroll* originated" (139).

[94] Stegemann, "Literary Composition," notes distinctive features of this section, which include its following Deuteronomy 12 – 26 in sequence and rendering it mainly word for word (139). He sees the author's incorporation of "an expanded version of the law code Deut. 12–26, not to outlaw its ancestor but to supplement it", such as Deuteronomy itself does and, later the parables of Matthew 13 supplements Mark 4 (140). Brooke, "Temple Scroll," adds the analogy of Chronicles and Kings (42). See also Philip R. Davies, "The Temple Scroll and the Damascus Document," in *Temple Scroll Studies: Papers Presented at the International Symposium on the Temple Scroll, Manchester, December 1987* (ed. George J. Brooke; JSPSup 7; Sheffield: JSOT Press, 1989) 201-10, who sees the *Temple Scroll* not as replacement for Torah nor as a supplement, but as "a more precise, more defined *torah*, which expands, abbreviates and rearranges in ways familiar from the Mishnah, although, unlike the Mishnah, it adheres largely to the biblical sequence" (207). See also Schiffman, "Temple Scroll and the Systems of Jewish Law," who notes that the author "maintains only a one-time revelation, at Sinai" (242).

where the author has given attention to the statement by relocating it,[95] but without any indication that the latter are unacceptable. It assumes divorce as a normal part of life.

In 60.9-21 the author cites Deut 18:5-14, in which 18:9-14 (60.16-21) contains warnings about divination and sorcery, but, unlike in the *Book of the Watchers*, there is no link made between sorcery and women or intermarriage. Women become the focus of attention briefly in 62.10 in a citation of Deut 20:8-18 (62.1-16), where they are listed among the booty to be spared and taken. This theme reappears in 63.10-15, concerned with captive women. The author cites Deut 21:10-14, but makes a significant addition concerned with purity. "She may not touch your purities for seven years, nor may she eat the peace offering until seven years pass; afterward she may eat".[96] The "purities" probably refers to pure food, as does the restriction on her participation in the meal of the peace offering. Why the restriction? To discourage marriage to foreigners? To wait until she becomes clean? More likely the assumption is that she must undergo a process of fuller integration. Lehmann argues that this refers to the marriage by priests on the basis that "the Temple Scroll addressed itself basically to priests" and sees here a reference to the priest's family eating תרומה, "heave offerings" and שלמים, "peace offerings".[97] He also draws attention to Yadin's interpretation, which sees a delay not of seven concurrent years, but fourteen years, who then relates it the probationary period for membership of the Qumran community.[98] Lehmann, instead, relates it to a tradition preserved in *Midrash Shemuel*, which links the requirement to seven years of conquest of the land and seven years of its division into tribal districts.[99]

---

[95] See Lawrence H. Schiffman, "The Law of Vows and Oaths (Num. 30:3-16), in the Zadokite Fragments and the Temple Scroll," *RevQ* 15 (1991) 199-214, 211-12.

[96] The author also changes the subject of the verbs in 53.12-13, so that the soldier, not the woman, cuts her hair, trims her nails, and changes her clothes. On this see Schiffman, "Laws Pertaining to Women," 218-19. In Schiffman, "Septuagint and the Temple Scroll," he notes that this variant is also reflected in the Septuagint of Deut 21:12, perhaps reflecting a common variant Hebrew text (290-91).

[97] Manfred Lehmann, "The Beautiful War Bride (יפה תאר) and Other *Halakhoth* in the Temple Scroll," in *Temple Scroll Studies: Papers Presented at the International Symposium on the Temple Scroll, Manchester, December 1987* (ed. George J. Brooke; JSPSup 7; Sheffield: JSOT Press, 1989) 265-71, 267. He sees a parallel in *m. Zeb.* 5.7.

[98] Yadin, *Temple Scroll*, 1. 367. See also Schiffman, "Laws Pertaining to Women," who while noting the parallels with Qumran, also points out that the *Temple Scroll* "makes no distinction here between solid and liquid food, a distinction prominent in the sectarian texts" (229).

[99] Lehmann, "Beautiful War Bride," 268-69.

It is striking that the extrapolation assumes the validity of (a person, let alone, a priest) taking a foreign woman as wife,[100] dangerous as this is according to the passage which the author cites in 2:1-15.[101] The author of *Jubilees* would not have tolerated such a concession. The provisions about taking a captive wife almost certainly also assume polygyny, something forbidden for the king. It is also interesting that the author found the need to make such an addition, an indication that it had relevance for his time, perhaps reflecting Maccabean conquests.

In 65.7-15 the author cites Deut 22:13-21, concerned with charges laid by a man against his recently married wife, that she was not a virgin. There are minor variations. These include use of ובעלה "and marries her" (7) instead of ובא אליה "has sexual intercourse with her" (Deut 22:13) under the influence of Deut 24:1, to clarify the legally married status and thus that the accusation is about breach of the marriage agreement.[102]

In 66.1-8a the author cites Deut 22:23-27, concerned with rape in the country and rape in the city, similarly with only minor changes. These include supplementary clarification of "in the field" by the words, "in a place far and hidden from the city", in 66.4-5. In 66:8b-11 the author cites Deut 22:28-29, concerned with the seduction of a virgin. In doing so he modifies the passage from Deuteronomy in the light of Exod 22:15-16, so that it speaks not of seizing her (ותפשה Deut 22:28), but seduction (יפתה Exod 22:16)[103] (and may understand ענה in 66.11 also not necessarily as rape, though it must imply seduction with violation as also in 66:3), and adds a proviso to ensure that any marriage would not contravene the laws of marriage and incest he is about to elaborate: "and she is permitted to him by the law" (66.9).[104] Wise sees this as reflecting the redactor's

---

[100] Lehmann, "Beautiful War Bride," points out that where this is espoused in later rabbinic discussion (see *b. Qid.* 21b), conversion is required (267-68).

[101] Cf. also 4QOrd[b]/4Q513 2 ii which appears to address the issue that daughters of priests marrying foreigners profane their fathers by such sexual liaisons (forbidden in Lev 21:9; see also Lev 22:12), which then lead to the whole family being forbidden to eat *teruma* or touch pure food. See also the concern about food and appropriate marriage in 4QHalakha A/4Q251 16 1-4. See the discussion of these texts on pp. 220-25 below.

[102] On this see Schiffman, "Laws Pertaining to Women," 221. See also the interpretations of this law offered in 4QOrd[a]/4Q159 2-4+8 8-10 and 4QD[f]/4Q271 3 12b-15 and the discussion on pp. 160-61, 216-19 below.

[103] See Moshe J. Bernstein and Shlomo A. Koyfman "The Interpretation of Biblical Law in the Dead Sea Scrolls: Forms and Methods," in *Biblical Interpretation at Qumran* (ed. Matthias Henze; Studies in the Dead Sea Scrolls and Related Literature; Grand Rapids: Eerdmans, 2005) 61-87, 69. They argue that by doing so the author shows that he believes that "seduction and rape are to be considered as identical offences and carry the same penalty" (69). Schiffman, "Laws Pertaining to Women," also suggests that ונמצא "and is discovered", enabled the author to envisage the girl as complicit (224).

[104] See Brin, *Studies in Biblical Law*, 115.

concern generally with proper marriages, which he finds also in the expansion of the incest laws at the conclusion of the document.[105] Schiffman notes that "the phrasing of this law would lead to the conclusion that the penalty of 50 shekels is to be paid even in cases in which a marriage cannot take place because it is consanguineous or otherwise prohibited."[106] It is a penalty, not a bride price. The provision includes the requirement that the man who is guilty of such seduction must marry the girl and "he cannot dismiss her לשלחה all his days". As Brin[107] observes, this depicts the prohibition of divorce as a punishment, and thus assumes the legitimacy of divorce otherwise, a stance which coheres with its use of Num 30:10 in 54.4-5 and with later writings of the sect and its revised version of Mal 2:16, which in 4QMinor Prophets[a]/4Q76 reads, כי אם שנתה שלח "for if you hate her, send her away".[108] Schiffman raises the question why the author of the *Temple Scroll* could not contemplate that the father be allowed to refuse the marriage, suggesting it reflects what he sees as the author's commitment to monogyny.[109] Alternatively, the author might have shared the values that lie behind Deut 24:1-4, which would assume the woman had been rendered thereby unclean for another man.

In 66.11b-12 the author then cites Deut 23:1 (MT),

לוא יקח 12 איש את אשת אביהו ולוא וגלה כנף אביה

A man shall not take his father's wife, and shall not uncover the garment of his father. (66.12)

Cf. ערות אשת אביך לא תגלה ערות אביך הוא

You shall not uncover the nakedness of your father's wife; it is the nakedness of your father. (Lev 18:8)

On the basis of the similarity to Lev 18:8 the author then adds to this statement, which stands in isolation in Deuteronomy, a further series of prohibitions drawn in

---

[105] Wise, *Temple Scroll*, 40-41. He also sees this concern as explaining the omission of all references to divorce and polygamy, thus Deut 24:1 and 25:5-10, and to prostitution as in Deut 23:18-19 (168). Divorce is however assumed in 54.4; 66:11 and polygyny implied in the instruction about the captive woman in 63.10-15.

[106] Schiffman, "Laws Pertaining to Women," 224.

[107] Gershon Brin, "Divorce at Qumran" in *Legal Texts and Legal Issues: Proceedings of the Second Meeting of the International Organisation for Qumran studies, Cambridge, 1995: Published in honour of Joseph M. Baumgarten* (ed. M. Bernstein, F. G. Martinez, J. Kampen; Leiden: Brill, 1997) 232-44, 239, 243.

[108] Brin, "Divorce," 234.

[109] Schiffman, "Laws Pertaining to Women," 225.

part from Leviticus 18 and 20, but reformulated to match the syntax of the initial statement, completed with a designation of the sin.[110]

לוא יקח איש את אשת
13 אחיהו ולוא יגלה כנף אהיהו בן אביה(ו) או אמו כי נדה היא

A man shall not take his brother's wife, and shall not uncover the garment of his brother, son of his father or his mother, because it is sexual impurity. (66.12-13)

cf. ואיש אשר יקח את אשת אחיו נדה הוא ערות אחיו גלה ערירים יהיו

If a man takes his brother's wife, it is impurity; he has uncovered his brother's nakedness; they shall be childless. (Lev 20:21)

ערות אשת אחיך לא תגלה ערות אחיך הוא

You shall not uncover the nakedness of your brother's wife; it is your brother's nakedness. (Lev 18:16)

לוא יקח איש את אחותו בת אביהו או בת אמו תועבה היא *vacat*

A man shall not take his sister, the daughter of his father or the daughter of his mother; it is an abomination. *Blank.* (66.14)

cf. ואיש אשר יקח את אחתו בת אביו או בת אמו וראה את ערותה
והיא תראה את ערותו חסד הוא

If a man takes his sister, a daughter of his father or a daughter of his mother, and sees her nakedness, and she sees his nakedness, it is a disgrace. (Lev 20:17; cf. also Lev 18:9 and Deut 27:22)

לוא 15 יקח איש את אחות אביהו או אחות אמו כי זמה היא *vacat*

A man shall not take the sister of his father or his mother; because it is depravity *Blank.* (66.14b-15) (cf. Lev 18:12-13; 20:19)

לוא 16 יקח איש את *vacat* בת אחיהו או בת אחותו כי תועבה היא *vacat*

A man shall not take *Blank* the daughter of his brother or the daughter of his sister, because it is an abomination. *Blank.* (66.15-16)

לוא יקח

A man shall not take … (66.17)[111]

---

[110] See Lawrence H Schiffman, "Prohibited Marriages in the Dead Sea Scrolls and Rabbinic Literature," in *Rabbinic Perspectives: Rabbinic Literature and the Dead Sea Scrolls: Proceedings of the Eighth International Symposium of the Orion Center for the Study of the Dead Sea Scrolls and Associated Literature, 7-9 January, 2003* (ed. Steven D. Fraade, Aharon Shemesh, and Ruth A. Clements; STDJ 62; Leiden: Brill, 2006) 113-25, 115.

[111] Puech, *DJD* 25, reconstructs the text of column 67, so that the prohibitions continue against taking the daughter of one's son or daughter, the wife of one's son, a wife and her daughter or the daughter of her son or daughter at the same time, and similarly, a woman and her sister (103-108). The column concludes with a citation of the provisions for Levirate marriage in Deut 25:3-10.

The use of the words לוא יקח איש "a man shall not take" indicates that the author is primarily addressing marriages rather than sexual intercourse as in Leviticus 18 and 20.[112] The placements of these prohibitions "at the very end of the Scroll serves to give them a certain emphasis".[113] The primary focus is appropriate marriages. In 66.13 the author retains from Lev 20:21 the declaration, נדה הוא "it is impurity". The word, נדה "impurity", is normally reserved for reference to menstrual impurity, but is used more broadly already in 45.10. He then appends a similar declaration to each of the prohibitions, in 66.14 and 16 using תועבה "abomination", applied in Lev 18:22 and 20:13 to homosexual acts and in 66.14 replacing the חסד הוא "it is a disgrace" of Lev 20:17. In 66.15 the author has taken זמה היא "it is depravity", from the prohibition against marrying a woman and her daughter in Lev 18:17 and 20:14. The supplementation of the citation of the single statement of Deut 22:30 by listing other incestuous marriages is natural enough, given the tendency elsewhere in the *Temple Scroll* to take into account material of a common theme, although it has not been the practice in the Deuteronomic paraphrase to this extent.

The sequence appears to be determined by beginning with the text which his paraphrase had reached, Deut 23:1. Normally the author would proceed to the next related material in Deuteronomy, namely 27:22 (against marrying one's sister, which parallels Lev 20:17 and 18:9), but first he inserts the prohibition against marrying the wife of one's brother from Lev 20:21 (parallelled in Lev 18:16), a prohibition which Deuteronomy does not contain, perhaps since it would conflict with the provisions of levirate marriage. Thereafter we have the prohibition about aunts, derived from Lev 20:19 (parallelled in 18:12-13), and the prohibition about nieces, which has no biblical parallel. One might then have expected the next prohibition, which breaks off unfinished, to have returned to Deut 27:23 (against marrying one's mother-in-law), unless the author had brought in more material from Leviticus, such as prohibitions of marrying grandchildren. While the author follows the formulation in Leviticus 20 closely, like Leviticus 18 it contains no indication of punishments.[114]

The syntax of this statement in 66.12 and of 66.13 creates an ambiguity about the meaning of each half of the statement, whether the second part is reinforcing the first or adding an additional dimension. Schiffman notes that Rabbi Judah and later the Targums Pseudo-Jonathan and Neofiti read Deut 23:1 in this way, as prohibiting sexual relations also with women whom the father had raped or

---

[112] See Brin, *Studies in Biblical Law*, who notes that this may explain why the author would not have included in the list the prohibitions of bestiality or homosexual relations (114).

[113] Himmelfarb, "Sexual Relations," 24.

[114] See Brin, *Studies in Biblical Law*, 123.

seduced (*m. Yeb.* 11.1; *t. Yeb.* 12.1).[115] The author would have disapproved also of these.

On the prohibition of a man marrying his brother's wife, Schiffman notes that the author would probably have made an exemption for levirate marriage,[116] but also that the ambiguity noted above remains unresolved, namely whether the second half of the statement reinforces the first or adds new dimensions.[117] This ambiguity does not arise with the remaining three prohibitions.

The prohibition in 66.16 of marriage to nieces seems to be understood as simply part of the supplementation, which clearly continued in the remainder of the column and into the next. It will have been seen as a logical consequence of the preceding prohibition against marrying one's aunt and is also the conclusion drawn by the author of D, the Samaritans, the early Christians, the Falashas, and the Karaites.[118] The prohibition is also assumed in *Jubilees*. Later, in D (5.7b-11a) and probably *4QHalakha A*/4Q251 17 2, 4-5, we see that the matter had become contentious.[119] Nothing here suggests the matter is contentious for the author of the *Temple Scroll.*

Within the range of chapters in Deuteronomy used by the author, 12, 13, 16:18 – 23:1, there are some passages which the author has not taken up. In some cases the reasons are obvious. The author has already dealt with the festivals and so passes over the material in 16:1-17. He has also passed over the preceding chapters, 14 – 15, which deal with pagan funeral rites (14:1-2; but see 48.8-10), clean and unclean foods (14:3-21, but see 48.1-5), tithes (14:22-29), the sabbatical year (15:1-18) and offering of the firstborn (15:19-23). More significant are omissions within the chapters which the author uses extensively, and, in particular, for our theme, material pertaining to sexuality. These include sections where the passages may well have formed part of the text but are among the sections missing at the beginning and ends of columns. This is apparent in the long citation which commences in 61.6 of Deut 19:15 and continues, apparently unbroken, until Deut 22:8 in 65.6.

---

[115] Schiffman, "Laws Pertaining to Women," 226.

[116] By contrast, Brin, *Studies in Biblical Law*, argues that the author by implication would have disapproved of levirate marriage (117). If we follow the reconstruction of Puech, *DJD* 25 and see 4Q524 16-22 as belonging to the final column of the *Temple Scroll*, then it includes a reference to Deut 25:3-10 on levirate marriage (16-22 6-10). See also Schiffman, "Prohibited Marriages," 123-25.

[117] Schiffman, "Laws Pertaining to Women," 226; Schiffman, "Prohibited Marriages," 117.

[118] See Schiffman, "Laws Pertaining to Women," 227; Schiffman, "Prohibited Marriages," 119.

[119] See the discussion of these texts on pp. 121-23, 225-27 below.

Deut 20:3b-7, part of the Rules of Warfare in Deut 20:1-20, are missing at the end of 61 and beginning of 62. It is very likely that they would have been cited in the missing portions of the manuscript. They include

> Has anyone become engaged to a woman but not yet married her? He should go back to his house, or he might die in the battle and another marry her. (Deut 20:7)

Deut 21:15-17, about the law of the firstborn, which begins with the words, "If a man has two wives ...", thus implying polygyny, is missing between the end of column 63 and the beginning of 64. We must assume it was part of the text and so would be an indication of the acceptance of polygyny unless there had been revisions to delete it. Similarly, the missing portions from the end of 64 and beginning of 65 probably included Deut 22:3-5, in which we find rules against transvestite behaviour:

> A woman shall not wear a man's apparel, nor shall a man put on a woman's garment; for whoever does such things is abhorrent to the LORD your God. (Deut 22:5)

The citation of continuous text begins again in 65.7 with Deut 22:13 and runs through to Deut 23:1 in 66.12. The author has omitted 22:9-12, which prohibits sowing another kind of seed in a vineyard, ploughing with ox and donkey together, weaving wool and linen together, and making tassels on one's cloak. He does, however, bring the prohibition of ploughing with ox and donkey (22:11) in 52.13. Elsewhere these texts about mixing are applied to intermarriage (*4QMMT* B 75-82; 4QD^f/4Q271 3 9-10), but that is not the case here. In the missing material between the end of 65 and beginning of 66 would have come Deut 22:19b-24a, which includes the text on adultery,

> If a man is caught lying with the wife of another man, both of them shall die, the man who lay with the woman as well as the woman. So you shall purge the evil from Israel. (22:22)

In all four instances of material which pertains to sexuality, betrothal and warfare, polygyny and the firstborn, transvestite behaviour, and adultery, now missing at the end or beginning of columns, it is likely that we have citations without elaboration, so that, beyond noting the author's obvious approval of what is contained in the text, we cannot identify specific attitudes.

Beyond that, the author has used selections of material from later in Deuteronomy earlier in his work, but mostly not as direct citations. Thus the author draws on Deut 23:10-11 (nocturnal emissions) in 45.6-12, Deut 23:12-14 (toilets) in 46.13-15, and Deut 23:21-23 (vows) in 53.11-13 (here as a direct quotation). He has not used the material in Deuteronomy 23 on attitudes to those born of illicit unions and foreigners (23:2-8), slaves (23:15-16), or female and male prostitutes (23:17-18). One wonders why.

The Deuteronomy paraphrase contains, or in the case of missing sections may be reckoned to have contained, a range of instructions and information pertaining to sexuality. Among the information which is incidentally present is the assumption that divorce (reflected in the oath of a widow and its prohibition as punishment for the man who seduced a virgin), polygyny (reflected in the teaching about a captive woman and about the rights of a firstborn), and even foreign wives (like the captive wife) are a normal part of life. The author will also have approved of Deuteronomy's instructions pertaining to adultery, transvestite behaviour, and a betrothed man and warfare. The author's main innovations are to be seen in providing a longer barrier of time before a foreign wife could be fully accepted into the community and share her husband's pure food and in adapting prohibitions of incest and provisions about seduction so that they reflected his concerns with appropriate marriage. The prohibition of marrying nieces seems not to have been treated as something requiring particular argument or emphasis. In this context the author employs language used in the context of impurity in P, in a non-ritual sense to describe the pollution caused by inappropriate marriages.

4 The Law of the King

Within the Deuteronomic paraphrase, the author cites Deut 17:14-18, in 56.16-21, changing it to the first person as usual, so that it presents the words of Yahweh directly. The final two verses in Deut 17:14-20 are missing, but were presumably to be found in the lost section at the beginning of the following column.

> *Blank* 12 When you enter the land which I give you, and take possession of it and live 13 in it and say: "I shall set a king over myself like all the peoples which surround me," 14 then you shall set over yourself a king /whom I shall choose./ From among your brothers you shall set over yourself a king; 15 you shall not set over yourself a foreign man who is not your brother. Only he shall not 16 multiply the cavalry to himself or make the people go back to Egypt on account of war in order to 17 multiply to himself the cavalry and the silver and gold. *Blank* And I told you, "You shall not 18 go back again on this path". He shall not multiply wives to himself, lest 19 they turn his heart away from me. He shall not multiply silver and gold; not too much. 20 *Blank* And when he sits upon the throne of his kingdom they shall write 21 for him this law according to the book which is before the priests *Blank*. (56.12-21; cf. Deut 17:14-18)
> [It shall remain with him and he shall read in it all the days of his life, so that he may learn to fear the LORD his God, diligently observing all the words of this law and these statutes, neither exalting himself above other members of the community nor

turning aside from the commandment, either to the right or to the left, so that he and his descendants may reign long over his kingdom in Israel]. (cf. Deut 17:19-20)[120]

The material from Deuteronomy addresses the king's marital behaviour in the words:

ולא ירבה לו נשים ולא יסור לבבו

and he shall not multiply wives for himself, or else/lest his heart will turn away. (17:17)

The author reads the text slightly differently:

ולוא ירבה לו נשים ולוא 19 יסירו לבבו מאחרי

and he shall not multiply wives for himself, lest they turn his heart away from me. (56.18-19)

The author or his source has read the *hiphil* 3rd person plural, יסירו, instead of the *qal* 3rd person singular, יסור, and has the additional word, מאחרי "from me". The difference lays the blame formally on the women, rather than on the king, and appears to be influenced by Deut 7:3-4, which warn against intermarriage:[121]

כי יסיר את בנך מאחרי ועבדו אלהים אחרים

for that would turn away your children from following me, to serve other gods. (Deut 7:3-4)

As Schiffman notes, "It is not simply the multiple marriages which constitute the problem; rather it is the deleterious influence of the women the king will marry".[122] Had the author only brought the citation, we would have again had to question whether we could say very much about its significance beyond these minor changes for determining the author's attitude beyond general approval.[123]

---

[120] Steudel, *Texte aus Qumran II*, notes that the text of Deut 17:19-20 is still too short to fill all seven lines at the beginning of the column (263 n. 127).

[121] So Schiffman, "Laws Pertaining to Women," 213, who points to a similar interpretation of Deut 17:17 in *m. Sanh.* 2.4 and *Sifre Devarim* 159. See also Casey D. Elledge, *The Statutes of the King: The* Temple Scroll's *Legislation on Kingship (11Q19 LVI 12 - LIX 21)* (Cahiers de la Revue Biblique 56; Paris: Gabalda, 2004), who notes influence from the language of 1 Kgs 11:2-6, 9, which condemns Solomon for his many foreign wives (89-90).

[122] Schiffman, "Laws Pertaining to Women," 212.

[123] Among the minor changes is the addition of למלחמה "on account of war" to "make the people go back to Egypt", which by implication allows other kinds of connections with Egypt such as trade and coheres with the generally positive attitude towards Egypt which characterises *Jubilees*. See also Moshe Weinfeld, "The Royal Guard

Instead, we have a substantial body of material which runs across three full columns in which the author purports to provide the instruction intimated in its reading of Deut 17:18,

וכתבו 21 לו את התורה הזואת על ספר מלפני הכוהנים *vacat*

> and they shall write for him this law according to the book which is before the priests. (56.20-21)

Again, the author, or his source, has slightly different readings from our text of Deut 17:18, which reads:

וכתב לו את משנה התורה הזאת על ספר מלפני הכהנים הלוים

> and he shall write for himself a copy of this law according to the book which is before the levitical priests.

The author has omitted **משנה** "copy" and changed the verb to the plural. He probably envisaged that the priests wrote the copy of the law and "this law" refers to what follows, not to the Torah as a whole or to Deuteronomy.[124] The author is probably alluding thereby to **משפט המלכה** "the law of the kingdom" which Samuel is said to have written and deposited before the Lord in 1 Sam 10:25.[125] He implicitly claims to provide the substance of this law in what follows[126] and probably does so as one who sees himself as heir to priestly heritage and authority.

In the elaboration, which reflects the language and themes of 1 Sam 8:11-18, Samuel's warning about future kings, we find extensive instruction about the king's army and about response to enemies at various levels of threat.[127] This can

---

according to the Temple Scroll," *RB* 87 (1980) 394-96, who notes parallels with the description of the royal guard in Diodorus Siculus. Maier, *Temple Scroll*, comments: "The close relations of the Oniads and the Tobiads to the Ptolemaic court could also have played a role when it came to actualizing the royal power described in Deuteronomy" (123-24).

[124] Maier, *Temple Scroll*, 124; Steven D. Fraade, "The 'Torah of the King' (Deut 17:14-20) in the Temple Scroll and Early Rabbinic Law," in *The Dead Sea Scrolls as Background to Postbiblical Judaism and Early Christianity: Papers from an International Conference at St. Andrews in 2001* (ed. James R. Davila; STDJ 46; Leiden: Brill, 2003) 25-60, 33. Elledge, *Statutes of the King*, 85.

[125] So Fraade, "Torah of the King," 33.

[126] So Heinz-Josef Fabry, "Der Begriff 'Torah' in der Tempelrolle," *RevQ* 18/69 (1997) 63-72, 70.

[127] On the extent to which the Law of the King as elaborated on the basis of Deuteronomy exegetes biblical passages and brings extraneous material see Serge Frolov, "'King's Law' of the Temple Scroll: Mishnaic Aspects," *JJS* 50/2 (1999) 298-307, who concludes that only a small part could have been produced by a purely exegetical process,

be seen in the broadest sense as an elaboration of the warning about increasing horses (56.16-17; Deut 17:16). There is also clarification of the role of the king in relation to the high priest. The king is bound to consult the high priest, who in turn consults the Umim and Thummim (58.18-21). Kingship is clearly envisaged as subordinate to the priesthood.[128] This reflects the dominance of priestly leadership during the Persian and Hellenistic period up to the time of Jonathan, who merged the two roles in himself. These instructions would have more relevance prior to his time. In 59.1-21 we find prediction about the future, in which the author reflects on history, reporting idolatry, breach of the covenant, dispersion and then hope, when Israel comes back to God "with all their heart and with all their soul, in agreement with all the words of this law" (59.9).

Early in his elaboration of royal law the author returns to the issue of marital behaviour.

vacat ואשה לוא ישא מכול 16 בנות הגויים
כי אם מבית אביהו יקח לו אשה 17 ממשפחת אביהו
ולוא יקח עליה אשה אחרת כי 18 היאה לבדה תהיה עמו כול ימי חייה
ואם מתה ונשא 19 לו אחרת מבית אביהו ממשפחתו

> *Blank* He shall not take a wife from among all 16 the daughters of the nations, but instead take for himself a wife from his father's house 17 from his father's family. He shall take no other wife in addition to her for 18 she alone will be with him all the days of her life. And if she dies, he shall take 19 for himself another from his father's house, from his family. (57.15-19)

This is an elaboration of "he shall not multiply wives for himself" (56.18; Deut 17:17). It begins by forbidding foreign wives. This corresponds to the instruction cited from Exod 34:16 in 2.14. There the warning is accompanied by the explanation that "their daughters who prostitute themselves to their gods will make your sons also prostitute themselves to their gods". In 56.18-19 (Deut 17:17) the warning also has an explanation: "lest they turn his heart from me". The author was probably reflecting on the corrupting influence of the wives of Solomon (1

---

whereas in the rest most exegesis "is either controlled or supplemented by eisegesis" and the provisions for the bodyguard and for conscription "have nothing or very little to do with the Hebrew Bible" (303). He notes similarities with the mishnaic exposition about the king in *m. Sanh.* 2.2-5 (304-305), which also begins with the Deuteronomy text and elaborates on it. See also Swanson, *Temple Scroll*, 117-73.

[128] See Fraade, "Torah of the King," who draws attention to the importance of this theme, including the elevation of the Levites (35-36). It is reflected also in *Jubilees* and the *Aramaic Levi Document*, where Levi and the Levites are elevated above Judah, and generally in Qumran where kingship is subordinated to priesthood (e.g. 1Q28a/1QSa 2.11-15) (drawn to my attention by Annette Steudel, email 4 October, 2006).

Kings 11:1-4; Ezra 9:12; Neh 13:25),[129] which led to the kind of idolatry that brought the disastrous situation described in the historical reflection in 59.

Here the focus is the king, not the rest of the population, where, despite the citation of Exodus 34, the author could contemplate that a man might marry a captive foreign woman, although that should be seen as exceptional.[130] The author probably assumes the prohibition on marrying Canaanites to apply to all Israelites, though not to the extent that he excluded that exception, to which he added further restrictions. Schiffman suggests that the focus may not be foreigners in general, but proselytes, whom the *Temple Scroll* would ban from the outer court for three generations (39.5-7). This, he notes, would cohere with the author's apparent intention to raise the level of sanctity required of the king to that of the high priest, who according to Lev 21:14 must marry a virgin from his people.[131]

Not only is the king forbidden to take a foreign wife. He is also forbidden to marry just any woman of Israel, whom he chooses. Instead, he must marry only a woman from מבית אביהו "from his father's house", which is then spelled out more precisely as ממשפחת אביהו "from his father's family", meaning his father's (not his mother's) extended family. It recalls Abraham's instruction about obtaining a wife for Isaac ממשפחתי ומבית אבי, "from my family and from my father's house" (Gen 24:40; cf. also Num 36:6).[132] That is very restrictive, even more so than Philo, who reports that the high priest was to marry a daughter of a priest (*Spec.* 1.110-112), but closer to Josephus, who specifies she must be from his tribe (*A.J.* 3.227, but cf. *Ap.* 1.31).[133] This may be the meaning of ἐκ τοῦ

[129] So Stegemann, "Literary Composition," who also mentions David (141).

[130] Schiffman, "Laws Pertaining to Women," notes the prohibition of marriage to Canaanites in Exod 34:16 and Deut 7:3-7, which was later expanded to include all foreigners, and also the significance of defining a Jew as one born of a Jewish mother (214).

[131] Schiffman, "Laws Pertaining to Women," 214-16.

[132] Elledge, *Statutes of the King*, notes the use of biblical texts from other legal contexts to supplement royal law (28). See also his discussion on pp. 149-50.

[133] Martha Himmelfarb, "Levi, Phinehas, and the Problem of Intermarriage at the Time of the Maccabean Revolt," *JSQ* 6 (1999) 1-24, interprets *Aramaic Levi Document* 6:4 / 17 as imposing this more narrow understanding (3-6); similarly Martha Himmelfarb, "Earthly Sacrifice and Heavenly Incense: The Law of the Priesthood in *Aramaic Levi* and *Jubilees*," in *Heavenly Realms and Earthly Realities in Late Antique Religions* (ed. Ra'anan S. Boustan and Annette Yoshiko Reed; New York: Cambridge University Press, 2004) 103-22, 105-106. She notes that similar restrictions which appear to have been imposed later on priests (marrying only the daughters of priests) and speculates that these may reach back to the early second century B.C.E. See also the discussion in relation to *4QMMT* B 75-82 on pp. 68-75 below.

γένους αὐτοῦ in Lev 21:14 LXX.[134] The restrictive meaning is more likely than to read "his family" as simply a reference to Israel as a whole.[135]

The words, "he shall not multiply", also receive a very restrictive interpretation, requiring monogyny on the king's part. It may well have resulted from a reading of Deut 17:17 together with Lev 18:18 which forbids a man marrying both a woman and her sister during their lifetimes.[136]

> ואשה אל אחתה לא תקח לצרר לגלות ערותה עליה בחייה
>
> And you shall not take a woman as a rival to her sister, uncovering her nakedness while her sister is still alive. (Lev 18:18)

If one understands by sister not a blood relative, but a fellow Israelite, then one could see in this text a prohibition of polygyny.[137] Monogyny appears, however, in the *Temple Scroll* to be a requirement specifically for the king, rather than an application to the king of a general rule,[138] as later became the case in the view of the author of *D* (4.20b-21). The reference to a man taking a captive woman (63.10-15) probably implies acceptance of polygyny as does the instruction about the

---

[134] See Fraade, "Torah of the King," 37.

[135] Cf. Schiffman, "Laws Pertaining to Women," who argues that the limitation to the house of the king's father and his clan should be understood not restrictively, but as referring simply to anyone born as a Jew from among the wider family of Israel (215). He notes that the use of בת אב and משפחה here match their usage in Gen 24:38 (recalling 24:3-4), where they are used loosely "with no technical connotation" (215). He notes that "alternatively, this passage may refer to a requirement that the king marry only a woman from his own family and clan, but such a measure seems to have no logical explanation". The explanation does exist if similar limitations were being applied to the high priest at the time. In favour of Schiffman's interpretation one could argue that the use of Lev 18:18 assumes a very broad use of sister matching the broad use of family

[136] So Heinz-Josef Fabry, "Levitikus in den Qumrantexten," 314.

[137] So Yadin, *Temple Scroll*, 1. 355-56; Maier, *Temple Scroll*, though he notes that the prohibition "should be understood not so much in terms of monogamy as of an extended sexual taboo" (127); and Schiffman, "Laws Pertaining to Women," who notes that the Karaites used Lev 18:18 against polygamy (217). See also Frolov, "King's Law," 302; David Instone-Brewer, *Divorce and Remarriage in the Bible: The Social and Literary Context* (Grand Rapids: Eerdmans, 2002) 71; Mayer Irwin Gruber, "Women in the Religious System of Qumran," in *Judaism in Late Antiquity, Part V: Section One: Theory of Israel* (ed. Alan J. Avery-Peck, Jacob Neusner, and Bruce D. Chilton; Leiden: Brill, 2001) 173-96, 185-89.

[138] Joseph M. Baumgarten, "The Qumran-Essene Restraints on Marriage," in *Archaeology and History in the Dead Sea Scrolls: The New York University Conference in Memory of Yigael Yadin* (ed. L. H. Schiffman; JSPSup 8; Sheffield: JSOT Press, 1990) 13-24, suggests that "the king as a role model for moral behavior was subject to supererogatory restrictions" (15).

right of the firstborn (Deut 21:15-17), which would have come between the end of column 63 and beginning of column 64. It would also be assumed in the cases of levirate marriage, which, as the previous section noted, may have been part of the paraphrase preserved in the final column. It is interesting that *m. Sanh.* 2.2 prohibits the king from engaging in levirate marriage. But even if we cannot determine the author's attitude towards levirate marriage, the other indicators support the view that what we have before us in the Royal Law is a requirement of monogyny for the king, but not for the people as a whole.

The insistence that the king have only one wife who remains with him all the days of his life could be read as excluding divorce,[139] but need not be read in that way. As we have seen, the *Temple Scroll* appears to assume the normality of divorce. It is presupposed as normal in 54.4-5, referring to vows of widows and divorcees, where the author cites Num 30:10 and has given it editorial attention, making it a section on its own,[140] and in 66.8-11, where in the citation of Deut 22:29 we find the imposition of prohibition of divorce as a punishment on the man who seduces a virgin.[141] If prohibition of divorce is being required of the king, we would again have an instance, like monogyny, of a special rule different from what applies to the general populace. It is far from clear, however, that such a restriction is implied here. Allowing a second wife only after the first one is deceased may be intended to reinforce the demand of monogyny rather than to make a point about divorce.[142]

The word עמו "with him" used here in 57.17 in relation to his wife stands in parallel to what is said of the bodyguard and the council, who are also to be עמו "with him" (57.6, 9, 12, 13): יהיו שומרים אותו מכול דבר חט "They shall guard

---

[139] As already Yadin, *Temple Scroll*, 1. 357. See also Elledge, *Statutes of the King*, 151-53; White Crawford, *Temple Scroll*, 60 and for a review of the issues of divorce in Qumran, see Vered Noam, "Divorce in Qumran in Light of Early Halakhah," *JJS* 56 (2005) 206-23, 206-10, who takes the *Temple Scroll* as forbidding divorce and so remarriage after divorce for the king, but otherwise argues that the sectarian stance was similar to the approach detected in some rabbinic halakhah of allowing divorce only on the grounds of adultery and should not be seen as distinctively sectarian (220).

[140] Yadin, *Temple Scroll*, 2. 242; Baumgarten, "Qumran-Essene Restraints on Marriage," 14; Tom Holmén, "Divorce in *CD* 4:20-5:2 and in *11QT* 57:17-18: Some Remarks on the Pertinence of the Question," *RevQ* 18/71 (1998) 397-408, 406-407.

[141] So Holmén, "Divorce," 407, who also draws attention to 4QOrd[a]/4Q159 2-4 8-10. He concludes cautiously, that "*11QT* 57.17-18 would thus appear as not putting forward any proscription of divorce, at least to the common man" (407).

[142] On remarriage after her death see Philip R. Davies, "Marriage and the Essenes," in *Behind the Essenes: History and Ideology in the Dead Sea Scrolls* (BJS 94; Atlanta: Scholars, 1987) 73-85, who observes: "It is not unlikely that the king is expected always to have a queen, and may therefore be obliged to remarry on the death of his previous wife" (78).

him from every act of sin" (57.10). This, in turn, reflects what is said of the Law ("this Law"), which is to accompany his reign according to Deut 17:19 (56.21) and to be עמו "with him" according to Deut 17:20 (though not preserved after 56.21).[143] Swanson notes that the language of taking a wife in 57.15 is not the usual לקח, but נשא, used only in Chronicles, Ezra and Nehemiah, where it often comes in the context of warnings against the sin of intermarriage (Ezra 10:44; 9:12; Neh 13:25), which "must be in mind … as one of the sins the guard keeps the king from".[144] This is perhaps more likely than Wise's suggestion that the author is reflecting on the account of David's sin with Bathsheba while his army was away, though this is not impossible.[145] Both suggestions relate to sexual wrongdoing and match the concerns of the section on marriage. On the other hand, מכול דבר חט "from every act of sin" could refer to potential actions of others against the king. In any case, all are to look after him. In relation to his wife, as Holmén notes, "his fidelity to her keeps him from sin".[146] Swanson draws attention to the image of the ideal wife in Prov 31:12, who does her husband "good, and not harm all the days of her life", גמלתהו טוב ולא רע כל ימי חייה.[147] Holmén suggests, therefore, that the emphasis in the *Temple Scroll* on her being with him all her days may reflect these ideals rather than concern with divorce.[148]

Nevertheless the text does preserve an emphasis not just on her, but on her, alone for all her life: כי היאה לבדה תהיה עמו כול ימי חייה "for she alone shall be with him all the days of her life" 57.17b-18a. This is still not enough, however, for us to conclude that the author is forbidding divorce to the king in situations where it might be deemed warranted.[149] Its ideal is that he have only one wife and that this relationship remain a good one throughout his life. It does not seek to deal with instances where the relationship might fail. In that sense we must conclude that it does not address divorce one way or other.[150]

On the other hand, the strict rules applied to the king do imply a value system according to which the highest ideal, to which, of all people, a king should aspire (and a high priest), is not polygynous, but monogynous marriage, and not marriage

---

[143] On this see Swanson, *Temple Scroll*, 128, 138; and see Holmén, "Divorce," 405.

[144] Swanson, *Temple Scroll*, 136.

[145] Wise, *Temple Scroll*, 105-106. Frolov, "King's Law," notes the reference to Solomon's bodyguard in Cant 3:7-8, but sees it as unlikely that the author would have drawn on that source (301). Cf. White Crawford, *Temple Scroll*, 59.

[146] Holmén, "Divorce," 406.

[147] Swanson, *Temple Scroll*, 138.

[148] Holmén, "Divorce," 406.

[149] So rightly Instone-Brewer, *Divorce and Remarriage*, 71-72.

[150] Schiffman, "Laws Pertaining to Women," suggests that the author may have agreed with the stance of the School of Shammai in insisting on a more literal interpretation of Deut 24:1 (216). Similarly Noam, "Divorce in Qumran," 220.

to whomever one chose, Gentile or Israelite, but marriage within one's own extended family.[151] As Gruber observes, "the records of the ancient Near East demonstrate that polygamy was generally confined to royalty and other wealthy and powerful men. Ordinary men could not marry more than one wife because of the economic hardship involved".[152] This situation is presupposed, for instance, in *1/4QInstruction*. Such ideals, even when not applied to the general population, would nevertheless exercise influence. The application of such restrictions by some to wider groups or to all people is, in one sense, a natural outcome. We see from the writer of D that this has occurred in his time and represents a view which he then vigorously propounds (4.20b-21).[153]

The Law of the King concludes with what must be an allusion by the author to his own time. Like the author of *Jubilees*, he identifies himself among those who return to God "with all their heart and with all their soul" (cf. *Jub.* 1:15, 23). This is common Deuteronomic language. The closest parallel in substance is in Deut 30:10, which also speaks of a time of return after disobedience:

> כי תשמע בקול יהוה אלהיך לשמר מצותיו וחקתיו הכתובה בספר התורה
> הזה כי תשוב אל יהוה אלהיך בכל לבבך ובכל נפשך
>
> when you obey the LORD your God by observing his commandments and decrees that are written in this book of the law, because you turn to the LORD your God with all your heart and with all your soul. (Deut 30:10)

---

[151] Instone-Brewer, *Divorce and Remarriage*, concludes: "It is impossible to know whether the Temple Scroll regarded monogamy as mandatory for all Jews, but they would at least have regarded the king as an example to look up to and probably to emulate" (64). See also his discussion in David Instone Brewer, "Nomological Exegesis in Qumran 'Divorce' Texts," *RevQ* 18/72 (1998) 561-79, 567-68.

[152] Gruber, "Women in the Religious System of Qumran," 187. She concludes that for the *Temple Scroll* and D "monogamy is not simply a matter of custom or economic necessity for the poor or middle class but also a principle that by divine decree applies to the wealthy and powerful" (187). At least this is so in relation to the king and, presumably, the high priest.

[153] On the relation of the *Temple Scroll* and D, see Lawrence H. Schiffman, "The Relationship of the Zadokite Fragments to the Temple Scroll," in *The Damascus Document: A Centennial of Discovery: Proceedings of the Third International Symposium of the Orion Center for the Study of the Dead Sea Scrolls and Associated Literature, 4-8 February 1998* (eds. Joseph M. Baumgarten, Esther G. Chazon, and Avital Pinnick; STDJ 34. Leiden: Brill, 2000) 133-45, who notes in relation to the *Temple Scroll*, that while "it is impossible to know if the prohibition would have extended to the rest of the people", the word בחייהם in D "should be understood to mean that one may not take a second wife as long as the first is alive, even in the event of divorce" and that "this same rule would probably have been intended by the Temple Scroll" (138). But see our discussion of D on pp. 111-19 below, where we argue that the concern is restricted to polygyny.

אחר ישובו 10 אלי בכול לבבמה ובכול נפשמה ככול דברי התורה הזואת

Afterwards they shall come back 10 to me with all their heart and with all their soul, in agreement with all the words of this law. (59.9-10)

The author clearly assumes that the *Temple Scroll* itself represents the basis for this return and renewal.[154] The people will return to the land, liberated, and then multiply and rejoice (59.12). Multiplying assumes a future where sexual relations form an integral part of the life of the people. The author continues in 59.13 with another biblical statement: "And I shall be their God and they shall be my people", then moves back to the theme of kingship. A similar sequence is evident in Ezek 37:23-24, which is also speaking of restoration, adding:

Then they shall be my people, and I will be their God. 24 My servant David shall be king over them; and they shall all have one shepherd. They shall follow my ordinances and be careful to observe my statutes. (Ezek 37:23-24)

For the author, however, the transition is not one of hope initially, but of warning:

And the king who 14 prostitutes (זנה) his heart and his eyes (removing them) from my commandments, shall have no-one who will sit on the throne 15 of his fathers, never, because I shall prevent for ever his descendants from governing again in Israel. (59.13b-15)

The image of prostitution had already featured in the citation of Exod 34:15-16 in 2.13-15. There it was used in relation to idolatry. Here the focus is probably wider. It is a metaphor, so need not have a particularly sexual connotation. The positive statements which follow, promise royal succession and victory over enemies, but, interestingly, not in terms of royal messianism. These final exhortations to observe this law and the promise of success echo the final words of Deut 17:14-20

19 It shall remain with him and he shall read in it all the days of his life, so that he may learn to fear the LORD his God, diligently observing all the words of this law and these statutes, 20 neither exalting himself above other members of the community nor

[154] So Fabry, "Der Begriff 'Tora'," 71. On the importance of the Law and the author's own work as a representation not a replacement of it, see Joseph M. Baumgarten, "Recent Qumran Discoveries and Halakhah in the Hellenistic-Roman Period," in *Jewish Civilization in the Hellenistic-Roman Period in Jerusalem* (ed. Shemaryahu Talmon; JSPSup 10; Sheffield: JSOT Press, 1991) 147-58, who notes the adaptations in the citation of Deut 17:10 about future teachers, so that in 56.3-4 it is qualified by accordance with the Torah, which would have been understood by the Qumran sect to include also *Jubilees* and the *Temple Scroll* (154-55).

turning aside from the commandment, either to the right or to the left, so that he and his descendants may reign long over his kingdom in Israel. (Deut 17:19-20)

It is interesting that this law, the *Temple Scroll*, should feature kingship so prominently. More seems to be at stake than moralising reflection on the failings of royalty in what, for the author, is past history, including accounting for their disappearance in the centuries after the exile and the emergence of a priestly leadership in their stead. As Stegemann notes, in this law "the king is no longer involved in cultic affairs, but is clearly subordinated to the priests in general and to the high priest in particular; the king himself is reduced to being a military leader, and to some extent, also a judge, but nothing else".[155] The concern of the author seems to relate to his own times. As with the instructions for the temple, so with the king, we are dealing with a blueprint to be implemented, presumably at some stage in the future by the author and his sympathisers when they establish their power within Israel. This would make sense in a time when there is some real prospect for reconstructing the temple and for having a monarchy. Frolov notes that "the non-Deuteronomic legal part of the document [the King's Law] is a curious mixture of eschatology and *Realpolitik*" which reflects a time when the royal and priestly offices are separate, but exercise of kingship was a real prospect, concluding that it "had most probably been written before autumn 153 when the high priesthood was taken over by Jonathan" and after the liberation of 164 B.C.E.[156] Alternatively, with Elledge, who dates the statutes to 143-125 BCE, we may see in them resistance to Hasmonean leadership which merged both roles.[157]

There is a major emphasis on warfare and defence. This has a footing in the negative comment in Deut 17:16 about not acquiring many horses, which the exposition turns into more positive instructions about a permanent bodyguard and the level of troop commitment in face of various degrees of danger. Such an emphasis would have practical relevance in the early to mid second century when the Maccabees assumed quasi-kingly roles, at least in a military sense, as here envisaged.

The extrapolation of the statement about not acquiring many wives goes in the opposite direction. The limit is set at one for a lifetime. While it envisages actual implementation at some stage in the future, there is no detail which suggests a particular historical context in which the author or his source is making the

---

[155] Stegemann, "Literary Composition," 142. He does not believe that the concerns arise from bad experiences with existing Jewish kings such as the later Hasmoneans.

[156] Frolov, "King's Law," 306-307. While expressing agreement, Annette Steudel (email 4 October, 2006) draws attention to the possibility that such discussion might have had no contemporary application, much as later rabbinic discussion of temple procedures at a time when the temple had long since ceased to exist.

[157] Elledge, *Statutes of the King*, 65-69.

statement and should certainly "not be reduced to simple polemical response to the specific behaviours of particular kings", as Fraade cautions.[158] It would begin to take on direct relevance as soon as the Hasmoneans began to assume princely leadership, which occurred some decades before they assumed the designation, king.

In relation to sexuality, the Rule of the King makes special demands on the king, reflecting his special role, similar but subordinate to the high priest. These include monogyny and marriage within his father's extended family. There was every reason given Israel's history of kingship to reject foreign wives and polygyny. The ideal was a king and his queen – and a replacement queen should she die. It is not clear that divorce would have been ruled out, although, given the high ideals, one can imagine that the author would contemplate it only in the case of serious breaches which required it. None of these values, rejection of marriage to foreigners, polygyny, divorce (which was permission to remarry), appears to have been seen as forbidden for people in general, although the first is apparently contemplated only within the exceptional circumstances of war booty and surrounded with increased restrictions. Once, however, people began to espouse notions of social or spiritual mobility, where they could contemplate that they might apply to themselves what applied to an elite, then possibilities emerged that these values would be espoused by (and for) people in general. In a similar way the mobility towards greater holiness would become the impetus for lay people to espouse values of groups located in a closer band to the centre of the circles of holiness. Such mobility was also potentially disruptive, especially where what once belonged appropriately within limited space and time, such as restrictions on nakedness and matters related to sexuality, came to be applied more widely.

5 Conclusion

The *Temple Scroll* is dominated by concern with the temple and above all with holiness. This informs its treatment of people who because of their gender or their various states of uncleanness must keep at a certain distance from the temple, either permanently or temporarily, until the state of uncleanness is relieved. The structure places women (and children and proselytes, and only in the fourth generation) at greater distance from the holy centre, than males, and, with even greater distance, than priests. Apparently only men over the age of twenty are to participate in the Passover meal.

Much of the concern with states of impurity pertains to sexuality. Generally the author takes the strictest position where there are differing alternatives within

[158] Fraade, "Torah of the King," 38.

the Torah and often extrapolates from them further. Thus it agrees with Numbers in banishing women during the time of menstruation or after childbirth, but adds their confinement in quarantine. There is a striking contrast in levels of strictness in the way the author handles discharges and seminal emissions. While the former are handled strictly and with additional ablutions, the latter receive far stricter treatment. In part this might still be seen as applying the strictest option among alternatives available in Torah. This includes extending the period of impurity from one to three days under the influence of Exodus 19, which, strictly speaking, deals with deliberate seminal emission in sexual intercourse, but can, for the author, be extended to all seminal emissions. The author also forbids sexual intercourse in the city, not a novel idea if by city we mean the temple where such behaviour is out of place anyway, but certainly new if, as is more likely, it refers to Jerusalem as a whole.

In these provisions relating to seminal emission the focus is not morality, nor the appropriateness of sexual intercourse in itself, which is elsewhere clearly assumed, nor the appropriateness of being male or female. It is the emission itself, seen as a normal part of life, just as are menstruation and childbirth, and needing to go to the toilet. The extreme provisions relating to the latter, which in effect forbid passing stool on the sabbath, an action which is simply part and parcel of normal human life, illustrate that such strictness has wider implications.

While not formally devaluing women, the effect of distancing them further from the centre of holiness and from Passover or quarantining them at certain times does influence the way they live and relate to others. It is not a major step from acceptance of one's difference within the divine order of things to sensing that the order brings unwarranted disadvantage. It is another order of reflection when *we* see such an order and recognise discrimination or disadvantage, whether or not this was felt by women at the time. The *Temple Scroll* made more acute and extreme a differentiation already present in Torah.

Much the same can be said of men and seminal emissions. These have their appropriate place (and *Jubilees* would say their appropriate time – not on the sabbath). The author assumes that in the right place seminal emissions are normal and natural occurrences and foresees sexual relations in the ideal future where God promises to multiply the people. In the case of sexual intercourse the author adopts the restrictions of his sources, sometimes without further comment. We can assume this for passages which have not survived at the beginnings or ends of columns, including disapproval of adultery and the requirement that a betrothed man give his marriage higher priority than his obligations to warfare. Among these are also disapproval of transvestite behaviour and provisions for the firstborn which assume polygyny. Polygyny appears to be assumed as normal as also the provision about the captive wife. The latter even allows marriage to a foreigner, despite the traditional warning embodied in Exodus 34, cited in column 2. Unlike there, where the citation is not elaborated, in the case of the captive woman it is, with the author adding restrictions, but thereby revealing that the basic notion of marrying a foreigner in these circumstances, which probably also entailed polygyny, could be deemed acceptable. Incidental references, such as the provision for oaths of a divorcee, also reflect an acceptance of the possibility of divorce, a right which as an additional punishment is withdrawn from the man who seduces a virgin.

The latter example also illustrates the author's particular focus on appropriate marriage. That man must marry the virgin – provided she is not in one of the forbidden categories of marriage. The scroll ends with a list of such forbidden categories, characteristically formulated as prohibitions about whom one might marry, not, as in its sources, prohibition of those with whom one may have sexual intercourse. We might not otherwise have noticed the converse of forbidding marriage to aunts, namely, forbidding marriage to nieces, as anything remarkable, had it not become a matter of dispute later in rabbinic times and then last century come to our attention as something for which the author of D had to contend. The shift from sexual relations to marriage is reflected also in a subtle change in the author's version of the man complaining that his wife was not a virgin.

Only some of these strictures relate to the temple space, but contravention of any of them created abomination or pollution. Within such strictures, however, appropriate sexual relations, probably perceived by the author as belonging solely within marriage, are assumed and valued as just as much as a part of life as the incidental excretions which also need careful attention. As with women, so with sexual relations between men and women, the restrictions can also be seen as the normal ordering of existence. That ordering does not formally devalue the sexual relations which entail seminal emissions in intercourse or the sexual being of males which produces seminal emissions (nocturnal – but there is surprising silence about other kinds of emissions, including through masturbation). It does, however, have the potential, to discriminate against or bring disadvantage to the people concerned, whether perceived as such by them or not. It also enhances a sense of tension between the holy and the sexual, which can, but need not, lead to the devaluing of the latter.

The tension between what is assumed in one setting as normal and in another as inappropriate comes to expression not only in relation to holy and secular space, but also in the special provisions imposed on the king, who must marry only one wife and from his father's family, thus ruling out marriage to foreigners and also polygyny, and may remarry another only after her death. We saw no convincing ground to lead us to conclude that it also excluded divorce. The author's version identifies women as a source of leading the king astray, though this relates in particular to their presence in numbers and probably to their including foreign women, as the concern with idolatry reflects, rather than with women as women.

The different standard applied to the king in these provisions has the potential for calling into question the "normal" values. This is all the more so, if normal people see such values as being of worth and themselves as worthy of aspiring to them. By the time of D the requirement of monogyny is being applied to all Israelites.

Compared with the early Enoch literature, we find nothing which links women and sorcery or which focuses on intermarriage with foreigners by Israelites or priests, a matter given serious attention in the *Aramaic Levi Document* and *Jubilees*. The exceptions are in the citation of Exodus 34 where the concern is idolatry and in the particular restrictions imposed on the king, where we may also see in a textual change a shifting of blame onto the women. The author obviously shares the disapproval which his sources express of various forms of sexual wrongdoing, but offers no indication that sexual wrongdoing is a major concern, such as we find especially in *Jubilees*.

As Milgrom notes,[159] the positions taken by the author of the *Temple Scroll* on a number of matters pertaining to sexuality coincide with positions taken in the later scrolls associated with Qumran. Thus the gradations of purity find their echo in 1QS/1Q28 6.16-21; the three day limit, in 1QSa/1Q28a 1.25-26; the prohibition of sexual intercourse in the city, in CD 12.1-2; the exclusion of women and physically impaired men matches the exclusions from the camp in the *War Scroll* (1QM/1Q33 7.3-5), which also shares a similar insistence on locating toilets at a great distance (2000 cubits; cf. 3000 in the *Temple Scroll*).[160] Himmelfarb notes, however, that *Jubilees* with its concern for sexual immorality and its tendency to conflate purity and morality, is closer to Qumran ideology than is the *Temple Scroll*.[161] While the latter has one instance of applying purity language to a moral issue (bribery defiles the House, 51.13-15), its primary concern is with impurity as the result of physical processes, which defiles the land, the city and the sanctuary,

---

[159] Milgrom, "Deviations," 166-67. He writes: "Thus, the rules of the Temple Scroll are compatible with Qumran law and undergird it" (167). He continues: "Judging solely by its impurity rules, it is an organic part of the Qumran literature". Other factors, however, such as the absence of polemic and distinctive sectarian features, suggest that the *Temple Scroll* belongs rather to the writings which the sectarian community saw as an authoritative resource, like *Jubilees*, rather than being a writing of the sect itself. See also his comment in Jacob Milgrom, "The Concept of Impurity in *Jubilees* and the *Temple Scroll*," *RevQ* 16 (1993) 277-84: "Whereas the *Temple Scroll* and *Jubilees* hope that their teaching will ultimately be accepted by all of Israel, the rest of Qumran has long despaired of this prospect: those outside the community are irretrievably doomed" (282). Similarly García Martínez, "Temple Scroll and the New Jerusalem," 445.

[160] On the relation to D, see also Schiffman, "Relationship of the Zadokite Fragments to the Temple Scroll," 138-40.

[161] Himmelfarb, "Sexual Relations" 35-36. On the alleged conflation of morality and purity at Qumran see Jonathan Klawans, *Impurity and Sin in Ancient Judaism* (Oxford: Oxford University Press, 2000) 75-88, and Harrington, *Purity Texts*, 27-30.

and with failure to observe purity laws, a stance it has learned from the Holiness Code.[162] *Jubilees* also stands under the influence of the latter but in a different sense: it expands the tendency evident in the incest prohibitions to see sexual immorality as something which defiles.[163] Thus, while the *Temple Scroll* and *Jubilees* have much in common, as Boccaccini emphasises,[164] and the former is seen by him as alluding to the latter in its statement in 51.6-7, "which I tell you on this mountain" (cf. *Jub.* 1:5; 4Q216),[165] their orientation is different. As Schiffman notes, the *Temple Scroll* is extremely conservative in its laws concerning women, while at the same time assuming marriage, sexual relations, and childbirth form part of properly ordered life. It shows no sign of ascetic or celibate tendencies; rather, the author "believed that the perfect society which he sought ... would be based on marriage and family, and that relations between the sexes are, as the Torah requires, to be conducted in sanctity and holiness", not only by priests but by "every man and woman in Israel".[166] The heightened focus on impurity through seminal emission, however, not least in the holy city, indicates a trend with the potential to develop in this direction.

---

[162] Himmelfarb, "Sexual Relations," notes that the intensification of purity laws in the *Temple Scroll* "brings ordinary Jews closer to priests by making the purity laws more elaborate and thus heightening their impact on both priests and lay people" (22). It applies the purity laws equally to priests and people, without blurring the distinction (23). By contrast, *Jubilees* "confers on all Jews the status of priests" (33) and "never stresses priestly prerogatives" (33).

[163] See also Klawans, *Impurity and Sin*, who contrasts the *Temple Scroll* and *Jubilees* thus: "Regarding its treatment of ritual and moral defilement, the Temple Scroll finds its mirror image in Jubilees. Jubilees is greatly concerned with the defiling force of idolatry and sexual sins, but not so concerned with ritual impurity per se. The Temple Scroll, by contrast, is greatly interested in ritual impurity legislation, but not so interested in moral impurity. What the two books share in common is that in neither is any fusion of these ideas presented", as he detects it in the sectarian literature of Qumran (51-52). The only innovation in relation to sources of moral impurity is to identify bribery as defiling in 51.11-15 (49-51).

[164] Gabriele Boccaccini, *Beyond the Essene Hypothesis: The Parting of the Ways between Qumran and Enochic Judaism* (Grand Rapids: Eerdmans, 1998) 98-104; see also Boccaccini, "Qumran and the Enoch Groups," 47.

[165] See Brin, "Connection," 108-109. Cf. Lyons, "Unauthorized Version," who, while noting that Boccaccini, *Beyond the Essene Hypothesis*, goes beyond Brin in posing dependence, argues that it is just as likely that the author may have made his own reference to the mountain in the missing opening column of the work (146).

[166] Schiffman, "Laws Pertaining to Women," 228.

CHAPTER TWO

Attitudes towards Sexuality in *4QMMT*/4Q394-399

The document known as *4QMMT*, *Miqṣat Ma'aśe Ha-Torah*, named after the author's own description of the substance of his writing, מקצת מעשי התורה "some of the works of the law" (*4QMMT* C 27),[1] has been reconstructed from around one hundred fragments from six fragmentary manuscripts, dated palaeographically from 75 – 50 BCE, found in cave 4 at Qumran (4Q394-399), and estimated to represent about 40% of the composite text.[2] The reconstruction by Elisha Qimron, which forms the basis of this discussion,[3] divides the document into three parts. *4QMMT* A is concerned with calendar. There is doubt about whether it originally belonged to the document,[4] but it has no bearing on our

[1] On the issue of translating as "works" rather than "precepts", as proposed by Qimron, see Florentino García Martínez, "4QMMT in a Qumran Context," in *Reading 4QMMT: New Perspectives on Qumran Law and History* (ed. John Kampen and Moshe J. Bernstein; SBLSym 2; Atlanta: Scholars, 1996) 15-27, 23-26.

[2] Elisha Qimron, "The Nature of the Reconstructed Composite Text of 4QMMT," in *Reading 4QMMT: New Perspectives on Qumran Law and History* (ed. John Kampen and Moshe J. Bernstein; SBLSym 2; Atlanta: Scholars, 1996) 9-13, 9.

[3] Elisha Qimron in *DJD* 10, 43-63. What follows uses the reconstruction and translation there, but for the manuscripts follows *DSSEL*, unless otherwise indicated.

[4] See the discussion in Lawrence H. Schiffman, "The Place of 4QMMT in the Corpus of Qumran Manuscripts," in *Reading 4QMMT: New Perspectives on Qumran Law and History* (ed. John Kampen and Moshe J. Bernstein; SBLSym 2; Atlanta: Scholars, 1996) 81-98, 82-86, who concludes that it was added by a scribe and "is to be considered extraneous to the original composition" (84).

investigation.[5] By contrast, *4QMMT* B contains comment about appropriate application of laws, among which we find a number which pertain to matters relating to sexuality.[6] This is also the case in *4QMMT* C, most of which takes the form of a direct address or exhortation to an individual, whom the author is seeking to persuade and whom he treats with considerable respect.[7] The writing lacks the frequently polemical tone characteristic of some literature at Qumran produced by the sectarian group.[8] That group appeared to have valued the work,

---

[5] But note that it assumes a solar calendar in 4Q394 3-7 i.2-3 / 4QMMT A 20-21.

[6] On the form of the document as different from both the *Temple Scroll* "which is formulated in the mode of legal material from the Hebrew Bible" and "other Qumran legal texts such as CD and its Cave 4 ancestors" see Moshe J. Bernstein, "The Employment and Interpretation of Scripture in 4QMMT: Preliminary Observation," in *Reading 4QMMT: New Perspectives on Qumran Law and History* (ed. John Kampen and Moshe J. Bernstein; SBLSym 2; Atlanta: Scholars, 1996) 29-51, 33. See also George J. Brooke, "The Explicit Presentation of Scripture in 4QMMT," in *Legal Texts and Legal Issues: Proceedings of the Second Meeting of the International Organization for Qumran Studies, Cambridge, 1995: Published in Honour of Joseph M. Baumgarten* (ed. Moshe J. Bernstein, Florentino García Martínez, and John Kampen; STDJ 23; Leiden: Brill, 1997) 67-88, who notes that "the very presence of explicit scriptural citations in MMT underlines that at least some of the scriptural texts of MMT are less far removed from scripture itself than they are in the Temple Scroll which belongs vaguely in the category of rewritten Bible" (84).

[7] In his literary analysis of style and language Miguel Pérez Fernández, "*4QMMT*: Redactional Study," *RevQ* 18/70 (1997) 191-205, points to indications that the author appears to have written the final section, but drawn on a collection of legal interpretations written for priests and revised by a different hand and reflecting a non-literary style and vocabulary.

[8] In a number of writings Schiffmann has argued that *4QMMT* reflects a Sadducean stance: Lawrence H. Schiffman, "The Pharisees and their Legal Traditions According to the Dead Sea Scrolls," *DSD* 8/3 (2001) 262-77, 273-74; Lawrence H. Schiffman, "Halakhah and Sectarianism in the Dead Sea Scrolls," in *The Dead Sea Scrolls in Their Historical Context* (ed. Timothy H. Lim et al.; Edinburgh: T&T Clark, 2000) 123-42, 135-38; and Schiffman, "Pre-Maccabean Halakhah," 354-57. See the critical discussion in Lester L. Grabbe, "4QMMT and Second Temple Jewish Society," in *Legal Texts and Legal Issues: Proceedings of the Second Meeting of the International Organization for Qumran Studies, Cambridge, 1995: Published in Honour of Joseph M. Baumgarten* (ed. Moshe J. Bernstein, Florentino García Martínez, and John Kampen; STDJ 23; Leiden: Brill, 1997) 89-108. He notes two or possibly three instances among the many interpretations of law by the author which coincide with positions later attributed to Sadducess, "those on streams of liquids (*m. Yad.* 4:6-8), on the red cow (*m. Para* 3:7), and perhaps those on the purity of hides and bones" (so Qimron, *DJD* 10, 132), but a number of positions which would have conflicted with their stance, including prohibiting Gentile sacrifice, dogs in Jerusalem, skins of clean animals in Jerusalem, priests marrying lay people (102-103). See also Eyal Regev, "Were the Priests all the Same? Qumranic Halakhah in Comparison with Sadducean Halakhah," *DSD* 12 (2005) 158-88, where he lists agreements and differences on p. 182.

preserving multiple copies, but its origins probably lie in the formative period of the life of the sect or in its pre-history, as did the writings with which it has much in common, the *Temple Scroll* and *Jubilees*, and perhaps also D.[9] It may, as its original editors suggested, be the work of the Teacher of Righteousness and be addressed to the Wicked Priest at an early stage in what became a vigorous conflict.[10] It may reflect a division within the movement which preceded the formation of the sect or derive from within its early years. We know too little to be sure. On the basis of its similarity of ethos with the writings mentioned above I consider it likely to have been composed sometime close to the mid 2nd century BCE. This appears more likely than that the work was a composition after the fact designed as an educational tool, though it is highly probable that it later served as a didactic instrument.[11] Given the limited information available to us, even that must be tentative. Its material pertaining to sexuality does at least preserve some indication of the attitude of one author and his associated group in these matters probably from within the 2nd century BCE, and we may assume, unless otherwise shown, that it reflects also the views of the community which preserved and valued the writing in the subsequent two centuries.

The following review will examine pertinent statements sequentially, especially because of the possibility that their immediate context may throw significant light on their interpretation, as appears to be the case in some instances. As Strugnell notes, "Most of these laws relate to the sanctuary, to things done there to the priesthood and to related questions of purity touching on priestly marriage, leprosy etc."[12] 4Q394 3-7 begins with some concluding comments about

---

[9] See García Martínez, "4QMMT in a Qumran Context," who concludes that the writing's eschatology and incipient dualism "favors a pre-Qumranic setting" (23); also Schiffman, "Place of 4QMMT," who speaks of "the early days of sectarian law" (98).

[10] Qimron, *DJD* 10, 117-21.

[11] On this see Steven Fraade, "To Whom it May Concern; 4QMMT and its Addressee(s)," *RevQ* 19 (2000) 507-26, who suggests that the work may have originated as a "'low-level' intramural pedagogical instrument for the teaching of candidates and/or neophytes to the community" (523). See also Maxine L. Grossman, "Reading '4QMMT': Genre and History," *RevQ* 20/1 (2001) 3-22, who suggests that the document may be an example of a document written after the event late in the life of the community as it retold its story, and cautions against confident use of its data to reconstruct history (19-22). Were this to be the case, one would expect to find the usual polemical tone and it would be unique in identifying the substance of the conflict which is notably absent in the later material, where, as we shall show, the conflict has moved from disputed interpretations to bedevilment of opponents.

[12] John Strugnell, "MMT: Second Thoughts on a Forthcoming Edition," in *The Community of the Renewed Covenant: The Notre Dame Symposium on the Dead Sea Scrolls* (ed. Eugene Ulrich and James VanderKam; Christianity and Judaism in Antiquity 10; Notre Dame: University of Notre Dame Press, 1994) 57-73, 63. On the importance of concern

what appears to be a 364 day solar calendar, a section attributed by Qimron and Strugnell to *4QMMT* A as lines 19 – 21.

4QMMT B is then seen to begin with the words, אלה מקצת דברינו "These are some of our rulings" (B 1).[13] The word, דברינו, might just as easily be translated, "our teachings, instructions, pronouncements, works, or practices".[14] The following context shows that the teachings do relate to laws.[15] Mostly the author introduces an issue with the preposition, על "concerning" or "on".[16] Within the fragmentary opening statement there is reference to purity (טהרת B 3). This already indicates that the teachings/practices relate to issues of purity and impurity. They are based mainly on Leviticus and Numbers.[17]

---

with laws relating to the purity of the temple see also Eyal Regev, "Abominated Temple and a Holy Community: The Formation of the Notions of Purity and Impurity in Qumran," *DSD* 10 (2003) 243-78.

[13] Strugnell, "MMT: Second Thoughts," notes: "Form-critically, the first words look extremely unlikely to belong to the incipit of a letter (though they could conceivably be the beginning of a section inside a letter); in fact, however, they look very like the incipit of a collection of laws—indeed, there is a very close parallel to them in another incipit of a collection of laws, the first verse of Deuteronomy: 'These are the words that Moses spoke to all Israel'" (62). Contrary to the *DJD* 10 edition he has come to prefer seeing *4QMMT* not as a letter or treatise, but as a collection of laws in analogy to Deuteronomy (62-63). He notes that this analogy would also cohere with seeing the final section of the document in the broadest sense as an exhortation and benediction rather than as the conclusion of a letter (67).

[14] On this see García Martínez, "4QMMT in a Qumran Context," who argues for "works, practices" (260).

[15] On its use in *4QMMT* see Qimron, *DJD* 10, 139. The word reappears in C 8, but there, too, the allusion could be to the particular practices being addressed in the context. Strugnell, "MMT: Second Thoughts," draws attention to the characteristic "that the laws are a written collection of pronouncements ascribed to the 'we'-community, not to God or to the angels nor even Moses as its source" (64). He also notes the absence of the term הלכה in the document and of the possible play on the word in the designation of opponents of the sect as דורשי חלקות "Seekers after Smooth Things" (65-66).

[16] On the use of על to introduce halakhic themes here and in D, and *4QOrdinances*, see Charlotte Hempel, "The Laws of the Damascus Document and 4QMMT," in *The Damascus Document: A Centennial of Discovery: Proceedings of the Third International Symposium of the Orion Center for the Study of the Dead Sea Scrolls and Associated Literature, 4-8 February 1998* (ed. Joseph M. Baumgarten, Esther G. Chazon, and Avital Pinnick; STDJ 34; Leiden: Brill, 2000) 69-84, 73.

[17] In his extensive discussion of biblical citations in *4QMMT* Brooke, "Explicit Presentation," observes that in *4QMMT* B the focus is on passages from Leviticus and Numbers and that the order is not dictated by the biblical text, whereas in *4QMMT* C the

1 The Problem of Gentiles

In B 3 the author moves directly to his concerns. The first three deal with: grain produced by Gentiles (B 3-5) (cf. *m. Par.* 2.1);[18] the purification offering (B 5-8) (cf. Lev 6:21; *m. Zeb* 11.6-8); and sacrifices by Gentiles (B 8-9)(cf. *m. Par.* 2.1). The third ruling argues from the analogy of sexual immorality.

8 ועל זבח הגוים [... זובחים]
9 אל הי[...]שא היא] כ[מי שזנת אליו

> And concerning the sacrifice of the gentiles; [we are of the opinion that they] sacrifice to the [...] that it is like (a woman) who whored with him. (B 8-9; 4Q394 3-7 i.11b-12a; 4Q395 3 – 7 i-ii.3b outlined)

The analogy is based on assumed disapproval of a woman seeking to commit an act of sexual wrongdoing with a man. Already here we should note that **זנה** is not to be construed in a narrow sense of acting as a prostitute,[19] but as in later occurrences of the word **זנות** in *4QMMT* (B 75, 82, C 5) of a woman engaged in illicit sexual relations. This broader use is already evident in *Aramaic Levi Document* and in *Jubilees*.[20] For a Gentile to bring a sacrifice, is as inappropriate

---

biblical source is Deuteronomy and the order does reflect the biblical text (assuming the order reconstructed by Qimron) (84).

[18] This depends on reconstructing the text to read Gentiles. See however the alternative reconstruction proposed in Yaakov Elman, "MMT B 3-5 and Its Ritual Context," *DSD* 6 (1999) 148-56, who argues that the issue is not grain brought by Gentiles, but grain brought by Levites and refers to the tenth of the tithe given to them which is in turn given to the priests (154-55).

[19] Erlandsson, S. "זָנָה," *TDOT* 4, 99-104. For its wider meaning in Qumran: Florentino García Martínez, "Man and Woman: Halakhah Based upon Eden in the Dead Sea Scrolls," in *Paradise Interpreted: Representations of Biblical Paradise in Judaism and Christianity* (ed. Gerard P. Luttikhuizen; Themes in Biblical Narrative, Jewish and Christian Traditions 2; Leiden: Brill, 1999) 95-115, 103-104.

[20] Loader, *Enoch, Levi and Jubilees*, 93-94, 98-101; 169, 174; see also Christine E. Hayes, *Gentile Impurities and Jewish Identities: Intermarriage and Conversion from the Bible to the Talmud* (Oxford: OUP, 2002), who notes that *Jubilees* and *4QMMT* share a similar understanding of intermarriage to foreigners (76-89). So already Ginzberg, *Unknown Jewish Sect*, 32; Joseph M. Baumgarten, and Daniel R. Schwartz, "Damascus Document (CD)," *PTSDSSP* 2, 29 n. 80; Similarly John Kampen, "The Matthean Divorce Texts Reexamined" in *New Qumran Texts and Studies: Proceedings of the First Meeting of the International Organisation for Qumran Studies, Paris 1992* (ed. G. J. Brooke; STDJ 15, Leiden: Brill, 1992) 149-67, 154; Aharon Shemesh, "Scriptural Interpretations in the Damascus Document and Their Parallels in Rabbinic Midrash," in *The Damascus Document: A Centennial of Discovery: Proceedings of the Third International Symposium*

as a woman seeking illicit sexual relations with a man.[21] Gentiles have no place offering sacrifices to God. It appears that they are excluded from that relationship, having, as it were, no covenant relationship with God.

Qimron notes the precarious state of the text, where even the word for sacrifice must be reconstructed, but considers that an allusion to prohibiting Gentile sacrifices is likely, given that this was a matter of controversy.[22] The rejection of sacrifices from Gentiles coheres with the first prohibition, if, indeed, that refers to accepting wheat produced by Gentiles. In the fragmentary text there is reference to touching and defiling. Probably the assumption is that such wheat renders people who touch it unclean. Therefore it is both not to be eaten (cf. Dan 1:8, Tob 1:10-11, and Jdt 10:5)[23] and also not to be brought into the sanctuary.

At least in the third ruling and possibly in the first we see the same exclusiveness in relation to Gentiles which appears later in the document in relation to marrying Gentiles. It is also possible that the second provision relates in some way to Gentiles if there is an association between copper/bronze vessels and Gentiles.[24] Carolyn Sharp suggests that already in these halakoth the issue of intermarriage to Gentiles both lies beneath the surface and is flagged by the analogy.[25] At least one could claim that one, but possibly all three, signal the issue

---

of the Orion Center for the Study of the Dead Sea Scrolls and Associated Literature, 4-8 February 1998 (ed. Joseph M. Baumgarten, Esther G. Chazon, and Avital Pinnick; STDJ 34; Leiden: Brill, 2000) 161-75, 164.

[21] Joseph M. Baumgarten, "The 'Halakha' in Miqṣat Ma'aśe Ha-Torah (MMT)," *JAOS* 116/3 (1996) 512-16, takes a different line of interpretation: "More plausibly it means, 'that it is as if you whored after him,' that is, by facilitating offerings to pagan deities a Jew is reckoned as if he himself had strayed after the strange gods. The wording recalls Exod. 34:15-16, 'for when they prostitute themselves to their gods and sacrifice to their gods (someone) will invite you, and you will eat of the sacrifice . . . and their daughters . . . will make your sons also prostitute themselves to their gods.' Thus, Damascus Document 12:8-9 forbids selling cattle or fowl to gentiles, lest they offer them as a (pagan) sacrifice. One cannot be sure what specific Jewish involvement with gentile sacrifices is banned by this fragmentary text, but it seems worthy of closer analysis" (§3).

[22] He refers to Josephus *B.J.* 2.409 and to traces of this view "attested in Karaite writings, in Pirqe Rab Eliezer and in other rabbinic sources", which otherwise took a contrary position, affirming Gentile sacrifices (Qimron, *DJD* 10, 150). See also Schiffman, "Place of 4QMMT," (92).

[23] So Qimron, *DJD* 10, 148.

[24] Cf. *m. Zeb* 11.6-8. Baumgarten, "'Halakha' in Miqṣat Ma'aśe Ha-Torah (MMT)," suggested as an alternative "that the law may relate to the mandatory separation between the offerings of the priests and the laity stressed in Ezekiel 46 and in 11QTemple 35 and 37" (§3), (noted also in Qimron, *DJD* 10, 149).

[25] Carolyn J. Sharp, "Phinehan Zeal and Rhetorical Strategy in *4QMMT*," *RevQ* 18/70 (1997) 207-22, 209-12, 218.

of separation from Gentiles and the analogy indicates that inappropriate sexual relations are a matter of concern to the author with inevitable consequences as part of the demand for separation.

In B 9-13 the author deals with cereal-offering (cf. Lev 7:15), arguing against the practice of not consuming it on the same day. There follows a statement of concern relating to purity and the red cow ritual (B 13-17; cf. Num 19), the hides of cattle [and sheep] (B 17-21), making things from unclean hides (B 21-22), the state of purity of those who carry carcasses of clean animals (B 22-24; cf. Lev 11:24-25, 27-28, 39-40, etc.), and an issue which cannot be identified (B 24-27). None of this pertains to issues of sexuality beyond illustrating the underlying concern with purity boundaries which also informs their treatment.

In B 27-35 the author proffers an opinion about the interpretation of Lev 17:3 which speaks of slaughtering animals "outside the camp". The author interprets the wilderness "tent of meeting" and "camp" as referring to the temple and Jerusalem, respectively.[26] This appears to match the view of the author of the *Temple Scroll*, where it informs the author's exclusion of those who have had a seminal emission from entry into the city until after three days' purification.[27] The writer of *4QMMT* repeats his assertion that Jerusalem is the camp in B 60-62. While not applied here to the area of sexuality, this enhanced sense of the sanctity of the city reflects a

---

[26] Hannah K. Harrington, "Biblical Law at Qumran," in *The Dead Sea Scrolls after Fifty Years: A Comprehensive Assessment* (ed. Peter W. Flint and James C. VanderKam, Leiden: Brill, 1998) 1.160-85, suggests "the sectarians derive Jerusalem's superior status from Deuteronomy, which often refers to the special 'place (מקום) which the Lord your God shall choose' (cf. Deut 12:11)" (174). See also her expansive treatment in Hannah K. Harrington, "Holiness in the Laws of 4QMMT," in *Legal Texts and Legal Issues: Proceedings of the Second Meeting of the International Organization for Qumran Studies, Cambridge, 1995: Published in Honour of Joseph M. Baumgarten* (ed. Moshe J. Bernstein, Florentino García Martínez, and John Kampen; STDJ 23; Leiden: Brill, 1997) 109-28. She notes "the three-day purification for impure persons before entering the sacred assembly or the holy city, respectively (1QSa 1:25-26; 11Q19 45:7-12)" (114), the banning of the physically impaired (11QT[a]/11Q19 45.12-14; 1QM/1Q33 7.3-5; *4QMMT* B 42-57); the prohibition of intercourse in the city (11QT[a]/11Q19 45.11-12; CD 12.1-2) and of hides of animals not slaughtered in the city (11QT[a]/11Q19 51.1-6; *4QMMT* B 21-26) (115). Correspondingly, she argues that the author, like 4Q400 and 11QT[a]/11Q19 38.5-9, viewed the whole temple as the holy of holies and applied to all priests what was required of the high priest (115). Cf. Bruno W. W. Dombrowski, "4QMMT after *DJD* X, Qumran Cave 4, Part 5," *Qumran Chronicle* 5/2 (1995) 151-70, who argues that the author is identifying the camp as the place where the addressees lived (154).

[27] Qimron, *DJD* 10, sees *4QMMT* as supporting Yadin's interpretation of the *Temple Scroll* that the sacred city means Jerusalem and not just the temple precincts (143-44). He says *4QMMT* differentiates four areas: temple, Jerusalem, settlements, and outside the settlements (145). See also our discussion of the issue on pp. 17-28 above.

stance which would have the kind of implications we see drawn in the *Temple Scroll*. In B 36-37 and B 37-38 (cf. Lev 22:28) the author addresses issues relating to eating pregnant animals and their foetuses.

2. "… and concerning the Ammonite and the Moabite …"

In B 39-49 the author returns to issues of exclusion. For the purpose of the discussion I have reproduced the Hebrew with indication of the different manuscripts, 4Q396 i.5 – ii.1 (base text); 4Q394 8 iii.9-19 (underlined text); and 4Q397 i.10-15 (outlined text). Where letters are not preserved in the base text they are enclosed in square brackets and where they are not preserved in any text but conjectured, they are in smaller font. The English translation is that of Qimron. The text is fragmentary and in Qimron/Strugnell's reconstruction reads as follows.

39 [ועל העמוני והמואבי והממזר ופצוע הדכה וכרו]ת השפכת שהם באים
40 [בקהל ונשים]ל[ו]קח[ים להיו]תם עצם
41 [אחת ובאים למקדש]
42 [טמאות ואף חוש]בים אנחנו
43 [שאין ואין לבו]א עליהם
44 [ואין לה]תיכם [ו]לעשותם
45 [עצם אחת ואין להבי]אם
46 [למקדש ואתם יודעים שמקצת] העם
47 [וה .. מ . . ים מתוכ]כים
48 [כי לכול בני ישראל ראוי להזהר מכול ת]ערובת [ה]גבר
49 ולהיות יראים מהמקדש

39 [and concerning the Ammonite] and the Moabite and the mamzer [and him whose testicles] have been crushed [and him] whose male member [has been cut off], who (nevertheless) enter
40 the congregation [and … … … … … and] take [wives to be]come one bone
41 [and enter the sanctuary … … … … … …]
42 [… … …] impurities. And we are of the opinion
43 [that one must not … … … and one must not cohab]it with them,
44 [… … … and] one must not let them be united (with an Israelite) and make them
45 [one bone … … … and one must not] let them en [ter]
46 [the sanctuary. And you know that] some of the people
47 [… … …] and become uni[ted].
48 [For all the sons of Israel should beware] of any forbidden unions
49 and be full of reverence for the sanctuary.

It interprets Deut 23:2-4 (ET 1-3).

2 לא יבא פצוע דכא וכרות שפכה בקהל יהוה
3 לא יבא ממזר בקהל יהוה גם דור עשירי לא יבא לו בקהל יהוה
4 לא יבא עמוני ומואבי בקהל יהוה גם דור עשירי לא יבא להם בקהל
יהוה עד עולם

> No one whose testicles are crushed or whose penis is cut off shall be admitted to the assembly of the LORD. 2 Those born of an illicit union shall not be admitted to the assembly of the LORD. Even to the tenth generation, none of their descendants shall be admitted to the assembly of the LORD. 3 No Ammonite or Moabite shall be admitted to the assembly of the LORD. Even to the tenth generation, none of their descendants shall be admitted to the assembly of the LORD.

From there it collates the categories: "[Ammonite] and the Moabite" (Deut 23:4); "the mamzer" (Deut 23:3); "[and him whose testicles] have been crushed [and him] whose male member [has been cut off]" (Deut 23:2)".[28] That the author puts the Ammonite and Moabite first on the list most likely reflects his concern to address the issue of Gentiles and intermarriage with them.[29] The author follows his usual pattern of using a participial construction to list the abuse or disregard of this law as he understands it.[30] The words שהם באים] בקהל (lit. "they entering the congregation"; B 39-40) reflect the formulation in Deut 23:2-4. The complaint is that this law is being disregarded and so this must mean that these people are "entering the congregation". From what follows it is evident that the author interprets this as referring to entering the people by marriage. Deut 23:1 had spoken of forbidden sexual relations (marriage), so that it would have been easy to read what followed as also pertaining to entry into the congregation by marriage. This is indicated by what is preserved in B 40, which has been reconstructed as ונשים]ל[ו]קח[ים להיו]תם עצם [אחת "and] take [wives to be]come one bone". The combination of ל[ו]קח[ים "taking" and עצם אחת "one bone" is an allusion to Gen 2:23-24 (ובשר מבשרי עצם מעצמי "and flesh from my flesh, bone from my bone" and והיו לבשר אחד "and they became one flesh") and indicates the theme of marriage, justifying the conjecture of ונשים before ל[ו]קח[ים. The use of Gen 2:23-24 is allusive rather than a citation and combines "bone" deriving from 2:23, with "one" from 2:24,[31] in a manner which needed no particular explanation and

---

[28] On the parallel texts, none of which has a list identical in all detail with *4QMMT*, but all of which have much in common see the table in Qimron, *DJD* 10, 146, and the discussion in Schiffman, "Place of 4QMMT," 91, 94.

[29] So Sharp, "Phinehan Zeal," 214.

[30] On the stylistic pattern which recurs throughout the halakhic section, see Qimron, *DJD* 10, 135-36.

[31] See Bernstein, "Employment and Interpretation of Scripture," 35.

so may have belonged to ways of speaking about marriage at the time.[32] It also makes it likely that the letters תם (40) include a third person plural suffix, alluding to people becoming one bone. Accordingly Qimron not unreasonably reconstructs להיו]תם, which reflects the והיו of Gen 2:24 to which the author is alluding. If ונשים is read before ל[ו]קח]ים, it would be reasonable to assume that the third person plural suffix is feminine, so that we would have a reference to males choosing wives.[33] Given that the focus is on what pure males should do, it is likely that the reference is not to males from among the forbidden categories, but to male Israelites and therefore to their taking wives from among the forbidden categories.

The interpretation needs to be considered also in the light of what follows. The word, טמאות "impurities" in B 42 reminds us of the underlying concerns of the author with separation. In B 43 and 44 we appear to move to the author's rulings designed to preserve Israel against this impurity. Qimron reasonably assumes a sexual reference in א עליהם and thus reconstructs ואין לבו]א עליהם. "No one", by implication, no male of the congregation of Israel, "is to go onto them", an allusion to the act of sexual intercourse.[34] In B 44, where we find ין לה]תיכם לעשותם, Qimron reconstructs ואין לה]תיכם [ו]לעשותם [עצם אחת, "and] one must not let them be united (with an Israelite) and make them [one bone", which would return to the Genesis allusion. This, too, appears to refer to sexual intercourse. The third person plural suffixes of לה]תיכם [ו]לעשותם are ambiguous. Strugnell, notes that they could be masculine, feminine, or common. He sees common as more likely in the light of the common gender of והיו in Gen 2:24, to which it alludes, rather than feminine as Qimron reads it.[35] Qimron reconstructs the same verb which he finds in לה]תיכם in B 44 also behind כים in B 47, which he reconstructs as מחוכ]כים. The verb is attested in C 81, מחוככים in a context where it also appears to describe illicit sexual relations. As Qimron observes, these words "seem to have the same meaning as the verb דבק in Gen 2:21-24".[36]

In his discussion of the verb, Strugnell, notes that Qimron derives it from a hypothetical and unattested verb, תוך, which in late Hebrew carries the meaning "to divide, mediate, compromise" and which Qimron connects with קרב "draw

---

[32] See also the extensive use of the Genesis passages in *1/4QInstruction* on pp. 300-12 below.

[33] Qimron, *DJD* 10, 159 n. 121.

[34] Qimron, *DJD* 10, 89.

[35] John Strugnell, "More on Wives and Marriage in the Dead Sea Scrolls (4Q416 2 ii 21 [Cf. 1 Thess 4:4] and 4QMMT§B)," *RevQ* 17/65-68 (1996) 537-47, 543. See also Dombrowski, "4QMMT after *DJD* X," 166.

[36] Qimron, *DJD* 10, 159 n. 122.

near, approach".[37] On the latter he observes that we would not expect with it a preposition like אל, עם, or ב. He rejects the proposal of W. Nebe, that the root is חכך "to bind, tie together"[38] on grounds of lateness and the spelling of the *Hiphil*. Instead, Strugnell suggests a possible derivation from נוך / ניך, widely attested in Semitic languages and meaning "to have impure (illegal) coitus". The absence of the *Nūn* he then explains by assimilation.[39]

B 46, reconstructed as ואתם יודעים שמקצ[ת העם] "And you know that] some of the people", would refer to the fact that this was actually happening and that the addressees would know about it. B 47 might contain a further allusion to illicit sexual intercourse, if we read מחוכ[כים. More secure is the text we find in B 48, מכול ת[ערובת [ה]גבר "of any forbidden unions". Ezra 9:2 uses the word, ערב "to mix/mingle", in the context of intermarriage with foreigners and Qimron conjectures it in B 80 in the context of intermarriage. The word [ה]גבר "male, men" after ת[ערובת "mixing, mingling, forbidden unions" may be a subjective genitive and refer to males engaging in inappropriate mixing[40] or it could be a regular absolute, a *nomen rectum*.[41] An objective genitive, producing an allusion to homosexual relations, is unlikely since we have no evidence that it was an issue.

Despite its fragmentary nature the text allows us to see the author interpreting Deut 23:2-4 as forbidding sexual relations/marriage between those listed and the (other) people of Israel. The primary focus is male Israelites engaged in illicit sexual intercourse and marriage with those from outside, who are not, in this way, to be brought into the congregation. The reference, however, to males in the opening list would also imply that the obverse is true: males are not to enter the congregation by marrying women of the congregation. The emphasis on intermarriage is striking compared with the way entry prohibitions are depicted in D (4QD^a/4Q266 8 i.6-9; cf. CD 15.15-17), which makes no mention of sexual categories; 11QT^a/11Q19 45.7-18, which is concerned with impurity through seminal emission; 1QSa/1Q28a 2.3-10, concerned with impurities and blemishes;

---

[37] Strugnell, "More on Wives and Marriage," 543. See also Dombrowski, "4QMMT after *DJD* X," 160, who notes that Qimron explains לה[תיכם on the basis of מתוככים in B. 81 and the restored reading מחוכ[כים in B 47 and as referring to the castigated promiscuity, whereas in the notes on p. 51 and p. 57 on B 44 and B 81, Qimron gives its meaning as "to cohere" which does not make sense in the context of B 80-81.

[38] W. Nebe, "Zwei vermeintliche Ableitungen von 'TWK' Mitte in Qumrân-Hebräischen," *Zeitschrift für Althebräistik* 5 (1992) 218-29.

[39] Strugnell, "More on Wives and Marriage," 544-45.

[40] So Qimron, *DJD* 10, who writes: "The word גבר appears to be a subjective genitive, as is זכר in למשכבי זכר 1QSa 1:10" (139 n. 47).

[41] So Strugnell, "More on Wives and Marriage," who translates: "for in the case of all male Israelites it is proper that a male should be [*sic* – surely to be omitted] keep from any improper sexual or marital contacts (obviously with a woman forbidden to him)" (541).

and 1QM/1Q33 7.3-6, concerned with blemishes and impurities, including seminal emission. 4QFlorilegium/4Q174, on the other hand, does include a similar list in a similar order of those who are not to enter the "house", but without a specific link to intermarriage.

הבית אשר לוא יבוא שמה
4 [... עד]עולם ועמוני ומואבי וממזר ובן נכר גר עד עולם כיא קדושו שם
... the house into which shall never enter a Ammonite or a Moabite, or a bastard, or a foreigner or a proselyte, never, because his holy ones are there. (1-2 i.3-4)

The language of taking wives, a formula for marriage,[42] also implies taking women and/by having sexual intercourse with them, and so can also mean sexual intercourse.

It is possible that the author also had in mind another prohibition which he finds in Deut 23:2-4, and which he claims is being flouted, namely entry of these people into the temple. This is conjectured by Qimron as implied already in B 41, when he reconstructs [ובאים למקדש] "[and enter the sanctuary]", but also in B 45-46, ואין להבי]אם [למקדש "and one must not] let them en[ter] [the sanctuary", and would then be implied in the concern expressed in B 49 of respect for the temple, ולהיות יראים מהמקדש "and be full of reverence for the sanctuary", where one can read it as the second major concern, the first being what immediately precedes: להזהר מכול ת]ערובת [ה]גבר "[beware] of any forbidden unions". The word טמאות "impurities, defilements" in B 42 would refer to both abuses. The reconstruction required to support the second concern is, however, far from secure.[43]

The author next moves on to consider two further categories of people who must not enter the sanctuary, the blind (B 49-50) and the deaf (B 51-54). In both cases the argument is not based on blindness or deafness as blemish, but on the pragmatic concern about their inability to comprehend and observe purity laws. This contrasts with the similar prohibition in the *Temple Scroll* where the assumption appears to be that their blemish makes them unfit (11QT[a]/11Q19 45.12-13).[44] There follows an argument against the view that a stream of liquid

[42] See Qimron, *DJD* 10, 85.

[43] See the criticism of Bernstein, "Employment and Interpretation of Scripture," who concludes that "the simple sense of MMT is that the subject under discussion is the law of marriage, not of the Temple" (38). Hayes, *Gentile Impurities*, sees it as referring to both (89).

[44] On this see Hempel, "Laws of the Damascus Document and 4QMMT," who notes a similar approach to *4QMMT* in 4QD[a]/4Q266 5 ii.1-3, which disqualifies priests with imperfect pronunciation because they may not communicate sufficiently accurately, in

cannot convey impurity to the liquid in a vessel from which it is poured (a dispute in which the author espouses a view later attributed to the Sadducees) (B 55-58). Matching the author's understanding of Jerusalem as "the camp", the author argues that there are to be no dogs in Jerusalem, who might eat flesh on bones from the temple (B 58-62).[45]

After a brief ruling about giving a tithe of fruit trees and herds and flocks to the priests (B 62-64)(cf. Num 15:30-39; Lev 19:23-25), the author addresses wrong practice in relation to lepers, in particular that some are entering houses with sacred food and eating it instead of waiting until sunset on the eighth day (B 64-72; cf. Lev 13:46; 14:8; Lev 4:13-14; 5:1-4; Num 15:27-31). He then offers a strict ruling about corpse impurity as including bones of the deceased (B 72-74; cf. Num 19:16-18).

3 "… and concerning the practice of illicit marriages …"

In B 75-82 (cf. Deut 23:2-4; Lev 21:7, 13-16) the author returns to the issue of marriage.

75 ועל הזונותי הנעסה בתוך העם והמה ב[ני זרע]
76 קדש משכתוב קודש ישראל ועל בה[מתו הטהור]ה
77 כתוב שלוא לרבעה כלאים ועל לבוש[ו כתוב שלוא]
78 יהיה שעטנז ושלוא לזרוע שדו וכ[רמו כלאים]
79 [ב]גלל שהמה קדושים ובני אהרון ק[דושי קדושים]
80 [וא]תם יודעים שמקצת הכהנים וה[עם מתערבים]
81 [46][ו]ה[ם]מתוככים ומטמאי[ם]את זרע[הקודש ואף]
82 את [זרע]ם עם הזונות כ[י לבני אהרון

75 And concerning the practice of illegal marriage that exists among the people: (this practice exists) despite their being so[ns] of holy [seed],
76 as it is written, Israel is holy. And concerning his (i.e. Israel's) [clean ani]mal

contrast to the stance in CD 15.15b-17a par. 4QD^{a}/4Q266 8 i.6-7 and 1QSa/1Q28a 2.4b-9, where the blind and the deaf are to be excluded because of the presence of angels (76).

[45] Sharp, "Phinehan Zeal," conjectures that the halakhoth in B 49-62 are also designed to function metaphorically, and so allude to those who fail to see and hearken to the dangers of intermarriage with Gentiles, and symbolise that danger through the reference to contamination of liquids and to forbidden dogs (219-20), but nothing in the text, itself, indicates a metaphoric intent.

[46] *DSSEL* reads וה[עם in B 79 and [ו]ה[ם] in B 80, compared with Qimron *DJD* 10, who does not read ה in either instance. Earlier Baumgarten, "'Halakha' in Miqṣat Ma'aśe Ha-Torah (MMT)," disputed even the ו: "The reading of the *waw* before the gap is not readily supported by the facsimile" (§17 n. 13).

77 it is written that one must not let it mate with another species; and concerning his clothes [is written that they should not]
78 be of mixed stuff; and he must not sow his field and vine[yard with mixed specie]s.
79 Because they (Israel) are holy, and the sons of Aaron are [most holy.]
80 But you know that some of the priests and the [laity mingle with each other] [as well as]
81 [And they] unite with each other and pollute the [holy] seed [as well as]
82 their own [seed] with women whom they are forbidden to marry. Since [the sons of Aaron should …]

The section is comparatively well preserved, the reconstruction based on two manuscripts 4Q396 iv.4-11 (base text) and 4Q397 ii.12-14 (outlined). We should not see this exposition as repetition, because B 39-49 dealt with marriage (sexual relations) in relation to particular categories of people as outsiders. On the other hand, this additional treatment indicates how important the issue of proper sexual relations/marriage was for the author. B 75-82 is to be considered as a whole, because the author mounts his arguments against illegal marriage in the context of forbidden mixing of kinds. He begins:

75 ועל הזונותי הנעסה בתוך העם והמה ב[ני זרע]
76 קדש משכתוב קודש ישראל

75 And concerning the practice of illegal marriage that exists among the people: (this practice exists) despite their being so[ns] of holy [seed], as it is written, Israel is holy.

The word, זנות, here as זונות "illicit sexual relations, illegal marriage",[47] has a wide range, as we have seen, and is not to be narrowed to prostitution. Its cognate זונות recurs at the end of this section, again not with the narrow meaning, "prostitutes", but as a reference to women with whom sexual relations (including marriage) are forbidden. The context must decide. In B 75-76 from קדש[ ]ב והמה Qimron reconstructs והמה ב[ני זרע] קדש "despite their being so[ns] of holy [seed]". The word והמה "and they" most naturally refers to what precedes, namely העם "the people", in whose midst and presumably by whom these acts of illicit sexual relations are being done. The identification of והמה with העם is further supported by the two-word citation of Jer 2:3 (קדש ישראל ליהוה "Israel holy to the LORD") in משכתוב קודש ישראל "as it is written, Israel is holy" (B

[47] On the form, זונות, ("illegal marriage"), attested also in CD 8.5 and possibly 7.1, see Qimron, *DJD* 10, 90. Cf. Dombrowski, "4QMMT after *DJD* X," who translates: "And regarding the prostitutes by force among your people" (168).

76).[48] This all makes the reconstruction ב[ני זרע] קדש "despite their being so[ns] of holy [seed]" plausible. The expression ב[ני זרע] קדש recalls Ezra 9:2, which also addresses intermarriage: והתערבו זרע הקדש בעמי הארצות "Thus the holy seed has mixed itself with the peoples of the lands", and finds an echo in the use of זרע "seed" which is attested in B 81, at the end of the section (and reconstructed in B 82).

While the context suggests illicit marriages, there is some debate about what kind of illicit marriages are in view. First, the author apparently shifts his attention to other matters, namely the prohibition of clean animals mating with species other than their own (Lev 19:19),[49] of wearing clothes of different kinds of fibres, and of sowing a field or vineyard with mixed species (B 76-78).

76 ועל בה[מתו הטהור]ה
77 כתוב שלוא לרבעה כלאים ועל לבוש[ו כתוב שלוא]
78 יהיה שעטנז ושלוא לזרוע שדו וכ[רמו כלאים]

And concerning his (i.e. Israel's) [clean ani]mal
77 it is written that one must not let it mate with another species; and concerning his clothes [is written that they should not]
78 be of mixed stuff; and he must not sow his field and vine[yard with mixed specie]s.

בהמתך לא תרביע כלאים שדך לא תזרע כלאים ובגד
כלאים שעטנז לא יעלה עליך

You shall not let your animals breed with a different kind; you shall not sow your field with two kinds of seed; nor shall you put on a garment made of two different materials. (Lev 19:19)

9 לא תזרע כרמך כלאים פן תקדש המלאה הזרע אשר תזרע ותבואת הכרם
10 לא תחרש בשור ובחמר יחדו
11 לא תלבש שעטנז צמר ופשתים יחדו

---

[48] So Bernstein, "Employment and Interpretation of Scripture," 45; Brooke, "Explicit Presentation," 74; and the translations of Geza Vermes, *The Complete Dead Sea Scrolls in English* (London: Penguin, 1997) 226; and Michael Wise, Martin Abegg Jr., and Edward Cook, *The Dead Sea Scrolls: A New Translation* (rev. ed.; San Francisco: HarperSanFrancisco, 2005) 460. Cf. Qimron, *DJD* 10: "Here the term כתוב can hardly introduce a quotation of Jer 2:3. It states rather that Israel is holy according to the Scripture" (55).

[49] Qimron, *DJD* 10, notes that rabbinic sources also compare illegal marriage with clean animals mating with different species: "If our restoration is correct, MMT restricts the law of *kil'ayim* (Lev 19:19) to pure animals; this is in contrast to the rabbinic view (*Sipra*, ed. Finkelstein, p. 401). The comparison of illegal marriages with *kil'ayin* is found in both rabbinic and Karaite sources (56).

You shall not sow your vineyard with a second kind of seed, or the whole yield will have to be forfeited, both the crop that you have sown and the yield of the vineyard itself. 10 You shall not plow with an ox and a donkey yoked together. 11 You shall not wear clothes made of wool and linen woven together. (Deut 22:9-11)

The author takes Lev 19:19 as his starting point, but supplements from Deut 22:9 and 11. Although the author begins each statement with the preposition על, with which he previously introduced new topics, he does not treat these as themes and so makes no comment about levels of their observance. Rather they are "mentioned here only as examples or by way of comparison"[50] and serve as proofs for his argument against illicit marriages. Kinds should not mix. The same applies to people.[51] The allusion to "mating" לרבעה is particularly apt.

B 79 then identifies two groups: the people and the sons of Aaron, and describes them both as holy, the one (even) more than the other:

[ב]גלל שהמה קדושים ובני אהרון ק[דושי קדושים]

Because they (Israel) are holy, and the sons of Aaron are [most holy.]

It could be that the author's concern is with priests marrying lay people, so that the comparison serves to enhance a boundary between the two, as Qimron suggests.[52] However it could be that the author is emphasising that both are holy, one more than the other, and that both, therefore, must not mix their holy seed with people whom they are forbidden to marry, such as foreigners or those whom the laws of incest forbid them from marrying. This would echo the emphasis of *Jubilees*, which highlights the people's holiness in order to argue against intermarriage and argues this especially in the case of priests (30:11-16; 23:21). A resolution depends in part on the reconstruction of what follows:

80 [ ]תם יודעים שמקצת הכהנים וה[ ]
81 [ ]ה[ ]מתוככים ומטמאי[ ]את זרע[ש]
82 את [ ]ם עם הזונות כ[

80 But you know that some of the priests and [ ]
81 [ ] unite (with each other?) and pollute the [ ] seed [ ]
82 their own [ ] with women whom they are forbidden to marry. Since [ ]

[50] So Qimron, *DJD* 10, 172. See also Schiffman, "Place of 4QMMT," 91-92.

[51] On the application of prohibition of mixing to marriages see Sir 25:8 and 4QD[f]/4Q271 3 9-11 and my discussion on pp. 157-59 below.

[52] So Qimron, *DJD* 10, 172; Kampen, "Matthean Divorce Texts Reexamined," 158-59; Himmelfarb, "Levi, Phinehas," 10.

Clearly B 80 now refers directly to priests. There is no verb. Instead we have the copula, making it very likely that another subject is being named and a reference to the other holy (but less holy) group is most likely. Qimron's reconstruction ו]העם (or now וה]עם as in *DSSEL*) makes good sense. These subjects now need a verb, which Qimron supplies as a participle (matching the author's pattern of describing existing behaviour in participial form): מתערבים "mixing". As Himmelfarb notes, this conjecture reflects (influence from) the language of Ezra 9:2 (והתערבו זרע הקדש בעמי הארצות "Thus the holy seed has mixed itself with the peoples of the lands"), whose likely influence (on the author) we have already noted above. The *hithpa'el* form could be reflexive and so mean that priests and people are intermarrying, as Qimron supposes, but it need not be reflexive. If it is not, but, rather, intransitive, then we may understand it as either standing on its own or as finding its complement later in the text.

The same issue arises in B 81, where the participle מתוככים is attested. We have already noted the use of this verb in B 45 to refer to illicit sexual intercourse. Again, one may read these illicit sexual relations as taking place between the priests and the rest of the people, or one may read the participle intransitively. According to Qimron it is a *hithpolel* participle from תוך, which he translates reflexively. Strugnell notes that the participle can be read reflexively, intransitively, or middle. In the light of the following phrase and the lack of an object he suggests that "the participle should be something like an intransitive, 'have sexual intercourse' or, conceivably, a transitive with an object, parallel to את זרע הקודש, understood; – but scarcely a reflexive or passive".[53] Taken in this sense it would refer to marriages between priests and laity (i.e. the sons of Aaron and Israel).

Accordingly, Qimron reconstructs from

ומטמאי[ ]את זרע[ ] [ש]

את [ ]ם עם הזונות

the words,

ומטמאי[ם]את זרע[הקודש ואף]

את [זרע]ם עם הזונות

and pollute the [holy]seed [as well as]
82 their own [seed] with women whom they are forbidden to marry.

Thus those who engage in sexual/marital relations across the divide between priests and the rest of the people defile (מטמאי[ם) the holy seed (את זרע] הקודש) and their own seed (ואף] את [זרע]ם). They do so "with acts of illicit sexual relations" (or "with forbidden women"). This reconstructed text assumes then a twofold effect of forbidden marriages between priests and people (the focus would

[53] Strugnell, "More on Wives and Marriage," 542.

be primarily on priests). They defile the "holy seed" (identified in B 79 as the people apart from the priests and in B 75 as the people generally). Thus they defile the people (in general or the lay people) and, to make matters worse, defile their own priestly seed. Such marriages would constitute the forbidden mixing of two different kinds, laity and priests.[54]

The rationale for the prohibition is not simply the mixing of kinds, but the need to protect the holiness of both priests and people. With regard to the basis of the halakhah, Qimron points to the similarity in vocabulary between Lev 21:15 ולא יחלל זרעו בעמיו lit. "and he shall not profane his seed among his peoples" and B 80-82: העם "people", זרע seed, offspring", טמא "defile". He points out that Lev 21:13-14 requires the high priest to take a wife מעמיו lit. "from his peoples", which has been understood as a reference to taking a wife from the people of Israel (as in Ezek 44:22), but, he notes, that "the plural noun, 'his peoples', scarcely fits this interpretation. Consequently, מעמיו was understood by several early sources as 'from his own family', i.e., paternal kin (or tribe), and the Samaritans even read מֵעַמּוֹ interpreting it as 'from his household'".[55] He contemplates "that the sectarians extended this law from the high priest to other priests, either by claiming that every priest may become the high priest, or by claiming that the sons of Zadok are descendents [sic] of the high priest, and should therefore follow the biblical laws directed to him,"[56] but considers it more likely

> that the sectarians deduced this halakha from their understanding of the root זנה. It is possible that זונה in Leviticus was understood as "a female outsider". In both Lev 21:14 and 21:7, the word זונה can hardly mean "harlot", and it may well have been interpreted by the sect as "a female outsider".[57]

He also cites 1 Chron 23:13 as providing a possible basis for seeing the priesthood as needing to remain separate (noting its use in 1QS/1Q28 9.5-6 and 8.5-11, which recalls the contrasts of *4QMMT*). In addition he refers to *Aramaic Levi Document* 6:3-4 / 16-17 on priestly marriage and cites 11QT[a]/11Q19 57.15-19, which rules that the king must marry a woman "from the house of his father"

[54] So also Bernstein, "Employment and Interpretation of Scripture," 46; Himmelfarb, "Levi, Phinehas," who argues partly on the basis that we have no independent evidence that intermarriage was a phenomenon of the early second century (15-24).

[55] Qimron, *DJD* 10, 172.

[56] Harrington, "Holiness in the Laws of 4QMMT," similarly speaks of an "expansive definition of holy persons" (117), and in Harrington, "Biblical Law", finds the restriction on marriage as derived from an extension of what applied in Lev 21:14 to the high priests, now in *4QMMT* to all priests (175). But then in her most recent work, Harrington, *Purity Texts*, speaks of B 75-82 as forbidding intermarriage with Gentiles (115).

[57] Qimron, *DJD* 10, 173.

and points to alleged references to limitations in priestly marriage in Philo and Josephus.[58] He also appeals to traditions about needing to marry into one's own tribe (Tob 1:9; 4:12; *Tg.* Ruth 3:10; Num 36:6-8),[59] but the concern here appears to be inheritance, rather than purity.

While the interpretation which sees in B 75-82 a concern with intermarriage between priests and lay people is possible, it depends rather heavily on conjectured reconstructions and must assume some inconsistencies in the passage, such as two different meanings for העם in the same passage, one referring to all the people (B 75) and the other as referring only to the laity (B 80).[60] The alternative interpretation, first proposed in a letter to Qimron by Joseph Baumgarten, and noted by Qimron, is that the passage is addressing intermarriage with Gentiles.[61] This appears to have stronger support from parallels and to offer a more coherent interpretation of the text.

Qimron's initial objection to reading מתוככים in the sense of, "mingle themselves with" (Gentiles), which is certainly possible, was that it would require something like בגוים "with Gentiles" on the same line and that there is no room for it.[62] Kugler questions this observation, noting that

> the left edge of this column is lacking; as a result we cannot be certain of the exact length of the column's lines. Moreover, lines in col iii of the same fragment run from a fully extant line of 40 spaces to a partially reconstructed line of 48 spaces. On the basis of material factors alone Baumgarten's suggestion is not without merit, and is not as impossible as Strugnell and Qimron make it seem.[63]

Hayes contests that, in any case מתוככים "mixing" need not require a בגוים "with Gentiles" immediately following, but is to be read with the prepositional phrase,

---

[58] Qimron, *DJD* 10, 174. He also refers to the work of Geiger in S. Poznanski (ed), *A. Geiger's Gesammelte Abhandlungen in hebräischer Sprache* (Warsaw: Tuschijah, 1910) 131-36, concerning sources (e.g., the LXX, Philo and Josephus) reflecting limitations on priestly marriages (172 n.181).

[59] Qimron, *DJD* 10, 174 n. 199.

[60] Baumgarten, "'Halakha' in Miqṣat Ma'aśe Ha-Torah (MMT)," §17. See also Robert A. Kugler, "Halakic Interpretative Strategies at Qumran: A Case Study," in *Legal Texts and Legal Issues: Proceedings of the Second Meeting of the International Organization for Qumran Studies, Cambridge, 1995: Published in Honour of Joseph M. Baumgarten* (ed. Moshe J. Bernstein, Florentino García Martínez, and John Kampen; STDJ 23; Leiden: Brill, 1997) 131-40, who speaks of העם בתוך as "the ambiguous phrase Strugnell and Qimron treat with unwarranted definiteness" (136).

[61] Qimron, *DJD* 10, 171 n. 178a. See also Grabbe, "4QMMT and Second Temple Jewish Society," 103; Harrington, *Purity Texts*, 115.

[62] Qimron, *DJD* 10, 171 n. 178a.

[63] Kugler, "Halakic Interpretative Strategies," 136.

עם הזונות "with women whom they are forbidden to marry", as complement in B 82, along with the two participles which follow מתוככים "mixing", or in association with them as parenthetical.[64]

In the explanatory comments of his view Baumgarten notes some further weaknesses in Qimron's reading.[65] With regard to alleged parallels to demanding priests marry only priests, he disputes the evidence cited from Philo and Josephus, who both clearly assume no such restriction, a conclusion later reinforced by Himmelfarb, who notes that, while both Philo and Josephus

> hold that the high priest may marry only a virgin from a priestly family (Philo, *Special Laws* 1.110; Josephus, *Antiquities* 3.277), ... Philo says explicitly that this rule does not apply to ordinary priests, who may marry any appropriate Israelite woman (*Special Laws* 1.111). In the passage in *Antiquities*, Josephus agrees with Philo.[66]

Referring also to *Ap.* 1.31, she shows that "in neither passage does Josephus require ordinary priests to marry women from priestly families", as Geiger assumed.[67]

Similarly, Baumgarten points out that the alleged parallel in *Aramaic Levi Document* 6:3-4 / 16-17 addresses marriage between priests and non-Israelite outsiders.[68] He finds a similar use of זנות to address marriage to outsiders in 4QOrd[b]/4Q513 and in *Jubilees* 30 and notes the analogical use of mixing halakhah to reinforce it in D. It is not insignificant that Qimron also suggests that זונה is best understood as referring to "a female outsider", better applicable to Gentiles than to fellow Israelite women.[69] Schiffman also notes that the concern in Ezek

---

[64] Hayes, *Gentile Impurities,* 84. She notes that even if one reads a disjunction between the participles, as the reconstruction והם in C 81 supposes, one can read what comes between מתוככים and עם הזונות as parenthetical (248 n. 75).

[65] Baumgarten, "'Halakha' in Miqṣat Ma'aśe Ha-Torah (MMT)," §17.

[66] Himmelfarb, "Levi, Phinehas," 9. Similarly Grabbe, "4QMMT and Second Temple Jewish Society," 103 n. 54.

[67] Himmelfarb, "Levi, Phinehas," 8-9.

[68] Cf. also Kugler, "Halakic Interpretative Strategies," argues that "4QMMT demonstrates the vitality of the interpretive tradition which treats זנה in Lev 21:14 as forbidden priestly marriage. But it is not *necessarily* in the same category as Aramaic Levi's narrow interpretation of זנה as priestly marriage with any non-virginal woman from outside the clan. Rather, it may reflect a first broadening among the sectarian scrolls of the law known from Lev 21:14 to include more cases than the one apparently covered there and certainly dealt with in Ar. Levi 16-17" (136). My own view is that *Aramaic Levi Document* is being equally broad and not just referring to priests, especially in the light of 4QLevi[b] ar /4Q213a 3-4 3a. See Loader, *Enoch, Levi, and Jubilees*, 91-94.

[69] Sharp, "Phinehan Zeal," 216 n.10.

44:22 about marriage partners for the daughters of priests is marriage to Gentiles not marriage to fellow Israelites.[70]

In addition, Sharp argues, "that the mixing in question is between Jews and non-Jews, rather than between priests and non-priests as Qimron and Strugnell suggest, is strongly supported by usages of ערב Hithpa'el in Ezra 9:2 and *Ps.* 106:35."[71]

כי נשאו מבנתיהם להם ולבניהם והתערבו זרע הקדש בעמי הארצות ויד השרים והסגנים היתה במעל הזה ראשונה

> For they have taken some of their daughters as wives for themselves and for their sons. Thus the holy seed has mixed itself with the peoples of the lands, and in this faithlessness the officials and leaders have led the way. (Ezra 9:2)

ויתערבו בגוים וילמדו מעשיהם

> but they mingled with the nations and learned to do as they did. (Ps 106:35)

Significantly, the passage from Psalm 106 follows the reference to Phinehas in 106:31. As Himmelfarb notes, however, the presence of מתערבים "mixing" in B 80 is conjectural.[72] She also sees a reference to intermarriage with Gentiles in *4QMMT* as "unlikely in the absence of evidence for the widespread occurrence of marriage between Jews and gentiles in the mid-second century".[73] But while this is true, for instance, of 1 and 2 Maccabees, the issue of intermarriage with Gentiles assumes a major role in *Jubilees* and *Aramaic Levi Document*, as we have shown. In addition, the influence of Ezra 9:2 does appear to be present elsewhere, in particular in the references to holy seed in B 75-76 and 80-81. This makes an allusion to intermarriage to foreigners much more likely as the focus of *4QMMT* here.[74]

Interpreting the passage as concerned with intermarriage to Gentiles also helps resolve another of the inconsistencies in Qimron's reading. The issue of intermarriage is one of contamination of the holy seed, Israel, as in *Jubilees* (e.g. 25:3, 12, 18).[75] The people as a whole are the holy seed, in B 82 as in B 75. Thus the inconsistency which Qimron must posit within B 75 or between B 82 and B 75 in the meaning of "holy seed" is removed. This makes better sense than to solve the inconsistency, as Qimron does, by reading "holy seed" as a reference to laity only in B 75, or, as Himmelfarb does, who with an alternative reconstruction

---

[70] Schiffman, "Prohibited Marriages," 121-22.

[71] Sharp, "Phinehan Zeal," 217. See also Hayes, *Gentile Impurities,* 85.

[72] Himmelfarb, "Levi, Phinehas," 8.

[73] Himmelfarb, "Levi, Phinehas," 8.

[74] So Hayes, *Gentile Impurities*, 85.

[75] See the discussion in Loader, *Enoch, Levi, and Jubilees*, 155-96.

argues that all references to holy seed refer to priestly seed.[76] Like *Jubilees* and *Aramaic Levi Document*, *4QMMT* also notes in B79 the special holiness of the priests and goes on to speak of defilement of both the holy seed and the most holy seed in B 80-82.[77] As Hayes notes, nowhere else where the holiness of the people is emphasised, such as in *Jubilees*, is the issue that of intermarriage between priests and lay people.[78] The harm comes to both – from intermarriage to foreigners. Thus she concludes:

> For Ezra, Jubilees, and 4QMMT, the designation of Israel as holy prefaces and justifies the application of certain priestly marriage laws to lay Israelites. In 4QMMT the law in question appears to be Lev 21:7: "They shall not marry a *zonah* . . . for they are holy to their God."[79]

> Israelite marriages with outsiders (*zonot*) defile the holy seed of lay Israelites as much as priestly marriages with outsiders defile their seed (i.e., the most holy seed of the priests). As holy seed and most holy seed, respectively, Israelite and priest alike are subject to the rule of Lev 21:7.[80]

---

[76] Himmelfarb, "Levi, Phinehas," offers an alternative reconstruction in B 75 reading ב[ני עם] קדש "sons of holy people" instead of ב[ני זרע] קדש "sons of holy seed", which enables one to limit the reference to priests. In B 81-82 she reads both את זרע[הקודש and את [זרע]ם עם as references to priestly seed on the analogy with *Aramaic Levi Document,* where she also interprets the concern as intermarriage of priests and lay Israelites (11). See my discussion of *Aramaic Levi Document* in Loader, *Enoch, Levi, and Jubilees*, 88-103, where I argue that intermarriage to Gentiles is also the concern there. On her reconstruction see the critical assessment in Hayes, *Gentile Impurities*, 85-86.

[77] Hayes, *Gentile Impurities,* argues that in any case "the mixing of the two seeds would in no way impair the status of the holy seed (the Israelite; though it may reduce the status of the most holy seed, i.e. the priests). Yet lines 81-82 make it clear that both the seed of the priests and the seed of the Israelites are being harmed by *zenut*" (83-84). On *Jubilees*, see my discussion in Loader, *Enoch, Levi, and Jubilees*, 174-76. Cf. Himmelfarb, "Levi, Phinehas," who argues that B 79 functions to draw a boundary between priests and lay people in order to reinforce the case against intermarriage between the two (10).

[78] Hayes, *Gentile Impurities*, writes: "When Israel is declared to be a kingdom of priests or holy (by H or D or Ezra or Jubilees), the result is always an equation of the two in some specific respect, not a distinction between them" (85). See also her discussion of the argument of Himmelfarb, "Levi, Phinehas," ("Phinehas" 10-11) that in B 81 "holy seed" refers not to lay Israel, but as in Lev 21:7 to male biology (85-86). Hayes makes the case that the point of establishing earlier that lay Israel is holy, is to ground the warning that intermarriage defiles the people.

[79] Hayes, *Gentile Impurities*, 85.

[80] Hayes, *Gentile Impurities*, 86.

Accordingly, we see the whole section as concerned with intermarriage to foreigners by any Israelite, but especially by priests, thus reading B 80 – 82 as follows:

80 [וא]תם יודעים שמקצת הכהנים ו[העם מתערבים]
81 [והם]מתוככים ומטמאי[ם]את זרע[הקודש ואף]
82 את [זרע]ם עם הזונות

[ ] you know that some of the priests [ ]
[ ] are having sexual intercourse and defil[ ] the [ ] seed [ ]
[ ] with forbidden women/illicit sexual relations [

which might be expanded (following Qimron) to read:

> And you know that some of the priests and the people are engaging in forbidden sexual relations and they are having sexual intercourse and contaminating the holy seed and their own seed with forbidden women/illicit sexual relations.

4 "… and concerning the women …"

B 82 renders the last surviving section of 4Q397 ii.6-13, which overlaps with fragments of 6-13 of 4Q396 up to B 81. Thereafter is a gap. In Qimron's reconstruction 4Q397 iv 14-21 then begins a third section of the document, which includes comment about the author and his group ("we have separated ourselves" C 7). His co-editor, Strugnell, however, places 4Q398 11-13 before this section.[81] We shall proceed on the basis of Qimron's order, but return to 4Q398 11-13 in the discussion.

The first lines of 4Q397 iv.14-21, C 1-3, are very fragmentary. In C 4-8 the author appears to continue with concerns about marriage and sexual relations.[82]

[81] See Qimron, *DJD* 10, 201, who notes the difference in placement. See also the discussion in Reinhard G. Kratz, "Mose und die Propheten: Zur Interpretation von 4QMMT C," in *From 4QMMT to Resurrection: Mélanges qumraniens en homage à Émile Puech* (ed. Florentino García Martínez, Annette Steudel, and Eibert Tigchelaar; STDJ 61; Leiden: Brill, 2006) 151-76, 162-66, who argues for Strugnell's order, but cautions that this is by no means certain.

[82] Thus Qimron, *DJD* 10, notes: "One should, however, recall that the section that follows B 82 is missing, and it is possible that the missing section (whose extent is difficult to estimate) contained further laws relating to marital status. This hypothesis finds further support in frg. 8 of the papyrus MS^{e}, in which the words תערוב 'sexual intercourse' … and האשה 'the woman' are found. The proper place of this fragment would seem to be in the gap at the end of section B" (131 n. 10).

4 ועל הנשי[ם החמ]ס והמעל[ ]
5 כי באלה[ ][83] בגלל [ ]החמס והזנות אבד[ו מקצת]
6 מקומות [ואף] כתו[ב בספר מושה שלו]א תביא תועבה א[ל ביתכה כי]
7 התועבה שנואה היאה [ואתם יודעים ש]פרשנו מרוב הע[ם ומכול טמאתם]
8 [ו]מהתערב בדברים האלה ומלבוא ע[מהם]לגב אלה

4 And concerning the women [… … … the malice] and the treachery
5 for in these […]because of [ ] malice and the fornication [some]
6 places were destroyed. [And it is] written [in the book of Moses] that you should [not] bring any abomination [into your home, since]
7 abomination is a hateful thing. [And you know that] we have separated ourselves from the multitude of the people [and from all their impurity]
8 and from being involved with these matters and from participating with [them] in these things.

Thus we have reference in C 4 to women in a form which in B introduced halakhic comment: ועל הנשי[ם ("and concerning the women").[84] It should be noted, however, that the text could be restored as ועל הנשי[א ("and concerning the prince"), as Kampen observed,[85] pointing to the reading ועל הנשי[א in CD 5.1. One might add that this could fit the theme of rulers, who feature later in what follows. The rulers mentioned, David and Solomon, were both ideals, but also both perpetrators of sexual wrongdoing. Thus the presence of והזנות in the following line need not require the restoration הנשי[ם. On the other hand, ועל הנשי[ם "and concerning the women" would follow well in Qimron's order after the last lines attributed to B, where these first lines probably belong, and the discussion which follows seems to make a distinction between those engaging in such behaviour (in relation to women and marriage) and the individual addressee ("you"), whom the author approaches with respect. As Schwartz notes, it is unlikely that the author would at the same time be accusing this addressee of violence, treachery and sexual immorality.[86] The following discussion proceeds on the basis of הנשי[ם

[83] So *DSSEL*. Cf. Qimron, *DJD* 10, who includes בגלל in the square brackets.

[84] On the formulae which the author uses to introduce halakhoth see Qimron, *DJD* 10, 135-37.

[85] John I. Kampen, "4QMMT and New Testament Studies," in *Reading 4QMMT: New Perspectives on Qumran Law and History* (ed. John Kampen and Moshe J. Bernstein;, SBLSym 2; Atlanta: Scholars, 1996) 129-44.

[86] Daniel R. Schwartz, "MMT, Josephus and the Pharisees," in *Reading 4QMMT: New Perspectives on Qumran Law and History* (ed. John Kampen and Moshe J. Bernstein; SBLSym 2; Atlanta: Scholars, 1996) 67-80, 77. He identifies the perpetrators of מעל and חמס as different from the addressee, the ruler addressed in *4QMMT* C, and from those administering the concerns addressed in *4QMMT* B, both of whom the author treats with respect and neither of whom he is accusing of מעל and חמס (77). These he identifies as the Hasmoneans and their Pharisaic backers who have introduced changes into temple law.

ועל "and concerning the women" as the reading, although with regard to our theme the implications are in the end similar.

From the end of C 4 we have ההחמ[ס והמעל] "[the malice or violence] and the unfaithful act". מעל "unfaithful act"[87] can refer to actions towards fellow human beings or towards God, and can be used of inappropriate sexual relations with kin, namely incest, as in CD 7.1. While ההחמס "malice, violence" is conjectured, the same word is preserved in C 5, where it stands in combination with the word for sexual wrongdoing: החמס והזנות "malice/violence and illicit sexual relations". The concern is again, as in B 39-48 and B 75-82, with הזנות, and here, as there, the word is not to be read narrowly as "prostitution", but as referring to illicit marriages/sexual relations.

This might support reading המעל "unfaithful act" in the previous line as also pertaining to sexual wrongdoing. The introduction, ועל הנשי[ם "and concerning the women", might suggest that the author is developing a different aspect of the theme. For some interpreters the author is thereby leaving what they see as the theme of B 75-82, namely, intermarriage between priests and laity. Qimron claims that the theme here is incest, though offers no further explanation.[88] The use of מעל could indicate this, given its use in that context in CD 7.1, although this is a rather slender thread on which to hang the determination of the theme of the passage. It may be an element within a broader concern, which seems also to have included a further attack on intermarriage with Gentiles.

The other words in C 4-5 beside הזנות, namely, המעל "unfaithful act" and החמס "violence", may suggest that more than sexual wrongdoing is at stake. Qimron notes that both pairs, המעל "unfaithful act" and החמס "violence", and הזנות "illicit sexual relations" and החמס "violence", commonly depict transgression in general in admonitions in the *Community Rule* and the *Damascus Document* (D),[89] but, as we have noted, מעל "unfaithful act" may well allude to sexual wrongdoing. It appears also in C 9, in what again appears as a stereotypical combination describing transgression of the law, מעל ושקר ורעה "unfaithful act and deceit and evil". Although the word could be referring to acts of treachery committed against other human beings (Israel, the temple) or to treachery against

---

He suggests that the multitude from whom the writer and his group have separated are the former Sadducean priests, reflecting a similar situation to that reported in the beginning of D (80).

87 Qimron, *DJD* 10, 85.

88 Qimron, *DJD* 10, 58.

89 Qimron, *DJD* 10, 58.

God (closer to sacrilege), and so could include a range of meanings from theft,[90] deceit, to offence against God (for disobedience to Torah), it may be focusing on illicit sexual relations. Hayes points out that מעל, for which she prefers the translation, "sacrilege", belongs to the vocabulary of Ezra where it belongs in the context of prohibiting intermarriage to foreigners (Ezra 10:2; Neh 13:27).[91]

The word, החמס "violence", is connected in content to the words which immediately follow והזנות "and illicit sexual relations" in C 5 and possibly in syntax according to Qimron's reconstruction:

[ ]. בגלל [ ]החמס והזנות אבד[ו מקצת] מקומות

[…] because of [ ] violence and illicit sexual relations [some] places were destroyed. (adapted translation)

That a deuteronomistic theology underlies this comment lies close to hand because the author will later return explicitly to its predictions of blessings and curses. The places (Qimron suggests מקצת "some of" them)[92] obviously indicate places which are valued, but, without further specification, it is difficult to know whether the author includes the temple, which one might have expected to have received separate mention, or simply other places, presumably cities or towns. The destruction of the temple lay some centuries back. It is more likely that the author is making a direct association between current or recent behaviour and recent destruction.

The accusation that this behaviour included violence may simply mean individual acts of violence.[93] If it refers to violence exercised in warfare, then we have an interesting conjunction of disapproval of military violence, disapproval of illicit sexual relations, and destruction of places suffered because of these, also in a military sense.

---

[90] So Schwartz, "MMT, Josephus and the Pharisees," 76. For this translation he refers to B. Bokser, "Ma'al and Blessings Over Food," *JBL* 100 (1981) 561-62. Schwartz points to CD 3 – 5 as a parallel and its allusions to "Eli's sons in 1 Sam 2:22 as polluting the sanctuary through iniquities with women" and points to 1 Sam 2:12-17, which highlights their abuse of temple property, as an even closer parallel to *4QMMT* (76). He notes also 1QpHab 1.6; 8.11 [?]; 9.3-9; 11.17 – 12.10 which speaks of מעל and חמס in relation to the "last priests of Jerusalem" (77).

[91] Hayes, *Gentile Impurities,* 87.

[92] Bernstein, "Employment and Interpretation of Scripture," who conjectures הרבה rather than מקצת at the end of C 5, notes the possible influence of Deut 12:2 (47), although it speaks of Israel destroying pagan shrines.

[93] If we were to understand מעל as theft, we would then have an association reflecting the prohibitions of the Decalogue: murder, theft and sexual immorality (as adultery).

The words which follow throw more light on what might be the author's concern.

6 [ואף] כתו[ב בספר מושה שלו]א תביא תועבה א[ל ביתכה כי]
7 התועבה שנואה היאה

[And it is] written [in the book of Moses] that you should [not] bring any abomination [into your home, since] 7 abomination is a hateful thing.

The allusion is to Deut 7:26

ולא תביא תועבה אל ביתך

Do not bring an abomination into your house.

Bernstein notes, that "this citation would be a fitting conclusion to the halakhic section" with the following lines understood as an epilogue.[94] The context in Deuteronomy 7 is foreign nations.[95] This coheres with the preceding context where the destroyers are doubtless Gentile nations. Within the broader context of concern with women, introduced in C 4, of disapproval of illicit sexual relations, violence and treachery or sacrilege, and of destruction through warfare, the author uses the Deuteronomy text to confirm his disapproval of bringing תועבה "abomination" into one's house. The word תועבה "abomination" appears to be related to something which might happen in such a context. It could refer to Gentile idols. Given the author's concern with women, however, it most likely refers to captive women, taken as booty in war. The translation, "Abomination is a hateful thing" (C 7), sounds tautologous, but makes good sense if it means bringing foreign wives into your house as something hateful to God.

Bernstein notes that it may well reflect the author's use of "Deut 12:31, which contains both תועבה and שנא, to explain or comment on the word תועבה in Deut 7:26".[96] It reads: כל תועבת יהוה אשר שנא "every abhorrent thing that the LORD hates". Strugnell/Qimron note that א[ל ביתכה might have been taken as referring to the temple,[97] but it makes better sense for it to refer to one's own house. As Hayes notes, in equating the idol with the idolator and thence with the forbidden woman, *4QMMT* reflects a parallel strategy to *Jubilees* which equates giving one's child to Molech to giving one's daughter to a foreigner in marriage.[98]

---

94 So Bernstein, "Employment and Interpretation of Scripture," 47.

95 Brooke, "Explicit Presentation," notes its use in association with Exod 34 in 11QT^{a}/11Q19 2.9 (76, 84). "It is especially notable that Deut 7:26 features in C 6 at the start of the hortatory material; it is used in 11QT^{a} 2:9-11, again as part of the opening redactional Deuteronomic framework" (84).

96 Bernstein, "Employment and Interpretation of Scripture," 47.

97 Qimron, *DJD* 10, 58.

98 Hayes, *Gentile Impurities,* 87.

If the author refers to taking captive Gentile women in the context of warfare as a form of entering an illicit relationship, this would stand in conflict with Deut 21:10-14. In the *Temple Scroll*, which cites this passage, we have seen that the author makes a significant addition which imposes a longer period of waiting before such a woman can be accepted into the congregation and eat the pure food (63.10-15). In *4QMMT* we would be seeing a further development which now forbids such marriages to Gentiles altogether.

In C 7-9 the author continues the theme, but now with a reference to himself and those associated with him.

7 התועבה שנואה היאה [ואתם יודעים ש]פרשנו מרוב הע[ם ומכול טמאתם]
8 [ו]מהתערב בדברים האלה ומלבוא ע[מהם]לגב אלה ואתם י[ודעים שלוא]
9 [י]מצא בידנו מעל ושקר ורעה כי על [אלה א]נחנו נותנים א[ת לבנו ואף]

7 abomination is a hateful thing. [And you know that] we have separated ourselves from the multitude of the people [and from all their impurity]

8 and from being involved with these matters and from participating with [them] in these things. And you [know that no]

9 treachery or deceit or evil can be found in our hand (i.e. in us), since for [these things] we give [... And]

The text of 4Q398 is underlined. The base text is still 4Q397 iv. The author describes himself and those with him as having separated themselves from the multitude of the people: ש]פרשנו מרוב הע[ם "we have separated ourselves from the multitude of the people".[99] The author then cites the ground for this separation. Two parallel statements are preserved in C 8. Qimron conjectures a third in C 7, [ומכול טמאתם] "[and from all their impurity]". At least the two following statements are well preserved:

[ו]מהתערב בדברים האלה

[and] from being involved sexually in these things (adapted)[100]

ומלבוא ע[מהם]לגב אלה

and from participating with [them]in these things

Thus he relates the separation to בדברים האלה "these things", which could look back on all the rulings reflected in the entire section, from *4QMMT* B (see B 4) onwards, but is better taken to refer to what immediately precedes and so to continue those concerns.[101] This warrants the translation of מהתערב in a sexual

---

[99] Cf. 1QS/1Q28 5.2 which also speaks of separation but uses the verb בדל.

[100] In his commentary Qimron, *DJD* 10, translates תערוב by "sexual intercourse" 131 n. 10.

[101] So Sharp, "Phinehan Zeal," 212; see also Schwartz, "MMT, Josephus and the Pharisees," who writes: "In this passage, the author claims that 'we' have separated from

sense "from being involved sexually", as תערובה in B 48. It certainly includes these concerns. In relation to B 75-82 we have already noted Hayes's observation, that in *4QMMT's* use of מהתערב we have probable influence from Ezra's discussion of intermarriage to foreigners.[102]

כי נשאו מבנתיהם להם ולבניהם והתערבו זרע הקדש בעמי הארצות ויד השרים והסגנים היתה במעל הזה ראשונה

For they have taken some of their daughters as wives for themselves and for their sons. Thus the holy seed has mixed itself with the peoples of the lands, and in this faithlessness the officials and leaders have led the way. (Ezra 9:2)

As noted above (p. 73), Sharp rightly draws attention also to Psalm 106 which, after celebrating Phinehas in 106:31, goes on to use the same language in 106:35 of illicit relations with the Gentiles:[103]

ויתערבו בגוים וילמדו מעשיהם

but they mingled with the nations and learned to do as they did. (Ps 106:35)

She notes that the second expression which the author brings, מלבוא ע]מהם [לגב, "from participating with them", occurs in *m. Yeb* 1.4 in relation to "intermarriage between groups with different purity standards".[104] It is very likely then that C 7 is explaining that the author and his group separated themselves from the multitude of the people over these matters. This need not exclude the other issues listed in *4QMMT* B, but the focus here is illicit sexual relations, in particular forbidden intermarriage with Gentiles, possibly with captive women.

In C 9 the word מעל "unfaithful act", reappears, in a combination describing transgression of the law, מעל ושקר ורעה "unfaithful act and deceit and evil". In the light of what has gone before it probably includes reference to sexual wrongdoing. The document continues with a personal appeal to the addressee to study Moses, the prophets and David, and in C 12 refers again to calamity as a result of disregard of Torah (as in C 6), in a citation of "Moses", derived from

---

the multitude of Israel because the latter is involved in crimes of fornication (זנות) and crimes of מעל" (76).

102 See also Jesper Høgenhaven, "Rhetorical Devices in 4QMMT," *DSD* 10 (2003) 187-204, who notes the use of the same word to describe forbidden sexual mingling in B 48 and 50.

103 Sharp, "Phinehan Zeal," 212.

104 Hayes, *Gentile Impurities,* 88.

Deut 31:29.[105] The author, then, continues with allusions to Deut 30:1-2, and the possibility of returning to God with heart and soul after experiencing the curses and blessings enunciated in Deuteronomy (C 13-17; similarly *Jub.* 1:15-16). The framework of thought is typically Deuteronomic. The addressee can learn from studying Moses, the prophets, and David that disaster follows when people neglect God's laws, especially in relation to illicit sexual relations and particularly about intermarriage to Gentiles. David and Solomon are stock examples.

According to Qimron's order these now come into view, but as he notes, the placement of C 18-24 is tentative.[106] These lines also allude to the curses and blessings of Deuteronomy,[107] referring to past history (Solomon, Jeroboam, Zedekiah), though without reference to specific sins, and also continue the motif of return. They appeal to the addressee to heed what happened to Israel's kings (C 23). C 24 concludes with reference to some who returned, whom it designates מבקשי תורה "seekers of the Torah". If we follow the placement proposed by Strugnell, then this section would come before the other material of C. It would then perform a similar function, except that part C would begin with the appeal to past history.[108] One of the major sins of Solomon was his taking foreign wives, also a theme earlier in the document. Although nothing within these particular lines makes that connection explicit, if not in the preceding material which is lost, at least both the end of B and what follows in C would surely bring it to mind.

According to Qimron's placement the final words of 4Q398 11-13 (*4QMMT* C 18-24), מבקשי תורה "seekers of the Torah", are followed by the first words of the fragment, 4Q398 14-17 ii (*4QMMT* C 25), [נשו]אי עונות "whose transgressions were [for] given." While the collocation of the fragments here and thus the statement about forgiveness is disputed,[109] what follows does, indeed, speak of David's forgiveness (cf. Sir 47:11).

---

[105] Bernstein, "Employment and Interpretation of Scripture," 48-49. On the abbreviated citations see also Brooke, "Explicit Presentation." 76-77. On the use of Deuteronomy see also Hanne von Weissenberg, "4QMMT – Towards an Understanding of the Epilogue," *RevQ* 21 (2003) 29-45.

[106] On C 18-24 Qimron, *DJD* 10, notes: "The text of these lines was taken from one of the large frgs. 11-13 of MSC. This text has no parallel in any of the other manuscripts and its placement is somewhat doubtful. In placing it here, we are following a suggestion put forward by M. Kister. The arguments in favour of this placement, as well as the objections to it raised by H. Stegemann, are set out in the Appendix." (60). See also Qimron, "Reconstructed Composite Text," 12-13.

[107] On this see Bernstein, "Employment and Interpretation of Scripture," 48-49.

[108] See the exposition of C on the basis of this reconstruction in Kratz, "Moses und die Propheten," 167-76.

[109] See García Martínez, "4QMMT in a Qumran Context," 18-19.

25 [נשו]אי עונות זכור [את] דויד שהיא איש חסדים [ו]אף
26 היא [נ]צל מצרות רבות ונסלוח לו

whose transgressions were [for] given. Think of David who was a man of righteous deeds and
who was (therefore) delivered from many troubles and was forgiven.
(C 25-26; 4Q398 14-17 ii, base text; 4Q399 i, outlined)

David's forgiveness was for his act of sexual wrongdoing. Given the theme of illicit sexual relations in the context, it is reasonable to suppose that its relevance would not be lost on the author or addressee or later hearers. Sexual wrongdoing in the form of taking foreign wives was also the main sin of Solomon beside idolatry (cf. Sir 47:19-21). This may be a better explanation of the presence of David and Solomon in the passage than that the addressee has comparable leadership responsibility, though this need not be excluded.[110] One could see the allusion to David as "a man of righteous deeds and who was (therefore) delivered from many troubles and was forgiven" as a diplomatic way of opening the issue of sexual wrongdoing engaged in on the part of the addressee, but nothing else suggests that the behaviour of the addressee is in focus. Schiffman notes the similarity to 11QT^a/11Q19 59.2-21, which also mentions a sequence of scattering of the people and their disgrace (probably because of the king's misdeeds) based on Deut 28:36-37, 48 and 64; the destruction of cities, based on Lev 26:31-32 and Jer 25:9; violation of the covenant, based on Deut 31:16 and Lev 26:15; then the people's repentance and God's response in rescuing them, following the deuteronomistic pattern.[111] In *4QMMT* the focus seems to be the deeds not of the individual being addressed, but of those whose behaviour he can prevent by what the author of *4QMMT* sees as a correct interpretation and application of Torah. This is, indeed, the focus of C 26-30.

We have (indeed) sent you
27 some of the precepts (works) of the Torah according to our decision, for your welfare and the welfare of your people
(מקצת מעשי התורה שחשבנו לטוב לך ולעמך). For we have seen (that)
28 you have wisdom and knowledge of the Torah. Consider all these things and ask Him that He strengthen

---

[110] Fraade, "To Whom it May Concern," challenges those who claim that the mention of the kings warrants "concluding that the addressee was himself a leader of royal (or near royal) status" (516), though without making the connection I propose here.

[111] Schiffman, "Place of 4QMMT," 96. See also the discussion in Steven D. Fraade, "Rhetoric and Hermeneutics in Miqsat Ma'ase Ha-Torah (4QMMT): The Case of the Blessings and Curses," *DSD* 10 (2003) 150-61, who notes the importance of the covenant festival at Qumran and its ritual of blessing and cursing, reflected in the *Temple Scroll*, the *Community Rule* and the *War Scroll*; and Kratz, "Moses und die Propheten," 169-73.

29 your will and remove from you the plans of evil and the device of Belial
30 so that you may rejoice at the end of time, finding that some of our practices (מקצת דברינו) are correct.
(C 26-30; 4Q398 14-17 ii.2b-6 base text; 4Q399 i.10b – ii.4a outlined)

The words, מקצת מעשי התורה, "some of the deeds/works/observances of the Law", serve appropriately as a designation of the document as a whole in the sense that it presents legal teachings about proper observance and introduced its concerns in similar terms: אלה מקצת דברינו "these are some of our rulings" (B 1; cf. C 30 מקצת דברינו).[112]

The document concludes with the words,

ונחשבה לך לצדקה בעשותך הישר והטוב לפנו לטוב לך ולישראל

And this will be counted as a virtuous deed of yours, since you will be doing what is righteous and good in His eyes, for your own welfare and
for the welfare of Israel.
(C 31-32; 4Q398 14-17 ii.7-8, base text; 4Q399 ii.4b-5, outlined)

They echo C 27 (לטוב לך ולעמך "for your welfare and the welfare of your people"), but more significantly, and typically, they conclude the exhortation with an allusion to scripture. While the words, ונחשבה לך לצדקה lit. "will be counted for you as righteousness", might be an allusion to Abraham's faith in Gen 15:6 (והאמן ביהוה ויחשבה לו צדקה "Abraham believed God and it was counted for

[112] On the significance of this passage for understanding Galatians 2, which also speaks of separation and being reckoned righteous on the basis of observing ἔργα νόμου "works of the Law", see James D. G. Dunn and James H. Charlesworth, "Qumran's *Some Works of Torah* (4Q394-399 [4QMMT]) and Paul's Galatians," in *The Bible and the Dead Sea Scrolls: The Princeton Symposium on the Dead Sea Scrolls: Volume 3: The Scrolls and Christian Origins* (ed. James H. Charlesworth; Waco, Tex.: Baylor University Press, 2006) 187-201; and earlier James D. G. Dunn, "4QMMT and Galatians," *NTS* 43 (1997) 147-53; Michael Bachmann, "4QMMT und Galaterbrief, מעשי התורה und ΕΡΓΑ ΝΟΜΟΥ," *ZNW* 89 (1998) 91-113; Martin G. Abegg, "4QMMT C 27, 31 and 'Works Righteousness'," *DSD* 6/2 (1999) 139-47; Martin G. Abegg, "4QMMT, Paul, and 'Works of the Law'," in *The Bible at Qumran: Text, Shape, and Interpretation* (ed. Peter W. Flint; Studies in the Dead Sea Scrolls and Related Literature; Grand Rapids: Eerdmans, 2001) 203-16; James D. G. Dunn, "Noch einmal 'Works of the Law'; the Dialogue Continues," in *Fair Play: Diversity and Conflicts in Early Christianity* (ed. Ismo Dunderberg, Christopher Tuckett, and Kari Syreeni; Leiden: Brill, 2002) 273-90.

him as righteousness"),[113] Sharp argues that the allusion is more likely to be to Phinehas in Ps 106:31 (ותחשב לו לצדקה ודר עד יולם "And it was counted for him as righteousness and his generation is forever").[114] She points out that the motif of Abraham would have no specific link with the context, either in part C or in the legal section B, where the issue of circumcision, so typically associated with Abraham and his faith, is entirely missing. An allusion to Phinehas' deed in Num 25:1-13 where he slays those who have married foreign wives is of immediate relevance for what precedes, especially if we see the author alluding to his last issue of concern, namely, "women" in C4, which, with the citation of Deut 7:26, best reflects concerns with foreign wives. In modification of Sharp's position Hayes plausibly suggests that the allusion might also include Abraham, given that *Jubilees* had connected the two, in a "remaking of Abraham along Phinehan lines" as a model separatist.[115]

The allusion to Phinehas and probably also to Abraham in the context of separateness from Gentiles makes excellence sense in the context of the exhortation in C 1-32, where, as we have seen, the author places major emphasis on the issue of intermarriage to Gentiles and cites it as a ground for him and his associates separating from the people over whom the addressee has, according to *4QMMT*, significant sway and influence. The author shows himself as standing in a tradition reaching through *Jubilees*, *Aramaic Levi Document*, Malachi, Ezra, Psalm 106 and Numbers, which was concerned with intermarriage to Gentiles.

Sharp goes further by suggesting that C 31-32 might well echo C 4-5, for which she offers an alternative reconstruction as follows,[116]

4 ועל הנשי]ם הנכריות החמ[ס והמעל] [

5 כי באלה]ים(ינו or)

4 And concerning the [foreign] women [… … the violence] and the treachery
5 for against Go[d (or: [our] Go[d).

She draws attention to the language of Ezra 10:2 and Neh 13:27, which she claims form the background both for the presence of מעל, which she would then take as treachery against God, and of הנכריות "foreign", which she conjectures as following ועל הנשי]ם, "and concerning women", and for באלה]ים "against God" (or באלה]ינו "against our God"), which becomes a direct reference to God.

[113] Bernstein, Employment and Interpretation of Scripture," mentions both Gen 15:6 and Ps 106:31, while apparently preferring the former (35-36). He notes the allusion to Deut 6:24-25 in the words, הישר והטוב "what is righteous and good"(35).

[114] Sharp, "Phinehan Zeal," 209-12.

[115] Hayes, *Gentile Impurities,* 88.

[116] Sharp, "Phinehan Zeal," 211.

אנחנו מעלנו באלהינו ונשיב נשים נכריות

we have acted treacherously against our God by marrying foreign women. (Ezra 10:2)

למעל באלהינו להשיב נשים נכריות

act treacherously against our God by marrying foreign women. (Neh 13:27)

She then suggests that the two alleged references to God in C 5 and C 31 (reading לפנו "before him" in C 31 and מלפנו "from before him" in C 28 as referring to God) function as an *inclusio*.[117] This would make good sense especially if with the allusion to Phinehas in the latter the common theme of concern with intermarriage also links them. A possible weakness in the conjecture is the apparent avoidance of the word, God, elsewhere in what survives of the document.[118]

Sharp also offers an interpretation of the halakhic section which she sees as concerned with intermarriage throughout. Thus she argues that the analogous use of mixing halakoth to address intermarriage in B 75-82 justifies looking for two levels of meaning throughout the halakoth section. She notes four passages which stand out from the rest because they "offer extrapolatory ideological characterizations in theologically freighted language that is quite unlike the general tenor of Section B"[119] (B 48-49; 70; 75-76; and 79). In addition she notes the expositions of the camp in B 29-31 and B 59-62 as having a different tone; they "provide the necessary parameters for the definition and justification of the sectarians' halakhic interpretations concerning holy space".[120] Of the four passages, B 48-49, B 75-76 and 79 are concerned with intermarriage, whereas B 70 is concerned with lepers. It "echoes Num. 15:30 in what is by far the sternest indictment of the entire document".[121] She suggests that "it is curious that this highly inflammatory polemical statement follows a passage concerning the appropriate length of time for a leper to be considered impure (B 64-68)", suggesting that its use here "is meant to flag a more substantive issue of concern

[117] Sharp, "Phinehan Zeal," 211.

[118] Fraade, "To Whom it May Concern," notes that "it appears that *4QMMT* avoids explicit reference to "God" (אל) (520 n. 47), which might count against Sharp's reconstruction here. He notes, however, "the use of third person singular pronominal suffixes referring to God, but without an explicit antecedent: C 15, C 28, C 31" (523 n. 59), but explains this within a theory that the writing is to be understood as a "'low-level' intramural pedagogical instrument for the teaching of candidates and/or neophytes to the community" (523). But here he is referring to the use of the document at the stage when the copies were in use, though in his view it was also its original purpose.

[119] Sharp, "Phinehan Zeal," 213.

[120] Sharp, "Phinehan Zeal," 214.

[121] Sharp, "Phinehan Zeal," 214.

without stating it directly".[122] That issue, she proposes, concerns the indictment of mixed marriages as contravening laws of purity and the failure of the priests to take responsibility for its enforcement.

Sharp notes that the first three halakhoth concern Gentiles. Here she sees the analogy between Gentile sacrifices and illicit sexual relations, כמי שזנת אליו "like (a woman) who whored with him" (B 9), as flagging the underlying issue in a direct way.[123] She sees the concerns with priestly failure in guarding people from sin (B 11-13; 25-27) as directly related to their failure by example in B 79 in improper sexual mixing. She thus sees the halakhoth concerning the cereal offering, the red heifer, and animal bones as functioning to illustrate priestly failure, though they remain issues in their own right.[124] She suggests that the halakhoth about the deaf and blind probably function at two levels, both literal, and metaphorical of "Jews who do not see or understand the error of their ways or of Gentiles themselves as inherently incapable of understanding the Law and so unfit for the congregation".[125] Similarly she interprets the halakhoth about liquids and about dogs as also containing a metaphorical allusion to sexual mixing with Gentiles (noting the parallel use in Mark 7:24-30). Thus about the halakhic material in *4QMMT* B, she argues, "What is determinative in this schema is that the selection of each halakha, whether on grounds of metaphorical connotation, analogical aptness, or simple illustrative power, has been made towards the end of illustrating a larger principle" and that that principle matches the concern of *4QMMT* C, namely intermarriage with Gentiles, which she then interprets in the context of Hellenisation.[126]

---

[122] Sharp, "Phinehan Zeal," 214, 216.

[123] Sharp, "Phinehan Zeal," 218.

[124] Sharp, "Phinehan Zeal," 218-19.

[125] Sharp, "Phinehan Zeal," 219.

[126] Sharp, "Phinehan Zeal," 220. Kenneth Atkinson, "4QMMT and Psalm of Solomon 8: Two Anti-Sadducean Documents," *Qumran Chronicle* 11 (2003) 57-77, makes the claim that "the purity regulations in 4QMMT … are all bracketed by statements that deal with illicit marriages among some priests" and comments that besides these "the other purity laws, mentioned in 4QMMT, which primarily deal with illicit combinations of items, are undoubtedly intended to be understood in the broader context of illegal priestly marriages" (69). These claims apply at most to *4QMMT* B 75-82, hardly to *4QMMT* as a whole. Though they recall Sharp's thesis, to which Atkinson refers (70 n. 34), he clearly reads the primary issue quite differently, namely, as intermarriage between priests and laity and even sees the allusion to Phinehas as just an illustration of this narrower concern (70-71), which he finds supported by *4QHalakhah A*/4Q251 17 7. His main purpose is to draw attention to the similarities between *4QMMT's* concerns and those of the later *Pss. Sol.* 8:8-13, listing fornication and theft from the temple among priests, suggesting both texts attack Sadducean priests and urge people to abandon the temple community (70-72, 74). It is not clear that *4QMMT* is urging the latter.

Sharp's metaphorical interpretation of individual halakhoth in relation to addressing concern with intermarriage to foreigners is speculative and depends on arguments from silence. On the basis of its role in Section C and the strength of the two halakhoth in *4QMMT* B which directly address this issue, there is a strong case at least for suspecting it may play a role in the other halakhic treatments, not least, in the concern with the failure of priests. But there is too little evidence from within the document itself that the author is using the halakhoth in the way Sharp suggests, despite the use of the analogy of mixing in B 75-82.[127] The assumption that the author is addressing the impact of Hellenisation is also speculative and would not, for instance, cohere with an interpretation that saw in *4QMMT* C the issue of captive foreign wives, though that, too, is not secure.

Returning to the concern with women, introduced in C 4, we can draw together aspects of the issue which survive in the text, at least into a question if not a solution. The issue is some form of illicit sexual relations (probably also alluded to as inappropriate sexual relations, using the word, מעל), but it is associated with violence and appears to be tolerated by priestly authorities who oversee the application of Torah, to a sufficient level to warrant the author and his group separating themselves. In addition, the community has suffered because of the destruction of some of its places, which the author interprets as signs of divine punishment for disregard of what he sees as an appropriate understanding of divine law. The allusion to bringing abomination into one's house appears directly related to acquiring foreign wives. It is not clear, however, how this fits together with violence on the part of the evil doers and the destruction of their places. Then one has to fit the addressee into the picture as well.

The combination of these factors would appear to reflect a situation where foreign wives have been taken, in a context which includes violence being done by some and being done to the community. That could include Gentile wives being taken as booty. This would fit a context of both military conquest and some defeat. To go beyond these observations is precarious. Conquest of Gentile lands is a feature of the reign of a number of the Hasmoneans, from Judas to Janneus. To a lesser extent the same could be said to be true of the sufferings of war, although this is more dramatic during the earlier period. It would certainly cohere with a dating of the document in the mid-second century BCE and the suggestions that the recipient might be Jonathan.[128] In such a context the reference to violence

---

[127] See the critical evaluation in Høgenhaven, "Rhetorical Devices," 195-97.

[128] For the view that the author addresses Jonathan at an early stage of his rule as part of a group that separated not on the basis of legal dispute but because of Hellenism, and that *4QMMT* is "The Law and the Torah" sent according to 4QpPsa (4Q171 1-10 iv.9) by the Teacher of Righteousness to the Wicked Priest, see Hanan Eshel, "4QMMT and the History of the Hasmonean Period," in *Reading 4QMMT: New Perspectives on Qumran Law and History* (ed. John Kampen and Moshe J. Bernstein; SBLSym 2; Atlanta: Scholars, 1996)

might intimate opposition to military warfare and so reflect disassociation from the Maccabean solution espoused by the Hasidim and *Jub.* 50:12 (cf. *Apoc. Mos.* 9:4-7). Whatever may have been the historical setting, the concern "about women" appears most likely to have been with Gentile wives, and may refer to captive foreign wives.[129]

5 Conclusion

4QMMT has come down to us in fragmentary form, which makes reconstruction both of its missing text and of its context difficult. In B 39-49 it addresses the issue of intermarriage to Gentiles, represented by its use of Deut 23:2-4, and by the pre-eminence given to Ammonites and Moabites, although it also lists other forbidden partners. It certainly concerns Israelite men taking foreign wives, but also assumes prohibition of men giving their daughters to Gentile husbands. While it interprets the prohibition of such people entering the congregation as a reference to entry by marriage, it appears also to have understood it as prohibiting their entry into the temple.

In B 75-82 we concluded that, here, too the most likely concern is with intermarriage to Gentiles, but here the theme is developed on the basis of Israel as holy seed, and the priesthood as even more holy, and that intermarriage is defiling for the holy seed of Israel, and when engaged in by priests, defiling of their especially holy seed. Here the author employs both the Ezra traditions of holy seed in a manner reminiscent of *Jubilees*, and also makes use of forbidden mixing among animal species, fibres in garments and crops in a field as analogies to support the argument. We saw this as more likely than that the author is concerned here with intermarriage between priests and the people.

A third time the author returns to the theme in the concluding exhortation. This is not only so in the early lines, at least from C 4 on, which in typical fashion identifies the theme as "concerning women", but also finds an echo in the concluding statement with its allusion to Phinehas (and perhaps also Abraham), by implication appealing to the addressee to prosecute issues of intermarriage with

---

53-65. See also Annette Steudel, "4Q448 – The Lost Beginning of MMT?" in *From 4QMMT to Resurrection: Mélanges qumraniens en homage à Émile Puech* (ed. Florentino García Martínez, Annette Steudel, and Eibert Tigchelaar; STDJ 61; Leiden: Brill, 2006) 247-63, who, noting common linguistic features between our document and 4Q448, contemplates whether the latter might have belonged to its opening.

[129] WAC set as their heading for C 4 "Ban on polygamous priestly marriages (?) (Deut. 17:17; 21:15-16)" (460), but the first text alludes to the rule of the king and the second to rules about children in a polygamous marriage and there are no verbal links.

the same strictness. The early treatment sets the issue in the context of treachery, violence, and destruction of warfare, and seems most likely to place intermarriage to Gentile women in that context. Acquiring a Gentile wife is to bring an abomination into one's house. The context of war may indicate that some of this has been happening in the taking of captive wives, in which case the author has used prohibition of Gentile marriage to override the provision for taking Gentile wives from the booty of war, taking the increased limitation evident in the *Temple Scroll* on the issue a major step further by prohibiting it altogether.

The threefold treatment of the prohibition of intermarriage warrants the conclusion that it was a major concern. It belonged within an overall stance evident in the halakhoth of section B, which is characterised by a strong emphasis on purity, both in relation to the temple and in relation to Jerusalem, which it identifies with the wilderness "camp", as does the author of the *Temple Scroll*. The boundaries relate both to places and to people, and to their relation to one another. As well as forbidding the entrance of certain groups, including Gentiles, into the temple, the author upholds a clear demarcation between holy Israel and the unholy, including Gentiles especially. This clear distinction explains how the author could liken Gentiles sacrificing, to people engaging in illicit sexual relations. There is no licit relationship or covenant between Gentiles and Israel's God. From this follows also that there can be no intermarriage.

Within the range of rulings relating to sexual issues it is interesting that only intermarriage with Gentiles features. We are not convinced that the author addresses intermarriage between priests and people, nor that he addresses incest, as has been suggested. Missing, too, is any reference to homosexual behaviours of various kinds (which the author might have used his analogy of mixing to address), bestiality, nakedness, intercourse during menstruation or pregnancy, purification after childbirth, masturbation, adultery, divorce, polygamy, or lustful attitudes or actions in general.

CHAPTER THREE

Attitudes towards Sexuality in the *Damascus Document*

The document, designated the *Damascus Document* (D), first came to light in modern times through the discovery of two medieval Hebrew manuscripts in 1896-1897 in the *genizah* of a Karaite synagogue in Cairo and was published in 1910 by Solomon Schechter.[1] Manuscript A contains 16 pages, Manuscript B, 2 pages, with substantial overlap, but some differences. The suspicion that they reflected a much earlier work was confirmed with the recovery of fragments of 8 copies in Cave 4 at Qumran (4QD^{a-g}/4Q266-272 and 4QpapD^{h}/4Q273) and a small number of fragments in Caves 5 (5QD/5Q12) and 6 (6QD/6Q15), the earliest of which, 4QD^{a}/4Q266, is dated on palaeographical grounds to the first half or middle of the first century BCE.[2] These have enhanced confidence in the reliability of the Cairo documents, with which the 326 lines of parallel material in the Qumran manuscripts exhibit less than thirty significant variants.[3]

In her review of research Charlotte Hempel proposes that D was composed probably towards the end of the second century BCE.[4] The situation is

[1] Solomon Schechter, *Documents of Jewish Sectaries* (Cambridge: Cambridge University Press, 1910).

[2] The Hebrew texts which forms the basis of the following discussion are based on *DSSEL*. For rendering the Hebrew into English I have sometimes sought to offer as close a translation as possible and indicate it with an asterisk, especially where the meaning depends on a particular interpretation of the Hebrew. In most cases I use the translations of Vermes (V) and *DSSSE* for CD, and *DSSEL* for QD, unless otherwise indicated.

[3] So Joseph M. Baumgarten, *DJD* 18, 6.

[4] Charlotte Hempel, *The Damascus Texts* (Companion to the Qumran Scrolls 1; Sheffield: Sheffield Academic Press, 2000) 23.

complicated by the fact that different recensions of the document later existed, as the Cairo manuscripts but also the surviving Qumran texts show,[5] and that the document, itself, may preserve older material, some of which could reach as far back as the third century BCE. There have been a number of attempts to identify what might have belonged to an original *Damascus Document*. Murphy-O'Connor, for instance, proposed the hypothesis that CD 2.14 – 6.1 was originally an Essene missionary document designed by returnees from Babylon to Palestine in the Maccabean period to make converts[6] and Philip Davies argues that the original document consisting of CD 1.1 – 7.9; 20.27b-34; and 9 – 16, belonged to the same religious context as *Jubilees* and *1 Enoch*.[7] Most recently Wacholder has argued that the document has a single author and, since it lacks any reference to the Antiochan persecution, is to be seen as "evidently going back to the third century B. C. E.".[8] While not denying that it has been redacted by the community at Qumran, we will operate on the assumption that it reflects a time early in the movement from which the sect at Qumran emerged.[9] It is, in any case, testimony to attitudes not only of its authors, but presumably also of those who treasured and copied it.

---

[5] See Hempel, *Damascus Texts*, 23-24, 77-79.

[6] Jerome Murphy-O'Connor, "An Essene Missionary Document? CD II,14-VI,1," *RB* 77 (1970) 201-29.

[7] Philip R. Davies, *The Damascus Covenant: An Interpretation of the "Damascus Document"* (JSOTSup 25; Sheffield: JSOT Press, 1983) 198, 203.

[8] Wacholder, *New Damascus Document*, 3. He also argues that the author is dependent on the books of *Enoch* and *Jubilees* and was, in turn, used as a source by the author of the *Community Rule* and the *Pesharim* (4). But this would require a much earlier dating of *Jubilees* than is generally supported by recent research.

[9] For a contrary view see Eyal Regev, "The 'Yahad' and the 'Damascus Covenant': Structure, Organization, and Relationship," *RevQ* 21/2 (2003b) 233-62, who on the basis of a comparison of the *Community Rule* and D concludes that the evidence of organisational structure, the relation of their penal codes and palaeographic dating point to the two works reflecting two different organisations, with D showing signs of being a later development, which "adopted certain precepts and concepts from S and revised them extensively", rather than the reverse. The reverse would suppose redactional revision in the light of the *Community Rule*, but leave unexplained why much that is central, such as the role of the assembly, is ignored (261-62). The fact that D's penal code still refers to sleeping or lying in the assembly and assumes communal meals, reflects use of the *Community Rule* or its sources (260-61). He suggests that some who had been members of the *Community Rule* community developed their separate organisation, which became the complex structure now reflected in D. He notes, however, that his proposal faces the difficulty of explaining the presence of so many copies of D at what he sees as the centre of the *Community Rule* community (262).

The material which has survived does not enable us to reconstruct the document as a whole. It does, however, enable us to recognise two major sections in the document:

I The Admonition
(CD 1.1 – 8.21; 20.1b-34; preceded by the fragmentary material preserved in 4QD^{a,b,c}/4Q266-268 and followed, similarly, by material in 4QD^{e}/4QD270; 6QD/6Q15)
with a bridging paragraph (4QD^{a}/4Q266 5 i.1-19 and 4QD^{b}/4Q267 5 ii.1-7) to:

II The Laws and Community Regulations
(CD 15.1 – 16.20; 9.1 – 14.22, preceded by material in 4QD$^{a, b, d, e, f, h}$/4Q266-267, 269-271, 273 and followed by material in 4QD$^{a, e}$/4Q266, 270).[10]

In what follows, material from CD will be identified only by columns and lines, but material from Qumran documents will also contain their document designation. The focus of our study is on matters pertaining to sexuality in the document. We shall consider the two sections of the document in sequence.

1 The Admonition

The Admonition proceeds by recounting the responses in history of Israel and people within Israel to God and God's commandments and by using them as a basis to urge obedience and right observance. That history, as retold by the author, encompasses a wide range, from the account of the Watchers in Genesis 6 to recent history in the time of the author. The author identifies himself with a community which is faithful and obedient, so that, in part, his writing serves to reassure its members by retelling their history as well as to exhort them to be faithful. As Albert Baumgarten puts it, "at least part of the purpose of the Damascus Document was to reassure its group of faithful that their minority situation was not unique; although truth had been trampled down from time immemorial, its ultimate victory was inevitable".[11]

That community traces its origins to a "remnant" (1.4; 2.11-13) whose recent history includes an initial act of repentance (1.8-9; 3.17 – 4.12); the formation of a covenant (3.12-16); some twenty years of groping existence before the emergence

---

[10] I shall follow the reconstruction of sequence set out in Hempel, *Damascus Texts*, based on the findings of current research (26-43).

[11] Albert I. Baumgarten, "The Perception of the Past in the Damascus Document," in *The Damascus Document: A Centennial of Discovery: Proceedings of the Third International Symposium of the Orion Center for the Study of the Dead Sea Scrolls and Associated Literature, 4-8 February 1998* (ed. Joseph M. Baumgarten, Esther G. Chazon, and Avital Pinnick; STDJ 34; Leiden: Brill, 2000) 1-15, 9.

of the leader, the Teacher of Righteousness, the interpreter of the law (1.9-11); the latter's death; and a subsequent period identified as forty years during which the author writes.[12] The "remnant" differentiates itself both from unrepentant Israel, whose temple was destroyed and who were taken into exile (1.3-4; 3.17-21), and from a group with whom it is in conflict, called among other things, "the seekers of smooth things" (1.12 – 2.1; 4.19), used later in 4QpNah/4Q169 of the Pharisees (3-4 i.2, 7; ii.2, 4; iii.3, 7; see also 1QH[a] x.15, 32; xii.10; 4QpIsa[c]/4Q163 23 ii.10). The latter group also has its own teacher, "the Liar" (1QpHab 2.1-2; 5.11; see also 20.15). There appear also to be some who have been part of their movement and have since left (8.1-2, 16).[13]

The measure of appropriate behaviour is not just a matter of loyalty to the author's group, but, in his eyes, of obedience to God's law and so faithfulness to the special covenant which governs that relationship. The section on Law gives specific instruction about what such faithful observance entails and also includes rules for life organised in special communities. The Admonition identifies specific instances which indicate what the author sees as acts of disregard for God's commands and which in part form the basis for their demarcation from other groups and from the people as a whole. It is within this context that we find matters pertaining to sexuality, which were clearly a concern.

The Admonition returns to the story of the community and its origins four times. In 1.1 – 2.1 the account begins with the destruction of the temple and the exile, identifies the community's beginning, reports its twenty-year wait before the Teacher of Righteousness (מורה צדק 1.11), and identifies the opposition group with their leader, the spouter of lies. A second account comes within 2.1-13, but its chief focus is to explain obedience and disobedience as something predetermined by God. The third account, 2.14 – 4.12a, begins with the fall of the Watchers and their offspring, following this with a brief run through history up to the exile, and an account of the remnant, their repentance, and their covenant with God.

All three sections begin with the words, "Now listen". The third section can also be understood as continuing in 4.12b – 5.19, since this section specifies areas over which the author and his community are in conflict with the other group and its leader, here designated as צו ("the precept" V). A significant part of this

[12] Cf. Wacholder, *New Damascus Document*, who sees the opening section as referring not to the past, but to the future, in that sense, entailing future predictions of considerable detail, including a future, new Damascus (141-52).

[13] On the use of the term, "seekers of smooth things" and its variants, including its probable association with those who gave emphasis to oral tradition, see James C. VanderKam, "Those Who Look for Smooth Things, Pharisees, and Oral Law," in *Emanuel: Studies in Hebrew Bible, Septuagint, and Dead Sea Scrolls in Honor of Emanuel Tov* (ed. Shalom M. Paul, Robert A. Kraft, Lawrence H. Schiffman, and Weston W. Fields; SVT 94; Leiden: Brill, 2003) 465-77.

section pertains to sexuality. A fourth account of the community's story (5.20 – 6.11a) begins directly with reference to "those who shifted the boundary and make Israel stray" (*DSSSE*) and the separation of the author's community under its leader, here designated as the Interpreter of the Law.

It is followed in 6.11b – 8.21b; 19 – 20 by specific instructions for the community, which include prohibiting participation in the temple or, perhaps, prohibiting inappropriate participation, warnings about riches, purity, sabbath and festival observance and sexual immorality, instruction for married people in camps, and severe warnings about those who abandon the community. 4QD^{e}/4Q270 and 6QD/6Q15 appear to offer further material belonging to the Admonition and include a list of acts of wrongdoing. Thus at a number of points the author enunciates his specific concerns and these include matters pertaining to sexuality. We shall examine each section in turn before drawing together the findings.

The Beginning 4QD^{a}/4Q266 1a-b 5a-25; 1 c-f?; 2 i.1-6a 4QD^{b}/4Q267 1 2-8; 4QD^{c}/4Q268 1 1-8

4QD^{a}/4Q267 contained the beginning of the document, but the opening words have not survived. The fragmentary text reflects issues which feature later in the document: "time of visitation"; "destruction"; "those who move the boundary"; "slander against the law"; "delaying festivals"; "moment of wrath for a nation that does not know him"; "precepts"; "perfect path"; "heard profound things"; "understood everything that happens before it comes upon them". The main parties are already recognisable: unfaithful Israel, the group with false interpretation of the Law, the author's group, and God who determines destiny. Nothing is preserved pertaining to sexuality.

The First Account CD 1.1 – 2.1; 4QD^{a}/4Q266 2 i.6b-25; 4QD^{c}/4Q268 1 9-17

The first of three sections beginning with "Listen" (echoing Prov 7:24), recalls Hosea in announcing God's dispute (ריב) with all flesh (Hos 4:1; cf. also Jer 25:31). While it tells the story of the community, it begins by telling the story of God, who "hid his face, … delivered them up, … remembering the covenant, … left a remnant, … caused a plant root to spring from Israel and Aaron" (V) (1.3-8). God's story responds to the story of "all flesh", narrowed then to Israel and further to a remnant in Israel. God's complaint is that they "were unfaithful and forsook him" (1.3), later described as "iniquity" (1.8). The community's story is set in contrast to "the congregation of traitors" (1.12), who "departed from the path" like a stubborn heifer (1.13-14). Their wrongdoing includes lying, leading Israel astray, "laying low the everlasting heights, abolishing the ways of righteousness and removing the boundary with which the forefathers had marked their inheritance" (V) (1.15-16). The motif of removing boundaries recurs throughout the Admonition and functions symbolically to refer to alteration of the limits set by Torah. This focus continues in 1.18-19, which claim that they

> sought smooth things and preferred illusions, and they watched for breaks and chose the fair neck (ויבחרו בטוב הצואר); and they justified the wicked and condemned the just, and they transgressed the Covenant and violated the Precept. (V)

and opposed the just and persecuted those who walked rightly, an allusion to the author's community.

Within these formal descriptions of the opponents' misinterpretation of Torah and its impact, there is really only one clue to the content of the false interpretation: ויבחרו בטוב הצואר "and they chose the fair neck" (V) (1.19). The only other occurrence of טוב הצואר comes in Hos 10:11.

> ואפרים עגלה מלמדה אהבתי לדוש ואני עברתי על טוב צוארה ארכיב
> אפרים יחרוש יהודה ישדד לו יעקב
>
> Ephraim was a trained heifer that loved to thresh, and I spared her fair neck; but I will make Ephraim break the ground; Judah must plow; Jacob must harrow for himself.

The link is confirmed by the reference to Ephraim as a "heifer", though for the latter CD 1.13 uses a different word, פרה, drawn from Hos 4:16, rather than עגלה. Campbell suggests that "Hos 10:12 is the source for מורה צדק [teacher of righteousness] in CD 1:11",[14] and that Hosea 9 – 11 "forms a wider background to this borrowing of scriptural language".[15] In the light of the following versions of the community's story in D, where sexual wrongdoing is one of the accusations made about the opponents, choosing the fair neck here is probably best taken as an allusion to sexual wrongdoing.[16] The mention of only this form of wrongdoing here reflects its importance for the author in defining the conflict. The expression, choosing the fair neck, may appear also in the list of rebukes against members of

---

[14] Jonathan G. Campbell, *The Use of Scripture in the Damascus Document 1-8, 19-20* (BZAW 228; Berlin and New York: de Gruyter, 1995) 62.

[15] Campbell, *Use of Scripture*, 62.

[16] Cf. Ginzberg, *Unknown Jewish Sect*, who argues that the passage should be translated, "and they wished for a stout neck", alluding to slavery to earthly pleasures, but focuses on gluttony (7). Campbell, *Use of Scripture*, writes: "its precise exegetical significance is not clear" (62 n. 25); similarly, Michael A. Knibb, *The Qumran Community* (Cambridge Commentaries on Writings of the Jewish and Christian World 200 BC to AD 200; v. 2; Cambridge: Cambridge University Press, 1987) 24.

the *Yahad* in 4QRebukes Reported by the Overseer/4Q477, where Eshel[17] reconstructs:

ואת חנניה בן שמ[עון הוכיהו]
10[אשר הואה וג]ם אוהב טובן הצואר]

And Hananiah son of Šim[ʿon was rebuked]
10 [because he al]so he chooses the fair[neck. (2 ii.9-10)

The parallel to Hosea and CD is insecure, since 4Q477 uses not a form of בחר ("to choose"), despite Eshel's translation, but אהב "to love", and the only shared word is the common, טוב "fair, good", but it is certainly possible.

The Second Account CD 2.1-13; 4QD^a/4Q266 2 ii.1-13a

This brief account emphasises that those who go astray are people whom God has not chosen, whereas those who turn to him are his chosen.[18] God knows and determines destiny. In this respect it is interesting that in speaking of the chosen remnant, the author declares that God's purpose is למלא פני תבל מזרעם "that the face of the earth might be filled with their seed" (V) (2.11-12; cf. also 1QS/1Q28 4.7). This assumes a community consisting of families and within this, sexual relations in the context of procreation. It would not make sense in a community of celibate people.

The Third Account
CD 2.14 – 5.19; 4QD^a/4Q266 2 ii.14-23; iii.5, 19-20; 3 i.1-7; ii.1-7a; 4QD^b/4Q267 2 1-3; 4QD^e/4Q270 1 i.1-3; 1 ii a-b; 6QD/6Q15 1 1-3; 2 1-2; 3 1-2

The third account begins with a warning to the hearers which specifies particular kinds of wrongdoing. It corresponds closely to what Jerome Murphy-O'Connor proposed was an "Essene missionary document".[19]

---

[17] Esther Eshel, *DJD* 36, 481.

[18] On the parallels with the treatise of the Two Spirits, which he sees as a source influencing the account here, see Armin Lange, *Weisheit und Prädestination: Weisheitliche Urordnung und Prädestination in den Textfunden von Qumran* (STDJ 18; Leiden: Brill, 1995) 242. He assumes dependence also on the *Community Rule* (1QS 10.21) and the *Thanksgiving Hymns* (1QH^a ix.9) and so concludes that CD must have been composed by the Qumran community (243).

[19] Murphy-O'Connor, "Essene Missionary Document?" 201-29.

History as a Story of Failure because of Sexual Wrongdoing 2.14 – 3.12

The warning includes the words:

ולא לחור במחשבות יצר אשמה וע(י)ני זנות

> and not to follow after the thoughts of a guilty inclination and eyes of sexual wrongdoing.* (2.16)

As Campbell notes,[20] the language reflects the influence of the commandment in Numbers about tassels:

והיה לכם לציצת וראיתם אתו וזכרתם את כל מצות יהוה ועשיתם אתם
ולא תתרו אחרי לבבכם ואחרי עיניכם אשר אתם זנים אחריהם

> You have the fringe so that, when you see it, you will remember all the commandments of the LORD and do them, and not follow the lust of your own heart and your own eyes (lit. follow/seek out your hearts and your eyes, that you might lust after them*). (Num 15:39)

Numbers 13-15 and Numbers 16 both bring accounts of rebellion, and play a significant role in D, Num 14:23 informing the language of CD 1.2.[21] Num 15:39 appears to use **זנים** "sexually lusting" in a metaphorical sense. Here in D, however, **זנות** is being taken in a literal sense as a reference to sexual wrongdoing. The word is not narrowed to prostitution, but includes all illicit sexual relations, as already its first example, the deed of the Watchers illustrates.[22] With the reference to "eyes", the author is perhaps also making a link with the opening Admonition of this section, "Hear now my sons and I will uncover your eyes" (V) (2.14).[23]

It is significant that sexual wrongdoing features again here, after being the only concrete sin apparently alluded to thus far in the document. The motif of lustful eyes has a long tradition both before and after its occurrence in this text.[24] It is also important to note the reference to **יצר אשמה** "guilty inclination". This apparently refers to an inclination which leads to sin and thus to guilt. It is thus closely associated here with "lustful eyes", though on its own it usually refers to

[20] Campbell, *Use of Scripture*, 73.

[21] Campbell, *Use of Scripture*, 73. See also Hermann Lichtenberger, *Studien zum Menschenbild in Texten der Qumrangemeinde* (SUNT 15; Göttingen: Vandenhoeck und Ruprecht, 1980) 150 n. 7.

[22] On the range of meaning of **זנות** see p. 57 n. 20 and pp. 361-62.

[23] So also Wassen, *Women*, 176.

[24] On lustful eyes see *Jub.* 20:4; 11QT[a]/11Q19 59.13-14; 1QS/1Q28 1.6; 5.4-5; 1QpHab 5.7; Sir 9:8; 26:21; 41:20-21; Sus 6-8; *T. Reub.* 3:10; 4:1; 6:1; *T. Iss.* 4:1-4; *T. Benj.* 8:2; Matt 5:28-30; and the discussion in William Loader, *Sexuality and the Jesus Tradition* (Grand Rapids: Eerdmans, 2005) 33-35. See also Kampen, "Matthean Divorce Texts Reexamined," 164.

the human inclination to sin. Nothing suggests that the author sees sexual desire in itself as evil or that inclination is to be equated with sexual desire. Here יצר "inclination" is negative through the addition of אשמה "guilt".[25]

The terms יצר and מחשבות appear together in the expression יצר מחשבות in 1 Chron 28:9, where it comes in David's address to Solomon:

כי כל לבבות דורש יהוה וכל יצר מחשבות מבין

for the LORD searches every mind, and understands every plan and thought.

Given Solomon's reputation for sexual wrongdoing, it could have easily been understood in this sense by subsequent hearers, but this need not be so. In 1 Chron 29:18 it relates to David's prayer for the people. The words יצר and מחשבות also appear together in Gen 6:5, which is the context from which the author begins his list of examples.

וירא יהוה כי רבה רעת האדם בארץ וכל יצר מחשבת לבו רק רע כל היום

The LORD saw that the wickedness of humankind was great in the earth, and that every inclination of the thoughts of their hearts was only evil continually.

In 2.16b the author of D turns to history in order to illustrate the dangers of "thoughts of a guilty inclination" and "eyes of sexual wrongdoing". As Ida Fröhlich observes, "the expressions יצר אשמה and עיני זנות serve as the keys to the meaning of the examples mentioned in the survey".[26] Thus the author continues: "For through them (בם) great men (רבים) have gone astray and mighty heroes (גבורי חיל) have stumbled from former times until now" (V). The preposition ב "in, by, because of" links together the list of examples which follow in 2.17 – 3.12, sometimes with a singular suffix בה "because of it" (3.1[2x], 2), referring to זנות "sexual wrongdoing", sometimes returning to the plural (3.4). The author also employs the word, רצון "pleasure/desire",[27] to describe this sexual lusting in 2.21; 3.3, (probably 3.7), 10, 11 (cf. רצה in 2.15 where it refers to what

---

[25] Lichtenberger, *Menschenbild*, 77-86, warns against equating יצר אשמה here with the later rabbinic teaching (150 n. 6). He notes that in using Num 15:39 the author replaces לבב "heart" by יצר "inclination".

[26] See also Ida Fröhlich, "'Narrative Exegesis' in the Dead Sea Scrolls," in *Biblical Perspectives: Early Use and Interpretation of the Bible in Light of the Dead Sea Scrolls: Proceedings of the First International Symposium of the Orion Center for the Study of the Dead Sea Scrolls and Associated Literature, 12-14 May 1996* (ed. Michael E. Stone and Esther G. Chazon; STDJ 28; Leiden: Brill, 1998) 81-99, 84.

[27] Wacholder, *New Damascus Document*, translates רצון in this passage as "passions" (31).

pleases God). From 3.9 onwards we therefore find בו "because of it", matching the masculine noun רצון "pleasure/desire" (3.9[3x], 10[2x]). In addition Qimron suggests that in 2.19 and 20 the two occurrences of the syntactically difficult כי "because" may be a graphical error for בו "because of it",[28] although perhaps בה would have been more likely given its occurrence in the preceding context. I have highlighted the extent of the use of the preposition ב "because of " and of other key words and expressions within the following translation of *DSSSE*.

> 2.14 And now, sons, listen to me and I shall open your eyes so that you can see and understand the deeds of 15 God, so that you can choose what he is pleased with (רצה) and repudiate what he hates, so that you can walk perfectly 16 on all his paths and not allow yourselves to be attracted by the thoughts of guilty inclination and lascivious eyes (ולא לחור במחשבות יצר אשמה וע[י]ני זנות).
>
> For many (or: great men רבים) 17 have gone astray (תעו) due to them (בם); brave heroes (גבורי חיל) stumbled (נכשלו) on account of them (בם), from ancient times until now. For having walked in the stubbornness 18 of their hearts (בשרירות לבם בלכתם)[29] the Watchers of the heavens fell (נפלו); on account of it (בה) they were caught, for they did not heed the precepts (מצות) of God. 19 And their sons, whose height was like that of cedars and whose bodies were like mountains, fell (כי נפלו) (because of it? בו or בה?). 20 All flesh which was there on the dry earth expired (כי גוע) (or because of it? בו or בה?) and they became as if they had never been, because they had realised their desires (בעשותם את רצונם) and had failed to keep their creator's precepts (מצות), until his wrath flared up against them.
>
> 3.1 Through it (בה), the sons of Noah and their families strayed (תעו), through it (בה), they were cut off. 2 Abraham did not walk in it (בה), and was counted as a friend for keeping God's precepts (מצות) and not following 3 the desire of his spirit (רוחו ולא בחר ברצון). And he passed (them) on to Isaac and to Jacob, and they kept (them) and were written up as friends 4 of God and as members of the covenant for ever. *Blank*
>
> Jacob's sons strayed (תעו) because of them (בם) and were punished in accordance with 5 their mistakes. And in Egypt their sons walked in the stubbornness of their hearts (הלכו בשרירות לבם), plotting against 6 God's precepts (מצות) and each one doing what was right in his own eyes (לעשות איש הישר בעיניו) and they ate blood, 7 and their males were cut off (יכרת) in the wilderness. (And he spoke) to them in

[28] Elisha Qimron, "The Text of CDC," in *The Damascus Document Reconsidered* (ed. Magen Broshi; Jerusalem: Israel Exploration Society, The Shrine of the Book, Israel Museum, 1992) 9-49, 13 n. 16.

[29] This phrase is not extant in 4QD^{a}/4Q266 2 ii.17, but is assumed. There the following line preserves עירי ה ("the Watchers"). 4QD^{e}/4Q270 1 3 apparently did not contain the words בלכתם בשרירות לבם נפלו "For having walked in the stubbornness of their hearts ... fell", though it retained the reference to the Watchers which follows. On this see Baumgarten, *DJD* 18, 141.

Qadesh: *Deut 9:23* "Go and possess (the land." But they preferred the desire) of their spirit (ויבחרו את רצון] רוחם]) and did not listen to 8 the voice of their creator, the precepts (מצות) he had taught them, and murmured in their tents. And the wrath of God flared up 9 against their congregation.

And their sons died through it (בו), and through it (בו) their kings were cut off (נכרתו), and through it (בו) their warriors (גבוריהם) 10 perished, and through it (בו) their land was laid waste.

Through it (בו), the very first to enter the covenant made themselves guilty and were delivered up 11 to the sword, for having deserted God's covenant and having chosen their whims (ויבחרו ברצונם) and having followed the stubbornness 12 of their heart בשרירות לבם, each one doing (what was) his desire (לעשות איש את רצונו). (*DSSSE*) (2.14 – 3.12a)

The author runs through history ("from ancient times until now") showing that following illicit sexual desire led to failure. The opening statement functions as a summary, speaking of "many" (רבים; perhaps "great ones") and "brave heroes" (גבורי חיל) and in both cases using בם ("because of them") as a reference back to either the lustful eyes or these and the thoughts arising from evil inclinations. Later in the list the term גבור reappears in association with kings and their failure, leading to the exile (3.9).

The author begins his history of failure with the myth of the Watchers, who fall בה "because of it", referring to the singular זנות (illicit sexual relations).[30] The phrase, בשרירות לבם "in the stubbornness of their hearts" occurs twice more in the history, in 3.5, also with the verb הלך "to walk" and with a reference to not heeding מצות "precepts", and in the concluding instance, in 3.11.[31] The author's depiction of the Watcher myth appears to be dependent on the *Book of the Watchers* or, more probably, on *Jubilees*, given the latter's influence in the following context. Accordingly, the author cites their fall and also the fall of their offspring, the giants. If we read בו or בה "because of it" in 2:19, this could be understood as implying that the offspring were also involved in acts of sexual wrongdoing, an element not present in the *Book of the Watchers* or in *Jubilees*, but it is more probably attributing their fall ultimately to the act of sexual wrongdoing of their parents. We note the absence of any reference to Adam and Eve,

[30] Cf. Gary A. Anderson, "Intentional and Unintentional Sin in the Dead Sea Scrolls," in *Pomegranates and Golden Bells: Studies in Biblical, Jewish, and Near Eastern Ritual, Law, and Literature in Honor of Jacob Milgrom* (ed. David P. Wright et al.; Winona Lake: Eisenbrauns, 1995) 49-64, who, considering בה as an isolated instance, suggests it refers to the phrase בלכתם בשרירות לבם "having walked in the stubbornness of their hearts" (62).

[31] On stubbornness of heart see Deut 29:18 and Jer 23:17 and Campbell, *Use of Scripture*, 73, 80.

presumably because the author found no ground there for seeing their fall as the result of illicit sexual lust.

The author then alludes to the flood (2.20-21), which it understands as God's judgement of humans for following their pleasure (רצונם). Like *Jubilees*, the author makes no specific link between the Watchers and their offspring and the flood. The reference to following their pleasure (רצונם) need not be narrowed to sexual wrongdoing, but probably includes it, especially if we read בו or בה. The word, רצון "pleasure/desire", becomes a key term is describing wrongdoing in what follows.

The author then lists Noah's sons and their kin who went astray בה "because of it", which appears twice (3.1). The reference is to זנות "sexual wrongdoing", as in 2.18. Fröhlich points to the sin of Ham in uncovering his father's nakedness, resulting in the curse of Canaan in Gen 9:18-27.[32] If, however, we take the likely influence from *Jubilees* into account, the sin probably refers to sexual wrongdoing in general (*Jub.* 9:15).

The author then notes that Abraham did not walk בה "in it" and so did not follow his רצון "pleasure/desire", described as not choosing "the desire of his spirit", ולא בחר ברצון רוחו (3.2-3a). The juxtaposition of בה "in it" and ברצון רוחו "the desire of his spirit" makes it very clear that רצון "pleasure/desire" is being used in relation to sexual pleasure. Abraham's resistance warrants his designation as "friend of God" (cf. also Isa 41:8; 2 Chron 20:7). The language, "friend of God", occurs in the context of intermarriage also in *Jubilees* 30, where it is applied to Levi's punishment of the Shechemites because of sexual wrongdoing.[33] In Ps 106:31 the actions of Phinehas are "reckoned to him as righteousness", like Abraham's act of faith in Gen 15:6, and *Jubilees* describes each as "friend of God" (*Jub.* 19:9; 30:20). Both Abraham and Phinehas uphold the precepts concerned with sexual wrongdoing, in particular, the prohibition of intermarriage. This suggests that the same association of ideas may be present here. Abraham, Isaac and Jacob, as 3.3 goes on to say, are "friends of God", because they uphold the precepts concerned with sexual wrongdoing.[34]

The reference to Abraham's handing down of commandments to Isaac and Jacob (3.3), of which Genesis reports nothing, is probably also drawing on *Jubilees*, which reports such instruction, in which sexual wrongdoing is a key

---

[32] Fröhlich, "Narrative Exegesis," 85-86.

[33] See Hayes, *Gentile Impurities*, who writes in relation to *Jubilees* and CD: "In CD the epithet 'friend of God' is attributed to Abraham because he guarded against miscegenation and so preserved intact the seed of Israel" (246 n. 52).

[34] See also the likely association of Abraham and Phinehas and the allusion to Gen 15:6 and Ps 106:31 in the context of concern with intermarriage in *4QMMT* C 31-32 and see pp. 84-85.

concern (20:3-6; 21:21-24; 22:14-20). *Jubilees* also offers background for the claims about Jacob's sons as sinning בם "because of them", namely because of the eyes of lust or these and the evil inclination (3.4-5a).[35] *Jubilees* rewrites the story of Judah (41:1-21) and offers a detailed elaboration of Genesis' mention in a single verse of Reuben's sin with Bilhah (33:2-9; cf. Gen 35:22; also 49:5). The reference to punishment according to their mistakes (3.5a) finds little basis in Genesis, but is addressed in *Jubilees*, where the author must explain why both were not executed but their sins dealt with less severely (41:24-28; 33:16). It seems very probable that *Jubilees* both informs the details of the author's list thus far and its emphasis on sexual wrongdoing, and probably also inspires the notion as a whole that sexual wrongdoing led to such failure throughout history.

The author then moves beyond the scope of *Jubilees* to report about the descendants of Jacob in Egypt that they "walked in the stubbornness of their hearts (הלכו בשרירות לבם), plotting against God's precepts (מצות) and each one doing what was right in his own eyes (לעשות איש הישר בעיניו)[36] and they ate blood" (3.5b-6). It is difficult to find evidence in the biblical record for these claims,[37] unless we understand the author to be referring both to the time in Egypt and to the period in the wilderness. This seems likely, given the reference to their males being cut off in the wilderness (3.7a), which appears to belong to what precedes. This means we need to include the reference to their refusal to follow the instruction at Kadesh, cited from Deut 9:23, that they go up to possess the land. On this basis it is possible to reconstruct the focus of the passage. The focus on sexual wrongdoing thus far makes it likely that this theme continues, rather than that it disappears or is treated now only as a metaphor. This is made all the more likely because of the recurring expressions. Walking in the stubbornness of their hearts (הלכו בשרירות לבם) recalls the deeds of the Watchers and their offspring. If with רוחם "their spirit", we reconstruct the words ויבחרו את רצון, so that in 3.7 we read, "and they preferred the desire of their spirit", this recalls the refusal of Abraham to walk in sexual wrongdoing, following ברצון רוחו "the desire of his spirit" (3.3). The reference to precepts and to God's wrath flaring up also recalls the sins of Noah's generation, who followed their desires (בעשותם את רצונם) and disregarded the precepts (מצות).

The passage also highlights further details: eating blood and the cutting off of their males. Eating blood, prohibited in Gen 9:4-5; Lev 17:10-14; Deut 12:23,

---

[35] Fröhlich, "Narrative Exegesis," points to Reuben's sin in Gen 35:22 (86).

[36] Campbell, *Use of Scripture*, notes the presence of this expression in Deut 12:8 (74).

[37] Knibb, *Qumran Community*, points to Ezek 20:5-9; 23:3 (which uses the metaphor of prostitution); and Josh 24:14, while noting the absence of such a notion from Exodus except for 5:20-21; 6:9, 12 (31), but the latter are very general, referring to resistance towards Moses. See also Campbell, *Use of Scripture*, 80-81.

seems unrelated to the theme of sexual wrongdoing and does not feature in the biblical material among Israel's sins in the time of Moses. It is, however, a major concern in *Jubilees* (cf. 6:7, 11-13), where it is alleged that such behaviour characterised both the generation of Noah and, by implication, that of Moses (6:18-19).[38] *1 Enoch* also identifies it as one of the sins of the offspring of the Watchers (*1 Enoch* 7:5; cf. *Jub.* 7:22-23, 28-29). Our passage continues, however, with a reference to the cutting off of males. This could simply allude in general terms to the generation which died in the wilderness, but more likely it refers to the slaying of males who according to Numbers 25 engaged in sexual relations with the Midianites against the precept prohibiting intermarriage, in which Phinehas becomes a hero. The juxtaposition with eating blood appears to make sense in this context. In Num 25:1-2 we read:

> While Israel was staying at Shittim, the people began to have sexual relations with the women of Moab. These invited the people to the sacrifices of their gods, and the people ate and bowed down to their gods.

Here we have illicit sexual relations associated with eating with Gentiles, which an author might easily conclude entailed eating blood. Accordingly, it seems very probable that the theme of sexual wrongdoing continues in the account of the sins of the people of Moses' generation. It is therefore unlikely that the author is shifting here to a metaphorical use of sexual imagery, as Fröhlich suggests.[39]

The next passage turns to "their sons", that is, the time of settlement in the land till the exile. Here we find a return to the prepositional phrase, בו "because of it", which appears four times. Its referent is most likely to be רצון "pleasure", understood in the light of the preceding context and the parallel prepositional phrases, as "pleasure" or "desire", particularly in a sexual context. The summary statement might well allude to the sexual wrongdoing of kings like David and Solomon, and warriors like Samson (who fell to sexual wrongdoing), but it is a

---

[38] See also Campbell, *Use of Scripture*, who draws attention to the link between eating blood and devastation of the land in Ezek 33:25, as here (81).

[39] Fröhlich, "Narrative Exegesis," 86. She draws attention also to the narratives of history in 4QCommGen A/4Q252 and the *Genesis Apocryphon*, noting the common theme of sexual transgression in all three. "Sins, prohibitions of biblical laws, are often mentioned in the texts, especially sins of זנות, either as the violation of sexual prohibitions or as idolatry. These sins are mentioned among the special prescriptions of the Mosaic law, the 'laws of the land,' i.e., prohibitions against sins which defile the land" (96). Cf. also Martha Himmelfarb, "Impurity and Sin in 4QD, 1QS, and 4Q512," *DSD* 8 (2001) 9-37, who speaks of the use of "damning metaphors" (13), but they are clearly more than this.

broad sweep,[40] judging that the devastation of the Babylonian conquest was the result of such sin.[41]

The final section (3.10c-12), again, uses the prepositional phrase, בו "because of it", referring to desire for sexual pleasure. It also forms an *inclusio* with the example with which the list began by referring to בשרירות לבם "stubbornness of heart", and strengthens the connections with what has gone before by twice making reference to רצון "pleasure" in ויבחרו ברצונם "and they chose their pleasure" and לעשות איש את רצונו "each one doing his pleasure/desire". The passage is referring to באי הברית הראשנים "the very first members to enter the covenant". Assuming the author is retaining a progressive sequence through history, these must refer not to the Mosaic,[42] Abrahamic or Noachic covenants, but to a covenant made some time after the devastation of the land. Most likely it refers to the first members of the covenant movement to which the author and his community trace their origins. It would then signal that some of those became guilty of sexual wrongdoing and suffered for it by being "delivered up to the sword". This will have taken place some time between the exile and the time of the author. One could place the reference in the context of the crisis with Antiochus Epiphanes, but this is speculative.

Seen as a whole, the section 2.14 – 3.12 is a remarkable portrayal of Israel's history under the rubric of sexual wrongdoing.[43] It is knit together by formal elements, such as the frequent use of the preposition ב "in, because of" to sustain the reference to sexual wrongdoing as the cause, by the use of רצון "pleasure, desire" in this sexual context, and by the repeated references to stubbornness of heart and to heeding precepts. The list appears at a number of points to stand under the influence of *Jubilees*, a work alluded to elsewhere in the document (citing it by title: CD 16.2). It stands behind the reference to the Watchers and their offspring,

---

[40] Knibb, *Qumran Community*, notes the similar cursory treatment made of the period from the settlement to the exile in 4 Ezra 3:23-27 and Nehemiah 9 (32).

[41] It is possible to see also in *4QMMT* C an allusion to the Babylonian conquest as the result of the sin of the kings, including Solomon, and with reference to marrying foreign wives. See p. 83 above. Cf. also 11QT[a]/11Q19 59.2-9, 13-15.

[42] Cf. Knibb, *Qumran Community*, who refers to הברית הראשנים in 1.4, which can be rendered, "the covenant with the first ones" (32). The temporal sequence makes the reference to the Mosaic covenant unlikely.

[43] Davies, *Damascus Covenant*, notes the "history" with its repetition of motifs, including rebellious "children", but makes no connection with the focus on sexual wrongdoing (79-81). Consequently when he then addresses the children's rebellion with the question, "In what do these divine commandments consist?" (81) his answer focuses primarily on issues of calendar and makes no mention of sexual wrongdoing. When he asks, "But what sin?" (88), in relation to the rebellion in the first and third account, he notes language of defilement and impurity, but not issues of sexual wrongdoing (88-89).

the flood, the sins of Noah's sons, Abraham as teacher of Isaac and Jacob, and friend of God, and Jacob's sons. A reference to sexual wrongdoing appears to be assumed in each instance, either directly or indirectly. The author does not appear to cross over at any point to a metaphorical use of sexual wrongdoing to depict unfaithfulness to covenant in general.

We noted above that the author repeats the exhortation, ועתה שמעו "Now listen" three times (1.1; 2.2; 2.14), in the third of which we find the fuller expression: ועתה בנים שמעו לי "Now, my children listen to me". As Wacholder notes, it recalls the identical exhortation in Prov 7:24 ועתה בנים שמעו לי (cf. also 5:7).[44] This is important because that context deals with sexual wrongdoing, namely the dangers of the strange woman. It makes it likely that רבים in 2.16b-17 also derives from that context: כי רבים חללים הפילה "because many she has caused to fall profaned" (Prov 7:26). The author appears, therefore, to have composed the section introduced by 2.14 (= Prov 7:24) in the context of the concern with sexual wrongdoing expressed in Proverbs. The use of the shortened phrase in 1.1 and 2.2 may indicate that already there the association of ideas is present.

Within the broader context of the document, the depiction of sexual wrongdoing as a major concern coheres with the emphasis in what follows, where, after identifying the faithful remnant, the author returns to identifying the work of Belial and focuses again on sexual wrongdoing in 4.13 – 5.19. Should Murphy-O'Connor be correct in arguing that 2.14 begins a source which once stood on its own, then it is all the more striking that the theme of sexual wrongdoing would have had such a prominent position.[45] This may explain why intermarriage appears to be in view here, whereas it is not a theme elsewhere in D.

From 3.12b the author then turns to the remnant, with whom, it declares, God "made his covenant with Israel forever, revealing to them hidden things (לגלות להם נסתרות) in which all Israel had gone astray" (V) (3.13-14; cf. Deut 29:28, הנסתרת ליהוה אלהינו והנגלת לנו, "The secret things belong to the LORD our God, but the revealed things belong to us"). The focus is no longer sexual wrongdoing, but falls on what follows: "his holy sabbaths and his glorious feasts" (3.14-15), the important issue of calendar. Beyond that, the author remains at a general level, speaking of righteousness (צדק), truth (אמת), the desires of his will (חפצי רצונו), "which a person must do to live by them" (cf. Lev 18:5), and a rich well (3.17), imagery developed further in 6.3-11 on the basis of Num 21:8. Of the remnant people the author reports:

---

[44] Wacholder, *New Damascus Document*, 175.

[45] On the importance of sexual sins in the depiction of Israel's history see also Wassen, *Women*, 183.

והם התגוללו בפשע אנוש ובדרכי נדה 18 ויאמרו כי לנו היא

and they had defiled themselves with human sin and unclean paths, and they had said, "This is ours". (*DSSSE*) (3.17-18a)

The author does not specify the nature of this sin.[46] It might relate to sexual wrongdoing, given what precedes, but we cannot be sure. The passage moves immediately to report God's atoning for their sin and forgiving their iniquities, again without specification (3.18b), and building a sure house for them, with eternal life and the glory of Adam as their future hope (3.19-20). The reference in 3.19 to "a sure house (בית נאמן) in Israel whose like has never existed from former times until now" (V) echoes the language of 1 Sam 2:35 concerning Samuel the priest: "I will build him a sure house (בית נאמן), and he shall go in and out before my anointed one forever".[47] The author then identifies them as the priests, "and the Levites, who joined them" (והלוים הם הלוים עמהם), a pun on Levi, used also in *Jub.* 31:16, but already in Gen 29:34; Lev 18:2, 4, and the sons of Zadok of Ezek 44:15 (3.21 – 4.6a),[48] promising a detailed list which never appears in the text.[49] In 4.6b-7 the author repeats that their sins were forgiven, repeated in 4.9-10, and underlines that their interpretation of the Law, acquitting the just and convicting the unjust (ויצדיקו צדיק וירשיעו רשע; cf. its opposite in 1.19 ויצדיקו רשע וירשיעו צדיק "they acquitted the wicked and convicted the just") is the basis of the community's teaching for all who join it subsequently (4.8-12a). It is interesting in the light of the emphasis in 2.14 – 3.12a that none of this returns to the issue of sexual wrongdoing, but remains at a general level with the exception of references to the calendar. This soon changes, the next time the author turns to specifics.

The Nets of Belial and Sexual Wrongdoing 4.12b – 5.19

After the discourse about the remnant in 3.12b – 4.12a, the focus moves to the present and returns to concerns about sexual wrongdoing. The author introduces imagery from Mic 7:11 about the wall which is built and the boundary which is removed:

נבנתה הגדר רחק החיק

The wall is built, the boundary far removed. (V) (4:12)

---

[46] On the probable allusion to Ezek 11:14-15 behind לנו היא, see Campbell, *Use of Scripture*, 81-82.

[47] On this see Campbell, *Use of Scripture*, 82-83.

[48] On the use of Ezek 44:15, see Campbell, *Use of Scripture*, 82-83.

[49] As Knibb, *Qumran Community*, notes, it is likely to have been "omitted because it was no longer of interest" (37).

יום לבנות גדריך יום ההוא ירחק חק

A day for the building of your walls! In that day the boundary shall be far extended. (Mic 7:11)

This imagery reappears in 4.19, בוני החיץ אשר הלכו אחרי צו, "the builders of the wall who have followed after Precept" (V), an allusion to Ezek 13:10.

יען וביען הטעו את עמי לאמר שלום ואין שלום והוא בנה חיץ והנם טחים אתו תפל

Because, in truth, because they have misled my people, saying, "Peace," when there is no peace; and because, when the people build a wall, they [the prophets] smear whitewash on it.

While in Micah the image of building a wall serves to express something positive, in the Ezekiel passage it is used negatively, particularly in relation to those who give false hope. Both images, building walls, and extending boundaries, recur frequently throughout the Admonition to describe the interpretation of the Law given by the opponents of the author and his group and presumed to influence Israel as a whole.[50] The image of moving "the boundary" (in 4:12 חיק;[51] but in 4QD[a]/4Q266 1a-b 4; CD 1.16; 5.20; 19.16; 20.20 גבול) seems directly applied to changing the Law and its interpretation (note the similarity of חיק "boundary" and חוק statute, which perhaps invited a play on words).[52] In 4.20, as elsewhere, the author identifies a particular teacher, here called "the Precept" (V) or "Zaw" (*DSSSE*) and described as preaching, an allusion to Micah 2:6. In 8.12 the author not only returns to the image of the builders of the wall, but also to that of whitewashing (cf. also Ezek 13:15). The allegation that in response to sexual wrongdoing teachers and interpreters alter the Law, features also in *4QWiles of the Wicked Woman*/4Q184, where we read that it leads some in response to the smooth-talking woman להשנות חוק "to alter the ordinance" (1.15; cf. also 1QS/1Q28, which speaks more generally about those who "bend the Law"; 11.2).

The conflict with this group and with the teaching given by its leader forms the background for the depiction of the present as a period during which "Belial will be set loose against Israel" (4.13). *Jubilees* also describes the present as the

[50] So García Martínez, "Man and Woman," who speaks of "the builders of the wall" as "rival group, but a group which is considered as representative of the whole of Israel outside the community" and "very prominent … that, if we take into account the halakhah of MMT, could even be identified with the Pharisees" (103). For the identification of the opponents as Pharisees see Schiffman, "Pharisees and their Legal Traditions," 271-72.

[51] CD-A reads חוק here as it does ההון in 4.17; in both cases we should read י not ו.

[52] It is interesting that 4QInstr[b]/4Q416 2 iv.6 depicts another man's adultery as an act of altering his boundaries (cf. also 2 iii.4).

time of Belial and depicts the future as one where satan will no longer exist (23:29; 50:5). The author continues in 4.14, depicting the present in the words of Isa 24:17,

פחד ופחת ופח עליך יושב הארץ

Terror, and the pit, and the snare are upon you, O inhabitant of the earth!

Picking up the imagery of Isaiah, but using a different word, מצידות "nets", the author provides an interpretation (פשרו, 4.14b) of the quotation as referring to "Belial's three nets about which Levi, son of Jacob spoke" (*DSSSE*) (4.15).

The passage is dense with allusion. Clearly the author is expounding the activity of Belial in the present. The reference to Levi may allude to the *Aramaic Levi Document* which warns against sexual wrongdoing, the major theme in what follows. Jonas Greenfield proposed that we have here an allusion to *ALD* 6:3 / 16.[53] In what survives of the *Aramaic Levi Document*, however, there is no reference to the imagery of nets, nor to what immediately follows, namely that Belial "catches Israel by setting them up as three kinds of righteousness (צדק)" (V) (4.16-17a). This statement recalls the allegation in 1.19, that the opponents ויצדיקו רשע וירשיעו צדיק "justified the wicked and condemned the just" (V), with its converse in 4.7, referring to the true interpreters of the Law who, by contrast, ויצדיקו צדיק וירשיעו רשע "justified the righteous and condemned the wicked" (V). The charge of persuading Israel to believe that three things are right when they are wrong, makes best sense in the context of dispute about interpretation of the Law.

In 4.17-18a the author then identifies the three nets.

הראשונה היא הזנות השנית ההין (= ההון) השלישית טמא המקדש

the first is sexual wrongdoing, the second, riches[54]; the third, defiling the temple.

It is consistent with the emphasis already given to sexual wrongdoing (זנות) that it comes first. This indicates its major importance for the author. It is also significant

---

[53] Jonas Greenfield, "The Words of Levi, Son of Jacob in Damascus Document IV, 15-19," *RevQ* 13 (1988) 319-22. See also Kugler, "Halakic Interpretative Strategies," 137. Cf. Henryk Drawnel, *An Aramaic Wisdom Text from Qumran: A New Interpretation of the Levi Document* (JSJSup 86; Leiden: Brill, 2004), who concludes the dependence is difficult to establish (19, 214).

[54] Joseph M. Baumgarten and Daniel R. Schwartz, *PTSDSSP* 2, translate ההין as "arrogance" and see it picked up again only at 5.12 in the reference to "blasphemies" (21). As we indicate, ההין makes good sense in its context and needs to be understood as having relevance already in the issue of polygyny. Cf. Greenfield, "Words of Levi," who suggests correcting ההין to פחז ("fornication") (322).

that this, the first net, receives primary attention in what immediately follows in 4.19 – 5.19a.[55]

The author then returns to the context of Isa 24:17, to use imagery from the following verse:

והיה הנס מקול הפחד יפל אל הפחת והעולה מתוך הפחת ילכד בפח

> Whoever flees at the sound of the terror shall fall into the pit; and whoever climbs out of the pit shall be caught in the snare. (Isa 24:18)

The author puts it in his own words:

העולה מזה יתפש בזה והניצל מזה יתפש 19 בזה

> The one who goes up from this is caught in that and whoever escapes from that is caught in the other.* (4.18-19a)

This suggests that the author sees the three issues as closely connected, an important perspective for when we consider the relation between the list and the exposition below. Before, however, proceeding to the exposition, or at least as part of its introduction, the author returns to the imagery of Mic 7:11 and especially Ezek 13:10. Thus he identifies "the builders of the wall who have followed after Precept" (V) (4.19), an allusion also to Hos 5:11, כי הואיל הלך אחרי צו lit. "He was determined to follow after Precept", as those responsible for creating these nets of Belial. They do so through their preaching, expressed through the words, הטף יטיפון, "they shall surely spout (V)/preach (*DSSSE*)", based on Mic 2:6, אל תטפו יטיפון, "Do not preach!"[56] Of these "builders of the wall" the author then declares:

הם ניתפשים בשתים בזנות לקחת 21 שתי נשים בחייהם

> They are caught in two (of them) in sexual wrongdoing by taking two wives during their (masc.) lifetime.* (4.20a-21a)

While one might expect that this is being alleged against Israel on the basis of their following the teachers, the text implicates the teachers, themselves. The word,

---

[55] Eileen Schuller, "Women in the Dead Sea Scrolls," in *The Dead Sea Scrolls after Fifty Years: A Comprehensive Assessment* (ed. Peter W. Flint and James C. VanderKam; Leiden: Brill, 1999) 2.117-44, notes that it is striking that the three instances, all of which involve women, "formed the core of the community's self-definition *vis-à-vis* the rest of the Jewish people who are accused of following corrupt practices on these points" (123-24).

[56] On the prophetic texts to which the passage alludes see Campbell, *Use of Scripture*, 127-29, but also his note about the possibility of influence from Exod 32:25 in the episode of the golden calf (125).

ניתפשים "they are caught", picks up יתפש "is caught", used twice in 4.18-19a. The word, בשתים "in two", would then seem to be best read closely with what precedes, referring to two nets.[57]

Alternatively, it could simply mean, twice or in two ways. If read in association with זנות "illicit sexual relations", then it could refer to two kinds of זנות "illicit sexual relations". These could be two aspects entailed in taking two wives. The presence of שתי "two" later in the sentence might suggest this, though it may be rhetorical effect rather than an attempt by the author to explain בשתים "in two". One could argue that there are two instances or aspects of adultery entailed in taking two wives, because from the perspective of monogyny its outcome is adultery committed against each, but this assumes an understanding of adultery as committed against women, not otherwise attested at the time.

Another way of reading בשתים "in two" in association with זנות "illicit sexual relations" is to see it referring to two instances of sexual wrongdoing. These might be the taking of two wives as one kind and either of the two further instances which follow in 5.6-7 and 5.7-11 (sexual relations with a menstruant and marrying a niece)[58] as the second kind, or both, taken together. Then one would need to read the words, הם ניתפשים בשתים בזנות as a separate statement, "They are caught in two ways in sexual wrongdoing", and what follows, לקחת שתי נשים בחייהם, as the first of the two kinds: "taking two wives in their lifetime", with the second kind coming some lines later. As the text currently stands, the second or third instances seem, however, too far away, if they are meant to illustrate the two kinds of sexual wrongdoing. There is the further complication that the second instance, while also pertaining to sexual wrongdoing, stands under the rubric of defiling the temple, not sexual wrongdoing.

If we read הם ניתפשים בשתים as a separate statement referring to being caught in two nets, "They are caught in two (of the nets)", which seems more likely, then the issue arises of how the author sees this happening. Some, for instance, identify the nets as זנות ("illicit sexual relations") and one or both of the second and third instances enunciated in the next column, usually the second, which explicitly mentions one of the nets, namely, defiling the temple. They, therefore, read the passage as saying: "They are caught in two (nets): in sexual wrongdoing … and they also defiled the temple …". This assumes that the author is indicating that they are caught in only two of the nets, not three, on the grounds

---

[57] So Rabin, *Zadokite Fragment*, 16-17; Davies, *Damascus Covenant*, 110, 114; García Martínez, "Man and Woman," 104.

[58] So Geza Vermes, "Sectarian Matrimonial *Halakhah* in the Damascus Rule" *JJS* 25 (1974) 197-202, who sees it as referring to the first and third instance (197). Similarly Wassen, *Women*, 120.

that the second, "riches", is not explicitly mentioned.[59] Such an assumption stands in some tension with what we find in the wider context, where wicked wealth features strongly among the author's concerns (e.g., 6.15 "wicked wealth which defiles").[60]

There is an awkwardness in the text, which many have noted, especially because of the mismatch between the three nets and the three instances which follow. Davies, for instance, declares that "any attempt at a complete correlation is futile, because there is no mention whatsoever of riches",[61] and suggests the use of sources by a redactor, who joins a tradition about the three nets with a list which was concerned originally only with sexual wrongdoing.[62]

---

[59] See the discussion in Davies, *Damascus Covenant*, 110-16. He notes that one way of explaining the redaction is to suggest that "riches" is replaced by a second matter of sexual irregularity (114). Another is to reduce the accusations to two and to read the reference to twofoldness in 4.20 as referring to (1) the first accusation and (2) the second and third taken together, even though defiling the temple is not elsewhere a major concern for the redactor, who retains it from his source because it matches the summary of wrongdoing (115-16). See also his discussion in Davies, "Marriage and the Essenes," 73-75.

[60] John I. Kampen, "The Significance of the Temple in the Manuscripts of the Damascus Document," in *The Dead Sea Scrolls at Fifty: Proceedings of the 1997 Society of Biblical Literature Qumran Section Meetings* (ed. Robert A. Kugler and Eileen M. Schuller; SBLEJL 15; Atlanta: Scholars, 1999) 185-97, notes the importance of wealth in CD 6 where it concerns vows and oaths related to sacrifices and offerings and so also pertains to defiling the temple (189-90).

[61] Davies, *Damascus Covenant*, 113.

[62] Davies, *Damascus Covenant*, sees the reference to defiling the temple as relating only to the second instance and as preserved from an earlier list by the author because of its correlation with the second net (115-16). He notes that the second instance lacks the biblical warrant which supports the first and third instance, but sees this as insufficient ground to treat it as a gloss (114). Adiel Schremer "Qumran Polemic on Marital Law and Its Social Background," in *The Damascus Document: A Centennial of Discovery: Proceedings of the Third International Symposium of the Orion Center for the Study of the Dead Sea Scrolls and Associated Literature, 4-8 February 1998* (ed. Joseph M. Baumgarten, Esther G. Chazon, and Avital Pinnick; STDJ 34; Leiden: Brill, 2000) 147-60, proposes a readjustment of the text on the basis that "marrying one's niece ... does not seem to be related to the accusation of defilement of the sanctuary ..., which precedes it, but in fact to the accusation of marrying two women, for both share the common subject of marital issues" (150). See her discussion, pp. 147-52. She suggests either a reordering or a deletion of the second accusation, resulting in what she sees as a text which makes better sense of the twofold sexual wrongdoing to which the text alludes. She also suggests that "the Tannaitic sources of tractate Yevemot reveal a social reality in which there were men who married their nieces while, at the same time, being married to another woman. This is exactly the situation which the author of the Damascus Document sees before his eyes" (156). Such parallels are not sufficient, however, to warrant the "surgery" (her word) she proposes, especially when, as we seek to show below, we can make sense of the text as it is.

There is, however, another way of reading the text as we have it which, while not ignoring the awkwardness of the text, makes good sense of the connections. This is to see in בשתים "in two" a reference to two of the three nets and to relate this not to all three instances which follow, but only to the first, namely, to the statement about taking two wives. In what two nets are people being caught who take two wives? Clearly one of the nets is sexual wrongdoing. But for people of the time, hearing the condemnation of polygyny, the identification of the second net would, I suspect, be obvious: riches or greed for wealth. One of the reasons for multiplying wives was greed, the acquisition of more dowries. Thus in their sexual wrongdoing by taking two wives they have been trapped in two nets: the net of sexual wrongdoing and the net of riches (i.e. greed). The association of sexual wrongdoing (זונות) and wealth (הון) occurs also in 8.5/19.17, "They have wallowed in the ways of sexual wrongdoing (בדרכי זונות) and wicked wealth (בהון הרשעה)".

This coheres well with the author's statement that the nets are of a kind that they operate together. We do not have a simple list of three instances matching the three separate nets, since sexual wrongdoing features in all three instances. In that sense the second instance also indicates an entanglement in two nets at the same time, defiling the temple and sexual wrongdoing, and the same applies, arguably, to the third instance. This makes more sense than to assume that the author simply ignores the second of the nets, riches, in his exposition.

The precise meaning of the allegation לקחת שתי נשים בחייהם, "by taking two wives during their (masc.) lifetime", has also been much debated.[63] If the masculine suffix is read exclusively, then בחייהם implies that throughout a man's whole lifetime he is forbidden to take a second wife. The plural would then correspond to the plural pronoun הם ("they") earlier in the line. Then, as Murphy-O'Connor argued, "the text does not forbid having two wives simultaneously. It goes much further and forbids two marriages in a single lifetime, be it after the death of a spouse or after divorce".[64] Some also saw this as implying a prohibition

---

[63] For the discussion of the various interpretations to the early 1970s see Vermes, "Sectarian Matrimonial Halakhah". For a discussion of recent research see Noam, "Divorce in Qumran," 206-209.

[64] Murphy-O'Connor, "Essene Missionary Document?" 220; similarly Davies, "Marriage and the Essenes," 75-85; 141-43; Abel Isaksson, *Marriage and Ministry in the New Temple: A Study with Special References to Mt. 19.13-22 and 1 Cor. 11.3-16* (ASNU 24; Lund: Gleerup, Copenhagen: Munksgaard, 1965) 60; Hartmut Stegemann, *Die Essener, Qumran, Johannes der Täufer und Jesus: Ein Sachbuch* (Freiburg: Herder, 1993), who argues that in any case the women married relatively late and died young (269-71); García Martínez, "Man and Woman,"105-109.

of divorce,[65] a reasonable conclusion when we bear in mind that divorce entailed permission to remarry.

Research in recent times has been able to take into account the publication of the *Temple Scroll* and, later, the fragments of D recovered from the caves at Qumran. Countering Murphy-O'Connor's interpretation, Yigael Yadin drew attention to the fact that the former contains a provision which restricts the king to having only one wife, but allowing remarriage after her death.[66] The *Temple Scroll*, as we have argued above, does not appear to apply such restrictions to the population at large, since it assumes both polygyny and divorce. If D is universalising what applied to the king, then it would be going in reverse direction in forbidding remarriage after the death of a spouse universally. The parallels are useful for comparison, but they do not allow us to assume that the author of D would have necessarily agreed. Much more weighty is the counter evidence from copies of hitherto unknown parts of the document itself.

Among the surviving D material from Qumran, 4QD^{f}/4Q271 3 12 now shows that D assumes that widows were free to remarry, so that the prohibition here in 4.20-21 almost certainly would not have applied to remarriage after the death of a spouse.[67] With the publication of 4QD^{a}/4Q266 9 iii.5 we can also now be certain, that, as many suspected on the basis of CD 13.16-17, D did assume divorce as an accepted part of life, so that earlier proposals that 4.20-21 targets divorce are also no longer tenable.[68]

Unless we assume with Schiffman that D "interpreted the biblical right of divorce to permit separation but not remarriage",[69] the assumption must be that

---

[65] So already Schechter, *Documents of Jewish Sectaries*, xvii; Joseph A. Fitzmyer, "The Matthean Divorce Texts and some new Palestinian evidence," in *To Advance the Gospel: New Testament Studies* (2d ed., Grand Rapids: Eerdmans, 1988) 79-111, who sees the prohibition as applying to both divorce and polygamy on the grounds that this is also forbidden to the king in the *Temple Scroll* (96).

[66] Yigael Yadin, "L'attitude essénien envers la polygamie et le divorce," *RB* 79 (1972) 98-99. Cf. Schiffman, "Relationship of the Zadokite Fragments to the Temple Scroll," who wonders whether the requirement might not apply to all also in the *Temple Scroll*, interpreting בחייהם as implying that "one may not take a second wife as long as the first is alive, even in the event of divorce" (138).

[67] Schuller, "Women in the Dead Sea Scrolls," 125.

[68] See the review of the evidence in Holmén, "Divorce in *CD* 4:20-5:2 and in *11QT* 57:17-18," 407. See also Noam, "Divorce in Qumran," who draws attention to evidence that divorce was accepted at Qumran, in 11QT/11Q19 54.4-5; 66.11; 4QOrd^{a}/4Q159 2-4; and the interpretation of Mal 2:16 in the version found in cave 4 (4Q76) (209-10).

[69] Lawrence H. Schiffman, *Reclaiming the Dead Sea Scrolls: The History of Judaism, the Background of Christianity, the Lost Library of Qumran* (New York: Doubleday, 1995), 130, in the context of affirming that marriage, divorce, and sexual relations were a regulated but accepted part of life in the sectarian community of the *Damascus Document* (129-33).

marriage after divorce was permitted. The apparent absence of reference to divorcees as potential brides need not suggest otherwise and is likely to be a misreading, as our discussion below will show. As Noam notes, the notion of divorce without permission to remarry would be highly problematic, given the widely attested practice in *m. Git.* 9.3, the Babatha Archive, Josephus, *J.A.* 4.293, the Elephantine documents, and not least Deut 24:1, of issuing a certificate which expressly allowed remarriage.[70] Accordingly, he argues that the reference here in 4.20 is to polygyny, not to divorce nor remarriage after divorce, nor to remarriage after death of a spouse.[71]

Thus what Murphy-O'Connor, for instance, argued was a straightforward reading of בחייהם "in their lifetime (masc)", needs extensive qualification. The marrying of widows assumes that at least for women a restriction to one spouse for an entire lifetime does not apply and this is likely to apply also to widowers. Similarly the acceptance of divorce also assumes licence to remarry for both partners. These contextual considerations require us then to reconsider the import of בחייהם "in their lifetime (masc)" in 4.20. If the restriction focuses on polygyny, then the meaning has to be limited to one's lifetime while married to a spouse.

Ginzberg noted the likely dependence of the formulation בחייהם "in their lifetime (masc)", on Lev 18:18.[72]

ואשה אל אחתה לא תקח לצרר לגלות ערותה עליה בחייה

And you shall not take a woman as a rival to her sister, uncovering her nakedness while her sister is still alive.

The author, he argued, interprets אשה אל אחתה "as a rival" or "in addition to her sister" as a reference not literally, to siblings, but to fellow Israelite women.[73] He assumed also, that as with the prohibition of marrying nephews, the author would apply Lev 18:18 equally to men, so that it applied to both the lifetime of the man

---

See also Schiffman, "Laws Pertaining to Women," 210-28; Schiffman, "Relationship of the Zadokite Fragments to the Temple Scroll," 138. Similarly Baumgarten, "Qumran-Essene Restraints on Marriage," who says it refers to the lifetime of the man and the woman and so prohibits both polygyny and remarriage after divorce (15).

70 Noam, "Divorce in Qumran," 211. See also Instone-Brewer, *Divorce and Remarriage*, 28-31, 75-84, 117-25; Wassen. *Women*, 117.

71 Noam, "Divorce in Qumran," 222.

72 Ginzberg, *Unknown Jewish Sect*, 19-20; Vermes, "Sectarian Matrimonial Halakhah," 198.

73 So also Aharon Shemesh, "4Q271.3: A Key to Sectarian Matrimonial Law," *JJS* 49 (1998) 244-63; Instone-Brewer, *Divorce and Remarriage*, 68-69; Instone-Brewer, "Nomological Exegesis," 561-79; Steudel, "Ehelosigkeit," 115-24.

and the lifetime of the woman in their marriage.[74] "The addition of בחייהם (=בחייהן) in our text is borrowed from Scripture and means only that this prohibition of marriage differs from all others in so far as it is in force only so long as a man lives with his first wife in marital union".[75] Thus, he argued, the author read Lev 18:18 as prohibiting polygyny.

While some have argued that the text should be emended to read בחייהן, "in their lifetime (fem)",[76] Steudel emphasises that there are many grammatical parallels to the possible use here of a masculine suffix with a feminine referent[77] and Mayer Irwin Gruber argues, that "it is now well known, the feminine dual is expressed by the pronominal suffixes *m/hm* as, for example, in 1 Sam. 6:10 where it is said of two female cows, 'they harnessed two of them (Heb.: *wayya'serum*) to a wagon, and they shut up in the house the calves belonging to the two of them' (Heb.: *we'et-benehem*)".[78] Read as feminine in its reference, בחייהם "in their lifetime" could still be taken to imply prohibition of taking one wife while the other is still alive (either simultaneously or after divorce), but given the constraints noted above, it, too, would also need to be understood in the restricted sense of the lifetime of the marriage. Then it makes just as much sense to read the suffix in the more common inclusive sense as referring to both the man and the woman, as Fitzmyer proposed.[79]

In relation to interpreting 4.20-21 and the possible absence of reference to divorcees as brides, Noam notes the significance of early tannaitic discussion, especially because it appears to be formulated over against an earlier more stringent view, reflected in halakha attributed to the school of Shammai.[80] This more stringent view made divorce conditional on a proven accusation of adultery against the wife, required rigorous judicial inquiry and attempted to prevent

---

[74] Ginzberg, *Unknown Jewish Sect*, 19.

[75] Ginzberg, *Unknown Jewish Sect*, 20.

[76] Emendation proposed by Rabin, *Zadokite Documents*, 16-17. Instone-Brewer, *Divorce and Remarriage*, points out that the emendation created new problems, such as the notion that remarriage is not allowed as long as the first wife is alive (65-66).

[77] Steudel, "Ehelosigkeit," 124, referring to Elisha Qimron, *The Hebrew of the Dead Sea Scrolls* (Atlanta: Scholars, 1986) 62.

[78] Gruber, "Women in the Religious System," 183. Cf. Davies, "Marriage and the Essenes," 80.

[79] Fitzmyer, "Matthean Divorce Texts," 96. Schiffman, "Laws Pertaining to Women," 217; Lawrence H. Schiffman, "Contemporizing Halakic Exegesis in the Dead Sea Scrolls," in *Reading the Present in the Qumran Library: The Perception of the Contemporary by Means of Scriptural Interpretations* (ed. Kristin De Troyer and Armin Lange; SBLSymS 30; Atlanta: SBL, 2005) 35-41, 39.

[80] Noam, "Divorce in Qumran," 211-19. The similarity to the house of Shammai was noted already by Schiffman, "Laws Pertaining to Women," 217.

marriage to a divorcee, who would on this view have to be an adulteress. He suggests that this might account for the absence of divorcees as possible marriage partners in 4Q271 3. He notes the use there of דבר "the thing" to refer a woman's engagement in illicit sexual relations.[81] If as Kampen suggests, we have here an allusion to ערות דבר "something shameful" (Deut 24:1),[82] then it must refer to an adulteress, and on the basis of this strict understanding, to a divorced woman. Thus 4Q271 3 would include the prohibition of marrying a divorced woman, at least, a woman divorced for adultery (i.e., who has had illicit sexual relations outside her father's house, that is, as a married woman).[83] It is accordingly followed by two further prohibitions: marrying an unchaste unmarried woman and an unchaste widow, building a comprehensive coverage of women forbidden because they have engaged in illicit sexual relations.

This is not the same, however, as prohibiting all divorcees from remarriage. Thus the apparent silence in 4Q271 3 with regard to divorcees in D's discussion of acquiring spouses or, better, the implied allusion to them as adulteresses, does not require that we should assume a peculiar understanding of divorce which omits the right of any divorcee to remarry, as, for instance, Aaron Shemesh proposes.[84] Prohibition of marrying adulteresses, including both prostitutes and women divorced for adultery, does not, therefore, amount to an absolute prohibition of remarriage after divorce. It does not imply that men who have divorced their wives may not remarry. It implies only that they and any other men are not to marry divorcees, that is, adulteresses. The exception would be, when a divorced woman is not deemed to be an adulteress, such as may be presumed to be the case in 4QD^{b}/4Q267 9 vi.4-5 which stipulates that a husband is expelled from the camp for engaging in illicit sexual relations with his wife and where the wife presumably remains in the camp.[85]

When Schuller observes that D offers no evidence of the existence of divorced women among those listed as receiving financial support from the community in CD 14.12-17,[86] this, too, need not mean that divorce never took place, since there clear evidence that it did. Rather it probably reflects the fact that it was rare, but more probably that that divorced women were considered to be adulteresses and so

---

[81] Noam, "Divorce in Qumran," 220.

[82] Kampen, "Matthean Divorce Texts Reexamined," 155-56.

[83] On 4QD^{f}/4Q271.3 and parallels see our discussion on pp. 156-63 below.

[84] So Shemesh, "4Q271.3," who sees this as evidence that remarriage by divorcees was forbidden (246, 248).

[85] So Brin, "Divorce at Qumran," 242-43.

[86] Schuller, "Women in the Dead Sea Scrolls," 125.

expelled.[87] Thus the evidence does not support reading 4.20-21 as attacking remarriage after divorce. It makes best sense, therefore, as a statement about polygyny.

Polygyny seems the primary focus also in the author's justification for his stance in what follows.[88] It begins with Gen 1:27, זכר ונקבה ברא אותם "male and female he created them" (4.21). The author appears to find support for his monogynous view in the occurrence of the singular nouns, זכר ונקבה "male and female". The missing steps in the reasoning appear to include the thought: this statement describes two individuals; it also describes marriage; therefore marriage consists of two individuals, a male and female.[89] The same kind of reasoning underlies the example of those who entered the ark in Gen 7:7-9, which also includes the words זכר ונקבה "male and female".[90] They entered in pairs. Pairs are what God wanted then and still wants. Therefore marriage consists of a pair, a man and a woman. Accordingly, this is the order of creation willed by God. Neither of these illustrations is so suitable for forbidding remarriage after divorce, let alone after death of a spouse. The same is true of the citation of Deut 17:17 in the next argument.

ועל הנשיא כתוב 2 לא ירבה לו נשים

And concerning the prince it is written, "He shall not multiply wives to himself". (V) (5.1b-2a)

In the *Temple Scroll* it is expounded in relation to the king, as in Deuteronomy (56.18; 57.15-19; cf. Deut 17:14-20). Here, however, it is applied generally.[91] The

---

[87] Stegemann, *Essener*, explains the absence of widows and divorced women from the list of those to receive care reflects the situation that women did not become full members and so retained property (262).

[88] On the importance of the rationale for interpreting the ruling see Vermes, "Sectarian Matrimonial Halakhah," 200-201.

[89] Cf. Davies, "Marriage and the Essenes," who sees the proof texts as referring to what is required for procreation, namely, only a pair (81-82). He cites Josephus' account of the Essenes to emphasise the focus on marriage only for procreation (83-84). It is not clear to me that the document reflects this concern with procreation.

[90] Noted already by Evald Lövestam, "Divorce and Remarriage in the New Testament," *Jewish Law Annual* 4 (1981) 47-65, 50.

[91] On the extent of polygyny at the time see Wassen, *Women*, who notes that "although it is impossible to know how common the practice of polygyny was, there is evidence that some men still took more than one wife in the late Second Temple period" (118). She cites Josephus *A.J.* 17.14; and the Babatha archives, which show that it occurred not only in royal circles. See also Instone-Brewer, *Divorce and Remarriage*, 59-60; Michael L. Satlow, *Jewish Marriage in Antiquity* (Princeton: Princeton University Press, 2001) 189-92; John J. Collins, "Marriage, Divorce and Family in Second Temple Judaism," in *Families in Ancient*

focus is clearly on having multiple wives at the same time. Multiplying wives was one of the notoriously negative aspects of both David's and Solomon's reigns, probably alluded to also in *4QMMT* C 12-26 and possibly already in CD 3.9 (cf. also Sir 47:19-21).[92] The issue was not remarriage. The explanation about David is interesting, for it exonerates David from any guilt on the grounds with regard to polygyny that he did not know that law (cf. 2 Kings 22 – 23), an excuse applied in *Jubilees* also to Reuben (33:16; cf. also 41:23-25 on Judah). It also alludes to the incident with Uriah. In the latter the focus is "blood", that is, murder, rather than lust or adultery, which we might have expected in the context, although these would surely have also been condemned.[93]

If we understand the allegation of sexual wrongdoing through polygyny as also implying a reference to the second net, riches, then it makes good sense that the author introduces his second instance by referring to the third net, pollution of the temple.[94] Thus we read:

> וגם מטמאים הם את המקדש אשר אין הם 7 מבדיל כתורה ושוכבים עם הרואה את דם זובה
>
> And they also defile the temple because they do not differentiate according to the Law and sleep with a woman who sees the blood of her discharge. (*DSSSE*) (5.6b-7a)

The allegation that they "lie with a woman who sees her bloody discharge" (ושכבים עם הרואה את דם זובה) most likely refers to sexual intercourse during

---

Israel (ed. Leo G. Perdue et al.; The Family Religion and Culture; Louisville: Westminster John Knox, 1997) 104-62, 121-22.

[92] See my discussion on p. 83 above.

[93] In her extensive discussion Jacqueline C. R. de Roo, "David's Deeds in the Dead Sea Scrolls," *DSD* 6 (1999) 44-65, argues plausibly that 5.5b-6a is best translated, "And the works of David were offered, except the blood (murder) of Uriah, and God left them to him" (ויעלו מעשי דויד מלבד דם אוריה ויעזבם לו אל). This assumes the cultic meaning of עלה "to offer", used metaphorically, and that ויעזבם "left them" means that they remained valid in God's memory to the benefit of later generations. Cf. Gary A. Anderson, "Two Notes on Measuring Character and Sin at Qumran," in *Things Revealed: Studies in Early Jewish and Christian Literature in Honor of Michael E. Stone* (JSJSupp 89; ed. Esther Chazon, David Satran and Ruth Clements; Leiden: Brill, 2004) 141-47, who understands עלה as "to weigh little" and so sees both parts of the verse speaking of forgiveness (145-46). See also Wacholder, *New Damascus Document*, who argues: "It grants the king absolution for all other misdeeds he may have committed, but makes him responsible for the blood of Uriah" (198). He was left to deal with it.

[94] Wacholder, *New Damascus Document*, finds a reference to defiling the temple through sexual intercourse in the temple city in 5.6b-11 (201), but the passage makes no mention of this. It comes to it only in 12.1.

menstruation, forbidden in Lev 18:19 and 20:18 and identified as causing impurity in 15:24. As Wassen argues, the absence of a biblical proof text probably reflects widespread recognition that this was forbidden and so needed no further warrant.[95] She notes that it could conceivably refer both to menstrual discharge and to bleeding at other times, drawing attention to the use of *zabah* to cover both categories in *4QTohorot A*/4Q274 1 i.4.[96] One could also point to 4QD[g]/4Q272 1 ii.7, where it is probably to be read as a title including a range of categories including נדה "menstrual impurity" in 4QD[a]/4Q266 6 and 4QD[g]/4Q272 1 ii (see the discussion on pp. 146-53 below).

Wassen goes further, however, arguing that such transgressions would be so unlikely among Jews of the time, that it is better to read the prohibition here in relation to marriage with foreign women who might not attend with such care to these matters. She cites concern with foreign women in *4QMMT* B 48-49 and 4QOrd[b]/4Q513 2 ii and 10 ii.3.[97] This is possible, but nowhere in the contexts which address the issue is this made explicit. It would, incidentally, be an indirect indication that D tolerates such marriages.

Many have noted that if one wanted to illustrate defiling the temple as a category distinct from sexual wrongdoing, there would be many stronger examples which could have been chosen.[98] As it stands, the text uses sexual intercourse with a menstruant (and possibly also the third instance, namely, marrying of nieces) to illustrate defiling the temple. This makes sense because for the author both nets are operating: sexual wrongdoing and defiling the temple. Failure to differentiate between purity and impurity leads to impurity which defiles the temple: אין הם מבדיל כתורה "none of them differentiates according to the Law" (5.6b-7a); similarly, ולהבדיל בין הטמא לטהור ולהודיע בין הקודש לחול "to differentiate between clean and unclean and to make known the difference between holy and unholy" (6.17b-18a; 12.19-21). It is interesting that the author sees the defilement as affecting not only the person, but also the temple. The context does not suggest that this refers only to priests who thus render themselves unclean and then enter the temple.[99] In line with *Jubilees* the author appears to see any such act by an Israelite (in the immediate context, by its would-be teachers and interpreters of the Law) as defiling the temple.[100] The connection between defiling the temple and intercourse with a menstruant may well be provided by

[95] Wassen, *Women*, 119.

[96] Wassen, *Women*, 119.

[97] Wassen, *Women*, 120.

[98] So Davies, *Damascus Covenant*, 116.

[99] Cf. Harrington, *Purity Texts*, who takes it as referring to priests (100).

[100] Cf. Kampen, "Significance of the Temple," argues that the focus, including on sexual wrongdoing, is not on Israel defiling the existing temple but members of the sect defiling the eschatological temple (190-96).

Leviticus, where the declaration about contracting impurity by having sexual intercourse with a menstruant in Lev 15:24 is followed by provisions about a *zabah* (15:25-30) (to which D also applies the same ruling in 4Q266 6),[101] and then immediately by the statement: "Thus you shall keep the people of Israel separate from their uncleanness, so that they do not die in their uncleanness by defiling my tabernacle (ולא ימתו בטמאתם בטמאם את משכני) that is in their midst" (15:31).

The third concern is with the laws of incest.

ולוקחים 8 איש את בת אחיה{ם}ו ואת בת אחותו *vacat*
ומשה אמר אל 9 אחות אמך לא תקרב שאר אמך היא
ומשפט העריות לזכרים 10 הוא כתוב
וכהם הנשים ואם תגלה בת האח את ערות אחי 11 אביה והיא שאר

> and each man takes as wife 8 the daughter of his brother and the daughter of his sister. *blank*
> But Moses said, "Do 9 not approach your mother's sister, she is a blood relation of your mother". The law of incest, 10 written for males, applies equally to females, and therefore to the daughter of a brother who uncovers the nakedness of the brother of 11 her father, for he is a blood relation. (*DSSSE*) (5.7b-11)

Here the author follows the line of converse logic in arguing that what applies to women and their nephews (Lev 18:13) must also apply to men and their nieces.[102] As Schwartz notes, this reflects a manner of approaching legislation which goes beyond citing authority, to engage in reasoned argument.[103] The opposing position

---

[101] See the discussion on p. 151 below.

[102] Wassen, *Women*, notes the inclusive reading also in dealing with the ruling in Deut 23:24 about oaths in 16.2-12 (121). One might also contemplate reading the first instance as reflecting an inclusive reading of Lev 18:18, as Ginzberg, *Unknown Jewish Sect*, suggested (19), although this would only make sense in relation to remarriage, not to polygamy, where the issue is only polygyny, hardly polyandry.

[103] Daniel R. Schwartz, "Law and Truth: On Qumran-Sadducean and Rabbinic Views of Law," in *The Dead Sea Scrolls: Forty Years of Research* (ed. D. Dimant and U. Rappaport; STDJ 10; Leiden: Brill, 1992) 229-40, who writes: "In other words, the union is not wrong because God forbade it, as a nominalist would say. Rather, God forbade it because it *is* wrong" (231). He sees the same operating in the arguments against polygamy, where he notes: "for those used to rabbinic halakha it is surprising to find anyone building a law out of a statement found in narratives concerning mankind's prehistory" (231). He also notes "the rabbinic refusal to grant normative importance to contemporary (since Sinai!) divine revelation, as opposed to Qumran which took it for granted. The latter position is, for religious people, simply a fact of realism: if religion consists of doing what God wants, whatever He wants, and whenever He announces it, it is included" (238), a contrast reminiscent to some extent of differences between traditional Catholic and Protestant perspectives. See also the critical discussion in Lutz Doering, "Überlegungen zum Ansatz der Halacha in den Qumrantexten," in *Qumran Kontrovers: Beiträge zu den Textfunden*

which limits the prohibition to women and nephews, but allows marriage of men and their nieces, became a norm in rabbinic exposition.[104] Here we have evidence that the issue was controversial. The author stands in line with *Jubilees* and the *Temple Scroll*, but the latter appears to assume it as uncontroversial. The prohibition reappears in the list of transgressions in 4QD^{e}/4Q270 2 ii.16, and may be alluded to in a general way in 7.1 and 8.6b-7a. It appears with some emphasis in *4QHalakhah A*/4Q251 17.2, discussed on pp. 225-27 below. In relation to the nets, it is clear that this third instance is a further example of the first net, sexual wrongdoing. The author may have intended that it also be read as a second way in which the temple was being defiled. Again, this need not imply that the focus is only on priests.[105] The perspective shared with *Jubilees*, which makes much of the sin of incest, would see the defilement as taking place as a result of any Israelite acting in this way.

Of the three nets, the first, זנות, "sexual wrongdoing", receives the greatest attention. This coheres both with the emphasis we have detected thus far in the Admonition and with much of the rest of D now preserved in the Qumran material. The author does not however ignore the other two nets. His statement that they are nets which function closely together indicates that he sees them as interrelated. Two of the nets are operating in the second instance, which specifically mentions defiling the temple in relation to having intercourse with a menstruant. But two are also operating in the first instance, which specifically mentions sexual wrongdoing in relation to polygyny, in which greed for riches plays a significant role. The third instance, also concerned with sexual wrongdoing probably functions similarly as an illustration of actions which defile the temple, thus involving two of the nets.

There is parallel material to these instances, in particular, in relation to defiling the temple in *Pss. Sol.* 8:9-12.

9 ἐν καταγαίοις κρυφίοις αἱ παρανομίαι αὐτῶν ἐν παροργισμῷ
υἱὸς μετὰ μητρὸς καὶ πατὴρ μετὰ θυγατρὸς συνεφύροντο
10 ἐμοιχῶντο ἕκαστος τὴν γυναῖκα τοῦ πλησίον αὐτοῦ
συνέθεντο αὐτοῖς συνθήκας μετὰ ὅρκου περὶ τούτων

---

vom Toten Meer (ed. Jörg Frey and Hartmut Stegemann with the collaboration of Michael Becker and Alexander Maurer; Einblicke 6; Paderborn: Bonifatius, 2003) 89-114, 105-10.

104 Ginzberg, *Unknown Jewish Sect*, 23-24. Schremer, "Qumran Polemic on Marital Law," argues that the third instance originally belonged closely with the first and reflects the practice evident in *m. Yeb* 1.2 of men taking their nieces as additional wives (155). It is not clear from D that the author is making such a link.

105 Cf. Davies, *Damascus Covenant*, who claims that to relate the third instance to defiling the temple would necessarily imply that it related to priests, but argues there is nothing to suggest that this accusation should apply only to a section of the population in this way (114).

11 τὰ ἅγια τοῦ θεοῦ διηρπάζοσαν
ὡς μὴ ὄντος κληρονόμου λυτρουμένου
12 ἐπατοῦσαν τὸ θυσιαστήριον κυρίου
ἀπὸ πάσης ἀκαθαρσίας
καὶ ἐν ἀφέδρῳ αἵματος
ἐμίαναν τὰς θυσίας ὡς κρέα
9 In secret places underground was their lawbreaking, provoking (him),
son involved with mother and father with daughter;
10 Everyone committed adultery with his neighbor's wife;
they made agreements with them with an oath about these things.
11 They stole from the sanctuary of God
as if there were no redeeming heir.
12 They walked on the place of sacrifice of the Lord,
(coming) from all kinds of uncleanness;
and (coming) with menstrual blood (on them),
they defiled the sacrifices as if they were common meat.

The main delict in common is defiling the temple with menstrual blood. The reference is to priests who engage in intercourse with, presumably, their wives during menstruation. In D the focus is not just priests but what applies to all Israel. It is, however, being alleged against the "builders of the wall", the would-be teachers of the people, presumably priests.

It is interesting to note that *Pss. Sol.* 8:9-11 also alludes to incest (between parents and children), as well as adultery, and stealing from the temple. Davies points to similar concerns also in *Jub.* 7:20 (sexual wrongdoing, impurity, and injustice).[106] As in *Jubilees*, such acts of sexual wrongdoing are understood to defile the temple. This is especially so of incest in *Jubilees*, the focus of the third instance in D, which *Jubilees* applies in a broader sense and not especially in relation to marrying nieces.

Jonathan Klawans notes that the emphasis in citing the sins of incest and sexual relations with a menstruant is not ritual defilement, but moral defilement, such as is reflected in Leviticus 18.[107] He notes that defilement of the land is a theme in the context of Isaiah 24:17 with which the passage began, pointing to

---

[106] Davies, *Damascus Covenant*, 110. See also Monika Pesthy, "The Three Nets of Belial from Qumran to the *Opus Imperfectum in Matthaeum*," in *Jerusalem, Alexandria, Rome: Studies in Ancient Cultural Interaction in Honour of A. Hilhorst* (ed. Florentino García Martínez and Gerard P. Luttikhuizen; Leiden: Brill, 2003) 243-53, 244, who, following a lead from Hans Kosmala, "The Three Nets of Belial: A Study of the Terminology of Qumran and the New Testament," *ASTI* 4 (1965) 91-113, then goes on to notice similar triads in the New Testament and beyond, including Eph 5:3; 4:19; Col 3:5; Mark 4:19-20; 1 John 2:16, and the fifth or sixth century Latin work, *Opus imperfectum in Matthaeum*, of pseudo-Chrysostom (245-50).

[107] Klawans, *Impurity and Sin*, 53-54.

24:5, "For the earth was defiled under its inhabitants".[108] He also notes that while here and in Leviticus the focus is defilement of the land, "the view of sexual sins as a source of sanctuary defilement was common in the late second temple period".[109] We have drawn attention to *Jub.* 30:15-16 in this regard which links sexual sin (intermarriage) with defilement of the people and the sanctuary (cf. also 23:21-23). Klawans makes a distinction however between these two sins and the first concerned with polygyny (and, as he sees it, also remarriage after divorce), because "this sin does not, presumably, violate the sex laws of Leviticus; if it did, CD would allude to them. Since it does not violate that code, it does not result in the moral defilement discussed in Leviticus 18:24-30".[110] If, however, we recognise an allusion to Lev 18:18 in the prohibition of polygamy, this conclusion needs revision. Then all three acts would produce such defilement. This counts in favour of reading all three as interrelated.

The prohibition of polygyny leaves some questions unanswered. These include what one should do about levirate marriage, which requires it. Sidnie White Crawford notes its absence in discussion of law in the documents at Qumran.[111] It is, however, assumed in *Jubilees*, for instance in the story of Judah and Tamar, and in the biblical sources, and also apparently in the *Temple Scroll*, if we consider that 4QT[b]/4Q524 represents the final column, as discussed above (p. 5). The prohibition also raises the status of concubines, captive women, and slaves. The fragmentary text of 4QD[e]/4Q270 4.19 (on this see pp. 155-56 below) appears to assume that sexual relations with slaves were acceptable and the possible allusion to the laws in Deut 21:10-14 about captive women may indicate that, as in the *Temple Scroll*, they might become wives, but then sole wives (cf. their acceptance in 11QT[a]/11Q19 63.10-15, but probable rejection in *4QMMT* C and the discussion of these above, pp. 30-31, 79-80).

After the exposition of the three nets in the context of concern with sexual wrongdoing, the author redirects his attention away from specific issues to more general criticisms of his opponents and their mode of interpretation. Thus in 5.12 he accuses them of blasphemy and of claiming that laws "are not certain". The accusation fits a situation where the opponents are seeking to offer more liberal

---

108 Klawans, *Impurity and Sin*, 55.

109 Klawans, *Impurity and Sin*, 56.

110 Klawans, *Impurity and Sin*, 56.

111 Sidnie White Crawford, "Not According to Rule: Women, the Dead Sea Scrolls and Qumran," in *Emanuel: Studies in Hebrew Bible, Septuagint, and Dead Sea Scrolls in Honor of Emanuel Tov* (ed. Shalom M. Paul, Robert A. Kraft, Lawrence H. Schiffman, and Weston W. Fields; SVT 94; Leiden: Brill, 2003) 127-50, 134.

interpretations of laws.[112] The author continues with warnings, based on God's actions "in ancient times" (5.15, 17), against associating with them, and with assertions about the people's lack of discernment (in following them). When the author refers here to the past, he does so within the framework of conflict with Belial, speaking of Moses and Aaron with the Prince of Lights in a struggle with Belial who raised up "Jannes and his brother" (5.18-19). This recalls the language of 4.13, which speaks of Belial being unleashed against Israel.[113] The author then appears to begin a new cycle of telling the story.

The Fourth Account CD 5.20 – 8.21a; CD 19.1 – 20.34; 4QD^a/4Q266 3 ii.7b-13; 4QD^b/4Q267 2 4-15; 4QD^d/4Q269 4 i.1-3; 6QD/6Q15 3 2-5

As 5:18-19 recall the reference to Belial in 4:13, so the motif of shifting the boundary in 5.20 recalls the image of the boundary in 4:12 (הגבול 5.20; cf. also 1.16 and החיק 4.12) to describe those who led Israel astray. There follows the account of God's raising up "from Aaron men of discernment and from Israel men of wisdom" (V) (6.2-3), which then moves into an exposition of Num 21:18 ("the well which the princes dug, which the nobles of the people delved with the stave"). An allusion to the history of the community appears to be encapsulated in the exposition in 6.3-11, and it may refer to the time before the coming of the Teacher of Righteousness. Then the author brings an exhortation to their successors, his community, to keep separate from others (6.11-14). It may enjoin them not to participate in the temple,[114] unless we translate with Davies,

> And all who have entered the covenant are not to enter the sanctuary "to light my altar in vain" unless they follow the observances of the law prescribed for the period of wickedness.[115]

---

[112] Cf. 1QH^a xii.17b-18, where the same words, "are not certain", are cited and other motifs from this context appear but without the specific reference to sexual wrongdoing. On this see the relevant discussion below (p. 240).

[113] On the background to the Jannes and Jambres figures see Lange, *Weisheit*, 416-20.

[114] This stands in tension with other parts which still assume participation in the temple cult and so may reflect the work of a later redaction.

[115] Philip R. Davies, "The Judaism(s) of the Damascus Document," in *The Damascus Document: A Centennial of Discovery: Proceedings of the Third International Symposium of the Orion Center for the Study of the Dead Sea Scrolls and Associated Literature, 4-8 February 1998* (ed. Joseph M. Baumgarten, Esther G. Chazon, and Avital Pinnick; STDJ 34; Leiden: Brill, 2000) 27-43, 35. See also his discussion in Philip R. Davies, "The Ideology of the Temple in the Damascus Document," in *Sects and Scrolls: Essays on Qumran and Related Topics* (South Florida Studies in the History of Judaism 134; Atlanta: Georgia, 1996) 45-60.

At this point the author returns to identify particular evils (beyond false teaching and interpretation in a general sense) (6.14b – 7.4). Here we find allusions to wicked wealth of various kinds which defiles: through vows and promises, through theft from the temple (cf. *Pss. Sol.* 8:11, cited above), and through stealing from the poor, widows, and orphans (6.15-17). The author goes on to address other issues, including the need to differentiate between clean and unclean (הטמא לטהור), holy and profane (הקדוש לחול), recalling 5.6b-7a; keeping the sabbath, the festivals, and the day of fasting in line with the teaching of the founders of the movement; setting apart holy portions (tithes); loving one's brothers; strengthening the hand of the poor, the needy and the stranger; seeking peace of one's brother; not being unfaithful toward a blood relative; refraining from sexual wrongdoing (זנות) according to the statute; reproving one's brother; and keeping oneself from uncleanness (6.17 – 7.4).

We note that sexual wrongdoing (זנות) again features here. While it appears as a single item among many, this may be misleading. It should probably be read closely both with what precedes and with what follows. It is immediately preceded by a statement about one's kin.

ולא ימעל איש בשאר בשרו

> And a man shall not be unfaithful to/act illegally/trespass in relation to his near relative.* (7.1)

This finds its echo in the list of transgressions in 8.4-8, where we read:

ויתעלמו איש בשאר בשרו 7 ויגשו לזמה

> And each man hid himself from/ignored (the status of?) his near relative, 7 but approached debauchery.* (8.6b-7a)

To trespass with regard to one's own kin (שאר בשרו) and ignore their status almost certainly alludes to incest, in the words of Baumgarten and Schwartz, "that is, they ignored the fact that certain relationships are incestuous".[116] The word מעל, used with the preposition ב "in relation to, towards", can carry the meaning "be untrue, violate one's legal obligations" and can also refer to taking what is banned. It need not have a sexual reference and has none in 1.3; 9.16-17; 20.4. Thus Davies takes it here as "applying to offence in respect of family obligations".[117] But the word appears in a context concerned with sexual wrongdoing in *4QMMT* C 4 and 9. Already Ginzberg pointed to the use here in 7.1

---

[116] Baumgarten and Schwartz, "Damascus Document", 29 n. 80. So already Ginzberg, *Unknown Jewish Sect*, 32; similarly Kampen, "Matthean Divorce Texts Reexamined," 154; Shemesh, "Scriptural Interpretations," 164; Wacholder, *New Damascus Document*, 232.

[117] Davies, *Damascus Covenant*, 131.

of the word שאר, which appears in a context concerned with incest in 5.7-11.[118] Interestingly, Davies cites with approval the findings of Murphy-O'Connor who points to the influence of the Holiness Code behind the list, including behind the item about trespassing with regard to kin, namely, Lev 18:6-7, which he then acknowledges in his parenthesis as having to do with "illicit marriages".[119] Our passage reflects the language with which Leviticus 18 introduces the list of prohibitions against incest: איש איש אל כל שאר בשרו לא תקרבו "None of you shall approach anyone near of kin" (18:6).

Shemesh notes the influence of Isa 58:5-7 on this list of transgressions, including ignoring one's kin, and sets the latter statement in relation to the *baraita* in *b. Yeb.* 62b which interprets ignoring one's kin in relation to not marrying one's niece, perhaps intentionally directed against the sectarian stance such as we find it in D.[120] It would make good sense of its position in both lists, immediately before another reference to sexual wrongdoing, if it is be read as referring to incest with nieces, a concern of the author.[121] It may, however, also include incest of other kinds, a major concern in *Jubilees*. A similar concern, expressed in similar language, appears to be among the charges against Hananiah in 4Q477, as we note below (pp. 232-33; cf. also Sir 23:16b).

Perhaps the reference to reproof without resentment in the following lines also has sexual wrongdoing, in particular, in mind, namely, reproof for transgressing laws pertaining to sexual wrongdoing, although this need not be the case. The same is to be said of the conclusion of the list:

> ולהבדל מכל הטמאות כמשפטם
> ולא ישקץ 4 איש את רוח קדשיו כאשר הבדיל אל להם
>
> to keep apart from every uncleanness according to the regulations, without anyone defiling 4 his holy spirit, according to what God kept apart for them. (*DSSSE*) (7.3-4)

---

[118] Ginzberg, *Unknown Jewish Sect*, 32 n. 82.

[119] Davies, *Damascus Covenant*, 133. Cf. Jerome Murphy-O'Connor, "A Literary Analysis of the Damascus Document VI,20 - VIII,3," *RB* 78 (1971) 210-32, 215-16. In his treatment of the list of accusations against the "princes of Judah", Davies cites 8.6 as referring to incest and sets it in parallel to 7.2 (163). Davies' table which correlates the accusations found in five sections of CD, identified as 4.13-19a; 4.19bff; 6.11ff; 8.3ff; 9 – 16, incidentally shows that only one item occurs in all five sections, "lust" and only one in four: "incest" (161-62).

[120] Shemesh, "Scriptural Interpretations," 164-67.

[121] Cf. A. Baumgarten, "Perception of the Past," who sees it as addressing lack of concern for kin and notes that this would set D apart from what Josephus reports as Essene practice (*B.J.* 2.134) and from 4Q477 (7-8).

The word, הבדיל ("to differentiate"), which appears here twice, featured in 5.6b-7a, in the context of the allegation of sexual relations with women in menstruation (אין הם מבדיל כתורה "for they did not keep apart in accordance with the law"). We also find a reference to defiling one's holy spirit immediately after the allegation of incest וגם את רוח קדשיהם טמאו "and also they defile their holy spirit" (5.11). The term הטמאות "uncleanness" almost certainly includes reference to sexual wrongdoing. Accordingly, the list of instructions may be read as having a focus on sexual wrongdoing in its final section, explicitly in 7.1b-2a, and probably in 7.1a, but also, at least, in part in 7.2b-4. This would cohere with the emphasis on sexual wrongdoing thus far in the document.

There follows in CD 7.4-6 a promise to

כל המתהלכים 5 באלה בתמים קדש על פי כל יסורו

all who walk 5 in these (precepts) in perfect holiness, according to all his teaching.* (7.4b-5a)

The form of the promise is slightly different in CD-A and CD-B.

ברית אל נאמנות להם 6 לחיותם אלף דור

The covenant of God shall be an assurance for them that they shall live for a thousand generations.* (CD-A 7.5b-6a)

נאמנות להם לחיותם לאלפי דורות

ככ שומר הברית והחסד 2 לאהב(יו) ולשמרי מצותי (מצותו) לאלף דור

assurance for them that they shall live for thousands of generations.

As it is written, "Keeping the covenant and grace with those who love (him) and keep (his) my commandments for a thousand generations".* (CD-B 19.1-2)

CD-B, which begins mid sentence, may represent an expansion, in which it cites the text which underlies אלף דור "a thousand generations", namely Deut 7:9 (cf. the citation of Deut 7:8 in 8.15). Alternatively CD-A abbreviates.

Baumgarten draws attention to the words of Pliny (*Nat. Hist.* 5.17), who speaks of the Essene celibates living by the Dead Sea:

Ita per saeculorum milia—incredibile dictu—gens aeterna est, in qua nemo nascitur. Tam fecunda illis aliorum vita paenentia est.

in this way this people has lasted – strange to say – for thousands of generations though no one is born within it. So fruitful for them is the penitence for life which others feel.[122]

---

[122] Baumgarten. "Qumran-Essene Restraints on Marriage," 19.

He notes

> the striking verbal parallels: saeculorum milia = *'lp dwr*; gens aeterna = *'m 'wlmym*. The word fecunda may be compared with *prwt zr'*, 'fruitfulness of seed', also used metaphorically in 1QS 4.6-7, while paenentia brings to mind the frequently used sectarian epithet *šby pš'*.[123]

Perhaps Pliny had access to Essene writings or to a source that knew them. Here in D the assumption could be that "those who walk in perfect holiness" will live for thousands of generations without procreation. The idea could be closely related to the hope articulated in *Jubilees* 23, where we find the assumption that sexual wrongdoing progressively reduced human lifespan and that in the future this would be reversed, but there the future state refers to living as infants and small children (23:28-29). Here, however, the assumption is that people will continue to live as adults. The thought is therefore closer to *1 Enoch* 5:7-9; 10:17, which promise long life, but assume the normal processes of marriage and birth. Earlier D has spoken of the seed of the remnant filling the land, also presupposing normal processes (2.11-12). Nothing suggests fruitfulness in these texts is just a metaphor. So the passage need not be read in the light of Pliny's comment as a reference to celibacy. The fact that it has been understood in this way, however, is related to what immediately follows.

There, after a *vacat* the document makes reference to married people who live in camps (7.6-9a).

> *vacat* ואם מחנות ישבו כסרך הארץ (only in CD-B 19.3 אשר היה מקדם)
> ולקחו 7 נשים (only in CD 19.3 כמנהג התורה) והולידו בנים
> והתהלכו על פי התורה *vacat* וכמשפט 8 היסורים כסרך התורה כאשר אמר
> בין איש לאשתו ובין אב 9 לבנו
>
> *Blank* And if they live in camps according to the rule of the land (as it was from ancient times)
> and take wives (according to the custom of the law) and bear children,
> they shall walk according to the law *Blank* and according to the regulation of the teachings according to the rule of the Law as it says:
> "Between a man and his wife and between a father and his son".* (cf. Num 30:17)

Elisha Qimron suggested that with this new beginning (ואם *vacat*) the author distinguished two groups, those who "walk in these (precepts) in perfect holiness" (7.5-6a) and those who live in camps.[124] The former "should not be worried about

[123] Baumgarten. "Qumran-Essene Restraints on Marriage," 19.

[124] Elisha Qimron, "Celibacy in the Dead Sea Scrolls and the Two Kinds of Sectarians," in *The Madrid Qumran Congress: Proceedings of the International Congress on the Dead Sea Scrolls, Madrid 18-21 March, 1991* (Vol 1; STDJ 11.1; ed. J. Trebolle

their continuity, since God will keep His promise and His covenant will keep them alive for thousands of generations (even though they have no women and children)".[125] Those not belonging to this group should marry. These two groups are commonly seen as belonging within a single movement, those who lived (permanently or for a period) in voluntary celibacy and those who did not. D is then often seen as "the rule for all Essenes living throughout Judaea, while the Community Rule applies only to those permanent dwellers at Qumran, who have chosen to pursue 'the perfection of holiness'".[126]

It is interesting that CD-B brings what appear to be expansions at this point or may reflect an earlier fuller text. As well as "and if they live in camps according to the rule of the Land" (7.6 = 19.2-3), it has: "as it was since ancient times" (מקדם אשר היה); and as well as "marrying" (7.6-7 = 19.3), it has: "according to the custom of the Law" (כמנהג התורה). This suggests the need to strengthen the warrant for this lifestyle.[127]

The transition from living for a thousand generations to the words, "and if they live in camps", may, however, suggest that the author envisages that those so living will also go on to live for a thousand generations. This is Wassen's view, who argues that the reference to those who live in camps is the result of a

---

Barrera and L. Vegas Montaner; Leiden: Brill, 1991) 287-94, 289-90. See also Baumgarten, "Qumran-Essene Restraints on Marriage," 18-20; White Crawford, "Not According to Rule," 146-47. See also Wacholder, *New Damascus Document*, who sees the document differentiating people who live in cities including Jerusalem – they are to be celibate – from the others who are to procreate (236-37).

[125] Qimron, "Celibacy," 290. He argues that the first group applied to themselves the rules they saw as appropriate to the temple and by extension to Jerusalem as a whole. Having left it (CD 6.11-12, 19), they now saw themselves as a substitute for the temple and as the camp of holiness in contrast to the other camps (290-91). In this he draws on Ginzberg, *Unknown Jewish Sect*, 32.

[126] White Crawford, "Not According to Rule," 149. See also Steudel, "Ehelosigkeit," 117-18; and Moshe J. Bernstein, "Women and Children in Legal and Liturgical Texts from Qumran," *DSD* 11 (2004) 191-211, who notes the substantial difference between "the community described in CD/4QD (and most other legal texts from Qumran) and that described by 1QS", which is "perhaps the exception among legal texts at Qumran in representing a society which does not include women" (211).

[127] On this see Steudel, "Ehelosigkeit," 117; Maxine L. Grossman, "Reading for Gender in the Damascus Document," *DSD* 11 (2004) 212-39, who notes that the data could support a plurality of historical constructions from the need to justify a new development to a need to defend an old one over against celibacy, but that both would assume "competing claims to a shared tradition" (235-36).

redactional addition,[128] and that it is not meant to make a distinction between the two, but to single out those who live in camps, "*from among the first group*, in order for the redactor to emphasise that the whole family, including women and children, should observe the laws and the community regulations".[129] If so, it certainly envisages not a form of celibacy, but marriage and, specifically, begetting children.

Whether the reference to those who live in camps is a redactional addition or not, it is certainly possible, indeed, preferable to read the text as it stands as referring not to two groups, but to a single group of people, "the men of perfect holiness", some of whom live in camps, while others do not. The latter might live in celibacy, a likely implication of the identification of others as marrying. But all are surely to walk in perfect holiness, whether in camps or, presumably, in a special single location, and all receive the promise that they will live for a thousand years. The implication of this inclusive reading of "those who walk in these things in perfect holiness" is that it breaks the nexus between celibacy and living for a thousand years, and so does not read that promise in the light of Pliny. Pliny, or Pliny's sources, may have constructed the promise of living a thousand generations with knowledge about celibacy, without understanding the background of the promise which neither in Deut 7:9 nor in D had anything to do with celibacy.

In support of reading the text in this way, we can note that in speaking of those who "walk in these matters in perfect holiness in accordance with all his teachings", the reference is to what immediately precedes, the list of appropriate behaviours in 6.14 – 7.4. These are just as applicable to people living in camps. Nothing in the context suggests two sets of standards, one for the men of "perfect holiness" and one for those who live in camps.[130] Nothing suggests that the description "perfect holiness" means something more than what the preceding stipulations require. The author's concern is how all of them live, namely, according to the Law. Within that framework of thought, therefore, the author attends to those living in families, reminding them by citing words of Num 30:17, "between and man and his wife and between a father and his son", originally about vows and oaths, that observance of Torah applies also to family relations. What appear to be supplements, or perhaps remnants of the fuller original text, in CD-B reinforce the validity of this way of life.

The longer ending to the admonition in CD-B goes on to make frequent mention of "the men of perfect holiness" (20.2, 5, 7) within the second of three

---

[128] Following among others Murphy-O'Connor, "A Literary Analysis of the Damascus Document VI,20 - VIII,3," 222.

[129] Wassen, *Women*, 127.

[130] Cf. also 1QS/1Q28 8.20 which uses the designation to refer to all members of the community.

sets of warnings against apostasy (20.1b-8a). It refers to someone who has entered עדת אנשי תמים הקדש "the congregation of the men of holiness" (20.2), who is slack and who is expelled, but may be received back again. The third warning (20.8b-13), like the first (19.33b – 20.1a), speaks of permanent exclusion for apostates, adding: "And neither for them nor their families (למשפהותיהם) shall there be a part in the house of the law (בבית התורה)" (*DSSSE*) (20.13). This can be taken as further evidence that those who belonged to "the house of the law" include men with families. In this context, too, it is not evident that a distinction should be drawn between "men of perfect holiness" and those who belong in "the house of the law". Alternatively, the reference to families would apply only to the third group.

Nothing in the text suggests, that if the difference lies not only in location but in attitude towards marriage and family, these aspects make those living in camps less worthy.[131] Accordingly, nothing suggests that marrying and bearing children is a kind of second class level of upholding the law. This would also apply if we were to read the reference to those who walk in "perfect holiness", exclusively, as a separate group who practised celibacy. But it would open the possibility, that some might use the distinction to assert the superiority of the first group and to identify marriage and family as something potentially negative. The same possibility would arise later when some Christians chose celibacy, but it was not a necessary conclusion then; nor is there evidence in D that marriage or sexual relations are seen negatively, despite what Josephus writes of the Essenes. The text, in fact, accords with Josephus' report that there were both married and celibate Essenes among those who as men of perfect holiness sought to live by the Law and looked forward to the promise of living a thousand generations. One might counter that living a thousand generations would mean marriage would no longer be relevant, but that is a view of marriage and sexual relations which limits its value to procreation (reflected in *1 Enoch* 15:5-7, but not at all in *Jubilees* and nowhere indicated in D).

The author then turns to speak of God's future judgement against those who despise God's Law, and, according to CD-A, cites Isa 7:17, which refers to the dividing of Ephraim and Judah (7.11-12). For CD-A that division indicates the time of the formation of his community, using the notion of a remnant who escaped to the north (7.13-14a). It then expounds this further by a creative use of Amos 5:26-27, which includes the citation of Num 24:17 (7.14b – 8.3). The point of the comparison of that event with the future is to warn that members of the

---

[131] Cf. Hannah K. Harrington, "Purity in the Dead Sea Scrolls: Current Issues," *Currents in Biblical Research* 4 (2006) 397-428, who speaks of "celibates as the 'men of perfect holiness' as opposed to the inferior holiness of those who have families (CD 7.4-9)" (398).

covenant who apostatise shall face destruction, as they did then (8.1b-2a). "They shall be visited for destruction by the hands of Belial" (V), understood as the day of God's visitation (8.2b-3a).

CD-B also preserves these warnings about apostasy (19.13-14 = 8.1b-3a), but reaches there via a different set of texts. Instead of Isa 7:17, Amos 5:26-27 and Num 24:17, it cites Zech 13:7, about someone striking the shepherd, scattering the sheep and turning his hand against the little ones. It then uses an expression from Zech 11:11, עניי הצאן השמרים אתי "the poor ones of the flock the ones revering me", to identify a remnant who escape. The others are to be destroyed when the Messiah of Aaron and Israel arises (19.10-11a). Only at this point does CD-B point to past history as a warning, speaking of what happened "at the time of the former visitation" (19.12) and citing Ezek 9:4 in support. The copies converge again in 19.13-14 = 8.1b-3a.[132] In what follows they turn to Hos 5:10, but differ in that CD-A brings only part of the text, whereas CD-B brings the full citation.

היו שרי יהודה כמסיגי גבול עליהם אשפוך כמים עברתי

The princes of Judah have become like those who remove the landmark; on them I will pour out my wrath like water. (Hos 5:10)

היו שרי יהודה אשר תשפוך עליהם העברה

The princes of Judah have become those upon whom wrath will be poured out.* (CD-A 8.3)

היו שרי יהודה כמשיגי 16 גבול עליהם אשפך כמים עברה

The princes of Judah have become like those moving 16 the boundary; on them I shall pour out my wrath like water.* (CD-B 19.15-16a)

In CD-A the reference to Judah recalls its interpretation of the split of Ephraim from Judah in its citation of Isa 7:17 in 7.11-12 and its interpretation in 7.12-14a. By citing the words, כמשיגי גבול "like those moving the boundary",

[132] On the possible relationship between the texts see Stephen Hultgren "A New Literary Analysis of CD XIX-XX, part 1: CD XIX:1-32a (with CD VII:4b-VIII:18b): The Midrashim and the 'Princes of Judah'," *RevQ* 21 (2004) 549-78, who proposes that "the A and B texts are both dependent on a common, older source that included the *Isaiah* midrash of VII:10-13b and the *Zechariah-Ezekiel* midrash of XIX:7-13b. The Isaiah midrash was accidentally omitted from the B text. The *Amos-Numbers* midrash of VII:13c-21a did not stand in the common source but was added to it by the redactor of the A text" (568). See his discussion (568-76). See also the review of research in Menahem Kister, "The Development of the Early Recensions of the Damascus Document," *DSD* 14 (2007) 61-76, who noting the common word נמלטו "they escaped" (7.14) and ימלטו "they shall escape" (19.10) argues that the B text is earlier and spoke of future deliverance, whereas the A text refers to fleeing to Damascus as an event in the past and that proof texts were chosen which fitted each understanding. B's text is more consistent in the tenses of its verbs; A's is more complex, reflecting the changes (69-73).

CD-B makes a connection with the use of that imagery to describe the false interpreters of the Law in 4.12, 5.19 and eslewhere. In both, the "princes of Judah" represent those who exercise influence through their teaching.[133] The manuscripts diverge again in describing them. CD-A reads: "For they shall hope for healing but he will crush them. They are all of them rebels, for they have not turned away from the way of traitors" (V) (8.4-5a), whereas CD-B reads: "For they entered the covenant of conversion, but have not turned away from the way of traitors" (19.16b-17a). The author then proceeds to list the sins of "the princes of Judah". The variants are minimal.

> They have wallowed in the ways of sexual wrongdoing (בדרכי זונות)
> and wicked wealth (בהון הרשעה),
> they have taken revenge and borne malice,
> every man against his brother, and every man has hated his fellow,
> and every man has hid himself from/ignored (the status of?) his near relative
> (ויתעלמו איש בשאר בשרו),
> but they have approached for debauchery (ויגשו לזמה)
> and have acted arrogantly for the sake of gain (להון).
> And they have done each one that which seemed right in his eyes
> and have chosen each one the stubbornness of his heart,
> and they have not kept apart from the people (CD-B adds: and from their sins)
> and have wilfully rebelled by walking the ways of the wicked. (8.5-9a / 19.17b-21)
> (V with modification)

Here again we see the prominence of sexual wrongdoing, the first sin listed.[134] As in the discourse about the nets, sexual wrongdoing is associated with the second net, wealth. The word זמה "debauchery" in 8.7 also refers to sexual wrongdoing and is best taken with the preceding statement, ויתעלמו איש בשאר בשרו "and every man has hid himself from/ignored (the status of?) his near relative", and

---

[133] Hultgren "New Literary Analysis of CD XIX-XX, part 1," has proposed that in שרי יהודה "the princes of Judah" שרי be read not as "princes" but as "those who depart from", deriving it from שור = סור, a word play on Isa 7:17 in 7.12, אפרים מיל יהודה סור "Ephraim departed from Judah" (558). He notes that Ephraim is used elsewhere as a codename for opponents, in particular, the Pharisees (4QpNah/4Q169 3-4 ii.2; 4QPsa/4Q171 1-10 ii.18; CD 1.13 – 2.1; 4.19) (559). Here he sees it referring "to apostasy from the pre-teacher movement" (559). He notes also that this makes sense of the similarity between the summary list in 6.11b – 7.4a and the criticisms in 8.3-12, because the latter details the sins of the renegades (560). These are then appropriately identified as the builders of the wall, namely, false teachers (563).

[134] Jerome Murphy-O'Connor, "The Critique of the Princes of Judah (CD VIII 3-19)," *RB* 79 (1972) 200-16, notes the close parallels in accusations against "the wealthy, corrupt upper classes found in the prophetic writings", citing Amos 2:6-7 (207).

understood as a reference to incest, just as in 7.1, ולא ימעל איש בשאר בשרו "And a man shall not be unfaithful to/act illegally/trespass in relation to his near relative", which stands in close association with a reference to sexual wrongdoing (זנות). As there, the reference is to incest, probably including marriage to nieces.

These are statements about the sins of those from whom the community originally separated and which still are matters of contention, hence the inclusion of sexual wrongdoing as in the discourse about the nets. The author continues in that historical frame in 8.11 = 19.24 by using Deut 32:33 to allude to "the head of the kings of Greece, who comes to carry out vengeance against them". One might think of Alexander, but the reference is more likely to Antiochus IV. So the author attributes a similar range of sins to the leaders then, from whom the founders of his group broke away, to those of the opponents in his own day. He then returns to his own time again, noting that "all these things the 'builders of the wall and those who daub it with plaster' have not understood" (V) (returning to the imagery of Ezek 13:10 cited in 4.19) (8.12). The author also returns to the imagery of Micah 2, to focus on the person who is currently their teacher, as a preacher of lies (8.13; cf. the slightly longer variant in 19.25-26). The analogy between the founding and the present continues in 8.14-21, as the author again attacks the "builders of the wall" (8.18) and warns against apostasy within his own community (8.18b-19).

In the longer conclusion, contained in CD-B, these warnings are extended. The first, 19.33b – 20.1a, partially in CD-A 8.21b, and the third, 20.8b-13, condemn apostates to permanent exclusion.[135] In the latter we noted the reference to families (למשפהותיהם; 20.13), which presumes members of "the house of the law (בבית התורה)" (20.10, 13) included married people. The second warning (20.1b-8a), which envisages possible return of apostates, speaks of "the men of perfect holiness" (20.2, 5, 7). In the present context it is possible by association with the third warning to conclude that "the men of perfect holiness" also included the married, a conclusion which would undermine the interpretation of 7.4-9 as depicting a celibate and a non-celibate group. Its different character has led some to claim that it represents a secondary interpolation.[136] Charlotte Hempel notes that it "has more in common with disciplinary legislation found in the Laws of the Damascus Document (cf. 4QD[a] 10 i.11 – ii.15 par.) and the Community Rule (cf. 1QS 6.24 – 7.25 par.) than the rest of the Admonition".[137]

---

[135] Knibb, *Qumran Community*, notes the three categories, each introduced similarly (19.33b; 20.1b; 20.8b) (71).

[136] On the possibility that 20.1b-8a is a secondary interpolation see Jerome Murphy-O'Connor, "A Literary Analysis of Damascus Document XIX,33 – XX,34," *RB* 79 (1972) 544-64, 554-55; Knibb, *Qumran Community*, 55.

[137] Hempel, *Damascus Texts*, 32. See also Knibb, *Qumran Community*, who draws attention to the similar material to 20.1b-8a in 1QS/1Q28 8.16b – 9.2 (55).

The passage also brings a further reference to Deut 7:9, which promises God's love towards those who love him for a thousand generations (20.22). Those who remain faithful will "prevail over the sons of the earth" (CD-B 20.34). 4QD^a/4Q266 4 7-13 appears to contain CD 20.33-34 and a few lines beyond it, which include a reference to God setting up a shepherd to feed his people, based on Ezek 34:23.[138] The longer conclusion bristles with detail which invites historical construction and speculation, which is beyond our task.[139] Within the longer ending there is no further mention of sexual wrongdoing. For hearers it might at most spring to mind in the accusation against the house of Peleg in 20.23-24a, that they יטמאו את המקדש "defiled the temple and turned back to the path of the people in some things" (*DSSSE*). "Some things" would surely recall the nets of Belial, including sexual wrongdoing with which defiling the temple is closely connected.

A Catalogue of Transgressions 4QD^e/4Q270 2 i.9 – ii.18; and 6QD/6Q15 5 1-5

Beyond CD-B further portions of the Admonition have survived among the fragments at Qumran. Thus 4QD^e/4Q270 2 i.9 – ii.18 and 6QD/6Q15 5 1-5 preserve fragments of a list of acts of wrongdoing. Charlotte Hempel notes that the catalogue "deals with issues raised elsewhere in the Laws of D, particularly in the halakhah stratum of the Laws, as well as in 11QT and MMT" and contemplates that either it derives from an originally independent document available also to the latter two documents or has been composed as "a kind of summary of topics dealt with in the Laws".[140] She sees the former as more likely, since its parallels are not to be found in the communal legislation, but only in the earlier halakhic stratum, and reflect a national perspective.[141]

Among the topics we find reference to a woman during her time of being a virgin, reconstructed as follows:

> או אשר עליה שם רע ב]בתוליה בבית 17 [אביה
> or who had a bad reputation during] her maidenhood in the house of [her father. (*DSSSE*) (4Q270 2 i.16-17a)

The reconstruction makes an assumption about the concern. It finds justification from 4QD^d/4Q269 9 6-7, with a parallel in 4QD^e/4Q270 5 20 (outlined) and 4QD^f/4Q271 3 12-13 (underlined), which appears to allude to the same issue with the same formulation:

---

[138] Baumgarten, *DJD* 18, 46-47.

[139] For recent discussion see the overview in Hempel, *Damascus Texts*, 60-64.

[140] Hempel, *Laws*, 168. See her fuller discussion, pp. 164-99.

[141] So Hempel, "Laws of the Damascus Document and 4QMMT," 81-82.

וכול אשה אשר עליה ש]ם רע בבתולי[ה] (7) [בבית אביה

and every woman who has had a b]ad reputation during [her] maidenhood 7 [in her father's house. (*DSSSE*) (4QD[d]/4Q269 9 6-7)

Accordingly, the concern relates to an unmarried woman gaining a bad reputation in her father's household, almost certainly through sexual wrongdoing. The formulation appears to reflect Deut 22:21, which speaks of an unmarried woman who has been engaging in illicit sexual relations in the house of her father: כי עשתה נבלה בישראל לזנות בית אביה "because she has committed a disgraceful act in Israel by engaging in illicit sexual relations in her father's house". The focus on sexual wrongdoing is confirmed by the context of the parallel statement cited above, where the instruction enjoins that there be "examination] by trustworthy [women] of repute selected by the command of the supervisor over 15 [the many" (4QD[f]/4Q271 3 13b-15a), presumably to confirm her virginity or otherwise. In the Catalogue of Transgressions the implication is that these people are to be condemned, whereas the passage in the Laws cited above, though also forbidding taking such a woman as a bride, at least provides for the testing of that reputation which might overturn the ban.

This is the first of three instances which we might identify under the heading of sexual wrongdoing in 4QD[e]/4Q270 2 i. Thus the next surviving words speak directly of sexual intercourse:

[או אלמנה אשר]ישכב אחר עמה

[or a widow] with whom someone else sleeps. (*DSSSE*) (4QD[e]/4Q270 2.i.17)

In a context of listing sexual wrongdoing, we may assume that the text implies that the אחר "someone else" refers to someone other than the husband. The issue could be straightforward adultery, but, as the reconstruction suggests, could refer to sexual intercourse with a widow after she became a widow, if we accept Baumgarten's conjecture in the reconstruction that אלמנה "widow" is the referent. This would receive support from 4QD[f]/4Q271 3 12 (base text), partially preserved also in 4QD[d]/ 4Q269 9 5 (outlined) and 4QD[e]/4Q270 5 19 (underlined), which speaks of sexual relations with widows after they have been widowed.

או אלמנה אשר נשכבה מאשר התארמלה

or as a widow who slept (with someone) after she was widowed.
(*DSSSE*) (4QD[f]/4Q271 3 12)

This comes earlier in the context which deals with women who had a bad reputation during their maidenhood in their father's house, noted above (4QD[f]/4Q271 3 11-12). Wassen, however, questions that the reference is to widows and argues that the reference to "another" man would be strange if the husband is deceased.[142] Instead she points to Deut 22:13-29 as the background for the passage, which deals with "a slandered virgin and three cases of women who engage in non-marital sexual relations: a wife, an engaged woman, and a non-engaged woman".[143] The allusion here would be to the second of these, introduced with the words, "If there is a young woman, a virgin already engaged to be married, and a man meets her in the town and lies with her …" (Deut 22:23). The influence on 2 i.16 of Deut 22:21, noted above (p. 137), makes the link with Deuteronomy 22 plausible. On the other hand, the parallel is not such that we can claim that the author is precisely matching those categories. The third instance, as we shall see, appears not to have adultery as its focus. Nevertheless, the connection with Deuteronomy 22 makes an allusion to an engaged woman possible. Accordingly, the second instance refers either to an unchaste widow or to an engaged woman, reflecting Deut 22:23.

The next instance focuses on a man who engages in illicit sexual intercourse within marriage:

[… או יק]רב אל אשתו ביום 19 […]

[… or who app]roaches his wife on the day of 19 […].
(*DSSSE*) (4QD[e]/4Q270 2 i.18-19)

The reconstruction does not indicate an interpretation in this instance. The text probably refers to intercourse on the sabbath (possibly also reflected in CD 11.5; 4QD[f]/4Q271 5 i.1-2; and 4QD[e]/4Q270 7 i.12-13; / 4QD[b]/4Q267 9 vi.4-5 and forbidden in *Jub.* 50:8)[144] or, perhaps, during menstruation (the issue in CD 5.7, though one might then expect the plural בימי), but probably not during pregnancy, because that becomes a topic later in the passage.

[142] Wassen, *Women*, 108.

[143] Wassen, *Women*, 108.

[144] So Joseph M. Baumgarten, "The Laws of the Damascus Document – Between Bible and Mishnah," in *The Damascus Document: A Centennial of Discovery: Proceedings of the Third International Symposium of the Orion Center for the Study of the Dead Sea Scrolls and Associated Literature, 4-8 February 1998* (ed. Joseph M. Baumgarten, Esther G. Chazon, and Avital Pinnick; STDJ 34; Leiden: Brill, 2000) 17-26, 19. In *DJD* 18, he also mentions the less likely possibility, that it refers to *Yom Kippur*, referring to *m. Yoma* 8.1 (144). See also Schuller, "Women in the Dead Sea Scrolls," 126; Wassen, *Women*, 109; Doering, "Purity Regulations," 604. He explains the strictness as reflecting the association of Exodus 19 and the Decalogue (605). He notes also that according to *b. Nid.* 38b-a some early Hasidim abstained from sex except on the 4th day – probably because semen is discharged for 3 days afterwards (so *m. Shab* 9.3), noting a similar ruling among the Samaritans (cf. *m. Ned.* 3.10), the Falasha and Karaites (605), in contrast to the rabbis who saw it as part of celebrating joy on the sabbath (606).

Column ii turns to tithes and apparent abuse of them ("defiling his holy spirit" ii.11), leprosy, and "one with an impu[re] discharge" (ii.12). The latter probably includes seminal discharge, but the context of the concern is not clear. There follows a warning about divulging "secrets of the people" (רז עמו) to Gentiles (לגואים), cursing one's people or preaching "rebellion against those anointed with the spirit of holiness", and slaughtering an animal carrying a live foetus. At the latter point 6QD/6Q15 (outlined) offers text which overlaps with 4QD^{e}/4Q270 (base text). The focus returns to matters pertaining to sexuality.

או אשר ישכב עם] 16 אשה הרה מקיץ דמ[ו

or who sleeps with] 16 a pregnant woman because of the heat (?) of [his] blood. (*DSSSE*) (4QD^{e}/4Q270 2 ii.15-16; 6QD/6Q15 5 2-3)

The issue is clear: sexual intercourse during pregnancy.[145] This became a matter of discussion in rabbinic tradition.[146] Here such intercourse is prohibited. *Genesis Apocryphon* also appears to assume this prohibition when it portrays Bitenosh as appealing to Lamech to remember their sexual pleasure, referring to the intercourse through which Noah was conceived (1QapGen/1Q20 2.9-10, 13b-14a), many months previously, but presumably (among) their most recent engagements to be in memory. Josephus reports that the Essenes practised such abstinence (*B.J.* 2.161), but alleging denial of pleasure as its basis, a stance not at all evident here.

With regard to the grounds for abstention, the translation above suggests the word מקיץ , rendered, "heat", derives from the stem קיץ, used in relation to heat and summer. The expression, "the heat of his blood", might then allude to sexual passion which the husband fails to control. The word מקיץ, however, is difficult. Qimron conjectures מקוץ דם "from the ceasing of blood".[147] But Wassen notes that the noun קיץ is nowhere else spelt with a *yod* in the document.[148] Baumgarten reads it as a *hiphil* participle from קוץ , "to awaken", suggesting that it may refer to bleeding caused by the pressure of sexual intercourse, and probably reflects concern with contracting impurity through contact with the blood.[149] Wassen,

[145] So Baumgarten, *DJD* 18, 146. Schuller, "Women in the Dead Sea Scrolls," 126.

[146] On this see Tal Ilan, *Jewish Women in Greco-Roman Palestine* (Tübingen: Mohr Siebeck, 1995; Peabody: Hendricksen, 1996) 107-108; and Joseph M. Baumgarten, "A Fragment of Fetal Life and Pregnancy in 4Q270," in *Pomegranates and Golden Bells: Studies in Biblical, Jewish, and Near Eastern Ritual, Law, and Literature in Honor of Jacob Milgrom* (ed. David P. Wright et al.; Winona Lake, Ind.: Eisenbrauns, 1995) 445-48, 447-48.

[147] Baumgarten, *DJD* 18, 146; so also Hempel, *Laws*, who notes that a *yod* may accompany a *sere* in Qumran Hebrew (167).

[148] Wassen, *Women*, 110.

[149] Baumgarten, *DJD* 18, 146.

accepting Baumgarten's translation "stirring the blood", prefers an earlier alternative mentioned by Baumgarten,[150] which saw the concern as bringing danger to the foetus.[151] Noting that according to modern knowedge pressure from sexual intercourse during pregnancy is no more likely to cause bleeding than at other times (though this is debatable especially where there is a history of miscarriage), she points to evidence in Greek and Roman medical sources. They reflect the view that blood plays a vital role for the foetus and that any loss of blood is therefore likely to reflect damage to the foetus, so much so that a few doctors urged restraint or even abstinence from sexual relations during pregnancy.

A second concern relates to a daughter.

או יקרב א]ל בת[אחיו

[or approaches] the daughter [of his brother. (*DSSSE*) (4QD^{e}/4Q270 2 ii.16).

The reconstruction plausibly interprets this as a reference to the prohibition of marriage to nieces, an issue addressed by the author in his exposition of the nets of Belial in 5.7-11, in which he declares that the restricted interpretation given by his opponents condones incest. The same concern is probably also being addressed in part in 7.1 and 8.6-7 and is one of the instances illustrating the three nets (5.7-11).

The third concern refers to homosexual intercourse, partially preserved in both 4QD^{e}/4Q270 (base text) and 6QD/6Q15 (outlined):

או ישכב עם זכר] (17) משכבי אשה vacat

or lies with a male] as one lies with a woman.
(*DSSSE*) (4QD^{e}/4Q270 2 ii.16b-17a / 6QD/6Q15 5 3-4)

The statement recalls ואת זכר לא תשכב משכבי אשה "You shall not lie with a male as with a woman" (Lev 18:22) and ואיש אשר ישכב את זכר משכבי אשה "If a man lies with a male as with a woman, ..." (Lev 20:13). Baumgarten notes that the formulation of the laws in Leviticus 20 with איש אשר ("a man who") presumably lies behind the repeated או אשר ("or who") in the list here in 4QD^{e}/

[150] Baumgarten, "Fragment of Fetal Life," 448. He also draws attention to the concern about the separate existence of the foetus of animals in the prohibition against slaughtering a pregnant animal in what immediately precedes (ii.15), an application of Deut 22:6, as in 11QT^{a}/11Q19 52.5, there, applied to sacrificial slaughter, and similarly in *4QMMT* B 36-38, and to 11QT^{a}/11Q19 50.10-19, according to which a mother contracts corpse impurity when her foetus dies (445-47).

[151] Wassen, *Women*, 110-11.

4Q270 2 i-ii.[152] This is the only clear instance in Qumran literature where homosexual relations are addressed.

The passage continues with warnings of destruction (להבעיר, "to destroy", 6QD/6Q15 5 4; cf. להעביר, "to remove", 4QD[e]/4Q270 2 ii.18) for those who transgress these provisions and further exhortations to obedience. Baumgarten now prefers the reading להעביר, "to remove", over להבעיר, "to destroy", seeing in the former a word play with עוברי "transgressors" in ii.17, which refers to those who defiled themselves by imitating the sexual practices of Canaan, against which Lev 18:24-25 warns, noting that because of it the land vomited out its inhabitants.[153] He draws attention to the importance of these moral limits also in 4QD[a]/4Q266 11 12-14. This fits the author's focus on sexual wrongdoing.

According to Hempel 4QD[e]/4Q270 2 ii.19-21 is "best taken as an introduction to an admonitory passage which has not been preserved".[154] She then sees the passage contained in 4QD[a]/4Q266 5 i.1-19 and 4QD[b]/4QD267 5 ii.1-7 as transitional to the section on Laws, which follows.

The "Catalogue of Transgressions" appears to have addressed illicit sexual intercourse by young women before marriage, probably during betrothal with another man, and within marriage, possibly on the sabbath. It also addressed sexual relations with a pregnant woman, offering a rationale which appears to take into account what is to be understood as potential damage to the foetus, and included prohibitions relating to marriage to nieces, and homosexual relations. It thus coheres with the preceding sections of the Admonition in emphasising the importance of sexual wrongdoing, although without giving it the same degree of prominence. It shares with it the concern about marrying nieces and possibly a reference to sexual intercourse during menstruation, though the reference is more likely to the sabbath. Polygyny, the first instance illustrating the nets of Belial, does not feature, perhaps because the list was compiled at a time when that was not yet seen as a sin, or perhaps because it was in a part of the fragmentary text which has not survived. The parallels are stronger with the Laws which follow, as the table below illustrates. At a formal level we note that while the texts are fragmentary, it does appear that the author has set his concerns out in two groups of three, echoing the structure within the exposition of the three nets of Belial in 4.15 – 5.11, which also includes reference to three aspects of sexual wrongdoing.

---

[152] Baumgarten, "Laws of the Damascus Document – Between Bible and Mishnah," 20.

[153] Baumgarten, "Laws of the Damascus Document – Between Bible and Mishnah," 20-21; cf. Baumgarten, *DJD* 18, 146.

[154] Hempel, *Damascus Texts*, 34.

Sexual Wrongdoing in the Catalogue of Transgressions and Parallels in D		
Catalogue of Transgressions	Admonition	Laws
A woman who gained a bad reputation in her father's house (4QD^e/4Q270 2 i.16-17a)		4QD^d/4Q269 9 6-7; 4QD^e/4Q270 5 20; 4QD^f/4Q271 3 12-13
A woman who has engaged in sex with someone other than her betrothed – (4QD^e/4Q270 2 i.17) (or a widow who has not remained chaste during her widowhood)		(4QD^f/4Q271 3 12, partially preserved also in 4QD^d/4Q269 9 5)
A man who has had sex with his wife on the day (sabbath?) (4QD^e/4Q270 2.i.18-19) (menstruation?)	(menstruation 5.7)	CD 11.5; 4QD^f/4Q271 5 i.1-2 ? 4QD^e/4Q270 7 i.12-13; 4QD^b/4Q267 9 vi.4-5 menstruation? 4QD^a/4Q266 6 ii.1-2
Sex with pregnant woman (4QD^e/4Q270 2 ii.15-16; 6QD/6Q15 5 2-3)		? 4QD^e/4Q270 7 i.12-13; 4QD^b/4Q267 9 vi.4-5
Marrying nieces (4QD^e/4Q270 2 ii.16)	5.7-11; 7.1 and 8.6-7	
Homosexual relations (4QD^e/4Q270 2 ii.16b-17a / 6QD/6Q15 5 3-4)		

In the second major section of D we find more specific detail about what right behaviour entails, including a number of laws pertaining to sexuality. Before we turn to these, we review our findings on the Admonition as a whole.

Conclusion

The Admonition which precedes the legal section in D is characterised by warnings and encouragement, given within the framework of a conflict between the author and his group (for whom he writes) and an opposing group who appear to have controlling influence, we may assume, in the temple and among the people. The author sometimes attacks his opponents by general allegations of lying and loose interpretation of the Law. The metaphors of building a wall and removing or moving boundaries are a common way of referring to the false teaching. The author also sets the conflict in the context of what he sees as history, particularly the time of the founding of his community, when it separated from the people and its leadership, with whom it was in conflict. The author draws an analogy between what happened then and what will happen in the future. Then the people and its leadership suffered at the hands of "the chief of the kings of Greece". Judgement will similarly come upon the false teacher and his community. The author seeks to inform his readers of the dangers and to ensure that they remain separate from that community, its leadership, and possibly also the temple.

Sometimes the author goes beyond these general allegations to identify specific areas of conflict. At a broad level, greed, lack of care about observing purity provisions and about celebrating the sabbath and festivals are among the concerns. The concern which receives greatest prominence, however, is sexual wrongdoing, mostly designated as זנות. "Choosing the fair neck" is the only specific wrongdoing mentioned in the first account of the community's story and may well already refer to sexual wrongdoing. In the third account sexual wrongdoing becomes a major focus of attention in two ways. Here the author appears to see himself as standing in the tradition of the warnings in Proverbs against the strange woman and sexual wrongdoing. First it is shown to be the major cause of failure throughout history, beginning with the Watchers and giants, the generation before the flood, Noah's sons, Jacob's sons in Egypt and in the wilderness, kings, and the founders of the community. This gives extraordinary significance to sexual wrongdoing. The focus in particular is on evil inclination and the following of sexual desire for pleasure in ways that are contrary to the law. The account stands under the influence of *Jubilees* and may reflect its concern with intermarriage to Gentiles. Nothing in the context suggests that sexual desire in itself or sexual pleasure is evil.

The author then follows this up by moving to his own time and his dispute with the other group. Here, too, sexual wrongdoing is at stake, the first of the three nets of Belial, but closely related to the other two, greed and the defiling of the temple. In fact the author elaborates only on the first, probably because he sees greed and defiling the temple as part of what sexual wrongdoing entailed. He rejects polygyny and espouses monogyny for all. The balance of evidence now available through the Qumran fragments favours limiting the concern in the first instance cited to polygyny, rather than reading the reference to "their lifetime" as precluding any second marriage, even after the death of a spouse, or remarriage after divorce. Divorce is best understood as entailing permission to remarry, but a strict interpretation of the grounds of divorce would mean that in most instances marrying a divorced woman, divorced as an adulteress, would be out of the question. The prohibition of polygyny goes far beyond the *Temple Scroll*, which makes it a requirement of the king, but not of the population as a whole. The second instance warns against sexual intercourse with a menstruating woman (as a matter of impurity which defiles the temple), a prohibition already contained in Lev 18:19 and 20:18 and identified as a source of impurity in 15:24. The third asserts that the incest laws (Lev 18:13) must be seen as forbidding marriage to nieces just as much as to nephews. Assumed as uncontroversial in the *Temple Scroll* and *Jubilees*, for D it had become an issue of contention with the opponents.

In the fourth account we find the author again listing a range of behaviours which should be followed and others which are to be avoided. Sexual wrongdoing features in these warnings, both in broad terms, but most probably also with reference to incest, including marriage to nieces. In the account of the sins of the leaders of the people at the time when the author's community and its founders left the people, sexual wrongdoing again takes first place, featuring twice in the list of accusations.

If we read all accounts together and ask about specific concerns, the three issues raised in the third account must be prominent. On the other hand, the references to the eyes of sexual lusting, including the depiction of it as the basis for failure across history, and the brief reference to choosing the fair neck, suggest that the concern is wider than the three cited instances of conflict. The three issues have a particular character as instances where the author's opponents are making improper rulings. The other references to sexual wrongdoing imply a much broader concern. They do not, however, enable us to identify particular details or aspects beyond those mentioned among the nets of Belial. The wider range of concerns becomes apparent when we turn to the section containing the laws, but are already visible in the Catalogue of Transgressions and include illicit sexual intercourse by young women before marriage, with another during betrothal, by married people probably on the sabbath and during pregnancy, and between males in the form of homosexual relations.

On the positive side, the second account appears to assume a future which includes normal human life, including marriage and begetting offspring, when it speaks of their seed filling the earth. The same may be present in the allusion to thousands of generations in the fourth account and appears to cohere with the instruction about married people in camps, where marriage and family are assumed as norms and the concern is that they live (and make vows) in accordance with the Law. One of the warnings about apostasy also assumes that married people belong to "the house of the Law" and, given the immediate context may lend support to the view that "the men of perfect holiness" also included those who were married, rather than being a distinctive celibate group, although D assumes that some, perhaps a large number, do not marry.

Before proceeding to discuss the Laws it is important to note the special character of the Admonition. While within the Laws it is not always easy to gauge the relative weight being given to regulations and prohibitions, in the Admonition we have the kind of material where emphases are more readily identified. The author is in the main not making lists, but engaging what he sees as particularly important. It is very clear that sexual wrongdoing is prominent, strikingly so, exemplified by the retelling of Israel's story under the rubric of sexual wrongdoing and the exposition of the nets of Belial. Where in the Laws the author very probably employs traditional resources (as already in the Catalogue of Transgressions), we need to read these in the light of the emphases set thus far in the work. There, too, we find that sexual wrongdoing receives considerable attention, and this, though perhaps existing in his sources, coheres with the emphases of the first part.

2 The Laws and Community Regulations

The material containing the laws, as distinct from the communal regulations, belongs, according to Charlotte Hempel, to a stratum of halakhah preserved in the document which is not sectarian, nor polemical, but written for the people as a whole with little sign of redactional activity or updating compared to the communal legislation.[155] She sees a second major literary stratum comprising communal legislation, in which there are "signs of extensive redactional activity and reworking". These include the addition of the Catalogue of Transgressions, material concerning the משכיל "Instructor", an expulsion rite, modifications reflecting the tenor of the *Community Rule*, and more allusions to *Jubilees*.[156] She concludes that "the communal legislation underwent a process of redaction in order to bring it into line with the community behind the Community Rule".[157]

Among the Qumran manuscripts are a number of fragments which appear to belong before the commencement of the material concerning laws in the Cairo document. These include a section on laws about disqualifying certain priests

---

[155] Hempel, *Laws*, 70-72, 187-89. Similarly, Martha Himmelfarb, "The Purity Laws of 4QD: Exegesis and Sectarianism," in *Things Revealed: Studies in Early Jewish and Christian Literature in Honor of Michael E. Stone* (ed. Esther G. Chazon, David Satran, and Ruth A. Clements; JSJSup 89; Leiden: Brill, 2004) 155-69, 169. Noting their extreme demands, she observes: "it is difficult to imagine their observance outside of a sectarian community or at least a community on a trajectory toward sectarianism" (169). See also Wassen, *Women*, 33-42, who compares the stratification proposed by Hempel, *Laws*, with that of Robert Davis, "The History of the Composition of the 'Damascus Document'," (Ph.D. dissertation; Harvard University, 1992). She notes significant overlap in what they determine as the earliest halakhic layer and their recognition of its general and non-sectarian nature, though preferring to see it emanating from a particular movement within the priesthood (39-40).

[156] Hempel, *Laws*, 189-90.

[157] Hempel, *Laws*, 191.

(4QD^{a}/4Q266 5 ii.1-16; 4QD^{b}/4Q267 5 iii.1-8; 4QD^{h}/4Q273 2 1-2; 4 i.5-11). This belongs to the early halakhic stratum of non-sectarian, non-polemical material.[158] Among the disqualifications we read of "sons of Aaron" who are said to have been אשר ישבה לגואים "captive among Gentiles" (4QD^{a}/4Q266 5 ii.5). The grounds are not given. The same concern appears in CD 14.15, which includes the description לאשר ישבה לגוי נכר "the captive taken by a foreign people". This assumes that something has happened to them during their captivity which continues to place them in a situation of need. This could include among other things sexual abuse or perhaps mutilation. In relation to disqualifying priests we are probably to think of an enduring condition, rather than something which might have rendered them ritually impure only for a time and for which there was purification.

Male and Female Discharges
4QD^{a}/4Q266 6 i-iii; 4QD^{d}/4Q269 7; 4QD^{g}/4Q272 1 i-ii; 4QD^{h}/4Q273 4 ii

This next section begins with skin disease, but then moves on, following the sequence of Leviticus 14-15,[159] to refer to male and female discharges and in that context to speak of sexual intercourse with menstruating women. This material also belongs to the early non-sectarian, halakhic stratum.[160] It assumes, for instance, participation in the temple cult through offerings. Both 4QD^{a}/4Q266 6 i.14 (base text) and 4QD^{g}/4Q272 1 ii.3 (outlined) preserve parts of the first heading,

ומ]שפט הזב את זובו

> [And the r]ule concerning one who has a discharge.
> (4QD^{a}/4Q266 6 i.14; 4QD^{g}/4Q272 1 ii.3)

The text continues:

כול איש א]שר זו]ב יז[וב] מבשר[ו

> Any man with a [dis]charge from [his] flesh. (4QD^{a}/4Q266 6 i.14; 4QD^{g}/4Q272 1 ii.3)

4QD^{g}/4Q272 1 ii.3-4 appears to lack זו[ב before יז[וב]. The following context speaks of seminal emission. It is therefore possible that this first statement also deals with seminal emission, probably emission during sleep, rather than abnormal discharge (cf. Lev 15:2). The passage continues:

---

[158] Hempel, *Laws*, 39-43; Hempel, *Damascus Texts*, 51.
[159] See Joseph M. Baumgarten, *DJD* 35, 87.
[160] Hempel, *Laws*, 43-50.

א]ו א[שר י]עלה [ע]ל[יו] מחשבת [זמ]ה או [אשר

o]r one [who] brings upon himse[lf lust]ful thoughts or [who
(4QD^{a}/4Q266 6 i.14; 4QD^{g}/4Q272 1 ii.3)

This is to be brought into relation to fluxes probably as a reference to masturbation.[161] Baumgarten, notes "that the Qumran exegetes associated *zab* impurity with sinful thoughts, in contrast with tannaitic halakha, which ... specifically exempted discharges resulting from sexual stimuli from this category".[162] For the contrast he points to the tannaitic halakha in *m. Zab* 2.2.[163]

The words או אשר "or who" will have introduced a third example (the author, as we have noted above, likes threes), but it has not survived. Himmelfarb suggests that the third example may well refer to sexual emission during intercourse. She also points out that the author thus clearly does not restrict the meaning of *zab* to abnormal discharge, but uses it to cover seminal emission as well, which strictly speaking is not a "flow", but was included under that heading already by the editors of Leviticus 15.[164] Accordingly the author could "find in Leviticus 15 three types of זב, the man with abnormal flow (Lev. 15:2-15), the man with a seminal emission outside of sexual relations (Lev. 15:16-17), and the man with a seminal emission in the course of sexual relations (Lev. 15:18)".[165] Alternatively, the first reference is also to seminal emission during sleep, covered also by Lev 15:16-17.

What follows in 4QD^{g}/4Q272 1 ii, which applies to all three concerns with impurity, makes reference to touch: מגעו כמגע ("his touch is like"; ii.5); הנוגע בו ("the one touching him" ii.7; cf. Lev 15:5) and to washing clothes (וכבס בג[ד]יו; ii.6; cf. Lev 15:13). It apparently summarises the rules in Lev 15:4-15 which relate to the *zab* with a discharge, but applies them to all three instances, and so "understood the more severe impurity of the man with a flow to apply to those

161 So Wassen, *Women*, 48.

162 Baumgarten, *DJD* 35, 88.

163 Baumgarten, *DJD* 35, 87-88.

164 Himmelfarb, "Impurity and Sin," 18. Himmelfarb, "Purity Laws of 4QD," 160, 163. Cf. Wassen, *Women*, who argues against the text's applying *zab* to all on the grounds that this happens neither in Leviticus 15 nor in the *Temple Scroll*. She notes that 11QT^{a}/11Q19 45.7-8, 11-12, 15-16 differentiates the length of time required by each for purification and argues that applying the requirement for sacrifices after impurity, to seminal emission would be unfeasible (48-49 n. 9). It is, however, problematic to assume that D would conform to the halakhah of the *Temple Scroll*. Certainly, as Wassen agrees, the provisions applying to a *zab*, if not that designation, are now being applied to the man with a seminal emission, but the author does place the three instances under the heading of the *zab*, and appears to follow it by another three under the heading of *zabah*, understood equally widely.

165 Himmelfarb, "Impurity and Sin," 18.

who had had seminal emissions".[166] This makes it likely that the first reference is not to an abnormal discharge, but also to seminal emission, thus making sense of what appears to be a comparison of all three to the man with the abnormal discharge, reflected in the words, מגעו כמגע ("his touch is like"; ii.5).

Wassen notes the focus of the passage on impurity contracted by touching any one of these. The author is making the requirements of purification after touching a *zab* apply also to those touching men impure from seminal emissions. "Accordingly, the ways by which a person impure from seminal emission transmits impurity are the same as those of a *zav*", and thus "it would make impurity from seminal emission more severe than the biblical stipulation in Leviticus 15".[167] She sees this as an instance of the halakhah clarifying what Leviticus had left unaddressed.

Himmelfarb notes that these laws are concerned with issues of purity and assume participation in the temple cult. They would have imposed severe restrictions on priests, but also on lay people wanting to bring sacrifices. She then goes on to suggest that these restrictions might be tolerable where sexual intercourse was allowed only for the purpose of procreation, such as Josephus reports of the Essenes (*B.J.* 2.160-61) and which she believes is assumed elsewhere in the document in its prohibition of sexual intercourse during pregnancy.[168] That assessment remains problematic, however, since it is not clear that D took such a restrictive view.

The next heading must be reconstructed, though its beginning is preserved in 4QD^{g}/4Q272 1 ii.7, and the reconstruction makes sense, following the ruling concerning male fluxes and in the light of what follows.

ו]משפט [הזבה

and] the law [of a woman who has a discharge.

The rule appears to begin by enunciating the length of the period of her menstrual impurity as 7 days in accordance with Lev 15:19a. The rest of column ii of 4QD^{g}/4Q272 1 is very fragmentary, but appears to include a reference to a person touching her ([הנו]גי בה[...]], 4QD^{g}/4Q272 ii.10). This probably derives from Lev 15:19b, "whoever touches her [the menstruant] shall be unclean until the evening". Wassen hypothesises that in analogy to the preceding discussion about males, which makes up for an omission in Leviticus 15 about what happens if someone

---

[166] Himmelfarb, "Impurity and Sin," 19. She notes that this contrasts with the position of the *Temple Scroll* which also treats seminal emission with greater severity by requiring a three day period for purification (45.7-12), but does not rule that touching such a man was defiling (19-20). See also Himmelfarb, "Purity Laws of 4QD," 161-62.

[167] Wassen, *Women*, 49.

[168] Himmelfarb, "Purity Laws of 4QD," 162-64.

touches a man who has had a seminal emission by applying the same rule that pertained to touching a *zab*, the author further "clarifies the biblical laws, by stating that the touch of a menstruant and the *zavah* is defiling".[169] 4QD^{g}/4Q272 ii has further lines, which include reference to waters of purification (ii.15; cf. also 13 and 17) and may reflect the treatment of the impurity of the *zab* as the equivalent of corpse impurity such as we find in *4QTohorot A*/4Q274 1 i.7-9.

In 4QD^{a}/4Q266 6, where column ii gives us more of the rule, we find reference to sexual relations. The concern is sexual relations with a menstruating woman. Its first provision is based on Lev 15:24.

האש[ה] [אשר י]קרב [ ] 2 [אליה ע]ון נדה עלו

[ ] the wom[an one who] approaches [her has the s]in of menstrual impurity upon him. (4QD^{a}/4Q266 6 ii.1-2)

ואם שכב ישכב איש אתה ותהי נדתה עליו

If a man lies with her, her menstrual impurity falls upon him. (Lev 15:24)

The rule adds ע]ון "sin" to the formulation in Lev 15:24, which Baumgarten interprets as adding a moral dimension to the purity concern. The moral dimension may also be implied by the use of קרב "approach" rather than שכב "lie". Himmelfarb again argues for differentiation between the moral and the impurity aspects.[170] "Nowhere in the course of Leviticus 15 does P prohibit sexual relations with a menstruant. It mentions such relations in order to lay out their implications for the purity of the man who engages in them".[171] Sexual intercourse with a menstruating woman is a concern in the Priestly material because the man contracts impurity. It is apparently not a moral problem. It is a moral problem, however, in the Holiness Code, where it is forbidden (Lev 18:19 and 20:18). Connecting the two sets of texts produces the עון "sin" here in 4QD^{a}/4Q266 6 ii.1-2. The menstrual impurity, itself, is not the sin. The rule thus repeats the prohibition cited in the exposition of the three nets as the second instance of sexual wrongdoing which the author's opponents allow (5.7).

The passage continues with reference to a woman who has a flow of blood outside the menstrual period, following the order in Leviticus (15:25-30). Depending upon the reconstruction it either goes on to place restrictions on her:

---

[169] Wassen, *Women*, 50.

[170] Himmelfarb, "Impurity and Sin," 21-22, 28.

[171] Himmelfarb, "Purity Laws of 4QD," 167-68.

ואם ראתה [עו]ד והיאה לו [בעת] 3 [נדתה] שבעת ימים
והיאה אל תוכל קודש

> If she ag[ain] sees (blood), and it is not [at the time of] 3 [her menstruation] of seven days, she shall not eat anything hallowed. (4QD^{a}/4Q266 6 ii.2b-3)

or, with Wassen,[172] it first refers to a man having sexual intercourse with her and becoming impure, and then goes on to place restrictions on her:

ואם ראתה [עו]ד והיאה לו[א עת נדתה טמא]שבעת ימים
והיאה אל תוכל קודש

> And if she sees (blood) ag[ain], and it is not [time of her menstrual period (and he has sexual relations with her) he shall be impure] for seven days. She shall not eat anything hallowed. (4QD^{a}/4Q266 6 ii.2b-3)

If we see here a reference to sexual intercourse, this matches what has just been said about the menstruant. According to Wassen, there are therefore two references to a man having sexual intercourse, the first with a menstruant,[173] the second, by extension, with a *zabah*. In both cases the man is unclean for seven days, thus applying to him in the first the law which in Lev 15:24 applied to sexual intercourse with a menstruant.[174] The designation of a woman as *zabah* after any appearance of blood is stricter than Lev 15:25, which specifies a discharge of "many days".[175]

The passage then continues:

והיאה אל תוכל קודש ואל ת[בו] 4 אל המקדש עד בו השמש ביום השמיני

> she shall not eat anything hallowed, nor come 4 into the sanctuary until sunset on the eighth day. (4QD^{a}/4Q266 6 ii.3b-4)

The text stipulates the restrictions on the *zabah*. Wassen shows that the restrictions match those imposed on a woman after childbirth according to Lev 12:4, further

---

[172] Wassen, *Women*, 51-52, who adapts the reconstruction of Ben Zion Wacholder and Martin Abegg, *A Preliminary Edition of the Unpublished Dead Sea Scrolls: The Hebrew and Aramaic Texts from Cave 4* (Fascicle 1; Washington DC: Biblical Archaeology Society, 1991) 13.

[173] So also Schiffman, "Zadokite Fragments and the Temple Scroll," 139.

[174] Wassen, *Women*, 52-53.

[175] Schuller, "Women in the Dead Sea Scrolls," notes that treating a woman with a flow of blood beyond the seven-day menstrual period as a *zabah* goes beyond the requirements in Rabbinic and Samaritan halakhah, "which did not invoke the category of *zabah* unless the bleeding continued for a longer period of time" (127). See also Harrington, *Purity Texts*, 48.

illustrating the systematising of Levitical law,[176] the reference to touching in Lev 12:4 understood as a reference to food.[177] Himmelfarb notes that the requirement of waiting until after sunset on the eighth day "clarifies or corrects Lev. 15:29, which leaves the impression that the offering of sacrifice restores the *zabah* to purity at any time on the eighth day" and brings it into consistency with what is required for men with seminal emissions and women who have had sexual relations.[178]

In the fragmentary remains of 4QD[a]/4Q266 6 ii the author departs from the order in Leviticus 15 which he has been following thus far to cite the provisions of Lev 12:2-8 about impurity after childbirth. The text is very fragmentary. It appears to offer a summary. What has survived includes reference to impurity after the birth of a male (6 ii.5), based on Lev 12:2. The words, "she shall not eat" (6 ii.9) will almost certainly refer to Lev 12:4, which forbids the woman from touching any holy thing or entering the temple. Here, as in the preceding instance which applies these prohibitions to the *zabah*, touching holy things is interpreted as eating holy food. In 6 ii.10 the death penalty for non-observance is probably based on Lev 15:31, which speaks of keeping the people from their uncleanness, lest they "die in their uncleanness by defiling my tabernacle that is in their midst".

Most striking, according to the reconstruction of of 6 ii.11 in Baumgarten, [הי]לד למנקת בטוה[רה "[the ch]ild to a wet-nurse (who can nurse it) in puri[ty", it makes a connection between the impurity of the woman and the infant, requiring that a wet nurse be used to prevent rendering the infant impure.[179] Thus Himmelfarb writes: "4QD concludes that during that initial period the infant she nurses would incur impurity by touching her, its clothes would require laundering, and it would require bathing daily in order to become pure again at sundown".[180] Schuller, too, notes that "the mention of a wet nurse suggests that the mother could not nurse during the period of her purification", though she acknowledges the

---

176 Wassen, *Women*, 53-54.

177 Wassen, *Women*, 54

178 Himmelfarb, "Impurity and Sin," 23. In making such stipulations neither D nor the *Temple Scroll* should be seen as being polemical (cf. *m. Par* 3.7) (24). Similarly, Himmelfarb, "Purity Laws of 4QD," on the reference to sunset on the 8th day (165).

179 Baumgarten, *DJD* 18, 57.

180 Himmelfarb, "Impurity and Sin," 26. She notes that in contrast to P, whose concerns are with priests and their families and lay people bringing sacrifices, "4QD's insistence on a nurse to replace the mother so as not to convey impurity to the newborn baby suggests a somewhat different point of view in which purity is valued for its own sake" (27)

fragmentary state of the text.[181] This assumes a communal arrangement and the availability of wet nurses. Wassen, however, questions this reading of the text. "The word בטוה]רה," she suggests, "may, in fact, begin a new sentence, in which case the mention of a wet-nurse does not necessarily relate to purity".[182] Pointing out that the next line deals with someone who cannot afford a lamb, based on Lev 12:6-8, she suggests that 6 ii.11 probably related to the requirements for the woman's purification and plausibly reconstructs as follows:

בטוה]רתה תביא כבש לילה ובן יונה או אור לחטאת[

At [her] purification, [she shall bring a lamb for a burnt offering and a pigeon or a turtledove for a sin offering].

She then suggests a number of other reasons why a wetnurse might be mentioned, including as a necessity where a mother cannot breastfeed or died in childbirth, or, even, as a prohibition against use of wetnurses.[183] In substance she argues also the impracticality and inappropriateness of preventing mothers from beginning to breastfeed (and then expecting them to begin long afterwards) and of finding surrogate nurses.[184] Given the fragmentary state of the text and the pragmatic concerns, there seems to be insufficient basis for finding here a reference to mothers rendering their infants impure.

The author has dealt with three instances under the general heading of *zabah* (a menstruant, a woman with a flow of blood outside her menstrual period, and a woman after childbirth), as he had under *zab*. The focus in both has been primarily on impurity. In the first, but possibly the first two instances, the woman's impurity is interpreted in relation to sexual intercourse and the resultant impurity which a man then contracts. One might even speculate that the third is concerned with contamination of another, namely the baby, but this is too uncertain.

Himmelfarb shows that in this section D has been offering "a close reading of Leviticus 12-15", treating its provisions as a system, following its logic stringently and resolving its difficulties.[185] Its method, unlike the *Temple Scroll* which lengthens periods of impurity, is to extend "the more stringent requirements of

---

[181] Schuller, "Women in the Dead Sea Scrolls," 127; similarly Harrington, *Purity Texts*, who interprets the danger as the mother bringing impurity to the infant through her milk and notes that this coheres with the view that already the foetus is a separate life (48).

[182] Wassen, *Women*, 57.

[183] Wassen, *Women*, 57-58. Wacholder, *New Damascus Document*, reconstructs, "And if she cannot nurse, she shall give the child to a nurse during her period of purification" (63). See his discussion on pp. 173-74.

[184] Wassen, *Women*, 56-57. She notes evidence of the use of wetnurses in the Roman world and in Egypt.

[185] Himmelfarb, "Impurity and Sin," 29; see also pp. 25-26.

certain types of impurity to other types".[186] There is, however, "nothing sectarian about them. The laws are directed at all Israel, not at a pious remnant. The same is, of course, true of the *Temple Scroll*", although their rules "are not only different from each other, but actually incompatible".[187]

The next section (4QD^{a}/4Q266 6 iii – iv; 4QD^{b}/4Q267 6 2-7; 4QD^{e}/4Q270 3 i.19-21; ii.12-21; iii.13-15; 4QD^{f}/4Q271 2 1-5) is concerned with agriculture and has nothing pertaining to sexuality. This is also the case with the following section (4QD^{d}/4Q269 8 i.3; ii.1-6; 4QD^{e}/4Q270 3 iii.19-21; 4QD^{f}/4Q271 2 7-13). At most we note its concern about contact with Gentiles. Both belong to the early halakhic stratum as do the following two sections.[188]

Women Accused of Adultery, and Intercourse with Female Slaves
4QD^{a}/4Q266 12 1-9; 4QD^{e}/4Q270 4 1-21

This next section is directly relevant. It deals with accusations of adultery against women, and with sexual intercourse with female slaves.[189] It is best preserved in 4QD^{e}/4Q270. The fragment begins:

[...]יבא איש אשה להאלותה

... a man bring a woman to have her tried by the curse. (4QD^{e}/4Q270 4 1)

The rule refers to the provisions in Num 5:11-31 for dealing with a woman accused of adultery. Again we are dealing with a summary exposition of a biblical law with some supplementation. The bringing reflects Num 5:15. The text is fragmentary. It goes on to refer to someone seeing.

[...]חרואה אם יראה אשה 3 [רעהו

[ ] who sees, if he sees [his neighbour's] wife. (4QD^{e}/4Q270 4 2-3)

This appears to have no parallel in the Numbers provision, which rather speaks of no one seeing. Baumgarten relates this to the parallel reference in *m. Sota* 1.1 about witnesses to the liaison even where there is no witness to the actual adultery.[190] Wassen argues on the basis of 4QD^{a}/4Q266 12 2 that the word עדים "witnesses" is to be read in 4 11, supporting a reference to witness, here.[191] In 4 2 the reference to the witness, the one seeing, is in the singular. This reflects some

---

186 Himmelfarb, "Impurity and Sin," 29.
187 Himmelfarb, "Impurity and Sin," 29.
188 Hempel, *Laws*, 50-70.
189 See the extended discussion in Wassen, *Women*, 59-68.
190 Baumgarten, *DJD* 18, 153.
191 So Wassen, *Women*, 64.

modification of the harsh provisions of Numbers 15. The same is true of what follows:

אם] אמרה אנוסה היתי

if] she said I was raped. (4QD^{e}/4Q270 4 3)

It assumes that the woman has the right to respond, a further indication of changes to the ordeal to increase the rights of women.[192] The text continues with reference to blood not coming forth:

[... לא יב]יאה כי אם דמה יצוא [לא יצא

[he shall not br]ing her unless her blood does [not] come forth. (4QD^{e}/4Q270 4 4-5)

If we follow the reconstruction with לא, proposed by Milik, we are dealing here with the case of a man suspecting his wife, which includes the evidence that she has not had her period, i.e. is pregnant.[193] This effectively limits the application of the law to women who have become pregnant, a further diminution of its severity.[194] Alternatively, without the negative, the blood might relate to the previous reference to rape.[195] These provisions reflect not theoretical elaboration, but issues of practical application, as Bernstein notes.[196]

The instructions concerning the priest's actions summarise the detailed provisions in Num 5:16-28.

ופרע 6 [הכהן את ראשה

[the priest] shall dishevel 6 [(the hair of) her head]. (4QD^{e}/4Q270 4 5-6) (Num 5:18)

והשביע את]האשה

and he shall impose an oath upon] the woman. (4QD^{e}/4Q270 4 6) (Num 5:19)

והשקה את [האשה את מי המרים המאררים]

and cause her to drink [the bitter water of the curse]. (4QD^{e}/4Q270 4 6-7) (Num 5:24)

The fragmentary lines which follow include reference to "giving", to "kings", and to some action "with a woman" (עם אשה 4 13), probably sexual relations. 4QD^{a}/4Q266 12 (outlined) appears to offer a parallel. The text of 4QD^{e}/4Q270 is thus reconstructed to read:

---

[192] So Wassen, *Women*, 65-66.

[193] So J. T. Milik, reported in Baumgarten, *DJD* 18, 153.

[194] So Wassen, *Women*, 66. She notes a similar limitation in *m. Sot.* 4.3, though there it is not as comprehensive.

[195] So Baumgarten, *DJD* 18, 154.

[196] Bernstein, "Women and Children," 202.

[...אל ישכב איש] עם אשה

let no man lie] with a woman. (4QD[e]/4Q270 4 13)

but without preserving the context. In view of the preceding context it is likely that "giving" refers to giving a daughter, and that "kings" refers to some application by example or extension from royal law, such as the requirement of monogyny. The following line mentions "the female slave" with an explicatory insertion by a scribe indicated below by superscript:

ה]שופחה [החרופה] ...

the] bondswoman who was designated. (4QD[e]/4Q270 4 14)

This makes it likely that these lines summarise the provision in Lev 19:20 about sexual relations with a woman who is a slave designated for another man.[197]

ואיש כי ישכב את אשה שכבת זרע והוא שפחה נחרפת לאיש והפדה לא נפדתה או חפשה לא נתן לה בקרת תהיה לא יומתו כי לא חפשה

If a man has sexual relations with a woman who is a slave, designated for another man but not ransomed or given her freedom, an inquiry shall be held. They shall not be put to death, since she has not been freed. (Lev 19:20)

The remaining lines cite biblical text (כאשר] אמר "as] he said", 4 15), which speaks of seven years, of taking a woman for oneself or for one's son, and of eating one's bread. The last surviving words, ישכב עם "sleep with", also refer to sexual intercourse. It is possible that we have reference to Lev 21:1-11, which deals with the release of slaves in the seventh year, but also with the woman sold as a slave, whom a master may take for himself or give to his son.[198] The allusion to eating one's bread (4 19) may be to Deut 21:10-14, which deals with the captive woman. We would then have another set of three instances, so typical of D: sexual intercourse with a slave woman designated for another man; sexual intercourse with one's own slave woman or by one's son; and, probably, sexual relations with a captive woman and her period of integration into the people. The *Temple Scroll* in dealing with the latter issues requires that

she may not touch your purities for seven years, nor may she eat the peace offering until seven years pass; afterward she may eat. (11QT[a]/11Q19 63.10-15)

---

[197] So Baumgarten, *DJD* 18, 154.

[198] Wassen, *Women*, notes: "The few preserved words of the fragments attest to the practice of using female slaves for sexual and reproductive purposes" (104).

Baumgarten notes the parallel but wonders how that provision fits the present context. "Perhaps the link is that in both cases a woman of pagan stock is ineligible as a member of the household before an extended period of purification." [199] Wassen draws attention to laws in 12.10-11 about masters selling slaves, who appear to have been non-Jewish in origin, and to have "entered with him into the covenant of Abraham".[200] The implication may be that D, or at least this legal provision, can contemplate marriage to a foreign captive woman. In the light of the prohibition of polygyny in 4.20-21 this could apply only to unmarried men. The text is, however, so fragmentary that the suggested allusions must remain tentative.

Dress, Finding Appropriate Marriage Partners, and Dealing with Slander
4QD^{b}/4Q267 7 1-7, 12-14; 4QD^{d}/4Q269 9 1-8; 4QD^{e}/4Q270 5 14-21;
4QD^{f}/4Q271 3 1-15

This section partly preserved in 4QD^{b}/4Q267 (italic); 4QD^{d}/4Q269 (outlined); 4QD^{e}/4Q270 5 14-21 (underlined); and 4QD^{f}/4Q271 3 1-15 (base text) also bears on attitudes towards sexuality. It is possible that the fragmentary text in 4QD^{f}/4Q271 3 3-4 is based on Deut 22:5.

אל [י]הי[ו כלי] 4 [גבר על איש ואשה] כאחת כי תועבה היא

Let not [the garments of a] 4 [male be worn by a man and woman] in common, for it is an abomination. (4QD^{f}/4Q271 3 3-4)

cf. לא יהיה כלי גבר על אשה ולא ילבש גבר שמלת אשה
כי תועבת יהוה אלהיך כל עשה אלה

A woman shall not wear a man's apparel, nor shall a man put on a woman's garment; for whoever does such things is abhorrent to the LORD your God. (Deut 22:5)

If this is the case, then this is a prohibition of transvestism.[201] Baumgarten points to the occurrence of כי תועבה היא "because it is an abomination" in the context of transvestism in 4QOrd^{a}/4Q159 2-4+8 7.[202] There, too, it comes immediately

---

[199] Baumgarten, *DJD* 18, 154.

[200] See Wassen, *Women*, 69-70.

[201] So Hempel, *Damascus Texts*, 36; *Laws*, 67.

[202] Baumgarten, *DJD* 18, 176. See also Charlotte Hempel, "4QOrd^{a} (4Q159) and the Laws of the Damascus Document," in *The Dead Sea Scrolls: Fifty Years after Their Discovery: Proceedings of the Jerusalem Congress, July 20-25, 1997* (ed. Lawrence H. Schiffman, Emanuel Tov, and James C. VanderKam; Jerusalem: Israel Exploration Society in cooperation with the Shrine of the Book, Israel Museum, 2000) 372-76.

before a discussion of slander against a bride, a sequence reflecting the order of Deut 22:5-21.[203]

The text relating to the responsibilities of a father who gives his daughter in marriage to another man is clearer. It comes in the context of concern with fraud in business transactions and insistence that the vendor carries responsibility for disclosing any faults in what is being sold. As Wassen notes, the text assumes that the "woman is seen as property in the marital transfer from the father to the husband ... She is not treated as a legal person but as someone fully dependent on her father".[204] Accordingly the father carries responsibility.

ואם 8 [את בתו יתן איש לאי]ש את כול מומיה יספר לו

> And if [a man gives his daughter to a m]an, let him disclose all her blemishes to him. (4QD[f]/4Q271 3 8)

The author reinforces this requirement by citing the curse in Deut 27:18 on those who lead the blind astray, which he uses metaphorically.[205] The passage continues with further aspects of the father's responsibility.

וגם אל יתנהה לאשר לוא הוכן לה

> Moreover he should not give her to one unfit for her. (4QD[f]/4Q271 3 9)

This, too, is followed by a biblical citation, Deut 22:10-11, incomplete in form:

כי 10 [הוא כלאים ש]ר המור לבש צמר (ו)פשתים יחדיו

> for 10 [that is *kil'ayim* (two kinds), (plowing with) o]x and ass and wearing wool and linen together. (4QD[f]/4Q271 3 9-10)

Shemesh proposes that the word, הוכן, should be taken in the sense of "prepared" and understood as "betrothed".[206] He sees the concern here, as with the following disqualified women, as a matter of preventing sexual relations which would count as adultery, on the assumption that sexual intercourse creates a marriage bond.[207] Sexual relations by a betrothed couple would also create a

---

[203] Wacholder, *New Damascus Document*, notes a certain ambiguity in the statement, which could be taken also to prohibit unisex clothing (259).

[204] Wassen, *Women*, 76. She also draws attention to parallel material concerned with such fraud in 4QInst[a]/4Q415 11 6-7 and *m. Qid.* 2.5 (74-75).

[205] On the metaphorical use see Bernstein and Koyfman, "Interpretation of Biblical Law," 83.

[206] Shemesh, "4Q271.3," 261-63.

[207] He sees the same assumption operating in 11QT[a]/11Q19 66.8-11, which requires that the raped girl remain with the man as his wife and omits the option that her father may refuse. See Shemesh, "4Q271.3," 248-49.

situation in which, were the man to marry someone else, that would constitute adultery because of the bond already established. He goes on to point out that the law of כלאים "two kinds" occurs in both Lev 19:19 and in Deut 22:9-11. In the former it "immediately precedes the pericope of the handmaid promised to a man (שפחה נחרפת – Lev. 19:20-22)" and in the latter, "the pericope dealing with accusations of premarital unchastity (Deut. 22:13-19)".[208]

Wassen rightly questions this view, since offering a woman to a man other than her betrothed partner would in any case be illegal.[209] She, in turn, draws attention to the parallel in *4QMMT* B 75-82, which cites Deut 22:9-11 and which, with Strugnell and Qimron, she takes as reference to marriage between priests and Israelites and argues that the reference here is to the need to marry someone within one's own kin.[210] She supports this with reference to Judith, Tobit, and *Jubilees* where endogamous marriage is important. It is far from secure, however, that the *4QMMT* text is about intermarriage between priests and other Israelites, rather than with Gentiles, a concern also prominent in *Jubilees*, and in any case our passage is not about marriage between priests and other Israelites. The use of Deut 22:10-11[211] does, however, suggest that the concern relates not just to individuals who are unsuitable but to categories of people.[212] Thus it might include marriage to Gentiles, as Deut 22:9-11 is applied in *4QMMT*, or marriage outside one's kin, although the metaphor of kinds does not suit this so well. The metaphor is even less suited to addressing incestuous marriages, such as marriage to uncles, addressed elsewhere.

The alternative is to interpret the metaphor in a way that it refers not to categories but to any unsuitable match. Then it might apply to others deemed unfit for various reasons, including those too young (cf. 1QSa/1Q28a 1.9-11, under twenty) or too old. The metaphor in Deut 22.9-11 of yoking an ox and an ass seems to be used in Sir 25:8b in this way to refer to the need for compatible individuals (having a "sensible" wife; 25:8a). What an original author intended, let alone what hearers and interpreters, including the final redactor, understood, must

[208] Shemesh, "4Q271.3," 263.

[209] Wassen, *Women*, 77.

[210] Wassen, Women, 77-79.

[211] Baumgarten, *DJD* 18, also draws attention to similar use in Josephus *A.J.* 4.229 (177). See also Bernstein and Koyfman, "Interpretation," 83.

[212] On this see Ida Fröhlich, "'Mamzer' in Qumran Texts – The Problem of Mixed Marriages from Ezra's Time: Law, Literature and Practice," *Transeuphratène* 29 (2005) 103-15, who writes: "This means that marriages of two Israelites could also be viewed as 'not matching' (*kil'ayim*); the marriage with an unsuitable partner meant for them the intermingling of two different categories. The biblical basis for this view is Lev 21:15 which teaches that a priest's marriage with an unsuitable (not necessarily impure) woman (for example widow, divorcee) profanes his seed or offspring" (111).

remain open to a range of possibilities. The use of the analogy does favour seeing the concern as one with categories of partners rather than personality traits.

The third issue addressed by the author is a woman who has had inappropriate sexual experiences, which he then divides into a further set of three concerns. It begins with the words,

אל יבא איש 11 [אשה בברית(?) הקו]דש

Let no man bring 11 [a woman into the ho]ly [covenant?]. (4QD[f]/4Q271 3 10b-11a)

It is not immediately clear what "the holy" קודש refers to here, but as Baumgarten observes, it probably refers to marriage, corresponding to a common usage of this stem in Mishnaic Hebrew.[213] He notes that "קודש and its cognates are employed in the context of a man's relationship with his wife and companion" in 4QpapRitMar/4Q502.[214] The usage appears also in 4QInst[a]/4Q415 2 ii 4.

The author then gives three instances of women with whom this should not happen.

אשר ידעה לעשות מעשה מדבר or בדבר
ואשר ידעה 12 [מעשה בבית] אביה
או אלמנה אשר נשכבה מאשר התארמלה

who has had sexual experience of doing the deed at large (or) the unseemly deed
or who has sexual experience of [the deed (while) in the household of] her father
or as a widow who has had intercourse after she was widowed.*
(4QD[f]/4Q271 3 11-12)

The first two may belong together, especially if we see ואשר "and/or who" as indicating that the second is further explication of the first. More probably we have another instance of three. The first might refer to sexual intercourse in the wilderness or open countryside (מדבר) in contrast to at home in her father's household, the second category. 4QD[e]/4Q270 5 18 preserves the two letters בד giving rise to the projected reading, בדבר. As Baumgarten notes, מעשה בדבר לעשות "to do the deed in the matter" and ידעה "know" are euphemisms for sexual promiscuity.[215] Read as מעשה בדבר "unseemly deed", it could as Kampen suggests, be related to ערות דבר Deut 24:1.[216] Given that the second category refers to a woman in the house of her father and the third, to a widow, the most likely category for the first instance is a woman who has committed sexual

[213] So Baumgarten, *DJD* 18, 177, who notes also the conjecture of supplying ברית "covenant".

[214] Baumgarten, *DJD* 18, 177.

[215] Baumgarten, *DJD* 18, 177; similarly Noam, "Divorce in Qumran," 220.

[216] Kampen, "Matthean Divorce Texts Reexamined," 155-56.

wrongdoing once she has left her father's house, i.e. as a married woman, most likely, therefore referring to an adulteress. In other words, under a strict reading of Deut 24:1, the woman would, therefore, be a divorcee.[217] As noted above in the discussion of divorce in the context of interpreting the three nets, Noam points out that a similar warning against marrying divorced women is to be found in early tannaitic traditions.[218] If we read מדבר "wilderness, countryside", as indicating "at large", in contrast to being in her father's household and so under its control, then the end effect is the same: it refers to illicit sexual intercourse once she has left her father's household, most likely, therefore, as a married woman, thus having committed adultery and been divorced.

In all three instances, the woman with sexual experience outside her father's house (either as a prostitute or, more probably, as an adulteress, who would then have been divorced, thus, probably a divorcee), the woman with sexual experience while still in her father's house, and the widow with sexual experience during her widowhood, the issue is that these are forbidden marriage partners. In an extensive discussion Shemesh argues that the rationale both for the prohibition of marrying a woman who has already had sexual experience (understood as a זונה) and a divorcee derives from Lev 21:7,

> אשה זנה וחללה לא יקחו ואשה גרושה מאישה לא יקחו כי קדש הוא לאלהיו
> They shall not marry a prostitute or a woman who has been defiled; neither shall they marry a woman divorced from her husband. For they are holy to their God. (Lev 21:7)

"While the biblical injunction is explicitly addressed to priests, sectarian halakhah characteristically broadens its scope, applying pentateuchal priestly law to the nation as a whole."[219] There is precedent for this both in *Jubilees*, a text significant for D, and in the *Aramaic Levi Document*.[220] Wassen notes that

> although the requirement of virginity for a young bride and chastity for a widow corresponds to general societal views, this conversion of general practice into codified law for all men – priests and laity alike – is unique.[221]

---

[217] So Shemesh, "4Q271.3," who sees this as evidence that remarriage by divorcees was forbidden (246, 248). But, strictly speaking, it forbids marriage to women divorced for adultery, not remarriage to or by other divorcees.

[218] Noam, "Divorce in Qumran," 211-19.

[219] Shemesh, "4Q271.3," 247. Wassen, *Women*, draws attention also to Lev 21:13-14a, the restrictions placed on the high priest, for whom a widow, divorced woman, defiled woman or prostitute are forbidden marriage partners. She rightly draws attention to the acceptability of widows in 4QD^f/4Q271 3 provided they have not engaged in illicit sexual relations, but she does not recognise an allusion to divorced women in 4Q271 3 (80-81).

[220] See also Loader, *Enoch, Levi, and Jubilees*, 93-103, 168, 174-75, 182-84.

[221] Wassen, *Women*, 81.

She notes that the honour and shame system of the ancient Mediterranean world form the background of such societal views.[222] But they also relate closely to notions of property and household.

The passage then turns to the case of the woman who a bad reputation while she lived in her father's household.

וכול 13 [אשר עליה ש]ם רע בבתוליה בבית אביה אל יקחה איש

And any 13 [woman upon whom there is] a bad [na]me in her maidenhood in her father's home, let no man take her. (4QD[f]/4Q271 3 12-13)

This matches the prohibition in the Catalogue of Transgressions (4QD[e]/4Q270 2 i.16-17a). The author then adds a proviso:

כי אם 14 [בראות נשים] נאמנות וידעות
ברורות ממאמר המבקר אשר על 15 [הרבים]

except 14 [upon examination] by trustworthy [women]
of repute selected by the command of the supervisor over 15 [the many.
(4QD[f]/4Q271 3 13b-15a)

The specific reference to the overseer indicates that these rules are being applied in the camps. This may well reflect adaptation of earlier material to become communal legislation.[223] The women, probably midwives,[224] are to inspect the woman, presumably to ascertain whether her hymen is intact. Should it be, then the author declares:

ואח]ר יקחנה ובלוקחו אותה יעשה כמ[ש]פט [ולוא] יגיד עלי[ה]

After]ward he may take her, and when he takes her he shall act in accordance with the l[a]w [and he shall not t]ell about [her]. (4QD[f]/4Q271 3 15)

In other words, members of the community are not to marry women who have engaged in illicit sexual relations before marriage. This coheres with what precedes, where this is the second category beside those who have engaged in illicit sexual relations in a previous marriage (by adultery and so are divorcees) or after becoming widowed. As Wassen notes, the inspection is a more satisfactory way of determining virginity than the display of blood stipulated in Deut 22:13-22 (and followed in 4QOrd[a]/4Q159), since first intercourse does not necessarily

---

[222] Wassen, *Women*, 81, 105.

[223] So Hempel, *Laws*, 69.

[224] Wassen, *Women*, 87. She notes that the plural may reflect the requirement of Deut 19:16 of two witnesses and that it also assumes women could act as witnesses, as do other sectarian writings at Qumran (88).

produce bleeding[225] and blood stains could be faked. Interestingly, 4QOrd^{a}/4Q159 also has an inspection, but only after the wedding takes place, raising questions about the purpose of the inspection (see the discussion on pp. 216-19 below). The rationale for the prohibition of sexual intercourse before the inspection is also to prevent unsuspected adultery taking place, should the woman already have had sexual intercourse with another man and so be already, in effect, married, according to the assumptions of the sect.[226] Thus the inspection is a way of avoiding that potential disaster, which would require the death penalty by stoning (so Deut 22:13-21).[227] It also shifts the responsibility from the husband to the community.

The prohibition of speaking about the inspected woman (probably formulated in allusion to Deut 22:14) probably relates to her bad reputation and thus offers her some limited protection. Wassen notes that, despite the amelioration through the inspection, the whole passage concerned with marital arrangements "typifies the double standard imposed on male and female sexuality", where the potential bride is subject to scrutiny and potential humiliation, whereas the potential husband faces no such examination.[228] Even at the point where women are empowered as inspectors, the "women midwives were agents in maintaining a legislative system that was oppressive to women".[229]

Wassen suggests that 4QD^{h}/4Q273 5 may belong here.[230] It speaks of taking a woman and the days of her blood:

אל יקח איש את האש]ה [5 [...] מימי ספרה את דם עד אשר י[

Let no man take a wom[an] 5 from the days she counted the blood of [ ] until [. (4QD^{h}/4Q273 5 4b-5)

She suggests it may refer to "marrying during the time of the woman's menstruation".[231] The reference to taking a woman belongs in the context which is concerned with taking a wife. Alternatively, it might fit in a context concerned with menstruation, such as in the discussion of the discharges in 4QD^{g}/4Q272 1 ii and 4QD^{a}/4Q266 6, but it is hard to see where there is space for it.

---

[225] On this see Wassen, *Women*, 83 and 85-87.

[226] Shemesh, "4Q271 3," 254-55; Wassen, *Women*, 85.

[227] So Wassen, *Women*, 84-85.

[228] Wassen, *Women*, 81, 105.

[229] Wassen, *Women*, 89.

[230] Wassen, *Women*, 89. She notes that there is an overlap with 4Q271 3.13 in the words, אל יקח איש "Let no man take a woman".

[231] Wassen, *Women*, 89; similarly Wacholder, *New Damascus Document*, 304.

Remaining Qumran fragments and the Beginning of the Laws Preserved in CD

4QD[a]/4Q266 7 i.1-5 contains a section concerned with holding grudges (similar to CD 9.2-8a, 18). The fragmentary passage preserved in 4QD[a]/4Q266 7 ii.1-10; iii.1-7; 4QD[b]/4Q267 4 i.6-7 refers to regulation, the camp and the overseer, but its issue has not survived. Neither passage preserves material relating to sexuality. They appear to relate to community organisation and so reflect communal legislation.[232]

All of the above passages precede the material found in the legal section of CD-A. Thereafter we have the unbroken text of CD-A, but with many additional witnesses to sections of it among the Qumran texts and some further material at the end which is not contained in CD-A. Hempel assigns the laws on oaths (16.6b-12), and freewill offerings (16.13-17a; 9.1; 4QD[a]/4Q266 8 ii.8-9; 4QD[e]/4Q270 6 iii.15-16), the material on reproof (9.2-8a), oaths (9.8b-10), the sabbath (10.14 – 11.18b), the purity of the altar (11.18c-21a), the purification of water (10.10b-13a), and relations to Gentiles (12.6b-11a) to the early, non-sectarian halakhic stratum.[233]

Most of the material preserved in CD-A has little to do with issues of sexuality. This is true of the main two sections in column 15, oaths and admission to the community. In 15.5 there is mention of admission of בניהם "their sons/children", which could refer exclusively to male children, but equally to both boys and girls, as Wassen argues.[234] It is notable that the list in 15.15-17 (4QD[a]/4Q266 8 i.7-9) of excluded people makes no reference to people in relation to their sexuality, unlike the similar list in *4QMMT* B 39-49. It is interesting that the ground for exclusion is the presence of angels in the congregation, derived from Num 5:3b or Deut 23:15. It is used elsewhere to ground provisions about purity and sexual abstinence before special gatherings (1QSa/1Q28a 2.8-9), limitations on who may enter the war camp (1QM/1Q33 7.6b-7), and restrictions on entering the new temple (4QFlor/4Q174 1-2 i.2-4). Here it is dealing with those who may be enrolled in the membership of the covenant community. This is not the same as all who are associated with the groups or camps, which would have included minors. The list of those excluded includes a נער, which might mean a "boy", leading to the conclusion that the congregation of the covenant consisted only of male adults, but here, too, Wassen argues for an inclusive sense. She notes that youth and women often occur together, such as in the list of those excluded from the war camp in 1QM/1Q33 7.3b and in *4QMiscellaneous Rules*/4Q265 3 3, and must include both male and female youths. Accordingly she sees the absence

[232] On this stratum of material in the document see Hempel, *Laws*, 73-148.

[233] Hempel, *Laws*, 30-38.

[234] Wassen. *Women*, 133-36.

of reference to women in the list here in D as a valid argument from silence to indicate that they were included.[235] The concluding section on admission, which comes in column 16, appears to cite the opening words of the book of *Jubilees* as literally definitive in terms of interpreting the Law (16.3-4; 4QD^{f}/4Q271 4 ii.5).[236] This coheres with what we have identified as its significant influence throughout the Admonition.

The rest of column 16 is concerned with oaths and vows and includes an interpretation of the biblical provision in Num 30:7-9 concerning oaths of women, to forbid annulment in instances of uncertainty. As Schiffman notes, "this passage affirms that sectarians, at least according to the Zadokite Fragments, are expected to marry and have children".[237] The column also includes warnings about illegitimate dedication of goods on which others have a claim.

Column 9, which properly follows 16, contains teaching about appropriate ways of dealing with conflict and avoiding resentment, further laws on oaths, and rules about loss of property and theft, and witnesses. The latter continue in column 10, which also sets up regulations for appointing judges. It, too, reflects influence from *Jubilees*, on 10.7b-10a (cf. *Jub.* 23:9-11).[238] It continues with rules about water and purification, and about the sabbath. The latter is an extensive section reaching well down column 11. It includes the following provision, attested also in 4QD^{f}/4Q271 5 i.1-2 (outlined),

אל יתערב איש מרצונו 5 בשבת

let no man engage in sexual intercourse for his pleasure 5 on the sabbath.* (11.5)

The word ערב "mingle" has sexual connotations in *4QMMT* B 48 (80?), C 8 (cf. Ezra 9:2 and *Ps.* 106:35)[239] and given that רצון "pleasure, desire" is also used in a

---

235 Wassen, *Women*, 153-54.

236 On this see James C. VanderKam, *Textual and Historical Studies in the Book of Jubilees* (HMS 14; Missoula, Mont.: Scholars Press, 1977) 255-58.

237 Schiffman, "Law of Vows and Oaths," 206. He notes the selective use of Num 30:3-16 in D compared to the *Temple Scroll*; the former deals only with oaths, not vows, and omits the vows and oaths of a man, of a minor woman, and of a widow or divorcee and a wife's vows or oaths of self-affliction (212). He sees the difference between the documents as best explained by different stages in development, with D reflecting "the later development of legal teachings which took place within the sect" (213). Wassen, *Women*, notes that the passage radically alters the provisions of Numbers 30, restricting a man's authority over women's oaths to those cases in which the fulfilment of a pledge taken by oath violates the covenantal law" (93). She notes that this empowerment of women "stands in sharp contrast to the legislation concerning women's oaths as found in 11QT and 4QInstruction^{b}" (93).

238 See Hempel, *Laws*, 102-103.

239 See pp. 63-64, 67, 73, 80-81 above.

sexual context in the Admonition (2.14 – 3.12a), we most probably have here a prohibition of sexual intercourse on the sabbath as in *Jub.* 50:8,[240] and I have translated accordingly. The word מרצונו "for his pleasure" might refer to an act of sexual intercourse just for pleasure. That might indicate approval of sexual intercourse on the sabbath only when it is for procreation. If, however, the rationale is impurity through seminal emission, as the following context suggests, then such a distinction is unlikely to be intended.[241] The ban is therefore more likely to be against any act of sexual intercourse. We noted above a further possible reference to prohibiting sexual intercourse on the sabbath in the Catalogue of Transgressions 4QD^{e}/4Q270 2 i.18-19.[242]

Specific provisions for removing impurity, with which the column ends, probably include dealing with impurity through seminal emission, though it is not named specifically.[243] Specific reference to impurity through seminal emission occurs, however, in what immediately follows at the top of column 12, where we read:

---

[240] See already Ginzberg, *Unknown Jewish Sect*, who observes: "From a linguistic point of view יתערב, 'mingle together,' might well be considered a euphemistic term for sexual intercourse, and as a substantive parallel one might refer to the Book of Jubilees, 50,8" (114-15). However he continues: "but the following מרצונו makes such an explanation impossible" (115). We argue to the contrary, that it makes it very likely. Understanding it as a reference to sexual intercourse, see also Elisha Qimron, "The Halacha of the Damascus Covenant – An Interpretation of 'Al Yitarev'," *Proceedings of the Ninth World Congress of Jewish Studies* D I (1986) 9-15; Qimron, *DJD* 10, 140; Doering, "Purity Regulations," though as referring to sexual relations among other things (607); and Wassen, *Women*, 94-95. For the suggestion that the affirmation of sexual relations on the sabbath in rabbinic tradition is formulated in deliberate contrast to such restrictions see Magen Broshi, "Anti-Qumranic Polemic in the Talmud," in *The Madrid Qumran Congress: Proceedings of the International Congress on the Dead Sea Scrolls, Madrid 18-21 March, 1991* (Vol 2; STDJ 11.2; ed. J. Trebolle Barrera and L. Vegas Montaner; Leiden: Brill, 1991) 2: 589-600, 596; Doering, "Purity Regulations," 606.

[241] Cf. Davies, "Judaism(s) of the Damascus Document," who concludes that "D's *torah* seems to view sexual relations as purely for procreation. Sexual activity apart from the legitimate bounds of a single lawful marriage is denounced as 'lust' זנות. Sexual intercourse is intrinsically unclean and may not take place in the 'city of the sanctuary' (12:1-2)" (34). The first statement appears to be an argument from silence and is not an implication of the statements which follow.

[242] So also Doering, "Purity Regulations," 604; Wassen, *Women*, 95.

[243] On the likely reference at the end of column 11 to houses of prayer given the same status as the temple which had been defiled, see Annette Steudel, "The Houses of Prostration: CD XI,21-XII.1: Duplicates of the Temple (I)," *RevQ* 16 (1993) 49-67, who argues that 12.1 attacks those who continue to defile the holy city, Jerusalem, by disregard of a sexual taboo (63).

אל ישכב איש עם אשה בעיר המקדש לטמא 2 את עיר המקדש בנדתם

No-one shall sleep with a woman in the city of the sanctuary to defile 2 the city of the sanctuary with their impurities. (CD 12.1b-2a)

The term, עיר המקדש, "city of the sanctuary", is capable of two meanings: the city, Jerusalem, in which the sanctuary is located,[244] or the temple precincts, i.e. that area within Jerusalem which counts as the temple precincts.[245] In the latter case the prohibition would simply reflect the common assumption that sexual intercourse is out of place in the temple and, as Wassen notes, would in that sense be "entirely redundant".[246] If, as is more likely, it refers to the city as a whole, then one has to assume that married members would not have lived in Jerusalem or, if and while they did for whatever period, abstained from sexual relations.[247] We noted a similar ambiguity in the *Temple Scroll* (45.11-12), where those who had had sexual intercourse are forbidden from entering the city of the sanctuary, which, therefore, also implies that sexual intercourse was forbidden in the city, itself. *4QMMT* appears to reflect the same understanding of Jerusalem when it identifies it as the equivalent of the wilderness camp in applying purity laws.

Wassen notes the differences between the *Temple Scroll* and D, in that the latter in not concerned to stipulate three days' waiting before entering the city, nor that impurity carriers be confined. "Since other types of impurities, such as *niddah*, in the city are of no concern in this document, unmarried men and women would still be able to live in Jerusalem; married couples had to refrain from sexual intercourse within the city".[248] Thus while a person who has completed purifications (*tebul yom*) could not enter the temple until after sunset, they could still enter the city the same day, unlike under the provisions of the *Temple Scroll*.

---

[244] So Yadin, *Temple Scroll*, 1.280; Harrington, *Purity Texts*, 103-104; Wassen, *Women*, 100-101; and see the discussion in the chapter on the *Temple Scroll*; Wacholder, *New Damascus Document*, 341.

[245] So Schiffman, "Laws Pertaining to Women," 211; Schiffman, *Reclaiming the Dead Sea Scrolls*, 131; Gruber, "Purity and Impurity," 73-74.

[246] Wassen, *Women*, 99.

[247] Similarly Davies, "Judaism(s) of the Damascus Document," who notes that the reference to marriage, divorce and children, implies that some, if not the majority do not marry and continues: "The hint of a celibate lifestyle among this group is apparently the product of concern for holiness and it seems to follow that if a D settlement existed in Jerusalem, its members were necessarily celibate" (34). See also Baumgarten and Schwartz, "Damascus Document," who conclude: "The effect of such stringency would be to make celibacy practically a norm for priests and others functioning in the sacred city of Jerusalem" (51).

[248] Wassen, *Women*, 102, similarly 104. She also notes that the purity concerns do not necessarily reflect "a negative view of sexual intercourse *per se*" (104).

Hempel notes that "a particular emphasis on the special status of Jerusalem … is on the whole absent from the Laws of D".[249] Accordingly she suggests that "CD 12,1b-2a constitutes an interpolation in the Laws of D which seems to have originated from the same milieu as 11QT[a] 45-47".[250] The alternative is that it belongs to the early halakhic stratum, as Wassen suggests.[251] It certainly coheres with a concern about impurity and resultant defilement of the temple which would have been consistent with an approach which extended its holiness to the city. Such regulations reflect a setting where Jerusalem remains central. At a later stage those who preserved copies of this document and perhaps its final redactors may have enjoined abandonment of contact with the city and the temple and have transferred the distinction to their own community, so that corresponding to Jerusalem, the core community was celibate, while those beyond the core group lived in non-celibate communities, such as we may assume from 7.5-9 / 19.1-5.

Column 12 continues with warnings about those who preach apostasy (linked with the figure of Belial), which it sets on the same level as necromancy and divining; defiling the sabbath and festivals (differing from both Exod 35:2 and Num 15:35 and also from *Jub.* 50:8, 12-13, in not requiring the death penalty); relations with Gentiles (concerned similarly to *4QMMT* with Gentile sacrifices, but also with killing Gentiles);[252] and further regulations concerning foods and purity. In the warning expressed in 12.4 about defiling the sabbath and the festivals (לחלל את שבת ואת המועדות) there may be an allusion to prohibiting sexual intercourse on the sabbath, as in *Jub.* 50:8, and on festivals.

Column 12 ends with provisions relating to the communities, beginning with

סרך מושב ערי ישראל על המשפטים האלה
להבדיל בין 20 הטמא לטהור
ולהודיע בין הקודש לחול

> the rule of the assembly of the towns of Israel according to these precepts
> that they may distinguish between 20 unclean and clean,
> and discriminate between the holy and the profane. (V) (12.19-20)

The words, המשפטים האלה "these precepts" seem best taken as a reference to the body of laws which precede. The following words match 6.17b-18a exactly. They recall the words of 5.6b-7a, אין הם מבדיל כתורה "none of them differentiates

[249] Hempel, *Laws*, 156.

[250] Hempel, *Laws*, 156. See also 154-62, 190.

[251] Wassen, *Women*, 98.

[252] On this see Schiffman, "Non-Jews," who sees this and the warning against plundering Gentile property as "a polemic against the Hasmonean rulers intended to prohibit the undertaking of campaigns designed only to add territory to their country or to accumulate spoils of war" (156).

according to the Law", where the focus is sexual wrongdoing. It may be assumed to be part of the concern also here.

The reference to the precepts by which the משכיל "Instructor" is to live are similarly brief (12.20b-22a). "The rule of the assembly of the camps" begins at the foot of column 12 and continues into column 13, where it stipulates the minimum constitution of the camp, the role of a priest who is to rule by the book of Hagy, or of a Levite in the absence of a priest, and his instruction by the Overseer (מבקר) (12.22 – 13.7a). There follows the rule for the Overseer (מבקר) (13.7b-19), which deals first with teaching and related pastoral responsibilities (13.7b-10). It then speaks of his examining members on the basis of their deeds and deciding on admissions (13.11-13). At this point the focus moves to commerce: he is to be consulted in all transactions of buying and selling (13.14-16a).

It is in this context that the instruction moves to dealing with marriage and divorce (13.16b-19). As Wassen notes, "these laws have been grouped together, since marriage and divorce – like business deals – involve transference of property".[253] The same association occurs in 4QD^{f}/4Q271 3 1-15, where a discussion of fair trade leads to the requirement that fathers are open about blemishes in the daughters they offer in marriage. Indeed the surviving documents about marriage from the period are dominated by the regulation of such concerns. The passage in 13.16b-19 is attested also in 4QD^{a}/4Q266 9 iii.4-9 (outlined) and 4QD^{d}/4Q269 10 ii 1-2 (underlined). It begins:

וכן] ל[כו]ל ל[וק]ח אש[ה] 17 וה[ואה] [... ב]עצה

> And likewise] with regard to [any]one who ma[rr]ies a wom[an] 17 and [...] in consultation. (*DSSSE*) (13.16b-17a)

CD appears to have an additional word after וה[ואה], not in the Qumran fragment. The laws articulated elsewhere about appropriate men for husbands and the quality of women offered to be wives (4QD^{f}/4Q271 3) would thus belong to this aspect of the Overseer's responsibility. That role also included receiving the assessment of midwives in the cases of determining the virginity or otherwise of women with a bad reputation. His responsibility is described here as עצה, best taken here as referring to "advice that carries the force of absolute authority".[254] That responsibility also entails dealing with divorce.[255] Here the texts are slightly different.

---

[253] Wassen, *Women*, 160, who notes the provisions outlined for the first instance, namely the need to inform the Overseer and act on his advice.

[254] Wassen, *Women*, 161.

[255] For earlier discussion, see Brin, "Divorce at Qumran", 238-39. He also points to 4QD^{b}/4Q267 9 vi 4-5, which in requiring expulsion of a man from the community for having illegal sex with his wife implies forced divorce (242-43).

וכן [256]{יבן} למגרש
והוא ייס]ר את בניהם [ובנותם (?)] 18 [וטפם ברוח]ענוה ובאהבת חסד
אל יטור להם[באף] 19 [ועברה על פ]שעיהם

> and likewise {he shall give counsel} with regard to anyone who divorces; he shall ins[truct their children ...] 18 [and their small children with a spirit of] modesty and with compassionate love. He should not bear resentment against them [in anger] 19 [and rage because of] their [s]ins. (*DSSSE*) (CD 13.17b-19a; 4QD[a]/4Q266 9 iii.6-9a)

For divorce it uses the word, גרש, attested in rabbinic Hebrew as the verb used in the *pi'el* for giving a letter of divorce, rather than שלח "dismiss/divorce", used in biblical Hebrew (Deut 22:29; 24:1).[257] This text clearly assumes marriage and accepts divorce as a normal part of life.[258] This counts against reading the earlier statement of the Admonition in 4.20-21 as forbidding divorce, that is, taking another wife while the divorced wife is still alive, especially if we understand by divorce the freeing of a woman to marry again. The passage makes clear, however, that divorce is not treated lightly, such as rabbinic traditions report of the school of Hillel, but makes it something which requires the scrutiny of the community through the Overseer. "A man was not free to divorce his wife at his own will".[259]

It is also interesting that the Overseer is to take responsibility for the children's instruction. If the reference is to children of the divorced marriage,[260] it probably assumes that the children would go with the mother, especially likely in the case of small children. Hence the role for the Overseer in instruction is in place of the father who would normally give instruction. This is more likely than that the Overseer is to take responsibility for all children, whatever the state of their parents' marriage, as, for instance, Albert Baumgarten assumes.[261] The exhortation

---

[256] Only in 4QD[a]/4Q266 9 iii 6.

[257] On this see Wassen, *Women*, 159.

[258] Davies, "Judaism(s) of the Damascus Document," reads the passage as implying that marriage was not the practice of many or most (34). It is not evident that the text implies this.

[259] Wassen, *Women*, 162. On women's possibility of divorcing their husbands see her brief review of the research (163 n. 103).

[260] So Holmén, "Divorce," 403; Bilhah Nitzan, "The Laws of Reproof in *4QBerakhot* (4Q286-290) in Light of the Parallels in the *Damascus Covenant* and Other Texts from Qumran," in *Legal Texts and Legal Issues: Proceedings of the Second Meeting of the International Organisation for Qumran studies, Cambridge, 1995: Published in Honour of Joseph M. Baumgarten* (ed. M. Bernstein, F. G. Martinez, J. Kampen; Leiden: Brill, 1997) 149-65, 154-55.

[261] Baumgarten, "Perception of the Past," 7; also Wassen, *Women*, who argues against taking it as instruction of only the children of the divorced marriage on the basis that the passage mentions only the man and that therefore the word for children should have masculine singular suffix (165). She then emphasises that the word about instruction should

to compassion is noteworthy and reflects a concern for the welfare of children. Wassen argues that the references to טפם "their infants" and בניהם "their children", should be read inclusively to refer to both girls and boys as in 1QSa/1Q28a 1.4-9.[262]

The instruction for the Overseer continues into column 14, where we also find the rule about the assembly of all the camps, about which the previous sections have been giving instruction. It is noteworthy that it includes proselytes beside priests, Levites and the people.[263] These laws also provide for collection and distribution of resources to the needy, including, as noted earlier, those who have been prisoners of Gentiles (and must have suffered some enduring harm), the girl who has no redeemer and the youth with no one to care for him (13.15-16). The absence of any reference to orphaned young children probably reflects an order in which they were cared for by the community in much the same way as the Overseer cared for the children of divorced parents. It became problematic when they reached an older age when the youth (נער) needed assistance to enter adulthood, including some resources for starting a marriage, and the young woman would need resources for a dowry, if she was to marry, which the text assumes would be normal. "By taking financial responsibility for young men and women, the community functioned as a surrogate family for them".[264] It is interesting that neither widows nor divorcees receive mention as especially needy, perhaps because there were few of the latter, given the strictness about divorce, and the former would remarry.[265] Women divorced for adultery would be expelled and those few from marriages where the husband was expelled were, like the widows, also likely to remarry. Column 14 breaks off at the beginning of a penal code. Fortunately, much of this is preserved in the Qumran fragments.

---

be seen as belonging within the broader framework of laws for the Overseer in relation to the community as a whole.

[262] Wassen, *Women*, 166.

[263] On גר as indicating "proselyte" here, see Davies, "Judaism(s) of the Damascus Document," 32.

[264] Wassen, *Women*, 170.

[265] So Wassen, Women, 170-71.

The Penal Code 4QD^a/4Q266 10 i – ii.15; 4QD^b/4Q267 9 vi.1-5; 4QD^d/4Q269 11 i.1-8; ii.1-2; 15 1-5; and 4QD^e/4Q270 7 i.1-15

The main statements in the Penal Code of interest to our study are those concerning nakedness found in 4QD^a/4Q266 10 ii.9-11 (base text) and 4QD^e/4Q270 7 i.1-3 (outlined).[266]

ואשר יהלך לפני רע]הו ערום בבית או בשדה הלך ערום לפני] 10 ה[ב]ריאות
והובדל ששה [חודשים ונענש שלושים יום

> And whoever walks [naked] in front of [his] fel[low in a house], or who walks naked in the field in front of] 10 the [cr]eatures, shall be excluded for six [months and shall be punished thirty days]. (*DSSSE*) (4QD^a/4Q266 10 ii.9-10a; 4QD^e/4Q270 7 i.1-2)

4QD^e/4Q270 has [ה]לך [ע]רום לפני הבריאות as a secondary insertion after בשדה. The prohibition against walking naked in front of one's fellow also occurs in 1QS/1Q28 7.14, though with the proviso, "without needing to". *Jubilees* strongly emphasises the importance of avoiding nakedness (3:30-32; 7:20-21). Originally 4QD^e/4Q270 made no reference to nakedness before animals, but simply to being naked in the house or in the field. The additional words create a chiasm, probably a secondary development. Nakedness before animals is an extension of the strictness.

The theme of nakedness is more specific in what follows.

ואשר] 11 [יו]צא את ידו מתחת בגד[ו והואה פוח ונראתה ערותו
והובדל שלו]שים 12 [יו]ם ונענש עשרה

> He who] 11 dr[a]ws out his hand from under [his] garment [and, being improperly clothed, his nakedness becomes visible, shall be excluded for thi]rty 12 [da]ys and be punished for ten. (4QD^a/4Q266 10 ii.10b-12a; 4QD^e/4Q270 7 i.3)

On the basis of the parallel in 1QS/1Q28 7.15b-16a Baumgarten conjectures that between בגד]ו "his garment" and והובדל "he shall be excluded" 4QD^e/4Q270 included the words: והואה פוח ונראתה ערותו "and, being improperly clothed, his nakedness becomes visible" (as above). It is probably better to take the addition as introducing not a further qualification of the first statement, but an alternative: "or being improperly clothed, his nakedness becomes visible". The first act is deliberate; the second is a matter of wearing inadequate clothing which exposes the nakedness. The "hand" is a common euphemism for the penis. This exposure receives only half the penalty of what is apparently full nakedness. The

266 Wacholder, *New Damascus Document*, draws attention also to the prohibition of דבר חבל "lewd speech" in 3, which may possibly have a sexual reference, noting that the same language is used in 10.17b-18a to describe what is prohibited on the sabbath (358).

parallel in 1QS/1Q28 7.14-16 has a prohibition of spitting between the command about nakedness in general and this provision. It describes the delict in the same words as 4QD^{e}/4Q270, including the two alternatives, but imposes a harsher penalty: punishment for thirty days, though without mention of exclusion.

Gesticulating with the left hand, a prohibition which follows shortly after in 4QD^{a}/4Q266 13-14 and 4QD^{e}/4Q270 5, and which is found also in the *Community Rule* (1QS/1Q28 7.17; 4QS^{e}/4Q259 i 14-15) has given rise to a number of explanations, including that the Therapeutae disapproved of an orator with their right hand (Philo *Contempl.* 77),[267] that Josephus mentions that the Essenes did not spit to the right,[268] or that mention of the left hand was to distinguish it from the euphemistic use in 11 where it refers to the penis.[269] A further possibility is that it reflects a culture in which the left hand was used in toileting and would be inappropriate to use in gesticulation (or in shaking hands, still widely observed in many societies today).[270]

The final piece of relevance relates to illicit sexual intercourse. It is found in 4QD^{e}/4Q270 7 i.12-13 (base text) and 4QD^{b}/4Q267 9 vi.4-5 (outlined).

> ואשר יקר[ב] 13 לזנות לאשתו אשר לא כמשפט ויצא ולא ישוב עוד [*vacat*
>
> and whoever approach[es 13 to have illegal sex with his wife, not in accordance with the regulation, shall leave and never return [*blank.*

Here illicit sexual intercourse with one's own wife might potentially refer to sexual intercourse during menstruation or in the days of impurity following childbirth,[271] or during pregnancy. Wassen points out, however, that the penal code does not contain biblical prohibitions elsewhere and therefore casts doubt on reading it in relation to menstruation or periods of impurity.[272]

---

267 A. R. C. Leaney, *The Rule of Qumran and its Meaning: Introduction, Translation and Commentary* (London: SCM, 1966) 207.

268 Leaney, *Rule of Qumran*, 207; Knibb, *Qumran Community*, 127.

269 Qimron and Charlesworth, *PTSDDSP* 1, 33 n. 188.

270 Wacholder, *New Damascus Document*, reads לשח here and לשוח in Gen 24:63 not as referring to gesticulation but to urinating, noting that urinating using the left hand is what the rabbis support (361).

271 So Kampen, "Matthean Divorce Texts Reexamined," 157

272 Wassen, *Women*, 178. See there her review of recent explanations. She rejects the suggestion that it may refer to illicit marriages, arguing, I think correctly, that these would not have been admitted in the first place. Cf. Angelo Tosato, "Su di una norma matrimoniale 4QD," *Bib* 74 (1993) 401-10.

This still leaves sexual intercourse during pregnancy.[273] Elsewhere the document grounds this prohibition on the basis of potential damage to the foetus (4QD[e]/4Q270 2 ii.15-16; 6QD/6Q15 5 2-3). While some read it from the perspective of reports in Josephus (*B.J.* 2.160), that Essenes do not engage in sexual intercourse except for procreation, that ruling makes no mention of it, but instead gives a different rationale.[274] The words, אשר לא כמשפט ("which is not in accordance with the regulation") suggest that the basis of the prohibition is not disapproval of sexual pleasure, but something more specific. Baumgarten notes its use in 4QD[f]/4Q271 3.15, where it apparently refers to the way the man engages in sexual intercourse with a bride who had needed to undergo inspection, and in 1QSa/1Q28a 1.10-11, where it refers to rules about marital life.[275] There it assumes that the woman would act as informant on her husband.[276] This is more likely to include something like sexual intercourse during pregnancy, but might also include other forbidden ways of engaging in sexual intercourse.[277] This could also include doing so at inappropriate times and places, perhaps also during a time

---

[273] In her detailed treatment she rejects this, but in her summary she writes: "I concluded that 'fornication', here primarily refers to sexual relations during a wife's pregnancy; underlying the prohibition is a rejection of non-procreative sexual intercourse combined with a belief that intercourse during pregnancy may be harmful for the foetus" (Wassen, *Women*, 203).

[274] See, however, Baumgarten, *DJD* 18, 165, who assumes it plays a role. In discussing 4QD[e]/4Q270 2 ii 15-16 Wassen, *Women*, acknowledges that it is not the primary reason for prohibiting intercourse during pregnancy, but then sees it playing a role here, explaining her contradiction by insisting that both may have been used as grounds (183). See also Gregory E. Sterling, "Was there a Common Ethic in Second Temple Judaism?" in *Sapiential Perspectives: Wisdom Literature in Light of the Dead Sea Scrolls: Proceedings of the Sixth International Symposium of the Orion Center for the Study of the Dead Sea Scrolls and Associated Literature, 20-22 May, 2001* (ed. John J. Collins, Gregory E. Sterling, and Ruth A. Clements; STDJ 51; Leiden: Brill, 2004) 171-94, who draws attention to the similar prohibition in *Ps. Phoc.* 189 and reads both as reflecting opposition to sexual intercourse other than for procreation (193)

[275] Baumgarten, *DJD* 18, 165. See also Kampen, "Matthean Divorce Texts Reexamined," who notes its occurrence in 7.1-2 (157 n. 31).

[276] See also Wassen, *Women*, 181-82. See also the discussion on pp. 207-208, about the possibility that 4Q249e may also have dealt with illegal sexual intercourse within marriage.

[277] Baumgarten, *DJD* 18, suggests "unnatural intercourse" (164-65), but without further explanation. Similarly Wacholder, *New Damascus Document*, who also considers that it might refer to failure to fulfil conjugal obligations as outlined in Exod 21:9-10 (364), but the passage seems to deal not with withholding sexual intercourse but conducting it in a forbidden way.

or in a place concerning which a regulation had required abstinence, such as during residence in Jerusalem or at the Qumran settlement,[278] or on the sabbath.[279]

The mark of its seriousness is permanent exclusion. The community took issues of sexual wrongdoing very seriously. It is noteworthy that the man is held responsible, not the woman. This is the converse of denying women a say, such as in the consultation with the Overseer about divorce.[280] It suggests a deliberate flouting of the authority of the community. The expelling of a husband would probably be understood as constituting a divorce, which means that some women divorcees would not be seen as adulteresses and so, like divorced men, would be able to remarry.

Permanent exclusion is also the penalty for despising the judgements of the Many or complaining against the Fathers of the community. The latter is addressed in what immediately follows, where we read of complaining against the Fathers and the Mothers, both honorific titles.[281] The comparative leniency with regard to complaints against the Mothers in 4QD[e]/4Q270 7 i.14, compared with the Fathers, is grounded in the observation that there is no רוקמה for the Mothers in the midst of the congregation.[282] The word רוקמה normally refers to embroidering, but probably refers here to an embroidered garment or cloth which symbolises

---

[278] So Shemaryahu Talmon, "The Community of the Renewed Covenant: Between Judaism and Christianity," in *The Community of the Renewed Covenant: The Notre Dame Symposium on the Dead Sea Scrolls* (ed. Eugene Ulrich and James VanderKam; Christianity and Judaism in Antiquity Series 10; Notre Dame: University of Notre Dame Press, 1994) 3-24, 9.

[279] Cf. also David Rothstein, "Women's Testimony at Qumran: The Biblical and Second Temple Evidence," *RevQ* 21 (2004) 597-614, who raise two further possibilities, that the statement speaks about fornication *against* one's wife (reading ל as against, in a similar sense to Mark 10:11), namely adultery, or that it refers to illegally returning to one's wife after adultery in contravention of Deut 24:1-4 (612-13 n. 68). Against the former possibility, it would make the אשר לא כמשפט "which is not according to statute" somewhat redundant. The latter alternative is difficult to imagine in a closed community, but not impossible.

[280] See Wassen, *Women*, 203.

[281] So Wassen, *Women*, 185-88, who notes the honorific phrase, אבות העדה "fathers of the congregation" in 4QMyst[a]/4Q299 76 3 and the honorific use of זקנות "Elders", similarly, in 4Q502 (186). On the latter see Sidnie White Crawford, "Mothers, Sisters, and Elders: Titles for Women in Second Temple Jewish and Early Christian Communities," in *The Dead Sea Scrolls as Background to Postbiblical Judaism and Early Christianity: Papers from an International Conference at St. Andrews in 2001* (ed. James R. Davila; STDJ 46; Leiden: Brill, 2003) 177-91, 180-83.

[282] On the significance of Mothers in the community see Baumgarten, *DJD* 18, 8, who draws attention to "Sisters" in 4QpapMarRit/4Q502.

authority.[283] This probably means that they do not have the same authority and status within the community, and that therefore complaints against them are correspondingly less problematic and more peripheral. It does, nevertheless, allow us to see that there were women with a designated role in some kind of leadership, however limited in status. The position of women in the community is, however, far from clear.[284]

The final portion of the document (4QD^{a}/4Q266 11 1-20; 4QD^{d}/4Q269 16; 4QD^{e}/4Q270 7 i.15-21; ii.11-15) contains a rite of expulsion, which would apply also to those having committed serious delicts, including illicit sexual intercourse with one's wife, mentioned above. It also contains the provision for the annual meeting of the camps. Nothing in this concluding section relates directly to matters of sexuality.

Review of Laws and Community Regulations

The following table sets out all the potential references to issues pertaining to sexuality in the section on Laws and Community Regulations and form the basis for the summary discussion below.

---

[283] Cf. White Crawford, "Not According to Rule", who sees in the enigmatic word, רוקמה, an allusion to authority, following J. F. Ewolde, "rwqmh in the Damascus Document and Ps 139:15," in *Diggers at the Well: Proceedings of a Third International Symposium on the Hebrew of the Dead Sea Scrolls and Ben Sira* (ed. T. Muraoka and J. F. Ewolde; Leiden: Brill, 2000) 65-83, 72. See also White Crawford, "Mothers, Sisters, and Elders," 179-80. Wassen, *Women*, argues against Ewolde that such a meaning is not evident in the widespread use of the word among the scrolls. Like George J. Brooke, "From Qumran to Corinth: Embroidered Allusions to Women's Authority," in *The Dead Sea Scrolls and the New Testament* (Minneapolis: Fortress, 2005) 195-213, 199-207; earlier, in *The Dead Sea Scrolls as Background to Postbiblical Judaism and Early Christianity: Papers from an International Conference at St. Andrews in 2001* (ed. James R. Davila; STDJ 46; Leiden: Brill, 2003) 157-76, but independently, she proposes that the reference is to an embroidered garment that signals a special status and may have links with mystical tradition, such as we find in the *Testament of Job* (185-97).

[284] On this see, Schuller, "Women in the Dead Sea Scrolls," 129-30, who notes that Stegemann, *Essener*, 262, questions whether they could become full members. This is not unrelated to the question of whether the document presupposes two groups, one, celibate (for a time), the other, not, and whether women could belong to the former (130-31).

Matters Pertaining to Sexuality in the Laws and Community Regulations of D		
Man with a flux (heading)	4QD^{a}/4Q266 6 i.14; 4QD^{g}/4Q272 1 ii.3	Lev 15:2
Man with a flux or seminal emission in sleep?	4QD^{a}/4Q266 6 i.14; 4QD^{g}/4Q272 1 ii.3-4	Lev 15:2-3 Lev 15:16?
Seminal emission – "lustful thought" – masturbation?	4QD^{a}/4Q266 6 i.15 4QD^{g}/4Q272 1 ii.4	
"or who" – seminal emission during intercourse??	4QD^{a}/4Q266 6 i.15-16 4QD^{g}/4Q272 1 ii.4-5	Lev 15:18
Touch and ablution	4QD^{a}/4Q266 6 i.16 4QD^{g}/4Q272 1 ii.5-6	Lev 15:4-15, 16b, 18b
Woman with a flux (heading)	4QD^{g}/4Q272 1 ii.7	Lev 15:19a
Menstruant – 7 day impurity	4QD^{g}/4Q272 1 ii.7b-9	Lev 15:19a
Touching a menstruant –impurity	4QD^{g}/4Q272 1 ii.10	Lev 15:19b-23
Sexual relations with menstruant contracts her impurity and is sin	4QD^{a}/4Q266 6 ii.1-2	Lev 15:24 Lev 18:19; 20:18
Woman with blood outside menstrual period: 7 day impurity;	4QD^{a}/4Q266 6 ii.2-3a	Lev 15:25-30
not eat holy food or enter temple	4QD^{a}/4Q266 6 ii.3b-4	Lev 12:4
Woman after childbirth – 7 day impurity for male	4QD^{a}/4Q266 6 ii.5-6	Lev 12:2
not eat [holy food] – capital offence	4QD^{a}/4Q266 6 ii.9-10	Lev 12:4
wet nurse: to avoid impurity?	4QD^{a}/4Q266 6 ii.11	
provisions for offering	4QD^{a}/4Q266 6 ii.12-13	Lev 12:6, 8
Accusations of adultery	4QD^{e}/4Q270 4 1-8	Num 5:13-31
Role of witness	4QD^{e}/4Q270 4 2-3	
Woman's response: rape	4QD^{e}/4Q270 4 3	
Blood: absent, so pregnant? Present, so rape?	4QD^{e}/4Q270 4 4-5	
? No intercourse during investigation?	? 4QD^{h}/4Q273 5	
The rite of testing	4QD^{e}/4Q270 4 5-8	Num 5:16-28
Sex with slaves Sex with another's slave	4QD^{e}/4Q270 4 13-14	 Lev 19:20-22
Sex with one's own slave?	4QD^{e}/4Q270 4 15-17	Lev 21:1-11
Sex with a captive woman?	4QD^{e}/4Q270 4 19	Deut 21:10-14
Cross-Dressing?	4QD^{f}/4Q271 3 3-4	Deut 22:5
Brides Giving away a daughter, not hiding blemishes (or cursed)	4QD^{f}/4Q271 3 8	 (Deut 27:18)
Giving away a daughter, not to unfit man: Gentile, outside kin?	4QD^{f}/4Q271 3 9-10	

Mixing kinds		Deut 22:10-11
Forbidden women as brides Adulteresses/divorcees? Unchaste daughters abroad?	4QD[f]/4Q271 3 11a	 Deut 24:1? Lev 21:7
Unchaste daughters at home	4QD[f]/4Q271 3 11b-12a	Lev 21:7
Unchaste widows	4QD[f]/4Q271 3 12b	Lev 21:7
Daughters of ill repute; women's inspection; then marriage; husband does not tell	4QD[f]/4Q271 3 12b-16	Deut 22:13-21
? Forbidding marriage during menstruation?	? 4QD[h]/4Q273 5	
No sex on the sabbath	CD 11.5; 4QD[f]/4Q271 5 i.1-2	
No sex in Jerusalem	CD 12.1-2	
Defiling the sabbath?	CD 12.4	
Marriage, Divorce, Children Oversight of marriage	CD 13.16a-17a; 4QD[a]/4Q266 9 iii.4-5a	
Oversight of divorce	CD 13.17b; 4QD[a]/4Q266 9 iii.5b	
Oversight of the children	CD 13.17b-19; 4QD[a]/4Q266 9 iii.6-9	
Former prisoners of Gentiles as needy (and disqualified as priests)	CD 14.15; 4QD[a]/4Q266 10 i.8. (4QD[a]/4Q266 5 ii.5)	
Virgin without kin	CD 14.15-16; 4QD[a]/4Q266 10 i.9	
Young man needing support	CD 14.16; 4QD[a]/4Q266 10 i.9	
Nakedness Nakedness before humans in the house	4QD[a]/4Q266 10 ii.9; 4QD[e]/4Q270 7 i.1-3	
Nakedness (before animals) in the field	4QD[a]/4Q266 10 ii.9-10; 4QD[e]/4Q270 7 i.1-2	
Exposing penis through clothes or their raggedness	4QD[a]/4Q266 10 ii.10-12; 4QD[e]/4Q270 7 i.3 (1QS 7.15b-16a)	
Gesticulating with left hand	4QD[a]/4Q266 10 ii.13-14; 4QD[e]/4Q270 7 i.5	
Illicit sex with wife (On the sabbath? In the holy city? During pregnancy?)	4QD[e]/4Q270 7 i.12-13; 4QD[b]/4Q267 9 vi.4-5	

The sections of D dealing with Laws appear to draw upon a tradition of interpretation, perhaps sources, which derive from a context where the exposition assumes the application of the laws to all Israel, rather than to a sectarian community. They are mostly derived from texts in Leviticus, Numbers and Deuteronomy. They regularly occur in sets of three instances, a pattern we noted also in the Admonition and the Catalogue of Transgressions. The exposition of the laws of flux follows Leviticus 15. In speaking of men, under the heading of "the man with a flux", it deals with seminal emission, probably covering the three main occasions of seminal emission: during sleep, as a result of masturbation and during intercourse. While there is awareness of moral sin in relation to lustful thoughts, the focus is impurity and the concern appears to be to provide a systematic exposition which compensates for absences or ambiguities in the Leviticus text by applying to all three instances the laws which apply to the *zab*. The result is both greater consistency and greater strictness.

The three instances gathered under the probable heading of "the woman with a flux" deal with the menstruant, the woman with an abnormal discharge of blood, and the woman after childbirth. Here, too, a similar tendency is apparent. It may include a case of applying the rules about touching a menstruant to touching a *zabah*, and about having sexual intercourse with a menstruant to doing so with a *zabah*, thus closing a gap in Leviticus. It homogenises the provisions relating to the *zabah* and the woman after childbirth by applying the prohibitions relating to the latter about food and entering the temple to the *zabah*. The outcome here is consistency rather than enhanced rigour, although the final instance adds the threat of the death penalty. While some have read the text as requiring that a woman in impurity forego breastfeeding and instead use a wet-nurse, this is far from secure in the text and would create insuperable difficulties for any kind of breastfeeding at all.

The exposition of the laws pertaining to accusation of adultery found in Num 5:13-31 in 4QD^{e}/4Q270 4.1-8 displays considerable development. It provides for calling on a witness (probably to the alleged liaison), for the woman to respond, for limiting the case to where pregnancy is confirmed (unless absence of blood relates to the claim of rape), besides apparently summarising the rite of Num 5:18. The effect is to render the law more workable and remove some of its potential abuses, although it still remains one-sided (only concerned with women) and oppressive.

The issues addressed in 4QD^{e}/4Q270 4 12-20 are scarcely decipherable, but may relate to sexual intercourse with slaves assigned to others (Lev 19:20-22), with one's own slave (Lev 21:1-11) and with captive women (Deut 21:10-14), but too little is preserved to be certain, let alone, to detect any tendencies. The fact that it is there probably indicates that sexual relations with one's female slaves and probably with captive women is allowed within a defined framework.

By contrast, the section dealing with brides is well attested and reasonably clear. It may be preceded by a prohibition of cross-dressing based on Deut 22:5. It comes to the discussion of brides after speaking of fair trade. While daughters were not sold, the transaction of marriage had significant financial implications and honesty was important about blemishes. Much of the discussion of brides and marriage partners is not an exposition of existing biblical legislation, but reflects application to the theme of some biblical material, beginning with a curse about lack of transparency about one's daughter. The section addresses inappropriate marriage partners from both sides, beginning with men not fit to be husbands. The text leaves us speculating what "unfit" means, but by its metaphorical use of the prohibition of mixing kinds in Deut 22:10-11, its probably refers not to individual traits in a man, but to men of a certain kind, such as Gentiles (as in *4QMMT*), perhaps also those outside one's kin. By contrast, unsuitable brides are clearly defined as those who have engaged in illicit sexual relations. They include women who have left their father's house for marriage and there engaged in illicit sexual relations, presumably adultery, and so are to be seen on the basis of strict reading of Deut 24:1 as women divorced for adultery; unmarried women who are not virgins; and widows who have not remained chaste. The biblical basis for these provisions appears to be a generalised application of what pertained only to priests in Lev 21:7, an expansionary move evident also in *Jubilees* and *Aramaic Levi Document*.

When the section considers the issue of ascertaining the virginity of a bride under suspicion, it effectively replaces the biblical provision set out in Deut 22:13-21. The changes have the inspection take place before the wedding and to be carried out by qualified midwives, thus preventing the husband being led unwittingly into adultery had she had intercourse with another, and removing the onus from the husband by giving the responsibility to the community and its Overseer. The latter detail allows us to see the way the provision worked in one of D's communities. Possibly the law may have once been applied outside the sectarian context. The provision in CD 13 for oversight of marriage, divorce and education of the children of divorcees also reflects D's communal setting, as do the instructions concerning caring for former prisoners of Gentiles, girls without a dowry and young men without backing; nakedness; and what appears to be a prohibition of sexual intercourse during pregnancy which assumes that a wife reports her husband to the community.

On the other hand, the prohibition of sexual intercourse in Jerusalem and probably on the sabbath, are likely to derive from earlier material, but of a kind which, like the restrictions on marriage partners, reflects an extension of the claims of observance of biblical laws, in relation to both space and time, just as it also extended to all Israel restrictions on who priests might marry.

The material from the sections dealing with the law thus indicate that the author of D and presumably his community stand in a tradition. That tradition included elaboration of biblical laws to enhance consistency, often resulting in greater strictness, but sometimes also to deal with practicalities, which resulted in revisions that put greater limits on potential abuses and to a limited degree improved the rights of the vulnerable, especially women. Beside these are laws which reflect an extension of the understanding of holy space and time to include the city and the sabbath and an extension of the requirements of priests to all people. We also find laws pertaining to sexuality which clearly have in mind the organisational structure of D's communities.

The Laws and the Catalogue of Transgressions

The partially preserved Catalogue of Transgressions condemns women with bad reputations in their father's house (almost certainly about sexual wrongdoing), women who are unfaithful to their betrothed (or, possibly, widows unchaste during their widowhood), men engaging in sex on the day of (? the sabbath; probably), the man engaging in sex with a pregnant women, a man marrying his niece, and homosexual acts. None of these is unambiguously attested in the law material. The laws in 4QD^{e}/4Q270 3 prohibit marriage to a woman reputed to be unchaste, but allow for testing which might exonerate her. They offer a parallel to the second instance, if it concerns widows, but not if its concern is with betrothed women, except that this might fit closely with the category of unchaste women. Illicit sexual relations with one's wife are mentioned also in the Laws: in Jerusalem, (probably) on the sabbath (probably), during pregnancy (less likely to be meant here because this receives separate mention earlier in the catalogue), during menstruation, and with a *zabah*. We do not know what "day" refers to in the catalogue. Sexual intercourse during pregnancy may find a parallel in 4QD^{e}/4Q270 7 i.12-13; 4QD^{b}/4Q267 9 vi.4-5. Prohibition of marrying nieces could be envisaged conversely in the warning not to give one's daughter to an unfit man, namely, an uncle, although this is less likely than that the latter refers to particular kinds of people with whom one should not mix. Prohibition of marrying nieces features in the Admonition, possibly three times. Nothing in the Laws addresses homosexuality, although the potentially related issue of cross-dressing is mentioned. The extant material in the catalogue does not, therefore, read like a summary of the Laws. It probably belongs to a tradition which the author has incorporated.

3 Conclusion

Considering the document as a whole, at least, all of what has survived, we have, on the one hand, traditions of law which expound biblical legislation, synthesising it, but also supplementing it to the point at times of replacing its provisions, and adapting it to communal needs. On the other hand, we have engaged exhortation which allows us to see particular emphases. While the extent of matters dealing with issues of sexuality in the Laws and communal legislation indicates that issues of sexuality played a significant part in the application of law and regulation, the emphases in the Admonition allow us to see that matters of sexuality were among the author's foremost concerns, especially in conflict with the rival teachers and their followers. In this context we can then see that some issues in particular received special attention. These are polygyny, sexual intercourse with menstruants, and marrying nieces. The surviving material about the laws contains no reference to the first. It may have been among the lost material. By contrast, the second issue is attested in the Laws, and the third issue, is attested not in the Laws, but in the Catalogue of Transgressions and probably in the warnings and exposition of the sins of "the princes of Judah".

Some of the laws appear to focus on issues of ritual impurity rather than issues of morality. Ritual impurity is at the forefront in discussions about the *zab*, especially seminal emission, and the *zabah*, the menstruant, and the woman after childbirth, but also sexual intercourse in the city and, it seems, on the sabbath. Ignoring any of these issues becomes itself a moral issue and some, like having sexual intercourse with a menstruant, are treated as both. In these contexts there is thus also explicit mention of moral concerns: lustful thoughts (though not elaborated) and sexual intercourse with a menstruant (or *zabah*) identified as sin. Matters relating to choosing appropriate spouses have a stronger moral focus. This applies also to the author's exposition of *zenuth* in relation to polygyny, sexual intercourse during menstruation, and marrying nieces, and with regard to charges of adultery, infidelity to one's betrothed, cross-dressing, homosexual acts, nakedness, and sexual intercourse during pregnancy.

Nothing suggests a negative attitude towards sexual relations in the proper context. There is some indirect evidence that not all members of the community married. It seems that among the men of perfect holiness some did and some did not, but nothing suggests that those who did were less worthy morally. The differentiation between those who engaged in sexual intercourse and those who were celibate appears to have been related to notions of appropriate space and time, reflected in the required abstinence in Jerusalem and on the sabbath. Presumably this formed the background for some choosing to be in a space and time where abstinence was appropriate and permanent.

Frequently the requirement of abstinence from sexual intercourse with a pregnant woman has been understood as reflecting what Josephus attributes to the Essenes, namely that they engaged in sexual intercourse only for procreation (*B.J.* 2.160-61).[285] Wassen assembles evidence of disapproval of sexual intercourse for

[285] Himmelfarb, "Purity Laws of 4QD," 162-64; similarly Schuller, "Women in the Dead Sea Scrolls," 127; Baumgarten, *DJD* 18, 165; Davies, "Judaism(s) of the Damascus Document," 34; M. Kister, "Notes on Some Texts from Qumran," *JJS* 44 (1993) 280-82; Harrington, *Purity Texts*, 47, 104; Wassen, *Women*, though she acknowledges that it is not the primary reason for prohibiting intercourse during pregnancy in 4Q270 2 ii 15-16 (183).

purposes other than procreation, noting that it appears to derive from "general influence of Hellenistic philosophy that often advocates moderation and self-control", citing Josephus, Philo, Pseudo-Phocylides, the *Testaments of the Twelve Patriarchs* and speaking generally of the "Pseudepigrapha".[286] More directly relevant are references in the early Enoch literature and the *Aramaic Levi Document*, documents found in the library at Qumran, but for D the case that it disapproves of sexual intercourse except for procreation is at most circumstantial and even then rather weak. The document reflects, for instance, great respect for *Jubilees*, which strongly affirms sexual relations as an expression of marital intimacy and not just for procreation. Where D addresses the prohibition of sexual intercourse during pregnancy, its reasons appear to be pragmatic concern for the foetus, not avoidance of pleasure or abstinence from intercourse except for procreation. The prohibition of engaging in the pleasures of sexual intercourse on the sabbath derives not from the pleasure but concern with the emission. Certainly sexual lusting receives prominence early in the document through the history of failures which it produced, but there the complaint was not against sexual desire, itself, but rather, inappropriate actions based on sexual desire. That is very different from a stance which sees sexual pleasure within licit relationships as in itself something evil.[287]

While sexual relations appear to have been seen as a normal part of life, in which some engaged and some did not, it is difficult to reconstruct the nature of the communities which the author has in mind. Much of the law tradition had been elaborated to apply to all people, but there are layers which relate to special communities and there are rules which apply specifically to them.[288]

Wassen, for instance, notes that "a large portion of the laws concern women".[289] She notes the androcentric perspective and the likely priestly origins of the halakhah, reflected in its concerns with purity and the temple, with laws of *sotah*, its prohibition of sexual intercourse in the city, its concern, as she sees it, with genealogy; and the extension of priestly laws to all in relation to marrying a *zonah*.[290] She also notes that some laws represent an improvement for women:

---

286 Wassen, *Women*, 179. See her discussion, 174-81. She also reads 1 Thess 4:4-5 as a reference to πορνεία (the equivalent of זנות) in marriage by translating σκεῦος as "wife", rather than as a reference to penis (a translation far from secure) (177).

287 Cf. Wassen. *Women*, who claims that D "reflects an underlying concern for the restriction of passions and desires" and points to the discourse in the Admonition on sexual wrongdoing (183). Even then she acknowledges that "D does not mirror the strong emphasis on controlling desires and emotions found in Philo, the Testament of the Twelve Patriarchs, or the ethical teaching of many Hellenistic writers" (183).

288 On the sociology of D, see Wassen, *Women*, 198-200.

289 Wassen, *Women*, 102.

290 Wassen, *Women*, 103.

women's oaths, limitations on *sotah*, and pre-marital inspection,[291] though she notes the irony that women are empowered to inspect, but only to serve control of women.[292] More controversial are her claims that at the level of the communities both young men and women were enrolled and had some access to the communal meetings, where according to 1QSa/1Q28a 1 11 they were expected to testify.[293]

Maxinbe Grossmann raises a number of significant issues which arise when one reads D with an eye to the constructions of gender, "the distinctions between practices and traits that are understood as 'masculine' and those that fall into category of 'feminine'".[294] She asks "how the text's presentation of gender reflects the makeup of a Damascus covenant community in its actual existence".[295] She also emphasises that the text needs to be seen as something that was read in communities, including over a period of time in which communities may have changed and within which competing readings may have been present, and so cautions against the assumption that textual differences need imply sectarian splits.[296] The matter is rendered even more complex by the possibility that a text itself has undergone revisions and expansions, a point which she illustrates by what she sees as additions in CD 19, which reflect some changing concerns. These might have been the need to defend a new idea over against an older order of celibacy or to defend an existing order against the celibacy order as something new – to name some possibilities.[297]

Her analysis identifies the androcentric perspective of the text, while noting some ambiguity because of the possible use of masculine forms to include reference to women. "Ambiguities of language thus construct a normatively-male covenanter, while leaving open the possibility of a female presence and female participation as a subset of that masculine norm".[298] She notes that legal references to women are constrained primarily to matters concerned with "marriage and divorce; the ordeal of the *sotah* and the reputation of the new bride; menstruation, birth, and post-partum purity; and proper sexual practices within marriage", the only exceptions being references to maidservants and to "mothers".[299] Women do not feature in the accounts of history nor as agents, except in examining for virginity, but then to report to men.

---

[291] Wassen, *Women*, 105-106.

[292] Wassen, *Women*, 105.

[293] Wassen, *Women*, 201.

[294] Grossman, "Reading for Gender," 214.

[295] Grossman, "Reading for Gender," 214.

[296] Grossman, "Reading for Gender," 215-16.

[297] Grossman, "Reading for Gender," 235.

[298] Grossman, "Reading for Gender," 218.

[299] Grossman, "Reading for Gender," 218-19.

She then demonstrates two possible readings of the text, depending on three different starting points which might have been shared by hearers. The first is an inclusive understanding of covenant, such as is reflected in Deut 29:9-10, which includes male Israelites, "wives" or "women" and male and female children. Accordingly, "the Damascus Document demonstrates an internalizing of deuteronomic identity" in its use of language and the retelling of its community story.[300] It assumes the presence of women (including their right to make oaths, though controlled by men), while men remain the principal actors. An inclusive reading of masculine forms can lead to the impression "that women may have participated as independent actors in the community, and not only in connection with their male protectors".[301] This receives support also from the fact that women have some leadership roles within the organisation of the community with some limited authority, such as in the case of the "mothers" and the women who examine for virginity. She then offers a reading based on what she sees are the more egalitarian values which she identifies in 4QpapRitMar/4Q502, to show that D "can be leveraged in that direction with surprising ease".[302]

Her counter example is a reading from the stance of *4QWiles of the Wicked Woman*/4Q184, noting that it, too, speaks of traps and of those who speak smooth words. The conceptual links based on shared vocabulary make possible a reading in which "men are part of the covenant, and they are righteous; women are separate from the covenant and a distinct threat to it".[303] Accordingly they would not be full members of the covenant and their everyday actions would need to "be closely controlled by patriarchal structures enforcing their piety, purity, and domesticity".[304] She notes that while "the inclusivity of a Damascus Document reading in the light of 4Q502 contrasts sharply with the misogyny of a reading that accepts the gender discourse articulated in the Wiles text ... all three texts were (most likely) present in the same social setting".[305]

While acknowledging the range of possible readings and the likelihood that multiple readings existed at any one time and over time, we are not thereby left without recourse to some controls. One could point out that some readings based on the Wiles text are a better fit than others. Our discussion of *4QWiles of the Wicked Woman*/4Q184 below argues, however, that it is a misreading to see the woman as somehow representative of all women. While D is ambiguous in relation to the possible inclusiveness in relation to its use of masculine forms, it clearly does see some women as trustworthy. On the other hand, while it clearly

---

[300] Grossman, "Reading for Gender," 225 and see 222-24.

[301] Grossman, "Reading for Gender," 227, and see 228.

[302] Grossman, "Reading for Gender," 230.

[303] Grossman, "Reading for Gender," 232, and see 230-33.

[304] Grossman, "Reading for Gender," 233.

[305] Grossman, "Reading for Gender," 238.

assumes a leadership role for "mothers", it strongly differentiates them from "fathers", in a manner which does not cohere well with an egalitarian stance. The paucity of references to women except for situations where they are potentially problematic for (and with) men reflects the dominant patriarchal society of the time against which the writings, especially of the sect, prove no exception.

In D attitudes towards sexuality play a significant role, both in the extent that its laws touch on pertinent issues and as a major focus of the author's concerns. In the Admonition it is striking that the author identifies sexual wrongdoing as a central aspect of the conflict and even portrays Israel's history from the perspective of failure because of the pursuit of the pleasures of sexual wrongdoing. The author's Admonition appears to have been influenced by *Jubilees*, which reflects a similar concern with sexual wrongdoing, but unlike *Jubilees* its focus is not marriage to Gentiles, but practices within Israel, itself. Concern with sexual relations with Gentiles may, however, be implied in the warning against mixing of kinds and Wassen, as we have seen, has suggested it makes best sense of the warning about sexual intercourse during menstruation,[306] though one could read the concern as being not with intermarriage, which it would assume, but practices within such marriages. The issue may in part underlie the history of failure in the early part of the Admonition, where it may reflect emphases of older tradition. Elsewhere in the document in contexts not pertaining to sexuality there is evidence that the author is concerned about Gentiles, so it is likely that it still plays a role in relation to sexuality even if not to the extent that the author names it directly as such. On the other hand, the apparent discussion about slaves and, possibly, captive women, assumes the likelihood of sexual relations with Gentile women and in the case of captive women, even of marriage, although the evidence is uncertain.

The three nets are rightly seen as indicative of the main issues: sexual wrongdoing, riches and defiling the temple. Thus the concerns are both moral and ritual purity, but like *Jubilees*, the author sees both as defiling the temple. Sexual wrongdoing, however, is the dominant concern, in particular, polygyny, sexual intercourse with menstruants and marrying nieces. Given the wide range of issues of sexual wrongdoing addressed in the document, it is noteworthy that the author should single these out and allege that they feature not just in the teaching of his opponents, but also in their practice. The association of such practice with alleged abuse of wealth and defilement of the temple makes it likely that those under attack belong to wealthy and influential families associated with the temple, probably including priestly families. Their designation, using the image of "princes of Judah", while not to be taken literally, nevertheless fits their identification as people of wealth and influence. It is possible that other aspects

[306] Wassen, *Women*, 120.

relating to sexuality were in dispute, but nothing in D's exposition of the laws indicates that this was so. Where the Admonition elaborates further, such as in the warnings of CD 6.14 – 7.4 and the allegations of CD 8.3-8, the references are to sexual wrongdoing as a general category and then, when specific, allude to incest, probably marriage to nieces. In other words, it seems that the areas of conflict focussed primarily on the three instances which expound the nets of Belial.

Aside from the author's own particular concerns, we can recognise a range of other important emphases reflected within the document in relation to sexuality. There is a major emphasis on restricting sexual intercourse to marriage (understood as monogynous). This appears however to embrace the notion that one may have sexual relations with slave women and captive women, perhaps as concubines, although the latter may well have been excluded as an option, and the possible allusion to captive women is to a context in Deuteronomy which speaks of marriage. D's condemnation covers all the options: unchaste virgins, unchaste widows, extra-marital sex and in relation to the latter probably assumes an interpretation of divorce law which restricted divorce to cases of sexual wrongdoing, normally adultery. While opposing marriage to adulteresses, it does not appear to espouse opposition to remarriage after divorce, just as it does not oppose remarriage of widows and widowers. The restricted interpretation of divorce law will have been part of a stance which limited abuse and so indirectly benefited women. Such amelioration is to be seen both in the procedure, however unscientifically based, for inspecting suspect virgins before marriage and letting the community rather than the husband decide, and in revising the procedure for testing allegations of adultery to include the role of witnesses, a possibility of response from the woman, and (probably) a limitation to when a woman has become pregnant. While remaining within a patriarchal framework and retaining many of the harsh processes, D also appears to espouse a stance of care and compassion, notably in relation to the children of divorcees, to caring for various members of the community, and in the concern for the foetus in relation to sexual intercourse during pregnancy. D does not denigrate sexual relations nor restrict sex to procreation. While in this sense it coheres with the positive stance towards sexuality in *Jubilees* as a normal part of life, it does not, however, go beyond treating it as normal to highlight its special value, as does *Jubilees*.

CHAPTER FOUR

Attitudes towards Sexuality in the Legal Texts

In the previous chapters I have discussed discrete documents, the *Temple Scroll*, *4QMMT*, and the *Damascus Document* (D). Partly that was because they most likely stem from the early period of the sect's history; partly, because they have a substantial amount of material pertinent to the theme. This is particularly the case with D. In the four chapters which follow I treat four groups of documents: *Legal Texts*, *Liturgical and Related Material*, *Biblical Exposition and Related Material*, and *Wisdom Texts*. Such classification is inevitably inadequate, since documents can include elements of all four aspects. It functions here only as a convenient way of grouping the material. Each document is considered in its own right,[1] and each has its own conclusion. I will not present a conclusion at the end of each of these chapters, but wait until the material of all four chapters has been discussed and then integrate the findings within a final chapter as a concluding assessment.

Inevitably we also face with these documents the problems of dating and of assessing the extent to which they are authored by the sectarian group or just preserved by them, as is, for instance, the case with biblical texts. Within the groups I have not attempted to divide the material further on the basis of such demarcation,[2] though I note relevant discussion where appropriate.

[1] Unless otherwise indicated the Hebrew text and translation follows *DSSEL*. An asterisk indicates my own translation.

[2] On the issue of demarcation between sectarian and non-sectarian writings see, for instance, the recent discussion in Devorah Dimant, "Old Testament Pseudepigrapha at Qumran," in *The Bible and the Dead Sea Scrolls: The Princeton Symposium on the Dead Sea Scrolls: Volume Two: The Dead Sea Scrolls and the Qumran Community* (ed. James H.

1 The *Community Rule* 1QS/1Q28; 4QS[a-j]/4Q255-264; 5Q11

The beginning of the *Community Rule* sets out the goal of the community under the Instructor as "to seek God with [all their heart and with al]l their soul" and "to do what is good and upright before him" (1.2) in accordance with Moses and the prophets (1.3). That includes loving everything which God elects and despising everything that God rejects, and keeping oneself at a distance from all evil, and becoming attached to all good works in order to do truth and justice and uprightness on earth (1.3-6; similarly 1.9b-11). Hating what God rejects and keeping distance from evil then comes to expression as:

ולוא ללכת עוד בשרירות לב אשמה ועיני זנות 7 לעשות כול רע

and no longer to walk in the stubbornness of a guilty heart and eyes of sexual wrongdoing to do all evil.* (1.6b-7a)

The statement recalls the words of D:

ולא לתור במחשבות יצר אשמה וע(י)ני זנות

and not to follow after the thoughts of a guilty inclination and eyes of sexual wrongdoing.* (2.16)

There, these words, especially עיני זנות ("eyes of sexual wrongdoing") become the basis for an account of Israel's history as a litany of failure because of sexual wrongdoing (2.16 – 3.12). Here, in the *Community Rule*, nothing suggests a particular focus on sexual wrongdoing. In what follows we read of concern with straying on matters of calendar (1.9a; similarly 1.14-15). The author seems satisfied to identify sexual wrongdoing as what belonged to a past life[3] and not to be concerned with it as an ongoing issue, let alone an issue of contention as we

Charlesworth; Waco: Baylor University Press, 2006) 447-67, who observes that "Qumran apocryphal and pseudepigraphic writings are marked by the absence of the distinctive sectarian terminology and organizational patterns" (460). Many, especially those "most heavily tinged with apocalyptic speculation", were composed in Aramaic, not Hebrew, the language of the sectaries (466). Among non-sectarian works in Hebrew are the various texts which rewrite the Pentateuch, prophets and the psalms, particularly those writings which deal with Sinai and post-Sinai traditions, reflecting the belief that Hebrew was publicly revealed to Israel (464-65).

[3] In 4QBarkhi Nafshi[b]/4Q435 2 i.2 = 4QBarkhi Nafshi[c]/4Q436 1 ii.1 we find the expression זנות עינים "sexual wrongdoing of the eyes", used similarly as referring to sexual wrongdoing as among the evils which which God has removed from the speaker. The association of eyes and sexual wrongdoing occurs also on a fragment of 4QBer[b]/4Q287 8 13, א]שמה ועיני זנות, but without a surviving context.

find in D. Similarly, while the reference in 1.18 to the time of the dominion of Belial recalls CD 4.13, 15, unlike in D, it does not become the basis for development of concern with sexual wrongdoing.

The expression which precedes the reference to eyes of sexual wrongdoing, namely שרירות לב "stubbornness of heart", is often used in D in relation to sexual wrongdoing (2.17; 3.5, 11; cf. also 8.8). In 1QS 2.26 and 3.3, however, where it appears in the context of condemning the person who refuses to enter the covenant, it is without a sexual association. This is also the case in 7.19, 24; 9.10; and in 4QS[d]/4Q258 1 i.4, to which we shall return below in discussing 1QS/1Q28 5.4-5. The term, שרירות לב "stubbornness of heart" appears without a sexual context also in 1QH[a] xii.15; 4QApocrJer[e]/4Q390 1 12; *4QCommunal Confession*/4Q393 3 3; and 4QpapSap B?/4Q487 1 ii.3, where in 2 7 we also find: לב אשמה "guilty heart". The expression, שרירות לב "stubbornness of heart" apparently derives from its use in Jeremiah (3:17; 9:13; 16:12; 18:12).

In the description of the liturgy which begins in 1.18b we find the Levites reciting "the iniquities of the children of Israel", but, similarly, nothing suggests that alludes to the kind of historical account of Israel's sins as caused by lustful eyes which we find in CD 2.16 – 3.12. The same apparent lack of interest in sexual wrongdoing is evident in the confession in 1.24 – 2.1a, and in the curses enunciated by the Levites against the lot of Belial in 2.4-9 and by both the priests and Levites in 2.11-17.

The Treatise on the Two Spirits

The next block of material of potential relevance is what is commonly identified as the *Treatise on the Two Spirits* in 3.13 – 4.26. It is absent from the earlier versions of the *Community Rule* in 4QS[d]/4Q258 and 4QS[e]/4Q259, though traces of it are found in 4QS[a]/4Q255 and 4QS[c]/4Q257. It appears to have been a later addition in the development of the document, but from an older source.[4] It is now widely

[4] See the discussion in Sarianna Metso, *The Textual Development of the Qumran Community Rule* (STDJ 21; Leiden: Brill, 1997) 135-40. She also reviews the debate of whether the passage is a unity or, itself, reflects development, suggested by what appears to be an earlier version of some parts in 4QS[a]/4Q255. She finds that the data supports the analysis that sees differences in vocabulary and thought between 3.13 – 4.14 and 4.15-26, the former using dualism within a cosmological, the second within an anthropological framework, following Peter von der Osten-Sacken, *Gott und Belial: Traditionsgeschichtliche Untersuchungen zum Dualismus in den Texten aus Qumran* (SUNT 6; Göttingen: Vandenhoeck und Ruprecht, 1969) 17-26. For a more differentiated view of the development of S tradition, see Charlotte Hempel, "The Literary Development of the S Tradition – A New Paradigm," *RevQ* 22 (2006) 389-401, who sees the documents as

regarded as stemming from a much earlier period and belonging with those works like *1/4QInstruction* and the *Visions of Amram*, which lack the distinctive vocabulary of Qumran, and arose in the pre- or proto-Essene period.[5] I discuss it, therefore, in its own right, before returning to its role in the context of the *Community Rule*.

It depicts humankind as potentially ruled by the רוח האמת "the spirit of truth" or רוח העול "the spirit of falsehood". While the same word, רוח, is used later in the exposition to explain the generation of psychological qualities in a person, for instance, רוח ענוה "spirit of meekness" (4.3) and רוח דעת "spirit of knowledge" (4.4), the focus is on the rule and influence of these spirits.[6] Accordingly, what they generate is described as originating from מעון אור "the dwelling of light" and מקור חושך "the fountain of darkness" (3.19). The two spirits are then identified as שר אורים "the prince of lights" and מלאך חושך "the angel of darkness" (3.19-21). Those who follow the one are called, בני אור "the children of light" (3.13), בני צדק "the children of justice" (3.20, 22, 24), and also בני אמת "the children of truth" (4.5, 6), and those who follow the other are called בני עול "the children of falsehood" (3.21).

This division is not a permanent fissure in reality, but part of the divine ordering (3.15-16; 4.16, 25), which includes setting a time limit after which those

---

reflecting "several complex and evolving processes" (401). See also the general introduction by Sarianna Metso, *The Serekh Texts* (London: T&T Clark, 2007) 15-20.

5 So Lange, *Weisheit*, 127-28; Jörg Frey, "Different Patterns of Dualistic Thought in the Qumran Library: Reflections on their Background and History," in *Legal Texts and Legal Issues: Proceedings of the Second Meeting of the International Organisation for Qumran studies, Cambridge, 1995: Published in Honour of Joseph M. Baumgarten* (ed. M. Bernstein, F. G. Martinez, J. Kampen; Leiden: Brill, 1997) 275-336, 296; Magen Broshi, "Predestination in the Bible and the Dead Sea Scrolls," in *The Bible and the Dead Sea Scrolls: The Princeton Symposium on the Dead Sea Scrolls: Volume 2: The Dead Sea Scrolls and the Qumran Community* (ed. James H. Charlesworth; Waco: Baylor University Press, 2006) 235-46, 237, 239-40. He notes also the reaction to this predestinarian dualism in Sir 43:6-7 and in 11QPs/11Q11 15.11-12 (241).

6 See the review of research on the dualism of the treatise in John R. Levison, "The Two Spirits in Qumran Theology," in *The Bible and the Dead Sea Scrolls: The Princeton Symposium on the Dead Sea Scrolls: Volume 2: The Dead Sea Scrolls and the Qumran Community* (ed. James H. Charlesworth; Waco: Baylor University Press, 2006) 169-94; Maxwell J. Davidson, *Angels at Qumran: A Comparative Study of 1 Enoch 1-36, 72-109 and Sectarian Writings from Qumran* (JSPSup 11; Sheffield: JSOT Press, 1992) 145-62; and for more recent discussion: Broshi, "Predestination," 235-46; and Bilhah Nitzan, "Evil and its Symbols in the Qumran Scrolls," in *Problem of Evil and its Symbols in Jewish and Christian Tradition* (ed. Henning Graf Reventlow and Yair Hoffman; JSOTSup 366; London: T & T Clark, 2004) 83-96.

who walk in darkness will face damnation and destruction at the hands of God's angels of destruction (3.23; 4.11b-14, 18-19).[7] For the children of light this will be the time when God will purify them, removing מתכמי בשרו "from the inward parts of his flesh" in each the spirit of perversity, sprinkling over them the spirit of holiness like waters of purification (4.20-22) and restoring them to the glory of Adam, where there will no longer be sin and injustice (4.23). The state of being is determined by God. *4QHoroscope*/4Q186, according to which "every human being is composed of nine parts – some parts of light and some of darkness",[8] shows us see how this might have been understood. Yet beside these explanations of divine ordering the passage assumes that human beings respond to the competing spirits which seek to lead them in their ways.

This dualistic scheme embodies a cosmic dualism, the opposition of two heavenly beings, whose realm comprises human beings; an ethical dualism, reflected in the list of virtues and vices; and a psychological dualism, which helps explain why the sons of light also commit sin (divine determinism of a person's lot or balance of parts of light and parts of darkness).[9] In the context of the *Community Rule* the implied identification with Belial in the preceding section and the emphasis on election gives greater attention to the statement as justifying the sectarian view of a division of humanity between the faithful members of the sect and the rest of humankind.[10]

The dualism may be compared with that found in the *Visions of Amram* and in the *War Scroll* which we shall consider below, since these share with the treatise the language of "light" and "darkness", and their children, and also assume an era of conflict of limited duration, followed by judgement (4Q544 1 9-15 = 4Q547 1-2 iii.9-13; 1QM/1Q33 1.1, 11, 13; 13.9-12). Yet these lack the ethical focus and the psychological dimensions and emphasise the sheer cosmic dualism or see conflict

---

[7] On the determinism reflected in the passage, which includes God's appointment of angels with diverse powers as in *1 Enoch* 6:7-8; 60:17-22; 82:11-12; *Jub.* 2:2, see Maxwell J. Davidson, *Angels at Qumran: A Comparative Study of 1 Enoch 1-36, 72-109 and Sectarian Writings from Qumran* (JSPSup 11; Sheffield: JSOT Press, 1992) 159-60; Nitzan, "Evil and its Symbols," 83-96, who points also to the parallel in 1QH[a] 9.10-20 (85). Similarly Broshi, "Predestination," who points also to 1QpHab 7.13-14 (238).

[8] Broshi, "Predestination," 238. Similarly, Nitzan, "Evil and its Symbols," 87.

[9] Frey, "Different Patterns," 290-95. Frey argues that "the sapiential idea of a predetermined order of creation, as documented in Sirach 33, is the ideological background of the teaching" in the treatise (298).

[10] See Frey, "Different Patterns," 301-303. He shows that this is also the emphasis it receives in CD 2.2-13 which in 2.7 cites 1QS/1Q28 4.22 (cf. also the possible citation of 1QS/1Q28 4.26 in 1QH[a] vi.11-12 and 4QAgesCreat/4Q181 1 ii.5) (303-307). On the possible influence of the treatise in D, see Lange, *Weisheit*, 132-33; 163; 241-42.

primarily as between God's people and others.[11] Frey sees this kind of dualism as reflecting an early emphasis with roots in the time of Daniel and in Persian dualistic tradition, and as then being used by the sect in preserving their identity, who could combine the sapiential dualism reflected in the *Treatise on the Two Spirits* with the more rigid cosmic dualism.[12] The dualism of the treatise also has much in common with *1/4QInstruction*, although as Tigchelaar notes, the correspondence is mostly with the middle section, 1QS/1Q28 3.18 – 4.14, not with 3.13-18; 4.14-26, suggesting that the latter may reflect a secondary development of the treatise.[13]

This complex dualistic discourse raises the question about the role human sexuality plays. There is a reference to sexual wrongdoing within the context of a list of sins which characterise the way of darkness (4.9-11). After listing greed, neglect of serving justice, falsehood, pride, deceit, arrogance, dishonesty, deception, hypocrisy, impatience, and folly, it speaks of sexual wrongdoing:

וקנאת זדון מעשי תעובה ברוח זנות
ודרכי נדה בעבודת טמאה

> arrogant zeal for[14] abominable acts[15] in a spirit of sexual wrongdoing
> and paths of impurity in serving what defiles.* (4.10)

---

[11] This is more so in the *War Scroll* than in the *Visions of Amram*, since in the latter the vision of the two opposing angels (4Q544 1 9-15 = 4Q547 1-2 iii.9-13) comes immediately after the prohibition on marrying a Canaanite (4Q543 4 2-4 = 4Q544 1 7-9 = 4Q547 1-2 iii 6-9a), thus perhaps implying an ethical dimension to what follows, though in the depiction of the vision, itself, the ethical element is absent. See the discussion on pp. 325-26 below.

[12] Frey, "Different Patterns," 308-31. See also Klaus Koch, "History as a Battlefield of Two Antagonistic Powers in the Apocalypse of Weeks and in the Rule of the Community," in *Enoch and Qumran Origins: New Light on a Forgotten Connection* (ed. Gabriele Boccaccini; Grand Rapids: Eerdmans, 2005) 185-99, who argues an Iranian background especially to the Aramaic opposites *qushṭa* (truth, righteousness) and *shiqra* (deceit) presupposed as antogonistic powers here and in the *Apocalypse of Weeks*.

[13] Eibert J. C. Tigchelaar, *To Increase Learning for the Understanding Ones: Reading and Reconstructing the Fragmentary Early Jewish Sapiential Text 4QInstruction* (STDJ 44; Leiden: Brill, 2001) 203, and see his discussion of the relationship, pp. 194-203, 207. For an analysis which both shows the structural coherence of the treatise and at the same time exposes the unevennesses in the text which call for some hypothesis of development, see Jean Duhaime, "Cohérence structurelle et tensions interns dans l'Instruction sur des Deux Esprits (1QS III 13 – IV 26)," in *Wisdom and Apocalypticism in the Dead Sea Scrolls and in the Biblical Tradition* (ed. Florentino García Martínez; BETL163; Leuven: Leuven University Press, Peeters, 2003) 103-32.

[14] וקנאת זדון may be treated independently from what follows, as "zeal of arrogance/ arrogant zeal".

[15] The first four words are partially preserved in 4QS^c/4Q257 5.8.

The list continues with reference to blasphemy, spiritual blindness and deafness, hardness of heart and having a stiff neck. Noting the concentration of cultic terminology (in the second line above), Klawans suggests that it "is being used to describe not specific violations of ritual purity law, but grave sinfulness in general".[16] This is probably too broad, since all other expressions in the list focus on a particular aspect. Sexual wrongdoing and cultic impurity are different, but closely related, so that we are best to see here a statement that recognises that sexual wrongdoing, itself, defiles, but that wrongdoing also entails ignoring avoidance of impurity, such as in having intercourse with a woman during her menstruation.[17]

The expression ברוח זנות "in a spirit of sexual wrongdoing", appears to derive from Hos 4:12, where it is used metaphorically, but here a literal application seems more likely since the focus is specific acts. Within the list sexual wrongdoing stands out as more elaborated and thus given more prominence, much as in the lists in CD 6.14 – 7.4 and 8.4-8, but there with greater specificity. This emphasis, not reflected elsewhere in the *Community Rule*, belongs to the older tradition. The following exposition in the treatise does not return to the sexual theme. The passage preceding the list, which depicts the way of the sons of light, speaks of a spirit which כול גלולי נדה "detests all impure idols" (4.5), that might also be translated "detests all impure ideas",[18] but need not have particular reference to sexual impurity or immorality.

With regard to further potentially relevant detail, nothing in the context suggests that what will be removed from the righteous, מתכמי בשרו, "from the inward parts of his flesh", according to 4.20-21 has anything to do with sexuality. Rather it is the spirit of perversity. Nor does the expression used in 1QS/1Q28 3.19, מקור חושך "the fountain of darkness", which uses the word מקור, found elsewhere sometimes referring to the penis (e.g., 1QM/1Q33 7.6; 4QOrd^c/4Q514 1 i.4), indicate a concern with sexuality. The image of the future glory of Adam is not depicted in a way that relates to sexual themes, such as one might expect if it

[16] Klawans, *Impurity and Sin*, 76.

[17] Duhaime, "Cohérence," notes: "elles sont construites suivant un parallélisme rigoureux qui évoque le comportement ('actions' // 'voies') en le qualifant ('abominables' // 'souillées') puis en indique la modalité d'exécution ('dans un esprit de débauche' // 'dans un service d'impurité')" (112) (Tr. "they are constructed according to a rigorous parallelism which highlights the behavior ('actions' // 'ways') by qualifying it ('abominable' // 'defiled') then indicates the way it is expressed ('in a spirit of sexual immorality' // 'in serving impurity'").

[18] So Takamitsu Muraoka, "The Community Rule (1QS), Column 4," in *Emanuel: Studies in Hebrew Bible, Septuagint, and Dead Sea Scrolls in Honor of Emanuel Tov* (ed. Shalom M. Paul, Robert A. Kraft, Lawrence H. Schiffman, and Weston W. Fields; SVT 94; Leiden: Brill, 2003) 335-46, 342-43.

entailed a return to paradise, understood as a temple, where, as in *Jubilees*, sexual relations would be inappropriate. Rather, the promise to those who are sons of light includes fruitfulness:

ופקודת כול הולכי בה למרפא 7 ורוב שלום באורך ימים
ופרות זרע עם כול ברכות עד ושמחת עולמים בחיי נצח
וכליל כבוד 8 עם מדת הדר באור עולמים

And the reward for all who walk in it will be healing, 7 plentiful peace in a long life and fruitful offspring with all everlasting blessings, eternal enjoyment with endless life, and a crown of glory 8 with majestic raiment in eternal light.
(*DSSSE*) (4.6b-8a) (partly preserved in 4QS^{c}/4Q257 5.4-5) (outlined)

This assumes that the sons of light will have children, i.e. will be married and live in families. Knibb[19] notes the similar image of future fruitfulness in *1 Enoch* 10:17-18. There is no indication that fruitfulness is only a metaphor.[20] There is some uncertainty about when these blessings eventuate, whether beginning in the present, or whether at a time in the future. The expression ופקודה, may be translated "and the visitation" rather than "and the reward", referring to the day of God's visitation which brings blessing for the sons of truth and wrath for the sons of deceit, as the passage goes on to declare.[21] In any case, even if the blessings of fruitfulness refer to this age, there is no indication that they then cease to be in the future. The imagery of light recalls the hope expressed in Dan 12:3, the reference to raiment implying some kind of embodied state in which one can be so clothed (cf. *1 Enoch* 104:2-6; *4QWiles of the Wicked Woman*/4Q184 1 8). For those with a majority of portions of light, "all the glory of Adam" is promised them (4.23) and this appears to assume their having spouses and children in "the new creation" (4.25). While such detail is incidental, it reflects assumptions about a place for marriage and sexuality. The passage is apparently cited in 4QpapRitMar/4Q502 16, in the context of what appears best understood as a marriage ritual (see pp. 258-59 below).

The dualism of this remarkable treatise, now incorporated in the *Community Rule*, does not therefore depict sexuality as particularly problematic, though it includes sexual wrongdoing as something generated by the angel of darkness. The

[19] Knibb, *Qumran Community*, 100.

[20] Cf. Baumgarten, "Qumran-Essene Restraints on Marriage," 17-18.

[21] So Émile Puech, *La croyannce des Esséniens en la vie future: Immortalité, resurrection, vie éternelle?* (EB 21-22; Paris: Gabalda, 1993) 426-40; Émile Puech, "Resurrection: The Bible and Qumran," in *The Bible and the Dead Sea Scrolls: The Princeton Symposium on the Dead Sea Scrolls: Volume 2: The Dead Sea Scrolls and the Qumran Community* (ed. James H. Charlesworth; Waco, Tex.: Baylor University Press, 2006) 247-81, 271.

dualism, itself, does not call human sexuality into question, but, rather, appears to affirm its place by assuming its role in the abundance promised in the glory of Adam.

The Remainder of the Community Rule

Returning to those sections of the *Community Rule* which follow the treatise, we find in the rule for those who join the community, which begins in column 5, another possible reference to sexual wrongdoing:

לוא ילך איש בשרירות לבו לתעות אחר לבבו
5 ועינוהי ומחשבת יצרו
(כ)יא אם למול ביחד עורלת יצר ועורף קשה
ליסד מוסד אמת לישראל ליחד ברית

> a man shall not walk in the stubbornness of his heart to go astray after his heart
> 5 and his eyes and the thoughts of his inclination,
> but is to circumcise in the community the foreskin of his inclination, and his stiff neck
> to lay a foundation of truth for Israel, for the community of the covenant.* (5.4b-5)

The reference to "eyes" and to "stubbornness of heart" recalls 1.6b-7a,

ולוא ללכת יוד בשרירות לב אשמה ועיני זנות 7 לעשות כול רע

> and not to walk in the stubbornness of a guilty heart and eyes of sexual wrongdoing to do all evil.*

and is similar to CD 2.16

ולא לתור במחשבות יצר אשמה וע(י)ני זנות

> follow after thoughts of a guilty inclination and after eyes of sexual wrongdoing.* (2.16).

The formulation, אחר לבבו ועינוהי "after his heart and his eyes" reflects the language of Num 15:39

ולא תתרו אחרי לבבכם ואחרי עיניכם אשר אתם זנים אחריהם

> and not follow your heart and your eyes in which you lust after them. (Num 15:39)

Even though Num 15:39 uses sexual language only metaphorically, given the echo of 1.6b-7a in 5.4b-5, it is likely that the latter does include reference to sexual wrongdoing. Like CD 2.16, it appears to connect sexual wrongdoing and inclination (יצר), without equating the two.[22] We shall return to the understanding of יצר, "inclination" in the context of the discussion of its use in the *Thanksgiving Hymns* below (pp. 246, 252). The metaphorical use of the image of circumcision reflects biblical precedents (Deut 10:16; Jer 4:4), and, as there, will not allude to issues of sexuality despite the preceding context. According to Carol Newsom, in 5.4-5. the "body imagery of heart, eyes, neck, and the erring will that they depict serve to represent the individual as naturally a creature of stubbornness and waywardness".[23] This coheres with the emphasis in the closing hymnic material, which we discuss below (11.9-12, 20-22).

On the other hand, we need to note that the text reads differently in 4QS^{b}/4Q256 and 4QS^{d}/4Q258, where it does not include these biblical allusions relevant to the theme.

> אשר]לא ילך איש בשרירות לבו לתעות כי אם ליסד מוסד אמת לישראל ליחד
>
> a man shall not walk in the stubbornness of his heart to go astray, but should establish a foundation of truth for Israel, for the Community.* (4QS^{d}/4Q258 i.4)

In 4QS^{b}/4Q256 the words which come before כי אם are not preserved, but the length indicates that it would have contained a similar number of words to 4QS^{d}/4Q258 i.4. Thus both manuscripts lack what gives 1QS/1Q28 5.4b-5 a potentially sexual reference. In her discussion of the differences Metso concludes: "The comparison between the manuscripts 1QS and 4QS^{b,d} indicates that 4QS^{b} and 4QS^{d} have preserved a more original text than has 1QS."[24] Accordingly, 1QS "has been expanded with a long phrase echoing several Old Testament verses (e.g. Num 15:39; Ezek 6:9; Deut 10:16; Jer 4:4)".[25] She identifies a process of redaction of the *Community Rule*, in which the self-understanding of the community is enhanced by "stressing the role of the community as the true temple and guardian of the covenant as well as the true keeper of the Law" and its scriptural legitimacy is emphasised.[26]

---

[22] Leaney, *Rule of Qumran*, notes that "uncircumcised" was one of the names for the *yetzer hara* in *b. Suk.* 52a (167).

[23] Carol A. Newsom, *The Self as Symbolic Space: Constructing Identity and Community at Qumran* (STDJ 52; Leiden: Brill, 2004) 138.

[24] Metso, *Textual Development*, 89.

[25] Metso, *Textual Development*, 78. See also Knibb, *Qumran Community*, 106.

[26] Metso, *Textual Development*, 89; see also 105 and 147 where she outlines what she sees as the stages of development. She shows that 4QS^{d}/4Q258 commenced with column 5 and was considerably shorter than 1QS (36-47, 67, 74). 4QS^{b}/4Q256 also contained a shorter text than 1QS. But see also Hempel, "Literary Development," who suggests that such differences may reflect diverse textual tradition rather than linear development.

Later in the passage we find reference to the need to dissociate oneself from someone who does not turn aside from sin, in the context of which it speaks of נדה "impurity" and טמא "defilement" (5.19b, 20a), used in a broad sense to depict what is unacceptable before God, rather than a narrow cultic sense, but nothing in the context suggests this need have a sexual reference, though the possibility should not be excluded. The same applies to the references to נדה "impurity" in 10.24 and 11.14.

As Martha Himmelfarb notes, the document applies to spiritual states what in P referred to physical states, and does so both with regard to states of impurity like H, but, unlike H, also with regard to the means of purification.[27] "Purity and impurity transformed into spiritual rather than physical categories, were central to the thought of 1QS"[28]. Casey Toews also notes that while 1QS assumes both ritual and moral impurity, it does not merge them, but does merge the means of purification, in a way that is unparalleled. "Lustrations now cleanse not only ritual impurity but moral impurity as well."[29]

Within the penal code we find reference to nakedness.[30]

ואשר יהלך לפני רעהו ערום ולוא היה אנוש ונענש ששה חודשים

And whoever walks about in front of his fellow naked, without needing to, he shall be punished for six months. (*DSSSE*) (7.14)

ואשר יוציא ידו מתוחת בגדו והואה 16 פוח ונראתה ונענש שלושים יום

And whoever takes out "his hand" from under his clothes, or if these are 16 rags which allow his nakedness to be seen, he will be punished thirty days. (*DSSSE*) (7.15-16)

והמוציא את יד שמאולו לשוח בה ונענש עשרת ימים

And whoever takes out his left hand to gesticulate with it shall be punished ten days. (*DSSSE*) (7.17)

The material is preserved also in 4QS^{e}/4Q259 i 9, 11-12, 14-15 and the first two provisions in 4QS^{g}/4Q261 5a-c 5-7, 8-9. These are also identical to what we find in the penal code of D, discussed on pp. 171-72 above, with minor exceptions (4QD^{a}/4Q266 10 ii.9-12; 4QD^{e}/4Q270 7 i.1-3, 5), and reflect a common concern with nakedness. 4QS^{e}/4Q259, reflecting an earlier version,[31] says the punishment in 7.14 is for sixty days (1 i.10), but in 7.8 it is more lenient.[32] On the various

[27] Himmelfarb, "Impurity and Sin," 30-31.

[28] Himmelfarb, "Impurity and Sin," 34.

[29] Casey Toews, "Moral Purification in 1QS," *BBR* 13 (2003) 71-96, 94.

[30] Toews, "Moral Purification," writes of "the Penal Code, 1QS 6:24—7:25" as "a series of sectarian rules dedicated entirely to the realm of moral impurity" (84). Concern with nakedness cannot, I believe, be contained in such a category, but reflects a complex of issues.

[31] Metso, *Textual Development*, 90.

[32] Metso, *Textual Development*, 70.

proposals to explain why gesticulating with the left hand is offensive see the discussion of the parallel statement in D.

Within the hymnic material with which the *Community Rule* ends (10.5 – 11.22) we find an anthropology which meets us more extensively in the *Thanksgiving Hymns*. In the *Community Rule* the individual asserts God's goodness and determining power in part by setting his own humanity and powerlessness in contrast to it.

> As for me, I belong to wicked humanity (לאדם רשעה)
> and to the foundation of iniquitous flesh (לסוד בשר עול).
> My iniquities, transgressions, sins with the perversities of my heart belong to the foundation of worms (סוד רמה) and those who walk in darkness,
> because man (אדם) does not (determine) his ways
> nor does a human being (אנוש) ordain his path,
> because to God belongs justification
> and by his power is the perfection of his way.* (11.9-11)

In 11.12 he writes,

> If I fall through iniquity of the flesh (אכשול בעוון בשר),
> my justification will be by the righteousness of God which stands forever,

and reports: יטהרני מנדת אנוש וחטאת בני אדם "he cleansed from defilement of the human being and the sin of man" (11.14-15). The column ends with similar statements of humility:

> What is a son of man (בן ה'אדם) among your wonderful works?
> As what can one born of a woman (ילוד אשה) stand before You?
> Kneaded from dust (מעפר מגבלו),
> his dwelling is the bread of worms (ולחם רמה מדורו);
> he is spit (מצירוק), moulded clay (חמר קורץ)
> – and to dust is his return[33] (ולעפר תשוקו).
> What shall clay (חמר) reply, one shaped by hand (יוצר יד)?
> What will he consider for the council?* (11:20b-22)

---

[33] I translate תשוקה as the equivalent of תשובה. This appears to be its meaning also in 1QM/1Q33 17.4 (cf. also 13.12; 15.10; 6Q18 2 4) and to be reflected in the LXX translation of Gen 3:16 which renders תשוקה by ἀποστροφή. On this see William Loader, *The Septuagint, Sexuality and the New Testament: Case Studies on the Impact of the LXX in Philo and the New Testament* (Grand Rapids: Eerdmans, 2004) 46-47; William Loader, "The Beginnings of Sexuality in Genesis LXX and Jubilees," in *Die Septuaginta – Texte, Kontexte, Lebenswelten* (ed. Martin Karrer and Wolfgang Kraus; WUNT; Tübingen: Mohr Siebeck, forthcoming 2007).

We shall return to these passages in our discussion of similar material in the *Thanksgiving Hymns* (pp. 243-54 below). Their relevance for assessing attitudes towards sexuality relates to the extent to which in connecting together the creation story and the processes of procreation to depict humanity in contrast to God, they imply something negative about sexuality.[34] For the present, we can observe that nothing in the hymnic material makes sexual wrongdoing an issue or addresses issues of sexuality in any positive sense. This appears to cohere with the emphases we have found throughout the document.

Conclusion

The *Community Rule* contains many references to wrongdoing and wrongdoers, especially those who are the community's enemy and those who abandon it or refuse to join it. This is also true of the series of instructions for the Community, its Inspector and Instructor, and the hymnic material with which the Rule ends. Demarcation is a primary concern.[35] It clearly envisages a demarcation and separation[36] during the dominion of Belial not only from sinners in general but also from errant teachers, probably designated as מעדת אנשי העול "the congregation of the men of injustice" (5.1-2; similarly, 5.10; 8.13; 9.17; cf. also 11.1-2) and אנשי השחת "men of the pit" (9.16; 10.19; cf. 9.22; CD 6.14-15). In 11:1-2 אנשי מטה may means "men of the bending (of the Law") (*DSSSE*), but it may refer to "stretching out" the finger in scorn. They are also said to err in rejecting revealed matters, possibly related to matters of calendar (5.11-12; cf. 1.14), but there is no indication of differences over issues of sexuality and, in any case the document forbids engaging with them in dispute (9.16; 10.19). Had sexual wrongdoing been a major concern, we might expect to find some indication of this

[34] In her analysis of group identity as reflected in the *Community Rule* Louise J. Lawrence, "'Men of Perfect Holiness' (1QS 7.20): Social-Scientific Thoughts on Group Identity, Asceticism and Ethical Development in the Rule of the Community," in *New Directions in Qumran Studies: Proceedings from the Bristol Colloquium on the Dead Sea Scrolls, 8-10th September 2003* (ed. Jonathan G. Campbell, William John Lyons, and Lloyd K. Pietersen; Library of Second Temple Studies 52; London: T&T Clark, 2005) 83-100, speaks of a virtuoso ascetic community and contrasts its optimism with the low anthropology of the individual in the *Thanksgiving Hymns* (97). This does not really cohere with the final form of the document where the hymn in 1QS/1Q28 10 – 11 reflects a similar anthropology, but it is true that the document reflects greater optimism, compared with the frequent sense of being under duress in the *Thanksgiving Hymns*.

[35] For a discussion of the role of purity language in protecting knowledge and forming subjectivity of the community see Colleen M. Conway, "Toward a Well-Formed Subject: The Function of Purity Language in the Serek ha-Yaḥad," *JSP* 21 (2000) 103-20.

[36] The verb used here is בדל; cf. *4QMMT* C 7 which uses פרש.

in the document. Instead there are only a few references and they refer to the past way of life. It is reasonable to conclude that in contrast to D, matters of sexual wrongdoing are incidental to the major concerns.

The language which echoes D and its concern with sexual wrongdoing appears to be used in an almost stereotypical way, such as we might expect had the *Community Rule* been composed in a context where the acute issues addressed in D were no longer a concern.[37] Sexual wrongdoing appears with significant emphasis in the list of deeds characteristic of the spirit of darkness in the *Treatise on the Two Spirits*, but is not developed. This matches its emphasis in the lists in D (CD 6.14 – 7.4 and 8.3-9). Perhaps the secondary expansion in 1QS/1Q28 5.4-5, where walking in the stubbornness of one's heart is linked to sexual wrongdoing as in 1.7, reflects some concern, but it appears only as a possibility within broader concerns. The penal code reflects a tradition shared by D which includes concern with nakedness, and the anthropology of the closing hymn may have implications for attitudes towards sexuality, but nothing in the context suggests sexuality itself is problematic.

It is also interesting to note what else is absent from the *Community Rule*. As Himmelfarb, notes "1QS has nothing to say about the sources of impurity so important to the Torah", but cautions that while "it delineates the special rules that govern the life of the community", it apparently assumes the laws of the Torah, so that "it would be a mistake to read any special significance into its lack of attention to purity laws".[38] Within the *Treatise on the Two Spirits* there may be an allusion to cultic impurity in relation to sexuality within the list in 4.10.

The only other detail of note is the hint that in incorporating the *Treatise on the Two Spirits* the document includes a vision of an embodied future which promised production of offspring and so assumes marriage, families, and a place for procreation and sexual relations.

---

[37] On the likelihood that the connection between D and the *Community Rule* is to be explained diachronically see John J. Collins, "The Yahad and 'The Qumran Community'," in *Biblical Traditions in Transmission: Essays in Honour of Michael A. Knibb* (ed. Charlotte Hempel and Judith M. Lieu; Leiden: Brill, 2006) 81-96, who notes such developments as the more complex admission procedures in the latter (95). Cf. Regev, "The 'Yahad' and the 'Damascus Covenant'". See also Sarianna Metso, "Whom does the term YAHAD identify?" in *Biblical Traditions in Transmission: Essays in Honour of Michael A. Knibb* (ed. Charlotte Hempel and Judith M. Lieu; Leiden: Brill, 2006) 213-35, who outlines the complexity of identifying the various groups people have identified in the *Community Rule* and D, given the equally complex nature of the development of these documents, themselves.

[38] Himmelfarb, "Impurity and Sin," 29. See also Toews, "Moral Purification," 93.

2 The *Rule of the Congregation* 1Q28a/1QSa; 4Qpap cryptA Serekh ha-ʿEdah/4Q249a-i

In this brief document, preserved in part also in cryptic script on papyrus fragments possibly from the early 2nd century BCE,[39] there are a number of features of interest.

It begins with "the rule for all the congregation of Israel at the end of the days" (1.1-5). In 1.4 the document speaks of an assembly which is inclusive. It uses the formula מטף עד נשים "from infants to women". The presence of men is presupposed. The concern is that all hear the precepts of the covenant. The passage is probably patterned on the inclusive gathering of the people for the renewal of the covenant in Deut 29:10 and the reading of the Law in Deut 31:9-13 (which mentions infants) and Neh 8:1-3. In relation to issues of sexuality this is important at least in the sense that it assumes a community of men and women where there are children, presumably from marriages, rather than solely adopted, and that this, in turn, assumes a place for sexual relations as a normal part of life.

It becomes important also for 1.11 where a woman is apparently to bear witness about her husband's adherence to the provisions of the Law, which she must first know, that is, have been taught. Before discussing this passage, we need also to note that there is difference of opinion about whether the intervening lines, 1.6-10, refer only to men or to both women and men (where the masculine plural form would need to be understood inclusively).[40] It is clear that 1.9b refers to a

[39] See Stephen J. Pfann, *DJD* 36, 515-74; Stephen J. Pfann, "Historical Implications of the Early Second Century Dating of the 4Q249-250 Cryptic A Corpus," in *Things Revealed: Studies in Early Jewish and Christian Literature in Honor of Michael E. Stone* (ed. Esther G. Chazon, David Satran, and Ruth A. Clements; JSJSup 89; Leiden: Brill, 2004) 171-86. Cautionary on the dating because of the limited amount of text: Charlotte Hempel, "The Groningen Hypothesis: Strengths and Weaknesses," in *Enoch and Qumran Origins: New Light on a Forgotten Connection* (ed. Gabriele Boccaccini; Grand Rapids: Eerdmans, 2005) 249-55, 254; Florentino García Martínez, "Response: The Groningen Hypothesis Revisited," in *Enoch and Qumran Origins: New Light on a Forgotten Connection* (ed. Gabriele Boccaccini; Grand Rapids: Eerdmans, 2005) 310-16, 314.

[40] For the proposed inclusive reading see Eileen Schuller, "Women in the Dead Sea Scrolls," in *Methods of Investigation of the Dead Sea Scrolls and the Khirbet Qumran Site: Present Realities and Future Prospects* (ed. Michael Wise et al.; Annals of the New York Academy of Sciences 722; New York: New York Academy of Sciences, 1994) 115-31, 123-24; the critique by Philip R. Davies and Joan E. Taylor, "On the Testimony of Women in 1QSa," *DSD* 3 (1996) 223-35, 229-30; the modified re-presentation of the inclusivity argument in Eileen Schuller, "Women in the Dead Sea Scrolls," in *The Dead Sea Scrolls after Fifty Years: A Comprehensive Assessment* (ed. Peter W. Flint and James C. VanderKam; Leiden: Brill, 1999) 2.117-44, (the work hereafter cited by the abbreviated title, "Women in the Dead Sea Scrolls," 1999) 131-32; and Wassen, *Women*, 141-42.

young man having sexual intercourse with a woman. There is no indication that what precedes has a different subject, although one might argue that the transition from 1.8 to 1.9-11 is not from discussing male issues to discussing a male at twenty, but from discussing male and female together to discussing each, a man and a woman, separately, as that stage of life requires, namely, the age for marrying. This would assume, however, that women were also to marry at age twenty.

It is more likely however that the age of twenty applies only to the young man and that 1.6-9a refer to the stages in life of a boy, up to the age of twenty. This is made all the more likely because 1.12-25 continue to address the life cycle of a man up to old age, including involvement in tasks assigned to males (like leadership in the armed forces). Thus 1.6 appears to make a new beginning after 1.4-5.[41] While it is possible to read 1.6-7 as referring to the instruction of all (both boys and girls), especially if we read 1.4-5 as applying to all assemblies (1.1),[42] the transition to 1.8-9a which begins addressing the life cycle of a male, and is continued to 1.25, does not indicate a change of subject.

The balance of argument, therefore, supports taking the instruction about life stages and roles as referring to males. This appears also to make best sense of the introduction in 1.6 especially if read וזה סרך לכול צבאות העדה literally as speaking of armies: "and this is the rule for the armies of the congregation". It remains, nevertheless, clear that both 1.4-5 and 1.11, as we shall see, assume that women also belonged in the assemblies and received instruction in the Law.

The "rule for the armies of the congregation" (1.6-25a) seems best understood, therefore, as relating to the males in the congregation. It outlines life stages. One is of a boy up to the age of twenty, who during his youth is to receive instruction in the Book of Hagy (1.6b-8a). The young man of twenty then joins the holy community as an adult (1.8b-9a). As Knibb notes,[43] this reflects the age of enrolment in the census in Exod 30:14; 38:26; Num 1:3; and 1 Chron 27:23. Here the document gives specific instruction about sexual relations.

---

[41] Schuller, "Women in the Dead Sea Scrolls" (1999), writes: "Although line 6 and following was once a distinct unit 'and this is the *serek* for all….,' in the final recension of the text it becomes subsumed under the introductory rubric (lines 1-5)" (132). In this she assumes the source critical study of Charlotte Hempel, "The Earthly Essene Nucleus of 1QSa," *DSD* 3 (1996) 253-69. See also Wassen, *Women*, 141 n. 37. She also argues that 1.8 assumes the same assembly as in 1.4-5 and so must be referring to both men and women (141 n. 38). The final recension, however, appears not to have changed the original male referent of the life cycle rules.

[42] So Wassen, *Women*, 142.

[43] Knibb, *Qumran Community*, 149.

ולוא י[קרב] 10 אל אשה לדעתה למשכבי זכר
כי אם לפי מילואת לו עש[רי]ם שנה בדעתו[טוב]
11 ורע ובכן תקבל להעיד עליו משפטות התורא ולהת[י]צב במשמע משפטים

> and he shall not [approach] 10 a woman to have sexual intercourse with her by lying with her as a male does
> until he has completed tw[en]ty years when he knows[good]
> 11 and evil; and on this she shall be received to testify about him in relation to the regulations of the law and to [st]and in the proclamation of the judgements.* (1.9b-11)

There is to be no sexual intercourse before the age of 20 and it also probably assumes not before marriage (as in *Jub.* 25:4), though that is not explicit. The descriptive formulation, י[קרב] 10 אל אשה לדעתה למשכבי זכר "approach a woman to have sexual intercourse with her by lying with her as a male does", reflects that found in Num 31:17, וכל אשה ידעת איש למשכב זכר "and every woman who has known a man by lying with him as a male" (similarly, Judg 21:12).[44] The reference to knowing good and evil (בדעתו טוב ורע) may reflect the formulation in Deut 1:39 ובניכם אשר לא ידעו היום טוב ורע "and you children, who today do not know good and evil". It might also echo the Eden story, which forbids eating מעץ הדעת טוב ורע "from the tree of the knowledge of good and evil" (Gen 2:17; cf. also 3:5, 22). There it includes an allusion to awareness of nakedness and so sexual consciousness.[45] The same expression appears in 2 Sam 14:17 and 1 Kgs 3:9 to indicate special expertise. Here in 1.10b-11 the focus is the age of responsibility. Knowing right and wrong would include matters pertaining to sexuality, but probably assumes something much wider, namely, knowledge of the law gained through the instruction in the Book of Hagy (1.7).

Borgen notes that identifying twenty as the age for entry into marriage has a parallel in *Abot* 5.21, which also divides life up into stages, but in greater detail.[46] It speaks of entering marriage at age eighteen. He also points to *Eccl. Rab.* 1.2, which has a similar set of stages and has entry into marriage at twenty.[47] Both are late, but may reflect a traditional view, a "different version of the same

---

44 So Knibb, *Qumran Community*, 149.

45 See R. Gordis, "The knowledge of Good and Evil in the Old Testament and the Dead Sea Scrolls," *JBL* 76 (1957) 126-138, 130. He interprets 2 Sam 19:36 similarly (136). See also Peder Borgen, "'At the Age of Twenty' in 1QSa," *RevQ* 10 (1961-62) 267-77, 267.

46 Borgen, "Age of Twenty," 269.

47 Borgen, "Age of Twenty," 269-70. He suggests that *Ecclesiastes Rabbah* is influenced by Eccles 12:1-8 and *Aboth* by Ps 90:10 (277 n. 21). He also mentions Philo, *Opif.* 103, about stages of a man's life.

stereotypical pattern".[48] He suggests that such patterns were ideal rather than realistic, which, he suggests, is reflected in the fact that some of them, for instance, do not speak of employment until even later and that such an age limit for marriage does not reflect rabbinic tradition elsewhere.[49] Accordingly, he cautions also against using 1QSa/1Q28a as a basis for claiming that Qumran limited marriage to men twenty years of age and over.[50]

In 1.11 תקבל "she shall be received" refers to the woman with whom the man has had sexual intercourse. Thc initial reaction to this reading, which implied a woman would have a legal function, was to propose an amendment of the feminine תקבל "she shall be received" to a masculine יקבל "he shall be received", and עליו "concerning him" to על פי "in accordance with". Baumgarten, who took up the proposal for amendment and argued it in detail,[51] has more recently changed his assessment, now seeing no need for an amendment.[52]

Davies and Taylor, in arguing against Baumgarten's defence of the original proposal, rejected the latter's contention that such a statement would be out of place, inappropriate in assuming a young girl could testify, and unlikely in a context in which few married and attitudes were misogynous. They pointed out that there is no sign of textual corruption and that the statement should be seen as having discrete application, and as implying attendance at judgement for a particular purpose.[53]

Some still see a problem that the passage assumes women under twenty might testify, a notion proposed already by Richardson.[54] Thus Borgen sought to interpret the feminine as a reference not to the woman, but to the family and congregation,[55] but this seems not to be the most natural referent in the context. Even Rothstein, who argues strongly for a translation which sees the woman testifying, acknowledges that the notion of a young woman under twenty testifying in this way remains a difficulty.[56] He nevertheless rejects Baumgarten's more

---

[48] Borgen, "Age of Twenty," 270.

[49] Baumgarten, "The Qumran-Essene Restraints on Marriage," notes that rabbinic tradition viewed the age of twenty as a terminus *ante quem* for marriage and assumes on the basis of 1QSa/1Q28a that at Qumran the opposite applied (14).

[50] Borgen, "Age of Twenty ," 271-72.

[51] Joseph M. Baumgarten, "On the Testimony of Women in 1QSa," *JBL* 76 (1957) 266-69. Similarly Lawrence H. Schiffman, *The Eschatological Community of the Dead Sea Scrolls: A Study of the Rule of the Congregation* (SBLMonSer 38; Atlanta: Scholars, 1989) 18-19 and Schiffman, *Reclaiming the Dead Sea Scrolls*, 134-35.

[52] Baumgarten, *DJD* 18, 165.

[53] Davies and Taylor. "On the Testimony of Women," 226-28.

[54] H. N. Richardson, "Some Notes on 1QSa," *JBL* 76 (1957) 108-22.

[55] Borgen, "Age of Twenty," 272-73.

[56] Rothstein, "Women's Testimony," 614 n. 73.

recent proposal,[57] to translate להעיד עליו on the basis of Jer 6:10 as "to warn him", rather than "to testify concerning him".[58] While acknowledging the former as a possibility, Rothstein points to the use of העיד with the meaning of testifying (as in rabbinic literature) in CD 9.20.[59] He draws attention to the requirement in the sect to report wrongdoing and that the kind of positive approach towards women reflected in *Jubilees*, the presence of "mothers" in the communal organisation in D (cf. 4QD[e]/4Q270 7 i.14), and the role of women's testimony in relation to virginity (cf. 4QD[f]/4Q271 3 13b-15a; 4QOrd[a]/4Q159 2-4+8 8-10), all make it feasible that here 1.11 envisages testimony by a wife about her husband's behaviour and that one should not approach the passage with assumptions based on the negative attitudes found in the Greco-Roman world and in some wisdom writings.[60] He points to the assumption that family members testify against each other already in Deut 13:7-10 about idolatry and in Deut 21:18-21 about rebellious sons.[61]

Rothstein argues, further, that a wife's testimony was not limited to marital relations, but might also include "less concrete offenses, such as excessive pride, and the like".[62] In this he contends with Davies and Taylor. Similarly, Wassen claims that the testimony was about communal regulations in general and could include here a reference to purity matters or to fornication or the ban on intercourse on sabbath (4QD[e]/4Q270 2 ii.15-16).[63] The context of 1.11, however, suggests that the requirement to testify relates to what immediately precedes, namely sexual relations, so that the testimony pertains to some form of wrongdoing within the context of sexual relations, and may imply no more than that women were expected to testify on such specific matters, as Davies and Taylor suggest.[64] As already noted, testimony for a defined area of special

---

[57] Baumgarten, *DJD* 18, paraphrases the meaning as: "she must promise to admonish her husband about the laws concerning sexual intercourse with which she is to familiarize herself by learning them and fulfilling them" (165).

[58] Rothstein, "Women's Testimony," 599; similarly Bernstein, "Women and Children," notes that "'to admonish' is an unusual translation of להעיד, which generally means 'to testify', and it is difficult to understand how the rest of the sentence, 'the laws of the Torah and to stand in the hearing of the laws,' pertains to the woman" (208). He suggests: "she shall take it upon herself to testify against him (according to?) the laws of the Torah and to be present at the proclamation of the verdict (?)"(208).

[59] Rothstein, "Women's Testimony," 601.

[60] Rothstein, "Women's Testimony," 602-605, 610-11.

[61] Rothstein, "Women's Testimony," 608-10.

[62] Rothstein, "Women's Testimony," 613. Rothstein assumes the sect forbad remarriage and so sees any such testimony as a big risk for a woman (613-14).

[63] Wassen, *Women*, 182.

[64] Davies and Taylor, "Testimony of Women," 229; White Crawford, "Not According to Rule," 139; Brooke, "From Qumran to Corinth," 205.

knowledge is sought also when expert women are commissioned to report on virginity in 4QOrd[a]/4Q159 2-4+8 8-10 before the marriage and in 4QD[f]/4Q271 3 12b-16 after it. The range of testimony envisaged in 1.11 is therefore probably also limited. The various prohibitions preserved in D discussed above (4QD[e]/4Q270 7 i.12-13; 4QD[b]/4Q267 9 vi.4-5; CD 11.5; 4QD[f]/4Q271 5 i.1-2; CD 12.1-2; 4QD[e]/4Q270 2.i.18-19; 4QD[e]/4Q270 2 ii.15-16; 6QD/6Q15 5 2-3) suggest it could include intercourse during menstruation, pregnancy, on the sabbath, in the holy city, all of which would constitute committing sexual wrongdoing with one's wife. It might possibly include polygyny, as Rothstein suggests,[65] although that broadens the focus beyond the immediate concern of the context. Contrary to the assumptions brought to the documents on the basis of Josephus, nothing suggests that the concern was intercourse for purposes other than procreation.[66]

The passage is therefore best understood as addressing marriage as coming also at the point where the man enters the community, but stressing that marital relations must remain within the law as understood by the community. In relation to the latter, then, there are matters on which only the woman had competence to report in the context of a hearing, and she is to do so. It might be seen as a digression, to be dealing with marriage at this point, but it belonged closely together with the man's turning twenty.

It is, however, interesting that in both of the surviving fragments of the *Rule of the Congregation* in cryptic script, as reconstructed by Pfann, which preserve this section of column one, the reference to the woman's testimony appears to be absent. This may suggest, that, as with the expansions of the *Community Rule* in 1QS/1Q28, so too 1QSa/1Q28a preserves an expanded text.[67] Alternatively, in one instance we may be dealing with an omission by *homoioteleuton*. The texts are as follows.

4 ובן עש]רים [שנה
5 יעבר (9) על הפקודים לבוא בתוך משפחתו] בגור[ל בעדת
6 קודש (13) ובן שלושים שנה (14) יתיציב ברואשי]אלפי [ישראל

4 Then at the age of twe]nty [years] 5 [he shall be subject (9) to the census; he shall enter in the midst of his clan]by lo[t to be united with] 6 [the holy Congregation. (13) Then at the age of thirty (14) he may be promoted to take his place among the chiefs of the]Thousands of [Israel].

(4Qpap cryptA Serekh ha-'Edah[d]/4Q249d 4b-6; 1QSa/1Q28a numbering in brackets)

The omission in 4Q249d by *homoioteleuton* because of the repetition of the words עדת קודש (outlined below in the text of 1QSa/1Q28a near the end of 1.9,

[65] Rothstein, "Women's Testimony," 612-13 n. 68.

[66] Cf. Davies and Taylor, "Testimony of Women," 331-32.

[67] So Pfann, *DJD* 36, 34.

and at the end of 1.12 and the beginning of 1.13) looks possible.[68] It would imply that the text of 1QSa/1Q28a, given below, is older than 4Q249d, which Pfann dates to the first half of the second century BCE.[69]

ובנ[ן] עשרים שנ[ה יעבר]
9 [על] הפקודים לבוא בגורל בתוך משפ[ח]תו ליחד בעד[ת] קודש ולוא י[קרב]
10 אל אשה לדעתה למשכבי זכר כי אם לפי מילואת לו עש[רי]ם שנה בדעתו[טוב]
11 ורע ובכן תקבל להעיד עליו משפטות התורא ולהת[י]צב במשמע משפטים
12 ובמלוא בו *vacat* ובן חמש ועשרים שנה יבוא להת[יצ]ב ביסודות עדת
13 הקודש לעבוד את עבודת העדה ובן שלושים שנה יגש לריב ריב
14 ומ[ש]פט ולהתיצב ברואשי אלפי ישראל

Then, at a[ge] twenty, [he shall be enrolled] 9 [in] the ranks and take his place among the men of his clan, thereby joining *the holy congrega[tion.]* He must not app[roach] 10 a woman for sexual intercourse before he is fully tw[en]ty years old, when he knows [right] 11 from wrong. From this time on she shall bear witness concerning him in relation to the statutes of the Law, and (he shall) ta[k]e his place among the ranks for the ceremonial proclamation of the ordinances. 12 And when he completes his *blank* At age twenty-five, he is eligible to ta[ke] his place among the pillars of *the holy* 13 *congregation* and to begin serving the *congregation*. When he is thirty years old, he may begin to take part in le[g]al disputes. 14 Further, he is now eligible for command, whether of the thousands of Israel …
(*DSSEL* adapted) (1QSa/1Q28a 1.8-14)

Thus 4Q249d appears to lack the lines 10b-12 and so the statement about marriage, and then to continue with an abbreviated form of 13, referring to the age of thirty years. 4Q249e, of similar age, is different again.

6 ובן שנא[יעבר (9) על הפק]ודים
7a] [ליח]ד [
7 לבוא בג]ורל בתו[ך משפחתו בעד]ת קוד[ש
8a ולוא יקר]ב (10) לאשתו
8 ובן חמ]ש ועשרי]ם שנה יבוא להתיצב ב]יס[ודות

6 Then at the age of twenty[he shall be subject (9) to the cen]sus: 7 [he shall enter by l]ot in the mid[st of his clan] to exist in uni[ty as a]Hol[y Congreg]ation.[

---

[68] The proposal that *homoioteleuton* has taken place is slightly complicated by the fact that the words following the second occurrence of עדת קודש "holy congregation", namely לעבוד את עבודת העדה "and to begin serving the congregation" are also missing, but that may relate to the occurrence of the word, העדה "congregation".

[69] Pfann, *DJD* 36, 534.

8a [And he shall not approa]ch (10) his wife[
8 [Then at the age of]twenty-fi[ve he will come to take his place among the]foun[dations].
(4Qpap cryptA Serekh ha-'Edah[e]/4Q249e 6b-8; 1QSa/1Q28a numbering in brackets)

4Q249e contains additions written above the line (7a, 8a). Read without them, it, too, appears to lack reference to the subject matter of 1QSa/1Q28a 1.10-11, namely, of a man's approaching a woman, and of her testimony, and also to cut off, like 4Q249d, after עדת קודש, "holy congregation", but, instead of going straight to age thirty, it continues with what the young man is to do at age twenty-five in its line 8. There is however a significant addition above line 8, reconstructed by Stephen Pfann as ולוא יקר]ב לאשתו "and he shall not approach his wife" (8a). He sees in these words, a reference not to marrying at age twenty, approaching a woman (1QSa/1Q28a has אשה not אשתו "his wife"), but to the beginning of a man's celibacy, suggesting that the modification in 1QSa/1Q28a expands the prohibition along the same lines to the effect of forbidding a man to approach any woman in the community.[70] To do so he must read כי אם not in its usual sense of "until" but as the equivalent of כי on its own, thus: "because, since". Hence, instead of "he shall not approach a woman ... until he is twenty years of age", he reads "he shall not approach a woman ... since he is twenty years of age". He also suggests that this requirement of celibacy reflects the view that "the genderless nature of the heavenly realm is jeopardized if the human priestly element engages in marital relations",[71] an assumption without support in the text, and argues that a woman's complaint against her husband would not make sense.

Leaving aside the issue of whether 1QSa/1Q28a represents an expanded version, or, as the *homoioteleuton* noted above might suggest, the earlier one, we might wonder whether it is credible that such a community would find the need to extend the prohibition to apply to sexual approaches to any woman and whether כי אם need mean anything other than "until" in the context. It is also not clear to me why the text would make no sense in requiring a woman to report on her husband in relation to sexual matters.

Assuming that before ב לאשתו, we read ולוא יקר, and that no words which followed qualified the statement significantly, we would have in 4Q249e a prohibition of a man having intercourse with his wife. At twenty he would be required to commence celibacy. This assumes he would have already been married, only for a very short time, but long enough to begin a family. One wonders whether this is really credible. If it were, it would be important evidence for the practice of celibacy which secondary sources attribute to some Essenes, but

---

[70] Pfann, *DJD* 36, 559.

[71] Pfann, *DJD* 36, 559.

would reflect a two stage process: marriage before twenty, sufficiently long before to produce children, then entry into celibacy at twenty. The closest parallel is in the account in the *History of the Rechabites*, which reports that among those on the island of bliss some marry, have intercourse only once, thereby produce twins, and thereafter remain celibate for the rest of their lives (11:6-8), but the parallel is remote.

4Q249e is, however, very fragmentary, and need not be read in this way. An alternative explanation may be that after לאשתו we read something like לזנות, "for sexual wrongdoing", as in 4QD^{e}/4Q270 7 i.12-13; 4QD^{b}/4Q267 9 vi.4-5, which reads ואשר יקרב לזנות לאשתו "and whoever approaches his wife for illicit sexual intercourse" (discussed on pp. 172-74 above). This would then simply be a variant way of expressing the same concern as in the more likely reading of 1QSa/1Q28a, namely that the young man not engage in sexual intercourse with his wife in illicit ways. One might speculate that 4Q249e could have begun with a defective text as apparently 4Q249d, and that a scribe, aware of the fuller text, supplemented it above line 8 with what was the original concern in the omitted lines, namely proper sexual relations in marriage.

After the long section on the life stages of a man from childhood to old age under the heading of the army of the congregation (1.6-25a), the document addresses preparation for a convocation. The members of the congregation are to sanctify themselves for three days before the convocation (1.26-27). This recalls Exod 19:13, which explicitly includes abstinence from sexual intercourse for the three days before the Lord appears at Sinai. Such abstinence is probably also to be assumed here, unless we assume the community was permanently celibate. Concern with purity also finds expression in the restriction on who may come to such a gathering. Excluded are all with deformities, but also any man "defiled by any of the impurities of a man".

> וכול איש מנוגע באחת מכול טמאו[ת] 4 האדם אל יבוא בקהל אלה
>
> and any man afflicted by any of the impurities of a man shall not enter the assembly of these.* (2.3b-4a) (cf. 1QM/1Q33 7.4b-5a)

These impurities probably include impurity caused through seminal emission, whether through intercourse (if practised) which we assume was forbidden in any case over the three days, or through nocturnal and other emissions. 11QT^{a}/11Q19 45.7-8 requires a three day period of purification for those with a seminal emission before entering the temple. The impurities might also include other discharges. Olyan notes that the formulation in 2.3-10 stands under the influence of Deut 23:2-9, especially 23:2. He suggests that the reference to male emissions was probably influenced by the reference to the crushed penis in 23:2.[72] The use of אדם (4) rather than זכר or איש is probably because of the contrast with the angels, for "the angels of holiness are in the midst of the congregation" (2.8-9). Presumably, equivalent restrictions would apply also to women. The reference to the presence of angels in 2.8-9 probably derives from either Num 5:3b or Deut 23:15.[73]

Restrictions on entry can apply to the temple, but also apply to the assembly (קהל) and to Israel – as *4QMMT* interprets Deut 23:1. Unlike *4QMMT* and 4QFlor 1-2 3-4 (which also mentions the presence of the holy angels as a rationale), 1QSa/1Q28a does not follow Deuteronomy 23 when it goes on to speak of *mamzerim* and non-Israelites, whom *4QMMT* excludes absolutely, especially by marriage. Instead, it picks up Lev 21:16-23, originally addressing the issue of priests excluded from practising, and uses it to create a list of people with blemishes (2.5-6; similarly 1QM/1Q33 7.4b-5a; CD 15.15-17; $4QD^a$/4Q266 8 i.7-9). The rule therefore applies to its convocation a combination of restrictions derived from the approach to Sinai (Exod 19:13), belonging to the congregation (קהל) of Israel (Deut 23:2); and participating in the temple as priests (Lev 21:16-23).[74] While not directly describing the convocation as such, it effectively has the status of the sanctuary. This means at the same time that we need to recognise in the document a distinction between the community and its special convocation for which special exclusions and preparations applied.[75]

The *Rule of the Congregation* preserves for us a window onto a community which included men and women, assumed marital relations, and affirmed sexual intercourse, while insisting it should be monitored so that a wife should report any wrongful sexual intercourse. The manuscripts which lack these provisions may preserve earlier versions or in one case be the result of *homoioteleuton*. 4Q249e can be read as requiring that at twenty years of age married men begin a life of celibacy, but this is unlikely. Beyond that, the document operated with a system of purity applied to special gatherings which were deemed special because of the presence of angels and for which one needed three days' consecration, probably including abstinence from intercourse after the model of Exodus 19. It constituted its assembly as the equivalent of the temple for which restrictions applied, including exclusions of people with deformities and men who had been rendered unclean by seminal emission (and by extension, doubtless also women in a state of impurity). Nothing in this indicates a negative attitude towards sexuality, but only

---

[72] Olyan, "Exegetical Dimensions," 43-44.

[73] Olyan, "Exegetical Dimensions," 45.

[74] See the discussion of 1QM/1Q33 and 4QFlor/4Q174, pp. 211-12, 269-70 below.

[75] On this see Aharon Shemesh, "'The Holy Angels are in their Council': The Exclusion of Deformed Persons from Holy Places in Qumranic and Rabbinic Literature," *DSD* 4 (1997) 179-206, 201-202.

that sexual relations were appropriate in the appropriate place and time and not otherwise. Any expansion of what constituted inappropriate place or time would impinge on sexual relations, as would any notion that the ultimately desirable place and time would be so sacred as to exclude sexual relations altogether, but nothing like this is indicated in the text. If we assume an allusion to celibacy, then the document would reflect a community in which people married and presumably lived in families and bore children, but then abstained from intercourse from age twenty.

3 The *War Scroll* 1QM/1Q33 4QM^{a-e}/4Q491-495; 4QpapM^{f}/4Q496

The absence of themes of sectarian conflict from both the *Rule of the Congregation* and from the *War Scroll* may indicate that they were composed long after such conflicts or before they became acute, more probably the latter.

The *War Scroll* contains little material pertinent to issues of sexuality. Where it comes to expression, the issue is purity rather than morality. We see this in 7.3b-7, which has a parallel in 4QM^{a}/4Q491 1-3. The column begins by specifying ages of those who are to be in the army (7.1-3a) in a way that recalls the prescriptions of what a man might do at various ages in relation to the army in 1QSa/1Q28a 1.6-25a, though differing substantially from the latter. It then states:

וכול נער זעטוט ואשה לוא יבואו למחנותם בצאתם
4 מירושלים ללכת למלחמה עד שובם

And no youth or woman shall enter their camp when they go out
4 from Jerusalem to go to battle until they return.* (7.3b-4a)

4QM^{a}/491 1-3 6 also includes ואשה ונער זעטוט "and a woman and a youth" in its list of those who are not to join with the army when it goes to battle. In relation to boys the reason will be about maturity. In relation to women it has most likely to do with the possibility that they might bring impurity into the camp through menstruation. It will also be related to the impurity brought through seminal emission in sexual intercourse.[76] The focus on male seminal emission is also present in what follows:

---

[76] White Crawford, "Not according to Rule," 136. See also Bernstein, "Women and Children," who speaks of "a level of purity in the camp which women and children were presumed not to be able to attain and maintain" (209).

וכול פסח או עוד או חגר או איש אשר מום עולם בבשרו או איש מנוגע בטמאת
5 בשרו כול אלה לוא ילכו אתם למלחמה

and any lame or blind or crippled person or a man with a permanent blemish in his flesh or a man afflicted by impurity
5 in his flesh, all these shall not proceed with them to battle.* (7.4b-5a)

The list is similar to the one in 1QSa/1Q28a 2.3-9, which also includes male impurity (similarly doubly emphasised; 1.26; 2.3-4; cf. 1QM/1Q33 7.4-5, and 6) as well as impairments (more extensively). There we find the exclusion expressed as, כול איש מנוגע באחת מכול טמאו[ה] האדם "any man afflicted by any of the impurities of a man", which is similar to the words איש מנוגע בטמאת בשרו "a man afflicted with impurity in his flesh", here in 1QM/1Q33. The list of impairments is also similar to that found in CD 15.15-17 (4QD^{a}/4Q266 8 i.7-9), which identifies who may not enter the congregation, but only in terms of impairments: "But no one who is a fool or insane may enter; and no simpleton or ignoramus or one with eyes too weak to see or lame or crippled (וחגר או פסח) or deaf or youth (נער זעטוט)". The inclusion of the under-age young (man?) person is shared with 1QM/1Q33. All three passages also share the same rationale: the presence of angels (1QM/1Q33 7.6; 1QSa/1Q28a 2.8b-9a; CD 15.17; 4QD^{a}/4Q266 8 i.9). The presence of angels also motivates such exclusion elsewhere (4QFlor/4Q174 1-2 i.3-5; cf. also *4QMMT* B 39-49; 11QT^{a}/11Q19 45.12-14).[77] It is also a way of expressing divine presence, recalling Deut 20:1, 4; 23:14, which speak of God being with the army.

The categories of impairment are drawn from the list in Lev 21:16-23, which deals with impediments to entering the priesthood. See also 2 Sam 5:8 which speaks of excluding the blind and the lame.[78] The overall framework of exclusion from the congregation is provided by Deuteronomy 23, especially 23:2. The passage in 1QM/1Q33 continues by stating that, conversely, they are all to be תמימי רוח ובשר "perfect in spirit and flesh/body" (7.5b). Clearly neither spirit nor flesh is something evil in itself.

The version in 4QM^{a}/4Q491 is more concise:

] ואשה ונער זעטוט וכול איש מנו[גע בטמאת בשרו]
7 המער]כה

and a woman and a youth and every man aff[ected by impurity in his flesh shall not

---

[77] On this see Shemesh, "Holy Angels," 179-206; Joseph A. Fitzmyer, "A Feature of Qumran Angelology and the Angels of 1 Cor 11:10," in Joseph A. Fitzmyer, *Essays on the Semitic Background of the New Testament* (SBLSBS 5; Missoula: Scholars, 1974) 187-204, 198-200.

[78] On the biblical texts influencing these passages see Olyan, "Exegetical Dimensions," 46-47, 49 and Shemesh, "Holy Angels," 193-97.

come near to the battle] line.* (1-3 6b-7a)

It lacks reference to the impaired, thus juxtaposing the mention of women and of men with impurity, but then adds categories not included in 1QM/1Q33.

ואנשי החרש [וה]מ[צ]רף ופקודים להיות אנ[שי ...]...

and the smiths [and the] sm[el]ters, and those enlisted to be [...].* (1-3 7)

The rationale here may well have to do not with purity, but with practical necessity, since these are vital to sustain weaponry.[79] 1QM/1Q33 (but not 4QM[a]/4Q491) then returns to male impurity and in doing so follows Deuteronomy 23, which addresses the issue of male impurity and the camp of the army.

וכול 6 איש אשר לוא יהיה טהור ממקורו ביום המלחמה לוא ירד אתם כיא מלאכי קודש עם צבאותם יחד

and any 6 man who is not clean from his "spring" on the day of battle shall not go down with them because the angels of holiness are together with their armies.* (7.5b-6)

Deut 23:9-10 stipulates that a man who has had a nocturnal emission is to be excluded from the camp of the army until he has undergone purification when he may return after sunset. Our passage mentions only the exclusion, not the return, because it deals with the day of battle.

The passage follows the sequence of Deuteronomy 23 also in moving to deal with toileting. Deut 23:12-14 requires people go outside the camp of the army with a trowel to a designated area in order to micturate and defecate, emphasising that no nakedness is to be exposed in God's sight. 1QM/1Q33 7.7 identifes this as "the place of the hand" (מקום היד) and stipulates a distance of two thousand cubits from the camp (also in the shorter version in 4QM[a]/4Q491 1-3 7-8). This recalls the provisions in the *Temple Scroll* which also speaks of מקום היד "the place of the hand", but specifies a distance of three thousand cubits (46.13-15). The stipulations conclude with the words

וכול ערות דבר רע לוא יראה סביבות כול מהניהם

and no immodest nakedness shall be seen in the surrounds of any of their camps. (*DSSSE*) (7.7)

---

[79] Jean Duhaime, *The War Texts: 1QM and Related Manuscripts* (London: T&T Clark, 2004) notes, that "these similarities and differences are better explained if two scribes are using a common source; the purity requirements are interpreted in a practical way in 4QM[a/b], whereas they apparently receive a sharper and more extended application in 1QM" (52).

וכול] 8 ערות לוא יראה סביבותיהמ[ה]

and nakedness is not to be seen in their surrounds.* (4QM^{a}/4Q491 1-3 7b-8a)

1QM/1Q33 10.1 also warns: ל[ה]שמר מכול ערות דבר רע "to keep ourselves from all immodest nakedness". The expression ערות דבר רע "immodest nakedness" describes inappropriate nakedness, which is therefore bad (רע). It does not imply that the naked human body in itself is bad. The issue of nakedness is about relations with others. It is therefore closely related to shame and modesty. Shame is not guilt, but a sense of something being out of place in the presence of others and therefore to be covered up. The word, ערות, carries both aspects of meaning: "nakedness", and response to nakedness in the presence of others, "shame". Here in 1QM/1Q33 two aspects play a role: nakedness, which should be avoided in the presence of others generally, but above all nakedness in places where God is especially present. The latter is both likely to be assumed because it is expressed directly in Deut 23:12-14, but also because the preceding lines of the column have emphasised the presence of the holy angels in the camp.

The *War Scroll* applies to the battle camp restrictions which originated in concern with the temple. Deuteronomy 23 provides some precedent for this in its requirements about toileting and concerns with nakedness. The author has taken the earlier section of Deuteronomy 23, concerned with who may enter the people of God, combined it with restrictions about entering the priesthood, as did the author of 1QSa/1Q28a, and applied it to the camp of the army. The rationale for prohibiting nakedness is exposure before God. The rationale for excluding those impaired and, with emphasis, those who are unclean through seminal emission (and women), is that angels are present.

This explanation is given elsewhere for excluding such people from the congregation when it is gathered and treated as the equivalent of the temple. Here in the *War Scroll* the focus is not the community as a temple, but the army and this appears to be an extension of Deuteronomy 23. It is a matter of being in a state of purity when engaging in battle. All people with seminal emission are excluded, and so also all sexual intercourse is forbidden. Deut 20:7 requires that a man "engaged to a woman but not yet married her" not join the battle.[80]

The notion that particular occasions such as battle and not only particular spaces like the temple and Sinai, require, by implication, sexual abstinence, need not imply that sexual relations at other times and places are inappropriate. In that sense the *War Scroll* is simply applying what was already implicit in the biblical tradition. On the other hand, any association between greater divine presence and

[80] David E. Aune, *Revelation* (3 vols; WBC 52; Nashville: Thomas Nelson, 1998) 2.820-21, points to Dio Cassius 60.24.3 as saying that law prevented men from marrying during military service.

greater abstinence from sexual relations has the potential to equate engagement in the latter as in some sense an act which greater proximity to God might call into question. It need not, however, do so. Finally, the dualism of light and darkness assumed throughout the work finds parallels in contexts where the battleground is the human person and where the conflict is strongly ethical. In the *War Scroll* the latter elements do not feature and so any potential relevance of sexuality as an arena of conflict is absent.

4 Other Legal Texts

4.1 11QSefer ha-Milḥamah/11Q14 // 4QSefer ha-Milḥamah/4Q285

Related to the War Scroll, either as a further revision or, as some conjecture, part of its lost ending,[81] the document preserved in 11QSefer ha-Milḥamah/11Q14 // 4QSefer ha-Milḥamah/4Q285 appears to promise a time of blessing after the great victory. There will be abundant harvest and freedom from sickness, disease, drought, blight, and miscarriage, and from wild animals and plague (11QSefer ha-Milḥamah/11Q14 1 ii.7-14a // 4QSefer ha-Milḥamah/4Q285 8 8). The document then explains that this will be so:

כיא אל עמכם ומלאכי
15 [קודשו מתיצבי]ם בעדתכם ושם קודשו נקרא עליכם

> For God is with you and the angels
> 15 [of his holiness are stand]ing in your congregation and his holy name is invoked over you. (11QSefer ha-Milḥamah/11Q14 1 ii.14b base text; 4QSefer ha-Milḥamah/4Q285 8 10-11 outlined)

The reference to miscarriage in 11 // 8 ואין משכלה "and no woman shall miscarry in your land" cites Exod 23:26 לא תהיה משכלה ועקרה בארצך "No one shall miscarry or be barren in your land". The text assumes that the normal processes of marriage, sexual intercourse and procreation, belong to the people's blessed future. It is interesting that here the presence of God and the angels is used to ground not temporary abstinence from sexual relations, but fruitful sexual relations.

[81] See the discussion in Duhaime, *War Texts*, 31-35.

4.2 *4QOrdinances[a]* 4QOrd[a]/4Q159

Fragments 2-4+8 of this document contain legal material.[82] It begins with the prohibition of selling an Israelite as a slave (1-3a, based on Lev 25:47-55),[83] and moves to judgement before a court of twelve (3b-6a; based on Deut 17:8-13). This assumes a form of the sectarian organisation, here of twelve men, including two priests (cf. CD 10.4-5, ten men, six from Israel, four from Levi; similarly 13.1; 1QS/1Q28 6.3 has 10). The passage then brings a prohibition of cross-dressing (6b-7; based on Deut 22:5) and an exposition of the law concerning complaints about a bride's virginity (8-l0a; based on Deut 22:13-21). These latter two themes occur in the same order in 4QD[f]/4Q271 (3 3b-4, 12b-15),[84] though at the beginning and end of a passage dealing with fraud in commercial transactions and in offering one's daughter in marriage, inappropriate mixed marriages, and women whom a man should not marry (4QD[f]/4Q271 3 5-12a). While both passages indicate a similar set of concerns based on exposition of biblical law, at least in the case of a wife's virginity the approach differs.

We begin first with the prohibition against cross-dressing. The allusion to the theme in 4QD[f]/4Q271 is so fragmentary that little can be discerned beyond the probable reference to Deut 22:5 as part of the exposition of the themes of Deuteronomy 22.[85] In 4QOrd[a]/4Q159 the passage reads:

---

[82] I follow the reconstruction of Moshe J. Bernstein in *DSSEL*, according to which the sequence of fragments is 1+9; 5; 2-4+8; 6; 7. On the placement of fr. 5 see Moshe J. Bernstein, "4Q159 Fragment 5 and the 'Desert Theology' of the Qumran Sect," in *Emanuel: Studies in Hebrew Bible, Septuagint, and Dead Sea Scrolls in Honor of Emanuel Tov* (ed. Shalom M. Paul, Robert A. Kraft, Lawrence H. Schiffman, and Weston W. Fields; VTSup 94; Leiden: Brill, 2003) 43-56.

[83] Francis Weinert, "4Q159: Legislation for an Essene Community Outside of Qumran?" *JSJ* 5 (1974) 179-207, raised the question whether the document can be from the Qumran community which forbad contact with Gentiles and whether cross-dressing and marriage issues would be relevant, suggesting the document is more like CD and not from Qumran itself (205-206). The document does not reflect typical sectarian language and most likely stems from early legal interpretation.

[84] See Baumgarten, *DJD* 18, 176 and the discussion in Hempel, "4QOrd[a] (4Q159)," who argues that the parallels in theme and sequence may be more extensive. She notes the standardisation of the bath and ephah based on Ezek 45:11 in 4QOrd[a]/4Q159 1 ii + 9 13 and 4QD[f]/4Q271 2, and the concern with poverty as a common factor in relation to selling an Israelite as a slave in 4QOrd[a]/4Q159 2-4+8 1-3a and 4QD[f]/4Q271 3.2, which deals with an impoverished Israelite. Both passages are based on Leviticus 25 (373), and both collections of laws move from Leviticus 25 to Deuteronomy 22 (375).

[85] See Baumgarten *DJD* 18, 175.

אל יהיו כלי גבר על אשה כול [וגבר אל]
7 יכס בשלמות אשה ואל ילבש כתונ[ת] אשה כיא [ת]ועבה היא

> Let there not be the clothes of a man on a woman. Any [and let a man not] put on a woman's cloak, and let him not wear a woman's tun[ic], for it is an abomination.* (2-4+8 6-7)

This is an expansion of Deut 22:5 by the addition of reference to the tunic.

לא יהיה כלי גבר על אשה
ולא ילבש גבר שמלת אשה
כי תועבת יהוה אלהיך כל עשה אלה

> The clothes of a man shall not be on a woman
> and a man shall not put on a woman's mantle,
> for it is an abomination before the Lord your God, anyone doing these things.
> (Deut 22:5).

Like 4QD[f]/4Q271, 4QOrd[a]/4Q159 follows the sequence of Deuteronomy 22, but unlike the former, passes over the concerns in Deut 22:9-11 about mixing, and moves directly to the theme of 22:13-21, slandering a virgin, which it briefly summarises:

8 כי יוצי איש שם רע על בתולת ישר[א]ל
אם ב[יום] קחתו אותה יואמר ובקרוה [נשים]
9 נאמנות ואם לוא כחש עליה והומתה
ואם בש[קר] ענה בה ונענש שני מנים [ואת אשתו לוא]
10 ישלח כול ימיו

> 8 Should a man malign an Isra[e]lite virgin,
> if on th[e day] of his taking her he says (it), then [women][86] shall examine her who are
> 9 reliable. If he has not lied regarding her, then she shall be put to death,
> but if he has testified against her fals[ely], he shall be fined two minas [and his wife] he shall [not]
> 10 divorce all of his days. (4Q159/4QOrd[a] 2-4+8 8-10)

This differs in some respects from both Deut 22:13-21 and 4QD[f]/4Q271 3 12b-15. The former deals with the matter in reverse order: false slander (22:13-19) and valid complaint (22:20-21), whereas 4QOrd[a]/4Q159 begins with the valid charge and then moves to the false charge. Deut 22:15-17 makes provision for the parents of the bride to bring evidence of their daughter's virginity to the elders who are hearing the complaint, namely blood-stained cloth. Neither 4QOrd[a]/

---

[86] **נשים** was conjectured by J. H. Tigay, "Examination of the Accused Bride in 4Q159: Forensic Medicine at Qumran," *JANES* 22 (1993) 129-34, before knowledge of the corroborating parallel in 4QD[f]/4Q271.

4Q159 nor 4QD[f]/4Q271 mentions this provision. Instead they provide for an examination to take place through trustworthy women (נשים נאמנות). They differ from each other with regard to when this examination takes place. In 4QD[f]/4Q271 the examination by the women takes place not in response to a husband's complaint nor after they have had sexual intercourse, but before they come together and because the woman has a reputation which raises questions over her virginity. The examination envisaged probably entailed physical examination on the widespread (and erroneous) assumption that a ruptured hymen necessarily indicated prior intercourse.[87] The women here and in 4QD[f]/4Q271 may be assumed to have been midwives, who had both the required expertise and the reputation of being competent and reliable witnesses in their field.[88]

Here in 4QOrd[a]/4Q159, however, we are dealing with the situation envisaged in Deut 22:13-21, namely complaint by the husband after consummation of the marriage. In this circumstance a physical examination might seem (on the basis of the assumptions of the time) to be able to contribute little to determining whether the woman had been a virgin, because, at least on the basis of their assumptions, the hymen would have ruptured at the consummation of the marriage. One might then suppose that the author of this passage knew both procedures (finding the cloth and examining the woman)[89] and chose the second without realising that it was ill-fitting. Or one could argue that the examination envisaged here was not physical, but rather consisted of interviewing the woman[90] (and perhaps her

---

[87] See the discussion of this passage on pp. 161-62 above.

[88] So Wassen, *Women*, who notes that אמן is used elsewhere of reliable witnesses (CD 9.21-23; 10.1-2) and that women's testimony is also assumed as trustworthy in 1QSa/1Q28a 1.11 (87-88).

[89] Cf. Wassen, *Women*, who, without drawing this conclusion, argues that the presence of the same word in both documents is striking and "presupposes literary or oral dependency" (84). See also Hempel, "4QOrd[a] (4Q159)," who writes: "It seems likely to me that the redactor/compiler responsible for the Laws of the Damascus Document in their present form drew upon a collection of traditional legal material not dissimilar to 4QOrdinances[a]" (376). She notes the similarities between the two identified by Baumgarten ("headings of the form 'Concerning x' (על plus x)", "use of clauses of the type אל plus jussive plus איש" and replacement of לא by אל in interpreting Deut 22:5 (375-76). See Joseph M. Baumgarten, "The Laws of the *Damascus Document* in Current Research," in *The Damascus Document Reconsidered* (ed. Magen Broshi; Jerusalem: Israel Exploration Society, The Shrine of the Book, Israel Museum, 1992) 51-62, 56; Baumgarten, *DJD* 18, 13. Hempel writes: "4Q159 does not reflect a particular organized community and frequently uses all-Israel terminology" and referring also to 4QD[f]/4Q271: "There is little evidence in either collection of laws warranting an association with a community that had separated from society at large" (376).

[90] Lawrence H. Schiffman, *PTSDSSP* 1, notes that one tanna saw it like that, but that most saw it as "examination of witnesses by the court to determine if an accident might

parents, though they go unmentioned). The notion that a physical examination would have no point is, however, not necessarily correct. The assumption of such an examination would have been the widespread (and fallacious) belief that at first intercourse the hymen would rupture. The examination after marital sexual intercourse would then be to detect evidence of a recent (fresh) rupture or injury, on the basis that if the hymen was recently injured it indicated recent loss of virginity rather than previous loss of virginity. Consultation with specialists in the field[91] has confirmed that where a sizeable recent rupture or tear of the hymen might have taken place, it would usually be possible to detect it within the next few days. This would then have enabled the examiners to conclude, on the basis of the medical assumptions of their time, that the woman would have been a virgin before the consummation of the marriage.[92]

The absence in the passage of mention of the cloth as evidence may reflect some awareness of the possibility of forgery.[93] Within the framework of knowledge of the time, one would have understood a physical examination to have been a more secure method. In her review of the evidence for how people understood the matter in ancient sources, Wassen notes that "the existence of the hymen was common knowledge in antiquity", attested to in both Greco-Roman literature and Jewish texts.[94] The focus on the rupture of the hymen also led to some awareness that this might have been occasioned by physical damage or injury of some kind other than sexual penetration (*m. Ket.* 1.1-7), and also that not all women bled at their first sexual intercourse (*b. Ket.* 10 a-b; *y. Ket.* 1.1, 25a). She also observes that such examination by midwives was opposed by Augustine,

---

have resulted in the loss of the physical signs of virginity or if testimony that she was not a virgin might exist" (157 n. 44). See also his "Laws Pertaining to Women," 221.

[91] I acknowledge the assistance of Rosemary Hudson Miller and Margaret Gleeson, experienced midwives, and Dr Maureen Philips, Co-ordinator, Medical/Forensic Services, of the Sexual Assault Referral Centre in Perth, who also referred me to relevant literature: Jeffrey S. Jones, Linda Rossman, Melissa Hartman, and Carmen C. Alexander, "Anogenital Injuries in Adolescents after Consensual Sexual Intercourse," *Acad Emerg Med* 10, 12 (2003) 1378-1383; and C. Lincoln, "Genital Injury: Is it Significant?" *MedSciLaw* 41.3 (July, 2001) 206-16. See, too, the discussion in Tigay, "Examination," 132-33, who also alludes to later rabbinic discussion and also practices in comparable cultures in recent centuries (82-84).

[92] Wassen, *Women*, 83, rightly points out the fallibility of such assumptions, but appears to reject the possibility that those conducting the examination might have believed that detection of a recently ruptured hymen would be evidence *for them* that the woman had been a virgin. Cf. Tigay, "Examination," 133; Shemesh, "4Q271.3," 254. On physical examination for virginity in the ancient world, see Wassen, *Women*, 85-88.

[93] On this possibility see Tigay, "Examination," 129-30.

[94] Wassen, *Women*, 85

Ambrose and Cyprian, although it is assumed in the *Protoevangelium of James* where Salome's inspection "confirms" Mary's abiding virginity (19-20).[95]

The man's fine is expressed as two minas in 4QOrd[a]/4Q159, which 1 ii +2 9 enables us to equate with the one hundred shekels of Deut 22:19, since it identifies 25 shekels as half a mina. In the reconstruction of Bernstein the final statement reads: ואת אשתו לוא 10 ישלח כול ימיו "and his wife he shall [not] divorce all of his days" (as Deut 22:19, ולו תהיה לאשה לא יוכל לשלחה כל ימיו "She shall remain his wife; he shall not be permitted to divorce her as long as he lives"). It assumes acceptance of divorce as part of normal life.

According to Brin, however, ישלח is to be read as a *pu'al*, "he shall be sent away", referring to the exclusion of the man from the community, effectively a divorce which leaves the woman in the community.[96] He argues for this on the basis of a missing direct object in the preserved text and points to the similar exclusions in CD 20.3-4; and 1QS/1Q28 8.21-23; 7.16-17; 4QS[g]/4Q261 4.2 (see also 4QD[e]/4Q270 7 i.12-13; 4QD[b]/4Q267 9 vi.4-5). This would then account for the presence of women divorced from their husbands in the community, but neither reading is certain.

There may be one further aspect of the document which pertains to issues of sexuality. According to Bernstein, 4QOrd[a]/4Q159 5 follows 1+9 and, in its interpretation (פשר) of an unidentifiable text, alludes to Exod 33:7 and to the response to the incident with the golden calf, which he suggests is preserved in 1.16-17.[97] In 5 2-3 it refers to punishment meted out by the sons of Levi (Exod 32:26-29) for the idolatry and revelry. According to Bernstein, the author of 4QOrd[a]/4Q159 apparently alludes to the withdrawal of his community from the camp(=Jerusalem) on account of perverse behaviour.[98] The context does not allow us to identify what kind of perversity the idolatrous eating and drinking and revelry would represent in his contemporary context. The emphases in *4QMMT* and D would prompt us to conclude that it included sexual wrongdoing (as Paul thought, 1 Cor 10:7-8), but that is not preserved here.

The two main elements preserved in 4QOrd[a]/4Q159 which are relevant to our theme consist of expositions of biblical law, similar to the legal material in D.

---

95 See Wassen, *Women*, 86.

96 Brin, "Divorce at Qumran," 240-42. In this he follows John Allegro, *DJD* 5, 6-8.

97 Bernstein, "4Q159 Fragment 5," 45-48. See earlier Joseph M. Baumgarten, "Scripture and Law in 4Q265," in *Biblical Perspectives: Early Use and Interpretation of the Bible in Light of the Dead Sea Scrolls: Proceedings of the First International Symposium of the Orion Center for the Study of the Dead Sea Scrolls and Associated Literature, 12-14 May 1996* (ed. Michael E. Stone and Esther G. Chazon; STDJ 28; Leiden: Brill, 1998) 25-33, who identified allusions to the golden calf episode in fragments 1 and 5 (29-30); similarly Baumgarten, *DJD* 35, 59.

98 Bernstein, "4Q159 Fragment 5," 54-56.

They are the prohibition of cross-dressing, a slight elaboration of an existing law, and an exposition of the law about slandering a virgin. The latter has changed the basis of evidence from display of bloodstained cloth to physical examination, which must assume it would be possible to determine whether the hymen had just been ruptured. If there is a progression of thought between this procedure and its relocation to before the wedding, as in 4QD[f]/4Q271, we may assume that this latter development took place both because it would be easier and because it would prevent the possibility of a man having intercourse unwittingly with an immoral woman.

The exposition also reveals that women, at least for a defined task, were treated as reliable witnesses, and that divorce was considered a normal part of life whether as something forbidden for the man to enact or as something imposed on him by his expulsion from the community to which his wife continued to belong and in which, one must assume, she would have been eligible for remarriage.

4.3 *4QOrdinances[b]* 4QOrd[b]/4Q513

In this related set of fragments (fragments 1-2 appear to relate to 4QOrd[a]/4Q159 1 ii), which appear to derive from a separate document,[99] there are references whose context seems irrecoverable, but which have potential relevance to issues of sexuality. In 2 ii there is reference in the context of impurity to sexual wrongdoing:

בעלות לבני הנכר ולכול הזנות אשר

> mistresses/wives for sons of foreigners and all the acts of sexual wrongdoing which… (2 ii.2)

The word, בעלות, could refer to wives or to women who usually as wives exercise authority over some in the household. The English word, "mistress", used in WAC, carries sexual connotations, often used to designate the female partner in an adulterous relationship. It is not evident that בעלה was used at the time in that sense. The reference appears to be to women who are in a marriage relationship with foreigners, probably best understood as Jewish women becoming wives of foreigners.[100] The association with הזנות indicates obvious disapproval and corresponds to its use elsewhere to refer to illicit marriages with foreigners. The passage would then relate to the prohibition of intermarriage with other peoples, as

---

[99] So Schiffman, *PTSDSSP* 1, who writes that the overlapping material "is not an indication of identity; rather the same ordinance appears here in different recensions" (148).

[100] See already, M. Baillet, *DJD* 7, 289, but who also draws attention to the possibility that בעלות derives from עלה "to go up", for instance, in war.

set forth in Exod 34:15-16 and Deut 7:3-4, which is also a major theme in *Jubilees*.

The context, however, suggests that the concern here is the priesthood and priestly families. Thus the preceding and following lines allude to food, including food from offerings and to making atonement. This makes it probable that we are dealing with issues of illicit marriage and access to food. The concern does not appear to be priests marrying foreign wives, prohibited in Lev 21:7 and Ezek 44:22, because the focus is on Jewish women and Gentile men. Therefore Baumgarten interprets the passage as referring to the daughters of priests who profane their fathers by such sexual liaisons, forbidden in Lev 21:9 (see also Lev 22:12), which would then lead to the whole family being forbidden to eat *teruma* or touch pure food.[101] This might also explain the reference to food in the following line.

Baumgarten points to possible influence from Mal 2:11 which speaks of Judah committing an abomination, profaning the sanctuary by marrying the daughter of a foreign god, and to a parallel concern in *Jub.* 30:16, although both of these assume a concern wider than priesthood.[102] Kugler concurs with Baumgarten and notes that *Aramaic Levi Document* 6:3-4 / 16-17 has similar concerns in focussing on priests marrying outside their clan and uses זנות to describe such illicit relations.[103] Both here and there, however, the concern is not just clan but intermarriage with Gentiles. That document also shows concern about priests' daughters, but, as we have argued elsewhere, appears, like *Jubilees* 30, to have broadened that concern to include all daughters of Israel, using Dinah as the prime example. In doing so it has taken what in Lev 21:9 referred to the daughters of priests and prostitution, and applied it to all Israelite women, and expanded זנות (originally "to ply prostitution") to refer to all illicit sexual relations, especially forbidden intermarriage with Gentiles.[104]

Here in 4QOrd[b]/4Q513, however, the concern appears to be focused directly on priestly families and on priests offering their daughters in marriage to Gentiles. The focus on illicit sexual relations and their implication for food continues in line 5 in the expression, הזנות מאכליהם "their food is of sexual wrongdoing".[105] The

---

[101] Joseph M. Baumgarten, "Halakic Polemics in New Fragments from Qumran Cave 4," in *Biblical Archaeology Today* (ed. J. Amitai; Jerusalem: Israel Exploration Society, 1985) 390-99, 392-95; following him Schiffman, *PTSDSSP* 1, 147 and 159.

[102] On the significance of the version of Malachi found at Qumran, see Arndt Meinhold, "Zur Bedeutung von 4QXII[a] für Mal 2, 10-16," in *Der Freund des Menschen: Festschrift für Georg Christian Macholz* (ed. Arndt Meinhold and Angelika Berlejung; Neukirchen-Vluyn: Neukirchener Verlag, 2004) 93-105.

[103] Kugler, "Halakic Interpretative Strategies," 137.

[104] See Loader, *Enoch, Levi, and Jubilees*, 93-94.

[105] So Schiffman, *PTSDSSP* 1, 159 n. 14.

words which follow speak of sin (עוון) and defiling (החל), in some way also continuing the same theme.

It is possible that the theme of intermarriage of priests may also lie behind the fragmentary allusion to mingling in 10 ii 3 ([...] . [ו]אין לערב בם "[and] not to mingle with [...]").[106] 10 ii.6 then refers to pure food and 11 1 to eating and 11.3 to depravity (זמה). One might imagine that this could cohere with a forbidding of intermarriage, especially by priests, but the material is too fragmentary. This is even more so in the numerous other references to sin, impurity and defilement in the other fragments (13 3, 5; 22 2, 3, 4; 30 1; 36 1).

The surviving fragments allow us to detect some concern with illicit sexual relations, apparently in the context of concern with intermarriage with Gentiles, specifically of Jewish women, and more specifically, daughters of priests. Much of the language appears to reflect priestly themes, so that the frequent mention of food may relate to consecrated food and so to priestly families. The document is important evidence of a continuing concern with such intermarriage. Concern with permission to eat food set aside for priests and their families, and with intermarriage come to expression also in 4QHalakhah A/4Q251 (see pp. 224-25 below) and intermarriage with Gentiles by priests recurs as a theme also in the *Apocryphon of Jeremiah*, the *Testament of Qahat*, and the *Visions of Amram*, documents which do not appear to be sectarian. Both 4QOrd[b]/4Q513 and the related 4QOrd[a]/4Q159 appear to belong to legal material which does not reflect sectarian concerns, but applies to Israel as a whole, like much of the legal material incorporated into D.[107]

4.4 *4QOrdinances[c]* 4QOrd[c]/4Q514

In the surviving fragment the first readable word is אשה ("woman"), but its context is irrecoverable. The following lines speak of a man's abstinence from eating and of counting seven days. Despite the allusion to a "woman" the uncleanness referred to in the following lines is not to uncleanness from seminal emission, for which the *Temple Scroll*, for instance, requires three days (45.7-8), but gonorrhea discharge, which requires seven days for purification (Lev 15:13). It uses the same language as the *War Scroll* in referring to the need for a man to be purified "from his spring" (ממקרו) (1 i.4; cf. 1QM/1Q33 7.6; Lev 12:7; 20:18), a term repeated three lines later in the same context of concern with purification and

[106] Baumgarten, "Halakic Polemics," takes it as "referring to the prohibition of mixing of priestly and sacrificial meat" (392). See also Schiffman, *PTSDSSP* 1, 165 n. 34.

[107] Thus Schiffman, *PTSDSSP* 1: "No direct tie for 4QOrd[a] or 4QOrd[b] to the sectarian practices exists" (148).

eating (1 i.7). The issue is again eating, but related to concern with purifications before access to food.[108]

4.5 *4QHalakhah A* 4Q251

This document also contains legal material, but is very fragmentary. Fragments 1-2 contain laws pertaining to the sabbath. There we read:

6 [ ]החיל [ ]מיא נדה בש[ר]ו ביום [ה]שבת
7 [ ]בי[ו]ם חששי בשר ער[וה]

[ ] profane(d) [ ] impurity of his fle[sh] on the sabbath day.
7 [...] on the sixth d[a]y the flesh of naked[ness]. (*DSSEL* modified) (1-2 6-7)

If with Baumgarten[109] one reads מיא נדה as מי נדה, one might see here with a prohibition of sprinkling "the waters" (מי) of purification mixed with the ashes of the red cow on the sabbath, as in 4Q265 7 3 (and *m. Pes.* 6.2), but the spelling מיא is unparalleled in the Qumran corpus.[110] They note also however that the preferred reconstruction as suggested by Milik of taking מיא as belonging to some form of טמא ("to defile") presents the difficulty that נדה follows without a preposition (ב or ל).[111] This makes attempts to identify the content of what is being said very precarious. One among many possibilities could be that it refers to defilement through engaging in sexual intercourse on the sabbath, especially if the verbs

---

[108] For the understanding which sees here a reflection of the requirement that all food be eaten in a state of purity and thus that the access to food after ablution on the first day refers to ordinary food, see Milgrom, "First Day Ablutions in Qumran," 568-69; and Jacob Milgrom, "4QTohora[a]: An Unpublished Qumran Text on Purities," in *Time to Prepare the Way in the Wilderness: Papers on the Qumran Scrolls by Fellows of the Institute of Advanced Studies in the Hebrew University, Jerusalem, 1989-1990* (ed. Devorah Dimant and Lawrence H. Schiffman; STDJ 16; Leiden: Brill, 1995) 59-68; Schiffman, *PTSDSSP* 1, 177; cf. Joseph M. Baumgarten, "The Purification Rituals in DJD 7," in *The Dead Sea Scrolls: Forty Years of Research* (ed. D. Dimant and U. Rappaport; Jerusalem: Magnes Press, 1992) 199-209, 205 n. 10; E. P. Sanders, "The Dead Sea Sect and Other Jews: Commonalities, Overlaps and Differences," in *The Dead Sea Scrolls in Their Historical Context* (ed. Timothy H. Lim et al.; Edinburgh: T&T Clark, 2000) 7-43, 22-23.

[109] Baumgarten, *DJD* 35, 71; similarly Joseph M. Baumgarten, "Theological Elements in the Formulation of Qumran Law," in *Emanuel: Studies in Hebrew Bible, Septuagint, and Dead Sea Scrolls in Honor of Emanuel Tov* (ed. Shalom M. Paul, Robert A. Kraft, Lawrence H. Schiffman, and Weston W. Fields; VTSup 94; Leiden: Brill, 2003) 33-41, 34.

[110] E. Larson, M. R. Lehmann, and L. Schiffman, *DJD* 35, 29, 30. They also mention that a reference to "waters of purification" could be read as prohibiting use of a mikveh on the sabbath (cf. *m. Beṣah* 2.2 as a view of the School of Shammai) (30).

[111] Larson, Lehmann, Schiffman, *DJD* 35, 30.

imply a state which might have been avoided (unlike nocturnal emission, for instance). The reference in the following line to naked flesh and the sixth day might relate in some way to justifying abstinence from sexual intercourse on the basis of Gen 1:27, where male and female are created on the sixth day. Doering notes that Exod 28:42 uses the phrase בשר ערוה ("naked flesh" or "flesh of shame") to refer to the genitals and may indicate a reference here to prohibition of sexual intercourse on the sabbath,[112] though, with Baumgarten, he considers it more likely to refer to purification of the whole body before the sabbath (as in 4QpapRitPur B/4Q512 36-38 iii.17 and 2 Macc 12:38).[113] At most one can say that the passage relates to the sabbath and to the male body and addresses (intentional) impurity and something about its nakedness[114] in a way that assumes the need for attention to avoid a breach of the sabbath as holy time.[115]

Fragment 12 (formerly 7) contains a prohibition of eating the foetus of a pregnant animal, a prohibition preserved also in 11QT^{a}/11Q19 52.5 and *4QMMT* B 36. Fragment 16 (formerly 11) deals with some issue of marriage.

1 [ואישה כי תהיה לכוהן ואכל]ה את לחם אישה
2 [קנין כספו ויליד ביתו ה]ם יאכלו בלחמו רק זונה
3 [וחללה לוא יאכלו את לחם הקודש] [ו]כל המעל אשר ימעל
4 [איש] לאכול כי תועבה

1 [when a woman is married to a priest, she may ea]t the food of her husband
2 [one purchased by him and one born into his household the]se] may eat of his food. An immoral woman
3 [or a profaned woman may not eat of the sanctified food. And] any offense which [a person] shall commit
4 [ ] to eat, for [it] is an abomination. (*DSSEL* modified) (16 1-4)

---

[112] Doering, "Purity Regulations," 601.

[113] Doering, "Purity Regulations," 602; Baumgarten, "Theological Elements," 35. He sees a link to the language of the *Thanksgiving Hymns* which speaks of the creature of clay (x.22) and of the *Community Rule*, which speaks of a foundation of wicked flesh (11.9) (35). See also Baumgarten, *DJD* 35, 93. For other suggestions and reconstructions (clothing which covers priests' nakedness or circumcision) see Larson, Lehmann, Schiffman, *DJD* 35, 30-31.

[114] Baumgarten, "Theological Elements," notes the concern with nakedness also in 4QpapRitPur B/4Q512 11 4, where it relates to priestly vestments (35).

[115] Eibert J. C. Tigchelaar, "Sabbath Halakha and Worship in *4QWays of Righteousness: 4Q421* 11 and 13 + 2 + 8 par *4Q264a* 1-2," *RevQ* 18 (1998) 359-72, draws attention to substantial teaching on the sabbath over two columns and seventeen lines in *4QWays of Righteousness*, but unfortunately much has been lost, including any possible rulings pertaining to matters of sexuality.

The issue is about "the right of a woman married to a priest to eat of the holy offerings allotted to him".[116] This food, derived from the *teruma* offerings, is to be eaten by the whole household according to Lev 22:10-13. The ruling in this fragment clarifies that this includes the wife who joins the household, and also the purchased slave and one born in the household, but excludes the two categories of women whom Lev 21:7 forbids a priest to marry: זונה, which had come to mean any woman engaging in illicit sexual relations (not just a prostitute) and חללה, someone born from a forbidden sexual relation between a priest and a woman.[117] The words כל המעל אשר ימעל translated, "any offense which [a person] shall commit", may have a more specific meaning in the context of the marital relationship, such as "unfaithfulness", a meaning possibly implied in *4QMMT* C 4, 9 (cf. also CD 7.1). In the context it may imply unfaithfulness of a man over against his wife, but unfortunately the extant text does not preserve the words which follow.

Finally fragment 17 (formerly 12) includes reference to incest prohibitions.[118]

1 על העריות
2 אל יקח איש את א[שת אביו ולא יגלה כנף אביו לא יקח איש]
3 את בת אחיו ואת בת א[חותו אל יגלה]
4 איש את ערות אהות א[מו או אביו זמה היא ואשה לא תהיה לאחי]
5 אביה ולאחי אמה[ ]
6 אל יגל איש ערות[ ]
7 אל יקח איש בתו נ[ערה לאיש זר]

1 Regarding forbidden sexual unions[

2 A man may not marry the w[ife of his father, so as not to uncover his father's 'hem'. A man may not marry]

3 the daughter of his brother or the daughter of [his] si[ster] A man [may not expose

4 the nakedness of the sister of [his] mo[ther or his father; it is a depravity. And a woman may not marry the brother of]

5 her father or the brother of her mother[

6 A man may not expose the nakedness of [

116 Larson, Lehmann, Schiffman, *DJD* 35, 44.

117 Larson, Lehmann, Schiffman, *DJD* 35, 44; similarly Harrington, *Purity Texts*, 61.

118 Aharon Shemesh, "4Q251: Midrash Mishpatim," *DSD* 12 (2005) 280-302 argues that the scroll interprets Ex 21:1 – 23:19 (293-94), which he sees the author treating sequentially in fragments 3, 4-7, 13 (which he reads as addressing the accidental striking of a pregnant woman during a fight, Exod 21:22-25), and 8, dealing with Exod 21:19-30, and 9, 10, 12 dealing with Exod 22:27-30. He then sees 17 belonging between these two groups to the exposition of Exod 22:15, which also precedes the discussion of forbidden marriages in $11QT^a$/11Q19 66.12-17 (281, 283, 290). See also Schiffman, "Prohibited Marriages," 113-25.

7 A man may not marry his un[married] daughter [to a stranger.
(*DSSEL* modified) (17 1-7)

Its introduction, על העריות "Concerning nakednesses", is reminiscent of the headings with על used in CD 9.8b; 10.14, *4QMMT*, and 4QOrd^{a}/4Q159.[119] Here its context is incest, understood as uncovering the nakedness of forbidden partners. Two different formulations are used, one using אל יקח איש את "a man shall not take" (17 2, 7), based on Deut 22:1, and the other using אל יגל איש ערות "a man shall not uncover the nakedness of" (17 6, 4), based on Lev 18:7-17.[120] The first prohibition reproduces Deut 23:1 in forbidding marriage to one's father's wife, also cited in 11QT^{a}/11Q19 66.11-12. The second prohibition forbids marrying a niece. In doing so it goes beyond CD 5.10, which mentions only the daughter of a brother, to include also the daughter of a sister, as in 11QT^{a}/11Q19 66 16-17, which it matches in both form and content. The listing of this prohibition as the first after the prohibition of marrying the wife of one's father and before the other prohibitions may indicate that the author is seeking to give it the kind of priority which we find in CD 5.7b-11a. The prohibition which follows, forbidding marriage to one's aunt (the sister of one's father or mother) (17 4) is based on Lev 18:12-13 and 20:19 (similarly 11QT^{a}/11Q19 66.15). In 4-5 the author returns to the niece-uncle marriage, but now formulating it from the female starting point, thus forbidding a woman from marrying her uncle (whether the brother of her father or of her mother). This again emphasises this particular prohibition.

The final line apparently refers to a man taking a husband for his daughter. What it prohibits is not clear.[121] Some have argued that it refers to a man who is a priest and forbids his giving of his daughter to someone who is not a priest. Qimron/Strugnell see this concern expressed in *4QMMT* B 75-82. Baumgarten sees the issue there as more likely to be the marriage of any Israelite to a non-Jew and our own analysis above (pp. 65-75) supports this. That is also likely to be what is being forbidden here, but, again, the state of the text prevents certainty.

The one secure finding from the review of this fragmentary text is that it preserves prohibitions of incest, formulated as in the *Temple Scroll*, but unlike the latter appears to give special emphasis to the prohibition of niece-uncle marriages, recalling the emphasis given this prohibition in D. It also addresses the issue of

---

[119] On this see Baumgarten, "Laws of the *Damascus Document*," (1992) 56; Baumgarten, *DJD* 18, 13; Lawrence H. Schiffman, "The Dead Sea Scrolls and Rabbinic 'Halakhah'," in *The Dead Sea Scrolls as Background to Postbiblical Judaism and Early Christianity: Papers from an International Conference at St. Andrews in 2001* (ed. James R. Davila; STDJ 46; Leiden: Brill, 2003) 3-24, 13-14; Hempel, "Laws of the Damascus Document and 4QMMT," 73.

[120] On this see Schiffman, "Prohibited Marriages," 115.

[121] See the discussion in Larson, Lehmann, Schiffman, *DJD* 35, 46-47.

who may eat the food of the offerings within a priestly household, clarifying that this included the wife, bought and born slaves, but not immoral women or their offspring. Less certain is whether it addresses appropriate marriage for daughters of priests or whether its concern is intermarriage of any Jewish woman to a non-Jew. Even less certain still is the connection between comments about male bodily impurity and nakedness, on the one hand, and the sabbath, on the other, which may relate to prohibiting sexual intercourse on the sabbath, but could also relate to broader concerns about impurity, nakedness and the sabbath.

4.6 *4QMiscellaneous Rules* 4Q265

This document contains a diverse range of themes and literary genres. Fragment 1 cites Isa 54:1-2 about the barren woman who has given birth. Its context is uncertain. It is probably metaphorical, but, given the attention to birth in fragment 7 and to women and children in fragment 3, it is not impossible that it might have some reference to celebrating birth. The words מדוע נבגוד איש באחיהו "Why are we unfaithful to one another?" (3 2) cite Mal 2:10. There may be traces of the earlier part of Mal 2:10 in the previous line. The quotation does not extend to Mal 2:10b, which speaks of "profaning the covenant of our ancestors", nor to 2:11-12 which relates unfaithfulness to intermarriage. Thus, though the citation might have had a broader application to relations between people, its focus could well be on marital relations and especially intermarriage with Gentiles. The latter might explain the seemingly abrupt transition in the next line to the exclusion of women and children from the celebration of the Passover, if, as Baumgarten notes, the accusation of unfaithfulness is part of an attack on lax observance in regard to exclusions.[122] Both *Jub.* 49:17 and 11QT[a]/11Q19 17.8-9 also restrict participation in Passover to males twenty years of age and over.[123]

Fragment 4 contains parts of a penal code in the first column and in the second deals also with the process of entry into the community, reflecting a sectarian context for the work. Fragment 7 begins with prohibition of sprinkling

[122] Baumgarten, *DJD* 35, 64. See also Baumgarten, "Scripture and Law in 4Q265," 30-32.

[123] 11QT[a]/11Q19 39.7-9 similarly excludes women and boys from the court of males and 1QM/1Q33 7.3 excludes them from the war camp. See the discussion in Baumgarten, *DJD* 35, 63. He notes that while according to Ex 12:3-4 Passover assumes participation of all members, it was then "fashioned in accordance with the deuteronomic centralization of all sacrifice in the Temple (Deut 16:5-7). The Levitical purity of all who partook of the paschal lamb was consequently a cardinal requirement" (63). Apparently, male only participation is assumed in Num 9:6 and 2 Chron 35:15, but by the time of Josephus only lepers, men with a discharge, menstruating women and people otherwise defiled were excluded (similarly *m. Pes.* 8.1) (64).

and laundering on the sabbath (7.3-4), forbidden also in 4QTohorot A/4Q274 2 i (and in *m. Pes.* 6.2, and in *4QHalakhah A*/4Q251 1 6 in one possible reconstruction). The fragment then goes on to mention a group of fifteen forming the council of the community, as in 1QS/1Q28 8 (cf. 12 in 4QpIsa^{d}/4Q164),[124] which it affirms as an atoning fragrance (7 7-9).

Somewhat unmediated, we then find in 7 11-17 an allusion to the garden of Eden.[125] The creation of Adam in the first week and then of the woman is used as a basis to explain purification requirements for a woman after childbirth, as in Lev 12:2-5, 7 days of impurity for a male child, followed by a further 33 days of remaining in her impurity, or 14 days for a female child, followed by a further 66 days. We find the same linkage between Eden and purification after childbirth in *Jub.* 3:8-14. In 7 11 we have an allusion to Adam's creation in the first week, as in *Jub.* 3:8, and in 7 12 we read that this took place before "he was brought to the garden of Eden". This matches the detail of *Jub.* 3:9. The reference in ii 12 to "bone [of his bones" alludes to Gen 2:23, but also matches the complex interpretation given in *Jub.* 3:8 according to which the woman was created in the second week on the sixth day, thus, on inclusive reckoning, on the fourteenth day of creation. The words, "[for] the garden of Eden is sacred and every young shoot which is in its midst is a consecrated thing" (7 14), correspond to the statement in *Jub.* 3:12 that the garden of Eden "is the holiest in the entire earth and every tree which is planted in it is holy".

Thus both passages treat the garden as the equivalent of the temple and then make the connection with the provisions about women after childbirth. In 7 14b-17 the fragment cites Lev 12:2b, 4a (abbreviating 4b), 5, bringing the missing part of Lev 12:4b about touching anything holy in 17. Similarly, *Jub.* 3:10-11 cites Lev 12:2, 4-5, but follows the order of Leviticus 12 and omits reference to menstruation, linking the time instead more directly to the weeks of creation.[126]

---

[124] On this see Baumgarten, "Scripture and Law," 26-27.

[125] See the discussion in Joseph M. Baumgarten, "Purification after Childbirth and the Sacred Garden in 4Q265 and Jubilees," in *New Qumran Texts and Studies: Proceedings of the First Meeting of the International Organization for Qumran Studies, Paris 1992* (ed. G. J. Brooke; STDJ 15; Leiden: Brill, 1994) 3-10; and in Baumgarten, *DJD* 35, 60-61, 70-72.

[126] Baumgarten *DJD* 35, notes that the focus of Leviticus is the mother whereas the traditional aetiology in both *Jubilees* and 4Q265 would be more applicable to the entry of a child, though that is not said (60). It is interesting in this regard that both omit Lev 12:3 which speaks of circumcision on the eighth day. Baumgarten also notes the observation by Michael Stone that in the *Life of Adam* cited by G. Syncellus in his Chronography, "Adam was brought into Paradise on the fortieth day of his creation, wherefore also they bring male children into the Temple on the fortieth day according to the Law" (60). He also notes that Luke 2:22 reflects the association of mother and child in the completion of purification (61).

It is interesting that both *Jubilees* and 4Q265 preserve this tradition. A concern with such purification is atypical of *Jubilees*, indicating that its author is probably using tradition. It may also account for the deletion of the reference to menstrual impurity in its citation of Lev 12:2, 4-5. By contrast 4Q265 cites Lev 12:2, 4-5 word for word. The references in 4Q265 to sectarian structures make it likely that it is the later work. The rationale linking the times of purification to the Garden of Eden is complex and worked out in *Jubilees* within the wider narrative, whereas 4Q265 seems dependent on that rationale without citing it.[127] Given that *Jubilees* is well attested by multiple copies at Qumran and was used as an authoritative source by the author of D, it is likely that we should identify its influence also here. The reference in 4Q265 to "every young shoot" may well be an elaboration of *Jubilees'* "every tree", and reflect influence from the elaboration of the metaphor in sectarian circles, such as we find in 1QH xvi.10-13.[128] Alternatively both may draw on an independent tradition.

If not independent testimony, 4Q265 7 certainly provides evidence of a tradition which saw the garden of Eden as a temple. This kind of thinking becomes important when Eden features in eschatology (cf. *Test. Levi* 18.10; Rev 22:1-2), especially with its potential for seeing the life to come as one without sexual activity. Brooke notes the association of the temple with a vineyard and with Edenic overtones in 4QpapBened/4Q500.[129] Michael Wise proposed that the reference to מקדוש אדם in 4QFlor/4Q174, which he translates as "the temple of Adam" alludes to an eschatological temple associated with Edenic hopes.[130]

The primary significance of *4QMiscellaneous Rules*/4Q265 for our theme is its attestation of the tradition found also in *Jubilees*, which sees the garden of Eden as a temple, a notion with implications for sexuality where this becomes an eschatological image. Beyond that, the exclusion of women and children from the

---

[127] James C. VanderKam, "Apocalyptic Tradition in the Dead Sea Scrolls and the Religion of Qumran," in *Religion in the Dead Sea Scrolls* (ed. John J. Collins and Robert A. Kugler; Grand Rapids: Eerdmans, 2000) 113-34, writes: "The fact that 4Q265 speaks of the first week when Adam was brought into the garden and that the garden is here called *holy* make it likely that *Jubilees* is the source for mooring this pentateuchal law in the story about the garden of Eden" (129). Similarly, García Martínez, "Man and Woman," 111.

[128] So Baumgarten, "Purification after Childbirth," 6-7.

[129] George J. Brooke, "4Q500 1 and the Use of Scripture in the Parable of the Vineyard," in *The Dead Sea Scrolls and the New Testament* (Minneapolis: Fortress, 2005) 235-60, 245 n.34.

[130] Michael Owen Wise, "That which has been is that which shall be: 4QFlorilegium and the מקדש אדם," in *Thunder at Gemini: And Other Essays on the History, Language and Literature of Second Temple Judaism* (JSPSup 15; Sheffield: JSOT Press, 1994) 152-85, 174-85. See also Joseph M. Baumgarten, "The Qumran Sabbath Shirot and Rabbinic Merkabah Traditions," *RevQ* 13 (1988) 199-213, 212-13; Baumgarten, "Purification after Childbirth," 8-9. See our discussion on pp. 269-70 below.

Passover is to be noted and may have been linked to strictures also on intermarriage, if the citation of Mal 2:10 implies awareness of that theme in its original context.

4.7 *4QPurification Rules A* 4QTohorot A/4Q274

The first fragment refers to uncleanness of a man with a gonorrhea discharge, requiring his isolation (1 i.1-4a).[131] The sequence moves from *zab* to *zabah*, following Leviticus 15, and forbids a woman in menstruation[132] to make contact with a *zab* or any vessel or seat he has touched, but provides for purification if she does (4b-5a).[133] In addition she is not to "mingle (אל תתערב) in any way" (5b). This might be understood in the broad sense of mixing as in 11QT^{a}/11Q19 45.4,[134] but might more specifically refer to sexual intercourse as in *4QMMT* B 48 (80?), C 8; 4QTQahat ar/4Q542 1 i.9 (cf. Ezra 9:2 and Ps 106:35), and probably CD 11.4.[135] The fragment also forbids a menstruant from touching a woman with permanent discharge (6). It continues by equating the contamination of menstrual blood and abnormal discharge (7-8a) and then includes reference to a man with an emission of semen, stating that for someone in the seven days' purification period to touch anyone with these impurities is the equivalent of contracting corpse impurity (8b-9).[136]

The reference to supplication at the beginning of the fragment is probably about restricting prayers during uncleanness, which has a parallel in the *Life AdEv* 6 and 4QpapRitPur B/4Q512 42-44 ii, where the *zab* recites blessings only after

---

[131] So Baumgarten, *DJD* 35, 101-102, who rejects Milgrom's conclusion that the citation of Lev 13:45-46, "Unclean, unclean!", indicates the subject is a person afflicted with skin disease. Cf. Milgrom, "'4QTohora^{a}," 61. Baumgarten notes that *Sifra Tazri'a* illustrates its use for all who are unclean and he notes that the reference to defiling bed and seat would refer to genital emission. See also his comments on the location to the northwest (102). See also Harrington, *Purity Texts*, 95.

[132] On the use of *zabah* here for a menstruant see Wassen, *Women*, 119.

[133] Baumgarten, *DJD* 35, 102. On the assumptions governing these concerns with purity see also pp. 87-88 and Harrington, *Purity Texts*, 96-97, where she produces a table showing contamination according to Tohorot texts.

[134] So Baumgarten, *DJD* 35, 102.

[135] On the prohibition of sexual intercourse during menstruation see 4QD^{a}/4Q266 6 ii.1-2; based on Lev 15:24; Lev 18:19; 20:18; and my discussion on pp. 149-50 above.

[136] See Baumgarten, *DJD* 35, 103 and 86-88, where he contrasts this severity with the much more lenient approach towards the *zab* in rabbinic literature. See also Harrington, *Purity Texts*, 102. See also 4QTohorot B/4Q277 1 ii.10-13 and the fragmentary 4QTohorot C/4Q278 which appears to be dealing with similar concerns.

purification.[137] This belongs also with the attitude which sees abstinence from sexual intercourse and so seminal emission, as commendable for a person wanting to devote themselves to prayer, as Paul presupposes in his advice to the Corinthians (1 Cor 7:5).

Fragment 2 deals with purification for those who touch a man's semen and reflects the extension of sprinkling with water mixed with ashes of the red cow, from corpse to genital impurity.[138] It also extends the effects of contamination from seminal impurity to touching any garment or vessel which semen has touched, thus applying to seminal impurity what Lev 15:10 applied only to abnormal discharge (2 i.4-6).[139] Similarly the contamination is extended to the man's bed and seat in 2 i.8. As Baumgarten notes, "the Qumran legists were inclined to magnify the defilement from seminal discharges by analogy to those of the *zab*".[140] We found a similar enhancement of the severity of seminal emission in the *Temple Scroll* in relation to the temple (see p. 26 above).

The document reflects thus an enhanced concern with the effects of seminal impurity, recalling similar emphasis in the *Temple Scroll* and raising the question why seminal emission, in particular, came to be seen in this way and what it might reflect about attitudes towards sexuality. The document may also allude to the prohibition of sexual intercourse during menstruation and apparently also reflects the view that prayer is best undertaken in a state of purity. This latter perspective is potentially significant where it might lead to an extension of such thought so that times and places of prayer, in the present and the future, require avoidance of actions which might create impurity, including sexual relations.

4.8 *4QRebukes Reported by the Overseer* 4Q477

While not a "Rule", this fragmentary document reflects application of law. It gives detail of charges laid against members of the *Yahad*. Some of the instances may

---

[137] So Baumgarten, *DJD* 35, 92-93, 102. See also Harrington, *Purity Texts*, who draws attention also to 4QRitPur A/4Q414 2 ii 5-6 and *Sib. Or.* 4.165-68 (29)

[138] Baumgarten *DJD* 35, draws attention to the use of sprinkling with ashes of the red cow from situations of corpse impurity to situations of impurity from genital discharges (83-87, 104). He also notes the ban in ii.2 on sprinkling on the sabbath (104).

[139] The text also contains some flexibility in allowing a man defiled by indirect contact with semen to keep wearing his garment if it was all he had to wear (2 i.6-7). On carrying the garment of a *zab* as defiling, see also 4QTohorot B/4Q277, which begins with a discussion of the sprinkling of waters of purification, insisting that it be done only by a priest properly purified, not by a child or ordinary Israelite (1 ii.2-7) and moves on in that context to discuss the *zab*, including contamination contracted by anyone carrying his garment (1 ii.13). On this see Baumgarten, *DJD* 35, 83

[140] Baumgarten, *DJD* 35, 105; see also p. 88; and White Crawford, "Not according to Rule", 135.

involve sexual wrongdoing. According to 2 ii.5-8 a certain Hananiah Nothos was condemned. The second name is interesting. It is Greek and could reflect either νότος, meaning "southerner" or νόθος, meaning "bastard", used in Greek texts also as a term for a sociological group of freemen with limited rights.[141] As for his wrongdoing, the charges appear to be threefold, but difficult to discern with any degree of certainty. The first is clear: he disturbed the spirit of the community, but also adds: ו]גם לערב א[ת, which could mean: "and also for mixing (possibly, sexually) with" (6); the second is irrecoverable (7), but the third is preserved and states: וגם אוהב את שיר בשרו "and he also loves his close kin" (8).[142] This recalls the language of D in condemning incest: ולא ימעל איש בשאר בשרו "And a man shall not be unfaithful to/act illegally/trespass in relation to his near relative" (7.1) and in 8.6b-7a, ויתעלמו איש בשאר בשרו ויגשו לזמה "And each man hid himself from/ ignored (the status of?) his near relative, but approached debauchery". It also matches the language of *4QApocJer* C^{b}/4Q387 fr. A, where we read:

בערותם לקרוב איש אל שאר בשרו

in their nakedness/shame, each man approaching his blood relative.

Cf. איש איש אל כל שאר בשרו לא תקרבו לגלות ערוה

None of you shall approach anyone near of kin to uncover nakedness. (Lev 18:6)

The document reports a second Hananiah, a son of Simon, on the grounds that וגם אוהב את טוב [הצואר] "he also chose the fair neck" (10). If the editor's reconstruction is correct,[143] we might have a further allusion to D, which in attacking the false interpretations of the law by its opponents singles out as an instance of wrongdoing: ויבחרו בטוב הצואר "and they chose the fair neck" (1.19). In both instances we are probably dealing with sexual wrongdoing. It is even possible to read the וגם as meaning, "he, too", in other words, emphasising that both Hananiahs were guilty of sexual wrongdoing. Of the two instances, the more secure is the allusion to what appears to be incest.

---

[141] Fröhlich, "'Mamzer' in Qumran Texts," 115.

[142] Cf. the earlier reconstruction of Robert H. Eisenman and Michael Wise, *The Dead Sea Scrolls Uncovered: The First Complete Translation and Interpretation of 50 Key Documents Withheld for Over 35 years* (Shaftesbury: Element, 1992), 269-73, who read שפך בשרו "his bodily emission", interpreting it as a reference to masturbation. See the critique of this reading in Joseph M. Baumgarten, "Zab Impurity in Qumran and Rabbinic Law," *JJS* 14 (1994) 273-77, 277.

[143] So Esther Eshel, *DJD*, 36, 481. However the only link is the common word טוב, "good, fair, attractive"; the verb is different, אהב, "love", not בחר, "chose", and the word, הצואר, "neck", must be supplied.

CHAPTER FIVE

Attitudes towards Sexuality in the Liturgical and Related Material

1 Purification Rituals

1.1 *4QPurification Liturgy* 4Q284

The fragments of this document, like *4QTohorot A*/4Q274, concern purification rites. Fragment 1 includes reference to the "waters of purification" מי נדה and seminal discharge (ש֯כבת הזרע[...]) (7-8). As Baumgarten notes, "The mention of semen after the 'water for sprinkling' is another indication that the latter was thought of as effective in purifying not only corpse defilement, but other forms of uncleanliness (see 4Q277 1 ii 9)".[1] From the remaining fragments, which are also poorly preserved, it is clear that the document concerns itself further with waters of purification (2 i.2-3; 3 3; cf. also; 6 1; 7 2), washing (2 i.4); and uncleanness (2 ii.1; 3 5). There might be a reference to menstrual impurity in 2 ii.1 if נדת is read in a narrow sense and in 3 1 if עתיה refers to "her times". The document also appears to cohere with the provisions outlined in 4QOrd[c]/4Q514 which prohibit eating food until after the initial purification and from the pure food of the community until after the immersion after seven days.[2]

[1] Joseph M. Baumgarten, *DJD* 35, 125.

[2] Baumgarten, *DJD* 35, 126; cf. also Harrington, *Purity Texts*, 63.

1.2 *4QRitual of Purification A* 4QRitPur A/4Q414

This document is also concerned with purification and, similar to 4QpapRitPur B/4Q512 discussed below, fragments 2 ii, 3, 4 reflect a pattern of purification by immersion on the first, third and seventh day, which matches that required in 11QT[a]/11Q19 49-50 (cf. also Tobit 2:9). It may, however, not be dealing with corpse impurity as there, but could include seminal impurity.[3] The initial immersion appears to have been understood as removing a layer of impurity which enabled the person to eat and the second probably removed a further layer, as reflected also in 4QOrd[c]/4Q514, *4QPurification Liturgy*/4Q284, and 4QpapRitPur B/4Q512.[4]

The language of purity and purification occurs frequently throughout this fragmentary text (1 ii-2 i 2; 2 ii, 3, 4 1, 4-5, 7-8; 7 6; 13 2, 4-5, 7; 22 1; 23 3; 27, 28 3). Occasionally there are references to specific impurities. In 7 11 we find נקבה והדו]ה "female and the menstruating woma[n".[5] Fr 17 also mentions a menstruating woman. Eshel finds the presence of יחד read as "community" in 5 7 and סוד אנשים "council of men" in 4QpapRitPur B/4Q512 (36-38 13), found similarly also in CD 14 8-10 and 1QH vi.18, to be indicative that 4Q414 and 4Q512 both probably originate in sectarian circles,[6] but יחד may mean "together" and סוד אנשים, "counsel of men" and the latter occurs without a context in 4Q512 and appears in the apparently non-sectarian 4QInstr[a]/4Q415 6 6.

1.3 *4QRitual of Purification B* 4QpapRitPur B/4Q512

The 232 fragments of this document mostly contain only one or two words, but it is clear that the overall theme is purification and liturgy, with frequent reference to purity, purification, washing, and sin. Eshel notes that the document includes three elements in the ritual of purification: confession of sin (29-32 18; 28 4; 99 2); request for forgiveness (34 15; 1-6 16) and thanksgiving (33; 35 729-32 7), and includes prayers both before and after immersion (1-6).[7]

---

[3] Esther Eshel, *DJD* 35, 138-39; see also Harrington, *Purity Texts*, 82.

[4] Eshel, *DJD* 35, 138-39; see also Harrington, *Purity Texts*, 64; Eyal Regev, "Yose Ben Yoezer and the Qumran Sectarians on Purity Laws: Agreement and Controversy," in *The Damascus Document: A Centennial of Discovery: Proceedings of the Third International Symposium of the Orion Center for the Study of the Dead Sea Scrolls and Associated Literature, 4-8 February 1998* (ed. Joseph M. Baumgarten, Esther G. Chazon, and Avital Pinnick; STDJ 34; Leiden: Brill, 2000) 95-107, 102.

[5] Reconstructed on the basis of *4QTohorat A*/4Q274 1 i.7. See Eshel, *DJD* 35, 144.

[6] Eshel, *DJD* 35, 139.

[7] Eshel, *DJD* 35, 136-37. Baumgarten, *DJD* 35, notes that in 10-11 x.2-5 the author assumes that the prayer is recited while the person is still in the water, but covered with his

In 36-38 iii.17 the text expresses gratitude for salvation מכול עדו[ת] בשרנו "from every nakedness/shame of our flesh". This might relate to human impurity in general, without any reference to moral sin,[8] though, as Himmelfarb observes, flesh is a euphemism for the genitals in Lev 15:2, 19 and ערוה "nakedness, shame" is used throughout the prohibitions of illicit sexual relations in Leviticus 18.[9]

In fr. 29-32 we find the words, פשעי ותטהרני מערות נדה "my transgressions and purified me from nakedness/shame of impurity" (vii.9). Harrington sees here "a clear mixture of ritual and moral impurity concerns", pointing also to "I sinned" in 28 viii.[10] Himmelfarb notes that נדה, originally a reference to menstrual uncleanness, is being used in a broader sense, the participants seeming all to be male.[11] In her discussion of 4Q512 she suggests that, like 4Q274, the document "purposely blurs the distinctions between the various categories of impurity found in the Torah", for instance, speaking of נגע נדה "affliction of menstrual impurity" (34 v.17; 1-6 xii.16), which combines terminology of skin eruptions and menstrual impurity and in 12 associates it with the language of corpse impurity.[12] "The thrust of the blessings in 4Q512 is not halakic definitions, but human imperfection".[13] She insists that here sin and impurity often stand side by side, but that they nevertheless remain distinct. "Sin and impurity are understood as two aspects of human finitude, corresponding to soul and body".[14] The latter bifurcation is potentially misleading, since there is no evidence in the sectarian texts that they distinguished body and soul in any absolute sense. Sin and ritual impurity are however aspects of human finitude in its vulnerability to impurity and its propensity to sinfulness.

---

garments (95). He draws attention to Josephus *B.J.* 2 161 who mentions the loincloth worn by Essenes and the dress by women, while bathing (95). See also Baumgarten, *DJD* 35, 92-93.

[8] So Harrington, *Purity Texts*, 65.

[9] Himmelfarb, "Impurity and Sin," 35.

[10] Harrington, *Purity Texts*, 28-29.

[11] Himmelfarb, "Impurity and Sin," 36.

[12] Himmelfarb, "Impurity and Sin," 35.

[13] Himmelfarb, "Impurity and Sin," 35.

[14] Himmelfarb, "Impurity and Sin," 36. Cf. Klawans, *Impurity and Sin*, who argues for a merging of moral and ritual concerns, which he identifies also in 1QS/1Q28 11.14-15; 1QM/1Q33 13 5; 1QH^{a} iv 19; ix 22; xix 11 (78, 87) and Baumgarten, "Purification Rituals," 200-201, who notes the penitential stance in 34. See also Harrington, *Purity Texts*, who interprets "hidden acts of guilt in 34 not as a reference to ritual impurity but to inadvertent sins (28).

In his edition of the text Baillet identifies sexual impurity as the theme of columns 3-7 and 9-11.[15] Over against Baillet, Baumgarten notes that בנגע נדה "affliction of impurity" occurs in 1-6 in relation to corpse impurity and that purification is linked to festivals in 29-32 and in 28 to sacrifices, contexts not related to sexual emission,[16] and therefore concludes: "It does not, therefore, appear that the confessional elements in the liturgy were limited only to sexual defilement".[17] On the other hand, in relation to 7-9 xi he suggests on the basis of Gen 39:10 to read line 4 as ולהיות עם [אשתו "to be with [his wife" as a reference to a *zab* and sexual relations with his wife (cf. such a person was quarantined according to 11QT^{a}/11Q19 48 15), rather than as Baillet, ולהיות עם [קודש "and to be a holy people".[18]

The document apparently contains more than references to seminal impurity among other impurities from which one is to be purified. It also includes purification from sin and that sin most likely includes sexual sin. This seems likely to be envisaged in references to shame and flesh, though within a broader framework of acknowledging human finitude. The question of the understanding of human finitude and of sexuality within it needs to be discussed in a broader context. It comes to its clearest expression in the *Thanksgiving Hymns* and the *Community Rule*, but also with significant precedents in *4QInstruction*.

2 The *Thanksgiving Hymns* 1QHodayot^{a}/1QH^{a}; 1QH^{b}/1Q35; 4QH$^{a\text{-}e}$/4Q427-31; 4QpapH^{f}/4Q432; (4Q471b?)

The Cave 4 manuscripts of the *Thanksgiving Hymns*[19] make it probable that there were various collections of such hymns, before and beside the major collection first known to us in 1QH^{a}, but now also in 4QH^{b}/4Q428, and that these existed alongside the major collection and continued to be copied separately.[20] 4QH^{a}/4Q427, for instance, appears to have been a smaller collection with a

[15] M. Baillet, *DJD* 7, 262-86, 263.

[16] Baumgarten, "Purification Rituals," 208. See also Doering, "Purity Regulations," who notes that 33+35 iv 1-5 reflects sanctification (להתקדש "to consecrate oneself") in water/immersion before sabbaths and festivals (600). He sees in להתקדש "to consecrate oneself" a play on Exod 19:10, 14 which also uses the root קדש, linked with the sabbath in the Decalogue (Exod 20:8) (601).

[17] Baumgarten, "Purification Rituals," 201.

[18] Baumgarten, "Purification Rituals," 204.

[19] I avoid possible confusion which can arise in the reconstructions from having columns but also numbered fragments not allocated to columns, by using Roman numerals to designate columns, and Arabic numerals to indicate fragments and lines.

[20] Eileen Schuller, *DJD* 29, 75.

different order. All of its preserved material contains what are regarded as community hymns. By contrast, apart from possibly an introductory hymn, what survives of 4QH^{c}/4Q429 preserves only material belonging to the "hymns of the Teacher", generally recognised as 1QH^{a} x.3-19; xii.5 – xiii.4; xiii.5-19; xiii.20 – xv.25; xvi.4 – xvii.36.[21]

The issue of authorship is complicated. A single author is unlikely, although some hymns may be the work of a single figure, conjectured to be the work of the Teacher of Righteousness.[22] Newsom notes that the "I" may function at times more as it does in the Psalms and so serve to shape the self of the hearer.[23] In her discussion of theories of authorial identity she concludes that she does not think "a definitive case can be made either for the hypothesis that the Hodayot of the leader be associated with the teacher of righteousness or the hypothesis that they be associated with an institutional role held by successive leaders".[24] On the other hand, she argues, the hymns, themselves, perform acts of leadership; "they serve to construct a figure who is a compelling object of loyalty".[25] In this sense they are also potentially important for our theme because they both reflect and shape identity and reinforce the values of the community which used them.

Conflict and Sexuality

Much of the material is dominated by a sense of conflict, in which the figure sees himself in opposition to those sometimes named as דורשי חלקות "seekers of smooth things" (x.15, 32), a term regularly used in depictions of the community's conflicts (CD 1.18; 4Qpap pIsa^{c}/4Q163 2-3 ii.10; 4QpNah/4Q169 3-4 i.2, 7; ii.2, 4; iii.7; *4QCatena^{a}*/4Q177 9 4),[26] but in opposition also both to those who threaten

[21] For a discussion of the Cave 4 manuscripts see Schuller, *DJD* 29, 74-75.

[22] So G. Jeremias, *Der Lehrer der Gerechtigkeit* (SUNT 2; Göttingen: Vandenhoeck und Ruprecht, 1963) 176-77.

[23] Newsom, *Self as Symbolic Space*, 204-208. See also John J. Collins, "Amazing Grace: The Transformation of the Thanksgiving Hymn at Qumran," in *Psalms in Community: Jewish and Christian Textual, Liturgical, and Artistic Traditions* (ed. Harold W. Attridge and Margot E. Fassler; SBLSymS 25; Atlanta/Leiden: SBL/Brill, 2003) 75-85, on the particular developments of the psalms compared to their canonical counterparts. Commenting on the community psalms, he notes that these are not psalms for specific occasions, but "rather, they give thanks for a state of being" (81).

[24] Newsom, *Self as Symbolic Space*, 299, and for the discussion see pp. 287-300.

[25] Newsom, *Self as Symbolic Space*, 345.

[26] Against the assumption that the expression, דורשי חלקות, the "seekers of smooth things", may be a play on הלכה, see John P. Meier, "Is there *Halaka* (the Noun) at Qumran?" *JBL* 122 (2003) 150-55, 154-55. See also Dennis Green, "'Halakhah at Qumran?' The Use of the Root הלך in the Dead Sea Scrolls," *RevQ* 22 (2005) 235-51, who,

his life and to those of his own community who have deserted him (xiii.22-25; 4 8). The focus of dispute relates to interpretation of the Law. Thus the author writes:

וכול יודעיך לא ישנו דבריך

all who know you do not change your words. (*DSSSE*) (vi.15)

זממו עלי {בי} בליעל להמיר תורתכה

they have plotted against me by Belial to change your law.* (xii.10)

משנים מעשי אל

have altered the deeds of God. (*DSSSE*) (xiii.36)

This recalls the accusations in the *Damascus Document* (D) about those who have shifted the boundaries (4QD^{a}/4Q266 1a-b 4; CD 4.12; 1.16; 5.20; 19.16; 20.24), in *4QWiles of the Wicked Woman*/4Q184 1 15, where some in response to the smooth-talking woman are led להשנות חוק "to alter the ordinance"; and also 1QS/1Q28, which may speak of those who "bend the Law" (11.2). This is overshadowed, however, by the sense of personal attack.

Within all these various reflections of conflict there is no indication, however, that sexual wrongdoing is a major concern, such as we find in D and the *Wiles of the Wicked Woman*. It is true there is little reference to anything specific in relation to dispute about the Law, although we do find mention of abuse of wealth and power (xviii.30). We also find some of the imagery associated with concern with sexual wrongdoing in D. The motif of nets and traps occurs a number of times, mostly to describe enemy strategies (x.29; xi.26; xii.12, "so that they may act like fools in their feasts so they will be caught in their nets", associated with Belial; and 3 4; cf. also xxi.10),[27] but sometimes in relation to temptation to sin, as in the nets of Belial in D, though never, as there, with reference to sexual wrongdoing.

This is particularly striking in xii.5-22, which shares some features with CD 4.13 – 5.12. It belongs to one of the hymns of the teacher. Within this passage, in which the author speaks of being driven from his land like a bird from its nest (xii.8-9), he declares that his enemies are:

---

noting the absence of the word הלכה in the extant documents and the widespread use of הלך in describing observance of law, concludes that it is most unlikely that the noun was understood in a technical sense in the sect and so deliberately avoided.

[27] The image is sometimes used to depict a strategy for dealing with sinners (x.8). Cf. also 4QpPs^{a}/4Q171 1-10 ii.10-11, which speaks of the poor ones being delivered from מכול פחי בליעל "all the traps of Belial".

והמה מליצי 10 כזב וחוזי רמיה
זממו עלי {בי} בליעל להמיר תורתכה
אשר שננתה בלבבי בחלקות 11 לעמכה

mediators 10 of fraud and seers of deceit.
they have plotted against me by Belial to change your law
which you engraved on my heart for smooth teachings 11 for your people.*
(xii.10, 11a)

The author continues in the following line with a reference to nets:

להתהולל במועדיה^ם להתפש במצודותם
כי אתה אל תנאץ כל מחשבת
13 בליעל ועצתכה היא תקום ומחשבת לבכה תכון לנצח
והמה נעלמים זמות בליעל

… so that they may act like fools in their feasts so they will be caught in their nets.
But you, O God, abhor every plan of
13 Belial and your counsel remains, and the plan of your heart persists endlessly.
But they, hypocrites, plot intrigues of Belial. (*DSSSE*) (xii.12-13)

In xii.16 we then hear of their "prophets of fraud attracted by delusion" and in xii.18 we read:

כי אמרו
18 לחזון דעת לא נכון ולדרך לבכה לא היאה

For they said
18 of the vision of knowledge: "It is not certain!" and of the path of your heart: "It is not that!" (*DSSSE*) (xii.17b-18)

In CD 4.13 – 5.12 we also have reference to Belial and to nets where we read of the opponents being תפש "caught" (4.16, 18) in the מצודות בליעל "nets of Belial" (4.13). We also hear of substantial changes to what the author sees as the Law (4.16 – 5.11), including the shifting of boundaries, of misleading prophets (4.19b-20), and of the response of some described as לאמר לא נכונו "saying, 'They are not certain!'" (5.12).

Despite these similarities, which may reflect some acquaintance with the passage in D on the part of the author, nothing in 1QH[a] xii.5-22 indicates that the issues at stake might be matters of sexual wrongdoing. "The nets" are not described. Part of the conflict may relate to issues of calendar, as the reference to "feasts" (xii.12) may suggest. There may be an allusion to foreign language and so to foreign influence, reflected in the accusations against the false prophets in xii.16 (= 4QH[d]/4Q430 4-5): "They speak to your people [with] stut[ter]ing lip and weird tongue", possibly reflected also in x.19 ("But they have changed them for an uncircumcised lip and a weird tongue of a people without understanding, and so they will be ruined by their mistake"). The author depicts his own past stay among foreign people as a time of danger in which God rescued him (xiii.5), but no specific evils are identified as belonging to this context. Nothing, in any case, suggests issues pertaining to sexuality are central to the conflict as in D.

What we have found in xii.5-22 is true of the rest of the collection. The absence of any reference to sexual wrongdoing is noteworthy. It would be all the more surprising if we were to assume, as some do, that the author also penned *4QMMT*. As in the *Community Rule*, the conflict is generally depicted as having become one between rival groups at enmity and not as a conflict focused on particular interpretations of the Law, as in D and even more so in *4QMMT*. While the hymns allude to conflict over law and probably still allude to this in the designation, "seekers of smooth things", the focus has moved to personal conflict. Thus where the hymns reflect conflict, the issue is not difference of opinion, but threat to the community and a sense of injustice and attack. As we shall see, this not only matches the perspective of the *Community Rule*, but also of the *Pesharim* which use biblical texts to explain the conflict.

Issues of sexuality in the broadest sense do however appear within the work, even if not as the focus of dispute or particular concern. Within the depiction of his beleaguered state in xi.1-18, for instance, the author employs the metaphor of childbirth in a passage which reflects a very positive appreciation of the normal processes of conception and birth. The image is combined with two others: a city under siege and a boat in rough seas. As Newsom notes, the imagery of labour, already used in Isa 13:7-8a; Ps 48:5-7; Jer 6:23-24; 49:4; and Isa 21:3, is employed by the hymn twice, depicting two pregnant women.[28] The passage employs a number of wordplays: משברים "womb, opening" and משברי מות "breakers of death"; חבלי שאול "labour pains" and "bonds"; כור "crucible", a pun on the word בכור "firstborn"; אפעה "serpent", linked also by pun with the words אפעה/אפע "nothingness".[29] There are allusions to biblical texts: כמו אות לדה "like a woman giving birth" from Jer 13:21; מבכריה "her firstborn" from Jer 4:31; כיא נהפכו ציריה "when her pains have come upon her" from 1 Sam 4:19; and וחבל נמרץ "and sharp pains" from Mic 2:10. While in each case the biblical texts speak of distress being suffered as the result of judgement on sin, in the passage "they hang in the air like a whisper of anxiety not even consciously acknowledged".[30] The labour pains leading to birth are described with great emphasis, using biblical images of the turbulence of threatening waves ("breakers

[28] Newsom, *Self as Symbolic Space*, 245-46.

[29] Newsom, *Self as Symbolic Space*, 246. On the word plays see also Knibb, *Qumran Community*, 174-76.

[30] Newsom, *Self as Symbolic Space*, 247.

of death")[31] and the "the pangs of Sheol" (2 Sam 22:5, 6), through which a wonderful child is born (cf. Isa 66:7; 9:5) from what is described as the woman's "crucible" (xi.7-12a; similarly 1QapGen/1Q20 6.1).

Juxtaposed to this first pregnant woman (xi.12a) is a second (xi.12b), who gives birth to a serpent, in what is similarly depicted as a process of severe labor pains, enhanced with the imagery of a storm-tossed boat, using Psalm 107:23-30 (xi.14-16a).[32] The focus then shifts to punishment of the spirits of the serpent and their return to the pit, Sheol and Abaddon (xi.16b-18). The serpent, here, alludes to the garden of Eden. The author then returns to give praise that he has been saved from the pit (xi.19). As Newsom notes,

> The whole symbolic economy of this composition is organized around the comparison and contrast of the two female figures. They are, in their pregnant state, quite alike. Specifically, both are subject to the pains and dangers of labor, described in similar terms. But for one, the outcome is the birth of extraordinary new life, while for the other the outcome is death.[33]

Specifically, the child of the first woman represents the knowledge and insight which the speaker treasures, whereas the monstrous serpent represents the opposition forces, who include would-be "wise men" (xi.14-15). The association with sin and judgement inherent in the biblical images of travail are thus transferred to the second woman.[34]

In all this, however, there is no negative slant on human sexuality. The depiction of childbirth shows a positive appreciation of what it entails. The image of being in pain like a woman in labor reappears briefly also in xiii.30-31a to depict the hymn writer's beleaguered state.

There is much else in the collection, however, beside a sense of conflict and persecution. This includes some material pertinent to our study, though largely incidental to its context. In xviii.33-36, for instance, the author speaks of his own anxiety, in which his "groaning reached down to the abyss, even searching through the caverns of Sheol". In this context he reports:

ואפחדה בשומעי משפטיכה עם גבורי
35 כוח וריבכה עם צבא קדושיכה ב[...]שה
36 ומשפט בכול מעשיכה וצדק ...[...].

I was terrified to hear your verdict against the powerful heroes,

[31] The metaphor of breakers and the connection with Sheol serves to describe the hymn writer's distress also in xvii.4 (cf. also xvi.31).

[32] The image also appears in xiv.22-24.

[33] Newsom, *Self as Symbolic Space*, 251.

[34] So Newsom, *Self as Symbolic Space*, 252.

> 35 your trial against the host of your holy ones. [...]
> 36 and judgment against all your creatures, and justice [...].
> (*DSSSE* modified) (xviii.34b-36)

This appears to allude to the Watcher myth. The term גבורי כוח "powerful heroes" appears as a reference to angels in xvi.11 (see also xiii.21; xiv.30). The word, קדושיכה "Your holy ones", using a common designation for angels, stands as a parallel. Both terms refer to the Watchers. The reference to ממזרים "bastards" in xxiv.15 and fr. 2 ii + 6.6 also reflects the Enochic tradition according to which the offspring of the Watchers and the women are designated in this way (*1 Enoch* 15:8-9). The particular theme of the Watchers' sexual wrongdoing, however, receives no attention. This coheres with what we have found elsewhere, namely, that the Watchers' act of sexual wrongdoing does not become the basis for either depicting their offspring's activity or their influence in terms of sexual wrongdoing.

Sometimes an author refers to his own birth, mentioning father, mother (her womb and breasts), and a wet nurse, reflecting a relatively wealthy family (xvii.29b-31), and also compares God's goodness to a father and a mother "who loves her child" and writes of God as a wet-nurse: "like a wet-nurse you take care of all your creatures on (your) lap" (xvii.36).[35] We also find the use of positive images of early infancy to describe an author's own role in positive terms, as a father, a mother and a wet-nurse:

> You have made me a father for the sons of kindness, 21 like a wet-nurse to the men of portent; they open their mouth like a chi[ld on the breast of its mother,] like a suckling child in the lap of 22 its wet-nurse. (*DSSSE*) (xv.20b-22a)

Self-Deprecation and Sexuality

One of the frequent motifs in contexts where authors give thanks for God's grace is that of human conception and birth. These belong within a piety which gives major emphasis to human creatureliness. Sometimes it is as simple as the author referring to himself or human beings as "flesh" (e.g. v.3, 4, 19), "dust" (e.g. xix.3; xxiii.4), or as "born of woman" (v.20; xxi.1), but usually it goes beyond that. The

[35] On the image of the wet-nurse and the possible play on words between אומן ("wetnurse") and אמן ("to be firm"; also: "Amen"), אמונה ("firmness"), and אמנה ("truly"), see Jacob Cherian, "The Moses at Qumran: The מורה הצדק as the Nursing-Father of the יחד," in *The Bible and the Dead Sea Scrolls: The Princeton Symposium on the Dead Sea Scrolls: Volume 2: The Dead Sea Scrolls and the Qumran Community* (ed. James H. Charlesworth; Waco: Baylor University Press, 2006) 351-61, 356-57, who also draws attention to similar imagery used of Moses in Num 11:12 (358).

author(s) make(s) regular use of a number of expressions which call for closer examination. They include:

building of dust (מבנה עפר) (v.21); formed from dust (יצרתה מעפר) (xi.21); creature of dust (יצר עפר) (xxi.16; 3 14); a heap of dust (מקוי עפר) (xx.25; 3 6); cf. kneaded from dust (מעפר מגבל) (1QS/1Q28 11.21); cf. my foundation of dust (סוד עפרי) (4QShir[b]/4Q511 28+29 3)

dust and ashes (עפר ואפר) (xviii.5); to dust he will return (לעפר תשובתו) (xviii.4; xx.26, 31; xxii.7; 4 11; 2 i.5); cf. to earth he will return (ואל אדמתם ישובון) (4QSap. Work B/4Q419 8 ii.8)

man? He is nothing but earth (אדם אדמה הוא) (xviii.3)

creature of clay (יצר החמר) (ix.21; xi.23-24a; xii.30; xix.3; xx.26; xxi.10b-11a; 3 5, 11, 18; xxii.7; xxiii.12); cf. moulded clay (חמר קורץ) (1QS/1Q28 11.21; 4QShir[b]/4Q511 28+29 4; probably also 1QH[a] xx.24); one shaped by hand (יוצר יד) (1QS/1Q28 11.22)

kneaded with water (מגבל מים) (v.21; ix.21; xi.24; xx.25); cf. kneaded from dust (מעפר מגבל) (1QS/1Q28 11.21); moulded (קורץ) (xviii.4; xx.24); cf. kneading from darkness (מחושך מגבלי) (4QShir[b]/4Q511 28+29 4)

building of sin (מבנה החטאה) (ix.22)

the spirit of flesh (רוח בשר) (v.20); spirit of iniquity (רוח נעוה) (v.21b-22a; xi.21); spirit of error and iniquity (רוח התועה ונעוה) (ix.22-23a)

foundation of shame (סוד הערוה) (ix.22); cf. my foundation of dust (סוד עפרי) (4QShir[b]/4Q511 28+29 3)

source/spring of impurity (מקור הנדה) (ix.22; xx.25)

oven/womb/crucible of iniquity (כור העוון) (ix.22)

nakedness of shame (וערות קלון) (v.21; xx.25)

spit(?) (מצירוק) (xx.32; 2 i.16)[36] ; cf. also 1QS/1Q28 11.21; creature of spit (יצר מצירוק) (4QShir[b]/4Q511 28+29 2-4)

guilt of unfaithfulness (באשמת מעל) (xii.30)

Mostly these descriptions occur in clusters.

However what is] the spirit of flesh (רוח בשר) to understand all these matters and to have insight in your wondrous and great counsel? What is someone born of woman (ילוד אשה) among all your awesome works? He is 21 a building of dust kneaded with water (מבנה עפר ומגבל מים), [ ] his foundation is the nakedness of shame (סודו ערות קלן) and a spirit of iniquity (רוח נעוה) rules over him.* (v.19b-22a)

I am a creature of clay, kneaded with water (ואני יצר החמר ומגבל המים), 22 a foundation of shame and a source/spring of impurity (סוד הערוה ומקור הנדה), an

[36] The photograph supports reading מצירוק in xxiii 2 i.16 with *DSSSE*, not מצידוק "from righteousness" as *DSSEL*.

oven/womb/crucible of iniquity and a building of sin (כור העוון ומבנה החטאה), a spirit of error and iniquity 23 without knowledge (רוח התועה ונעוה בלא בינה), terrified by your just judgments.* (ix.21b-23a)

And I, from dust (עפר) [I] have been gathered, [and from clay] I have been [mou]lded 25 to be a source/spring of impurity ([קו]רצתי למקור נדה) and nakedness of shame (וערות קלון), a pile of dust, kneaded with [water, …] (מקוי עפר ומגבל] מים) a lodging of 26 darkness. The creature of clay must return to the dust (ותשובת יצר המר לעפר) at the time of … […] in the dust (עפר), 27 to the place from which he has been taken. …
31 He who returns to the dust (עפרו)…32 …. spat saliva a creature of clay (מצירוק יצר החמר) (xx.24-27, 31-32)

Such statements occur regularly within a context which is extolling God's greatness. They are appropriately described as "Niedrigkeitsdoxologien", "self-deprecating doxology",[37] in which the depiction of humanity in the basest of categories (earth, dust, clay, ashes) serves to contrast God's glory and grace. This usually happens in association with the motif of judgement, but may also occur independently of the context of praise as "Elendsbetrachtungen", "seeing oneself as wretched".[38] Commenting on ix.21-27, Becker notes that the contrast is not between God's saving acts for Israel and Israel's failures, as in the biblical tradition, but between human "Nichtigkeit und Sündenverfallenheit" ("nothingness and capitulation to sin") and God's acts and goodness in creation.[39]

Many of the formulations take the shape of rhetorical questions and echo the spirit and form of Psalm 8:4 ("What are human beings that you are mindful of them, mortals that you care for them?") (v.20; vii.21; xi.24; xii.29; xv.32; xviii.3, 12; xix.3; xx.27, 31-33; xxi.6). The references to dust, clay, earth, water and spit (?) serve to reinforce the humble nature of human beings and so to highlight God's generosity in showing compassion. The same is implied in the designation of human beings simply as בשר "flesh". The language in such designations reflects the second creation story in Genesis according to which

וייצר יהוה אלהים את האדם עפר מן האדמה
The Lord God formed man/human being from the dust of the ground. (Gen 2:7)

---

[37] So Heinz-Wolfgang Kuhn, *Enderwartung und Gegenwärtiges Heil: Untersuchungen zu den Gemeindeliedern von Qumran mit einem Anhang über Eschatologie und Gegenwart in der Verkündigung Jesu* (SUNT 4; Göttingen: Vandenhoeck und Ruprecht, 1966) 27-28; see also Jürgen Becker, *Das Heil Gottes: Heils- und Sündenbegriffe in den Qumrantexten und im Neuen Testament* (SUNT 3; Göttingen: Vandenhoeck und Ruprecht, 1964) 139; Lichtenberger, *Menschenbild*, 73-74; Lange, *Weisheit*, 223.

[38] Kuhn, *Enderwartung*, 27.

[39] Becker, *Heil*, 139.

This explains not only יצר "creature", אדם "man/human being" with the play on אדמה, "earth, ground", used in xviii.3, and עפר "dust", but also חמר "clay" and מים "water", as the product and agent for making something from dust, for which the process is not only described using the verb יצר "to form", but also the words גבל "to knead", בנה "to build" (cf. Gen 2:22), and קרץ "to mould". There are also many echoes of the Genesis declaration that human beings return to dust (xviii.4; xx.26, 31; xxii.7; 4.11; 2 i.5; cf. also 1QS/1Q28 9.22):

כי עפר אתה ואל עפר תשוב

because you are dust and to dust you shall return. (Gen 3:19)

In his discussion of the language Lichtenberger notes that יצר is widely used in the Hebrew scriptures for a work of creation, often in association with the image of the potter (e.g. Ps 103:14; Gen 2:7).[40] He notes that it is also used for action or thought, which can be negative, but need not be (so 1 Chron 28:9; 29:18; Gen 6:5). He points to the common use in the Hebrew scriptures of יצר עפר "creature of dust" where the focus is the act of creation (Gen 2:7), and of clay יצר החמר "creature of clay" where the focus is on shaping and moulding, and that the former often occurs, as in Gen 3:19, in association with the motif of humankind returning to dust (e.g. Ps 104:29; Job 10:9; 17:16; 21:26).[41] He also notes that in the *Thanksgiving Hymns* the reference to humankind being shaped from clay is not part of an appeal to God's sympathy as the maker, as in the use of the image in Job, but simply a way of focussing on human creatureliness.[42]

While the creation story forms the primary background for the imagery, some elements suggest that the author(s) may have also had procreation in mind. P. Wernberg-Møller suggested that the unusual word, מצירוק, derives from two words מצי רוק and appears to mean "spit, spat saliva".[43] This could still fit the creation story, but the image would be more fitting as a euphemism for ejaculated semen. It would be possible to hear such an allusion at a secondary level also in the references to water. Wernberg-Møller, who suggested the allusion to semen,[44] pointed to parallels in Wisd 7:2; *Aboth* 3.1; and the Koran. Accordingly Otto Betz spoke of a sequence of self-description in the sect's anthropology, from below to

---

[40] Lichtenberger, *Menschenbild*, 77-78.

[41] Lichtenberger, *Menschenbild*, 79-81.

[42] Lichtenberger, *Menschenbild*, 79-80.

[43] P. Wernberg-Møller, *The Manual of Discipline* (STDJ 1; Leiden: Brill, 1957) 43, 39, 155.

[44] Wernberg-Møller, *Manual of Discipline,* 155.

above, starting with the genitals.[45] Against this approach Lichtenberger argues that the author is not describing parts of the body, but speaking of the whole.[46] He disputes the derivation of מצירוק from מצי רוק on the basis that it is written as one word and such combinations are very rare in Hebrew.[47] In addition he suggests that the word used with water, מגבל (kneaded"; v.21; ix.21; xi.24; xx.25), expressing the notion of forming, does not fit an allusion to doing something with semen. It better fits the idea of creation and is used in this way in later rabbinic texts (so *Lev. Rab.* 29.1).[48] The juxtaposition, however, to other expressions which do have potentially sexual connotations, such as ערות "nakedness, shame", נדה "impurity", מקור "spring, fount (penis)", and כור "crucible (womb, vagina, birth canal?)", terms discussed below, makes the possible, additional level of allusion to procreation likely at a secondary level, although creation is the primary source of the imagery. Even if a reference to procreation is uncertain, it would still be seen, like the references to earth, dust, clay and water, not as something negative in itself. While using them to emphasise lowliness, nothing suggests that the author sees either the substances or the processes of creation or of procreation as something evil or dirty.

The issue is more complicated, however, when in these same contexts the hymns also use expressions like:

> his foundation is the nakedness of shame (סודו ערות קלן) and a spirit of iniquity (רוח נעוה) rules over him. (v.21-22a)

> a foundation of shame and a source/spring of impurity (סוד הערוה ומקור הנדה), an oven/womb/crucible of iniquity and a building of sin (כור העוון ומבנה החטאה), a spirit of error and iniquity 23 without knowledge (רוח התועה ונעוה בלא בינה). (ix.22-23a)

> I have been [mou]lded 25 to be a source/spring of impurity (קו[רצתי למקור נדה) and nakedness of shame (וערות קלון). (xx.24b-25)

---

[45] Otto Betz, *Offenbarung und Schriftforschung in der Qumran Gemeinde* (WUNT 5; Tübingen: Mohr Siebeck, 1960) 123; similarly G. Maier, *Mensch und freier Wille: Nach den jüdischen Religionsparteien zwischen Ben Sira und Paulus* (WUNT 12; Tübingen: Mohr Siebeck, 1971) 180-81.

[46] Lichtenberger, *Menschenbild*, 75-76.

[47] Cf. Lichtenberger, *Menschenbild*, who suggests the word may derive from the Aramaic stem טרק meaning to mix (82-83 n. 33).

[48] Lichtenberger, *Menschenbild*, 83, referring to Jonas C. Greenfield, "The Root 'GBL' in Mishnaic Hebrew and in the Hymnic Literature from Qumran," *RevQ* 2/6 (1960) 155-62, 157-58. Lichtenberger also refers to *Gen. Rab.* 14.2 which makes a close connection between the אד of Gen 2:6 and the act of Gen 2:7 (83-84).

The designation of people as sources of נדה "impurity" and ערות קלון "nakedness of shame" raises a number of questions. Is this a reference to ritual impurity such as belongs to being human and has no moral significance or is it referring also to moral impurity? Lichtenberger notes that ערות "nakedness, shame" is used primarily in relation to the area of sexuality in 1QS/1Q28 7.14; CD 5.10; and 1QM/1Q33 7.7 and 10.1 and has this meaning here, where it highlights sexual/seminal impurity (not moral impurity).[49] The same may be said of נדה "impurity", which in sectarian documents usually carries a broader meaning than menstrual impurity. In the expression מקור הנדה "source/spring of impurity" (ix.22; xx.25), the word, מקור "spring, fount", used elsewhere as a euphemism for the penis (e.g. 1QM/1Q33 7.6; 4QOrd[c]/4Q514 1 i.4), will also have sexual connotations, but probably also refers to ritual impurity as in 1QM/1Q33 7.6. Lichtenberger notes that כור "oven, crucible, womb" might contain a sexual allusion, since Aramaic כורא means "weibliche Scham" ("female pudenda") and כור "crucible" occurs in 1QH xi.8, 10, 12 as a reference to the body of pregnant women (see also 1QapGen/1Q20 6.1).[50] In none of this do we find the implication that sexual organs, male or female, or sexual activities or seminal emissions are wrong in themselves,[51] but they certainly belong to those aspects of being human where issues of ritual purity arise. Nothing links nakedness/shame to sin, such as in the Eden story which sees awareness of nakedness as its consequence; nor are the impurities of being human signs of sinfulness. Rather, they are indications of human creatureliness which must be attended to in order to be able to approach a holy God.

Similar language occurs in the *Community Rule* with similar implications:

> What, indeed, is a son of man (בן ה׳אדם) among your wonderful works? 21 As what can one born of a woman (ילוד אשה) be considered in your presence? Kneaded from dust (מעפר מגבל), his dwelling is the bread of worms (ולחם רמה מדור); he is spit (מצירוק), 22 moulded clay (חמר קורץ) – and to dust is his return[52] (ולעפר תשוקתו). What shall clay (חמר) reply, one shaped by hand (יוצר יד)? What will he consider for the council?* (11:20b-22)

---

[49] Lichtenberger, *Menschenbild*, 84. See also the discussion on pp. 363-65 below.

[50] Lichtenberger, *Menschenbild*, 86.

[51] So rightly Lichtenberger, *Menschenbild*: "Es wird jedenfalls nicht von der Unreinheit der Sexualorgane gesprochen, sondern von der Unreinheit des Menschen (ואני!)" (tr. In any case what is spoken of is not the impurity of the sexual organs, but the impurity of human beings [ואני!]) (85).

[52] I translate תשוקה as the equivalent of תשובה. See 198 n. 33 above.

Some motifs or combinations appear here which are not found in the *Thanksgiving Hymns*. These include, מעפר מגבל "kneaded from dust"; ולחם רמה מדור "bread of worms"; יוצר יד "shaped by hand"; and חמר קורץ "moulded clay" (this is conjectured in xx.24, but the import is the same). The differences are quite striking considering the common motifs and indicate a composition in a different context of discourse from where the *Thanksgiving Hymns* were composed.

In v.21 and ix.22 these designations are juxtaposed to further descriptions which are, however, clearly moral in character: "a spirit of iniquity (רוח נעוה) rules over him" (v.21-22a); "an oven/womb/crucible of iniquity and a building of sin (כור העוון ומבנה החטאה), a spirit of error and iniquity without knowledge (רוח התועה ונעוה בלא בינה)" (ix.22). They also belong within a string of designations which begins with the language of creation and also speaks of ritual impurity. We may find a similar juxtaposition in the hymn in 1QS/1Q28 11, which moves from human sinfulness in 9-11 to juxtaposing sin and ritual impurity in 14-15, to creatureliness in 20-22; and in 4Qpap RitPur B/4Q512, which juxtaposes purification מכול ערו[ת] בשרנו "from every nakedness/shame of our flesh" (36-38 iii.17)[53] and forgiveness of transgressions, though without confusing the two.[54]

There seem, therefore, to be three levels of reality in a human being which the hymn writer addresses: the lowliness of human life reflected in the substances and process of its creation (and possibly procreation); the (non-moral) impurity which belongs to the natural experience of being human; and human sinfulness. While the second is entailed in the first, the question arises whether the third is also in some sense innate. Taken to an extreme that could call into question both procreation and creation as acts responsible for evil and so evil in themselves. This would certainly have implications for attitudes towards sexuality.

The juxtaposition of statements about lowly substance, being a source of impurity, and having a propensity to sinfulness, necessarily implies an element of self-deprecation which goes beyond simple lowliness. Newsom speaks of the "masochistic sublime", contrasting it with the language of self-abasement found in the Psalms, which is not self-loathing.[55] She notes how in ix.1-39 the typical

---

[53] Similarly, ותטהרני מערות נדה, "and purified me from nakedness/shame of impurity" (29-32 vii.9).

[54] Other references which express impurity as inherent in the human condition include: נדה בשרו "impurity of his flesh"; בשר ערוה "flesh of nakedness/shame" (4QHalakhah A/4Q251 1-2.7); טמאת בשר "defilement of [belonging to] the flesh" (1QSa/1Q28a 2.3-4); and טמאת האדם "defilement of [belonging to] humankind" (1QM/1Q33 7.4-5; cf. ערות דבר רע "shamefulness/nakedness of a bad thing", referring to setting toilets at a distance from the camp (1QM/1Q33 7.7).

[55] Newsom, *Self as Symbolic Space*, 220.

juxtaposition of lofty statements of praise followed by self-disqualification threatens also to call into question even that knowing which praise assumes.[56] The author, she argues, allows the paradox to be, "insisting on the contradiction: the simultaneous recognition of nothingness of the self and the powerful voice of knowledge with which it speaks", only to be resolved by the assertion of an act of divine grace in granting knowledge, and so "discourages the desire for autonomy and offers as desirable an existence that is measured, governed, and subjected by the divine autonomy".[57] Similarly, of 1QH[a] xviii.2-5 she writes: "Through the language of paradox, it is the insistence on the negative that provides the validation of the subject. The more the negation of the self is insisted upon, the more the self is grasped as the site of divine activity".[58]

The paradox is even more seriously one of reconciling self-deprecation and belief in divine creation. It is not resolved by attributing human sinfulness to a primeval fall by Adam[59] or by angels,[60] or to evil spirits,[61] nor by alleging contaminating influence from some external force such as Belial, who does feature elsewhere in the depictions of conflict. Nor, as some have suggested, does בשר "flesh" depict a sphere of evil power in the quasi-apocalyptic sense that underlies Paul's later use of σάρξ.[62] The problem is not external to humanity or something acquired in the course of time, but inherent in being human. The references to the spirit of flesh (רוח בשר) (v.20); spirit of iniquity (רוח נעוה) (v.21b-22a; xi.21); and the spirit of error and iniquity (רוח התועה ונעוה) (ix.22-23a) are anthropological, not a reflection of demonology. They speak of the human spirit. This is also therefore different from the dualism in the *Treatise on the Two Spirits*, which combines the psychological with a notion of two angelic powers, the prince

[56] Newsom, *Self as Symbolic Space*, 226-28.

[57] Newsom, *Self as Symbolic Space*, 229.

[58] Newsom, *Self as Symbolic Space*, 230.

[59] When hope is expressed in 1QS/1Q28 5.15 as inheriting "all the glory of Adam", this does not appear to be interpreted as reversing the effects of a fall.

[60] Lichtenberger, *Menschenbild*, 90.

[61] Lichtenberger, *Menschenbild*, who notes that even the spirit of depravity is anthropological, not about a spirit outside of humanity (90). Nor is spirit a separate part of a human being (91).

[62] Cf. Jörg Frey, "Flesh and Spirit in Palestinian Jewish Sapiential Tradition and in the Qumran Texts: An Inquiry into the Background of Paulinian Usage," in *The Wisdom Texts from Qumran and the Development of Sapiential Thought: Studies in Wisdom at Qumran and its Relationship to Sapiential Thought in the Ancient Near East, the Hebrew Bible, Ancient Judaism, and the New Testament* (ed. Charlotte Hempel, Armin Lange, and Hermann Lichtenberger; BETL 159; Leuven: Peeters-Leuven University Press, 2002) 367-404, who, referring to בעוון בשר in 1QS/1Q28 11.12, writes: "Flesh seems to represent an evil sphere or even power that causes human sin and causes the pious to stumble" (384). Similarly Becker, *Heil*, 112.

of light and the angel of darkness. As we shall see below in our discussion of 4QShir[a,b]/4Q510, 511, it was possible to combine this language of self-deprecatory ideas with demonology, but this is not what we find in the *Thanksgiving Hymns*.

The location of the problem in humanity is evident in the following statement:

> Who is flesh (בשר) compared to this? What creature of clay (יצר החמר) can do wonders? He is in iniquity (בעוון) from his mother's womb, and in guilt of unfaithfulness (באשמה מעל) right to old age. (xii.29-30)

The writer speaks in the same breath of God's act of creation and of human sinfulness from birth, indeed, from before birth. The idea and, in part, the language (עוון) seem dependent on Psalm 51

> הן בעוון חוללתי ובחטא יחמתני אמי
> See, in iniquity I was brought forth and in sin my mother conceived me. (51:7; E: 51:5)

This should caution against weighing the statement too heavily as a declaration of ontology.[63] The same allusion reappears in 4QPrFêtes[a]/4Q507 1.2-3. The framework of thought within the *Thanksgiving Hymns* which makes such an apparently paradoxical statement possible is not a dualism which assumes two opposing forces at work in creation, let alone some kind of evil associated with human sexuality, but theistic predestination. As Newsom puts it in depicting the hymn writer: "Predestined for his fate, he is in a sense simply an effect of God, not so much a protagonist in a cosmic drama as a sign of divine activity".[64] That divine grace according to v.24-25 can rectify the situation: "And I, your servant, have known thanks to the spirit you have placed in me". This stands in contrast to the spirit of flesh (רוח בשר) earlier in the passage (v.20). Elsewhere we read of God apportioning to each human being propensities for good or evil (1QS/1Q28 4.24-26). This is already assumed in *1/4QInstruction* which also speaks of the spirit of the flesh and of divine predestination (4Q416 1 11; 4Q417 1 i.17; 4Q418 81+81a 1b-3a). *4QHoroscope*/4Q186 even depicts human beings as made up of nine parts variously distributed between light and darkness. Thus here in vii.13 the writer affirms: "in his hand is the inclination of every spirit". After the negative

---

[63] In relation to ix.21-27 Becker, *Heil*, observes: "Aber wird hier nicht darüber reflektiert, wie die Sünde in die gute Schöpfung kam, d.h. des Menschen Sündenverfallenheit wird nicht genetisch abgeleitet, sondern es wird nur konkret bekannt" (tr. There is no reflection here about how sin came into creation, which is good; in other words, human failure in sin is not derived genetically, but simply confessed in a basic kind of way") (138).

[64] Newsom, *Self as Symbolic Space*, 276.

assessment in ix.22 the writer gives thanks in ix.32 that God has "strengthened the spirit of man" (רוח אנוש). Similarly, following the negative and seemingly hopeless situation depicted in xii.29-30, cited above, the author can affirm: "the path of man is not secure except by the spirit which God creates for him" (xii.32).

The same juxtaposition occurs in the hymn appended to the *Community Rule*, where the author affirms his belonging לאדם רשעה "to evil humankind" and לסוד בשר עול "to the assembly of unfaithful flesh" (11.9) only to assert a few lines later, that, if he falls בעוון בשר "in the sin of the flesh" (11.12), God's goodness will deliver him and enable him to walk rightly.

Another common term used to depict human propensity to sin is the word, יצר, "inclination". It usually occurs with a qualifier indicating sinful inclination, reflecting the negative use in Gen 6:5,

וכל יצר מחשבת לבו רק רע כל היום

and every inclination of the thoughts of their heart was wicked continually.
(Gen 6:5; cf. also 8:21)

Thus it appears already in 4QInstr^{c}/4Q417 1 ii.12 in an exhortation to avoid being led astray. *4QParaphrase of Genesis and Exodus*/4Q422 speaks of יוצר רע "an evil inclination" in association with human disobedience in the garden of Eden (i.12). Nothing indicates that to have an inclination is bad in itself, but the assumption appears to be that the human being inclines to sin and so must resist the inclination when it is so directed. Indeed in 1QH vii.13 the author declares that the יצר, "inclination" of every spirit is in God's hand, as part of his determinism, which thus may be either positive or negative. Similarly xv.13 speaks of God knowing the יצר "inclination" of every creature and xiii.6, of not having been abandoned to the "plottings" of his inclination (בזמות יצרי), which assumes the human inclination is towards sin. The assumption in xix.20 is also that human "inclinations" are towards sin. Apparently a good יצר is also possible.[65] In xv.16 the author appeals to God's knowledge of his "inclination" in a positive sense. Thus in 3 10 the author holds out the hope that in the future "there will be no more inclination of injustice nor works of deception". Nowhere do the hymns associate an evil inclination with sexual desire, nor, as in CD 2.16, with illicit sexual desire as a way in which it might express itself. In none of these instances do we find particular reference to sexual wrongdoing, but rather the author appears to be speaking of human frailty and propensity to sin.

---

[65] In ix.35 the writer exhorts the wise to be יצר סמוך (also in x.9, 36), which could mean "of steadfast inclination", but more probably means "trustful creature", an allusion to יצר סמוך (Isa 26:3). So Muraoka, "Community Role," who describes the phrase as "a key phrase in Qumran anthropology" (339).

A certain paradox remains. On the one hand, human beings are seen as having a propensity to sin from the womb (or is it even more inevitable than that?), and that God, not one's being flesh and blood in itself, determines the direction of one's inclination. There is then the prospect of a day when this will no longer be so, that is, when people's inclinations will be towards good, but this, too, will be God's doing. On the other hand, the hymns also assume the possibility of change in the present and of choice for change. The lowly human creature is a source of wrongdoing – but need not be. If anything, the authors appear to play on human frailty, but assume that, as in their own present state, human frailty need not make sin and ignorance inevitable, especially if one belongs to those destined to be righteous now and in the future. The resolution of the paradox appears to lie in depicting that belonging not simply as human choice but as divine predestination.

While one's lot is determined by God and this means that for some there is escape from the propensity of human beings to sin and hope if they succumb,[66] nothing in the document suggests that one's sexuality is to blame for one's condition. The evil inclination nowhere appears, for instance, as uncontrollable sexual urge. Even though sexuality is to the fore in highlighting impurity and probably in highlighting creatureliness (assuming allusions to procreation as well as creation), there is no indication that it is more than that and that one's sexuality is something evil. The author does not, indeed, focus on sexual wrongdoing in his depiction of human failure, let alone on human sexuality as its source. If there is an allusion to semen, there appears to be no attempt to disparage either the processes of procreation or the substance, any more than God's work of creation is disparaged. Clay is clay and dust is dust, semen is semen – not evil substances, only lowly ones.

A piety which affirms creation, extols God, and in order to do so, deprecates self, and does so in poetry, is almost bound to stretch logic to its limits and beyond. Such doxological affirmations can embrace contrasting and at times incompatible assertions. In reverse, coming to terms with rejection can employ similar notions of election and determinism to provide a rationale for that rejection, while at the same time paradoxically embracing the possibility that enemies may change.

Outside the rhetoric of praise and self-assurance, however, such statements have the potential to develop a life of their own. In the case of the self-deprecating assertions of the hymns, these could easily be detached from their context which affirms divine creation and become the inspiration for more pessimistic assessments of humanity. Pushing the logic of statements asserting human

---

[66] Forgiveness is central to the hymnwriters, who look back on sin from which they have been rescued: בנדה התגוללתי "I wallowed in impurity" (iv.18); "great offence" (xi.21); "the plottings of my inclination" (xiii.6).

sinfulness already from the womb could lead to questioning the integrity of creation and the creator.

It is not far from such pessimism to reach the conclusion that humans need a salvation not only from their own being (or part of it) but also from their creator. In such developments sexuality, already exposed as a source of shame in a ritual sense, would be vulnerable to being made to bear significant blame. The paradox of the hymns' anthropology is held together in tension, unresolved. Despite the negative plight, there is hope and grace, if only for the predestined, and neither human creation nor human procreation, in process or substance, nor human sexuality is demonized.

The *Thanksgiving Hymns* are remarkable for their lack of focus on matters pertaining to sexuality in the context of their many references to conflict and to opponents. At the same time they make creative use of experiences generally related to human sexuality, including a graphic description of the pangs of childbirth as a metaphor for the experience of being beleaguered, but also of the intimacy of nursing and parenthood as an image of God. They know the myth of the Watchers' sexual wrongdoing and their punishment, but do not turn attention to sexual wrongdoing in their own time. Their extraordinary affirmations of God's glory and wisdom are achieved in part through a contrasting deprecation of human life and human sinfulness, but the pessimism in asserting the latter never denies God's involvement in creation and never disparages either the process or the substance of creation – or procreation. Human sexuality is an aspect of that creation which also entails living with impurity, but never appears as in itself a source of evil or as something to be despised.

3 *4QBlessings* 4QBer^{a-e}/4Q286-90

In 4QBer^{a-e}/4Q286-90, which appears to be "one version of the sectarian community's annual covenant renewal liturgy",[67] blessings are followed by curses, but in neither is there reference to matters pertaining to sexuality. The participants are to curse Belial במחשבות משטמתו "in his hateful plans" (4QBer^{a}/4Q286 7a ii b-d.2) and כול רו[חי גו]רלו במחשבות רשעמה "all the spirits of his lot in their wicked plans" (3). What follows elaborates further: מחשבות נדת [ט]מאתמה "their plans of defiling impurities" (4). The curse of "the angel of the pit and spirit of Abaddon" speaks of מחשבות יצר א[שמתכה "the plans of your guilty inclination" (7a-8a). Clearly these forces are being made responsible both for moral sin and for plans which lead to ritual defilement in a way that is culpable. Though not using the language of battle, the passage assumes

[67] James R. Davila, *Liturgical Works* (Grand Rapids: Eerdmans, 2000) 41.

that the individual human being is caught in conflict with the spirits of Belial and looks forward to the day of their defeat, which lies in the future. While not using the language of "bastards" or "spirits of bastards", the anthropology is similar to that of 4QShir[a,b]/4Q510, 511; and *4QIncantation*/4Q444 discussed below, in depicting the human plight not primarily as psychological creatureliness, but as being caught in the schemes of demonic forces.

In 4Q287/4QBer[b] 8 13 we find the words,]א[שמה ועיני זנות ופעולת "g]uilty [ ] eyes of sexual wrongdoing". This recalls similar expressions in D: יצר אשמה וע(י)ני זנות "guilty inclination and eyes of sexual wrongdoing" (2.16), the *Community Rule*: לב אשמה ועיני זנות "guilty heart and eyes of sexual wrongdoing" (1.6-7) and *4QBarkhi Nafshi* (4Q435 2 i.2, immediately below).[68] Unfortunately the context is not preserved.

4 *4QBarkhi Nafshi[a-d]* 4Q434-438

In 4Q434 2 6 the document uses the image of a bridegroom with his bride to depict the joy that God will bring to Jerusalem. The image is based on Isa 62:5. The editors' translation, "as a bridegroom on (על) a bride",[69] suggests an explicitly sexual image, an act of sexual intercourse, but it is just as likely to be metaphorical, meaning "over/about/because of". Even then, part of that delight will be sexual. The use of the image indirectly reflects affirmation of human sexual love and certainly no sense that it would be inappropriate in an image speaking of God.

In 4Q435 2 i.1-2 (= 4Q436 1 i.10; ii.1) we have references to change in the individual. 4Q435 reads:

> … and you have set a [p]ure [heart] in its place.
> 2] The evil inclination (יצר רע) you have driven with rebukes far from me
> and the spirit of holiness you have set in my heart. Sexual immorality of the eyes (זנות עינים)
> 3 [you have removed from me and it gazed upon] all your [w]ays.
> (*DSSEL* modified) (2 i.1-3a)

4Q436, which preserves the preceding context, enables us to see that the author is giving thanks for a number of things which God has done. Immediately before the

[68] Nitzan, "Laws of Reproof," draws attention to the application of the laws of reproof of Lev 19:17-18 in these texts, reflecting the provisions in CD 9.3-4, 17-19 (see also 4QD[a] /4Q266 18 ii) and 1QS/1Q28 5.24-25; 6.1, and also draws attention to the list of rebukes against members of the *Yahad* in 4QRebukes Reported by the Overseer/4Q477 (150-53).

[69] M. Weinfeld and D. Seely, *DJD* 29, 280.

words above we find the (partially reconstructed) words: "[the heart of stone] you have [dri]ven with rebukes far from me" (1 i.10a). The "heart of stone" (assuming the conjecture), the "evil inclination", and "sexual immorality of the eyes", are not equated, but belong to a list of things which God has removed, which include "stiffness of neck", "wrathful anger", "haughtiness of heart and arrogance of eyes", and "spirit of deceit", as the passage goes on to enumerate (3b-5). The human state is portrayed here not as the battleground against the bastard spirits, but as a psychological reality which can be changed. That psychological reality includes illicit sexual desire, expressed typically with the word זנות "sexual wrongdoing" in combination with עינים "eyes" (cf. CD 2.16; 1QS/1Q28 1.6-7; 4QBer^{b}/4Q287 8 13).

Apart from its possible allusion to sexual joy and its use of the imagery of eyes of sexual wrongdoing, the document reflects dualism of the psychological type, which, as elsewhere, does not depict sexuality as problematic in itself.

5 The *Words of the Luminaries* 4QDibHam^{a-c}/4Q504-506

This document consists of a collection of daily prayers. In 4Q504 i.4-12 it alludes to the creation of humanity, including that they were fashioned in the image of God's glory, given the breath of life, placed in the garden of Eden, and that they are flesh and return to dust. The column ends by referring to human wrongdoing and the shedding of blood (13-14). Sin and forgiveness is a constant theme throughout these prayers, but at no point enunciated in relation to matters of sexuality except perhaps in 4Q504 xvi.12-20. There we find reference to Moses and the prophets and to evil which would ensue, including something about מלכינו "our kings" (16) and about taking our daughters (לקחת בנות) (17) and acting pervertedly or destroying (ישחתו) (18), but the context is not preserved. The mention of זרע ישראל "the seed of Israel" (20) may indicate that the context is intermarriage. Baillet sees it as referring to the problem of intermarriage at time of Ezra and Nehemiah.[70] Alternatively, it might refer to the Watchers or, better suited to the reference to "our kings", to Solomon's taking many wives, including foreigners (Deut 17:17; 1 Kgs 3:1; 11:1-8).[71]

---

70 Maurice Baillet, "Un recueil liturgique de Qumrân Grotte 4: Les Paroles de Luminaires," *RB* 68 (1961) 95-250, 220; Davila, *Liturgical Works*, 258.

71 Noted by Davila, *Liturgical Works*, 258.

6 *4QFestival Prayers*[a,b] 4QPrFêtes[a]/4Q507 and 4QPrFêtes[b]/4Q508

4QPrFêtes[a]/4Q507 makes reference to human frailty, the theme strongly present in the *Thanksgiving Hymns*.

ואנו בעולה מרחם ומשדים בא[שמה
ועד היותנו צעדינו עם נדה יב]

> and we are in evil from the womb and from the breasts in gu[ilt]
> and as long as we live our steps with impurity … (1 2-3)

This, in turn, recalls 1QH[a] xii.29b-30, which speaks similarly of the "creature of clay":

והוא בעוון 30 מרחם ועד שבה באשמת מעל

> And he is in iniquity from the womb and to old age in the guilt of unfaithfulness

The idea and, in part, the language (עוון) seem dependent on Psalm 51

הן בעוון חוללתי ובחטא יחמתני אמי

> See, in iniquity I was brought forth and in sin my mother conceived me (51:7; E: 51:5)

The self-deprecation is not, therefore, to be understood as positing a theory about the origins of sin in humanity, let alone, as denigrating sexual intercourse and conception. It appears to belong to the psychological dualism noted above in the *Thanksgiving Hymns*.

4QFestival Prayers[b] 4QPrFêtes[b]/4Q508, mentions in its Prayer for the Day of Atonement that God knows יצרנו "our inclination" (2 5; similarly 1QH[a] xv.13), but otherwise brings nothing pertinent to our theme.

7 *4QpapRitual of Marriage* 4QpapRitMar/4Q502

Of the 343 published fragments of this document, most consist of no more than a word or two. Some are more substantial but nevertheless poorly preserved and very fragmentary. In fragment 1 enough words survive for us to recognize that the text has some relation to issues of sexuality. These include:

3	האדם] ואשתו ל[	a man] and his wife for[
4	]לעשות זרע[	]to produce descendants[
7	] רעייתו אש[ר	] his spouse wh[o

[עינת ש] 9	] intercourse of [

Material apparently pertaining to marriage appears also in the following:

[ת לו בת אמת ומתהל]כת	] to him a reliable woman who wal[ks (2 6)
א]ביהו א[	] his [f]ather [
ש]מחת יח[ד	j]oy of being togeth[er
[משיל]	] rule[(4 2-4)
מ]עיו לפרי ב[טן	his [b]elly for the fruit of the w[omb (20)
[כבדם א]	] their glory [
[טים לשמחת]יחד	] for the joy of [togetherness (22 2-3)
א]בי הנערה ו[	f]ather of the girl [(108 3)

Fragment 24 speaks of a woman standing in the assembly (24.4). There are a number of references to sons and daughters, adults, and elders. **בטן** "womb" appears in fr. 180, **פרי בטן** "fruit of the womb", and in 163 (cf. also 50 2);[72] **בניהם** "their children" in 308; and **אשתו** "his wife" in 309.

Baillet, who first edited the document, identified the document as a wedding ritual.[73] In 6-10 3 and 8 the document speaks of a "time of joy" and apparently of a "festival" **מועד**. Baillet's view was challenged, however, by Baumgarten, who argued that the reference to a time of joy and festival, and the frequent mention of the whole community (also reading **יחד** as "community" rather than as "together"), and especially of seniors and long life reflect a wider festival of some kind, perhaps associated with *Sukkoth*, not unlike the festival which Philo describes of the Therapeutae (Philo *Contempl.* 68 – 89).[74] Noting that what he saw as a festival included men and women, including formerly married men and women, and gave particular deference to the elderly, Baumgarten pointed to similar inclusivity ascribed to the Therapeutae (Philo *Hypoth.* 11.13). He noted in fr. 16 a citation of the *Treatise on the Two Spirits* (1QS/1Q28 4.6-8), where, he argued, **פרות זרע** "fruitful offspring" is "used in a decidedly figurative fashion", and suggested that this may also apply in 4QpapRitMar/4Q502.[75] In 2 6 he saw the expression **בת אמת** "daughters of truth" as the equivalent of "sons of truth" in 1QS/1Q28 4.6, and not as a reference to reliable spouses.[76] Nor, he argued, need

[72] Also in 4QpapPrQuot/4Q503, 183 and 221.

[73] Baillet, *DJD* 7, 81-105.

[74] Joseph M. Baumgarten, "4Q502, Marriage or Golden Age Ritual?" *JJS* 34 (1983) 125-35, 128, 130-31. Johann Maier, *EncDSS*, also notes the allusion to the palm branches of *Sukkoth* in fr. 99 (2.783). See also the alternative suggestion in Michael L. Satlow, "4Q502 A New Year Festival?" *DSD* 5 (1998) 57-68.

[75] Baumgarten, "Qumran-Essene Restraints on Marriage," 17-18.

[76] Baumgarten, "4Q502, Marriage or Golden Age Ritual?" 128.

fr. 24, which has a man and a woman alternate in invoking blessing on each other, refer to marriage partners; rather it reflected the kind of choral responsive liturgy which Philo attests of the Therapeutae.[77] He pointed out that references to long life are also to be found independently of any wedding context in 4QpPs[a]/4Q171, 1QH[a] iv.3-15 and CD 6.11 – 7.6.

On the other hand, Baumgarten observes that the document is, nevertheless, important evidence for the inclusion of men and women and shows that they

> had an integral role in the communal life of the Qumran sect. … since 4Q502 alludes positively to *'dm w'štw*, "a man and his wife", and expresses thankfulness for the "seed of blessing" seen in the joining of young and old of both sexes, we may infer that Qumran ideology had a great deal more tolerance for the affirmation of family life characteristic of rabbinic Judaism than was previously thought.[78]

Schuller notes that "there seems to be some link to the *yaḥad* of 1QS which makes the inclusion of women all the more unexpected".[79] White Crawford notes that in 19 2, 24 4 (and possibly 107 1) זקנות implies women elders and that אחיות "sisters" in 96 1 may also designate female members.[80]

Reviewing the alternative proposals, Davila demonstrates that the original suggestion that we have before us fragments from a festival celebrating a wedding still has most to support it.[81] It is a certainly a joyful occasion. "Fruitfulness of seed" need not be figurative. Producing seed (as in fr. 19) is a literal blessing,[82] which need not stand in conflict with 1QS/1Q28 4.6, which it appears to echo, for the latter, in depicting future hope, also envisages abundant progeny. The motifs of creation and fruitfulness recall the themes of the wedding prayer in Tob 8:6-7, as Baillet already noted.[83] Davila points out that the word רעיה "darling" (1 7) is used elsewhere only in Canticles, where it refers to Solomon's beloved (1:9, 15; 2:2, 10, 13; 4:1, 7; 5:2).[84] He notes that יחד can be mean "together" as well as "community" and argues that in 1 9 עונה (translated, "intercourse" above) probably alludes to sexual intercourse as a conjugal duty in Exod 21:10.[85] Nothing,

---

[77] Baumgarten, "4Q502, Marriage or Golden Age Ritual?" 128; Baumgarten, "Qumran-Essene Restraints on Marriage," 17.

[78] Baumgarten, "Qumran-Essene Restraints on Marriage," 12-13.

[79] Schuller, "Women in the Dead Sea Scrolls," 137.

[80] White Crawford, "Mothers, Sisters, and Elders," 181-83. See also Edward Cook "A Liturgy of Thanksgiving" in WAC, 182-83, who suggests the document presents a liturgy to accompany youths into the *yahad* when they came of age.

[81] Davila, *Liturgical Works*, 182, 189.

[82] Davila, *Liturgical Works*, 182, 189, 197.

[83] Baillet, *DJD* 7, 81.

[84] Davila, *Liturgical Works*, 189.

[85] Davila, *Liturgical Works*, 190.

he argues, suggests that the reference to virgins in fr. 19 entails that they are old, as Baumgarten's interpretation assumes.[86] He sees the reference to length of days in 20 2 as being like the prayer in Tob 8:7 ("grant ... that we may grow old together") and the references to "womb" as pertinent to the wedding theme, noting also that the word "spread out" (יצע) (20 4) is also used for couch or bed, and marriage bed in particular, in Gen 49:4 and 1 Chron 5:1.[87] In fr. 24 he sees a possible wishing of long life for the bride and in fr. 31, where we may have a reference to twins, an indication of fertility.[88] In fr. 95 and 96 he notes also the word, חבב "cherish", used in rabbinic Hebrew of passionate sexual desire.[89] The mention of "the father of the girl" in 108 fits a wedding context and recalls Deut 22:16,19.[90] Finally, the reference to *lulavs* in fr. 99 need not imply *Sukkoth* exclusively, because their use is attested also for other occasions of celebration, so that it is also best to see the seven day period alluded to in fr. 97 as the period of a wedding celebration.[91]

Assuming the document does belong in the context of a wedding, then it is important evidence not only of the place of women in the community, which would still be reflected at least in the communal event described, but especially for the place of marriage and family. The fragmentary remains still allow us to see joy in the coming together of man and woman, including allusions to the joy of sexual intimacy. In what is preserved there is no evident note of disapproval or constraint.

8 The *Songs of the Sage* 4QShir^{a,b}/4Q510, 511

In 4QShir^{a,b}/4Q510, 511 the Instructor asserts God's splendor and radiance in order to frighten "all the spirits of the ravaging angels and the bastard spirits (רוחות ממזרים), demons, Lilith, owls and [jackals ...] and those who strike unexpectedly to lead astray" (4Q510 1 4-6 = 4Q511 10 1-2).[92] The allusion to "bastards" reflects the Enochic tradition that the giants were bastards and their

86 Davila, *Liturgical Works*, 197.

87 Davila, *Liturgical Works*, 198-99.

88 Davila, *Liturgical Works*, 201-203.

89 Davila, *Liturgical Works*, 204, referring to Michael L. Satlow, "'One Who Loves His Wife Like Himself': Love in Rabbinic Marriage," *JJS* 49 (1998) 67-86, 70, 72.

90 Davila, *Liturgical Works*, 207.

91 Davila, *Liturgical Works*, 205-206.

92 For the possibility that the image of Lilith as winged and horned influences 4Q184, see Joseph M. Baumgarten, "On the Nature of the Seductress in 4Q184," *RevQ* 15 (1991) 133-43, 139-41. On Lilith see also Isa 34:14, where she is associated with goat-demons in desolate places. See also the discussion of 4Q184 on p. 329 below.

corpses the source of evil spirits (*1 Enoch* 15:8-9).[93] The designation, "bastards", appears in this sense also in 4QShir[b]/4Q511 2 ii.3; 35 7; 48, 49 + 51 2-3; and 182.

In 4QShir[b]/4Q511 the author underlines his frail humanity by speaking of himself in language which echoes the *Thanksgiving Hymns*

וא[ני אודכ]ה כיא למען כבודכה
3 [ש]מתה דעת בסוד עפרי ה[ללכה] ואני מצירוק יצר
4 [חמר]קורצתי ומחושך מגב[לי]ה יה ועולה בתכמי בשרי

> and I [shall thank yo]u that, for the sake of your glory,
> 3. you [pl]aced knowledge in my foundation of dust so that I might p[raise You.] And I am a creature of spit (?).
> 4. I was moulded [of clay] and [my] kneading was from darkness [ ] and injustice is in the filth/innards of my flesh.* (28+29 2-4)

While it uses the same vocabulary: סוד "foundation"; עפר "dust"; צירוק "spit?"; יצר "creature"; קורץ "moulded"; מגבל "kneaded"; בשר "flesh", the combinations, סוד עפרי "foundation of dust"; מצירוק יצר "creature of spit"; מחושך מגב[לי "kneading from darkness"; עולה בתכמי בשרי "injustice … in the innards of my flesh", and possibly חמר]קורצתי "moulded of clay", are surprisingly not paralleled in the *Thanksgiving Hymns*.

We find רוח עולה בתכמי בשרו "spirit of injustice in the innards of his flesh" in the *Treatise on the Two Spirits*, 1QS/1Q28 4.20b-21a, and the expression בתכמי בשר "in the innards of his flesh" in 1Q36 14 2 and 4Q444 1-4 i +5 3, and later in this document at 4Q511 48-49+51 ii.3-4. The word, בתכמי, need not necessarily be disparaging, "filth", but rather be another way of speaking of what is deep within the human person, here using the image of innards or bowels. The words מצירוק יצר "from spit, creature" appear in 1QH[a] xx.29, but within the expression, מצירוק יצר חמר "from spit, creature of clay". Both here and in 1QH[a] xx.24 editors conjecture חמר "clay" before קורצתי "moulded", as 1QS/1Q28 11.22. There may be traces of the expression, "dust and ashes" also in 126 2, which preserves only the letters פר of what may have read עפר ואפר "dust and ashes".

Thus far we appear to be dealing with a similar anthropology of self-deprecation to what we found in the *Thanksgiving Hymns*. This is called into

[93] On this see Baumgarten, "Nature of the Seductress," 134; Esther Eshel, "Genres of Magical Texts in the Dead Sea Scrolls," in *Die Dämonen/Demons: The Demonology of Israelite-Jewish and Early Christian Literature in Context of their Environment* (ed. Armin Lange, Hermann Lichtenberger, and K. F. Diethard Romheld; Tübingen: Mohr Siebeck, 2003) 395-415, 408-409.

question, however, by what we find in 4Q511 48, 49 + 51, for here the document brings together a reference to the bastard spirits and human frailty:

ובפי יפחד [כול רוחות]
3 ממזרים להכניע[ ]טי טמאה כיא בתכמי
4 בשרי יסוד [ד וב]גויתי מלחמות

and by his mouth he frightens [all the spirits]
of the bastards to subdue [ ] impurity because in the filth/innards
of my flesh is the foundation [and in] my body are battles.* (48-49+51 ii.2b-4)

We read of the frightening of the spirits of the bastards already in 4QShir[a]/4Q510 1 4-6 = 4QShir[b]/4Q511 10 1-2 and in 4QShir[b]/4Q511 35 7, but in the passage above we find what appears to be a close connection between these spirits and the human flesh. Whether we translate בתכמי as referring to human flesh as "filth" or as referring to its "innards", as is more probable, the statement makes the human flesh and human body the location of conflicts which involved the spirits of the bastards. This goes beyond the psychological dualism reflected in the *Thanksgiving Hymns* by interpreting the human condition in the context of demonology. It also differs from the dualism of the *Treatise on the Two Spirits* in 1QS/1Q28 3.13 – 4.24 by moving beyond a controlled theism which predetermines the rule of opposing spirits, the prince of light and prince of darkness, and by attributing the human plight to the wild demonic spirits let loose on the world from the offspring of the Watchers. The author clearly sees his work of praising God's power and upholding God's statutes as part of the weaponry to defeat these forces. Within this different anthropology we still find nothing which suggests that the body, itself – including its sexuality, which gives rise to issues of impurity – is, beyond that, problematic.

9 *4QIncantation* 4Q444

As noted above we find also in *4QIncantation*/4Q444 a reference to בתכמי בשר "innards of the flesh" (1-4 i +5 3). Here it stands in parallel to במבניתי "my structure", apparently referring to the human body. The passage assumes conflict: ויהי רוחי ריב במבניתי "and they became spirits of controversy in my structure". This recalls the depiction of conflict in the *Treatise of the Two Spirits*, where we read: עד הנה יריבו רוחי אמת ועול בלבב גבר "Until now the spirits of truth and deceit contend in the hearts of humankind" (1QS/1Q28 4.23b). The spirits in *4QIncantation*/4Q444 are of two kinds. On the one hand, they include God's gift of "true knowledge" (1), "truth" (2), "knowledge and understanding, truth and righteousness" (3). On the other hand, they include the "spirits of wickedness".

Thus the passage urges the hearer: "strengthen yourself by the laws of God, and in order to fight against the spirits of wickedness" (4). It is also similar to the anthropology we noted in the *Songs of the Sage*/4Q510, 511, above, confirmed through the allusion to the bastard spirits in what follows. For the passage goes on to speak of a curse and apparently to look forward to תום ממשלתה "the end of the dominion" of the ממזרים ורוח הטמאה "bastards and of the spirit of impurity" (8) and of תועבה "abomination" (11). Again we have before us an allusion to the myth of the Watchers and their bastard offspring, from whom the evil spirits emerged (*1 Enoch* 15:8-9).[94] Referring to תום ממשלתה "the end of the dominion", Esther Chazon observes: "The entire phrase would then refer to the apocalyptic idea of the limited duration of the dominion of evil and its culmination in the eschaton".[95]

Again, nothing suggests that human sexuality is problematic. Nor does use of the Watcher myth suggests its use to explain or to expose sexual wrongdoing.

10 *4QExorcism ar* 4Q560

4QExorcism ar/4Q560 contains words of exorcism addressed to demonic spirits. It makes reference to male and female in the afflictions they bring as they enter human bodies. This is not sexual, but demonic penetration. The words refer to particular kinds of demons in the light of their effects: "the male Wasting-demon and the female Wasting-demon"; the "Fever-demon and Chills-demon and Chest Pain-demon" and the "male Shrine-spirit and female Shrine-spirit".[96] Within a framework of thought informed by the Watcher myth, these are the demons who emerged from the slain body of the Watchers' offspring to afflict humanity with illnesses (*1 Enoch* 15:9-12).[97] Despite tracing their origins to an act of sexual wrongdoing, that of the Watchers, their behaviour, like that of their parents, the giants, is not depicted in sexual categories, but as doing harm and bringing illness..

---

[94] So also Esther G. Chazon, *DJD* 29, 377; Eshel, "Genres of Magical Texts," 409.

[95] Chazon, *DJD* 29, 377

[96] On this see Esther Eshel, "Genres of Magical Texts," 397; Hermann Lichtenberger, "Qumran and the New Testament," in *The Changing Face of Judaism, Christianity, and Other Greco-Roman Religions in Antiquity: Presented to James H. Charlesworth on the Occasion of his 65th Birthday* (ed. Ian H. Henderson and Gerbern S. Oegema with the assistance of Sara Parks Richter; SJSHZ 2; Gütersloh: Gütersloher Verlagshaus, 2006) 103-29, 125-26.

[97] On this see Esther Eshel, "Genres of Magical Texts," 404; Loader, *Enoch, Levi, and Jubilees*, 31-32 and also Eibert J. C. Tigchelaar, *Prophets of Old and the Day of the End: Zechariah, the Book of Watchers and Apocalyptic* (OTS 35; Leiden: Brill, 1996) 204-207.

11 *11QApocryphal Psalms* 11QapocPs/11Q11

The first four columns of this document appear to have depicted the time of judgement against demons carried out by God's angel who will consign them to darkness (cf. 1QS/1Q28 4.11b-14).[98] In column 5 we then find words belonging to an incantation or curse, which address the demons:

מי אתה [הילוד מ]אדם ומזרע הקד[ושי]ם

Who are you, [offspring of] humankind and the seed of the h[oly one]s?* (5.6)

This alludes to the Enoch myth according to which the giants and the spirits which emerged from their bodies were the offspring of the Watchers and human women and thus matches the designation elsewhere of the spirits as "bastards".[99]

12 *4QHoroscope* 4Q186

This extraordinary document warrants mention because it gives particular attention to the human body and to the time of birth or conception as indicative of the proportions of parts of light and parts of darkness in a human being.[100] Of significance for our discussion is that there is no particular emphasis given to sexual genitalia in any of the material which survives. This coheres with the dualisms elsewhere in the Qumran documents, which do not depict human sexuality as problematic.

---

[98] On this see Nitzan, "Evil and its Symbols," 89.

[99] Baumgarten, "Nature of the Seductress," 134; Eshel, "Genres of Magical Texts," 404.

[100] On this see Nitzan, "Evil and its Symbols," 87; Broshi, "Predestination," 238.

CHAPTER SIX

Attitudes towards Sexuality in Biblical Exposition and Related Material

1 *Pesharim*

1.1 *4QPsalms Pesher[a]* 4QpPs[a]/4Q171

Among the *Pesharim*, 4QpPs[a]/4Q171 interprets Psalm 37 and then the beginning of Psalm 45 in relation to the conflict of the community. At no point have we any indication of the substance of the conflict other than that the Man of the Lie led people astray, and, therefore, no indication that issues of sexuality might have played a role. This is despite reference being made to the congregation of the poor ones being delivered from מכול פחי בליעל "from all the traps of Belial" (1-10 ii.10-11), an expression recalling מצודות בליעל "the nets of Belial" used in CD 4.15. The depicting of the conflict is thus closer to the tone of the *Community Rule* and the *Thanksgiving Hymns* than to the *Damascus Document* (D). It shares with the latter the image of living for a thousand generations (1-10 iii.1-2a and, apparently 1-10 iv.3; cf. CD 19.1-2; Deut 7:9). It brings an eschatology which entails possessing the land and the city (1-10 iii.10-11) and uses Adamic imagery (1-10 iii.1b).[1] While making no reference to resurrection, it assumes future blessing in an embodied state. It also assumes marriage, sexual relations and the begetting of children since it promises "the inheritance of Adam" not only to those who return, but ולזרעם עד עולם "also to their seed forever" (1-10 iii.1-2a).

[1] On the link between Adamic expectation and Jerusalem-focused hope, see Wise, "That which has been," who notes the linking of these expectations in Ezekiel (17:23; 20:40; 40 – 48) (181-83).

1.2 *Habukkuk Pesher* 1QpHab

The *Habukkuk Pesher* is also concerned primarily with conflict, but, in addition, with the impact of the cruel Kittim as an instrument of punishment. At a number of points it cites rejection of the Law as the issue of conflict between the community of the poor and its opponents (1.11; 5.11-12; 8.1, 10, 17; cf. 12.4-5). The conflict is also about their rejection of the instruction of the Teacher of Righteousness (2.2, 6), which included predictions about the future. Apart from the allegations of violence and injustice towards the community, the transgressions include greed and violence generally. These are alleged, in particular, against the Wicked Priest, who apparently began well but then "his heart became proud, he deserted God and betrayed the laws for the sake of riches. And he robbed and hoarded wealth from the violent men who had rebelled against God. He seized public money, incurring additional serious sin"(*DSSSE*) (8.8-12). Reference to accumulating wealth through pillaging other nations occurs in 9.5. The description in column 8 continues with the words:

ודרכי 13 ת[וע]בות פעל בכול נדת טמאה

> And he performed re[pul]sive acts of every type of defiling impurity. (*DSSSE*) (8.12b-13a).

This is the closest we come to a potential allusion to sexual wrongdoing, but it is not explicit. In 12.8 the author speaks in similar words in expounding Hab 2:17:

פשרו הקריה היא ירושלם 8 אשר פעל בה הכוהן הרשע
מעשי תועבות ויטמא את 9 מקדוש אל

> Its interpretation: the city is Jerusalem 8 in which the /Wicked/ Priest performed repulsive acts and defiled 9 the Sanctuary of God. (12.8b-9a)

Beyond that, the misdeeds are primarily depicted as acts against the community and the Teacher of Righteousness, including pursuing the latter on the Day of Atonement (11.5-8), reflecting calendrical disputes. There might be an allusion to dispute about sexual wrongdoing in the assertion that the Teacher and his community

לוא זנו אחר עיניהם בקץ 8 הרשעה

> have not engaged in sexual wrongdoing following their eyes in the time of wickedness.* (5.7b-8a)

It recalls the words which form the rubric for the depiction of Israel's failures in D:

ולא לתור במחשבות יצר אשמה וע(י)ני זנות

and not to follow after the thoughts of a guilty inclination and eyes of sexual wrongdoing* (2.16)

1.3 *4QUnidentified Pesher Fragments* 4QpUnid/4Q172

The unidentified pesher fragments of 4Q172 contain an allusion to Gomorrah in the context of sexual sin. Tigchelaar transcribes fr. 4 as follows:[2]

1]כן ויזנו עמם[
2]העול ברחו[
3]פחז עמורה[
4]בוערת וגם כ [
5]לבבם *vacat* [
6] איתי בח[

1] thus and they committed sexual wrongdoing with them[
2] iniquity (they) fled[
3]sexual immorality of Gomorrah[
4]burning and also as[
5]their hearts [
6]with me in ..

In his discussion[3] he draws attention to many uncertainties in the text, both in identifying letters in the first and last lines, and in reconstructing incomplete words. Thus in 2, ברחו[could be the beginning of ברחובות "on the squares" and in 6, איתי might be part of ראיתי "I saw". Nevertheless, the motifs of sexual wrongdoing, iniquity, (possibly) fleeing, and Gomorrah, all cohere well with the biblical story and reflect an interpretation which sees it judged for sexual wrongdoing. Tigchelaar notes some shared vocabulary with *4QWiles of the Wicked Woman*/4Q184: עול "iniquity" (used with the article other than in this fragment only in 1QS/1Q28 5.2, 10; 8.13; 9.17); פחז "sexual immorality";[4] and (possibly) ברחובות "on the squares".[5]

---

[2] Eibert J. C. Tigchelaar, "Sodom and Gomorrah in the Dead Sea Scrolls," in *Sodom's Sin: Genesis 18-19 and Its Interpretations* (ed. Ed Noort and Eibert J. C. Tigchelaar; Themes in Biblical Narrative 7; Leiden: Brill, 2004) 47-62, 51.

[3] Tigchelaar, "Sodom and Gomorrah," 50-52.

[4] On this meaning of פחז see also 4QApocJer A/4Q383 fr. A; *4QWiles of the Wicked Woman*/4Q184 1 2, 13, 15; 4Q202 3.1 (*1 Enoch* 8:2) (ἐπόρνευσαν Codex Panopolitanus); *Aramaic Levi Document* 6:3 / 16 (פחז συνουσιασμοῦ); Sir 23:5; 19:2; 41:17; and Gen 49:5. There פחז כמים can mean not "unstable as water", but "wanton in water", according to James L. Kugel, "Reuben's Sin with Bilhah," in *The Ladder of Jacob: Ancient Interpretations of the Biblical Story of Jacob and His Children* (Princeton: Princeton

1.4 Other *Pesharim*

Issues relating to sexuality are absent in what survives from the fragmentary 1QpPs/1Q16 and 4QPs[b]/4Q173. The *Micah Pesher* (1QpMicah/1Q14) also offers nothing concrete related to our theme, and, similarly, the *Hosea Pesher* (4QpHos[a]/4Q166). Its interpretation makes nothing, for instance, of the allusion to nakedness in Hos 2:11-12 (2.8-13) or of the image of marriage (1:15-16) in relation to our theme, nor is enough preserved in 4QpHos[b]/4Q167 to discern its use of Hos 6:9-10 ("they commit a monstrous crime [זמה עשו]. In the house of Israel I have seen a horrible thing; Ephraim's whoredom [זנות] is there, Israel is defiled"), except that the interpretation relates it to the "nations" (10, 26 1-3).

In 4QpNah/4Q169 we find the quotation:

> Because of the countless debaucheries of the prostitute, gracefully alluring, mistress of sorcery, who sells nations through her debaucheries, and peoples through her sorcery, I am against you, says the LORD of hosts, and will lift up your skirts over your face; and I will let nations look on your nakedness and kingdoms on your shame.
> (Nah 3:4-5; 4Q169 3-4 ii.7)

However, the document uses these references to prostitution and sexual immorality metaphorically to describe false teaching (3-4 ii.7-11a). It assumes that the conflict includes matters of interpretation of the Law, designating the opponents as דורשי החלקות "seekers of smooth things" (3-4 ii.4, iii.3, 6-7),[6] but gives no indication of the substance of disputes, let alone that they might relate to any sexual issues.

The *Isaiah Pesher* is occupied with hope of victory over the Kittim, but also with conflict with those whom it also identifies as דורשי החלקות "seekers of

---

University Press, 2006) 81-114, 85-90. See also Jonas C. Greenfield, "The Meaning of פחז," in *Studies in Bible and the Ancient Near East, Presented to Samuel E. Loewenstamm, on his Seventieth Birthday* (ed. Y. Avishur and J. Blau; Jerusalem: E. Rubenstein, 1978) 35-40.

[5] Tigchelaar, "Sodom and Gomorrah," 51-52.

[6] On the historical allusions see the recent discussion in Shani Berrin, "*Pesher Nahum, Psalms of Solomon* and Pompey," in *Reworking the Bible: Apocryphal and Related Texts at Qumran: Proceedings of a Joint Symposium by the Orion Center for the Study of the Dead Sea Scrolls and Associated Literature and the Hebrew University Institute for Advanced Studies Research Group on Qumran, 15-17 January, 2002* (ed. Esther G. Chazon, Devorah Dimant, and Ruth A. Clements; STDJ 58; Leiden: Brill, 2005) 65-84, 72-73; James H. Charlesworth, *The Pesharim and Qumran History: Chaos or Consensus*. (Grand Rapids: Eerdmans, 2002) 97-98.

smooth things" (4Q163/4QpIsa[c] 23 ii.10), but again giving no indication of issues in dispute.

2 *4QFlorilegium and 4QCatena[a]* 4QFlor/4Q174 and 4Q177

4QFlor/4Q174 expounds 2 Samuel 7, Nathan's prophecy to David, in order to speak of the future temple, which will replace the defiled temple of Israel, and of the future messiah. In 1-2 i.21 2b-4 it brings a list based partly on Deuteronomy 23 about who should be excluded from the temple and, as in similar lists of exclusion, brings the rationale: "because his holy ones are there" (cf. CD 15.15-18 / 4QD[a]/ 4Q266 8 i.6b-9; 1QM/1Q33 7.6; 1QSa/1Q28a 2.3-9; *4QMMT* B 39-49; 11QT[a]/ 11Q19 45.12-14). Accordingly, Ammonites, Moabites, and bastards, but beyond Deuteronomy 23 and under the influence of Ezek 44:6-9, the foreigner (בן נכר) and proselyte (גר) are also to be excluded,[7] and Ammonites and Moabites excluded not for a set period of years but forever.[8] The document does not take up from Deuteronomy the "man with a crushed testicle", nor relate the restrictions to issues of intermarriage as does *4QMMT*. Of the parallel lists only the *Temple Scroll*, which does not really offer a list, deals as our document does with exclusions from the temple and appears to mean by this, like the *Temple Scroll*, a temple to be constructed to replace the defiled temple (1-2 i, 21 2-6), but not yet equated with the temple which God will finally establish at the end of time (cf. 11QT[a]/11Q19 29.8-10). The others deal with entry into the community, as in Deuteronomy 23, or participation in special assemblies, except for the *War Scroll* where the restrictions are about the army camp.

"Temple" may however equate to community in the document. This depends in part on how we understand the expression מקדש אדם "temple of Adam/ humankind" in 6b. It might refer to the community as a temple (cf. 1QS/1Q28 9.4-5), which would bring it into line with the focus on entry restrictions in D.[9] Wise

---

[7] On this see Joseph Baumgarten, "The Exclusion of *Netinim* and Proselytes in 4Q Florilegium," in *Studies in Qumran Law* (SJLA 24; Leiden: Brill, 1977) 75-87.

[8] Wise, "That which has been," notes that 4QFlor shares this exclusion of all foreigners, including proselytes with the *Temple Scroll*, 167. 11QT[a]/11Q19 40.6 bans them from the male court, restricting them to the third court with the women. See also Shemesh, "Holy Angels," 198.

[9] For the earlier discussion see George J. Brooke, *Exegesis at Qumran: 4QFlorilegium in its Jewish Context* (JSOTS 29; Sheffield: JSOT Press, 1985) 184-93, who concludes that "the whole description is concerned with identifying the sanctuary proleptically with the Qumran community and its role in the latter days" (193) and speaks of "the identification of מקדש with קהל, which is implied in the indirect quotation of Deut 23:2-4" in what follows (193).

and Baumgarten have argued that it is probably best translated as "temple of Adam", and understood as referring to the future temple. It reflects the widely held view that the end will be restored as at the beginning, evident in the allusions to inheriting "all the glory of Adam" in CD 3.20 and 4QpPs[a]/4Q171 1-10 iii.1-2a (cf. also 10-11).[10] Brooke makes a strong case that we have before us some polyvalence in the expression מקדש אדם. He sees two principal meanings, a sanctuary made up of human beings, a designation of the community, but with a proleptic reference to the sanctuary of Adam to be established by God as a restoration of "what was originally intended".[11] Sulzbach notes, however, that place (מקום) needs to be given its full weight (as in Deut 12:11), so that we are probably dealing with a reference to an interim, divinely sanctioned site for worship.[12] It belongs in any case to evidence of an approach to sacred space linked with Eden imagery.[13] Issues of the place of sexuality might then potentially arise, especially if linked with notions of a future in a temple garden paradise. There is, however, no trace of those issues here.

4QCatena[a]/4Q177, sometimes linked with 4QFlor/4Q174,[14] has in 1-4 a cluster of potentially relevant references. In 1-4 2 there appears to be an allusion to Deut 7:15 about God protecting the people from sickness. The following line may preserve an allusion to the nations: נהיה כמש[פחות הארצות] "let us be like the tr[ibes of the nations]". This would fit the context of Deuteronomy 7, which is concerned to urge annihilation of the nations of the land and to prohibit

---

[10] See the discussion in Wise, "That which has been," 174-85.

[11] George J. Brooke, "Miqdash Adam, Eden and the Qumran Community," in *Gemeinde ohne Tempel/Community without Temple: Zur Substituierung und Transformation des Jerusalemer Tempels und seines Kults im Alten Testament, antiken Judentum und frühen Christentum* (ed. Beate Ego, Armin Lange, and Peter Pilhofer; WUNT 118; Tübingen: Mohr Siebeck, 1999) 285-301, 288-89. In this he goes beyond Wise who restricts the meaning to an eschatological temple as depicted in the *Temple Scroll*, to be built before what God will finally construct. See Brooke's critique, pp. 289-91. See also Annette Steudel, *Der Midrasch zur Eschatologie aus der Qumrangemeinde (4QMidrEschat[a.b]): Materielle Rekonstruktion, Textbestand, Gattung und traditionsgeschichtliche Einordnung des durch 4Q174 ("Florilegium") und 4Q177 ("Catena A") repräsentierten Werke aus den Qumranfunden* (STDJ 13; Leiden: Brill, 1994) 166-67.

[12] Sulzbach, "Of Temples," 175-79.

[13] See Sulzbach, "Of Temples," on the role of Eden imagery in temple tradition (169-71).

[14] See Steudel, *Midrasch zur Eschatologie,* who sees them as belonging to the same document, which may well also have included 4Q178, 4Q182 and 4Q183. See also the discussion in Jonathan G. Campbell, *The Exegetical Texts* (London: T&T Clark, 2004), who concludes that Steudel's proposal should be seen as possible rather than probable, because there exist no overlapping texts among the documents which would make the case for their belonging together more secure (53-54). Similarly Jacob Milgrom, *PTSDSSP* 6B, 287.

intermarriage with its inhabitants (7:2-3). After reference to the last days, to the rising up of a man, and to fire (5-6), the passage may then speak of פוח]זים "wan[ton men" (7), if so, probably alluding to sexual wrongdoing.[15] The fragments continue with reference to mourning in the time of Belial in contrast to the blessing which is to come (8-9).[16] This blessing is then connected to information about epochs, years and numbers recorded "on the tablets" (10-12). Apparently refering to what was on the tablets, the document speaks of the ספר התורה שנית, "the book of the second Law" (*DSSEL*, *DSSSE*) or "the book of the Law again"[17] (14), apparently advocated by a leader, but rejected by others, for which they are apparently punished by "the sword of their enemies" (14-16). If the reference is not simply to the Torah, but another document,[18] then the allusion to tablets, the apparent concern with sexual wrongdoing, and with relations (possibly intermarriage) with the nations might suggest the book of *Jubilees*.

Like a number of other *pesharim* the document also refers to "the seekers after smooth things" (9.4). In 12-13 i.5 it mentions having "ten righteous men in the city", an apparent allusion to Genesis 18, the destruction of Sodom and Gomorrah (cf. also 4QCommGen A/4Q252 iii.2-6). On the basis of reconstructing 4QCatena[a]/4Q177 19 in the light of its parallel in 4QBéat/4Q525 22, it is possible to see an allusion to Sodom and Gomorrah also in this fragment. The references to עו[שי זמה "disgusting acts", possibly התלוננו יחד "spend the night together" and יתגוללו "wallow", a term used of sexual wrongdoing in CD 8.5 / 19.17, would then allude to sexual wrongdoing in those cities.

Tigchelaar notes that both *4QCatena[a]*/4Q177 12-13 i.5 and 4QCommGen A/ 4Q252 iii.2-6 appear to allude to Genesis 18. Both use the unusual expression בני בליעל "children of Belial", found elsewhere only in Deut 13:14.[19] Accordingly, he proposes that if one reads 4Q177 + 4Q174 (as one, with Steudel) and 4Q252 together, both works reflect a sectarian discussion of Jerusalem as Sodom. "Both texts (4Q252 and 4Q174+4Q177) express the idea that when the children of Belial will be annihilated, the city of Jerusalem will be saved on account of ten or more righteous ones in the city".[20]

---

[15] On the use of פחז to designate sexual wrongdoing see p. 267 n. 4 above.

[16] Cf. also 4QPsalms[f]/4Q88 x.10, which, like *Jubilees*, looks forward to a time when in Judah Belial will be no more.

[17] John Strugnell, "Notes en Marge du Volume V des 'Discoveries in the Judaean Desert of Jordan'," *RevQ* 7 (1970) 163-276, 238; Steudel, *Midrasch zur Eschatologie*, who draws attention to similar allegations of rejection of Torah in 1QpHab 5.9-12 and 4QpIsa[c]/4Q163 23 ii.14a (109); similarly Milgrom, *PTSDDSP* 6B, 291.

[18] See John Allegro, *DJD* 5, 68.

[19] Tigchelaar, "Sodom and Gomorrah," 61-62.

[20] Tigchelaar, "Sodom and Gomorrah," 62.

While the text of 4QFlor/4Q174 and *4QCatena*[a]/4Q177 is fragmentary, there do appear to be allusions to sexual wrongdoing, probably to intermarriage. This coheres with what also appears to be an allusion to *Jubilees* where this is a major concern. Two further references to sexual wrongdoing link it to Sodom and Gomorrah. Taken together as a whole, there is a strong focus on the future, including an eschatological temple with strict provisions about who may enter it. One might imagine that the issues of intermarriage and of Sodom and Gomorrah's sexual wrongdoing played a role in contrast to a future hope for Jerusalem, its temple of Adam, and restoration of primeval paradise, but in the surviving texts nothing that is said about the future indicates the place of sexuality in such visions. There appear to be close connections with the ideas of *Jubilees*, the *Temple Scroll* and D. This coheres with a similar focus on sexual wrongdoing in contrast to those sectarian documents where this focus is lacking. On the other hand, its Adamic eschatology finds an echo in 4QpPs[a]/4Q171 (1-10 iii.2b, 10-11).

3 *4QAges of Creation* 4QAgesCreat A-B/4Q180-181

4QAgesCreat A-B/4Q180-181 comprise two fragmentary documents which exhibit overlap and may be part of one work, though some see them as "two similar – but not identical – works".[21] They comment on material found within Genesis 6 – 22. In what appears to have been the beginning of the document 4QAgesCreat A/4Q180 reads: פשר על הקצים "Pesher/interpretation concerning the times" and continues in a manner which recalls *Jubilees* (and *4QCatena*[a]/4Q177) to speak of God setting the times of all that is to come and recording them on tablets. The first incident to which the document refers in offering interpretation (פשר) is the myth of the Watchers:

7 [ו]פשר על עזזאל והמלאכים אש[ר באו אל בנות האדם]
8 [וי]לדו להם גברים ועל עזזאל]

[and] interpretation concerning Azazel and the angels wh[o came to the daughters of humankind]
8 [and gave] birth for themselves giants. And concerning Azazel (4Q180 1 7-8)

What follows is not well preserved, though it may have some relation to judgement (cf. משפטים ומשפט סוד; "judgments and judgment of the council"). The summary description reflects a version of the story in which Azazel has come to be seen as the leader of the angels who had sexual relations with human women and produced giants as offspring, reflecting the emphasis on Asael in *1 Enoch* 12 –

[21] Campbell, *Exegetical Texts*, 67.

16, rather than his distinctive role in *1 Enoch* 6 – 11 (echoed in the *Animal Apocalypse*, *1 Enoch* 86:1-3), where the leader is Shemihazah. It is interesting that it speaks of Azazel, as in the *Book of the Giants* and the *Parables of Enoch* (*1 Enoch* 54:5; 44:4), rather than Asael, and also that it uses פשר "interpretation" apparently in relation to the *Book of the Watchers*, indicating its authoritative status.[22] As VanderKam notes, "the Azazel version of the story is already joined with the one in which the angels mate with women and father giants from them".[23]

The sin of the angels in producing giants as offspring comes to expression also in 4QAgesCreat B/4Q181 as part of what appears to refer to the beginning of another period of time:

1 [לאברה]ם [עד הולי]ד ישחק]
2 [בנות]האדם וילד[ו] להמה גברו]ים

to Abraha]m [till he bega]t Isaac [
the [daughters of] humankind and [they] begat for them giant[s.* (4Q181 2 1-2)

The document makes further reference to the Watchers in the context of a statement about sins and their effects:

1 לאשמה ביחד עם ס[רי] עמ[ו
ו]ל[התגולל] ל בחטאת בני אדם
ולמשפטים גדולים ומחלים רעים
2 בבשר לפי גבורות אל ולעומת רשעם
לפי{סוד נדתם} טומ^א^תם

[22] So George W. E. Nickelsburg, "The Books of Enoch at Qumran: What We Know and What We Need to Think about," in *Antikes Judentum und frühes Christentum: Festschrift für Hartmut Stegemann zum 65. Geburtstag* (ed. Bernd Kollmann, Wolfgang Reinbold, and Annette Steudel; BZNW 97; Berlin and New York: de Gruyter, 1999) 99-113, 106-107. See also *Apoc. Abr.* 13:7-14; 14:6; 23:12-13.

[23] VanderKam, "Apocalyptic Tradition,"123. Cf. Armin Lange, "The Essene Position on Magic and Divination," in *Legal Texts and Legal Issues: Proceedings of the Second Meeting of the International Organisation for Qumran studies, Cambridge, 1995: Published in honour of Joseph M. Baumgarten* (ed. M. Bernstein, F. G. Martínez, J. Kampen; Leiden: Brill, 1997) 377-435, 414 n. 129, who, noting that they are called Watchers in 4Q180, concludes that it must be a different version of the myth than what we find in CD 2.17-21. Following Carol A. Newsom, "The Development of 1 Enoch 6 – 19: Cosmology and Judgment," *CBQ* 42 (1980) 310-29, he believes this reflects a myth where there is no divination and Azazel is head of the angels. On the rendering of Asael עשאל as Azazel עזזאל in the *Book of the Giants* and here in 4QAgesCreat A/4Q180 1.7-10, which loses the allusion to technical skills implied in עשה, see Annette Yoshiko Reed, *Fallen Angels and the History of Judaism and Christianity: The Reception of Enochic Literature* (New York: Cambridge University Press, 2005) 96-98.

מסיר בני [שמים] וארץ ליחד רשעה עד
3 קצה

for guilt in the community with the stub[born] ones of his] people,
and for [wallowi]ng in the sin of the sons of Adam
and for great judgements and grievous illnesses 2 in the flesh,
according to the mighty deeds of God and corresponding to their wickedness
according to {the foundation of their impurity} their impurity, which turned aside the sons of [heaven] and earth to a community of wickedness until 3 its time.
(*DSSEL* supplemented) (4Q181 1 ii.1-3a)

The text appears to reflect the tradition according to which "the sons of heaven" are now condemned to wait until the judgement.[24] In that sense, with the wicked of earth who have died, they form a community of wickedness awaiting trial. The hope of the righteous is to join the holy ones, a common motif in many writings found at Qumran. The designation, "sons of heaven", a likely conjecture given the size of the lacuna (the האלוהים "God" of Gen 6:2 would be too long) matches *1 Enoch* 6:2. The subject of מסיר "delivering, turning aside, removing" is most likely God. The passage speaks apparently of התגולל "wallowing", used elsewhere of sexual sins (though nothing indicates this here), of illnesses of the flesh (perhaps alluding to the myth that spirits emerged from the bodies of the giants and brought sickness to humanity; *1 Enoch* 15:11-12), and the language of impurity used in a moral sense: לפי{סוד נדתם} טומ°אתם "according to {the foundation of their impurity} their impurity". The context makes a moral reading of טומ°אתם and also of the erased סוד נדתם likely. As in the *Book of the Watchers*, the consequences of the Watchers' sexual wrongdoing, are not themselves depicted in terms of sexual wrongdoing.

Campbell, noting that "the fall of the angels is prominent in 4QAges of Creation A-B", observes that "the appearance of similar traditions in narrowly sectarian texts like 4QAges of Creation A-B confirms the importance of these ideas for the Qumran community in general and for its distinctive emphasis on matters angelic in particular".[25] This holds, even if the focus of the documents may have been to deal with problematic texts concerned with the nature of angels and of God, as Tigchelaar proposes.[26]

[24] So also Frey, "Different Patterns," 306 n. 116.

[25] Campbell, *Exegetical Texts*, 75.

[26] Tigchelaar, "Sodom and Gomorrah," 57. Cf. also Devorah Dimant, "The 'Pesher on the Periods' (4Q180) and 4Q181," *IOS* 9 (1979) 77-102, who suggests that the author is interested in the theme of sin and punishment (91-99). She also notes that the period from the birth of Shem to the birth of Isaac, and the descent of the Watchers to the destruction of Sodom and Gomorrah, matches the second week (93:4) in the *Apocalypse of Weeks* (*1 Enoch* 93:1-10; 91:11-17).

In 4Q180/4QAgesCreat we also find reference to the sin of Sodom and Gomorrah. It depicts God's concern to examine whether it deserved annihilation (2-4 ii.5-9; as in Gen 18:20-21). The passage does not identify the nature of the sin.

While the text is fragmentary, what survives makes clear reference to the sins of the angels, the sons of heaven, in having sexual relations with human women and thus producing giants, but like the early traditions does not appear to interpret the wickedness which ensued in terms of sexual wrongdoing.

4 *4QCommentary on Genesis A* 4QCommGen A/4Q252

This document, sometimes referred to as *Genesis Pesher*,[27] reproduces select passages from Genesis 6 – 49 with brief comment in six columns.[28] A number of the incidents to which they refer have potential relevance in the search to identify matters pertaining to sexuality.[29] Accordingly, I will review each briefly in the sequence in which it appears in the document (which also matches the sequence of the passages in Genesis).

In i.1 – ii.5a the document cites passages from the account of the flood in Genesis 6 – 8 (citing parts of 6:3a; 7:10-12, 24; 8:3-6, 8-14, 18), offering a concise retelling of the events and giving particular attention to timing.[30] The document begins with reference to "the four hundred and eightieth year of Noah's life" when, it continues,

1 [ב]שנת ארבע מאות ושמונים לחיי נוח בא קצם לנוח ואלוהים
2 אמר לא ידור רוחי באדם לעולם
ויחתכו ימיהם מאה ועשרים
3 שנה עד קץ מי מבול

[27] Shani Berrin, "Qumran Pesharim," in *Biblical Interpretation at Qumran* (ed. Matthias Henze; Grand Rapids: Eerdmans, 2005) 110-33, writes: "It is now generally agreed that 4Q252 is a sort of 'commentary' comprised of sections of biblical interpretation in various genres, including one in the *pesher* genre (col. iv: 3-6), a comment on Jacob's blessing of Reuben, which includes the formula פשר" (131 n 81).

[28] On the compass of the document see George J. Brooke, *DJD* 22, 187-90; George J. Brooke, "The Thematic Content of 4Q252," *JQR* 85 (1994) 33-59, 36-38.

[29] Eisenman and Wise, *Dead Sea Scrolls Uncovered*, write: "There is a collateral interest in sexual matters reflecting the condemnation of 'fornication' which one finds in other Qumran documents like that in the 'three nets of Belial' section of the Damascus Document" (81).

[30] Brooke, "Thematic Content," notes: "In fact only a few verses with chronological information are excluded" (39). Joseph L. Trafton, *PTSDSSP* 6B, notes its "exclusively calendrical concern" (205).

1 In the four hundred and eightieth year of Noah's life their end came for Noah and God
2 said, "My spirit will not dwell among humanity forever"
and their days were determined as "one hundred and twenty
3 years" until the time / end of (the) waters of (the) flood. (i.1-3a)

The passage cites parts of Gen 6:3. The word קצם "their end" might allude therefore to wicked humanity, but it may allude to the offspring of the Watchers, as Gen 6:3 is interpreted by both *1 Enoch* 10:10-11 and *Jub.* 5:8. Brooke and Fröhlich assume a reference to the sin of the Watchers, and in particular to their sexual wrongdoing, though, as Brooke concedes, this is confined to the rather unmediated קצם "their end" in what was the opening line of the document, leaving no room for an actual account of the Watchers to precede it.[31]

As Bernstein notes, the account of the flood, which follows, appears concerned to show that "no event in the narrative took place on the sabbath and that Noah's stay in the ark was a perfect 364-day year (1+3 ii 3)".[32] This entailed the innovation of adding two additional days to the Genesis scheme in order to have his calendar reckoning match the Genesis account which has the ark come to rest on the seventeenth of the seventh month.[33] Thus the account appears designed to explain what otherwise might have been seen as a problem. It does not mention the sinfulness to which the flood is a response of judgement and so also makes no reference to sexual wrongdoing.

In ii.5-6 the document cites Gen 9:24-25 (also partly preserved in 4QCommGen C/4Q254 1), but adds an explanation for the curious detail that God cursed not Ham, but his son, Canaan: "for God had blessed the sons of Noah" and allowed Ham's descendants, apart from Canaan, to dwell in the tents of Shem

---

[31] Brooke, "Thematic Content," 36-37; George J. Brooke, "The *Commentary on Genesis A* and the New Testament," in *The Dead Sea Scrolls and the New Testament* (Minneapolis: Fortress, 2005) 177-94, 182; Ida Fröhlich, "Themes, Structure and Genre of Pesher Genesis: A Response to George J. Brooke," *JQR* 85 (1994) 81-90, 88.

[32] Moshe J. Bernstein, "Pentateuchal Interpretation at Qumran," in *The Dead Sea Scrolls after Fifty Years: A Comprehensive Assessment* (ed. Peter W. Flint and James C. VanderKam; Leiden: Brill, 1998) 1.128-59, 152.

[33] Brooke, "Thematic Content," 39. He notes that the events are rewritten to fit a solar calendar, though differently from in *Jubilees* (40). See also George J. Brooke, "Biblical Interpretation at Qumran," in *The Bible and the Dead Sea Scrolls: The Princeton Symposium on the Dead Sea Scrolls: Volume 1: Scripture and the Scrolls* (ed. James H. Charlesworth; Waco: Baylor University Press, 2006) 287-319, 308-309; Brooke, "Commentary on Genesis A," 179-80

(ii.6b-7; cf. Gen 9:1, 27). The focus appears to be the cursing of Canaan instead of Ham, not the nature of the offence, which is assumed, but goes unmentioned.[34]

In ii.8-9 the focus moves to Abraham's move from Ur to the land of Canaan (citing Gen 11:31b, but also 2 Chron 20:7) with particular attention given to the counting of years, thus again dealing with complex issues of chronology.[35] It continues with reference to the covenant ritual in Gen 15:9a, 17b and Abraham's departure from Canaan, but the end of the column is not preserved. In the fragmentary remains of the next column we recognize allusions to the destruction of Gomorrah (Gen 18:31-32) in combination with Deut 13:7 and 20:11, 14 about destroying cities and taking booty (iii.1-6). It was perhaps an attempt to relate the two consistently, but too little is preserved for us to know whether the text included some reference to the sin of Gomorrah or its nature. If this instance follows the emphasis of the preceding instances, then the focus was probably on explaining coherence.

The next episode, also poorly preserved, refers to the sacrifice of Isaac (iii.6b-9), apparently citing from Gen 22:10-12. Only fragmentary allusions survive in iii.12-13 to Isaac's sending of Jacob to find a wife (Gen 28:3-4), with no indication of the theme beyond that. The next preserved allusion is to Timna, concubine of Eliphaz, son of Esau, and her giving birth to Amalek (Gen 36:12a). The document then cites Saul's destruction of Amalek (based on 1 Sam 14:48; 15:3, 7) and Deut 25:19 about the need to destroy the memory of Amalek (iv.1-3a). From there it jumps to Jacob's blessing of Reuben (Gen 49:3-4), where it explains (פשרו "its interpretation, explanation") Jacob's disapproval by cross-referencing it with the account of Reuben's sleeping with Bilhah (Gen 35:22) (iv.3b-7). In v.1-7 the document moves to the blessing of Judah, where, again, it offers a cross-reference, associating Jer 33:17 (the promise of an occupant of the throne of David) with the blessing in Gen 49:10. There it identifies the "staff" with kingship, and proceeds to identify a reference to "thousands" with "the standards" in Gen 49:10, which it then interprets in relation to the community. The last column of the document appears to allude to the blessings of Asher and Naphtali (vi.1-2; Gen 49:20-21).

Brooke argued that the document appears to deal with unfulfilled blessings and curses, especially about sexual misbehaviour and the possession and purification of the land. He notes in regard to the allusion to Deut 13:13-19 and 20:10-20, that they relate only to cities given to Israel as inheritance, so that the document assumes, in line with Ezek 47:15-20, that the destruction of Sodom and

[34] Cf. also 4QCommGen C/4Q254 which mentions the cursing of Canaan, but without further comment preserved (1 1-4).

[35] So Brooke, "Thematic Content," 44-45; Brooke, "Commentary on Genesis A," 184.

Gomorrah was to be seen as part of the purification of the land.[36] In particular he notes the connection of the Genesis passages with sexual wrongdoing: the Watchers, to whom he sees an allusion in the opening lines, the curse of Canaan, Gomorrah, the Amalekites, and Reuben.[37] He refers to Pseudo-Philo, which connects Judges 19 and Genesis 19, in support of including the Amalekites under this concern.[38] He sees a parallel interest in sexual wrongdoing in CD 2.16 – 3.2, noting that both texts refer to Abraham as God's friend (אהב, ii.8; CD 3.2).[39] There, as we have shown above, the focus on sexual wrongdoing is clear and continues beyond 3.2 to 3.12. The parallels to the present passage are, however, not extensive. They include a possible reference to the Watchers, although our document probably alludes to their offspring (also mentioned in D), and the reference to Abraham noted above. While the myth of the Watchers depicts an act of sexual wrongdoing, one should differentiate this from the wickedness which ensued, promoted primarily by their offspring. Their actions are not, in fact, depicted as acts of sexual wrongdoing. The wickedness of humanity, however, doubtless included it.

Fröhlich also argued the centrality of sexual wrongdoing in the document, suggesting that it presents contrasting pairs where the first is connected to sexual wrongdoing: the Watchers with Noah; Canaan's curse with Abraham's entry and covenant; Gomorrah with Abraham's willingness to sacrifice Isaac; the annihilation of Amalek and the sin of Reuben with the blessing of Judah and his brothers.[40]

In response to Brooke, Bernstein observed that the document does not, in fact, focus on acts of sexual wrongdoing,[41] and our review of the material confirms this. There may have been some focus on sexual wrongdoing in the context of the fragmentary references to Gomorrah, to Isaac's instruction to Jacob to seek a wife (against intermarriage; cf. Gen 28:1), and implied in the word, קצם "their end", in the first line, should that refer to the Watchers and not primarily to wicked humanity, but these are arguments from silence and as noted above, the Watchers' offspring are nowhere depicted as engaging in sexual wrongdoing. In those texts which are well preserved there is also no indication that this is a concern.

---

[36] George J. Brooke, "The Genre of 4Q252: From Poetry to Pesher," *DSD* 1 (1994) 160-79; Brooke, "Thematic Content," 59; George J. Brooke, "4Q252 as Early Jewish Commentary," *RevQ* 17 (1996) 385-401, 388-89. See also Brooke, *DJD* 22, 185-207.

[37] Brooke, "Thematic Content," 47, 56; "Commentary on Genesis A," 182.

[38] Brooke, "Thematic Content," 52.

[39] Brooke, "Thematic Content," 57; similarly Fröhlich, "Narrative Exegesis," 84-86.

[40] Fröhlich, "Narrative Exegesis," 89.

[41] Moshe J. Bernstein, "4Q252: Method and Context, Genre and Sources: A Response to George J. Brooke," *JQR* 85 (1994) 61-79, 67, 74. See also Trafton, *PTSDSSP* 6B, 205.

Some of the passages have as their focus the resolution of exegetical conundrums. This is apparent in the passages about the flood and about Ham and Canaan, where each concludes with a solution. It is probably also the case with the reference to Reuben (explaining why he loses the blessing of being firstborn, where פשרו appears to mean: "its explanation", rather than an interpreting application to the present) and to Gomorrah, where some explanation is being given also through the cross-references to the laws of war and the idolatrous city in Deuteronomy. Cross-referencing is used as an exegetical tool also in the reference to Judah and the promise of Davidic messiahship, linked to אנשי היחד "the men of the community" (v.5).

Accordingly, the document appears best understood as a series of "responses to various difficulties in the text of the Hebrew Bible".[42] While, therefore, it has been interpreted in a way that would have made it significant for our theme, closer examination, especially of the flow of argument in those sections which are well preserved, indicates that this does not appear to be the focus of the document. At most we can note that a number of the passages with which it deals originally pertained to sexual wrongdoing in some way, but in none of them does the document address it as a theme. Its purpose seems, rather, to explain what are sensed as problematic texts. In dealing with apparently problematic texts, issues of sexuality are not treated as problematic or given particular attention.

5 Other Reworked Biblical Material and Exhortations

The material which has potentially relevant allusions to sexuality in this section is mostly very fragmentary and without sufficient context to discern particular trends or values.

5.1 *Reworked Pentateuch* 4QBibPar[RP^{a}]/4Q158; 4QRP^{b-e}/4Q364-367

Much of these documents consists of word for word copying of the biblical texts, but sometimes there are significant additions, omissions and combinations.

In recounting Jacob's wrestling with the divine visitor (Gen 32:24-32) 4QBibPar[RP^{a}]/4Q158 adds the substance of the visitor's blessing which includes

[42] Bernstein, "Method," 79; see also Bernstein, "Pentateuchal Interpretation," 152-54; so also Tigchelaar, "Sodom and Gomorrah," 60. The counter argument of Brooke, "4Q252 as Early Jewish Commentary," that the Akedah appears not to address such a conundrum (387-88) is not cogent because of the fragmentary nature of the text. It is also not difficult to imagine that text presenting problems which might have been addressed in the missing material.

the words: "May the Lord make you fruitful and multiply you" (1-2.7). In 7-8.1-2 the document cites a selection of commands from the decalogue: the command to honour parents, the prohibition against false testimony, and the prohibition of coveting the wife of a neighbour (Exod 20:12, 16, 17), but not the other prohibitions, including the one against adultery. The same fragments preserve traces of Exod 21:10, which deals with taking a second wife, but not diminishing the food, clothing, or marital rights (sexual intercourse) of the first wife (7-8 15).

4QRP[b]/4Q364 brings Gen 25:18-21, reporting Isaac's taking Rebecca as his wife and successfully seeking God's help because of her barrenness, so that she conceived (1a-b). In 2 there are traces of the story of Isaac's attempts to pass Rebecca off as his sister before Abimelech, as in Gen 26:7-8. In 4b are traces of Gen 30:8-14, the story of the mandrakes. In 7 we have a reference to Shechem, probably citing Gen 34:2. In 9a-b we find traces of Gen 38:14-21, from the story of Tamar and Judah. In 4QRP[c]/4Q365 we find remains of Gen 21:9-10, Sarah's decision to have Hagar expelled (1). 4QRP[e]/4Q367 brings Lev 11:47 – 13:1, including the provisions for purification after childbirth (1a-b). In 3 3-4 it cites Lev 20:13 condemning homosexual acts between men as an abomination.

While a number of the fragments bring portions of the Pentateuch relevant for issues of sexuality, none brings interpretation or gives indication of particular emphasis by addition, omission or placement. At most one might note the added blessing in the story of Jacob as emphasizing fruitfulness and the omission of some parts of the decalogue, including prohibition of adultery, as at least indicating that the compiler did not see them as relevant enough to cite at that point.

5.2 References to Eden

4QParaphrase of Genesis and Exodus/4Q422 includes an allusion to the story of Eden (i.9-10), including mention of the act of disobedience as forgetting, and of a יוצר רע "evil inclination" (i.12), but without further detail. In *4QMeditation on Creation A*/4Q303 we find reference to Adam, knowledge of good and evil and his wife as a helper (8-11), but the text is too fragmentary to discern the context or focus of the passage. *4QRenewed Earth*/4Q475 speaks of the future in terms of all the world becoming like Eden (כול תבל כעדן) (5). It assumes a future of embodied existence like other developments of eschatology related to Eden.

5.3 *4QPseudo-Jubilees* 4QpsJub[a]/4Q225 and 4QpsJub[c]/4Q227

4QpsJub[a]/4Q225 preserves a version of the sacrifice of Isaac which reflects the account in *Jubilees*, including the involvement of Mastema (משטמה) and his angels (2 ii.6, 13, 14) and Belial (*Jub.* 17:15-18). It also reflects a common concern of *Jubilees* in the first words preserved in 1.1, מעוון הזנות "from the sin of sexual wrongdoing", but unfortunately the context is not preserved.

In 4QpsJub[c]/4Q227 we find reference, as in *Jubilees*, to an angel and his colleagues, including from his statement the words: "E]noch after we taught him" (2.1). The fragmentary text which follows has the words, א]רץ אל תוך בני האדם "ear]th to among the sons of humankind", probably referring to the presence of the Watchers, followed by, "and he testified against all of them" and after a gap on the next line: "and also against the Watchers" (2 2-4), an allusion to Enoch's testimony against the Watchers reflecting *1 Enoch* 12 – 16, but nothing more is preserved. The text is too fragmentary to decide whether it speaks of Enoch testifying against two groups or just the same group, mentioned a second time after intervening words, which would make sense of the וגם "and also".

5.4 *Apocryphon of Jeremiah* and *Pseudo-Ezekiel*

4QApocrJerC[a-f]/4Q385a/387/388a/389/390/387a[43] also reflects the language and concerns of *Jubilees*, though it deals with the period beyond what *Jubilees* covers, yet still as God's instruction to Moses. There is a concern about עבדי נכר "those who serve what is foreign" (4Q385a 5a-b 9 = 4Q387 3.6; 4Q387a 4 7), and about neglect of sabbaths and festivals (4Q385a 3a-c 6 = 4Q388a 3 5; 4Q390 1 8; 2 i.9-10):

ואת מקדשי יטמאו 10 [את שבתותי יחללו]את[מו]עדי יש[כח]ו
ובבני[נכר]יחלל[ו]את זר[ע]ם

> And they will defile my Temple, 10 [they will profane my sabbaths], they will for[ge]t my[fes]tivals
> and with the sons of fo[reign]ers [t]he[y] will profane their offspr[ing.
> (4Q390 2 i.9-10)

This reflects the ethos and emphasis of *Jubilees*. In relation to matters of sexuality, this includes an attack on intermarriage of women to foreign men. Its concern with profaning the sabbath could include doing so through having sexual intercourse. Similarly, defiling the temple, could, as in *Jubilees* (e.g. 30:12-15), include doing so by sexual wrongdoing of various kinds. In 4Q387 fr. A we find reference to issues of nakedness, linked probably with the profaning God's name, which precedes it, and to incest:

---

[43] I follow the titles and renumbering of Devorah Dimant, *DJD* 30, 91-260. On the confusion and complexity of the various designations of 4Q383-91, see Monica Brady, "Biblical Interpretation in the 'Pseudo-Ezekiel' Fragments (4Q383-391) from Cave Four," in *Biblical Interpretation at Qumran* (ed. Matthias Henze; Grand Rapids: Eerdmans, 2005) 88-109, 88-94.

]בערותם לקרוב איש אל שאר בשרו

] in their nakedness, each drawing near to his close kin.

The allusion is to Lev 18:6.[44] In language reminiscent of *Jubilees* the author speaks also of the angels of Mastemot (4Q390 1 11), of abominations (תעבות) perpetrated by priests in Jerusalem (4Q388a 7 ii 7; 4Q389 8 ii.1), or by "three who will rule" (4Q388a 7 ii.8).

This document, which shows no marks of being sectarian has affinities with *Jubilees* and its concerns with intermarriage, incest, and defilement of the sabbath (possibly through sexual intercourse).

In 4QApocJer A/4Q383 fr. A we find the accusation:

2]שה מחללי הברית מט]מא

3]אבותם בוזזי אמותם הפוחזים [

2] those who profane the covenant, who de[file

3] their fathers, despoilers of their mothers, who act in a depraved way.*

It is possible that these accusations are all of a sexual nature, in which case they would include an allusion to incest. פחז "act in a depraved way" is used in a sexual sense in 4QpUnid/4Q172 4 3; 4QEn^{b} ar/4Q202 3 1 (= *1 Enoch* 8:2); *Aramaic Levi Document* 6:3 / 16 (see also Gen 49:5).

4QpsEzek^{b}/4Q386 speaks of a son of Belial who will lead to a multitude being defiled (הטמא) (1 ii.4), but says nothing of the nature of the defilement, though it clearly assumes a culpable deed.

5.5 Material Related to the Flood

4QNoah ar/4Q534, which may not relate to the flood, includes a prediction which compares someone's deed or building in the future with that of the Watchers, clearly associated in the context with sin, but without further specification: וכל[א׳[ן יתבנון כעירין עובדה "and enclose[ur]es shall be built, its work/deed/building will be like the Watchers" (1 ii +2 15-16). Unfortunately, it is not clear to whom it refers nor to what particular deed or work, or whether it may pertain to sexual wrongdoing. A few lines earlier there appears to be a reference to virgins, [ ]לא ובת[ו]לן יתבן די "and virgins will dwell without", perhaps a vision of security, maybe of virgins unsullied by seductive Watchers, but the text is too fragmentary except to note that it is part of the positive side of a prediction.

4QExhortation Based on the Flood/4Q370 refers to the sin punished in the flood using the expression, כמחשבות יצר לבם ה]רע "according to the thoughts of

[44] See Brady, "Biblical Interpretation," 102-103.

the [evil] inclination of their hearts" (1.3), but without specific reference to sexual wrongdoing. In 2.3-4 the text apparently refers to purification of people from iniquity and evil which consisted in or is related in some way to knowledghe of good and evil, an allusion to Gen 2:17.

5.6 Material Related to Exodus, the Entry and the Exile

1QApocrMoses[a]?/1Q22 brings a prediction to Moses by God that the people would abandon God (following the reconstruction of Tigchelaar):[45]

וילכו א]חר[שקוצי ה]גו[ים ותו]עבתיהם [ואחר גל]וליהם[עבדו]את
8 אלו[היה]ם והיו לפ[ח ל]מוקש ויע[זבוני
וישכחו ה]דש ושבת ו[יובל]וברית

> and follow the abominations of the nations, and their offences and their idols; and they will worship 8. their gods and they will be a snare and a trap; and they will abandon me and forget new moon and sabbath and jubilee and covenant (1.7-8) (outlined = 4QDM = PAM 43,686)

The focus appears to be idolatry, although an allusion to sexual wrongdoing should not be ruled out, given that the parallel material in *Jub.* 1:9[46] is understood in this way in its broader context. The motif of trap and snare (פח מוקש) occurs in CD 4.14-15 in the context of the nets of Belial (מצוד פחד פח) which it interprets with a primary emphasis on sexual immorality, though nothing indicates that this is its focus here.

4QapocrPent A/4Q368 cites Exod 34:11-24 about not making covenant with the inhabitants of the land (2 3-4), but without making any link to issues such as intermarriage.

4QapocrJosh[a]/4Q378 makes reference to "their daughters" in 10 1 and on the following line: "[and] you take some of the[ir] daughters[", possibly relating to the prohibition against intermarriage with Canaanites.

4QapocrLam A/4Q179 compares the city's suffering to "a w]oman naked, like one suffering, and like one abandoned [by her husband]. All her fortifications[like] a barren and impoverished woman" (2.6-7).

---

[45] Eibert Tigchelaar, "A Cave 4 Fragment of *Divre Mosheh* (4QDM) and the Text of 1Q22 1:7-10 and *Jubilees* 1:9, 14," *DSD* 12 (2005) 303-12, 303-306.

[46] On this see Tigchelaar, "Cave 4 Fragment," 306-308, who reconstructs the Hebrew of *Jubilees* and sees the 1Q22 as earlier. See also my discussion in Loader, *Enoch, Levi, and Jubilees*, 216-19.

5.7 *4QDanSuz? Ar* 4Q551

4QDanSuz? ar/4Q551 refers to an old man, to a son of Jonathan, son of Joshua, son of Ishmael, and all the men of the city gathering round a house demanding of a man that he bring someone out, to which the man replies, addressing them as brothers and urging that they not act wickedly. The fragment then makes reference to peace and a tantalising "[because o]f this". Milik proposed that the incident alludes to the story of Susanna and the elders, hence the naming of the document.[47]

An allusion to Judges 19 seems much more likely.[48] There we also read of an old man who gave hospitality to a traveller (19:16-21). The men of the city gather around the house and demand that the man bring out the guest so that they could have sexual relations with him (male-rape), to which the host responds, addressing them as brothers, and similarly urging that they not act wickedly (19:22-24). The host then surrenders the Levite's concubine to their lusts and the Levite later dismembers her to call Israel to war against Benjamin. The story also has intertextual connections to the incident in Gen 19:1-11, where the men of Sodom want to male-rape Lot's (angelic) guests. Similarly Lot addresses them as brothers, urging them not to act so wickedly, offering them his two virgin daughters. None of these stories speaks of a "son of Jonathan, son of Joshua, son of Ishmael", so that we are most likely dealing with a retelling of the Gibeah incident with additional detail. What survive are snippets of narrative, but not the consequences associated with "[because o]f this" (ל[דנה), nor an evaluation, although we may assume the event was viewed with outrage.

5.8 Two Narrative Works

The fragmentary text, *4QNarrative A*/4Q458, contains a reference to הזנות "sexual wrongdoing" (2 i.6), but without a clear context beyond mention of angels executing judgement, someone fleeing and reference to uncleanness (הטמאה) (2 i.5), followed by a report of someone destroying an army, devouring the uncircumcised and an ascent and an anointing with the oil of kingship (2 ii.3-6). In 17 we read the words, נעל ראובן "Reuben abhorred", probably an allusion to his sexual wrongdoing, but nothing more is preserved beyond an isolated reference to Judah in the preceding line and Joseph on the next, possibly reflecting Genesis 49.

---

[47] J. T. Milik, "Daniel et Susanne à Qumrân," in *De la Tôrah au Messie: Mélanges Henri Cazelles* (ed. M. Carrez. J. Doré, and P. Grelot; Paris: Desclée, 1981) 337-59; see also Peter W. Flint, "Noncanonical Writings in the Dead Sea Scrolls: Apocrypha, other Previously Known Writings, Pseudepigrapha," in *The Bible at Qumran: Text, Shape, and Interpretation* (ed. P. Flint; Grand Rapids: Eerdmans, 2001) 80-126, 114.

[48] So WAC, 555; George W. E. Nickelsburg, "4Q551: A Vorlage to Susanna or a Text Related to Judges 19?" *JJS* 48 (1997) 349-51.

4QNarrative C[a]/4Q462 uses the image of a woman whose face will change to brilliance and refers also to her menstruation (עדה) and clothes and her being loathed, and in impurity (טמאה), apparently as a way of speaking of hope for Jerusalem (1.15-19).

6 The *Genesis Apocryphon* 1QapGen ar/1Q20

This work contains a rewriting of much of Genesis 6 – 14, supplemented by traditions some of which are known to us from elsewhere in early Enoch literature and *Jubilees*.[49] It exists in a single copy found in cave one at Qumran and does not appear to be sectarian.[50] The scroll dates to around the turn of the millennium and Fitzmyer concludes the original is likely to have been composed not long before in the first century BCE.[51] Much of the document is poorly preserved. The first column with substantial content, column 2, commences in the course of a narrative about the conception of Noah.

The two preceding columns, which at first circulated independently of the rest of the document, and were later identified as belonging to it, are numbered 0 and 1.[52] While fragmentary, they allow us to recognize that they included reference to the myth of the Watchers as found in *1 Enoch* 6 – 16. The narrative in column 2 assumes that the hearer has already been informed of the Watchers' deeds, since it portrays Lamech as concerned his wife's pregnancy may have resulted from their actions. The presence of some likely allusions to the myth (in Genesis and *1 Enoch* 6 – 16) as identified by Fitzmyer in 0.4, 8, 17; and 1.1[53] (and there are more as we shall see below) supports the conclusion that "the fragmentary lines of columns 0

---

[49] The Aramaic text and English translation of Genesis Apocryphon are based on Joseph A. Fitzmyer, *The Genesis Apocryphon of Qumran Cave 1 (1Q20): A Commentary* (3d ed.; Biblica et Orientalia 18/B; Roma: Pontificio Istituto Biblico, 2004). See also Matthew Morgenstern, Elisha Qimron, and Daniel Sivan, "The Hitherto Unpublished Columns of the Genesis Apocryphon," *Abr-Nahrain* 33 (1995) 30-54.

[50] So Fitzmyer, *Genesis Apocryphon*, 22-25.

[51] Fitzmyer, *Genesis Apocryphon*, 28.

[52] Moshe J. Bernstein, "From the Watchers to the Flood: Story and Exegesis in the Early Columns of the *Genesis Apocryphon*," in *Reworking the Bible: Apocryphal and Related Texts at Qumran: Proceedings of a Joint Symposium by the Orion Center for the Study of the Dead Sea Scrolls and Associated Literature and the Hebrew University Institute for Advanced Studies Research Group on Qumran, 15-17 January, 2002* (ed. Esther G. Chazon, Devorah Dimant, and Ruth A. Clements; STDJ 58; Leiden: Brill, 2005) 39-63, notes that it "is unwise to presume that the *Apocryphon* began with column 1 or even column 0" (44).

[53] Fitzmyer, *Genesis Apocryphon*, 117-20.

and 1 must have been devoted to a description of the depraved state of humanity before the flood as a result of the conduct of 'the daughters of men' and 'the sons of God' (Gen 6:2-4)".[54]

One of the distinctive features of the document is that different individuals speak in the first person in each section. The "we" in columns 0-1 "are imprisoned" (0.8, 13) and the object of God's anger. The allusion is almost certainly to the Watchers, who according to *1 Enoch* 10:4-6, 11-15; 14:4-5 and *Jub.* 5:6, 10 were bound until the judgement. Thus the document in these columns reports words of Watchers. This helps make sense of the fragmentary substance of the columns, though much must remain tentative.

In 0.2 Fitzmyer translates]די בכול נקבל גיור, "for in every (way) we shall welcome an adulterer", noting that in *Tg. Neofiti* of Exod 20:14 and Lev 20:10 גיור means "adulterer".[55] This would cohere with the nature of their crime and associate them with adulterous activity. Indeed, this will be Lamech's fear. If, with Wise in *DSSEL*, one understands it as "stranger" or "alien", the focus may be on inappropriate mixing, another way of designating their crime. In 0.5-6 God is addressed directly in the second person singular. The Watchers speak of God's anger using a rhetorical question which begins מן הוא "Who is there ..." and concludes חמת רגזך "the heat of your anger", inviting the conjecture that the missing words included reference to some one being able to withstand it. God's anger is highlighted also in 0.7, which speaks of quivering and trembling. The theme of God's anger returns in 0.11 ברגזך "in your anger" and 0.12 indicates that judgement is imminent: וכען קריבה ידך למחה "and now your hand (is) near to smite". The Watchers are facing the prospect of judgement (cf. *1 Enoch* 10:6, 12-13; 14:4; *Jub.* 5:10).[56] In 0.8 they describe their lot: אנחנא אסירין "we are prisoners" and in 0.13 indicate that their time of imprisonment (אסרנא) is coming to an end. The reference to fire (נור) also reflects judgement (cf. *1 Enoch* 10:6, 13).

In 0.15 Fitzmyer translates ומתמחין מן אחיהון "and they are being smitten by their brothers".[57] Within the context of the Watcher myth this most likely refers to the giants killing each other (*1 Enoch* 10:9, 12; 12:6; 14:5; *Jub.* 5:9). In 0.17 he translates אן מתחתנין "that they would not ally themselves by marriage", a further allusion to the Watcher myth (*1 Enoch* 6:1-2; 7:1; 12:4; 15:3-4; *Jub.* 5:1).[58]

[54] Fitzmyer, *Genesis Apocryphon*, 117.

[55] Fitzmyer, *Genesis Apocryphon*, 117.

[56] See Bernstein, "From the Watchers to the Flood," 44-45. Cf. Fitzmyer, *Genesis Apocryphon*, who understands the anger as directed at human depravity (117).

[57] Fitzmyer, *Genesis Apocryphon*, where he disputes Milik's reading מן אחרהון "because that suffixal form of the prep. is impossible" (118).

[58] Fitzmyer, *Genesis Apocryphon*, 118-19.

He notes also that מרה עלמא "eternal Lord" (0.18) reflects the language of Enoch literature (cf. 4QEn^{b}/4Q202 1 iii.14).[59] Column 1 appears to continue with the Watcher myth, the first line preserving the words, ועם נקבתא "and with the women/females". Unfortunately it is not clear what רז רשעא "mystery of evil" (1.2) or רזא "mystery" (1.3) refer to, though it doubtless relates to the myth in some way and could refer to forbidden knowledge, the "stolen mystery", passed on to women by the angels (*1 Enoch* 15:3).[60] The reference to סמין כשפין וח]רשין "medicines, magicians and sooth[sayers" in 1.11 most likely reflects the detail in the myth about the Watchers' teaching forbidden knowledge, especially to women (*1 Enoch* 7:1; 8:1; 9:6, 8; 16:3). Further general allusions to the myth are reflected in 1.13 (עובדא די עבד]ו "deed which [they] did") and 1.14 (ובישתא "and the evil"). Apparently part of line 20 was left blank, which may have indicated a new section about to begin.

Despite its fragmentary state 0.1 – 1.20 seem best understood as an account in which the Watchers, shortly before their judgement, bound in the depths, describe the fearful prospect of God's anger. Either they or a narrator also make mention of the mutual destruction of their offspring, their own deeds of illicit sexual relations with women and their passing on to them the secrets of sorcery and divination. The motifs of their being bound till the final judgement, the mutual self-destruction of their offspring, and their passing on forbidden knowledge to the women, all derive not from Gen 6:1-4, but from the myth as recounted in *1 Enoch* 6 – 11.[61]

The myth of the Watchers by no means disappears from view in the succeeding sections of the work. This is true both of Lamech's story and of what follows. Thus in 1.22 אסיר תקיף "strong prisoner" or אסור תקיף "strong bond" probably refers to the imprisonment of the Watchers. In 1.25 we find ולקלל לכול בשרא "and as a shame (or curse) on all flesh". This is probably

---

[59] Fitzmyer, *Genesis Apocryphon*, 119. He referred, however, to 4Q529 1.6, 7, 11, 12, in the document now identified as 4QWords of Michael ar.

[60] George W. E. Nickelsburg, "Patriarchs Who Worry about Their Wives: A Haggadic Tendency in the *Genesis Apocryphon*," in *Biblical Perspectives: Early Use and Interpretation of the Bible in Light of the Dead Sea Scrolls: Proceedings of the First International Symposium of the Orion Center for the Study of the Dead Sea Scrolls and Associated Literature, 12-14 May 1996* (ed. Michael E. Stone and Esther G. Chazon; STDJ 28; Leiden: Brill, 1998) 137-58, sees it referring to "the watchers' revelations in 1 Enoch 8:1-4; 16:3" (142).

[61] Fitzmyer, *Genesis Apocryphon*, appears to give insufficient weight to the centrality of the myth in these columns when he writes that they "must have been devoted to a description of the depraved state of humanity before the flood" (117) and "the depraved state of humanity and God's reaction to it" (120), similarly p. 17. The focus seems to be the state of the angels rather than the state of humanity.

referring to the impact of the Watchers and their offspring on humanity, namely the increase in human wickedness (Gen 6:3, 5; *1 Enoch* 9:1).[62] The next two lines, which contains the words ובמשלחן לכון שלח הוא "and by messengers he sent to you" (1.26), and לארעא ולמחת לה "to the earth, and to go down to it" (1.27), may well refer to that version of the myth found in *Jubilees* which understood the Watchers as having been sent to earth on a divine errand (*Jub.* 4:15; 5:6; 7:21). The remaining words of the column return to the plight of humanity, as apparently not knowing what to do and to something having impact on all flesh. This would certainly make sense as part of a description of the plight in which humanity found itself as a result of the Watchers' deed, to which the four angels draw attention in *1 Enoch* 9:1-3.

The depiction of humanity's plight is probably part of the introduction of Lamech's story. It continues across the columns to the end of column 5, of which the column preserved best by far is column 2. There we find Lamech speaking in the first person about his concerns about his wife's pregnancy. The story has close parallels with *1 Enoch* 106-107, where Lamech's response comes after Noah's birth (106:4).[63] This makes it likely that *Genesis Apocryphon* must have also contained some reference to Noah's appearance and behaviour at his birth before column 2 begins.[64] In 5.5 and 7 the account of Enoch's response assumes this because it speaks of Lamech being afraid at Noah's appearance and in 5.12-13 reports about the child, that "his eyes shone like the su[n]" and that "this child (is) a flame," perhaps recalling the lost description (cf. *1 Enoch* 106:2, "When he opened his eyes, the house shone like the sun"; 106:5, "His eyes are like the rays

---

[62] So Fitzmyer, *Genesis Apocryphon*, 121.

[63] On the two accounts see Loader, *Enoch, Levi, and Jubilees*, 71-76; George W. E. Nickelsburg, *1 Enoch 1: A Commentary on the Book of 1 Enoch Chapters 1-36, 81-108* (Hermeneia; Minneapolis: Fortress, 2001) 541-42; and Nickelsburg, "Patriarchs Who Worry about Their Wives," 138-47. He calculates that the account in *Genesis Apocryphon* is 3.74 times longer than *1 Enoch* 106-107 (139).

[64] So Fitzmyer, *Genesis Apocryphon*, 122; similarly Nickelsburg, "Patriarchs Who Worry about Their Wives," 138. See also Bernstein, "From the Watchers to the Flood," who notes that "from the standpoint of the narrative, it is significant that there is not a great deal of space within which Lamech could be introduced (unless he was mentioned in the fragmentary portions of column 0, 1, or earlier, lost material), and for the birth and marvelous nature of the child to be described" (46). But see also by contrast Eileen Schuller, "Response to 'Patriarchs Who Worry about their Wives: A Haggadic Tendency in the *Genesis Apocryphon*," in *George W.E. Nickelsburg in Perspective: An Ongoing Dialogue of Learning* (2 vols; ed. Jacob Neusner and Alan J. Avery-Peck; JSJSup 80; Leiden: Brill, 2003) 1. 200-12, who provides evidence that the "initial section with the description of the extraordinary child might have been somewhat longer in the *Genesis Apocryphon* than in *1 Enoch*" (205) and shows that this is also the case in the description given Methuselah (205).

of the sun"; similarly 106:10). The description in *1 Enoch* 106:2-3 speaks of him as having a "body whiter than snow and redder than a rose" with hair "all white and like white wool and curly", eyes that made the house shine like the sun, standing up and praising God already in the hands of the midwife, like the angels in heaven (106:4-5). Noah's legendary features are described also in 1QNoah/1Q19 3 5: they "[illuminated] the rooms of the house like rays of the sun", and in 4QAramaic N/4Q535 3 3, which gives the baby's weight as "three hundred and fif[ty] shekels".[65]

Lamech's fear is informed by the Watcher myth, just presented.[66] So he contemplates די מן עירין הריאתא ומן קדישין זרעא ולנפיל[ין] "that the conception was from the Watchers or that the seed was from the Holy Ones, or (belonged) to Nephil[im]" (2.1). Here "Watchers" and "Holy Ones" are equated. The third element: לנפיל[ין] "belonged to the Nephil[im", reflects the myth that after the women conceived by the Watchers they produced extraordinary offspring. Unlike in *1 Enoch* 106 where Lamech ran off to his father, Methuselah, *Genesis Apocryphon* first has Lamech confront his wife, Bitenosh (2.3-18). She reassures Lamech and reminds him of the erotic pleasure of their sexual intercourse:

יא אחי ויא מרי דכרלך על עדינתי א]
(10) [בחו]ם ענתא ונשמתי לגו נדנהא

O my brother[67] and my lord, recall my pleasure .[ ]
10 [in the hea]t of the time, and my breath in the midst of its sheath. (2.9-10)

Fitzmyer explains: "The body is understood to be a sheath, and the panting breath is like a sword moving back and forth within it. It is thus an expressive figure for emotional panting during intercourse".[68] The sexual imagery is striking. She returns to this reassurance a few lines later: [דכרלך] עדינתי "recall my pleasure" (2.13b-14a), ... "this seed is from you; from you is this conception, and from you the planting of [this] fruit [ ], and not from any stranger, or from any of the Watchers, or from any of the sons of hea[ven" (2.15-16). The erotic

---

[65] Fitzmyer, *Genesis Apocryphon*, 258, 123.

[66] In Matthew's account of Jesus' birth Joseph harbours similar anxieties, only to be told, by contrast, that his child is of the Holy Spirit (Matt 1:19-20; similarly Luke 1:31-35 but in relation to Mary and the visit of the angel Gabriel). See also Nickelsburg, *1 Enoch 1*, 540; Nickelsburg, "Patriarchs Who Worry about Their Wives," 145-46.

[67] On the use of "brother" to refer not to a first degree sibling, see Fitzmyer, *Genesis Apocryphon*, who draws attention to similar usage in 4QTob[b]/4Q197 4 i.12 and 4 iii.12-13 (130).

[68] Fitzmyer, *Genesis Apocryphon*, 131. He notes the metaphor of sheath for the body also in Dan 7:15 and *b. Sanh.* 108a.

elaboration reflects the view that conception is more likely to occur where there has been highly intense and pleasurable sexual intercourse.[69] It certainly assumes a very positive attitude towards sexual relations and its pleasure within the context of marriage. In addition, Bitenosh's reply would barely make sense unless it assumes that during pregnancy sexual intercourse had ceased. This is probably being assumed here as the rule, as also in 4QD^{e}/4Q270 2 ii.15-16; 6QD/6Q15 5 2-3 (cf. also Josephus, *B.J.* 2.161).[70]

No such exchange occurs in the account in *1 Enoch* 106-107. It is probably best seen as an embellishment in keeping with what appears to be the author's special interest, which is reflected in similar additions to the story of Abram and Sarai in Egypt.[71] The embellishments appear to reflect that *Genesis Apocryphon* is using either *1 Enoch* 6 – 11[72] or a related tradition. In 2.19 *Genesis Apocryphon* then returns to the storyline found in *1 Enoch* 106:4-7. Unlike the latter it does not have Lamech give detail about the child's appearance, but instead uses the summary statement, "I told him everything", and has Lamech ask his father to seek Enoch's wisdom. In *1 Enoch* 106 – 107, Enoch, himself speaks in the first person. Both accounts report Enoch's response, but little of what must have been a substantial reply remains in columns 3-4, and column 5 is also fragmentary. Already the reference to "the days of Jared, my father" in 3.3 belongs to Enoch's reply (as in *1 Enoch* 106:13). The reference will be to the descent of the Watchers (*1 Enoch* 6:2-6; *Jub.* 4:15). Little that is decipherable in columns 3 and 4 tells us the substance of the speech. Perhaps the words, "evil" (4.3) and "justice" (4.11) and "on/against them" (4.14) explain the deeds of the Watchers and their offspring, and their judgement.

When we come to column 5, we happen to reach a point in the speech where Enoch gives a response to the specific question. He assures Methuselah that the child is "not from the sons of heaven, but rather from Lamech" (5.3). In the fragmentary remains of the column we can see that Enoch, himself, appears to have seen the child, who lifted his face to him "and his eyes shone like the su[n

[69] For a modern discussion of this notion see Joann Ellison Rodgers, *Sex: A Natural History* (New York: Times Books, 2002) 325-32, who writes: "Studies show that women retain more sperm – about 70 percent more than usual – if they have an orgasm" (327), noting factors like the release of oxytocin during female orgasm which facilitates the movement of male sperm.

[70] This makes sense of what Nickelsburg, "Patriarchs Who Worry about Their Wives," sees as "a bit obscure", namely the relevance of their pleasure when they made love (143).

[71] Nickelsburg, "Patriarchs Who Worry about Their Wives," 158. See also Bernstein, "From the Watchers to the Flood," who emphasises that "vivid dialogue" is a pervasive characteristic of the document (47).

[72] Nickelsburg, "Patriarchs Who Worry about Their Wives," 140-41, 158. See also Nickelsburg, *1 Enoch 1*, 542.

] 13 this child (is) a flame" (5.12-13). Unlike in *1 Enoch* 106 – 107, Enoch's predictions appear to relate only to the time of Noah, not a time of even stronger iniquity in the future, but as there, the words to Methuselah and so to Lamech (and so to the hearer) are disclosed as a רז "mystery" (5.25). While the story of Lamech is closely connected to the preceding story of the Watchers, its rationale remains unclear. In part it enhances Noah's status. It may however also be countering traditions which saw Noah as belonging to the category of giants, such as we find in Pseudo-Eupolemus.[73] If so, it concedes the wondrousness, but not the origins, showing on the contrary that Noah came to counter the consequences of Watchers' deeds, not to continue them.

Somewhat mysteriously the column ends with the words, כתב מלי נוח "the book of the words of Noah" (5.29), perhaps indicating use of a different source for what follows.[74] Again we have a narration in the first person, this time in the person of Noah. Possibly the reference to the book simply refers directly to what follows,[75] so that we might imagine that a similar statement preceded each of the other sections presented in the first person. Unfortunately, the relevant lines where this might have been preserved are not extant.

Inspired by Gen 6:9, which reports that in his generation Noah was איש צדיק "a righteous/upright man", the account repeatedly refers to Noah's קושט "uprightness", six times in the first six lines (6.1-6). These lines appear to be poetically structured and to describe Noah's birth בכור "in the crucible" and מעי "the womb" of his mother to his adulthood and walking in the way of truth and rejecting falsehood and darkness, a dualism also reflected elsewhere.[76] This emphasis seems closely related to Noah's approach to marital law. It is a prime example of his uprightness. He acts כדת חוק עלמא "according to the eternal law" (6.8). Noah describes this eternal law as having been given by God to human

---

[73] On this see Loren T. Stuckenbruck, "The Origins of Evil in Jewish Apocalyptic Tradition: The Interpretation of Gen 6:1-4 in the Second and Third Centuries B.C.E.," in *The Fall of the Angels* (ed. Christoph Auffarth and Loren T. Stuckenbruck; Themes in Biblical Narrative 6; Leiden: Brill, 2004) 87-118, 93-98, who points to the description of Noah's grandson, Nimrod, in Gen 10:8-9, as a גבר "mighty one", γίγας "giant"; cf. Gen 6:4). See also Loren Stuckenbruck, *The Book of Giants from Qumran: Text, Translation, and Commentary* (TSAJ 63; Tübingen: Mohr Siebeck, 1997) 32-39.

[74] So Michael E. Stone, "The Books Attributed to Noah," *DSD* 13 (2006) 4-23, 6. He concludes: "It seems to us more than likely that a Book or Books of Noah existed in the third century BCE or earlier. Some material drawn from this document is preserved in ALD, *Jubilees*, and the Genesis Apocryphon" (18).

[75] So Fitzmyer, *Genesis Apocryphon*, 144-45.

[76] On this see Bernstein, "From the Watchers to the Flood," 52.

beings, without saying when or how (6.9).[77] In accordance with this law Noah had his sons marry the daughters of his brothers and has his daughters marry their sons (6.8). In 6.10 he appears to repeat a reference to his sons' taking wives for themselves, perhaps indicating that it was a completed task or perhaps repeating the earlier statement.[78]

If we ask what this highlighting is meant to exclude, it could be the marrying of nieces or possibly the marrying outside the family, and especially Gentiles. Within the world of the narrative the second alternative is, however, problematic, because as an option it had ceased to exist after all others had drowned in the flood. But within the world of the hearers this option would have been real. VanderKam draws attention also to the list that Noah gives of Shem and his children in 12.9-12, noting that in comparison with Genesis there are as many daughters as there are sons. This ensures they have no need to marry outside their family (the text assuming that marrying siblings was a necessary exception at this new beginning as it was in the first human family).[79] This was not the case with Ham and Japheth who had four sons and seven daughters and seven sons and four daughters respectively and where intermarriage was thus a necessity and did not matter. As in *Jubilees*' depiction of the early generations of humankind, the author is apparently making clear that in the restart of humanity after the flood, the particular chosen line of Shem maintained purity of line uncontaminated by intermarriage.[80] VanderKam notes that this occurs to an extent that goes beyond *Jubilees* which in the first generation allows intermarriage with the acceptable line of Japheth. The attention given the matter in 12.9-12 suggests then that the author's intent in 6.8-9 relates to the purity of the chosen line and so was concerned with intermarriage outside the chosen line.[81] For the hearers of the *Genesis Apocryphon*, Noah is a model father whose action in arranging appropriate marriages, sets an example over against those who engage in intermarriage with Gentiles. There is also no marrying of nephews or of nieces. In addition, in the author's mention of the name of Noah's wife, Imzera, absent from Genesis, we see also another interest shared with *Jubilees* as the author identifies and gives greater prominence to women.[82]

---

[77] Fitzmyer, *Genesis Apocryphon*, draws attention to a similar attribution of marriage law to divine origin in Tob 6:13, 18; 7:12 (148).

[78] So Bernstein, "From the Watchers to the Flood," 54.

[79] James C. VanderKam, "The Granddaughters and Grandsons of Noah," *RevQ* 16 (1994) 457-61.

[80] On this see Betsy Halpern-Amaru, *The Empowerment of Women in the Book of Jubilees* (JSJSup 60; Leiden: Brill, 1999) 9-31; Loader, *Enoch, Levi, and Jubilees*, 155-57.

[81] So also Bernstein, "From the Watchers to the Flood," 53-54.

[82] On this see Bernstein, "From the Watchers to the Flood," 53.

The Watcher myth makes another appearance in 6.11 where Noah reports that in a vision he is informed בעובד בני שמין "about the conduct of the sons of heaven". A Watcher then informs him of what is to come. In 6.19 we find reference to the violence of the Nephilim (as *1 Enoch* 7:1-6; *Jub.* 7:23, 25) and in 6.20 to the "holy ones who were with the daughters of m[en". The words of the Watcher continue until 7.7 and appear to have included information about the impending flood. The following text in this and the following column is mostly lost. In 8.1 there is probably a reference to Noah's wife (as Gen 7:13). Nothing survives of column 9. By column 10 the account has reached the end of the flood, the disembarkation and the sacrifice of the he-goat. In 11.13-14 Noah blesses God for destroying all who do violence, evil and deceit. In 12.13 we find the beginning of the account where Noah planted a vineyard, dated as in *Jub.* 7:1-2, but it is not clear whether Noah went on to recount Ham's indiscretion.

Columns 13 – 15 report a vision of Noah about trees. It reports attacks, especially on the trees. Those doing so include animals, some described as of gold, silver, and iron (13.9-10), and the sun, moon, and stars (perhaps an allusion to heavenly beings?). A second scene of assaults follows, this time against an olive tree (13.13-17; cf. Zech 4:3-14; Ezek 31:3-9) which the four winds destroy. Then, after a gap of some lines, Noah is addressed as being a great cedar with apparently three others sprouting from it, identified as Noah's three sons. Then 14.16 reports what appears to be a problem: that some boughs of one of these trees "enter into the boughs of the first one" (repeated in 14.17). If, as is likely, the first is Shem (identified as the people of Noah in 14.11-12), then the vision may allude to Canaan's intrusion into Shem's space, as reported in *Jub.* 10:29-34.[83] Alternatively it might be saying something about inappropriate mingling, especially through intermarriage. A fourth scene of assault begins with the assertion that most people will turn to evil. It pictures someone coming from the south with a sickle (15.1-20; cf. Rev 14:14-19), apparently a figure of judgement.[84] This detail indicates that the author sees himself as part of a minority over against a majority who do evil: "they will turn aside, the majority of them will be evil" (15.9), a stance which would be quite compatible with someone wanting to identify with the perspective of the sectarian authors of Qumran or authors who preceded them, though it also fits Noah's own situation in humanity. The overlapping of the story of Noah's generation and a writer's generation is also a feature of *1 Enoch* 10.

In 16 – 17 we finally reach an account of Noah dividing the land among his sons. Nothing survives about the allotment to Ham, but since his lands are referred

[83] The view expressed in personal correspondence from Esther Eshel, August 2007 and James M. VanderKam, October, 2007.

[84] So Fitzmyer, *Genesis Apocryphon*, 169. On the significance of the south in Enochic tradition see Kelley Coblentz Bautch, *A Study of the Geography of 1 Enoch 17-19: 'No One Has Seen What I have Seen'* (JSJSup 81; Leiden: Brill, 2003), 120-25, 204-205.

to in 19.13, it was probably mentioned in column 18.[85] Nothing is preserved of column 18, although it must have also included the transition to the new narrative: Abram's story.

In 19.13 begins the account of Abram's stay in Egypt, based on Gen 12:10-20. The story has been enhanced by adding that Abram had a dream about two trees (19.14-17a). In contrast to Noah's vision which stretches over three columns, Abram reports his dream over four lines - but also using the image of trees, seeing himself as a cedar (used of Noah in 14.9). Men wanted to cut down the cedar and keep only the beautiful date palm, which pleaded a stay of execution.[86] The application is obvious, but, depicted as given to him in a dream, Abram's strategy is thus given the status of divine insight and plan,[87] better for Abram's image than any notion that his ploy was simply crude self-interest.

The author has also embellished the story with emotional interaction between Abram and Sarai, reminiscent of the embellishment of the Lamech story. Sarai weeps when she hears Abram's request (19.21). Abram weeps at the prospect of Sarai being in danger (20.12).[88] The account reverses the advice from Abram's saying Sarai is his sister as Gen 12:13 to Sarai saying Abram is her brother (as in Gen 20:13). Perhaps this, too, is designed to help Abram's image. His image is further reinforced when he is depicted teaching wisdom to Pharaoh's men from "the book of the words of Enoch" (19.25). The emphasis on Enoch coheres with the emphasis given by the document to its seminal myth about the Watchers.

In Column 20 we then find ourselves in line 2 in the midst of a description of Sarai's beauty which continues to reflect the author's sensitivity to such matters. So, beside the personal and warm interchange between the marriage partners, we also have a celebration of Sarai's femininity: her face, her hair, her eyes, her nose, her radiance, her breasts, her whiteness, her arms, her hands, her palms, her

---

[85] Alternatively it was already in the missing lines of column 15, as Fitzmyer, *Genesis Apocryphon*, proposes (171).

[86] Fitzmyer, *Genesis Apocryphon*, draws attention to Ps 92:13 as the source of the image: "The righteous flourish like the palm tree, and grow like a cedar in Lebanon", noting that later rabbinic tradition applied it to Abram and Sarai in Gen 21:17, citing *Gen. Rab.* 41.1; *Tan. Lekh* 4; *Zohar* on Genesis 12. He also mentions the possibility that Canticles may be a source which uses cedar of the young man and palm of the girl (5:15; 7:7-8) (185)

[87] So also Fitzmyer, *Genesis Apocryphon*, 184; Bernstein, "Pentateuchal Interpretation," 147; Sidnie White Crawford, "The Rewritten Bible at Qumran," in *The Bible and the Dead Sea Scrolls: The Princeton Symposium on the Dead Sea Scrolls: Volume 1: Scripture and the Scrolls* (ed. James H. Charlesworth; Waco: Baylor University Press, 2006) 131-47, 147.

[88] Nickelsburg, "Patriarchs Who Worry about Their Wives," notes the psychological interest (148).

fingers, her feet, her legs! (20.2-6).[89] "There are no virgins or brides who enter a bridal chamber more beautiful than she" (20.6). The accolade continues: "Yet with all this beauty there is much wisdom in her" (20.7). These, we hear, are the words of Hyrcanus[90] reporting to the Pharaoh (20.8). While this all serves to enhance the drama of the story, it also reflects a positive appreciation of female beauty and an affirmation that women may also be celebrated for their wisdom. The approach both to women and to marital relations coheres with the emphases of *Jubilees*.

The narrative then has Pharaoh respond to the report by desiring her and then marvelling at her once she appeared. It is clear from what follows that the statement, that Pharaoh נסבהא לה לאנתא "took her to himself as wife" (20.9) and Abram's comment later, דברת אנתתי מני בתוקף "my wife has been taken away from me by force" (20.14), do not mean that Sarai was raped nor that sexual intercourse took place. Abram assures us that in response to his prayer, "May he not be able to defile (לטמיא) my wife tonight" (20.15), Pharaoh "was not able to approach (למקרב) her;[91] nor did he have sexual intercourse (ידעהא) with her, though she was with him two years" (20.17). Pharaoh reinforces this by his own admission that he had not known (ידעהא) her and had not defiled (טמיהא) her (20.30). The word "defile" reflects the view that had this happened she would have become unclean for Abram, as Bilhah became for Jacob after Reuben's intercourse with her (*Jub.* 33.9), and as reflected in Deut 24:1-4.[92] The language of her being taken by force also appears twice in *Jubilees'* terse retelling of the story (*Jub.* 13:11, 13), where it also cannot mean that intercourse let alone forced intercourse took place.[93]

The story retains the element of deception, though first reported in action when Sarai was already with the king and in the form that, as requested, Sarai says that Abram is her brother (20.10). Like *Jubilees*, the account suppresses the detail that Abram received benefit from Sarai's being with Pharaoh (cf. Gen 12:16). It may derive from *Jubilees* the detail that Sarai was with Pharaoh for two years (*Jub.* 13:10). It greatly embellishes the reference in Gen 12:17 to plagues afflicting Pharaoh and his household. These come apparently in response to Abram's prayer and, apart from rendering Pharaoh impotent, strike not only his household but all

---

89 On the poetry of the passage see James C. VanderKam, "The Poetry of 1QApGen XX, 2-8a," *RevQ* 10 (1979-81) 57-66; and Fitzmyer, *Genesis Apocryphon*, 193.

90 On the possibility that this is a play on one of the Jewish rulers of that name, see Fitzmyer, *Genesis Apocryphon*, who favours Hyrcanus II (198-99).

91 Fitzmyer, *Genesis Apocryphon*, notes that this draws on Gen 20:4 (205).

92 See also Fitzmyer, *Genesis Apocryphon*, 203.

93 Otherwise the account in *Jub.* 13:11-15 differs significantly already from the Genesis account. It lacks reference to Sarai's beauty, to Abram's worry about his survival because of Sarai, to the ruse about Abram and Sarai being siblings, to Abram's receiving benefit from Pharaoh because of Sarai, and to Pharaoh's confrontation of Abram.

his physicians, magicians and wise men summoned to cure him (20.16-21). The elaboration continues with the intervention of Hyrcanus, inspired by a dream to seek Abram's help to pray for the king, lay hands on him and heal him, and with Lot's release of the vital information at the source of the problem, who accordingly reports Sarai's true status to his master (20.21-26a).

The story returns then to Pharaoh's confrontation of Abram, but this, too, reflects elaboration as Pharaoh asks for prayer and exorcism, is healed, lavishes gifts on Abram and reassures him on oath that no sexual intercourse occurred (20.26b-31a).[94] Significantly it adds that Pharaoh also gave gold and silver and garments of fine linen and purple to Sarai – "and Hagar, too" (20.31-32a). The additional attention to Sarai, and even to Hagar, is remarkable. Far from being expelled as a *persona non grata*, Abram is sent off with special escort (20.33), along with Lot and his newly acquired Egyptian wife (20.34). The motif of prayer and the more favourable response of the king stand under the influence of the parallel episode in Gen 20:1-18 concerning Abraham and Abimelech. As in *Jubilees*, marriage to Egyptian women is unproblematic. The remaining columns which survive are a free rendering of what follows in Genesis 13 and then a very close rendering of Genesis 14.

The expansive retelling of the story over at least 52 lines reflects not only the conventional art of the story-teller, but also some significant values. These include a concern to remove potentially negative traits from Abram's image, who now appears as divinely guided sage, healer, and exorcist, learned in the "book of Enoch". They also include a valuing of marital partnership, including at an emotional level, but also sexual purity. No intercourse, let alone rape took place, which was important to protect Sarai directly and her image, but also Abram who can receive her back knowing that she is not forbidden for him. The story also reflects a valuing of women, including Hagar, but especially Sarai, whose femininity is celebrated, but also her wisdom, and who is also graced with honouring gifts from Pharaoh. While their versions of this story differ markedly, *Genesis Apocryphon* and *Jubilees* share the valuing of marital partnership and of women, both their femininity and their wisdom. Though in different ways, they also both remove potentially negative aspects of Abraham's image.

Both the story of Abram and Sarai and that of Lamech and Bitenosh reflect the valuing of marital intimacy. In the latter story this includes the pleasure of sexual intercourse as something positive and, interestingly, associated with the widespread belief that thereby the likelihood of conception is enhanced. At the same time the story apparently reflects the practice of abstaining from sexual

---

[94] Nickelsburg, "Patriarchs Who Worry about Their Wives," notes as background to the notion of sickness caused by demons, the aetiology of demons and sickness reflected in *Jub.* 10:1-13 and *1 Enoch* 15:11 – 16:1 (149).

intercourse during pregnancy. Attention to marriage is central to the author's depiction of Noah's uprightness: it showed in his choice of marriage partners for his children. This may well be in reaction to forbidden marriages, such as we find in D's designation of niece marriages as one of the nets of Belial. It is more likely, however, to allude to intermarriage with foreigners. If the merging of boughs in Noah's vision relates to marriage, then a reaction against intermarriage may also be found there. Concern with marital purity informs the clarifications in the story of Abram and Sarai that no intercourse took place.

While the reference to reading the book of Enoch could simply belong to the fiction of the embellishment of the story, it is more likely to reflect what the author actually saw as an ideal and practised. The evidence for this comes in the "books" or sections on the Watchers, Lamech and Noah, where the myth as told in *1 Enoch* 6-11 is fundamental. If there is an allusion to their descent by divine command, then we may have to assume access to a version of the myth such as we find in *Jubilees*, where the Watchers' deed occurred while they were on a divine commission on earth, and not as a wanton act which included abandoning their heavenly posts. In what survives their deed is never described in those terms. As in both the *Book of the Watchers* and in *Jubilees*, their deed appears not to be portrayed as generating a succession of such acts to which intermarriage would belong, though this can be said only of the little that survives.

This reading is in contrast to Nickelsburg who argues a connection between the story of Lamech and that of Abram in *Genesis Apocryphon*, on the one hand, and *1 Enoch* 6 – 11, on the other, where the issue is: women having illicit relationships with forbidden others. He concludes that "the author of the *Apocryphon* is concerned about some kind of miscegenation. The sexuality of Israelite women is seen to constitute a danger".[95] *1 Enoch* 6 – 11 does not, however, single out Israelite women, but, if anything, sees dangers in marriages by men to foreign women who would be the bearers of sorcery and illicit knowledge, though this is never made explicit nor was the myth understood in this way by those who subsequently used it within the early Enoch literature or in *Jubilees*. The issue of potential danger in women's beauty is another issue, but here in contrast to *1 Enoch* 6 – 11 it is not an issue of blame or regret but something positive and celebrated and therefore making women vulnerable to men's desires.

---

[95] Nickelsburg, "Patriarchs Who Worry about Their Wives," 150, and see pp. 150-54. The parallels between the Watchers and Pharaoh (both see, desire, take as wife, prayer and judgement) are not strong. Significantly, between Pharaoh and Sarai no intercourse takes place, which is the focus in the Watchers' story, and in the latter, prayer arises more because of the impact of the offspring. See the critical discussion of Nickelsburg's attempt to find the theme of intermarriage in the document, in Schuller, "Response to 'Patriarchs who Worry'," 207-209.

CHAPTER SEVEN

Attitudes towards Sexuality in the Wisdom Texts

1 *1/4QInstruction*$^{a\text{-}f?g}$ 1Q26, 4Q415-418, 418a,c?, 423

This major work,[1] whose importance for the keepers of the collection is attested by the multiple copies,[2] is generally considered to be a non-sectarian writing.[3] Its

[1] The text and translations are based on John Strugnell and Daniel J. Harrington, *DJD* 34 (and *DSSEL*), unless otherwise indicated, but I have put the translation into contemporary English and removed italics and capitalization within sentences.

[2] While multiple attestation is usually taken as indicating the value of the work to the community which housed the collection, it is also possible that it may rather reflect the number of copies brought to Qumran by individuals, in other words, reflect a sign of its popularity elsewhere, not necessarily at Qumran. On the nature of the library whose function included being an archive of shared property see Armin Lange, "The Qumran Dead Sea Scrolls – Library or Manuscript Corpus," in *From 4QMMT to Resurrection: Mélanges qumraniens en homage à Émile Puech* (ed. Florentino García Martínez, Annette Steudel, and Eibert Tigchelaar; STDJ 61; Leiden: Brill, 2006) 177-93, 192.

[3] See the review of evidence in Armin Lange, "Die Weisheitstexte aus Qumran: Eine Einleitung," in *The Wisdom Texts from Qumran and the Development of Sapiential Thought: Studies in Wisdom at Qumran and its Relationship to Sapiential Thought in the Ancient Near East, the Hebrew Bible, Ancient Judaism, and the New Testament* (ed. Charlotte Hempel, Armin Lange, and Hermann Lichtenberger; BETL 159; Leuven: Peeters-Leuven University Press, 2002) 1-30, 23-24. He points also to the characteristic combination of Torah wisdom and eschatology in *1/4QInstruction*, *4QMysteries*, and the *Treatise on the Two Spirits* (25-26). See also John Strugnell, "The Sapiential Work 4Q415ff and Pre-Qumranic Works from Qumran: Lexical Considerations," in *The Provo International Conference on the Dead Sea Scrolls: Technological Innovations, New Texts,*

editors suggested a date somewhere between Proverbs and Ben Sira for its composition, while others have dated it with greater probability to at least the early second century.[4] We consider it here in its own right and also because it formed part of the collection which sectarian authors also read. Its material is extensive. The following discussion focuses on those parts which pertain or might potentially pertain to matters of sexuality.

In the very fragmentary 4QInstr[a]/4Q415 2 i + 1 ii.4-6 we find reference to זרע קודשכה "your (sg.) holy seed" and that לוא ימוש זרעכה מנחלת "your seed will not depart from the inheritance of (something)", and adding, תשיש בפרי "you shall rejoice in the fruit of" (2 i + 1 ii.4-6; cf. also 8 3; 21 2). Agricultural metaphor appears to continue in what follows where the word יפרח "blossom" is preserved (8). The reference to seed could potentially relate to the issue of intermarriage and the purity of the seed, but, the surviving material is insufficient to determine if this is so.[5] It may be an allusion to the garden of Eden, whose

---

and Reformulated Issues (ed. Donald W. Parry and Eugene C. Ulrich; STDJ 30; Leiden: Brill, 1999) 595-608; Matthew J. Goff, *Discerning Wisdom: The Sapiential Literature of the Dead Sea Scrolls* (VTSup 116; Leiden: Brill, 2007) 62-63.

[4] Matthew J. Goff, *The Worldly and Heavenly Wisdom of 4QInstruction* (STDJ 50; Leiden: Brill, 2003) 230-31; Goff, *Discerning Wisdom*, 65-66; Puech, "Resurrection," 265 n. 24; Lange, *Weisheit*, 47; Lange, "Weisheitstexte," 24, who reports on the basis of personal communication from A. Steudel that the manuscript evidence existed at Qumran in at least two versions, 4QInstr[b]/4Q416 1 preserving the beginning of one, 4QInstr[c]/4Q417 1 preserving the beginning of another, apparently older version (17). See also Strugnell and Harrington, *DJD* 34, 19. For the complex issues of textual reconstruction see Tigchelaar, *To Increase Learning*, of whose work Daniel J. Harrington, "Recent Study of 4QInstruction," in *From 4QMMT to Resurrection: Mélanges qumraniens en homage à Émile Puech* (ed. Florentino García Martínez, Annette Steudel, and Eibert Tigchelaar; STDJ 61; Leiden: Brill, 2006) 105-23, writes that it "should be regarded as a supplement to DJD XXXIV" (106). See also Benjamin Wold, *Women, Men, and Angels: The Qumran Wisdom Document* Musar leMevin *and its Allusions to Genesis Creation Traditions* (WUNT 2.201; Tübingen: Mohr Siebeck, 2005) 30-38. Tigchelaar concludes that the "grounds for regarding 4Q417 1 I as the first column of 4Q417 are not cogent" (247).

[5] In relation to 4QInstr[d]/4Q418 103 ii.6-9, where prohibitions against mixing from Deut 22:9-11 function as an analogy, but not, it seems, in relation to intermarriage, Tigchelaar, *To Increase Learning*, notes the following, which is equally applicable here in relation to 4Q415 2 i. + 1 ii.4-6: "In post-exilic texts 'holy seed' is used predominantly in sections dealing with intermarriage, but nothing in the preserved text suggests this is the issue at stake here" (229). He draws attention to *Aramaic Levi Document* 14-22 and *4QVisions of Amram*[c]/4Q545 4 17 about priestly seed (230).

imagery also appears in 4QInstr[g]/4Q423, which speaks positively of eating from the trees of the garden as a metaphor for gaining wisdom.[6]

Instructions to a Married Woman and a Married Man

In 4QInstr[a]/4Q415 2 ii we find a passage apparently addressed to a married woman.[7] The words preserved in the first line, כאב כבדי "Like a father honour", are best taken as an exhortation to a married woman concerning her attitude towards her husband,[8] rather than towards her "father-in-law", as the editors propose.[9] This gains support from what follows, where the next line addresses the woman, אל תמישי בלבבך "Do not remove in your heart", and in the following line reads: כול היום ובחיקו "Every day, and in his bosom".[10] This would seem more appropriate as a reference to the husband than to the father-in-law. The following lines then appear to speak of marriage as a covenant (as also in Prov 2:17; Mal 2:14)[11] and of the breakdown of marriage:

פן תפרעי ברית קוד[ש
ואויבה לנפשך ובו[

> 4 lest you neglect the hol[y] covenant (or: the covenant of marri[age) [
> 5 and one (a woman) hated by your soul, and [.* (4QInstr[a]/4Q415 2 ii.4-5)

---

6 On this see Wold, *Women, Men, and Angels*, 82-83, who also draws attention to similarities with 1QH[a] xvi, where imagery of Eden is employed metaphorically.

7 On the possibility of reading masculine plurals rather than imperative feminine singular, see Strugnell and Harrington, *DJD* 34, 48. Their translation assumes the latter. See also Tigchelaar, *To Increase Learning*, 229; Goff, *Worldly and Heavenly Wisdom*, 219, 229. There is no need to see the address to women as envisaging how husbands should address their wives on the grounds that women were not likely to be literate, as Wold, *Women, Men, and Angels*, suggests (243), since the document will have been read aloud to be heard, not composed primarily for private reading.

8 Wold, *Women, Men, and Angels*, 88, 200, who points to a parallel application in Philo *Q.G.* 1.27 (200); Goff, *Discerning Wisdom*, 49.

9 Cf. Strugnell and Harrington, *DJD* 34. See also Tigchelaar, *To Increase Learning*. Observes that the traces after כבדי would be consistent with ח[ותנ]ך[, "your father-in-law" (33).

10 Wold, *Women, Men, and Angels*, conjectures that the line may have ended as בחיקו בר]אך or בחיקו בר]א or בחיקו בר]אשיתך (201), i.e. with reference to "her creation" or "creation" or "her beginning", as part of what he sees as the document's emphasis on woman's origin from man as basis for its ethical teaching (202-203).

11 The word ברית "covenant", in the sense of marriage, may occur already at the end of line 3 if one conjectures בר]ית. See Strugnell and Harrington, *DJD* 34, 46, who also note the use of ברית "covenant" in this sense is unique to 4QInstruction among the 227 occurrences of the word in the 1-11Q concordances.

The use of קודש may have specifically marital connotations as in 4QD[f]/4Q271 3 11 (see also 4QpapRitMar/4Q502 1 6; cf. Prov 2:17).[12] The words אויבה לנפשך "one hated by your soul" most likely refer to a woman who threatens the marriage from outside. It is less likely to refer to a rival within a polygynous relationship, because that need not entail the breakdown of the marriage and a woman's returning to her father's house,[13] if that is the meaning of what follows, nor does the document assume polygynous marriage elsewhere, a situation largely impossible among the poor anyway to whom it is addressed. The reference in 7 to בבית מכו[רותיך] "the house of [your] orig[ins,]" could allude to returning to her parents' house after breakdown of a marriage, or it might relate to good reputation, as in what follows, which speaks of the woman in her marriage "covenant" (ובבריתך "and in your covenant") being a focus of praise among all men (7-8). This echoes the theme of the praise of virtuous women in Prov 31:28, 31.[14] The final line preserves a further reference to the house of origin, in the expression, מבית מולדים "from the house of birth", but its relation to what precedes cannot be determined.[15]

4QInstr[a]/4Q415 9 appears to be addressed to a married man and to refer to the womb of his wife conceiving children: להורות בטנכה לכ[ה "so that your (masc) womb (i.e. wife) should conceive for you" (2).[16] The masculine, "your womb", reflects the marital relationship and assumptions of ownership, and is the equivalent of "your wife" (similarly, in the reference in 4QInstr[g]/4Q423 3a: בפרי בטנו "with the fruit of his womb"). In 6-7, בה הכינה כיא היאה תכון["on it (or her) he has established it (or her), for it (she) is the foundation"* might allude to wisdom, but in the light of what follows more probably refers to the wife. The following line contains the words: יחד ממשל זכר את נ[קבה "together the dominion of the male over the fe[male ...]" (7) and the next line, רוחה המשל בה

[12] So Strugnell and Harrington, *DJD* 34, 49, who suggest it could mean, "your bond of betrothal"; Goff, *Discerning Wisdom*, 50.

[13] So Goff, *Discerning Wisdom*, 49.

[14] So Strugnell and Harrington, *DJD* 34, who also point to Gen 21:15 and Cant 6:9.

[15] Wold, *Women, Men, and Angels*, takes it with the other allusion to "house" as a reference to women's origin (85-86, 122), namely in creation. See also Matthew Morgenstern, "The Meaning of *byt mwldym* in the Qumran Wisdom Texts," *JJS* 51 (2001) 141-44, who argues that the background is astrological, referring to the constellations at the time of one's birth. This appears to be its meaning also in 4Q299 3a ii-b 9-16 and 5 5, where it describes celestial phenomena. On this see Eibert J. C. Tigchelaar, "Your Wisdom and Your Folly: The Case of 1Q – 4QMysteries," in *Wisdom and Apocalypticism in the Dead Sea Scrolls and in the Biblical Tradition* (ed. Florentino García Martínez; BETL 163; Leuven: Leuven University Press, Peeters, 2003) 69-88, 88.

[16] Tigchelaar, *To Increase Learning,* disputes לכ[ה, arguing that the visible text favours למ[ן (35).

"her spirit make to rule over her" (8). These suggest that the author is alluding to Gen 1:27 and 3:16 (והוא ימשל בך "and he shall rule over you"). The remaining text may speak of מחסורמה "their deficiency" or of "their poverty"[17] The former might be part of a rationale for male rule within the context of a contrast between male and female (נקבה in 11):]זה מז "this one from (less than) that [one 9" (cf. וכמוזני "and according to scales" 11), but the text is too uncertain to be clear.

In 4QInstr[a]/4Q415 11 (base text) and 4QInstr[d]/4Q418 167b (outlined), the document appears to allude to the giving away of a daughter in marriage to a future husband;

> כ]ול מומיה ספר לו ובגויתיה הבינה]ו ...[
>
> [A]ll her blemishes recount to him, and make [him] understand her bodily defects […]. (4QInstr[a]/4Q415 11 6; 4QInstr[d]/4Q418 167b 6)

The instruction about declaring blemishes recalls the *Damascus Document's* (D) instruction in 4QD[f]/4Q271:

> ואם (8) [את בתו יתן איש לאי]ש את כול מומיה יספר לו
>
> And if (8) [a man giv]es [his daughter to a m]an he shall recount to him all her blemishes (4QD[f]/4Q271 3 8; 4QD[e]/4Q270 5 14 underlined)

Both have the phrase, כול מומיה יספר לו, "he shall recount to him all her blemishes", in common.[18] In their introduction Strugnell and Harrington note that at first sight the passage moves across a number of themes: weights and measures (1-3); an "address on spirits and other miscellaneous topics" (4-5); "on stumbling stones" (6-10) and an address to the instructor on "how he should treat his wife when she bears children".[19] They then affirm Qimron's observation, that the whole passage can be seen as reflecting a single theme: "giving advice to the maven … on one subject, namely on marrying off his daughter; she should not be esteemed according to her looks (or bodily defects), but it is rather according to her spirit that the bridegroom should 'weigh' her".[20] This makes good sense of the context. Already in 4 the marital theme appears in the reference to beauty and in the two references to togetherness in 4 and 5.[21] They note that behind both texts is the

---

[17] Strugnell and Harrington, *DJD* 34, translate with the former but indicate that "'poverty, need' is more likely here" (56).

[18] Strugnell and Harrington, *DJD* 34 suggests that 4Q271 "seems to quote" from this passage (59).

[19] Strugnell and Harrington, *DJD* 34, 59.

[20] Strugnell and Harrington, *DJD* 34, 59.

[21] With Wold, *Women, Men, and Angels*, reading יחד in 5 as not about public examination but expressing: "you established them together" 227.

warning in Deut 27:18 about misleading the blind, which they see coming into 4Q271 via *1/4QInstruction*. The former cites it directly, however, whereas the latter assumes it in its more discursive statements about stubbing one's foot in the darkness. In 7 it contains the image of the woman as a stumbling block, probably alluding to Eden, and in 8 to either God's or the man's response of anger.[22] A negative image of women's vulnerability to sin is implied.

In 11 the text is very difficult.

> ואם נפרדה בהריתכה קח מו[לדיה
>
> If she is divided (?) when she is pregnant for you, take the offs[pring of her. (4QInstr[a]/4Q415 11 11)

The editors propose that the statement might refer to a caesarean childbirth in which the woman dies.[23] Wold proposes that that "divided" alludes not to caesarean birth, but to the woman's separation from her parents (cf. Gen 2:24).[24] The word פרד "to separate" is used with this specific reference also in 4QInstr[b]/4Q416 2 iv.3 and 4.[25] Accordingly, the line could be proffering advice that once you have married the woman and she has become pregnant, then you should undertake something; but what? The motif of acknowledging offspring might occur also in 4QInstr[b]/4Q416 2 iii.20. But there, too, the translation of מו[לדיה is uncertain. In both, and also in 4QInstr[a]/4Q415 2 ii.9 and 4QInstr[c]/4Q417 2 i.11, the expression מולדי seems better translated as "origins/birth-time of", so that then the phrase קח מולדי would mean "take notice of the origins/birth-time of".[26] The imperative קח is used in this sense also in 4QInstr[d]/4Q418 77 4 in relation to taking notice of רז נהוה "the mystery to come".[27] Accordingly, the line could be proffering advice that once you have married the woman and she has become pregnant, find out when she conceived. But Wold also suggests that בהריתכה might be seen as deriving not from the root meaning to conceive, but from the root meaning "instruction".[28] The line would then refer to the need in the context of instruction to find out about the woman's time of birth. If, however, we take מולדי as a reference to "origins", then the exhortation could mean that the man should take notice of the fact that as woman

---

22 So Wold, *Women, Men, and Angels*, 228.

23 Strugnell and Harrington, *DJD* 34, 62.

24 Wold, *Women, Men, and Angels*, 229-30.

25 The verb, פרד, is used in this technical sense in later Hebrew and Aramaic, though not in biblical Hebrew. So Strugnell and Harrington, *DJD* 34, 127.

26 So Wold, *Women, Men, and Angels*, 229.

27 Wold, *Women, Men, and Angels*, 94-95.

28 Wold, *Women, Men, and Angels*, 228-29.

she was taken from man (Gen 2:21-23) and from this flow the consequences for marital advice and instruction. That appears also to make good sense of the similar statement in 4QInstr^{b}/4Q416 2 iii.19-21, to be discussed below. The following two lines also refer apparently to the woman, but what is preserved is too fragmentary to enable the context to be discerned.

In 4QInstr^{b}/4Q416 2 i.7 / 4QInstr^{c}/4Q417 2 i.12 היה בעל ריב לחפצכה can be translated: "Be an opponent of your desire", as *DSSSE*, which could refer to sexual desire, but this cannot be confirmed from the context and is in any case uncertain. The editors translate: "Be an advocate on behalf of thy (= your) own interests",[29] but acknowledge that "it could express a Pythagorean asceticism as much as a Jewish or Christian one".[30] The immediate context warns against perversity (נעויה) (13) and sin (פשע) (14), so that בעל ריב לחפצכה may be speaking of the need to exercise control over the struggle which the enticement of pleasure brings, but nothing implies this is necessarily sexual or ascetic.

As part of a series of isolated instructions 4QInstr^{b}/4Q416 2 ii.21 (see also 4QInstr^{c}/4Q417 2 ii.26 outlined) declares: וגם אל תקל כלי [ח]יקכה "Moreover do not treat with dishonour the 'vessel' (or 'wife') of your [bo]som".[31] Immediately beforehand it had warned against inappropriate estimation of oneself. The editors note that an alternative reading is כלי חוקכה "lawful wife", but that the parallel in iv.5 and its parallels in Deut 13:7 and 28:56 suggest כלי חיקכה "wife of your bosom" is preferable.[32] The word, כלי, means "vessel, utensil, weapon". They note that the extension of meaning to include the sexual organs of either sex, "and then, by a *pars pro toto* metonomy, to men or women ... is commonplace and ubiquitous (cf. e.g. in Greek σκεῦος, in Latin *Vas*, and in many modern languages)".[33] It is used in the feminine sense in *b. Meg.* 12b. The usage here is accordingly to be understood simply as a reference to wife, not with a

---

[29] Strugnell and Harrington, *DJD* 34, 176.

[30] Strugnell and Harrington, *DJD* 34, 183.

[31] For a review of research see Wold, *Women, Men, and Angels*, 191-97.

[32] Strugnell and Harrington, *DJD* 34, 108. Strugnell argues that the author is expanding the Decalogue command to love father and mother to include wife. In seeking the connection between the prohibition of cursing one's father and mother in Deut 27:16 and the term, "wife of his bosom" found in Deut 13:7 (about idolatry) and 28:54 (about neglect of family). George J. Brooke, "Biblical Interpretation in the Wisdom Texts from Qumran," in *The Wisdom Texts from Qumran and the Development of Sapiential Thought: Studies in Wisdom at Qumran and its Relationship to Sapiential Thought in the Ancient Near East, the Hebrew Bible, Ancient Judaism, and the New Testament* (ed. Charlotte Hempel, Armin Lange, and Hermann Lichtenberger; BETL 159; Leuven: Peeters-Leuven University Press, 2002) 201-20, points to Deut 27:15 which is concerned with idolatry (209).

[33] Strugnell and Harrington, *DJD* 34, 108.

particular emphasis on her sexual being or sexual organs. In an excursus[34] the editors note Benoit's suggestion that the passage could throw light on the use of σκεῦος in 1 Thess 4:4, where it might refer to a person's wife or to a man's sexual organ. 4QInstr[b]/4Q416 shows that it could refer to the wife and that Paul may have intended κτᾶσθαι in the same sense as χρῆσθαι, sometimes used interchangeably, to mean "treat" and so with ἐν ἁγιασμῷ καὶ τιμῇ "in holiness and honour" as the equivalent of אל תקל "do not treat with dishonour", with the meaning of the *pi'el* of כבד, "treat with honor". They also note the similarity in formulation, raising the possibility that Paul may have known the document.

Elgvin has challenged the view that the reference here is to "wife", rather than "penis", as in 1 Sam 21:6.[35] He argues that elsewhere the word for wife is used directly, and that the reference to wife without further elaboration is too isolated in its context (there is only a small gap to the beginning of the next column). A reference to the penis he sees as more likely in this context which concerns manners and so reads it as addressing the need for modesty, as in 1QS/1Q28 7.12-14; 4QD[a]/4Q266 10 ii.9-12; 4QD[e]/4Q270 7 i.1-3.[36] On this interpretation חיקכה must mean something like "your lap".

The context, however, deals with behaviour towards those who are not a man's equal, so a reference to one's wife need not be unexpected. The use of חיקכה "your bosom", not so far away in the following context with reference to wives, makes such an allusion here more probable. Wold emphasises in addition that חיקכה "your bosom" is not so much an allusion to intimacy as to the origin of woman from man as in Gen 2:20-25.[37] He also explores further possible allusions to men and women and sexuality in the preceding context. Wold notes possible relevant references in 4QInstr[b]/4Q416 2 ii to rule over women (3, if reconstructed as המשול בה "to rule over her"), to covering one's shame (3), to not touching and

---

[34] Strugnell and Harrington, *DJD* 34, 109-10.

[35] Cf. Wold, *Women, Men, and Angels*, who notes that כלי is not used there in the construct (194).

[36] Torleif Elgvin, "To Master His Own Vessel: 1 Thess 4.4 in Light of New Qumran Evidence," *NTS* 43/4 (1997) 604-19, 607-609. See also Jay E. Smith, "Another Look at 4Q416 2 ii.21, a Critical Parallel to First Thessalonians 4:4," *CBQ* 63 (2001) 499-504, who suggests an allusion here to 2 Sam 6:20 where Michal accuses David of bringing dishonour to himself by exposing himself to slave girls (503). Menahem Kister, "A Qumranic Parallel to 1 Thess 4:4? Reading and Interpretation of 4Q416 2 II 21," *DSD* 10 (2003) 365-70, proposed a different reading which removes any allusion to a woman or to a penis: "And do not be disgraced by (living) not according to your prescribed portion (בלי חוקכה or בלו)" (366). See the critical discussion in Florentino García Martínez, "Marginalia on 4QInstruction," *DSD* 13 (2006) 24-37, who disputes the palaeographical basis for reading בלי instead of כלי.

[37] Wold, *Women, Men, and Angels*, 195-96.

causing a woman to stumble (16), and to not drinking wine where there is no covering (19).[38] This make a reference to one's wife more plausible.

An Exposition of Marriage

In 4QInstr[b]/4Q416 2 iii.15b we have the beginning of a major section concerned with family and marriage, reaching to iv.13. It begins with an exhortation to the hearer to honour father and mother (iii.15b-19a), offering as support that "as God is to a man, so is his own father; and as the lords (אדנים) are to a person, so is his mother; for they are the 'womb that was pregnant with you'" (16-17a).[39] The plural noun, אדנים, "lords", suggests not a second, parallel, reference to God, but a reference to angels.[40] The involvement of angels in creation is presumed also in 4QInstr[c]/4Q417 1 i.17, and based on a reading of Gen 1:26 which speaks in the plural, "Let us make".

In 4QInstr[b]/4Q416 2 iii.19b-21 we then find the beginning of a discussion related to marriage. The passage is also preserved in 4QInstr[d]/4Q418 10 (outlined).[41]

19 ואם רש אתה כשה]
20 בלוא חוק *vacat* אשה לקחתה ברישכה קח מולדי[
21 מרז נהיה בהתחברכה יחד התהלך עם עזר בשרכה[

19 And if you are poor as we[re . . . just as . . .]
20 without statute *vacat* (?), you have taken a wife in your poverty, Take her offspring [in your lowly estate. But take care lest you be distracted]
21 from the mystery that is to come while in your relations with her together, walk with the helper of your flesh[. (4QInstr[b]/4Q416 2 iii.19-21)

The first line picks up the motif of poverty, commonly assumed throughout the document and apparently reflecting the likely state of the hearers.

---

[38] Wold, *Women, Men, and Angels*, 218-222.

[39] Strugnell and Harrington, *DJD* 34, 113, adapted to contemporary English. Wold, *Women, Men, and Angels*, notes that the text assumes activity of both God and angels in creation (149-50, 154-55) and goes on to show instruction includes veneration of angels (155-79).

[40] See the discussion in Wold, *Women, Men, and Angels*, 149-55.

[41] Strugnell and Harrington, *DJD* 34, note that בה]המשילכה להתהלך "he has set you in authority over her for her to walk" occurs both in 4Q416 2 iv.7 and 4Q418a 18, but observe that "the text surviving in 4Q418a 18 can neither be identified with the surrounding preceding text in 4Q416 nor be easily fitted into the very narrow lacunae there" (491), so that 4Q418a 17 and 18 are to be seen as further statements about marriage independent of the passage we are considering. Cf. Tigchelaar, *To Increase Learning*, who argues that the fragment does represent a parallel (133-34).

Unfortunately the sentence is incomplete and has sections missing within it. The meaning of כשה is unclear; it may be a form of the relative.[42] The precise reference of בלוא חוק "without statute" is also uncertain. If it relates to the discussion of marriage, which follows, it may be referring to some aspect that is illegal. It may relate to what precedes and have nothing to do with marriage. The reference to taking her offspring (קח מולדי), as the editors read it, is similar to how they read 4QInstr[a]/4Q415 11 11 (קח מו]לדיה), which they take as referring to death in childbirth. Here the focus would be on acknowledging and by implication caring for the children, rather than disowning them presumably because of poverty or because there is something about the marriage that is "without statute".

The smaller lacuna between lines 20 and 21 also poses problems. The *mem* before רז נהיה "the mystery of existence", a common expression in the document, but here brought into relation with marriage, suggests separation from, perhaps in the context of warnings. In their translation cited above, the editors conjecture that some warning about distraction occurred in the gap between 20 and 21 and assume hesitancy about marriage against a background of commitment to celibacy, which they conjecture.[43] One might read בלוא חוק as implying that marrying is in some sense exceptional, but a supposed allusion to celibacy is read into the context and one does not get the impression either from this passage or from elsewhere in the document that marriage is treated as something exceptional or in a concessionary way. The passage appears to affirm marriage and the acknowledgment, and presumably upbringing, of children in a family.

A different interpretation follows if we read מולדי as referring not to offspring, but to the wife's time of birth or her origins, reading it in the light also of מולדי ישע in 4QInstr[c]/4Q417 2 i.10-12 and similar terms in 1QMyst/1Q27 1 i.5 and 4QHoroscope/4Q186 1 ii.8; 2 i.8.[44] The concern would then be about elect status reflected in time of birth. Accordingly Goff, for instance, translates: "get [her] birth times ([מולדי[כ) ... from the mystery that is to be when you associate yourself (with her)".[45] The passage would then reflect an astrological perspective about appropriate times for conception and birth. Alternatively one might see here not a reference to birth times, but to origins, in particular, the origin of woman from man according to Genesis and the consequences of this for understanding

[42] Strugnell and Harrington, *DJD* 34, 122.

[43] Strugnell and Harrington, *DJD* 34, 113, 123.

[44] So Torlief Elgvin, "An Analysis of 4QInstruction" (Diss. Hebrew University, 1997) 231; Goff, *Worldly and Heavenly Wisdom*, 76 n. 174; Daryl F. Jeffries, *Wisdom at Qumran: A Form-Critical Analysis of the Admonitions in 4QInstruction* (Gorgias Dissertation Near Eastern Studies 3; Piscataway: Gorgias, 2002) 250; Wold, *Women, Men, and Angels*, 187-88.

[45] Goff, *Worldly and Heavenly Wisdom*, 76.

marital relations, teaching which we can assume belonged to "the mystery to come". The exhortation then amounts to a call to look carefully at Genesis refracted through the exegetical wisdom alluded to in "the mystery to come". The context then does precisely that. It would then carry a similar meaning to what was said in 4QInstr[a]/4Q415 11 11.

The verb חבר, "to associate with", most likely refers to sexual intercourse in this context. The phrase עזר בשרכה "the help or helper of your flesh" (also 4QInstr[e]/4Q418a 16b+17 3) merges together the thought of woman made as the man's helper (as Gen 2:20) and the notion that through intercourse they have become one flesh (as Gen 2:24).[46]

The passage continues in the next column with a direct citation of Gen 2:24, את אביו [ו]את אמו ודב[ק באשתו והיו לבשר אחד] "his father [and] his mother and clin[g to his wife and they shall become one flesh]" (4QInstr[b]/4Q416 2 iv.1 / 4QInstr[d]/4Q418 10 5). It then picks up the language of Gen 3:16,

אותכה המשיל בה

He has set you in authority over her.
(4QInstr[b]/4Q416 2 iv.2; 4QInstr[d]/4Q418 10 5 outlined)

והוא ימשל בך (Gen 3:16)

And he shall have authority over you.

The principle of male authority, noted above, is asserted also in 4QInstr[c]/4Q417 1 i.9; 4QInstr[a]/4Q415 9 7-8; 4QInstr[d]/4Q418 228; 4QInstr[e]/4Q418a 18 4.[47] The following line then speaks of someone who does not have authority over her, probably a reference to the father. It then refers also to separation from the mother. This appears to be an interpretation of Gen 2:24, although that text speaks of the man leaving father and mother, not the woman. Such clear delineations and transfers of authority would have been important to emphasise and are reflected in this extrapolation. The document continues the interpretation of Gen 2:24 in association with Gen 3:16 in the words,

ואליכה [תשוקתה ותהיה] 4 לך לבשר אחד

and towards you [shall be her desire; and she shall become] 4 for you one flesh (4QInstr[b]/4Q416 2 ii.3b-4a)

---

[46] On the reflection of Gen 2:18 and 2:23, see Frey, "Flesh and Spirit," 390; and on the echoes of Genesis 2-3 generally in the passage, see Brooke, "Biblical Interpretation," 213; and the extensive treatment in Wold, *Women, Men, and Angels*, of allusions to Genesis 1 – 3 throughout the document (81-123).

[47] On this see Wold, *Women, Men, and Angels,* 203-204.

The male is addressed here. The conjectured text would thus represent a further application of Gen 3:16, already used to speak of male authority over the woman.[48] Here it would speak of her תשוקתה, best understood here as her sexual desire.[49] It is noteworthy that the author appears to assume that the woman becomes the man's flesh. This matches the thought above that the woman is designated as "the help of your flesh" (iii.21) and that the document can speak also of the man's womb (4QInstr[a]/4Q415 9 2; 4QInstr[g]/4Q423 3a). It also coheres with an understanding that interprets Gen 2:24 and the bringing back to the man that part of him which had been removed according to Gen 2:21-22.

The passage continues with reference to offspring. God will "separate" a daughter for another man, and a son, probably for the daughter of a neighbour (4). This further expands the interpretation of Gen 2:24. It is interesting that the passage then returns to the original couple:

> ואתה ליחד עם אשת חיקכה כיא היא שאר ער[ותכה]
>
> and you shall be made into a unity[50] with the wife of your bosom, for she is the flesh of ['your] nak[edness']. (4QInstr[b]/4Q416 2 iv.5)

This is affirming marriage and also probably assumes monogyny, at least, as practical monogyny. The expression, אשת חיקכה, "wife of your bosom", is possibly not just an expression of marital intimacy, but also an allusion to the creation of woman from man's side (bosom), as Wold suggests.[51]

The passage then addresses what interference from other men would mean:

---

[48] Tigchelaar, *To Increase Learning,* reconstructs on the basis of his assumption that 4Q418a 18 provides a parallel with the words: ואליכה [לבבו והיא תהיה] "and to you [is his heart and she shall be]" (48, 133).

[49] The word appears in 1QS/1Q28 11.22 in the sense of "return", as the LXX translators read it, confirmed by the use of תשובה in the same expression in 1QH[a] x.4 and 6QpapHymn/6Q18 ii 4. It occurs again in 4Q418 168 3, but without a clear context. See Strugnell and Harrington, *DJD* 34, 127. See also my discussion in Loader, "Beginnings of Sexuality," where I show that "return" is the likely meaning of the word also in 1QM/1Q33 17.4; 15.10.

[50] For alternative readings which take יחד as "community" or as an adverb with the preposition עם see Strugnell and Harrington, *DJD* 34, 128.

[51] Wold, *Women, Men, and Angels*, 189-90. "The creation of the female in the use of this epithet could be used to raise issues of her derivation to provide ethical instruction both *to* her and *in regard to* her" (190). He also suggests that in iv.5 it is better to read ער[ומכה] "nakedness", a closer echo of Gen 2:25 (191)

ואשר ימשול בה זולתכה הסיג גבול חייהו

And whoever, apart from you, tries to rule over her "has displaced the frontier of his life". (4QInstr^b/4Q416 2 iv.6)

This will surely include adultery. Moving boundaries derives from language about property (Deut 27:17; 19:14), implying that one man has trespassed on another man's property.[52] Authority includes sexual control. The association of control and women's sexual desire is already present in Gen 3:16 and is assumed here. This is more likely than that the text alludes to a second marriage, assuming divorce.[53] The document then pursues the issue by emphasising the right of the husband to have (sole) dominion over his wife.

ב[רוחה] 7 המשילך להתהלך ברצונכה

Over her spirit 7 he has set you in authority, so that she should walk in/according to your pleasure. (4QInstr^b/4Q416 2 iv.6b-7)

The noun רצון probably includes sexual pleasure or desire, as in CD (2.21; 3.3, 10, 11), given the apparent association with adultery which precedes. It will also be more than that, since what follows speaks of a husband's control also of his wife's vows, offerings, and oaths, which he has the power to annul (7-9), and where the word רצון is repeated.[54] This must be its context in the exhortation, השב רוחכה לרצונכה "Turn her spirit to your good pleasure" in 8 and similarly in 9. The issue of rash or excessive vows appears to continue in 10-12 where there is also mention of a man's inheritance, probably as something potentially endangered by a wife's vows, but this is not clear. In 13 we have a further reference to חיקכה אשת "the wife of your bosom" (cf. iv.5). The editors suggest that it probably introduces a new section about women and sexual relations, rather than a continuation of the theme of vows and oaths.[55] Inheritance is endangered also, for instance, by adulterous liaisons.

What emerges from this important passage is a strong emphasis on marriage, probably assuming the practical monogyny which would be the norm among the hearers as poor people, but also understood within a strongly patriarchal framework to the extent that the woman is understood to become one flesh with

[52] On this see Lawrence H. Schiffman, "Halakhic Elements in the Sapiential Texts from Qumran," in *Sapiential Perspectives: Wisdom Literature in Light of the Dead Sea Scrolls: Proceedings of the Sixth International Symposium of the Orion Center for the Study of the Dead Sea Scrolls and Associated Literature, 20-22 May, 2001* (ed. John J. Collins, Gregory E. Sterling, and Ruth A. Clements; STDJ 51; Leiden: Brill, 2004) 89-100, 90.

[53] Cf. Strugnell and Harrington, *DJD* 34, 129.

[54] On the control of oaths here, see Schiffman, "Halakhic Elements," 90-91.

[55] Strugnell and Harrington, *DJD* 34, 131.

her husband, thus becoming his flesh and being under his sole authority. It also assumes a strong commitment to marriage in the marrying of offspring, including an emphasis on being open about a daughter's blemishes, not, of course, a son's![56] The foundation for the teaching is clearly the account of creation in Genesis. As Wold puts it, "The manner in which both wives and husbands live with and think about one another is derived from the nature of their creation".[57] The author clearly follows his own advice, "Take notice of her origins", in making the Genesis material the basis for his instruction.

The remaining references pertinent to our theme are few and limited. 4QInstr^{c}/4Q417 1 i.27 warns the hearer: "You shall not *go astray* afte[r] you[r] heart and ^{after} your e[y]es[", probably including the use of the eyes in sexual wrongdoing. 4QInstr^{d}/4Q418 101 ii.2-5 appears to focus on sin, and possibly on sexual wrongdoing in particular.

> 2. sin[ ]
> 3. And do not (let her/it not be) in his house (אל תהי בביתו) For [ ]
> 4. he shall [not] be sparing of his wealth; Be [ ]
> 5. his kin. He shall not do harm to (or act unfaithfully against or inappropriately toward) his own kin (לוא ימעל בבשרו [ ]. (modified)

One might see references to sexual wrongdoing in אל תהי בביתו if read as: "let her not be in his house" (a prostitute or immoral woman, for instance?) and also in the final line, if read as an allusion to incest, since similar phraseology occurs in CD 7.1 (ולא ימעל איש בשאר בשרו "And a man shall not be unfaithful to/act illegally/trespass in relation to his near relative") with that as its apparent meaning (see pp. 126-27 above and cf. also 4Q477 8 and 4QApocrJerC^{b}/4Q387 fr. A). 4QInstr^{d}/4Q418 127 1-4 may also address sexual wrongdoing, if its first recoverable word, מקורכה, is a reference to the penis, since there follow warnings against wrongdoing, including judgement apparently on those who ד]רשי חפץ "se]ek pleasure" (cf. also 4QInstr^{d}/4Q418 81+81a 18). A similar disapproval may be reflected in the instruction היה בעל ריב לחפצכה in 4QInstr^{b}/4Q416 2 i.7 and 4QInstr^{c}/4Q417 2 i.12 if translated: "Be an opponent of your desire".

4QInstr^{d}/4Q418 86 uses the image of a father and his daughters in relation to God's anger (1) and perhaps contains a reference to days allotted to her (2). In 4QInstr^{g}/4Q423 1, 2 1 the document contains some reflections of the garden of

---

[56] Goff, *Worldly and Heavenly Wisdom*, notes the differences between *4QInstruction* and D (224). While sharing some similar legal concerns (e.g., a husband's control of his wife's vows; 4Q416 2 iv.8-9; CD 16.10-12; cf. Num 30:6-15), the former's focus is primarily ethical. It shows no concern with matters of forbidden marital relations nor about structures for gaining permission to marry or divorce. D never relates marriage to poverty.

[57] Wold, *Women, Men, and Angels*, 234.

Eden and the expulsion, and mentions, presumably, Eve, giving birth, but without further relevant detail. It employs the images metaphorically, including the notion that the trees offer the good fruit of knowledge and wisdom, and assumes male authority over the garden.[58] As Wold notes, the document nowhere makes anything positive out of the woman being first to eat of the tree of knowledge of good and evil, but rather assumes her disobedience.[59] Eating the trees for knowledge and eating that particular tree seem not to be confused. 4QInstr^{g}/4Q423 3 1-5 / 1QInstr/1Q26 2 2-4 apparently looks to the future promising abundant offspring and 4QInstr^{g}/4Q423 3a mentions "the first fruits of his womb" בטנו (meaning "his wife", as in 4QInstr^{a}/4Q415 9 2), but without further substance of significance. 4QInstr^{g}/4Q423 4 1 / 1QInstr/1Q26 1 5 refers to a woman honouring her husband more than God.

Other potentially significant references whose context has largely been lost include 4QInstr^{b}/4Q416 9.1 "on her that is pregnant"; 4QInstr^{d}/4Q418 103 ii.6-8 about mixing of kinds, but literally and not related to sexuality or intermarriage; 4QInstr^{d}/4Q418 127 4 about punishment of those who seek their own pleasure (חפץ); 4QInstr^{d}/4Q418 178 about covering shame, addressed to a woman; 4QInstr^{d}/4Q418 183 a+b 2; [תעזוב שכבת זרע] "you/she shall give up sexual inter[course"; 4QInstr^{d}/4Q418 211: בכל עוברותמה "in all their pregnancy"; 4QInstr^{d}/4Q418 236: אם נקבה "if a female"; 4QInstr^{d}/4Q418 243: "a woman abounding in folly"; 4QInstr^{d}/4Q418 251: "inheritance of Adam"; and 4QInstr^{g}/4Q423 3 "inheritance in the sons of Adam". In 4QInstr^{c}/4Q417 1 i.9 the words פרש את אושה may allude to the creation of woman from man, "he separated woman", if one reads אושה as אישה, but that would be the single instance of this spelling at Qumran.[60] These indicate that the document contained much more about issues of sexuality than what has survived.

Dualism and Sexuality

Beyond these specific references to issues pertaining broadly to sexuality, the document also embodies a dualism which must be examined for its potential relevance. Two of the main passages have been identified as coming early in the document, at least one of which formed the beginning of one of the versions. This has significance since they establish values through which the whole document is then viewed.

In a passage which recalls 4QMyst^{b}/4Q300 3, 4QInstr^{b}/4Q416 1 begins with statements about God's dominion over creation, heavenly hosts, luminaries and

[58] So Wold, *Women, Men, and Angels*, 203-204.

[59] Wold, *Women, Men, and Angels*, 205.

[60] See the discussion in Wold, *Women, Men, and Angels*, 98-99.

humankind, and moves on to judgement.[61] It speaks of a time of God's judgement, but also of reward for God's בני אמתו "faithful children", lit. "sons of truth" (10) and rejoicing for the "sons of heaven" (12). The expression, "sons of heaven", here, probably refers to angels, as it does in 4QInstr[d]/4Q418 69 ii.12. This may also be so of "sons of truth", as Tigchelaar suggests. Alternatively, the latter refers to human beings. A mark of "the righteous" is that they can distinguish good and evil (15; cf. also 4QInstr[c]/4Q417 1 i.8; 4QInstr[d]/4Q418 78 1). The passage speaks of the destruction by God of כל רוח בשר "every spirit of flesh" (12) and of כל אשר התגללו בה "all who defiled themselves in it (sc. wickedness)" (11).

If we follow Tigchelaar's suggestion, however, that בני אמתו "sons of his truth" may refer to angels,[62] then it would be possible to relate the passage more directly to the Watcher myth.[63] Accordingly, the statement, "all who defiled themselves in it (sc. wickedness)" (11) would refer to the Watchers who defiled themselves with women. The allusion to fear and dread in 11 and 12 may refer to the guilty or could simply indicate awe at God's punishment of the Watchers whose engagement with women was an act of defilement (similarly 1QH[a] xviii.34b-36; 1QapGen/1Q20 0.7). It would then juxtapose the punishment of the Watchers and their offspring with the punishment of human beings, כל רוח בשר "every spirit of flesh" (12). It also speaks of the יצר בשר (16) which, as we noted above, may mean "inclination", but could just mean "creature" of "flesh", indicating here those to be condemned.

If there is an allusion to the Watcher myth here, as seems likely, we note the depiction of their sin as an act of defilement, but also that there is no further link made to sexual wrongdoing in relating their fate to human beings or their deeds. The expression, כל רוח בשר "every spirit of flesh" (12), makes no such connection. It is, however, otherwise a matter of contention among interpreters. Frey, for instance, reads "every spirit of flesh" as a reference to a second group of humans beside the "son of truth", and so finds here a usage of "flesh" to designate

---

[61] Goff, *Worldly and Heavenly Wisdom*, notes the similarities to *1 Enoch* 2 – 5, which moves from order and creation to judgement (5).

[62] Tigchelaar, *To Increase Learning,* 180.

[63] Tigchelaar, *To Increase Learning*, also notes the parallel between 4Q416 1 1-10 and the nature homily in *1 Enoch* 2 – 5 (183-84). See also Loren T. Stuckenbruck, "4QInstruction and the Possible Influence of Early Enochic Traditions: An Evaluation," in *The Wisdom Texts from Qumran and the Development of Sapiential Thought: Studies in Wisdom at Qumran and its Relationship to Sapiential Thought in the Ancient Near East, the Hebrew Bible, Ancient Judaism, and the New Testament* (ed. Charlotte Hempel, Armin Lange, and Hermann Lichtenberger; BETL 159; Leuven: Peeters; Leuven University Press, 2002) 245-61, who discusses possible links, concluding that they reflect independent parallels, not dependence.

a particular group.[64] Thus he writes: "It is obvious, however, that not all human beings are characterized as בשר"[65] and goes on to differentiate this dualistic use from the *Thanksgiving Hymns* where the authors can also speak of themselves as בשר. He then traces the origin of the dualism to sapiential self-deprecatory texts such as Job 4:17-21; 14:1-4; 15:14-16, which include sinfulness, into which the term בשר has been introduced.[66] Alternatively, the term is meant inclusively to refer to all human beings, the only exceptions being those to whom revelation has been given.

The issue comes to the fore also in the second major passage which reflects dualism, 4QInstr[c]/4Q417 1 i. The column begins with an exhortation to study רז נהיה "the mystery that is to come" (2, 3, 6), which contains information about the order of creation, truth and iniquity, wisdom and foolishness, and their predetermined punishments. This resource, variously revered as ספר זכרון "the book of memorial" (15-16; cf. Mal 3:16; CD 20.19), חזון הגוי "the vision of Hagu" (16; cf. CD 10.6; 13.2; 14.7-8; 1QSa/28a 1.7),[67] and רז נהיה "the mystery that is to come" (2, 3, 5, 18), gives the hearer true understanding. The ordained lot and fate of all human beings, of "all the sons of Seth (בני שות)" (15) is engraved in it. The passage then declares that God gave this treasure of wisdom and knowledge as an inheritance.

וינחלונו לאנוש עם עם רוח
כ[י]א 17 כתבנית קדושים יצרו
ועוד לוא נתן הגוי לרוח בשר

[64] Frey, "Flesh and Spirit," 391-92.

[65] Frey, "Flesh and Spirit," 392.

[66] Frey, "Flesh and Spirit," 397-98, 400. Matthew J. Goff, "Reading Wisdom at Qumran: 4QInstruction and the Hodayot," *DSD* 11 (2004) 263-88, says that flesh means all human beings in *Hodayot* and is part of "Niedrigkeitsdoxologie" (self-deprecating doxology), but that for *1/4QInstruction* there is never a problem in being a human being and flesh refers only to the wicked spirit (282). He notes positive references to *enosh* in 1QH[a] xix:10-14 (283); but notes that unlike *Hodayot* there is no joining with angels in prayer and no reference to creatures of dust in *1/4QInstruction* (283-84); similarly Goff, *Worldly and Heavenly Wisdom*, 95.

[67] On the relationship between the vision of Hagu and the "book of Hagy" (CD 10.6; 14.6-8; 1QSa/1Q28a 1.6-7), see Goff, *Worldly and Heavenly Wisdom*, 80-83. See also Cana Werman, "What is the *Book of Hagu*?" in *Sapiential Perspectives: Wisdom Literature in Light of the Dead Sea Scrolls: Proceedings of the Sixth International Symposium of the Orion Center for the Study of the Dead Sea Scrolls and Associated Literature, 20-22 May, 2001* (ed. John J. Collins, Gregory E. Sterling, and Ruth A. Clements; STDJ 51; Leiden: Brill, 2004) 125-40, who concludes that הזון ההגוי means "meditated vision" and does not yet carry the meaning of ספר ההגוי "the Book of Hagu" (137-41).

כי לא ידע בין 18 [טו]ב לרע כמשפט [ר]וחו

> and he gave it as an inheritance to אנוש with a people of spirit
> because 17 they were fashioned after the structure of the holy ones
> and no longer/still/again he did not give Hagu/meditation/knowledge to the spirit of flesh, because it does not know (how to distinguish) between 18 good and evil in the judgement of its spir[it].* (4QInstr^{c}/4Q417 1 i.16b-18a)

The passage bristles with exegetical difficulties.[68] The word אנוש can be interpreted in three main ways, which then have implications for interpreting the rest of the passage. It could refer to Enosh, son of Seth, and reflect a tradition according to which God gave revelation to Enosh (cf. Sir 49:16), who then transmitted it.[69] In his time the Watchers were active and in 15 it is possible to see in בני שית a reference to the "sons of Seth", depicted as wicked.[70] Then the "people of the spirit" might refer either to human beings or to angels, heavenly spirits.[71] If the reference is to human beings, then it could be read as those special human beings who continue to study the precious resource which Enosh received.

The two major alternative readings are to see in אנוש not a name, but a reference either to the first human being, Adam,[72] or to humankind. The reference to בני שית is then usually taken as an allusion to Num 24:17, a popular text in writings of the time, which speaks of the coming of a star from Jacob and a sceptre

---

[68] See the extended discussion in Lange, *Weisheit*, 49-92; John J. Collins, "In the Likeness of the Holy Ones: The Creation of Humankind in a Wisdom Text from Qumran," in *The Provo International Conference on the Dead Sea Scrolls: Technological Innovations, New Texts, and Reformulated Issues* (ed. Donald W. Parry and Eugene C. Ulrich; STDJ 30; Leiden: Brill, 1999) 609-18; John J. Collins, "The Mysteries of God: Creation and Eschatology in 4QInstruction and the Wisdom of Solomon," in *Wisdom and Apocalypticism in the Dead Sea Scrolls and in the Biblical Tradition* (ed. Florentino García Martínez, BETL163; Leuven: Leuven University Press, Peeters, 2003) 287-305; Strugnell and Harrington, *DJD* 34, 163-65; Daniel J. Harrington, *Wisdom Texts from Qumran* (London: Routledge, 1996) 55; Goff, *Worldly and Heavenly Wisdom*, 81-126; Goff, "Reading Wisdom," 279-80; Wold, *Women, Men, and Angels*, 124-49.

[69] Lange, *Weisheit*, 86-88; "Weisheitstexte," 19-20; Brooke, "Biblical Interpretation," 213; Frey, "Flesh and Spirit," 393; cf. Wold, *Women, Men, and Angels*, 101-102.

[70] Frey, "Flesh and Spirit," Frey sees behind the passage the myth of the "mythological tradition of the fall of the angels during the time of the sons of Seth" (393).

[71] Lange, *Weisheit*, who suggests it refers to angels not to people (88-89). Similarly, Frey, "Flesh and Spirit," 393. Referring to Enosh, he writes: "So this primeval father and the עם רוח, i.e. the obedient angels, gained the heavenly memorial as an inheritance". Enosh and his successors constitute one part of humanity; those designated as the רוח בשר "spirit of flesh" constitute the other, who are wicked (393).

[72] Collins, "Likeness," 612.

from Israel and of God's judgement on the wickedness of "the sons of Sheth".[73] This is usually then associated with taking "people of the spirit" as also a reference to human beings. The meaning would then be that the resource was given to either Adam and to people of the spirit, or to humankind and, with further specification, people of the spirit among them.

The reference to the holy ones in the explanatory clause which follows could refer to human beings, but more probably refers to angels. It thus reflects an interpretation of Gen 1:26 according to which humankind is created in the image of אלוהים, understood not as a reference to God, but to angels.[74] If the explanatory clause introduced by כ[י]א "because, that" about the angels relates to what precedes, then it is telling us why God entrusted these human beings with the resource. The assumption appears to be that they must share with the angels the capacity to understand and obey it.[75]

A further complication arises in the words which immediately follow. They speak of God not giving the resource to the spirit of flesh. The difficulty lies in the two words, ועוד לוא, which, understood in a temporal sense, mean "and/but no longer",[76] but could be construed as, "and yet", in the sense: "even though". The latter is not well supported and the former, the more usual meaning. The difficulty then attaches to the identity of "people of the spirit" and "spirit of flesh". There is little doubt that they are being set in contrast. Collins, who favours a non-temporal sense for ועוד לוא, understands them to refer to two separate humanities, which he then sees as reflecting use of the two creation accounts in Gen 1:26-27 and 2:7 to describe creation of two different kinds of human beings.[77] Accordingly, some human beings are created in the image of angels according to Gen 1:26-27 "Let us make humankind in our own image" and so qualify to receive the revelation;

---

[73] Collins, "Likeness," 611-12.

[74] So Collins, "Likeness," 612-15; Goff, *Worldly and Heavenly Wisdom*, 94-97.

[75] It might be possible to construe the explanatory clause about the angels as providing a rationale for what follows, namely God's refusal to give humankind the revelation because having been created by angels and not just by himself, human beings are faulty. If the allusion to angelic structure is an attempt to (dis)qualify human beings and point to their fallibility, this understanding of angels may be influenced by the Watcher myth which exposes such fallibility. But this view attested in Philo shows no trace otherwise in the document which holds angels in high esteem.

[76] So Strugnell and Harrington, *DJD* 34, 166; see the discussion of this option in Crispin H. T. Fletcher-Louis, *All the Glory of Adam: Liturgical Anthropology in the Dead Sea Scrolls* (STDJ 42; Leiden: Brill, 2002) 115; Goff, *Worldly and Heavenly Wisdom*, 99, who notes it as a possibility. Arguing that it is the most expected meaning: Wold, *Women, Men, and Angels*, 140-41.

[77] Collins, "Likeness," 616-17; similarly Collins, "Mysteries," 302; Goff, *Worldly and Heavenly Wisdom*, 94-99; Goff, *Discerning Wisdom*, 34.

others, by implication created according to Gen 2:7, do not. Thus he posits an ontological dualism underlying the anthropology of the document. This approach also underlies Frey's assumption that 4QInstr^{b}/4Q416 also spoke of two different humanities. This notion of a fixed dual creation of humanity would be a radical form of dualism leaving no chance of change.[78]

Collins sees in אנוש a reference to the first Adam, supporting his hypothesis in part by pointing to the use of אנוש in the *Treatise on the Two Spirits* (1QS/1Q28 3.13, "He created אנוש to rule over the world"), which he takes as referring to Adam, and to Philo's use of the two creation accounts to depict two kinds of humanity, although there are significant differences between Philo's understanding and what Collins prposes here.[79] A difficulty in Collins' proposal about use of the two creation stories is that the explanatory clause alluding to the first also uses language of the second, namely יצרו "his fashioning", suggesting a merging of Gen 1:27 and Gen 2:7 ("The Lord God fashioned וייצר *adam* from the dust of the ground").[80] There are further problems with his proposal. As Wold notes, it is far from clear that אנוש in the *Treatise on the Two Spirits* (1QS/1Q28 3.13) refers to Adam, and not humanity in general, which is the meaning of the word elsewhere in *1/4Q Instruction* (4QInstr^{d}/4Q418 55 11; 77 3).[81] Wold also points to Collins' note in comparing *1/4QInstruction* with the Book of Wisdom that both conceive of all humanity possessing immortality and this is based on Gen 1:27. That would appear to exclude the notion of a separate creation.[82]

If however we understand ועוד לוא in a temporal sense, then it suggests that what God once did, he no longer does. In other words, having stated that God gave revelation to humankind (or to Adam), a people of spirit, made in the image of angels, he now no longer does so. "People of spirit" may be interpreted in apposition to אנוש understood as humankind generally, which is how one would

---

[78] John J. Collins, "The Eschatologizing of Wisdom in the Dead Sea Scrolls," in *Sapiential Perspectives: Wisdom Literature in Light of the Dead Sea Scrolls; Proceedings of the Sixth International Symposium of the Orion Center for the Study of the Dead Sea Scrolls and Associated Literature, 20-22 May, 2001* (ed. John J. Collins, Gregory E. Sterling, and Ruth A. Clements; STDJ 51; Leiden: Brill, 2004) 49-65 writes: "the distinction between righteous and wicked is a permanent one" (52).

[79] On this see Wold, *Women, Men, and Angels*, 141-48.

[80] So Elgvin, "An Analysis of 4QInstruction," 91. Collins, "Mysteries," acknowledges the difficulty, but rejects the conclusion that the contrast must be not between two humanities, but between two times, a time before sin and a time after (302). One could read יצרו as meaning "his inclination", but then the allusion to creation is lost. On the case for reading יצרו as a reference to fashioning, rather than inclination, see Wold, *Women, Men, and Angels*, 148.

[81] Wold, *Women, Men, and Angels*, 131.

[82] Wold, *Women, Men, and Angels*, 134; Cf. Collins, "Mysteries," 303.

probably have read it more easily before the scribe added עם "with, along with". Now it seems more like a supplement beside אנוש, with the sense of either humankind among whom were spiritual people,[83] or Adam, along with the rest of humankind, people of spirit. The assumption appears to be that all human beings were created after the image of angels.[84] The temporal sense suggests that what once was given to all is no longer given to all. That need not reflect a particular historical event, such as sin in the garden,[85] but the contention that human beings have not realized the potential which they have by their creation, but rather have chosen to ignore God's revelation and live according to what became common human ways, or, translated into the language of predestination, not all prove to be God's elect.[86] All should have, but in the course of time with the corruption of humanity only a few are now recipients of revelation.

Against this view Goff counters that "to maintain that 4QInstruction taught that all people were given revelation but that it was taken away from some at a later point is a tremendous claim that relies on a brief expression, ועוד לוא of 4Q417 1 i.17".[87] But it is also a big claim to suggest it teaches the creation of two humanities. To assert that humanity once had revelation, even if only Adam or only in its beginnings, and no longer has it, except for a few, need not imply that it was taken away from some, nor should the details be pressed into representing a specific "fall" or made to represent a precise numerical explanation. Language of election and predestination is notoriously imprecise and functions here in a way that declares that only a few have revelation and others do not and they remain just people of flesh, whereas this was not always the case.

On balance, the second reading seems to me more probable, not least because the notion of two separate creations goes far beyond anything we find in related

---

[83] Apparently the view of Wold, *Women, Men, and Angels*, who writes: "The 'spiritual people' are not the only ones formed in the likeness of the holy ones; but rather, the subject of the pronominal suffix of יצרו in line 17 refers to all humanity" (148).

[84] Wold, *Women, Men, and Angels*, 116-17, who points out that Goff also appears to read 4Q423 in this way (119).

[85] So rightly, Wold, *Women, Men, and Angels*: "Reading 'no more' in 4Q417 1 I does not necessitate reading a fall of humanity rooted in Adam's sin" (119). Eden is a metaphor in 4Q423 and 4Q417 of the condition of the addressees (119). While there are now two groups, there were not originally (139). This is the result of "a subsequent failure of a segment of humanity to know and adhere to a pursuit of wisdom" (140). A segment of humanity has accordingly lost the revelation (179).

[86] On the tradition that human beings were created to know good and evil in Sir 17:7, see Fletcher-Louis, *Glory of Adam*, 116; Collins, "Likeness," 616; Esther G. Chazon, "The Creation and Fall of Adam in the Dead Sea Scrolls," in *The Book of Genesis in Jewish and Oriental Christian Interpretation: A Collection of Essays* (ed. Judith Frishman and Lucas van Rompay; Traditio Exegetica Graeca 5; Leuven: Peeters, 1997) 13-24, 18.

[87] Goff, *Discerning Wisdom*, 34 n. 99.

literature and does not seem to have been an idea which those who treasured the document espoused or learned from it. In addition, the hearers are addressed not only as the righteous but also as people capable of failing. This is evident in the contrast with the angels in 4QInstr^{d}/4Q418 55, which declares: "[As for the holy angels], are they like Man? (No,) for he (i.e. man) is sluggardly. And are they like a son of man? (No,) for he comes to an end" (11). It reflects a similar kind of tension to the later, though slightly different predestinarian dualism of the *Thanksgiving Hymns*, in the sense that all humanity is beset with the propensity to sin and ignorance, but that at the same time some are chosen to receive revelation (in reality, when they respond).

We have before us, in any case, an anthropology that assumes that only certain human beings, those whose future is engraved in the revered book will be able to appreciate it and be its custodians. They are to gaze in it on "the mystery that is to come" (18-19). Similarly 4QInstr^{d}/4Q418 77 2-4 apparently speaks of a weighting determined by God which affects human destiny and judgement. The others, the רוח בשר "the spirit of flesh", have no such knowledge because they are not able to distinguish between good and evil. While, as Tigchelaar notes,[88] this is depicted here as a failure of knowing and therefore as warranting judgement, the use of the term, רוח בשר "the spirit of flesh", in 4QInstr^{b}/4Q416 1 12 assumes a culpability which warrants Frey's conclusion that they are sinful.[89] This does not, however, mean that the "spirit of flesh" is necessarily sinful in itself. The document assumes that the hearer still has the capacity to respond positively or negatively.[90]

4QInstr^{d}/4Q418 81+81a 1-6 throws further light on the anthropology. Having extolled the addressee's role in blessing the angels and praising God, it speaks of his being separated from the רוח בשר "spirit of flesh":

[א]ז הבדילכה מכול 2 רוח בשר
ואתה הבדל מכול אשר שנא
והנזר מכול תעבות נפש [כי]א הוא עשה כול
3 ויורישם איש נחלתו

[88] Tigchelaar, *To Increase Learning,* 188.

[89] Frey, "Flesh and Spirit," 390-91. So also Goff, *Worldly and Heavenly Wisdom*, who comments, "the expression should not be understood as a reference to the human condition per se, but rather as a designation for people who are not among the elect" (95).

[90] Cf. also Goff, *Worldly and Heavenly Wisdom*, who notes elsewhere: "Although the addressee is predisposed to righteous behavior, being in the lot of the angels, he must nevertheless choose to live in this way … He can turn to wickedness despite his elect status" (221). Wold, *Women, Men, and Angels,* also notes the exhortations about tiredness in 4QInstr^{d}/4Q418 55 11, cited above (181).

> The]n he has separated you from[91] every 2 spirit of flesh
> so that you might be separate from (or: and you, be separate from) everything which he hates
> and hold yourself aloof from all that (his) soul abominates,
> because he has made everyone 3 and has made them each to inherit his own inheritance (81+81a 1b-3a)

The parallelism enables us to see that "spirit of flesh" is being used here not as a description of human embodiment – the writer is still embodied – but as something connected to what opposes God and what God hates and holds to be abominable. One might simply equate the two, so that "spirit of flesh" is seen as a designation of all who oppose God and draw the conclusion that this is directly implied here in the use of the term "flesh".[92] That would cohere with the view that sees "spirit of flesh" as a designation of a second set of human beings created beside the "people of the spirit". On the other hand, one need not assume an exact parallel nor that a dual creation is involved. The document appears to be speaking of the addressee's having separated himself from those to whom he once belonged.[93] The imagery of the preceding context and of what follows ("he has appointed you as most holy one"* 5) might indicate that this is about separation for a priestly role. Thus Tigchelaar points to the allusion in 3 to Num 18:20, and to Num 8:14 and 16:9, which speak of the Levite being separated from the congregation of Israel.[94] Alternatively, it refers to separation from the rest of humanity along with others who have done the same. Then the "spirit of flesh" is, in itself, a neutral designation for humankind, except by association. Thus Tigchelaar, who concludes that in none of the four occurrences is it "undisputedly negative", points to a similar usage in 4QInstr[b]/4Q416 2 ii.2-3 // 4QInstr[c]/4Q417 2 ii.4 "If he closes his hand, then the spirit of all flesh רוח כל בשר will be gathered in" (cf. Job 34:14-15).[95] Neither the word "spirit" nor the word "flesh" is negative; nor is the expression, "spirit of flesh", except that humankind has generally not chosen to follow the way of God.

---

[91] I follow Tigchelaar, *To Increase Learning,* in reading מכול not בכול, which has no justification in the original (95).

[92] See Frey, "Flesh and Spirit," 390-91.

[93] So Wold, *Women, Men, and Angels*: "lines 1-2 describe the addressee as separated from 'all flesh' at a point in the past as opposed to a separate creation" (163).

[94] Tigchelaar, *To Increase Learning,* 187; earlier Armin Lange, "Determination of Fate by the Oracle of the Lot," in *Sapiential, Liturgical and Poetical Texts from Qumran: Proceedings of the Third Meeting of the International Organization for Qumran Studies Oslo 1998: Published in Memory of Maurice Baillet* (ed. D. K. Falk, F. García Martínez, and E. M. Schuller; STDJ 35; Leiden: Brill, 1999) 39-48, who sees here a reference to Aaron or Aaronic priests (40). See also Fletcher-Louis, *Glory of Adam*, 178-85.

[95] Tigchelaar, *To Increase Learning,* 188.

Overall, the use of "flesh" to depict humanity opposed to God, while it may imply an inherent vulnerability due to the participation in the act of creation, does not mean that human embodiment in itself is sinful or that the flesh, let alone any part of it such as the sexual genitalia, is sinful or evil.

In one instance we apparently find the term יצר רע:

> 12. Let not the thought of an evil inclination מחשבת יצר רע mislead you[ ]
> 13. you shall faithfully seek. Let not the th[ought of an evil inclination] mislead you[ ]
> 14. without his appointing the understandings of the flesh. Let not there lead y[ou] astr[ay]. (4QInstr[c]/4Q417 1 ii.12-14)

Derived from Gen 6:5, the expression here more likely refers to human thought and planning than to an aspect of human creation. The expression יצר בשר appears in 4QInstr[b]/4Q416 1 16 = 4QInstr[d]/4Q418 2 8, where it may mean "inclination of the flesh", but could just as easily mean "creature of flesh". As Strugnell and Harrington note, references to "evil inclination" are without any talk of a corresponding good inclination as in later rabbinic writings and without the psychological and metaphysical dualism of the two spirits.[96] Nor is there any trace of the self-deprecatory anthropology of the *Thanksgiving Hymns* and related parallels, which use the substances of creation and procreation to emphasise the lowliness of the human creature, though the use of both בשר "flesh" and יצר "inclination" appears to be similar. The work does use, in particular, the option of human beings' return to the dust, but in a distinctive way related to a belief in life beyond the grave as it speaks of return to the pit in which the person will find accusers: "You were fashioned [by the power of G]od, but to the everlasting pit shall your return be. For it (sc. the pit) shall awaken [to condemn] you[r] sin, [and the creatures of] its dark places [ ] shall cry out against your pleading" (4QInstr[d]/4Q418 69 ii.6-7).[97]

---

[96] Strugnell and Harrington, *DJD* 34, (33); cf. Frey, "Flesh and Spirit," who finds evidence in *1/4QInstruction* of both the good and the evil inclination, linked with the spirit of the flesh (395). On the relevance of these texts for the background and development of the concepts of the two inclinations, see also Johann Cook, "The Origin of the Tradition of the יצר הטוב and יצר הרע," *JSJ* 38 (2007) 80-91, 88-90.

[97] On the "eternal pit" in the document see Goff, *Worldly and Heavenly Wisdom*, 200-202.

Conclusion

In conclusion, the dualism represented in the document seems best understood as based on an understanding of humankind as created in the image of angels, but as having closed itself to the gift of wisdom offered by God and apparently represented in the Vision of Hagu. While all human beings are flesh, those who have closed themselves off from this wisdom follow only the spirit of flesh and its propensity to sin, its evil inclination, and are without hope and these are then referred to as the "spirit of flesh" (= those who go the way of most human beings). This seems more likely than that the author sees them as a separate creation from the beginning, although one cannot be certain. Those who have not gone the way of the "spirit of flesh" (or apparently who have ceased from doing so) belong to "the people of the spirit". As is common in contexts which assume a determining theism, such people are understood not only to have made responsible choices and to be needing to stick with them (the point of the constant warnings), but also as those predestined to be people of the spirit.

Within this dualism nothing suggests that human sexuality is part of the problem, nor that "flesh" or "inclination" have a specifically sexual reference. Those who follow the teachings of *1/4QInstruction* clearly engage in marriage and sexual relations as something positive.

The document includes strong affirmation of marriage, based on an understanding rooted in a particular interpretation of Genesis 1 – 3, and probably understood as refracted through the vehicle of wisdom described as "the mystery to come". In particular it appeals to women's origin in that story, possibly encrypted in the allusion to "the wife of your bosom", namely the wife taken from your side, as the basis for instruction about sexual union, male authority, women's weakness and inferiority, control over vows and oaths, ownership and resistance of adulterers, honouring one's wife, her being the foundation for the family and the man's own(ed) womb and flesh, leaving one's parents, marrying off one's sons and daughters, the latter without hiding blemishes, and, addressed to wives, honouring their husband like their father, remaining in intimate love and so countering rival women and avoiding marriage breakdown. There also appear to be warnings against illicit desire and lustful eyes, and immoral women (prostitutes?). Altogether the instruction assumes that the people of the spirit engage in marriage, enjoy sexual relations, produce children, live in hierarchically ordered marriages which include respect for wives but in which husbands rule. Nothing suggests celibacy. Issues of polygyny and monogyny are not addressed, presumably because among the poor only monogyny was practical anyway. Nor is there any indication that future hope might be disembodied or devoid of such relationships.

2 *1/4QMysteries* 1QMyst/1Q27; 4QMyst^{a-c}/4Q299-301

This extensive, poorly preserved work, which like *1/4QInstruction* appears to be a wisdom writing emanating from non- or pre-sectarian circles, has little directly related to our theme.

The expression בית מולדים "house of birth" (4QMyst^{a}/4Q299 1 4; 3aii-b 13) probably refers to time of birth, understood in an astrological sense and used in the second passage in the context of divine predestination (cf. also 5.5). The issue of birth must also have been the focus in 28, but the context is not preserved. In 8.7 יצר בינה "inclination of understanding" appears also determined by God. The word, יצר "inclination, creature", appears also in 8.6 and 33. The document is concerned with transgression, special knowledge/wisdom (mystery), including about future hope and judgement, but in nothing which survives does it relate these to issues of sexuality. 4QMyst^{b}/4Q300 3 2-3 mentions a purpose expressed as "in order that they would know (the difference) between g[ood and evil, and between falsehood and truth, and that they might understand the mysteries of transgression] (3) all their wisdom. But [they] did not know [the mystery of that which was coming into being, and the former things they did not consider", but aside from possible allusions to maturity or to the tree of knowledge of good and evil, there is nothing specific. There are some indications of a self-deprecating anthropology: "what is dust [and ashes …?" (4QMyst^{c}/4Q301 4 3) and "wh]at is flesh that […?" (4QMyst^{c}/4Q301 5 3). 4QMyst^{c}/4Q301 2b 5 mentions תבנית זכר "the image of a male", but its significance is not preserved.

3 The *Testament of Qahat* and the *Visions of Amram* 4QTQahat ar/4Q542 and 4QVisions of Amram$^{a-f?}$ ar/4Q543-49

These two works seem best understood, as also the *Aramaic Levi Document*, as belonging to priestly instructional tradition or wisdom, as has been argued recently by Henryk Drawnel.[98]

[98] Henryk Drawnel, "The Literary Form and Didactic Content of the *Admonitions* (*Testament*) *of Qahat*," in *From 4QMMT to Resurrection: Mélanges qumraniens en homage à Émile Puech* (ed. Florentino García Martínez, Annette Steudel, and Eibert Tigchelaar; STDJ 61; Leiden: Brill, 2006) 55-73, who writes: "The *Levi Document*, *Admonitions of Qahat* and *Visions of Amram* are three compositions that belong to priestly didactic lore of the Second Temple period and stem from the didactic priestly milieu" (72). See also Drawnel, *An Aramaic Wisdom Text*.

3.1 The *Testament of Qahat* 4QTQahat ar/4Q542

In the so-called *Testament of Qahat*, Qahat refers to himself and his father, Levi, as not having engaged in "[min]gling" (ע[רב]ובר), probably an allusion to intermarriage with Gentiles (1 i.9).[99] It is most likely related closely to the warning a few lines earlier: "Do not give your inheritance away to strangers/Gentiles (לנכראין), nor your inheritance to half-breeds (לכילאין)" (5-6a). This is not about giving gifts, but about engaging in intermarriage and so threatening the inheritance of priests of Levi by contaminating their line. Drawnel notes that "the Aramaic term, כילאין 'half-breed,' is best explained by the reference to the Hebrew dual form כלאים, 'two kinds,' indicating types of animals, seed or textile that cannot be mixed (Lev 19:19; Deut 22:9)".[100] When fr. 3 alludes to זנותא "illicit sexual relations" (ii 12), the concern is probably similar, though the context has not survived. Concern with priests intermarrying with Gentiles is also a theme of the *Aramaic Levi Document* with which this document has affinity.[101]

3.2 The *Visions of Amram* 4QVisions of Amram[a-f?] ar/4Q543-49

The document, the *Visions of Amram*, refers to marriage in two different ways. It refers to Amram giving his daughter Miriam in marriage to his younger brother, Uzziel, when she was thirty years old (4Q543 1a-c 5-6 = 4Q545 1a i.5-6 = 4Q546 1 3-4). The document shows no indication that this marriage was problematic, even though it contravened the prohibition of marrying nieces, enunciated in the *Temple Scroll*, D, *4QHalakhah A*/4Q251 and elsewhere. The reference to Miriam being 30 years of age is somewhat surprising since this is the normal age for men to marry, not women. If this is an attempt to ameliorate the anomaly, it is not clear how it should do so. Nor does the document reflect any sensitivity about the marriage by Amram himself to his aunt Jochabed, his father Qahat's sister, which contravenes the provisions of Lev 18:12-14; 20:19. Like Exodus 6:20 and Num 26:59 and the *Aramaic Levi Document* (which nevertheless ameliorates it somewhat by having them born on the same day; 12:3 / 75), this document assumes that marriage to be unproblematic.[102]

---

[99] So Drawnel, "Literary Form," 70.

[100] Drawnel, "Literary Form," 69.

[101] On this see my discussion in Loader, *Enoch, Levi, and Jubilees*, 87-112.

[102] Cf. *Jubilees*, which omits all reference to the marriage. See also Sidnie White Crawford, "Traditions about Miriam in the Qumran Scrolls," in *Women and Judaism* (ed. L. J. Greenspoon, R. Simkins, and J. Cahan; Studies in Jewish Civilization 14; Omaha: Creighton University Press, 2003) 33-44, 38-39; and Loader, *Enoch, Levi, and Jubilees*, 273.

Aside from noting the apparently unproblematic uncle-niece and aunt-nephew marriages, we should also observe the positive portrait both of the seven days of wedding festivities ("Then he gave a feast lasting seven days and he ate and drank at the feast and rejoiced" 4Q543 1a-c 6b-7) and of the relationship between Amram and Jochabed. Amram is portrayed as affirming his relationship to Jochabed, his wife, even though he had had to move to Palestine while she was in Egypt. Accordingly, he assures us that when he was forced to stay in Hebron, cut off from Egypt to which his father, Qahat, and Jochabed had returned, he "did not take another wife", though "there were many women in Canaan", indicating his special love for her, and that he desired to see her face when he returned to Egypt (4Q543 4 2-4 = 4Q544 1 7-9 = 4Q547 1-2 iii 6-9a).[103] It does not appear to assume monogyny as a norm, but, if anything, reinforces the prohibition against intermarriage with Canaanites and all foreigners. This positive stance towards friendship and love in marriage and the rejection of intermarriage recall the book of *Jubilees* where these are important features. Intermarriage with Gentiles is also a theme in the related *Testament of Qahat*, noted above, and the *Aramaic Levi Document*.

It may be significant that it is precisely in the context of affirming his love for his wife that Amram then goes on directly to report his vision, in which he sees the two opposing angels who vie for human allegiance (4Q544 1 9 = 4Q547 1-2 iii.9). Visions come to those who are faithful children of light and uphold proper marriage, but, more importantly, Amram's decision to remain faithful to his wife and not take a foreign wife reflects obedience to the angel of light. The language used here, children of light and children of darkness, and the two opposing angelic figures (4Q548 1 ii-2 9-16; 4Q544 1 9-15), is close to the terminology of the *Treatise on the Two Spirits* in 1QS/1Q28 3.13 – 4.26, which also depicts two heavenly beings, שר אורים "the prince of lights" and מלאך חושך "the angel of darkness", commissioned to compete for control over humankind, who thus divide themselves into בני אור "the children of light" (3.13), בני צדק "the children of justice" (3.20, 22, 24), and בני אמת "the children of truth" (4.5, 6), or בני עול "the children of falsehood". Here, in addition, one of the two is named: "Malkiresha" (4Q544 2 13), and described as having the appearance of a snake (כפתן), a possible allusion to the snake of Eden (though in Genesis a different

[103] On this see Betsy Halpern-Amaru, "Burying the Fathers: Exegetical Strategies and Source Traditions in Jubilees 46," in *Reworking the Bible: Apocryphal and Related Texts at Qumran: Proceedings of a Joint Symposium by the Orion Center for the Study of the Dead Sea Scrolls and Associated Literature and the Hebrew University Institute for Advanced Studies Research Group on Qumran, 15-17 January, 2002* (ed. Esther G. Chazon, Devorah Dimant, and Ruth A. Clements; STDJ 58; Leiden: Brill, 2005) 135-53, 147-52.

word (נחש) is used),[104] and as wearing colourful clothing (4Q544 1 13). The colourful clothing probably alludes to clothing worn by women and deemed seductive, such as we find in 4Q184 1 4-5 14-15.[105] Nitzan notes that despite the similarities to the *Treatise on the Two Spirits*, here in the *Visions of Amram*, there is no mention of God nor any concern to explain the struggle between the two spirits in terms of divine ordering. She explains this as reflecting Persian influence.[106] Nor does our passage reflect the kind of psychological extrapolations found in the treatise.

4Q549, which probably belongs to the same document, then assumes that Amran and Jochabed have been reunited, reports first her death, and then that of Amram. Its fragmentary remains go on to refer to the birth of children to Uzziel and Miriam, of Mishael, Elizaphan and Sithri, and to Hur, and to Aaron and Elizabeth.

The *Visions of Amram* shares with the *Testament of Qahat* and the *Aramaic Levi Document* a concern with intermarriage with Gentiles, and with the latter a more liberal understanding of the laws of incest. Beside its concern with intermarriage, its positive stance toward marital partnership recalls a similar emphasis in *Jubilees*, though in relating the same incident of Amram's absence from Jochabed *Jubilees* makes no mention of marital issues (46:10). The striking dualism of the vision does not take up issues of sexuality, although it may be significant that Amram's choice to love Jochabed and resist marrying a Canaanite is the immediate context for relating the struggle and doubtless models appropriate resistance against the angel of darkness. Its depiction of Malkiresha's appearance reflects motifs which belong to the image of the strange woman, the seductress.

4 The *Wiles of the Wicked Woman* 4Q184

One of the initial difficulties in dealing with this manuscript is the text. John Strugnell subjected the edition of John Allegro in *DJD* 5 to severe criticism.[107] While *DSSEL* reproduces Allegro's text, I have chosen to use the text (and its translation) reproduced in *DSSSE* which takes the critique of Strugnell into account.

[104] Apart from noting the possible allusion to Genesis, Nitzan, "Evil and its Symbols," notes also the use of the image in 1QH^a xiii.26-29 (from Deut 32:33); and also in CD 8.9-12 =19.22-24; and 1QH^a xi.12, 18 (93-94).

[105] So Nitzan, "Evil and its Symbols," 95.

[106] Nitzan, "Evil and its Symbols," 87.

[107] Strugnell, "Notes," 263-58. See also Jean Carmignac, "Poème allegorique sur la secte rivale," *RevQ* 5/19 (1965) 361-74, 364 n. 6.

The textual issues begin already with what Allegro conjectured was the first word: הזונ[ה "the prostitute", which Strugnell declares to be impossible because of space and because one would have seen traces of the *nun.*[108] In substance Allegro's conjecture was not wide of the mark inasmuch as the poem[109] is portraying a woman engaged in activity depicted as immoral and dangerous, though no specific mention is made of prostitution or monetary payment.[110] The first two lines clearly use feminine singular verbs and focus primarily on the woman's speech.

> She [...] utters futility (הבל) and in [...].
> She is always looking for (תשחר) depravities (תועות),
> [and] whets the word[s of her mouth, ...]
> 2 and implies insult (וקלס תחל[י]ק (or: and she flatters/uses smooth speech in derision)
> and is [bu]sy (להליץ or: to scoff) leading the community (יחד or: together?)[111] astray with non[sense.] (1.1-2a) (*DSSSE* supplemented)

The motif of speech is a common feature of depictions of the immoral woman. Thus Prov 2:16, להצילך מאשה זרה מנכריה אמריה החליקה "You will be saved from the strange woman, from the foreign woman with her smooth/flattering word"; similarly 7:5. Prov 5:3 says: וחלק משמן חכה "and her speech is smoother than oil" (cf. Prov 6:24 מחלקת לשון נכריה "from the smooth tongue of the foreign woman"; 7:21; Sir 9:2).[112] Already her loose and bold speech

---

[108] Strugnell, "Notes," 264. See also the discussion in Melissa Aubin, "'She is the Beginning of all the Ways of Perversity': Femininity and Metaphor in 4Q184," *Women in Judaism: A Multidisciplinary Journal* 2.2 (2001) 1-23, 11-13.

[109] On the poetic form of the document see Aubin, "She is the Beginning," 3-9; Rick D. Moore, "Personification of the Seduction of Evil: 'The Wiles of the Wicked Woman'," *RevQ* 10/40 (1981) 505-19, 509-12; and earlier Carmignac, "Poème allegorique," 362-63, who describes it as monotonous and lacking the poetic creativity of the author of the *Thanksgiving Hymns* (363).

[110] So rightly Goff, *Discerning Wisdom*, 108. He provides an introduction to the document as a whole (104-21).

[111] For "together" see John Strugnell, "The Smaller Hebrew Wisdom Texts Found at Qumran," in *The Wisdom Texts from Qumran and the Development of Sapiential Thought: Studies in Wisdom at Qumran and its Relationship to Sapiential Thought in the Ancient Near East, the Hebrew Bible, Ancient Judaism, and the New Testament* (ed. Charlotte Hempel, Armin Lange, and Hermann Lichtenberger, BETL 159; Leuven: Peeters-Leuven University Press, 2002) 31-60, 40.

[112] See Scott C. Jones, "Wisdom's Pedagogy: A Comparison of Proverbs VII and 4Q184," *VT* 53 (2003) 65-80, 75. On the deliberate contrast between sharpness and smoothness see Aubin, "She is the Beginning," 13.

contravenes the (male) cultural models of appropriate behaviour for women and reveal her as a transgressor of norms.

As Aubin observes, the language in this opening section also has parallels with sectarian writings describing conflict. Thus she notes that תועות "depravities" occurs in 1QH^{a} ix in descriptions of apostasy.[113] A clearer example is to be found in CD 20.11. She also notes that the juxtaposition here of smooth speech (תחליק) and scoffing (להיליץ) occurs in depictions of apostasy in 1QH^{a} x.13-15, 31-32; xii.7-10.[114]

The focus then moves from her speech to her body. Moore notes a progression in the poem which moves from the woman's head, her speech, to her torso, to her hands and feet, and then down to the netherworld, matching the journey of those who succumb to her wiles.[115]

Her heart weaves traps (פחין),
her kidneys (כליותיה) n[ets (מק]שות).
Her eyes] 3 have been defiled with evil,
her hands grasp the pit,
her feet descend to act wickedly,
and to walk in crimes.
[…] 4 (are) foundations of darkness,
and there are plenty of sins in her wings (בכנפיה or: in her hems/skirts).
(1 2b-4) (*DSSSE* supplemented)

The motif of nets and traps is employed also in Prov 7:23 in depicting the strange woman: כְּמַהֵר צפור אל פח "like a bird rushing into a snare". The motif appears in the context of sexual wrongdoing also in CD 4.14 which cites the word play of Isa 24:17, פחד ופחת ופח עליך יושב הארץ "Terror, and the pit, and the snare are upon you, O inhabitant of the earth!", and goes on to speak of the three nets (מצודות) of Belial. Instead of פחין "traps" Allegro reads פחוז "wantonness", a word also used in the context of sexual wrongdoing in 13 and 15 (also in fr. 3; and 4QpUnid/4Q172 4 3; 4QEn^{b} ar/4Q202 3 1 = *1 Enoch* 8:2; *Aramaic Levi Document* 6:3 / 16; cf. also Gen 49:5).[116]

The reference to feet in 3 רגליה להרשיע ירדו recalls the words of Prov 5:5 רגליה ירדות מות "her feet go down to death". Aubin raises the possibility that

---

[113] Aubin, "She is the Beginning," 14.

[114] Aubin, "She is the Beginning," 15.

[115] Moore, "Personification," 509-10. See also Aubin, "She is the Beginning," 8.

[116] On the "perversity" of Allegro's translation, "In perversion they seized the fouled (organs) of passion, they descended the pit of her legs to act wickedly", see Strugnell, "Notes" 264.

"feet" may also be an allusion to her sexual genitalia.[117] "In her hems/skirts" appears to be a more appropriate translation of בכנפיה than "wings", given the subject matter, and forms a more fitting transition to what follows, which goes on to speak of her attire and dwelling. It also fits the downward progression of the description. Aubin refers to Gaster's suggestion that the hem of the skirt may have served as a money pouch (then potentially a reference to prostitution).[118] She also considers that "foundation of darkness" may have a double reference, including to the woman's genitalia.[119] "The simultaneity of both valences, then, creates a *double entendre* in this phrase. Her genitals are filled with transgressions, presumably sexual deviance, and her garments are filled with transgressions, the ways of sin generally."[120] On the other hand, Baumgarten argues that כנף is not used of women's attire, and so must refer to wings.[121] He sees this as part of the image of the woman as being like the demon Lilith, depicted as closely connected to the underworld, a central theme in what follows.

Her [...] (are) night gloom (תועפות לילה horns of the night?)
and her clothes [(are) ...
5 Her veils are shadows of the twilight
and her adornments diseases of the pit.
Her beds [her couches] are couches of the pit (שחת),
[...] 6 (are) deep ditches (מעמקי בור).
Her lodgings are couches of darkness
and in the heart of the nigh[t] (באישני ליל[ה] in the pupil of the night) are her tents.
In the foundations of gloom 7 she sets up her dwelling,
and camps in the tents of silence, in the midst of the eternal fire.
(1 4b-7a) (*DSSSE* supplemented)

This passage operates at two levels. References to clothes, veils, adornments, couches, lodgings, night[122] and darkness, will all be literal, yet at the same time at the least the latter two suggest more than that. Baumgarten also suggests that the words תועפות לילה "horns of the night" might well continue the image of the woman as being like Lilith, sometimes depicted as having horns.[123] Adornments

[117] Aubin, "She is the Beginning," 16.

[118] Aubin, "She is the Beginning," 17; T. H. Gaster, *The Dead Sea Scriptures* (New York: Anchor Press, 1976) 495.

[119] Aubin, "She is the Beginning," 17.

[120] Aubin, "She is the Beginning," 17.

[121] Baumgarten, "Nature of the Seductress," 139.

[122] On the expression באישני לילה "in the pupil of the night" see Prov 7:9.

[123] Baumgarten, "Nature of the Seductress," 140. On demonic horns see also 11QApPsa/11Q11 5.7, which, however, uses the word קרן.

can be positive, but are frequently depicted as instruments of seduction,[124] as already in the myth of the Watchers (*1 Enoch* 8:1-2). The expression, "the tents of silence", is a way of speaking about death (cf. Ps 94:17).[125] The reference to the pit and deep ditches reflects Prov 23:7, כי שוחה עמקה זונה ובאר צרה נכריה "For a prostitute is a deep ditch; a foreign woman a narrow well" (cf. also 22:14). Quite possibly the reference has double meaning, referring both to the woman's vagina and to the destiny of those who go there.

The next section sets her in relation to others to whom she poses a danger.

> She has no inheritance among all 8 those who shine [.] brightly.
> She is the start of all the ways of wickedness.
> Alas! She is the ruination of all who inherit her,
> and calamity for a[ll] 9 who grasp her.
> For her paths are paths of death,
> and her roads are tracks to sin.
> Her trails lead astray 10 towards wickedness,
> and her pathways to the guilt of transgression.
> Her gates are the gates of death,
> In the entrance to her house Sheo[l] proceeds.
> 11 A[l]l [those who go to her will not] come back,
> and all those who inherit her will descend to the pit. (1 7b-11a)

Here we find an extension of the imagery of light and darkness (cf. Prov 4:18-19). The words, "those who shine brightly", probably reflect an eschatology not unlike Dan 12:3 according to which the righteous will shine like the stars (cf. also *1 Enoch* 104:2-6; 1QS/1Q28 5.8).[126] The words, והיאה ראשית כול דרכי עול "and she is the start/beginning of all the ways of wickedness", echo what is said of Behemoth in Job 40:19 הוא ראשית דרכי אל "it is the first of the ways of God", but, significantly also what is said in Prov 8:22 of Wisdom, which God created as ראשית דרכו "the beginning of his way",[127] and Prov 9:10 (and Ps 11:10), "fear of Yahweh is the beginning of Wisdom".[128] Not only is the woman depicted using

---

[124] Aubin, "She is the Beginning," notes that they may be "associated with portraits of both chaste women (2 Samuel 1:24; Jeremiah 2:32; Ezekiel 16:11; Isaiah 49:18, also 1QM 19:7) and personifications of wayward Israel as harlot", as in Jer 4:30 and Ezek 23:40 (18).

[125] So Carmignac, "Poème allegorique," 367 n. 24.

[126] So Harrington, *Wisdom Texts*, 33.

[127] Strugnell, "Notes," 266, who contrasts 11QPs[a]/11Q5 18; also Strugnell, "Smaller Hebrew Wisdom Texts," 40; see also Harrington, *Wisdom Texts*, 34; John J. Collins, *Jewish Wisdom in the Hellenistic Age* (Louisville: Westminster John Knox, 1997) 115.

[128] So Aubin, "She is the Beginning," 18. See also Moore, "Personification," who assumes the entire document is represented in fragment 1, arguing for a symmetrical structure with this statement at its centre (509); similarly Aubin, p. 8.

motifs from the strange woman in Proverbs, but, as there, she is constructed in part in the light of her opposite, the wise woman. "Starkly polarized, these figures provide an ideal template upon which the 4Q184 author can distinguish his group from a demonized 'other'."[129] The possible allusion to Behemoth may intend to depict her as like a devouring monster.

The destiny or inheritance of those who turn to her is sin and through sin, death and the pit of Sheol. The notion of post-mortem judgement is expressed through the words, "eternal fire" (7).[130] In the words כ[ו]ל[באיה בל]ישובון "all who go into her will not come back" (11) we have an allusion to Prov 2:19a כל באיה לא ישובון "all who go into her will not come back", possibly an allusion to a common expression in Babylonian mythology to describe the netherworld.[131] Baumgarten, noting the links with the underworld here and in Proverbs, points out that the poem alludes eleven times to the underworld and portrays the seductress "not merely as leading her victims to the netherworld, but as herself being a resident and creature of that dark realm".[132] The preceding verse, Prov 2:18 reads, כי שחה אל מות ביתה ואל רפאים מעגלתיה, "because her house leads to death and her paths to the shades", and may well have influenced 10: שעריה שערי מות בפתח ביתה תצעד שאול "her gates are gates of death, and in the doorway of her house Sheol walks". This motif appears also in Prov 7:27, דרכי שאול ביתה ירדות אל חדרי מות "Her house is the way to Sheol going down to the chambers of death" (cf. also 9:18). As Aubin observes, the poet appears also to merge the ideas of the woman's body and her house, so that to enter the one is to enter the other, and simultaneously to enter the gates of Sheol.[133]

The next section describes her behaviour.

She hides in ambush in secret places,
[…] 12 al[…]
In the city squares she veils herself,
And in the gates of the village she stations herself,
and there is no-one who can ke[ep her] 13 from her incessant [fornicat]ing (מה[זנו]ת תמיד).

---

[129] Aubin, "She is the Beginning," 15.

[130] So Strugnell, "Notes": "le contraste est entre une vie parmi les feux (ténébreux) de l'enfer et l'immortalité parmi les astres (ou les anges)" (tr. The contrast is between life among the fires [darkness] of hell and immortality among the stars [or angels]) (266).

[131] Baumgarten, "Nature of the Seductress," 141.

[132] Baumgarten, "Nature of the Seductress," 139.

[133] Aubin, "She is the Beginning," observes: "Playing on these Proverbs elements, the poet conflates the Seductress's home with her body, and indeed, Sheol. This is not a great interpretive leap, in a language for which 'house' can mean 'womb,' and the womb, in turn, determines womanhood. With the turn of a phrase her body and her dwelling merge." (20).

Her eyes scan hither and thither,
and she raises her eyebrows impudently (בפחז or, more probably: in sexual wantonness). (1 11b-13) (*DSSSE* supplemented)

Veiling belonged to the attire of the prostitute (Gen 38:14; cf. Cant 1:7). The depiction here reflects Prov 7:12, פעם בחוץ פעם ברחבות ואצל כל פנה תארב "Now in the street, now in the squares, and at every corner she lies in wait" (cf. also 27:28; Cant 3:2, 5:7; and possibly 4QpUnid/4Q172 4 5). The behaviour matches what we know of the behaviour of prostitutes from other sources, but, as in Prov 7:12 "is strikingly similar to the location of Wisdom in Proverbs 1:20-33 and in Proverbs 8".[134] Thus "the author heightens the difference between Wisdom and her 4Q184 antithesis by tacitly evoking and reversing Wisdom imagery".[135] The reference to her eyes recalls Prov 6:25 (cf. also Sir 26:9). By contrast, according to Prov 31:10-31 the good woman remains focused on her household and has no place in the city squares or their gates; her husband is the public face. The use of בפחז here (as in 15 below, 3 5 and possibly 1 2, as already noted above) is best taken as a reference to "sexual wantonness".

The final section in the major fragment focuses on her purpose:

to spot a 14 just ma[n] and overtake him,
and a [no]ble man, to trip him up (ותכשילהו);
the upright to turn (from) the path,
the righteous chosen ones 15 from keeping the precept,
to make those with a steady [mind] ridiculous with recklessness (בפחז sexual wantonness),
and those who walk uprightly to alter the ordin[na]nce (להשנות חו[ו]ק).
To make 16 the simple rebel against God,
to turn their steps off the paths of justice,
to bring presumpt[uous]ness into their [hear]t,
so that they do not walk 17 in the paths of uprightness.
To sidetrack man into the ways of the pit,
and seduce the sons of men with smooth words (חלקות).
(1 14-17) (*DSSSE* supplemented)

The language of stumbling, used in a sexual context, occurs also in sayings attributed to Jesus (Mark 9:42-48). The aims listed in this passage function as a warning to the hearer, scarcely as an accurate description of the real aims of the immoral woman envisaged in the text or, for instance, of those who plied

[134] Aubin, "She is the Beginning," 19.

[135] Aubin, "She is the Beginning," 19. This is already apparent in the opening lines where we find the description of the woman as "looking for" (תשחר), just as the wise woman does in Prov 1:28; 8:17 (11).

prostitution, which probably included the need to make a living. Thus the document seeks to alert the just, noble, upright, righteous, and stable to the dangers which the woman poses. Of particular note is the reference to her leading such men להשנות חוק "to alter the ordinance", suggesting that her activity has led men to propose interpretations of the Law with which the author disagrees, because they alter/change its meaning. In this regard the allusion to חלקות "smooth words" (17 and 2) recalls the use of this term to describe those who according to D seek to alter the Law by their interpretations, but, as noted in relation to 2 above, it was also a standard feature of the depiction of the strange woman in Proverbs.

Among the other fragments, where little text is preserved, fragment 2 makes reference to the Law, ובתור[ה "and in the La[w" (2), and to ורום עינים ולב ערל "haughtiness of eyes and uncircumcised heart". The reference to eyes fits the sexual imagery implied in fragment 1. Similarly in fragment 3 עם אישוני פחז "with pupils (eyes) of sexual wantonness" (5) continues the sexual theme. In fragment 4 מע]ל "unfaithfulness" may also reflect the sexual theme, which probably underlies the few words of fragment 6: ברחובותי[ה "in her squares" and probably אל תבוא "do not enter".

The simplest reading is to see in the document a warning against the dangers posed by the immoral woman, much as we find in Prov 2:16-19; 5:3-20; 6:23-35; 7:1-27; and Sir 9:3-4, 6-7. This is so even if her portrait is, as Jones notes,[136] less erotically charged than the strange woman of Proverbs. That danger is depicted in two main ways. It leads to death and apparently beyond death to eternal fire of judgement. It also leads the upright to abandon or alter the Law (15). This suggests interpretation of the Law by men in a way which rationalises their behaviour. The document may be indicating more than a general danger in this regard. It could possibly have particular people or a particular group in mind, although the tenor of the document does not suggest that the dangers coming from the wicked woman affect only some opposing group. For the poem assumes that the hearers will identify themselves, not some other group, as among the upright. It differs from Proverbs 7 also in that it is not addressed primarily to a son or young man,[137] but to all, including the simple and, obviously, people in a position to interpret or misinterpret statutes. D attacks those who alter or interpret the Law in a way which allows what it sees as sexual wrongdoing, namely, polygyny, intercourse with

---

[136] Jones, "Wisdom's Pedagogy," 12; see also Goff, *Discerning Wisdom*, who notes that "there are, however, erotic aspects of her portrait" (109). "The woman of 4Q184 is immoral and can easily be read as sexually active" (110). He notes also that her marital status is not an issue as in the depiction of the strange woman in Proverbs 7 (111).

[137] So rightly, Goff, *Discerning Wisdom*, who emphasises that unlike Proverbs 1 – 9 this text is not focused on teaching sexual ethics to young men (110-11).

menstruants, and niece marriages (4.13 – 5.11). None of these specific categories, however, fit what is being depicted here: going to immoral women.[138]

The simplest reading is able to account, therefore, for all the detail which lies before us in the document and so should not be abandoned without strong counter evidence.[139] Soon after its publication there were, indeed, attempts to give more complex explanations of the purpose of the document. Already in his advance publication of the text before it appeared in *DJD* 5, John Allegro wrote: "one suspects that the wicked woman is figuratively used here for some other object of the writer's polemic, perhaps, as in Revelation, Rome".[140] Dupont-Sommer then speculated that the focus was not the danger of prostitutes, but of women generally, as in Ben Sira and Philo.[141] Neither adequately explained the concerns with changes to the Law. Carmignac then interpreted the document as an attack on a rival sect with whom the author disagreed and whose behaviour it stigmatises as being like the behaviour of prostitutes.[142] He sees in the motif of "smooth" talk in 2 and 17 and of "the community" in 2 important clues which enable the document to be read in the context of the conflict with "the seekers of smooth things" referred to in the *Thanksgiving Hymns*, the *Pesharim*, and D.[143]

Strugnell proposed that the document be read as a depiction of Dame Folly, the counterpart of Dame Wisdom, as depicted in 11QPs[a]/11Q5 18, and sees it not

[138] Grossmann, "Reading for Gender," notes how the concerns of D and 4Q184 can be heard together, so that "the traps of the wicked woman in fact *are* the sexual transgressions described in the Damascus Document" (232).

[139] It is striking that Moore, "Personification," begins his article with the statement: "Every scholarly treatment of *The Wiles of the Wicked Woman*, a short sapiential poem of Qumran's fourth cave, is in agreement that the work is to be understood allegorically" (506). This is now no longer true!

[140] John M. Allegro, "The Wiles of the Wicked Woman: A Sapiential Work from Qumran's Fourth Cave," *PEQ* 96 (1964) 53-55, 53.

[141] A. Dupont-Sommer, "Le Psaume CLI dans 11QPs(a) et le probleme de son origine essenienne," *Sem* 14 (1964) 25-62, 54-55; see also Gaster, *Dead Sea Scriptures*, who questioned that the sect would be worried about urban street walkers and saw here a reflection of alleged Essene misogyny (495); see also Magen Broshi, "Beware the Wiles of the Wicked Woman: Dead Sea Scroll Fragment Reflects Essene Fear of, and Contempt for Women," *BAR* 9/4 (1983) 54-56. Cf. Harrington, *Wisdom Texts*, 33; Goff, *Discerning Wisdom*, 118.

[142] Carmignac, "Poème allegorique," 372-74; Johann Maier, "Wiles of the Wicked Woman," *EncDDS*, 2.976.

[143] Carmignac, "Poème allegorique," 365 n. 10. See also A. M. Gazov-Ginzberg, "Double-Meaning in a Qumran Work: The Wiles of the Wicked Woman," *RevQ* 6/22 (1967) 279-85, who sees the document addressing all hostile outsiders, including Jewish and Macedonian authorities; and H. Burgmann, "The Wicked Woman: Der Maccabäer Simon?," *RevQ* 8/31 (1974) 323-59, who argues that it depicts Simon. Cf. Collins, *Jewish Wisdom*, who argues that it is too narrow to see the focus being on false doctrine (115).

as sectarian nor as engaging with another sect, though it uses some Essene language reflected also in the Qumran sect.[144] While affirming Strugnell's identification, Baumgarten introduces the importance of the demonic dimension. Accordingly, he argues, 4Q184 "is the description of the seductive demoness who resides in the darkness of the netherworld but issues forth stealthily to lure the unsuspecting to apostasy and perdition".[145] White Crawford, for whom "4Q184's subject, Dame Folly, is beyond doubt",[146] notes that both in Proverbs 1 – 9 and here "the sin contemplated is clearly fornication".[147] On the other hand, she argues, the motifs associated with Lilith, whose sins in folklore are also sexual, mean that "Dame Folly has ceased to be simply human and has become demonic".[148] What she designates the "catastrophization" of Dame Folly makes the depiction similar to the struggle between the angel of darkness and the prince of lights in the *Treatise on the Two Spirits*.[149]

Collins, noting that in Proverbs 9 "'the foolish woman' (or 'Lady Folly') is clearly the antitype to Lady Wisdom, an allegorical representation of foolishness rather than a mere prostitute", [150] concludes that "it is probably safe to say that something more is intended than a warning against adultery" also in 4Q184.[151] "What is at issue here is not just sexual transgression but a whole way of life, of which sexual transgression is only a representative instance."[152] Grossmann similarly writes: "As a metaphor and catchall term, the wicked woman represents all the sins that a covenanter must avoid".[153] Similarly, Moore had spoken of the poem as a work of "hamartiology".[154] At the same time Grossmann draws attention to the values implicit in the image, contrasting it with positive images of

---

[144] Strugnell, "Notes," 266-67. In agreement A. S. van der Woude, "Wisdom at Qumran," in *Wisdom in Ancient Israel: FS J. A. Emerton* (ed. J. Day, R. P. Gordon and H. G. M. Williamson; Cambridge: Cambridge University Press, 1995) 244-56, 247; Harrington, *Wisdom Texts*, 31-35.

[145] Baumgarten, "Nature of the Seductress," 143. See also Sidnie White Crawford, "Lady Wisdom and Dame Folly at Qumran," *DSD* 5 (1998) 355-66, 361, but also the cautionary note of Lange, "Weisheitstexte," who sees Baumgarten's description as going beyond the intention of the text (10 n. 45).

[146] White Crawford, "Lady Wisdom and Dame Folly," 360.

[147] White Crawford, "Lady Wisdom and Dame Folly," 360.

[148] White Crawford, "Lady Wisdom and Dame Folly," 361.

[149] White Crawford, "Lady Wisdom and Dame Folly," 361-62. On this see also Collins, *Jewish Wisdom*, who notes that it shares with that treatise the notion of punishment after death in fire (1QS/1Q28 4.13) (115-16).

[150] Collins, Jewish *Wisdom*, 114.

[151] Collins, Jewish *Wisdom*, 115.

[152] Collins, Jewish *Wisdom*, 115.

[153] Grossman, "Reading for Gender," 230.

[154] Moore, "Personification," 507.

women in D as "silent, obedient, and often invisible; ... on the sidelines, except in matters of marriage, procreation, and child-rearing".[155] By contrast "the wicked woman is pictured as walking about in public, whether stealthily or shamelessly, in search of men with whom to fornicate. And worse than walking, this woman talks, leading men astray with 'smooth words'".[156]

Aubin's analysis emphasizes what she calls "the signature premise of the text, its emphatic link between femininity and apostasy".[157] Accordingly "the feminine figure is viewed as a gendered expression of the 4Q184 author's notion of heresy".[158] In this she effectively returns to the thesis of Carmignac. Thus she reads the document as reflecting the use of women by men, and especially sexual infidelity, as a way of depicting apostasy, as in Isa 1:21; Nah 3:4-7; Prov 2:16-19; 5:6, and particularly in relation to marriage: pointing to Jer 2:20, 25; 3:1-13; Ezek 16:23; Hos 1-3.[159] She concludes: "In 4Q184, the symbol of heretical woman functioned socially to mediate conflicts between men, orthodox and heterodox. Constructed for a male spectator, masculinist politics are inscribed on feminine bodies".[160]

In his comparison of Proverbs 7 and 4Q184 from a pedagogical perspective Jones notes that, whereas the former evokes awareness of ambiguity to enable the student or son to develop skills of discernment, 4Q184 portrays the wicked woman unambiguously and emphasizes her connection with the underworld. Its description of the upright man reflects the values of the *Treatise on the Two Spirits*.[161] "While her sexual dimensions cannot be denied, 4Q184 combats more than just sexual transgression, but the whole way of life which this Wicked Woman represents."[162] Similarly Goff concludes that the woman serves "as an allegory for wickedness and folly"[163] and "as a kind of 'floating signifier' representing wickedness in general".[164] As we shall see, such generic abstractions fail to account for the nuances of the text.

---

155 Grossman, "Reading for Gender," 231.

156 Grossman, "Reading for Gender," 231. At the same time she notes that in D "the only significant references to women in the text are those that focus on sexually-related subjects: marriage, divorce, reputation, procreation, and menstrual purity" and where in the "gendering of thematic domains" women are associated with "sex and transgression" (233).

157 Aubin, "She is the Beginning," 1.

158 Aubin, "She is the Beginning," 3.

159 Aubin, "She is the Beginning," 13.

160 Aubin, "She is the Beginning," 22.

161 Jones, "Wisdom's Pedagogy," 78-79.

162 Jones, "Wisdom's Pedagogy," 78.

163 Goff, *Discerning Wisdom*, 111.

164 Goff, *Discerning Wisdom*, 121.

At the very least the document allows us to see what an author understands are the dangers posed by a woman who does not conform to his male ideal of womanhood. The danger is seduction by word, appearance, and behaviour. Whatever additional levels of meaning may be intended or reflected in the text, they depend for their efficacy on the negative stereotype. Even remaining at this literal level of disapproval of the seductive woman, there is use of double meaning, so that terms like feet, foundation, ditch, house, pit, appear with reference both to external realities and as reference to sexual genitalia. The fact that such women were active at night enhanced the possibilities to use darkness metaphorically. In addition imagery of the demonic may have informed the image. The literal concern with the seductive woman is present also in Proverbs, on which the author draws heavily, and in Ben Sira. The same literal concern appears to be reflected in the additional small fragments.

The case for arguing that something more is intended depends partly on internal elements within the document and partly on external elements. Already in Proverbs, beside the literal concern with the seductive woman, there is evidence of the use of the wise woman and the seductress to depict wisdom and goodness, on the one hand, and foolishness and evil, on the other. This connection, highlighted by Strugnell, makes it at least possible that something similar operates here. There are certainly examples in the Qumran material of depictions of wisdom as a woman. They always come in contexts, however, where the application is very clear, such as where they are accompanied by exhortations to be wise in various ways.[165] The element of exhortation is missing, however, in 4Q184, where no such generic exhortations appear. There also appears to be too much concentration on the detail of the wicked woman for her to be functioning just as a symbol. A literal reading makes better sense of the presentation. It depicts the real dangers of sexual wrongdoing.

There are, however, some other elements which might suggest a more specific concern. The final section gives considerable focus to what might happen if the woman has her way. The wise and good man would turn from God's law.[166] While this could allude to disobedience in a generic sense, it more likely alludes to succumbing to the woman's sexual temptation. Of particular significance is the note that it might also lead the upright to change the statute (להשנות חו[ו]ק). This suggests a specific concern about interpreting the Law.

The presence in the document of concern about changing the Law and of language used in sectarian documents of apostasy, "smooth" talk and "scoffing"

[165] E.g., 4QSapWork/4Q185 1-2 ii 8-15; 11QPs[a]/11Q5 18 and 21 (Sira 51:13-19), where the teaching-learning application is explicit (14).

[166] Goff, *Discerning Wisdom*, notes the frequency of language reflecting the motif of path (113). He also notes that the victims are depicted not as simple ones and fools as in Prov 7:7; 9:16, but the upright (116).

(already noted by Carmignac), raises the possibility that the poem is, indeed, concerned with some who were seeking to change the statutes. D, as we have seen, provides the closest parallel to what may be at stake, albeit with significant differences. There, certain behaviours in the sexual realm have apparently led some teachers to give interpretations of the commandments which the author sees as illegitimate, who then attacks such teachers using the language of smooth speech and scoffing. The behaviours cited there do not entail engaging with immoral women, but in a general sense the concerns are similar and relate especially to sexual wrongdoing. These teachers shift the boundaries (of the Law) (playing on the similarity between חיק "boundary" and חוק "statute", 4.12; cf. also 1.16; 5.20; 19.16; 20.20). They revile "the statutes of God's covenant, saying, 'They are not certain'" (CD 5.12). The opposition group is identified in CD as being men of scoffing who dispute laws (20.11) or as following the scoffer (1.14) and as being seekers of smooth things, who seek to change the Law (CD 1.18).

Accusations of changing divine law are also to be found in *1 Enoch* 99:1 ("Woe to you who alter the true words"; similarly 98:14-15) and 104:9 ("Do not err in your hearts or lie, or alter the words of truth, or falsify the words of the Holy One"; similarly 10-11), but without particular reference to sexual wrongdoing. They also find their echo later in similar contexts. "They are not certain" reappears in 1QH[a] xii.18, though without an explicitly sexual context, which also speaks of those who change God's words (vi.15; cf. xii.10). The *Community Rule* possibly speaks of those who bend the Law (11.1-2). The language of scoffing in association with disputing the law appears in 4QpIsa[b]/4Q162 ii.6, 10; 4QBéat/ 4Q525 23.8, also that of going down to the pit and stumbling. The designation of opponents who seek to change the Law as "seekers of smooth things" is widespread (1QH[a] xii.10; x.15, 32; 4Qpap pIsa[c]/4Q163 23 ii.10; 4QpNah/4Q169 3-4 i.2, 7; ii.2, 4; iii.3, 7; *4QCatena[a]*/4Q177 9 4; 4Q185 1-2 ii.9).

Carmignac used the parallels with speaking smoothly and scoffing to argue that the woman functions as a symbol of the rival group, so that the issue is resisting its intrusions and teachings, by alleging that heeding them is as bad as succumbing to the wiles of a wicked woman. The problem with that construction is that those who seek to change the law are the seduced, not the smooth speaking seductress. The descriptions of those who face the danger posed by the woman (just, noble, upright, righteous chosen ones, those with a steady mind, those who walk uprightly, the simple, 14-16) may be assumed to be appropriate self-descriptions of the author and those with whom he identifies. They are certainly not designations of an opposing group. If we see in 4Q184 a literal concern with immoral women and the impact they have, then that concern is being addressed to the author's own people (though, by implication, pointing to the negative example of some who have already failed). There is no hint here of separated opposing groups. Rather, the author envisages that his own people are in danger. The profile of those addressed appears, however, not only to include some who do fall to sexual wrongdoing, but also those who rationalize it by changing the law. Again, however, nothing suggests that this is being done by another group. It is, rather, something happening among people otherwise recognized as upright and who should stay that way.

What then are we to make of the allusions to "smooth talk" and "scoffing" and their parallel with descriptions of those who sought to change the statute in D? Such "smooth talk" is attributed in 4Q184 not to the interpreters of the law, but to the woman; and there it clearly derives from the images of Proverbs. This means that any attempt to make a link between this image and its use to describe people who alter the law must suppose that the author intends a double allusion. It would have to look something like: the woman with her smooth talking leads by implication to similar smooth talking by the teachers who use it, in turn, to rationalize departure from the law. This assumes some subtlety on the part of the author, although it is not impossible. But even without this, the document clearly addresses a moral danger and the resultant perversion of the Law's interpretation by some who succumb to it.

The advantage of seeing the document as addressing the danger of sexual wrongdoing and the way it has led some to change the meaning of the Law is that it does not require that the woman become just a symbol. Rather, the issues of sexual wrongdoing remain paramount, and that is what gives greater substance to the parallel to D. Since the author sees this danger as also existing among his own, the document probably reflects a stage in the conflict where there is still engagement over differences in interpretation of the Law, and not yet a time of clear sectarian division or even of the more developed estrangement evident in D. For the difference from D is that the latter clearly demarcates an opposing group, even though its articulation of the conflict retains reference to the substance of the dispute, which, as here, is about sexual wrongdoing and attempts to change the Law to accommodate it. 4Q184 appears to fit better in a non- or pre-sectarian setting, where within the community as a whole, doubtless the community in Jerusalem, including the priests, some are succumbing to the "wiles of wicked woman" or more generally to the sexual wrongdoing she represents, and among them are some who are teachers and who rationalize their responses with interpretations of the law which the author disputes. One such area of dispute was intermarriage with foreign women, closely associated with the stereotype of the strange woman and prostitution.

We appear therefore to be dealing not with sectarian demarcation, but with concerns within the community as a whole. The focus on the detail of the woman's seduction appears also to suggest that she cannot be reduced to a symbol of something else, like false teaching. If the woman represents the dangers seen in immoral women, and those dangers include not only sin and the eternal fire of judgement, but also distortion of the statutes, we have before us a situation broadly analogous to what we find in D, but also in some other early documents.

The poem appears to have been composed at a time when an issue such as this was seen by some as causing apostasy from true faith and adherence to Torah. That issue is addressed by a number of documents generally believed to be either non sectarian, such as *Jubilees*, *Aramaic Levi Document*, *Testament of Qahat*, *Visions of Amram*, *Apocryphon of Jeremiah*, or from the early days of the sectarian movement, such as *4QMMT*. The depiction of the woman, while still primarily focused on sexual immorality, connects her to the demonic and the netherworld in a manner which by implication also taints all who fall to her wiles. Thus one could see sources here for the kind of demonizing of the opposition group evident in the *Thanksgiving Hymns* and the *Pesharim*, but the document, itself, seems to belong to the earlier stage which we see reflected in D, where the actual issues of dispute have not been left behind.

Rather than see the document as dealing generically with sin by employing the metaphor of the wicked woman, it seems more likely that we have before us a document which really is concerned with sexual wrongdoing. In particular, the focus is on the dangers posed by seductive women and the impact they are having, not just in leading people to sin, but also in causing some in positions of authority (interpreters of the law) to change their application of the law in ways which this author, like the author of D, and, in milder terms, the author of *4QMMT*, sees as error and apostasy.

CHAPTER EIGHT

Attitudes towards Sexuality in the Dead Sea Scrolls: Concluding Assessment

My aim in this section is to offer a synthesis of the findings of the previous discussion of individual documents. This assessment will not repeat the detailed arguments in relation to contentious or obscure points, but seek to discern overall tendencies and themes. One of the difficulties in attempting to do this is the diversity of the documents and relative uncertainty about the provenance, including, in many cases, whether they belong to the writings produced by members of the *Yahad* or just to its library or repository of documents, assuming that is what was found in the caves. The Hebrew scriptures belonged to that library as well as early Enoch literature, *Jubilees*, and the *Aramaic Levi Document*, discussed in a previous volume, all of which precede the foundation of the community. The range of literature which remains is, nevertheless, immense, and the discussion of its theme will be undertaken with an awareness of these other documents and their potential significance.

1 Conflict and Sexuality

The *Damascus Document* (D) addresses issues of sexual wrongdoing in the context of conflict with opponents whom it accuses of seeking to shift the boundaries by changing the Law, especially in relation to sexual wrongdoing. The issues pertaining to sexual wrongdoing are both explicitly itemised in 4.15 – 5.11 and given emphasis in the list of wrongdoing attributed to the "princes of Judah", which must include reference to its opponents, in 8.3-9 / 19.15-21 (cf. also 6.14 –

7.4) and in the depiction of history as a story of succumbing to sexual wrongdoing and wanton pleasure (2.16 – 3.12). The allegation that the congregation of traitors "chose the fair neck" (1.19) is probably already identifying sexual issues as belonging to the heart of the dispute.

Much of the language of conflict found in D reappears in the *Pesharim* and among the *Thanksgiving Hymns*. The enemies are "seekers of smooth things". They are in the view of the writers false teachers of the law, who reflect the dominion of Belial. But, unlike in D, the conflict is not explained in these documents in relation to rejection of particular interpretations of the Law and especially, in that regard, matters relating to sexual wrongdoing. Rather the conflict is depicted as one in which the authors are disputing not interpretations but the legitimacy and integrity of their opponents.

Thus the *Pesharim* read biblical texts as predicting and portraying the story of the community and its leader. Aside from allusions to violence and greed, the focus is on the enemies of the community and, as an external player, the cruel Kittim, who variously become God's agents of vengeance and need finally to be destroyed, themselves. The focus is not on the substance which might have originally formed the basis of the conflict. It is on people and groups and their leaders.

This is also the case in the *Thanksgiving Hymns*. Here we find some statements in the first person, which also reflect conflict. Some speak of persecution. They will have functioned in many ways like the psalms which portray dispute and conflict, providing a vehicle for people facing their own distress. But some of them probably reflect actual conflict which the author and a community faced and conflict within the community itself. There is reference to changing God's words (vi.15; cf. xii.10). Here, too, however, the focus is not on disagreement over actual substance as in D and *4QMMT*, but on competing claims to authority. This is so even in $1QH^a$ xii.5-22, which contains language that echoes CD 4.13 – 5.11, in which the author confronts the false teaching of his opponents, accuses them of changing the Law and identifies their captivity in the nets of Belial, strongly connected to sexual wrongdoing. In the passage in $1QH^a$, however, no such connections are made with matters of the substance of the dispute when designating the opponents as people of Belial and as caught in traps. There is also no hint that it had anything to do with sexual wrongdoing. This is the case throughout the collection of hymns. The author can even employ sexually related motifs such as the two pregnant women in the pangs of childbirth to depict, on the one hand, the suffering of his community and, on the other, the monstrous birth of a serpent which represents his opponents, but nothing suggests that the conflict, itself, has any relation to matters pertaining to sexuality. This is in contrast to *4QMMT* and D, where the separation and conflict are shown to be directly related to such matters.

The same is also true of the *Community Rule*, which, while lacking some the typical terms related to the conflict, such as the "Teacher of Righteousness" and the "seekers of smooth things", also clearly emphasises separation from the men of injustice (5.1-2, 10; 8.13; 9.17) and the men of the pit (9.16; 10.19), who are possibly said to bend the Law (11.1-2) and err. At most there is a hint that one issue is the calendar (5.11-12; cf. 1.14), but in any case the focus is not dispute with opponents, which is here expressly forbidden (9.16; 10.19), but separation and denial of their authority.

In these documents, however, there may still be some traces of what appear to have been the earlier disputes. D makes עיני זנות "eyes of sexual immorality" the basis for a depiction of history which shows it as constantly the source of failure (2.16 – 3.12). The same expression occurs in the *Community Rule* as one of the designations of the evil from which the community members had turned away (1.6),[1] but even then it receives no special emphasis and no elaboration. Similarly, the *Habakkuk Pesher* asserts that the community and its leader, the Teacher of Righteousness, have לוא זנו אחר עיניהם בקץ הרשעה "not lusted after their eyes in the time of wickedness" (5.7b-8a), and speaks of the Wicked Priest in Jerusalem who performed מעשי תועבות ויטמא את 9 מקדוש אל "repulsive acts and defiled the temple of God" (12.8b-9a). These acts may have been sexual in nature. These may reflect memory of the kind of dispute which is reflected in D, but there is no further elaboration; the document puts primary emphasis on acts of violence committed against the community and its leader and on disputing the opponents' status and authority.

Despite these few references, it remains the case that the depictions of conflict in the *Thanksgiving Hymns*, the *Pesharim*, and, to a lesser degree, the *Community Rule*, the documents which speak most of conflict between the community and others, lack reference to specific disputes of interpretation of the Law and, in particular, do not make sexual wrongdoing a major issue, as do D and, much more politely, *4QMMT*. In the former documents what is disputed is not interpretation, but the interpreters' authority. It looks very much like a development has taken place where what was once disagreement over interpreting what is authoritative, namely Torah, has become a direct conflict between the authorities, themselves, the interpreters and their two groups, one of whom, at least, is bedevilling the other. It is a familiar pattern in escalation of conflict from fighting issues to fighting people.

Some documents, which also clearly reflect conflict and use standard terms to designate opponents do appear to focus on sexual wrongdoing. Thus 4QFlor/ 4Q174 and *4QCatena*[a]/4Q177 speak of "seekers of smooth things" and "the

---

[1] Also *4QBarkhi Nafshi*[b]/4Q435 2 i.2 = *4QBarkhi Nafshi*[c]/4Q436 1 ii.1; and cf. 4QBer[b]/4Q287 8 13).

Interpreter of the Law", and at the same time appear concerned with intermarriage. Their affinity with the *Temple Scroll*, *Jubilees*, and D, places them closer to the latter than to the *Community Rule*. *4QWiles of the Wicked Woman*/4Q184 most likely also reflects conflict over changes to the Law or its interpretation in the area of sexual wrongdoing, which the woman represents (1 15). Less certain is that its use of the motif of smooth speaking reflects this language of conflict, since it derives primarily from the image of the strange woman in Proverbs. But it, too, appears to belong with what seem to be the earlier stages of the conflict. Like D, *4QMiscellaneous Rules*/4Q265 also reflects a particular community with its community rules and is concerned with sexual wrongdoing, although it lacks polemic.

Concern that some with claims to teaching authority are changing the Law appears also in the *Epistle of Enoch* (*1 Enoch* 98:14-15; 99:1; 104:9-11), though there, as later in 1QS/1Q28 11.1-2; 1QH[a] vi.15; xii.10, with no connection to sexual wrongdoing. But elsewhere, such as in *Jubilees*, the major emphasis on sexual wrongdoing very likely forms part of the author's conflict with such authorities, as reflected in *Jubilees* 23. In these instances we are probably dealing with texts which reflect conflict within the broader community among religious leaders or teachers, doubtless with groups of associates, but not yet closely defined or polarised to the point of separation. This may well be the conflictual setting in which issues of sexual wrongdoing play a role also in the *Apocryphon of Jeremiah* C, which seems close to *Jubilees*, sharing among other things its focus on intermarriage and incest. The emphasis given the prohibition of incestuous marriage in *4QHalakhah A*/4Q251 most likely reflects awareness of contrary viewpoints and so potential conflict, which is expressed in acute form in D.

Some documents which focus in particular on the sexual relations of priests indicate a situation of conflict. This appears to be the case in *4QOrdinances*[b], but the conflict is arguably still within the community as a whole. Concern with intermarriage of priests is an issue in both the *Testament of Qahat* and the *Visions of Amram*, as earlier in the *Aramaic Levi Document*, but not apparently in the context of conflict.

The surviving material is an inadequate basis for attempting to reconstruct a history of such conflicts, both because of its diverse settings and because we have no way of knowing how representative it is of what was being written in the period. On the other hand, some patterns emerge which suggest some lines of development. It is noteworthy, for instance, that almost all of the documents which deal with sexual wrongdoing in the context of conflict belong to what are broadly recognised as non- or pre-sectarian writings and that in those which are clearly sectarian, the *Community Rule*, the *Pesharim* and the *Thanksgiving Hymns*, conflict focuses not on issues of interpretation, but on issues of authority, where the focus of rejection is now people, a group and its teacher/s, rather than particular ideas. The exception to this is D (and perhaps also 4Q174/177), where we witness both: attacks on the rival group and attacks on its particular teachings. It would appear to have been composed in a sectarian context but where it was still meaningful to focus on differences in interpretation. Though much more conciliatory in tone, *4QMMT* appears also to reflect a sectarian context in which a leader gives grounds for the separation on the basis of differing biblical interpretation, in particular concerned with intermarriage with Gentiles.

In this regard it is interesting to note the particular topics in dispute. *Jubilees* is concerned with intermarriage of both priests and ordinary Israelites with Gentiles, and in doing so reflects the emphasis of Ezra and Nehemiah, though expressing the concern as fear of immoral influence. The emphasis on intermarriage with Gentiles is also represented in *Aramaic Levi Document*, though with a particular focus on priesthood, reflected then also in *Testament of Qahat* and the *Visions of Amram*. Whether that concern was already being expressed in the *Book of the Watchers*, encoded in the myth of angelic priests engaging in illicit relations, is uncertain because we have no evidence of subsequent tradition seeing such a connection in the myth. Possibly *4QWiles of the Wicked Woman*/4Q184 represents the temptation of intermarriage, but nothing focuses on foreignness in her description. *4QMMT* continues the concern with intermarriage. By contrast, intermarriage with Gentiles does not appear to be an issue in D, which otherwise covers so much relating to sexuality. One fragmentary text of D appears, as does the *Temple Scroll*, to affirm marriage to captive women, who would be foreign, and if the attack on sexual intercourse during menstruation has Gentile women in mind, as Wassen suggests, this would also assume acceptance of such marriages. At least one may conclude that nothing which has survived of D indicates that they were an issue.

The situation is slightly different with regard to the other major concern of *Jubilees*, namely, incest. It features generically in two lists in D and in a specific form in the prohibition of marriages to nieces, a prohibition nowhere enunciated in *Jubilees*, but certainly significant enough for the author of the latter to reconstruct some biblical relationships accordingly. The Levi literature, by contrast, seems quite unconcerned about this. It is possible but unlikely that major discourses of *Jubilees* about incest are primarily directed against niece marriages.

While D makes use of *Jubilees* as authoritative, it also has an important precursor in the *Temple Scroll*, sharing with it the special sanctity of Jerusalem, concern with polygyny and with marriages to nieces, and probably a tolerance still towards people marrying captive (Gentile) women. But whereas in the *Temple Scroll* polygyny is forbidden only to the king and prohibiting marriage to nieces is asserted as unproblematic, D shows the former being generalised to all and the latter as an issue of contention. In this sense D relates closely to what has gone before, especially *Jubilees* and the *Temple Scroll*, and has affinities with the *Wiles of the Wicked Woman*, but is also at some remove from them as it is also from *4QMMT* in tone and thematic concern (intermarriage). At the same time it does not belong with the emphases of the *Community Rule*, the *Thanksgiving Hymns*, and the *Pesharim*. It reflects a time (and/or a place) where intermarriage is not a paramount issue, but where disputing the opponents' teaching remains relevant and where the focus is particular acts of sexual wrongdoing, polygyny, sexual intercourse with menstruants, and marriage to nieces.[2]

Overall, there appears to be a pattern according to which those documents most concerned with issues of sexual wrongdoing belong to pre- or early sectarian writings, whereas sexual wrongdoing in the later sectarian documents plays only a minor role and their depictions of conflict do not make it central, preferring to depict conflict not as debate about particular issues of interpretation but as consisting in rival claims to authority by groups and their leaders. D, which contains most about issues of sexuality, appears to reflect a stage in that conflict where particular issues remain disputed, but where bedevilling opponents as a group has emerged, foreshadowing later developments where the latter becomes the dominant focus.

Not all discussions of sexuality occur within a context of controversy and conflict. This is also true of intermarriage, as we shall see, below. It is also the case in much of the legal material where conflict may be implied but is not expressed.

2 Purity Laws, Human Embodiment, and Discharges

In dealing with conflict we have the advantage of common language and themes which help in identifying sectarian documents. In dealing with legal rulings we cannot necessarily assume coherence nor that documents are sectarian. In discussing D above we noted the likelihood that it incorporated an older collection

[2] While I am inclined to see in D a text which represents an earlier stage in the conflict than the *Thanksgiving Hymns*, the *Pesharim* and the *Community Rule*, and a later stage than *4QMMT* and than those texts concerned especially with intermarriage, it might be possible to see it as reflecting a later stage, namely the situation just before the conquest of Pompey in 63, especially if one understands *Pss. Sol.* 8:8-12 as sharing the same concerns. It speaks of priests coming to temple service defiled by menstrual blood and of incest and adultery. But only menstrual blood is a true parallel. Incest in *Pss. Sol.* 8:9 is not about marrying nieces but about sexual relations between fathers and daughters and mothers and sons, and adultery does not feature significantly in D. In addition the palaeographical dating of the 4QD manuscripts would have them produced very close to what would have been the time of the autograph, a likelihood their diversity probably excludes. On their dating see the discussion in chapter 3, above.

of laws which assume application to all Israel and not primarily to a sectarian community. Some of the other documents dealing with law may also reflect such a stage of development.

A number of texts deal with impurities which belong to the natural processes of human embodiment and its sexuality and are not moral in character. They include the man with a gonorrhea discharge,[3] the woman in menstruation[4] and after childbirth,[5] as well as the man with a seminal emission.[6] The *Temple Scroll* quarantines them all, together with those suffering with leprosy and related diseases, to a place outside cities, based on what Num 5:2 required of the camp (48.14-17). *4QTohorot A*/4Q274 deals with contact among people with these impurities, forbidding a menstruating woman from touching a man with a discharge or a woman with an abnormal discharge (1 i.4b-5a, 6; similarly 4QD^{g}/4Q272 1 ii.10 about touching a menstruating woman), treating a menstruating woman and a woman with a discharge equally seriously and then declaring that anyone in a seven day purification period touching any of these contracts the equivalent of corpse impurity (1 i.7-9).

This helps explain the application of the ritual of sprinkling with water mixed with the ashes of the red cow not only in cases of corpse impurity, but also for these impurities, reflected, for instance, in 2 i.1.[7] *4QTohorot B^{b}*/4Q277, insists that such sprinkling be undertaken only by a properly purified priest, perhaps in reaction to the practice attested later of it being done by a child or ordinary Israelite (1 ii.2-7). 4QRitPur A/4Q414 apparently applies the provisions concerning corpse impurity in Num 19:16-19 and expounded in 11QT^{a}/11Q19 49.5-21 to other impurities, including seminal impurity. It apparently assumes that the first of the three immersions, on the first, third and seventh day, cleanses people sufficiently to enable them to eat. 4QOrd^{c}/4Q514 is also concerned about purification before partaking of food (1 i.7). Here it interesting also to note that in applying Num 5:2-3 to Jerusalem the *Temple Scroll* replaces those who have contracted corpse impurity with those who have become impure through seminal emission (46.17-18).

4QTohorot A/4Q274 applies to the man with a seminal emission the provisions which belong to the man with the gonorrhea discharge, namely that the man's garment and the vessel he touched also carry defilement (2 i.4-6; cf. Lev 15:10), extending it even further to include his bed and seat. Similarly, 4QD^{g}/272 1 ii.3-7a applies the provisions of Leviticus 15 relating to gonorrhea discharge to

---

3 11QT^{a}/11Q19 45.13; 4QOrd^{c}/4Q514 1 i.2-3; *4QTohorot A*/4Q274 1 i.1-4a.

4 4QD^{a}/4Q266 6 ii.1-4; 4QD^{g}/4Q272 1 ii.7-10.

5 4QD^{a}/4Q266 6 ii.5-10.

6 4QOrd^{c}/4Q514 1 i.4, 7; 1QM/1Q33 7.6; *4QPurification Liturgy*/4Q284 1 7-8.

7 Also *4QTohorot B^{b}*/4Q277 1 ii.8b-9; *4QPurification Liturgy*/4Q284 1 7-8; 4QD^{g}/4Q272 1 ii.15.

what are probably three instances of seminal emission (by masturbation, in sleep, and in sexual intercourse). While this is in part an instance of a tendency to homogenise the laws, it also reflects an enhanced concern with seminal impurity such as we noted in the *Temple Scroll*. There we find even greater strictness, with the requirement of a three day period before they can re-enter the temple, including washing their clothes, and bathing on the first and third day at sunset. This reflects a homogenising of Lev 15:16-18 with Exod 19:10-15, the rules of approach to Sinai. The closest parallel to this in the other documents we have examined is in 1QSa/1Q28a, where the three day rule is applied before the special assembly as including abstention from sexual intercourse (1.25-26). A similar process of homogenisation in the direction of strictness and clarity is reflected in D's application of the purification requirements of a woman after childbirth, to a *zabah*, and the specification that her impurity lasts until sunset on the eighth day ($4QD^a$/4Q266 6 ii.3-4; cf. Lev 12:4; 15:29). One possible interpretation suggests that D considers a woman so unclean after childbirth that to avoid contaminating the child, a wet nurse is required, but this is unlikely ($4QD^a$/4Q266 6 ii.11). The only other reference to purification after childbirth comes in the extraordinary interpretation of the creation of Adam and Eve in *4QMiscellaneous Rules*/4Q265, paralleled in and probably derived from *Jubilees*, where their entry into the garden as a temple is made to match and then provide the rationale for the 40 or 80 days purification after birth of a boy or a girl.

Issues of ritual purity appear a major concern in the largely fragmentary material of a legal character. In many instances we have only a few words signalling a theme, but without further content, such as the references to menstruation in *4QPurification Liturgy*/4Q284 2 ii.2; 3 1; and 4QRitPur A/4Q414 7 11; 17. At times it is not clear whether the text is dealing with seminal impurity or corpse impurity, as in 4QpapRitPur B/4Q512 3-7 and 9-11.

None of these legal determinations appear, however, to be driven by controversy. This is so even in the legal material in D, in contrast to its Admonition. While accusations against opponents there and in other sectarian documents appear to include allegations of wrongdoing in relation to impurity generally and not just moral impurity, none of the legal expositions which broadly pertain to (non moral) sexual impurity appears polemical.

Ritual and Moral Impurity

In some other areas the issues of ritual impurity and moral impurity lie close together. Failure to address ritual impurity is already a culpable act. Equally, acts of moral wrongdoing, including sexual wrongdoing, brought defilement to the temple, the people and the land. These assumptions, with their roots in the biblical tradition and enunciated in *Jubilees*, inform the documents before us. Sexual intercourse with menstruants, for instance, is said in CD 5.6-7 to defile the temple (cf. also 4.18), perhaps applying also to marriage to nieces (5.7b-11a). Forbidden marriages by priests and people with outsiders defile the seed of both according to *4QMMT* B 81-82.

Some issues which may be seen as moral contain broader elements of impurity. These include issues of nakedness, cross-dressing, intermarriage, incest, sexual intercourse during menstruation, virginity, restrictions of access to sacred space or community, and restrictions of sexual behaviour in sacred space and time. We shall discuss these further below.

One of the key terms which carries a wide range of meanings in these documents is נדה. It occurs a numbers of times referring to menstrual impurity[8] and in the expression, מי נדה, "waters of purification".[9] It is also used of male ritual impurity in 11QT^a/11Q19 45.10 (of impurity through seminal emission), *4QPurification Liturgy*/4Q284 2 ii.1 (cf. also CD 12.2) and in the *Thanksgiving Hymns,* which allude to seminal impurity in the expression: מקור הנדה "source/spring of impurity" (ix.22; xx.25). The H tradition of Leviticus had used נדה of incest in 20:21 (similarly 11QT^a/11Q19 66.13). In 4QpapRitPur B/4Q512 we find it used in association with language which belonged to leprosy: 34 v.17; 1-6 xii.16, where it refers to corpse impurity.

נדה is clearly used to designate what is unacceptable before God also in a moral sense and has warranted judgement.[10] It is also used of the evil spirits and their judgement.[11] It is thus used not only of non-culpable ritual impurity, but also of culpable, that is, moral impurity, which encompasses all acts of disobedience, whether related to moral or non-moral issues, e.g., 1QpHab 8.13; and 4QAges Creat/4Q181 1 ii.1-3a, where the Watchers' defiling deed is being depicted as culpable. In the *Treatise on the Two Spirits*, the words ודרכי נדה בעבודת טמאה "and the ways of impurity in the service of defilement" (4.10; cf. CD 3.17) belong within a list of moral categories including: greed, neglect of serving justice, falsehood, pride, deceit, arrogance, dishonesty, deception, hypocrisy, impatience, and folly. Here נדה includes sexual wrongdoing, and clearly has a moral reference. 4QRitPur A/4Q414 links "impurity" directly with guilt (2 ii, 3, 4 8).

---

[8] *4QMiscellaneous Rules*/4Q265 7.15; 4QD^g/4Q272 1 ii.8; *4QTohorot A*/4Q274 1 i.7, 8; 4QRP^c/4Q367 1a-b 7; 4QD^a/4Q266 6 ii.2; cf. also *4QPurification Liturgy*/4Q284 2 ii.1; iii.1.

[9] 1QS/1Q28 3.4, 9; 4.21; 4QD^f/4Q271 2 12; *4QTohorot B^b*/4Q277 1 ii.5-9; *4QPurification Liturgy*/4Q284 1 7; 3 3; cf. also 4QpapRitPur B/4Q512 1-6 xii.2.

[10] CD 2.1, 3.18; 4QpNah/4Q169 3-4 1; 4Q374 2 ii.3; 4QApocrJerC^d/4Q389 69 2; 1QS/1Q28 5.19.

[11] 1QM/1Q33 13.5; 4QBer^a/4Q286 7a ii b-d 4; 4QShir^b/4Q511 43 7.

Similarly in the *Thanksgiving Hymns* נדה is spoken of as something for which one is to blame and needs forgiveness (iv.19; xix.11).

In 1QS/1Q28 11.14-15, the words יטהרני מנדת אנוש וחטאת בני אדם "cleansed from defilement of the human being and the sin of man", may well be juxtaposing ritual impurity and moral sin, but might possibly be using impurity in a moral sense. In some other contexts the possibility of a double reference is also uncertain. For instance, when 4QPrFêtes[a]/4Q507 decries human frailty in the words, ואנו בעולה מרחם ומשדים בא[שמה] ועד היותנו צעדינו עם נדה יב["and we are in evil from the womb and from the breasts in gu[ilt] and as long as we live our steps with impurity …" (1 2-3), impurity may still speak of human sin or may mean the human being as a source of ritual impurity. In 4QpapRitPur B/4Q512 29-32, on the other hand, where we read, פשעי ותטהרני מערות נדה "transgressions and purified me from the shame of impurity" (vii.9), the context then speaks of offering, making it likely that here ערות נדה "shame of impurity" has connotations of ritual impurity. This same is likely with מכול ערו[ת] בשרנו "from every nakedness/shame of our flesh" (36-38 iii.17). In 4QSapWork B/4Q419 1 11 the "abomination of impurity" may also focus primarily on ritual impurity. In 4QD[a]/4Q266 6 ii.1-2 the author reformulates Lev 15:24 which deals with contracting ritual impurity through sexual intercourse with a menstruant, but adds עון "iniquity" to it, thus linking it with the moral prohibitions of Lev 18:19 and 20:18, though without equating moral and ritual impurity.

The use of נדה to some extent mirrors a wider issue, namely whether these documents might not only see moral sin as defiling, but also see ritual sin as, itself, morally culpable, merging both kinds of impurities together. We have not found evidence supporting such a conclusion.[12] Those passages which deprecate humankind because of its substance and its being a constant source of ritual impurity, to which we return below, do not appear to confuse these two aspects with culpable sin, which it attributes to the propensity to sin. One reading of 4QD[g]/4Q272 1 ii.3-4 has been to see it indicating that a *zab* is morally responsible for his plight through his lustful thoughts,[13] but, as we argued above, all three references are likely to be to forms of male seminal emission and the second

[12] See also the discussion in Himmelfarb, "Impurity and Sin," of the *Community Rule* (29-34), who notes that "physical states that P designates as impure do not play a role in its rules", but that "purity and impurity, transformed into spiritual reality rather than physical categories, were central to the thought of 1QS" (34); and of 4QpapRitPur B/4Q512 she concludes: "impurity as an indication of human imperfection is not the same as impurity as a result of sin or impurity as in and of itself sinful" (36).

[13] So Baumgarten, "Zab Impurity," who also points to the listing of lepers and those with a discharge along with transgressors in 4QD[e]/4Q270 2 ii.12 (275). It is not however clear that the juxtaposition implies that they are transgressors or simply that they are inadmissible.

emission to be about masturbation. While there are some points where it is not absolutely clear whether "impurity" refers to moral or ritual impurity, there is no instance where ritual impurity is clearly designated as sinful. Sinfulness would be to neglect it, to fail to avoid it where possible, and not to undertake the prescribed rites of purification.

Klawans suggests

> five ways in which the identification of ritual and moral impurity manifests itself in the sectarian literature of Qumran. First, very frequently, sins – and not just those enumerated in Leviticus 18, but all sins – are described as impurities. Second, outsiders, who by definition sin, are assumed to be ritually [im]pure. Third, insiders are not to sin, and those who do are likewise considered defiling. Fourth, initiation involved not only moral repentance, but ritual purification. Finally, instances of ritual defilement among insiders seem to be assumed to result from sin: the ritual purification of insiders involves repentance too.[14]

He notes the extension of נדה "impurity" and also תועבה "abomination" to cover moral as well as ritual sin beyond the semantic ranges they carry not only in the Pentateuch but also in the *Temple Scroll* and *4QMMT*.[15] The first four points seem well founded. The fifth is not convincing. The evidence he brings for it is 4QpapRitPur B/4Q512 29-32 vii.8-9 which juxtaposes thanksgiving for forgiveness and purification, which he takes unnecessarily as an equation of the two.[16] The other text to which he appeals is *4QTohorot A*/4Q274 which he suggests indicates "that the sectarians assumed ritual defiling disorders to come about as a result of sin", noting the penitential stance required of the impure in 1-4.[17] These texts, however, are still some distance from equating ritual impurity with sin.

3 Sexuality and Order

Some of the material pertinent to sexuality and order comes in the legal documents. The most comprehensive coverage by far is to be found in D. Its Catalogue of Transgressions (4Q^{e}/4Q270 2 i.9 – ii.18; and 6QD/6Q15 5 1-5) covers a number of matters related to sexual wrongdoing. It includes a woman who gained a bad reputation in her father's house (4QD^{e}/4Q270 2 i.16-17a); a woman who has engaged in sex with someone other than her betrothed (or

---

[14] Klawans, *Impurity and Sin*, 75.

[15] Klawans, *Impurity and Sin*, 77-79.

[16] Cf. Himmelfarb, "Impurity and Sin," who notes that both in this passage and also in 34 v.15-17, "while impurity and sin stand side by side, they remain separate" (36).

[17] Klawans, *Impurity and Sin*, 87.

possibly a widow who has not remained chaste during her widowhood) (4QD^{e}/4Q270 2 i.17); sexual intercourse with a pregnant woman, grounded by an argument about potential damage to the foetus (4QD^{e}/4Q270 2 ii.15-16; 6QD/6Q15 5 2-3), and on "the day" (probably the sabbath) (4QD^{e}/4Q270 2 i.18-19); marriage to nieces (4QD^{e}/4Q270 2 ii.16); and homosexual acts (4QD^{e}/4Q270 2 ii.16b-17a / 6QD/6Q15 5 3-4).

Abstaining from intercourse during pregnancy appears to be assumed also in *Genesis Apocryphon*, where it makes sense of Bitenosh's reminding Lamech of their pleasurable intercourse through which Noah was conceived, presumably some nine months or so earlier. Similarly its narrative of the abduction of Sarai by Pharaoh also reflects a legal provision, namely the rule of Deut 24:1-4 according to which having had sexual intercourse would have made Sarai unclean for Abram, as Bilhah became for Jacob (Gen 35:22; *Jub.* 33:7), and so has Pharaoh declare that he had not known (ידעהא) her and had not defiled (טמיהא) her (20.30).

In its legal section D includes an exposition of Num 5:13-31 about accusations against a wife that she has committed adultery (4QD^{e}/4Q270 4 1-8). It also deals with sexual relations with what appear to be three categories of slave women: another's slave, one's own, and a captive woman (4QD^{e}/4Q270 4 13-19), reflecting exposition of Lev 19:20-22; 21:1-11; and Deut 21:10-14. These assume approval of sexual relations with one's own slaves, reflecting a widespread practice of sexual exploitation in the ancient world (cf. also CD 12.10-11 which assumes Gentile slaves who also become part of the covenant of Abraham). So little of the relevant text is preserved, however, that the allusions remain tentative. If we assume a reference to captive women, this would entail marriage, and so raise other issues discussed below in relation to both polygyny and marriage to Gentiles.

Cross-dressing may well be addressed in 4QD^{f}/4Q271 3 3-4, more clearly attested in 4QOrd^{a}/4Q159, which specifies that Deut 22:5 is to be applied to both the outer- and the undergarment and perhaps also to unisex clothing. The issue of giving away brides and finding suitable partners receives extensive attention in 4QD^{f}/4Q271 3 8-16 and includes that a father be honest about her blemishes and choose a suitable partner. This may well be an allusion to not marrying Gentiles, which would be singular in D for whom it is otherwise not an issue. Its proof text Deut 22:10-11 is used in that context in *4QMMT* B and elsewhere. It may, however, have broader, generic reference here. The three categories of women one is forbidden to marry are the immoral unmarried woman, the immoral woman beyond her father's house, probably meaning the adulteress (therefore, divorced), and the widow who has not remained chaste. The obverse is probably to be assumed: namely, that marriage to an unmarried woman, a divorcee who is not an adulteress (such as one whose husband the community has expelled for illicit intercourse, probably reported by her), and the chaste widow, is acceptable.

The passage then deals with the situation where there is uncertainty about the status of the unmarried woman. It expounds Deut 22:13-21, the rules about dealing with a husband's complaint that his wife was not a virgin, but shifts the focus to the time before the wedding, providing that "expert women" inspect the woman before the wedding. This bypasses the unreliable biblical provision about showing bloodstains and also obviates the danger that the husband might unwittingly be rendered unclean, should she have had sexual relations already with another. 4QOrd[a]/4Q159 also testifies to attempts to find a more satisfactory handling of the situation and also proposes a panel of expert women inspectors, but they perform their task after the wedding, apparently on the basis that such an inspection would enable them to discern evidence of her having been a virgin.

Polygyny

D gives particular prominence to polygyny, sexual intercourse with a menstruant, and marriage to nieces, as constituting sexual wrongdoing, one of the nets of Belial and closely related to the other two, greed for wealth and defiling the temple (CD 4.15-18a). The second, and possibly the third (and potentially all three) defile the temple, inasmuch as sin defiles the temple. Greed will doubtless have played a role in the practice of polygyny, an option under any circumstances only for the rich. This is probably why *1/4QInstruction* appears always to assume monogynous marriage, while never espousing monogyny as such. While the *Temple Scroll* proscribes polygyny for the king, it does not appear to do so for the rest of the population. In elaborating the provisions about the captive wife (63.10-15), it tacitly assumes polygyny for some (unless it restricted that practice to unmarried men, of which it gives no indication), and it probably cited Deut 21:15-17 in the lost lines between columns 63 and 64, in which provision is made for the offspring of polygynous marriages. Similarly, Amram reports that his decision not to take a Canaanite wife, while cut off from Jochabed, was evidence of his love (*4QVisions of Amram*/4Q543 4 2-4 = 4Q544 1 7-9 = 4Q547 1-2 iii.6-9a), the assumption being, apparently, that there would otherwise not have been a problem in taking another wife. D represents a stance in which what once was seen as required for the king, has become a model and requirement for all. It, too, however apparently assumes that a man may take a captive woman as wife, but presumably this would be permissible only for an unmarried man.

Sexual Intercourse with a Menstruant

Its second instance of sexual wrongdoing, intercourse with a menstruant (CD 5.6b-7a), is, by contrast, unambiguously supported in biblical law, both as an issue of impurity (with apparently no guilt attached) according to P (Lev 15:24), and as something directly forbidden according to H (Lev 18:19 and 20:18). Thus the author of D needs no justification to assert his claim. It is possible that the prohibition is aimed at intercourse also with a woman with an abnormal discharge (as in 4QD^{a}/4Q266 6 ii.2b-3). That it must have only foreign women in mind, since Jewish women would allegedly be observant, is questionable. Some see an allusion to this prohibition in the Catalogue of Transgressions 4QD^{e}/4Q270 2 i.18-19 which forbids a man to approach his wife on "the day", but the more likely reference there is to intercourse on the day of sabbath. Similarly the warning in the penal code in 4QD^{e}/4Q270 7 i.12-13 and 4QD^{b}/4Q267 9 vi.4-5 forbidding illicit sexual intercourse within a marriage probably does not have intercourse during menstruation in mind, since the penal code does not elsewhere repeat biblical prohibitions. On the other hand, the exposition of provisions relating to the *zabah* in 4QD^{a}/4Q266 6 ii clearly prohibits sexual intercourse with a menstruant, citing Lev 15:24, modified to make it a moral prohibition (4QD^{a}/4Q266 6 ii.1-2), but apparently also with a woman with an abnormal discharge (6 ii.2b-3). It may be in mind in 1QSa/1Q28a 1.11 as one of the things for which a wife is obliged to report her husband. We may have reference to prohibiting sexual intercourse by a woman who is menstruating also in *4QTohorot A*/4Q274, if that is the primary focus of the reference to "mingling" (אל תתערב) (1 i.5b). There may be a reference to a *zab* having sexual intercourse with his wife in 4QpapRitPur B/4Q512 7-9 xi.4, but, if so, it refers to the time after his purification when he may also eat and drink in the cities.

Incest

The third instance of sexual wrongdoing is incest, in particular, marriage between a man and the daughter of his brother or of his sister, where it is argued on the basis that it is implied in the matching biblical prohibition of marriages between a man and his mother's sister (CD 5.7b-11a; cf. Lev 18:13). As noted above, the catalogue of transgressions in D also briefly lists the prohibition of a man approaching "the daughter of his brother" (4QD^{e}/4Q270 2 ii.16). The same prohibition appears in *4QHalakhah A*/4Q251 17, which while not offering a rationale as in D, nevertheless appears to give it special emphasis, both by formulating it in both possible variations (marrying the daughter of a brother or sister and marrying the brother of one's mother or father), but also by its prominent placement in the list of other prohibitions of incest. This stands in contrast to the listing of the one variant at the conclusion of the *Temple Scroll* where it apparently receives no special emphasis. The *Temple Scroll* does, however, exhibit some concern with incest generally, when discussing seduction of a virgin in 66.8b-11, based on Deut 22:28-29, read alongside Exod 22:15-16. For there the author specifically adds to the provision that the man is forced to marry the raped girl, the proviso that this applies only if "she is permitted to him by the Law" (66.9).

Prohibition of marriage to nieces already informs the values of *Jubilees* to the extent that the author rewrites biblical material to ensure it is not implied of anyone of note.[18] While *Jubilees* does not address this prohibition explicitly, it does depict the angel as giving great emphasis to the prohibition of incest in general in the expositions that follow the story of Reuben and Bilhah and Judah and Tamar (*Jub.* 33:9-20; 41:23-26). It is possible to read such concern as also reflecting concern about marrying nieces, but one would have expected some direct reference if that had been so. *Genesis Apocryphon*, which stands under *Jubilees*' influence, portrays Noah as a model in setting up the marriages of his offspring, since he acts according to eternal law. Noah is shown as having an equal number of grandsons and granddaughters (12.9-12) and ensuring that they marry appropriately (6.6-10). The point of the author's emphasis may have included that none of the arranged marriages contravenes the law of incest: there is no marrying of nephews or nieces; but its primary concern was probably forbidden intermarriage outside the chosen line.

The more general concern with incest appears in the context of sexual wrongdoing in the list of sins in CD 6.14 – 7.4b (linked also with the need for reproval) and 8.3-9, which speak of a man acting illegally or inappropriately (ימעל 7.1)[19] or ignoring status (ויתעלמו 8.5b-6a) in relation to a near relative (בשרו שאר). Similar behaviour appears to be in mind in the rebukes in 4Q477 8, probably referring to incest: וגם אוהב את שיר בשרו "and also he is a lover of his near relative". Likewise 4QApocJer C^{b}/4Q387 fr. A expresses concern that each one is approaching his near relative (בערוהם לקרוב איש אל שאר בשרו). There may also be a reference to incest in the words of 4QInstr^{d}/4Q418 101 ii. 5: לוא ימעל בבשרו "He shall not do harm to (or act unfaithfully against or inappropriately toward) his own kin". 4QApocrJer A/4Q383 fr. A may allude to incest between parents and children (an evil addressed in *Pss. Sol.* 8:9-11). Reuben, whose incestuous deed is explained in 4QcommGen A/4Q252, appears to function as a negative example also in *4QNarrative A*/4Q458.

Strikingly, the document, *4QVisions of Amram*, seems to ignore incest laws in depicting the marriage of Miriam, Amram's daughter, to his younger brother, as it

[18] See the discussion in Loader, *Enoch, Levi, and Jubilees*, 156, 245-46, 250, 255, 274.

[19] On the possibility that in *4QMMT* C מעל carries this sense, see p. 77 above.

does the incontrovertible breach of incest laws in the marriage of Amram himself to his aunt, Jochabed. This suggests a measure of tolerance among those who included the books of the Levi tradition, *Aramaic Levi Document* (which also reports Amram's marriage), the *Testament of Qahat*, and the *Visions of Amram*, in the collection, presumably because their values lay elsewhere, at least in warning against intermarriage with Gentiles.

Other Forbidden Marriages, including to Gentiles

The issue of permission to eat food set aside for priests and their families, *terumah*, comes to expression in *4QHalakhah A*/4Q251, which affirms that a wife whom a priest has married and brought into his household from another family may eat, as may a slave and a slave's child born in the household, but not a זונה or a חללה, two categories identified in Lev 21:8 as forbidden for a priest to marry, best understood here as a woman who engages in illicit sexual relations, including a prostitute, but others as well, and the offspring of such relations. Issues of a woman's eating sacred food appear also in D's treatment of women with a discharge, to whom it applies the restriction in Lev 12:4 concerning women after childbirth, that they not "touch any holy thing", which it interprets as "food" (4QD^{a}/4Q266 6 ii.2b-3). It goes on to repeat the application to women after childbirth, even prescribing the death penalty for non-observance (ii.10).

The *Temple Scroll* alludes to captive women, citing the provisions of Deut 21:10-14, which apparently affirms priests' taking them as wives (63.10-15), but with the significant proviso: "She may not touch your purities for seven years, nor may she eat the peace offering until seven years pass; afterward she may eat" (63:14b-15). This assumes acceptance of marriage of priests to such women, who may be assumed to be Gentiles, and, at most, indicates sensitivity to the dangers and therefore adds the restriction, but no prohibition. This stands in contrast to *4QMMT* C 6-7, which seems to use the warning in Deut 7:6 about bringing an abomination into one's house to attack such marriages.

The issue of priestly families and food, and the impact of illicit sexual relations, appears also to receive attention in 4QOrd$^{b?}$/4Q513, where the concern is expressed initially in relation to priests' daughters marrying the sons of foreigners. The *Apocryphon of Jeremiah C*, also concerned with foreigners, speaks of people debasing their offspring with the sons of foreigners (4QApocrJer C^{e}/4Q390 2 i. 10), where the context, which refers to priests, suggests that the issue is again that priests are allowing their daughters to marry foreigners. This emphasis is also present in *4QTestament of Qahat* and *4QVisions of Amram*, which concern priests, and where the former targets intermarriage both with Gentiles and "half-breeds" (כילאין, reflecting the prohibition of mixing of kinds in Lev 19:19; Deut 22:9, i.e., children of mixed marriages).[20] The same concern about priests marrying Gentiles is present in the *Aramaic Levi Document*.

Some see a reference to concern about priests marrying outside of priestly families in *4QMMT* B 75-82, though I consider that a reference to intermarriage of both priests and people with Gentiles is more likely to be the focus. The concern that both priests and lay people are marrying Gentiles comes to expression already in Ezra and Nehemiah (Ezra 9:1-2; Neh 10:28-30). Some have seen an allusion to the dangers of intermarriage of priests with Gentiles in *1 Enoch* 12 – 16, where the Watchers are depicted as priests who have abandoned their heavenly temple, but, if so, subsequent writers do not show signs of having read it that way. The focus there seems rather on foreign women as sources of forbidden knowledge and, if intended, the concern about intermarriage would apply more generally.

The issue of intermarriage in *4QVisions of Amram* reflects the broader prohibition of marrying Canaanites and so extends its focus beyond priestly families. Amram's love and goodness is shown in his not taking a Canaanite wife, when cut off from Jochabed. *Aramaic Levi Document*, while also primarily concerned with educating priests, seems best understood as forbidding all marriage with Gentiles for both priests and people, as did *Jubilees*. Intermarriage is a key theme in *4QMMT*. In B 39-49 it addresses the issue by expounding Deut 23:2-4 in a way that deleted the time limit and so removed all possibility of Ammonites and Moabites, men and women, ever joining the congregation by marriage. In B 75-82 it approaches the issue from the perspective of its defiling both Israel's seed and that of the priesthood and uses the prohibition of mixing animal species, fibres in garments and crops in Lev 19:19 and Deut 22:9-11 to bolster the argument. Its third assault (C 4-32) may focus especially on foreign wives taken as booty and urges the zeal and faith of Phinehas and Abraham to justify strict rejection. The latter emphasis matches one of the expositions in *Jubilees* of the theme, following the account of Dinah's rape, which it made the basis for attacking both intermarriage to Gentiles and existing mixed marriages (30:7-23). The references to David and Solomon in *4QMMT* C 18, 25 may include an allusion to their notoriety, particularly Solomon's, for taking foreign wives and being corrupted by them (cf. also Sir 47:19-21). The author may already have intermarriage with Gentiles in mind when he compares the acceptance of sacrifices from Gentiles as the equivalent of entering an illicit sexual relationship (B 8-9). They have no place in the covenant and so certainly no place as spouses of the seed of Israel.

When *Genesis Apocryphon* depicts Noah carefully choosing partners for his children and ensuring that they marry appropriately (6.6-10) and lists the sons and daughters of Shem as being equal in number (12.9-12), it offers a model against intermarriage. The same concern may be expressed in Noah's vision where the

[20] Drawnel, "Literary Form," 69.

boughs of one tree mingle inappropriately with the first tree (14.16-17). The trees represent two of Noah's sons and their families and the mingling with the first tree would target intermarriage by Shem's line with the others, but it may instead relate to Canaan's land claims. It is possible to see in *4QWiles of the Wicked Woman*/4Q184, an allusion to a foreign woman, but the poem nowhere makes this explicit. It is then fully absent in other documents reckoned to be sectarian, perhaps, at least, because such marriages were less likely to be a prospect for closed communities.

In view of the attention given by D to sexual wrongdoing of various kinds, it is surprising that it does not address the issue of marriage to Gentiles. One might see it in the warning about unsuitable partners in 4QD^{f}/4Q271 3 9-10 which alludes to the prohibition in Deut 22:10-11 of mixing animal species and fibres, but it is not explicit. There may be allusions to it in the "history" of failure through sexual wrongdoing in 2.16b – 3.12a. The designation of Abraham, Isaac, and Jacob as "friends of God" in this account of sexual wrongdoing may evoke the associations so strongly laid out in *Jubilees*, which the author values, with Phinehas and the prosecution of intermarriage to Gentiles as sexual wrongdoing (cf. *Jub.* 19:9; 30:20). Similarly the reference to the wilderness generation eating blood may have been associated with the occasions in Numbers 25 where eating with Moabites and marrying them and then a marriage to a Midianite provoked God's wrath and in the latter case made Phinehas a hero and friend of God, whose deeds were reckoned as righteousness (cf. Ps 106:31). Intermarriage may also have been seen as the main way in which according to 3.9-10 the kings were guilty of sexual wrongdoing. These would all be indirect references to intermarriage, which is otherwise never addressed explicitly. Wassen has suggested that the prohibition of sexual intercourse with a menstruant probably assumes marriage to Gentile women who might ignore such scruples.[21] That would, nevertheless, imply acceptance of the marriages, themselves. Perhaps more significantly, D appears to have included reference to marrying captive women, who would have been Gentiles. This practice is assumed in the *Temple Scroll* (though presumably not for the king) which imposes additional restrictions on it though it is still seen in the context of polygyny, unlike in D, where the option would be open to only the unmarried man. The latter document may, thus, accept the prospect of marriage to Gentiles. This, in turn, would explain its absence as an issue to be addressed among its many concerns with sexual wrongdoing.

The issue of marriage to Gentiles may surface in some other documents, though their fragmentary state makes any certainty difficult. The last preserved line of *4QHalakhah A*/4Q251 17, for instance, appears to address it as an issue affecting every Israelite, like the incest prohibitions which it immediately follows,

---

[21] Wassen, *Women*, 120.

though some argue, to my mind unconvincingly, that it applies only to priestly families. *4QMiscellaneous Rules*/4Q265 cites Mal 2:10 about Israel's unfaithfulness and may imply that such unfaithfulness entails intermarriage with foreigners if the author intended that concern expressed in Mal 2:11-12 to inform its use. A concern with such restrictions might explain the transition to the theme of excluding women and children from the Passover in the following line as remaining with the theme of exclusions. Similarly there may be an allusion in *4QCatena*[a]/4Q177 to the concern with intermarriage in Deuteronomy 7, if the citation of Deut 7:15 in 1-4 and the allusion to being like the tribes of the nations implies this context. If the reference to the tablets and the second Torah refer to *Jubilees*, this would cohere with a concern with intermarriage, a major concern of that work. 4QapocrPent A/4Q368 uses Exod 34:11-24 about not making covenant with the people of the land, but without any surviving reference to the concern there about intermarriage though it is probably implied. 4QapocrJosh[a]/4Q378 probably alludes to the prohibition of intermarriage with the inhabitants of the land. In 4QDibHam[a-c]/4Q504-506 the juxtaposition of references to kings, to taking daughters in marriage, and to seed in xvi.12-20, has suggested to some a concern with intermarriage.

Returning to the *Temple Scroll*, while it appears to contemplate marriage to Gentiles, including by priests, it sets severe limits on the king. He is to marry only within his father's extended family, so certainly no Gentile. Its rendering of Deut 17:17 which forbids the king having many wives lest his heart turn away from God, 11QT[a]/11Q19 56.18 changes the verb יסור "turn away", referring to his heart as the subject, to יסירו "they turn away", now referring to the wives as the subject and his heart as the object, and adds מאחרי "from me". These may well stand under the influence of Deut 7:3-4 which warns against intermarriage with Canaanites lest: יסיר את בנך מאחרי "they turn your child(ren) away from me". Part of the responsibility of his minders who are to "guide him against every act of sin" (57.10) is to guard him against contracting such foreign marriages (57.16-19). The author is therefore addressing marriage to Gentiles, but only in relation to the king. While in 11QT[a]/11Q19 2.12-15 it cites Exod 34:15-16 about relations with Canaanites, which uses sexual language as a metaphor to describe idolatry, and forbids intermarriage, nothing suggests that the author focuses here on intermarriage, itself.

The Myth of the Watchers

The myth of the Watchers to which a number of documents allude and to which we return in more detail below would have allowed itself to be used as a model to warn either against priests marrying outside their families or marrying non-Jews, or against intermarriage in general. Some have indeed speculated that this concern was implied in the *Book of the Watchers*. Nothing in the documents we have considered preserves such an interpretation. The myth is cited however as an example of sin and future judgement.

It is the first instance in D's history epitomised by sexual wrongdoing, according to which the Watchers stumbled in sexual sin and fell and their offspring as high as cedars and large as mountains, also fell (2.17-19). In the fragmentary remains of its first columns we see that *Genesis Apocryphon* told the story of the Watchers' sin with women and its implications in some detail. They report their imprisonment, facing the dread prospect of judgement, their sin both in having sexual relations with human women and in passing on to them forbidden mysteries, and the mutual destruction of their offspring. While reflecting detail preserved primarily in *1 Enoch* 6 – 16, for instance, about forbidden knowledge, the account may be dependent on a form of the myth present also in *Jubilees*, according to which the descent in the days of Jared was not part of the act of sin as in *1 Enoch*, but a divine commission to come to earth to offer appropriate teaching during which, however, they turned to seducing women. Poor Lamech fears his wondrous child might be the fruit of the Watchers' seduction of Bitenosh.

1/4QInstruction may allude to their prospect of fearful judgement (4Q416 1 10-12). One of the hymn writers in the *Thanksgiving Hymns* also speaks of being terrified to hear of God's judgement against the holy ones and their offspring (1QH[a] xviii.34b-36), though without mentioning the particular nature of their sin.[22] *4QAges of Creation*, on the other hand, twice mentions their delict with the daughters of humankind (4Q180 1 7-8; 4Q181 2 1-2), describing them as under the leadership of Azazel, and also reporting the future judgement of the "sons of the heavens" along with wicked human beings (4Q181 1 ii.1-3a). Similarly 4QpsJub[c]/4Q227 refers to their activity and to Enoch's testimony against them (2 2-4). 4QNoah ar/4Q534 compares someone's evil deed or building in the future with that of the Watchers, but without detail (1 ii +2 15-16). Some see an allusion to the Watchers in the word, "their end", in the opening line of 4QcommGen A/4Q252, but the reference there is more probably to their offspring and probably also to the generation of human beings destroyed in the flood, thus not to the sexual exploits of the Watchers.

We shall return below in discussing dualisms to the numerous references to the bastards or bastard spirits, who also belong to the Watcher myth, as the spirits that emerged from the Watchers' offspring. As in the *Book of the Watchers* and *Jubilees*, the activity of the Watchers' offspring and their spirits in the material we have surveyed is not portrayed as sexual wrongdoing, but rather as violence and harm.

---

[22] Cf. also 1QHymns/1Q36 16, in which there is reference to מש]פט אף ונפילי "judgment, wrath, and Nephilim" (16 3).

Other Instances of Sexual Wrongdoing, including Homosexual Acts

There were a number of instances of sexual wrongdoing in the Hebrew scriptures beside that of the Watchers which might have inspired writers of the documents. Some interpret the mention of Ham, Gomorrah, the Amalekites, Reuben, and possibly the Watchers, in 4QcommGen A/4Q252 as indicating an intention to give special focus to sexual wrongdoing, but where enough of the context is preserved to indicate special interest this seems to have to do not with issues of sexuality but exegetical conundrums.

There are allusions to Sodom and Gomorrah in the context of warnings. 4QUniden/4Q172 makes a specific connection between sexual wrongdoing and Gomorrah. In iv.10 *4QCatena*^{a}/4Q177 appears to allude to the story and may be referring to it also in 9 (par. 4QBéat/4Q525 22), which speaks of disgusting acts, spending the night together and wallowing. This is probably to be taken as an allusion to homosexual acts, otherwise addressed only briefly in the prohibition in the catalogue of transgressions in 4QD^{e}/4Q270 2 ii.16b-17a / 6QD/6Q15 5 3-4 and indirectly in the prohibition of cross-dressing in 4QD^{f}/4Q271 3 3-4 and 4QOrd^{a}/4Q159. The explicit prohibition, which is based on Lev 18:22-23, may be associated in 4QD^{e}/4Q270 2 ii.17b-18 (cf. 6QD/6Q15 5 4) with an allusion to the warning in Lev 18:24-25 about defiling oneself by imitating the sexual practices of Canaan and being vomited out of the land. 4QAgesCreat/4Q180 reports God's concern to check whether Sodom and Gomorrah's sin warranted their destruction (2-4 ii.5-9; cf. Gen 18:20-21), but nothing is preserved concerning the nature of the sin. 4QDanSuz? Ar/4Q551 paraphrases the similar incident of attempted male rape in Judges 19.

In D concern with sexual wrongdoing is a high priority. Already the allusion to choosing the fair neck in CD 1.19 should probably be understood in this context, since this becomes the primary focus of the accusations which follow. The image may well be employed similarly in 4Q477. The image of the immoral, foreign woman in Proverbs leaves it mark in D's admonition, where the appeal, "Listen, my sons, to my words" (Prov 7:24; CD 1.1; 2.2, 14), underlines the link and the depiction of sexual wrongdoing shows some signs of dependence on the model. We shall consider the counter model of Lady Wisdom in discussing Ben Sira/Sirach in a future volume. The most direct influence of the negative model comes in *4QWiles of the Wicked Woman*/4Q184, where, as in its use in Ben Sira,[23] the concern is with the sexual dangers which the woman presents[24] and the impact

[23] 9:3,4, 6-7, 8-9; 23:18-26; 25:2d; 26:10-12, 19-22; 41:20b(22a), 21c(23b); 42:8b.

[24] Possibly 4QInstr^{d}/4Q418 101 ii.2-5 alludes to the entry of an immoral woman or prostitute into someone's house. 4QInstr^{d}/4Q418 127 1-4 appears to allude to the seeking of sexual pleasure; possibly also 4QInstr^{d}/4Q418 81+81A 18; 4QInstr^{b}/4Q416 2 i.7 and 4QInstr^{c}/4Q417 2 i.12, if translated, "Oppose your desire".

it has been apparently having, including among interpreters of the Law, who have sought to alter the Law in response to their seduction. That motif of altering the Law in relation to sexual wrongdoing is a significant theme also in D's portrait of the teachers whom it attacks, and finds an echo, as we saw above in the discussion of conflict, in the *Thanksgiving Hymns*, the *Community Rule*, and the *Pesharim*, but now independent of the original sexual context.

The Range of זנות *"Sexual Wrongdoing"*

The most common designation of sexual wrongdoing in the documents is זנות. The word, זנות, is used in D to designate polygyny, sexual intercourse during menstruation and incest (an uncle with a niece) (4.17, 20). Having earlier designated prostitution, it now covers a wider range of illicit sexual relations. This matches the wider use of the word to be assumed in *Jubilees*, the use of the Aramaic word, זנות, in *Aramaic Levi Document* (6:3-4 / 16-17), in both of which it relates to forbidden marriages (intermarriage with Gentiles) and is associated with a broader application of the prohibition of priest's marrying prostitutes and their daughters engaging in prostitution (Lev 21:7, 9; cf. *Jub.* 30:7; 4QLevi[b] ar/4Q213a 3-4 3a).[25] It also matches the broader use of the word in *4QMMT* where it refers to illicit sexual relations (*4QMMT* B 75, 82, C 5; cf. also B 8-9).

D's use of the word in 2.16 also includes the range of acts of sexual wrongdoing listed in its litany of failures (2.16 – 3.12). These include the deed of the Watchers. The same broader meaning is to be assumed in the repetition of the phrase, עיני זנות "eyes of sexual wrongdoing", in 1QS/1Q28 1.6 and 4QBer[b]/4Q287 8 13; (cf. CD 2.16), and in the related expressions also linked with eyes: לתעות אחר לבבו ועינוהי "to go astray after his heart and his eyes" in 1QS/1Q28 5.4b-5a (based on Num 15:39 with sexual allusions); זנו אחר עיניהם "lusting after their eyes" in 1QpHab 5.7; and זנות עינים "sexual immorality of the eyes" in *4QBarkhi Nafshi*/4Q434-438 (4Q435 2 i.2).[26] References to וכול הזונות "and all the acts of sexual wrongdoing" in 4QOrd[b?]/4Q513 2 ii.2 and to the זונה "immoral woman" and, as reconstructed, the "profaned woman" חללה in *4QHalakhah A*/4Q251 16 2-3, concern illicit sexual relations of priests. The reference to ויזנו עמם "and they commit sexual wrongdoing with them" in 4QUnid/4Q172 apparently alludes to sexual sin at Gomorrah, as does the parallel word for sexual immorality, פחז, two lines later (used also in *4QWiles of the*

[25] Its use probably lies behind *1 Enoch* 10:9-10; see also the *Book of the Giants*, 4Q203 8.9.

[26] See also 4QInstr[c]/4Q417 1 i.27 which speaks of going astray after one's heart and one's eyes. Cf also 4Q184 3 5: עם אימוני פחז "with pupils (eyes) of sexual wrongdoing".

Wicked Woman/4Q184 1 13, 15; 3 5). The broad sense of illicit sexual relations is probably also to be presupposed in: רוח זנות "spirit of sexual immorality" in 1QS/1Q28 4.10 (based on Hos 4:12); מעוון הזנות "from the sin of sexual wrongdoing" in 4QpsJub[a]/4Q225 1 1 and הזנות "sexual immorality" in *4QNarrative A*/4Q458 (2 i.6).

Sexual Wrongdoing as an Issue

Thus sexual wrongdoing remains an issue in many documents, but in sectarian documents largely as one of the sins to be avoided or from which one has been delivered. In none of them does it have the prominence which it receives in *Jubilees*, but also in *4QMMT* and D. This coheres with our observation in the first section, where we noted that it had also disappeared as a major issue in the depiction of opponents and conflict. Incest appears to remain a concern, at least as a matter of discipline within the community. We may assume legal issues pertaining to sexuality had continued relevance. The Watchers' deed functions largely in the context of warnings of judgement, not as paradigmatic of intermarriage nor as aetiological of sexual wrongdoing in particular. Even their offspring, the bastard spirits, have no particular bent towards sexual wrongdoing. The sin of Sodom and Gomorrah, apparently understood as sexual, and Reuben's sin, function as warnings against sexual wrongdoing. Intermarriage, to which some allusions are more certain than others, features in a number of documents with close affinities to *Jubilees* and the *Aramaic Levi Document*, often, though not exclusively, in relation to priests, but does not appear as a concern in documents recognised as sectarian.

4 Sexuality in Time and Space

Sacred space and sacred time play a major role in determining the appropriateness of engaging in sexual relations.

Nakedness

There is a sense in which nakedness also belongs to a category affected by appropriateness of context. Nakedness is an area of concern in many documents (cf. already *Jub.* 3:30-32; 7:20-21). The word, ערוה, carries a range of meaning, from literal "nakedness" to the "shame" felt or imputed when nakedness is inappropriately exposed, to "shame" in response to any inappropriate or sinful act.

Thus the penal code in the *Community Rule* stipulates punishments for being naked in someone's presence, exposing one's penis and gesticulating with the left hand (1QS/1QS28 7.14, 16-17). Similar prohibitions appear in D (4QD[a]/4Q266 10 ii.9-12a; 4QD[e]/4Q270 7 i.1-3). Nakedness is also an issue in the prohibition in the *War Scroll*, where the concern is to keep nakedness away from the war camp (1QM/1Q33 7.7; 10.1). In that concern the issue is not just exposure before others, but above all before the holy angels who are present in the camp. Therefore no inappropriate nakedness is to be seen around the camp and for that reason toilets are required to be 2000 cubits from the camp, recalling the stipulation of 3000 cubits distance of toilets from the holy city in the *Temple Scroll*.[27]

The concern is nakedness in the wrong place. Nakedness or exposure of the sexual genitalia is the primary concern. The implication is not that the naked human body is something bad. Rather nakedness is to be covered in relationship to others and in special places with special presences. Apart from these passages, we have reference to Ham's sin and the curse of Cain in 4QcommGen A/4Q252, but the focus there is not the sin, but explaining why Canaan and not his father is cursed.

In the *Thanksgiving Hymns* the expressions ערות קלון "nakedness of shame" (v.21; xx.25) and סוד הערוה ומקור הנדה "a foundation of shame and a source/spring of impurity", (ix.22) focus on shame, probably with ritual impurity in mind which necessarily accompanies the embodied human person and the discharges of their sexual genitalia. Nowhere is this designated as sin. This is probably also the focus in 4QpapRitPur B/4Q512 where moral sin and the shame of ritual impurity are juxtaposed in the statement whose beginning has been lost: פשעי ותטהרני מערות נדה "transgressions and purified me from nakedness/ shame of impurity" (29-32 vii.9). The shame of ritual impurity is probably also intended in the expression מכול ערו[ת] בשרנו "from every nakedness/shame of our flesh" (36-38 iii.17).

When incest laws speak of the nakedness (עריה) in a relationship, the concern is also sexual genitalia and the distinction is made between nakedness in a relationship, sexual intercourse, which is appropriate, and nakedness which is inappropriate, partly because it belongs in another relationship. Thus Lev 20:11 explains: "The man who lies with his father's wife has uncovered his father's nakedness"; it is the nakedness appropriately exposed only in the relationship between his father and mother. Similarly 4QInstr[b]/4Q416 2 iv.5 speaks of sexual union with one's wife: היא שאר ער]ותכה, "she is the flesh of your nakedness" . In these contexts we find עריה used both to describe exposure of sexual genitalia and as a term to describe deliberate inappropriate exposure, which is moral sin. Both senses are evident in *4QHalakhah A*/4Q251 which puts prohibited incestuous relationships under the heading: על העריות "Concerning forbidden sexual relations" and goes on to speak of incest as uncovering the nakedness (עריה) of

[27] Note also the concern with covering excrement in *4QHalakhah C*/4Q472a.

someone, meaning their genitalia, and thereby engaging in sexual intercourse in an inappropriately close relationship, the language already of Leviticus 18 (similarly 11QT[a]/11Q19 66.12-16; CD 5.7b-11a). The context of incest also explains its use in 4QApocJer C[b]/4Q387 fr. A בערותם לקרוב איש אל שאר בשרו "in their nakedness, each man drawing near to his blood relative".

In *4QHalakhah A*/4Q251 there is also reference to inappropriate nakedness on the sabbath. This raises the issue of sexuality in relation to special times and places.

Sexual Intercourse in Sacred Time

The concern with inappropriate nakedness on the sabbath in *4QHalakhah A*/4Q251 probably relates to prohibiting sexual intercourse on the sabbath, as already expressed clearly in *Jub.* 50:8 (cf. also 2:25-27). The concern in these instances is less likely to be nakedness, itself, than deliberate seminal emission involved in what would otherwise be an appropriate relationship in which to uncover nakedness and engage in sexual intercourse. The issue is sacred time.

There are a number of other passages where there may be an allusion to prohibiting sexual intercourse on the sabbath, but where, as in *4QHalakhah A*/4Q251, we are reduced to speaking of degrees of probability. It is very likely that the prohibition of a man approaching his wife "on the day of" in 4QD[e]/4Q270 2 i.18-19 refers to sexual intercourse on the sabbath. It would be consistent with the author's respect for *Jubilees* where the prohibition is unambiguously identified as one of the ways in which people defile the sabbath (*Jub.* 50:8). In CD 11.5 (4QD[f]/4Q271 5 i.1-2) the author prohibits "sexual intercourse for pleasure" on the sabbath, an expression which does not reflect a demarcation between procreation and pleasure, but implies blanket disapproval of indulging in the pleasure of sexual intercourse, apparently because of the impurity of seminal emission. This raises the possibility further that the injunction in CD 12.4 against defiling sabbaths and festivals may also include a reference to sexual intercourse (cf. also the reference in 12.1 to prohibiting sexual relations in the holy city). A similar reference to defiling sabbaths and the temple and forgetting the festivals, appears in 4QApocrJer C[e]/4Q390 2 i.9-10, a work that reflects the ethos of *Jubilees*. It is closely linked to a charge that priests are debasing their offspring with sons of foreigners. This may suggest a sexual component in what precedes, but that is uncertain.

Prohibition of sexual intercourse on the sabbath may also be at least part of what is being targeted in the penal code in 4QD[e]/4Q270 7 i.12-13; 4QD[b]/4Q267 9 vi.4-5, where we find the warning about approaching one's wife for illicit sexual intercourse. A similar concern about illicit marital intercourse appears to be present in 1QSa/1Q28a 1.11, which requires that a wife report on her husband. The shorter form of the text in 4Q249e may indeed have read much like the formulation of the penal code.

Sexual Intercourse in Sacred Space

Concern with sacred time is closely related to sacred space. We see this in the *Temple Scroll's* exclusion of women and under-age boys from the Passover in 17.8-9 (similarly *Jub.* 49:17; *4QMiscellaneous Rules*/4Q265 3.3), reflecting a similar delineation between the court of the male Israelite over 20 years of age and that of the women, children, and proselytes (after the third generation; 40.6-7) in the new outer court.

The two converge indirectly in the requirement in the *Temple Scroll* that toilets be located 3000 cubits from the city and in the *War Rule* that they be 2000 cubits from the camp, noted above in discussing nakedness. Where distance of travel on the sabbath is limited to 1000 cubits (CD 10.21), the effect is to ban defecation on the sabbath. Josephus notes this as a distinctive characteristic of the Essenes (Josephus *B.J.* 2.147-149). One wonders how this could be sustained. On the other hand, *4QMiscellaneous Rules*/4Q265 allows a man to walk 2000 cubits to accompany grazing animals on the sabbath and this might allow us to assume that, had the prescription of the *War Scroll* been followed, people would just "make it".

More significantly, holy space has implications for sexual relations. *4QMiscellaneous Rules*/4Q265 shares the tradition with *Jubilees* which saw the garden of Eden as a holy sanctuary which modelled the prescriptions for the period of waiting after giving birth (*Jub.* 3:8-14). *Jubilees* also presumes that no sexual intercourse took place during the stay in the garden. There was nothing unusual in the assumption that sexual intercourse was out of place in the temple. It is striking, however, that this ban is extended by implication in the *Temple Scroll* and explicitly in D to "the holy city", which is best understood not as another term for the wider temple precincts, but to Jerusalem itself. This matches also the way the restrictions about the tabernacle and the camp are applied in *4QMMT*. The implication is not that only men were to live in the city, but that both men and women living or temporarily staying there were to practice sexual abstinence. The issue is not sexual intercourse in itself, let alone women, or human sexuality, but voluntary seminal emission. People with involuntary discharges, men and women, were similarly forbidden to enter or remain in the holy city. The *Temple Scroll* also provided for quarantining such people from ordinary cities, although it seems to make a distinction between the holy city and all other cities in that it does not impose on them the ban on those who have sexual emissions, and so by implication ban on sexual relations (48.14-17).

Restricted Entry

A number of documents enunciate entry restrictions based on Deuteronomy 23 and parts of Leviticus. The versions vary both in whom they restrict and what it is to which entry is restricted. While not offering a list like the others, the *Temple Scroll* imposes restrictions on who may enter the temple. These include all who are in a state of impurity, all lepers or infected persons as well as the blind (45.7-18). Women, boys under 20, and proselytes (after three generations) are restricted to the outer court (39.7; 40.6-7). 4QFlor/4Q174 similarly refers to restrictions on entry into a future temple, basing its list partially on Deuteronomy 23. Thus from there it bans Ammonites, Moabites, and *mamzerim*, but also foreigners and proselytes. Unlike Deuteronomy 23, which makes provision for entry of Ammonites and Moabites after the tenth generation, the ban here is total. Such a total ban appears also to be envisaged in the use of Deuteronomy 23 in *4QMMT* B 39-49. This coheres with its statement earlier that allowing Gentiles to sacrifice is like sanctioning illicit sexual relations (B 8-9). They have no business offering sacrifices to God, since they have no place in the covenant relationship. It also bans the blind and deaf from the temple, but on grounds that their disability would prevent them from being able to observe the Law correctly (*4QMMT* B 49b-54), though they may still have access to sacred food (54b). The primary application in *4QMMT* B 39-49, however, is on entry into the congregation, reflecting the original focus of Deuteronomy. This is also how the provisions are interpreted in D and the *Rule of the Congregation*, and, some have argued, also metaphorically in *4QFlorilegium*.

Before turning from the spatial to the communal emphasis, it is important to note that the restriction in relation to space is found in the *War Scroll*, which bars certain people from the camp: people with disabilities (in 4QM[a]/4Q491 also craftsmen who were essential for sustaining weaponry), men in a state of uncleanness (because of discharge or seminal emission), and boys and women (1QM/1Q33 7.3-5). People with disabilities were barred from the temple anyway, so this text extends the restriction to the war camp. Excluding women probably related both to their natural propensity to become unclean through menstruation, and probably also because it would prevent at least one avenue of seminal impurity. These detailed restrictions largely reflect the application of biblical restrictions about war camps.

Beside *4QMMT* B 39-49, which is concerned primarily with intermarriage with Gentiles and their consequent entry into the congregation of Israel, two further texts contain related lists also with a focus on people rather than place. Thus D is concerned with its community: "the fool or insane may not enter; and no simple[ton or]ignoramus or one with eyes too weak to [see or lame or crippled or deaf] or m[ino]r child" (CD 15.15-17; 4QD[a]/4Q266 8 i.7-9). It does not exclude proselytes, who are listed as a fourth category of those who belong (CD 14.4, 6, like *4QFour Lots*/4Q279 5 2-6, which describes them as a "fourth lot") and whose care also belongs to the responsibilities of the righteous (CD 6 21).

The list of banned people in the *Rule of the Congregation* relates not to the community, but to special gatherings: "and if there is a convocation for all the congregation for judgement or for the community council or for a convocation of war" (1QSa/1Q28a 1.25b-26a). The list includes a range of people with disabilities, including also the faltering elderly, as well as any man in a state of impurity through discharge or seminal emission. The document does not apply such restrictions to everyday life, but only to particular gatherings.

These diverse lists represent extrapolations of biblical restrictions, partly based on Deuteronomy 23, but also using lists of disabilities originally applying to restrictions about who may perform as priests in Lev 21:16-23 (also 2 Sam 5:8). Common to all restrictive lists is the rationale pointing to the presence of the angels of God. This gives the special place or people a special sacredness. The meaning is straightforward when applied to the temple. There the exclusion, among others, of those with seminal emission makes sense. This is so also in relation to the camp and seems to be the background for the restrictions in the *Rule of the Congregation*. There, as in the *Temple Scroll*, we have the requirement that no one enter who is unclean from seminal emission for three days and by implication that all abstain from sexual intercourse in those days of preparation, reflecting Exod 19:11-13. The *Rule of the Congregation* offers us therefore a clear instance where special gatherings call for temporary celibacy since they are to be treated as the equivalent of the temple or, at least, understood as places where God's angels are present. The restrictions applied to entering the congregation, as distinct from its special gatherings, which we find in *4QMMT* B have a different focus: exclusion of Gentiles and intermarriage. Neither its list nor the list in D focuses on issues such as seminal emission.

The change from temporary to permanent exclusion of Gentiles, including, apparently, proselytes, in *4QMMT* and *4QFlorilegium* coheres with a strong stance reflected in *Jubilees* against intermarriage with foreigners and matches also, to some degree, the strictures of the *Temple Scroll* in relation to the male court of the temple. The exclusions of people with disabilities reflects biblical restrictions about entry of priests to the temple, but their extension to the assembly of the people is an innovation which makes special claims about the community in assembly. The same applies to banning those in states of impurity from the assembly. The exclusion of women from the war camp is a special case, but reflects existing biblical provisions.

In so far as these matters pertain to attitudes towards sexuality the shifts are of three different kinds: towards exclusion of Gentiles and so against intermarriage; towards expanding the holy space to include the city and the camp, thereby restricting acts which produce seminal emission; and towards sacralisation of the community in assembly in a way that transfers to it some provisions originally related to the temple.

5 A Place for Sexuality?

This process of sacralisation and restriction raises a number questions. What impact might the additional restriction on sexual intercourse (associated with an enhanced emphasis on the impurity brought about by seminal emission) have on attitudes towards sexuality generally? What impact might the restrictions on women have on women and their participation and on marriage? At one level, the answer must be that it is a matter of time and space. There is room for human beings, male and female, whose embodiment necessarily entails times of ritual impurity which excludes them from sacred spaces. Application of temple imagery to the community must also assume there is place for such normal human beings, but that their times of impurity bar them not from the community as such, but from its special gatherings. The fact that the *Temple Scroll* (and the Herodian temple) demarcates ritually clean men and women, in itself raises questions whether such demarcations were transferred to the community and its holy gatherings. This raises the question of women's participation, but also of the place of celibacy.

The issue of women's participation is much wider than the scope of our research can cover and has been extensively treated.[28] The texts appear to reflect divergent positions, from *4QMiscellaneous Rules*/4Q265 and the *Temple Scroll* which ban women and children from Passover to the *Rule of the Congregation* which strongly affirms their presence in the community. Our focus is both narrower and broader: it is looking at attitudes towards sexuality and matters pertaining to sexuality, and these relate to men as well as women, though, as Grossman noted, most of what we hear about women seems concerned with issues of sexuality.[29]

Celibacy

Do the restrictions leave a place for sexuality or are there signs that it is something to be restricted also in ordinary space and time and even, by some, to be avoided. The accounts of the Essenes in Philo, Josephus, Pliny and Hippolytus all suggest

---

[28] See especially Schuller, "Women in the Dead Sea Scrolls"; Gruber, "Women in the Religious System of Qumran"; White Crawford, "Not According to Rule"; Wassen, *Women.*

[29] Grossman, "Reading for Gender," 218-19.

an answer in the affirmative to the second alternative, if the documents belong to the Essene movement, while Josephus reports that some Essenes married and others did not.[30]

In *Prob.* 75-91 Philo cites as an example of "virtue" (καλοκἀγαθίας) those who are called "Essaeans" (Ἐσσαῖοι), a word which he conveniently derives from "holiness" (ὁσιότητος). We then hear of the virtues and values which Philo praises as he describes their way of life. They prefer to purify their minds rather than offer sacrifices, reject lawless city life (ἀνομίας) to live in villages, where they work in the fields or in crafts and reject accumulation of wealth, war and commerce. They also reject slavery, believing nature has made all equal. Philo sums up their devotion to strict observance of the sabbath and sabbath gatherings and of the law as upholding "love of God, love of virtue, and love of people" (φιλοθέῳ καὶ φιλαρέτῳ καὶ φιλανθρώπῳ). He illustrates this with reference to their rejecting oaths and falsehood, sharing financial resources, houses, food, and clothing, and caring for the sick. This ideal account makes no reference to marriage or issues of sexuality, so that one might normally assume that Philo is speaking of people who also marry.

In *Apologia Pro Judaeis* (*Hypothetica*), however, where he also speaks of the Essenes, he notes beside these qualities, that the members are "mature men approaching old age, no longer tossed about by the emissions of the body or driven by passions" (τέλειοι δ' ἄνδρες καὶ πρὸς γῆρας ἀποκλίνοντες ἤδη, μηκέθ' ὑπὸ τῆς τοῦ σώματος ἐπιρροῆς κατακλυζόμενοι μηδ' ὑπὸ τῶν παθῶν ἀγόμενοι) (3). He mentions that while they have no children, they are fathers to children, presumably by adoption, who then care for them in old age not out of obligation but spontaneously. Philo's adulation continues with the statement that they banned marriage and observe "celibacy" (ἐγκράτειαν), which he lauds at great length as avoiding the dangers which women's sensuality and selfishness pose.

Behind this extravagant celebration of Philo's own values and prejudices, there may be some reliable information about, at least, some Essenes not marrying and about their enlisting children as carers. Philo's goal of persuasion would not work if this were not true of at least some, but we should exercise great caution about generalising these claims to all Essenes, particularly because this is not supported by the other major witness, Josephus. The misogynist explanation for their celibacy is entirely Philo's and probably has no basis in Essene reality. Nothing in the documents we have considered suggests such an approach to women, though they know the dangers which immoral women pose. The same

[30] The texts are conveniently collated in Geza Vermes and Martin D. Goodman (ed.), *The Essenes according to the Classical Sources* (Sheffield: JSOT Press, 1989).

applies to his negative stance towards the natural sexual desires of younger men, which may also call into question his report that the Essenes were older men.

Philo's ideals are also apparent in his depiction of the Therapeutae in *Contemp.* 1-2, 11-40, 63-90, whose focus is the study of the Law, prophets, and psalms, who live in isolation (χωρὶς ἕκαστοι μονούμενοι παρ' ἑαυτοῖς) (30), but meet together on the sabbath in gatherings which include women, but segregated "to preserve the modesty appropriate to women's nature" (τοῦ τε τὴν αἰδῶ τῇ γυναικείᾳ φύσει διατηρεῖσθαι) (33). Similarly at the Feast of Weeks they recline, but separately, men on the right, women on the left, among whom, Philo tells us, are many women who have chosen to remain virgins in their pursuit of wisdom (68). Their living in isolation as individuals implies celibacy. Women committed to celibacy and modesty are deemed here to be acceptable.

In the case of Josephus, beside incidental reference to individual Essenes, we have in *B.J.* 2.119-161 an equally tendentious account of the Essenes (Ἐσσηνοί),[31] which makes historical evaluation difficult.[32] Josephus is probably playing to the values of his hearers when he attributes to the Essenes renunciation of "pleasure" (ἡδονᾶς) and the "passions" (πάθεσιν) (120).[33] He, too, notes their celibacy and is more explicit about the adoption of children (120). His cautionary note that they do not reject marriage and procreation for others comes with a rationale for their own celibacy which is close to Philo's misogyny: women are dangerous because of their "licentiousness" (ἀσέλγεια)[34] and cannot be trusted to

---

[31] On the variations in designating the Essenes as to be expected and not as indications of different groups or sources, see Stephen Mason, "What Josephus Says About the Essenes in his Judean War," in *Text and Artifact in the Religions of Mediterranean Antiquity: Essays in Honour of Peter Richardson* (ed. S. Wilson and M. Desjardins; Waterloo, ON: Wilfrid Laurier University Press, 2000) 423-55, 426.

[32] On Josephus' endeavour to shape his narrative to appeal to Roman readership, countering the view that Jews are unstable and troublesome, see Mason, "What Josephus says," 433-35. Cf. the more positive assessment in Todd S. Beall, *Josephus' Description of the Essenes Illustrated by the Dead Sea Scrolls* (SNTSMon 58; Cambridge: CUP, 1988) 37-42. His alleged parallels to Josephus' report of rejection of pleasure in CD 2.16, 4.17 – 5.11 and *4QWiles of the Wicked Woman*/4Q184, are about rejection not of sexual desire or women, but of sexual wrongdoing and immoral women. See also Boccaccini, *Beyond the Essene Hypothesis*, who in his discussion (38-46) gives credence to the accounts of Philo and Josephus, speaking of "Essene misogyny" (41).

[33] Mason, "What Josephus says," writes: "In all of its aspects, this could hardly be more typical of Josephus's presentation of Judean ideals. Mastery of passions was of course basic popular philosophy and with a strong dose of misogyny admixed, reflected the conservative values of Rome that were so fondly attributed to Cato (Plutarch, *Cat. Ma.* 1-9)" (434).

[34] Mason, "What Josephus says," notes: "As for women's allegedly wanton behaviour, this is one of Josephus's instinctive *topoi*" (434).

remain faithful (121).[35] In many other details Josephus agrees with Philo, while adding considerably more. This includes a note that an "order" (τάγμα) of Essenes exists who do marry and consider it wrong not to propagate the species (160-61).[36] According to Josephus wives are put under surveillance for three years before marriage and monitored through three menstrual periods to confirm that they are capable of bearing children. Consistent with his positive rationale for marriage, namely childbearing, and his negative stance towards sexual desire and pleasure, Josephus declares that they abstain from sexual intercourse during pregnancy, "showing that they do not marry for "pleasure" (ἡδονήν), but because it is necessary to have children" (161).[37] In a much shorter account in *A.J.*18.18-22, Josephus offers a summary, which baldly states, "they take no wives", adding a rationale: "as leading to discord" (21).

Pliny's brief summary of the Essenes (*Esseni*) in *Nat. Hist.* 5.17.4 (73) is also a work of adulation, in which he notes that they are "a unique people and admirable beyond others in the whole world, without any women and renouncing love entirely" (*gens sola et in toto orbe praeter ceteras mira, sine ulla femina, omni venere abdicata*). This race, he reports, has existed for thousands of years without anyone being born into it.

While all three accounts are blatantly idealistic and bizarre,[38] they do provide sufficient evidence for us to conclude that some Essenes did not marry. It is doubtful that one can claim much more with regard to what they say about marriage and marital relations beyond that. At most the reference to adopting children and the comment about abstention from sexual intercourse during pregnancy may reflect actual practice, though with regard to the latter probably not

---

[35] Hippolytus, *Refutatio* 9.18-28, echoes Josephus, and perhaps is dependent on him or a similar source, in noting the Essenes' practice of "control" (ἐγκράτεια), rejection of "all desire" (πάσης τε ἐπιθυμίας), even of hearing of such things, renunciation of marriage, while not rejecting it for others, though another order does marry, but engages in sexual intercourse only for procreation, not for pleasure. On this see also Steudel, "Ehelosigkeit," 122.

[36] Cf. Mason, "What Josephus says," who suggests that the account of a marrying order of Essenes may be Josephus's invention to account for his own links with the movement and the discrepancy that he had had a number of marriages (448)."He made them up as a device to broaden their representative character to include people such as himself" (449).

[37] Mason, "What Josephus says," shows that these are typical of the values which Josephus wants to claim for all Jews (*Ap.* 2.199, 202) (435).

[38] Strugnell, "More on Wives and Marriage," writes: "Philo's and Josephus' apologetic witness on Essene celibacy, if not idealized, can perhaps be explained as part of their colouring of their picture of the Essenes for Greek readers with traits drawn from contemporary religio-ascetic groups; as ethnographers each interprets as a general practice of celibacy some of the Jewish purity-restrictions on marriage mentioned in *MMT*" (547).

for the reasons given, which are so blatantly part of Josephus' own value system. Neither the disparagement of women, nor the negative evaluation of sexual desire, nor the insistence that sexual intercourse take place solely for purposes of procreation[39] finds agreement in the documents we have considered.

The likelihood that these external witnesses do provide reliable evidence about celibacy, at least of some, in the movement raises the expectation that we should find traces of this in the Qumran documents, if they belong to the Essene movement. It is not possible within this discussion to pursue the vexed question of whether this is where they belong or whether they belong to a similar, but not the same, movement.[40] Pliny's identification of what was probably the community at Qumran as Essene[41] and the considerable degree of overlap[42] in areas other than sexuality and marriage between the reports of Philo and Josephus and the documents have made the hypothesis plausible. If we assume it, then a number of observations are possible. The documents, however, must be allowed to speak for themselves.[43] The primary question, given the minimal historical worth of the

---

[39] Cf. Joseph M. Baumgarten, "Celibacy, " in *EncDSS*, 122-25, who speculates that the young wife in 1QSa/1Q28a 1.11 is to report on non-procreative sex (123).

[40] As Albert I. Baumgarten, "Who Cares and Why does it Matter? Qumran and the Essenes, Once Again!" *DSD* 111 (2004) 174-90, 188. See the recent discussion of Groningen hypothesis and the Enochic hypothesis in *Enoch and Qumran Origins: New Light on a Forgotten Connection* (ed. Gabriele Boccaccini; Grand Rapids: Eerdmans, 2005) 249-435. Common to both hypotheses is the view that Qumran is not the centre of the Essene movement, but a splinter from it; yet none of the secondary sources suggests a split and the primary sources indicate no tension between those living in camps and marrying and those living elsewhere. On this, see the contribution of John J. Collins, "Enoch, the Dead Sea Scrolls, and the Essenes: Groups and Movements in Judaism in the Early Second Century B.C.E.," in *Enoch and Qumran Origins: New Light on a Forgotten Connection* (ed. Gabriele Boccaccini; Grand Rapids: Eerdmans, 2005) 345-50. The situation is complicated by the archaeological evidence indicating settlement at the site only from the end of the second century at the earliest, whereas some sectarian documents are older than that, and by the range of material found in the caves, which includes what may be described as sectarian, proto-sectarian, and non-sectarian material. In addition multiple copies sometimes vary considerably, indicating complex compositional history. We cannot assume that our external sources are speaking of a uniform movement, let alone one centred on Qumran, itself, of which neither Philo nor Josephus make any mention.

[41] The proximity of an Essene settlement is also attested by Dio of Prusa according to Synesius, *Dio* 3, 2.

[42] See the summary of overlaps in James C. VanderKam, and Peter Flint, *The Meaning of the Dead Sea Scrolls: Their Significance for Understanding the Bible, Judaism, Jesus and Christianity*. (London: HarperCollins, 2002) 242-50. See also A. Baumgarten, "Who cares?" who points to discrepancies, e.g. the location of a toilet on the site at Qumran (186).

[43] Similarly, Qimron, "Celibacy," 288.

accounts in what they say about marriage, must be whether the testimony that some Essenes practised celibacy finds any confirmation in the surviving material.

Firstly, the documents never address the issue directly. The best trace of an assumed celibacy occurs in D, where a differentiation is made among members of the community, the men of perfect holiness, who uphold the Law (6.14 – 7.4a), between those who live in camps, marry and have children, on the one hand, and the rest, on the other, who evidently do none of these things (7.4b-9a / 19.1-5a).[44] Its motif of living for a thousand generations finds a garbled echo in Pliny's account where it is linked with celibacy. But the text in D assumes that this promise applies to all, not just those not living in camps, just as all are assumed to be upholding the Law.

Beyond this, the evidence is at most indirect. Pfann's proposal to read what survives of 4Q249e 8a ב לאשתו as belonging to a statement requiring celibacy: ולוא יקר]ב לאשתו "And he shall not approach his wife",[45] is fraught with difficulty, partly on textual grounds, since we cannot know what followed, which could have referred to illicit sexual intercourse as in the penal code of 4QD[e]/4Q270 7 i.12-13; 4QD[b]/4Q267 9 vi.4-5, and partly on substantial grounds, because it would assume that a man was already married before he turned twenty and had presumably already had children.

Steudel suggests that the imagery of the temple and holy of holies, applied to the house of Aaron (1QS/1Q28 8.4b-7a; 9.5-6), would imply that a "priesterliche Sondergruppe" (tr. special priestly group) would need to remain in a state of impurity, which would preclude marriage, at least for the priests.[46] This is certainly possible, depending how much of the metaphor is transferred. Qimron similarly conjectured that such a development would carry with it the prohibition implied in the *Temple Scroll* on sexual intercourse within the camp of the city, so that those of the camp would have to be celibate.[47] It is very likely that notions of holy space and time played a significant role in this, as D's distinction between those in camps and those not in camps, and not asceticism of which we find no trace. Certainly, as we have noted in discussing holy space and holy gatherings above, temporary abstinence is envisaged. The *Temple Scroll* and D apparently see Jerusalem as requiring such abstinence, both from residents and from visitors.

---

[44] So also Baumgarten, "Qumran-Essene Restraints on Marriage," 18-19; Hempel, "Earthly Essene Nucleus," 91; White Crawford, "Not According to Rule," 132, 148; Grossmann, "Reading for Gender," 235-37; Steudel, "Ehelosigkeit," 117-18. See the discussion on pp. 129-31 above.

[45] Pfann, *DJD* 36, 559.

[46] Steudel, "Ehelosigkeit," 119; similarly ; Fletcher-Louis, *Glory of Adam*, 132-33.

[47] Qimron, "Celibacy," 290-93; and Baumgarten, "Qumran-Essene Restraints on Marriage," 19.

Others have suggested that the constraints which the legal documents impose with regard to purity and monogyny might have made celibacy a practical option for some. However, while a practical choice for celibacy, permanently or temporarily, based on age, being widowed or divorced, or on the difficulties of strict observance may have played a role,[48] the contrast being made in the best documentary evidence, namely D, suggests a religious motive and is probably best understood in relation to a choice for a life of more stringent purity,[49] an emphasis recurrent within the documents.

Assuming a connection between the collection of scrolls and the settlement at Qumran, we need also to take into account the complex archaeological data from the cemetery.[50] Although the details are yet to be fully published and the sample of graves explored is very small (43 of relevance out of nearly 1200, of which only four appear to be female),[51] there appears to be enough evidence to suggest that the settlement was predominantly male and, perhaps more importantly, did not contain families. Otherwise, given the high infant and child mortality rates and the findings at comparable sites, one would have expected to have found infants and children among the burials.[52] It need not have been exclusively male, though so-called gendered items do not reflect what one would normally expect in a mixed community.[53] From over 150 years of habitation only one spindle whorl and five beads have survived.[54] The indication of a predominantly male settlement and the absence of anything indicating family housing and family life,[55] would be

---

[48] So Baumgarten, "Qumran-Essene Restraints on Marriage," 15-16; Baumgarten, "Celibacy," 125; White Crawford, "Not According to Rule," 135, who also mentions the widowed, unmarried, and divorced (147).

[49] So Steudel, "Ehelosigkeit," 124.

[50] See the review of the data in Magness, *Archaeology*, 163-87; White Crawford, "Not According to Rule," 140-44; A. Baumgarten, "Who Cares?" 180-85; Robert Kugler and Esther Chazon, "Women at Qumran: Introducing the Essays," *DSD* 11 (2004) 167-73; Joseph E. Zias, "The Cemeteries of Qumran and Celibacy: Confusion Laid to Rest?" *DSD* 7 (2000) 220-53; Hanan Eshel, Magen Broshi, Richard Freund, and Brian Schultz, "New Data on the Cemetery East of Khirbet Qumran," *DSD* 9 (2002) 135-65; Joan Taylor, "The Cemeteries of Khirbet Qumran and Women's Presence at the Site," *DSD* 6 (1999) 285-323.

[51] A. Baumgarten, "Who cares?": "There were women buried at Qumran, and the remains of at least four of these women have been definitely identified" (185); Kugler and Chazon, "Women at Qumran": "So in all, one can at most say that there is evidence for perhaps three females among the remains removed from the 43 tombs excavated by de Vaux" (169-70). See also Magness, *Archaeology*, 172.

[52] Magness, *Archaeology*, 173, 185.

[53] See White Crawford, "Not According to Rule," who notes that this makes their presence difficult to prove while not ruling it out absolutely (141-42).

[54] Magness, *Archaeology*, 175-78.

[55] Baumgarten, "Celibacy," 123.

consistent with the site having been populated largely by those who did not live in camps and marry.

Many questions remain unanswered, such as whether the celibacy was lifelong or of limited duration, for instance, only during one's stay in a special place like Qumran or during set times (at least, prior to and during assemblies as in 1QSa/1Q28a 1.25 – 2.9),[56] whether celibacy was an early or late development in the movement,[57] whether the documents, themselves, might reflect different locations or different times. For instance, it has been common to interpret the absence of reference to women in the *Community Rule* as indicating that it was written for the celibate members[58] and D for those living in camps.[59] But the latter appears to be inclusive of both and the former may not fit such a narrow focus, as we indicate below.[60]

While I consider that the report of Josephus about two kinds of Essenes does find some confirmation in the documents which have survived, these do not support the emphasis which he or the other secondary authors have given celibacy, just as they do not support the rationales they admiringly portray. But for CD 7, one might not even have considered celibacy a practice in the community, had we not had the secondary reports. The documents exhibit rather a generally positive attitude towards marriage and sexual relations within it, and, significantly envision it as part of their future hopes and not as something which that holy time and space will exclude.

Marriage and Sexuality in the Future and the Present

One important source for understanding the values relating to human life expressed in these documents is to identify how they envisage the future. In the *Treatise on the Two Spirits*, the *Community Rule* promises to those who walk in the spirit of light: "healing and a spirit of peace in length of days and fruitful offspring (פרות זרע) with all everlasting blessings, eternal enjoyment with endless life, and a crown of glory 8 with majestic raiment in eternal light

[56] So Torleif Elgvin, "The *Yaḥad* is More Than Qumran," in *Enoch and Qumran Origins: New Light on a Forgotten Connection* (ed. Gabriele Boccaccini; Grand Rapids: Eerdmans, 2005) 273-79, 277.

[57] Grossmann, "Reading for Gender," 235-36; cf. also Steudel, "Ehelosigkeit," 117-18.

[58] Qimron, "Celibacy," 293-94.

[59] White Crawford, "Not According to Rule," 149.

[60] See also Baumgarten, "Celibacy," 124, who points to the shared penal code. On this see also Steudel, "Ehelosigkeit," 119.

(עם מדת הדר באור עולמים)" (4.6b-8) (partly preserved in 4Q257 5.4-5).[61] This implies a form of radiant embodiment in which glorious state people give birth to offspring, thus are married and have sexual relations. CD 2.11b-12a similarly speaks of a future for the remnant where God will fill the face of the world with their offspring (למלא פני תבל מזרעם). A similar thought comes to expression in the *Pesher on Psalms* (4QpPs[a]/4Q171), which promises to those who return that they will live for a thousand generations and that the inheritance of Adam will be given to them, but also ולזרעם עד עולם "to their seed forever" (1-10 iii.1-2a). The following context then speaks of their repossessing the holy mountain (1-10 iii.10-11). As noted above, the promise of living for a thousand generations is also to be found in CD 7.6 / 19.1-2, for all who are faithful, as in 1QS/1Q28 and 4QpPs[a]/4Q171. The promise echoes *1 Enoch* 10:17-18, which speaks of the righteous escaping: "they will live until they beget thousands, and all the days of their youth and their old age will be completed in peace". 4QInstr[g]/4Q423 3 1-5 / 1QInstr/1Q26 2 2-4 also assumes a future promising abundant offspring. The *Temple Scroll* also envisages a future in which the people will return to the land, liberated, and then multiply and rejoice (59.12). Similarly *11QSefer ha-Milḥamah*/11Q14 1 ii.11 // *4QSefer ha-Milḥamah*/4Q285 8 8 takes up the promise of Exod 23:26, that there will be no miscarriage in the time of future blessing, clearly assuming that marriage, sexual relations, and procreation are a normal part of life in the future as in the present. Its rationale for guaranteeing such fruitfulness is notably, that God and the holy angels will be with them, a reason not for abstinence, but for fertility! (ii.14b // 8 10-11). Multiplying assumes sexual relations in a community where people marry and bear children. It means that this would also have been seen as normative in the present.

The relevance of statements about future hope for our question is complicated to some degree by uncertainty about how the writers understood such life. This includes whether they envisaged resurrection and of what kind, and whether, with or without resurrection, they envisaged future life as being in an embodied state of some kind. In particular, this relates both to sexual relations and to procreation. At a number of points in the *Thanksgiving Hymns* we read of future life. In xi.19 the writer speaks of being delivered "from the pit and from Sheol of Abaddon", which may, as in the psalms, mean being rescued from dying, but it continues: "You have raised me up to an everlasting height, so that I can walk about on a limitless plain" (xi.20). The assumption appears to be that such elevation entails assurance of everlasting life. The passage goes on to speak of taking one's place with the angels as one's eternal destiny, understood as something which is a present and

---

[61] There is no need to interpret this metaphorically as in Wis 3:13. Cf. Baumgarten, "Qumran-Essene Restraints on Marriage," 17-18; Baumgarten, "Celibacy," 123; Steudel, "Ehelosigkeit," judging it irrelevant to the issue because it deals with the eschaton (123).

continuing reality. It then sets this in contrast to what appears to be a description of future judgement (xi.25-36), which the writer will now survive. Nothing is said about what that future state of being looks like, so that the natural assumption is that it continues to be in some embodied state as now. At most we read that the writer will "walk" (xi.20).[62]

In xix.11-12 we read similarly of a writer reporting his joining the sons of truth and the lot of the holy ones, but also of being raised from the dust as the worms of the dead to an everlasting community,.[63] In xii.20-22 we again find the juxtaposition of judgement against "deceitful men" and the assurance that those in harmony with God will, as it puts it, "stand before you forever and … be secure forever more". Puech argued that these statements imply a future resurrection,[64] but it is not explicit in the text. As Collins observes,

> The main eschatological focus of these hymns is on life with the angels, which is experienced as a present reality. This does not necessarily mean that there was no place for resurrection in the eschatology of the Dead Sea sect. But it does mean that resurrection language was not the primary vehicle of eschatological hope in the sect, nor even a necessary one.[65]

Collins, therefore, also doubts the reliability of the report in Hippolytus that Essenes believed in resurrection, arguing that it is a reading in of Christian belief.[66] While, in relation to the reports of the Essenes, Collins concludes that "the belief in immortality of the soul seems … a reasonable approximation of the

---

[62] See also the discussion in James H. Charlesworth, "Prolegomenous Reflections Towards a Taxonomy of Resurrection Texts," in *The Changing Face of Judaism, Christianity, and Other Greco-Roman Religions in Antiquity: Presented to James H. Charlesworth on the Occasion of his 65th Birthday* (ed. Ian H. Henderson and Gerbern S. Oegema with the assistance of Sara Parks Richter; SJSHZ 2; Gütersloh: Gütersloher Verlagshaus, 2006) 237-64, 248-50.

[63] John J. Collins, "The Essenes and the Afterlife," in *From 4QMMT to Resurrection: Mélanges qumraniens en homage à Émile Puech* (ed. Florentino García Martínez, Annette Steudel, and Eibert Tigchelaar; STDJ 61; Leiden: Brill, 2006) 35-53, cautions that the expression, "raise from the dust the worm of the dead", need not be based on belief in a future bodily resurrection, but may function only metaphorically (49).

[64] Puech, C*royance des Esséniens en la vie future*, 363-66. See also the discussion in George J. Brooke, "The Structure of 1QH[a] XII 5 – XIII 4 and the Meaning of Resurrection," in *From 4QMMT to Resurrection: Mélanges qumraniens en homage à Émile Puech* (ed. Florentino García Martínez, Annette Steudel, and Eibert Tigchelaar; STDJ 61; Leiden: Brill, 2006) 15-33, who argues that a belief in future resurrection has informed the author's depiction of his present relationship with God (26-33).

[65] Collins, "The Essenes and the Afterlife," 51.

[66] Collins, "The Essenes and the Afterlife," 40, 52. See his extensive discussion of the sources and the history of their investigation (35-45).

Scroll's affirmation of eternal life, translated into Greek idiom",[67] this still leaves open whether future life was understood to be embodied.[68] Such embodiedness need not entail belief in resurrection of one's corpse without remainder, as Paul and the gospel writers assume, but could simply be presumed to be the case wherever post-existence is understood to involve more than a kind of resting survival. *Jub.* 23:31, for instance, depicts a form of existence in which those on high can look down on their former bodies. Forms of belief in the nature of future existence were diverse, and even among those espousing a resurrection of the body without remainder, the new embodiedness is far from a replication of flesh and blood, but can appear, disappear, shine, and be properly designated spiritual, as later Christian texts about the resurrection of Jesus and of believers illustrate (1 Cor 15:35-49; Luke 24:31).

Émile Puech argues that, far from having a realised eschatology or belief in an immortal soul, the Essenes of Qumran "awaited the arrival of a messianic kingdom at the end of the eschatological war at the finish of the final Jubilee, the Day of the Lord or the Last Judgement" which assured "the resurrection of the just dead and the transformation of the living just into the glory of Adam upon an earth purified by fire and renewed, in the company of angels in the presence of God".[69] Puech emphasises however that such resurrection was not understood as a return to former life, but as a transformation, closer to the notion of a glorified body known from Zoroastrianism and Dan 12:3 and included the notion of an intermediate state, already reflected in *1 Enoch* 22.[70] He argues for the influence of Daniel 12 on 4QDibHam[a]/4Q504, *4QMessianic Apocalypse*/4Q521, the *Community Rule*, and the *Thanksgiving Hymns*, and suggests that its concepts also underlie *1/4QInstruction* (where he finds both post mortem individual judgement and universal judgement), the *War Scroll*, D, and *Pseudo-Ezekiel*, where he sees it in the use of Ezekiel 37.[71] Much of the evidence we considered above in relation to future fruitfulness presupposes a kind of embodiment. Frequently this is associated with the imagery of light. Thus 1QS/1Q28 4.5 speaks of being clothed in a raiment

---

[67] Collins, "The Essenes and the Afterlife," 48. He notes that what Josephus says of the Essenes appears not to match his own beliefs which included both belief in an immortal soul which faces judgement and in bodily resurrection, as reflected in his report of his own speech in Jotapata ("in the revolution of the ages, they return to find in chaste bodies a new habitation" *B.J.* 3.374-375) (42-43).

[68] Collins, "The Essenes and the Afterlife," notes in relation to the *Treatise on the Two Spirits*: "Some of the rewards of the righteous would seem to require a corporeal state, but the body in question may be a spiritual rather than an earthly body" (46). He suggests that the rule books assume that the righteous receive their reward immediately after death (47).

[69] Puech, "Resurrection," 279.

[70] Puech, "Resurrection," 270-71.

[71] Puech, "Resurrection," 263-76.

of light. *4QWiles of the Wicked Woman*/4Q184 speaks of "those who shine brightly", reflecting the astral imagery of Dan 12:3 and *1 Enoch* 104:2-6.

The question in relation to sexuality is the extent to which such embodiment included or excluded sexual activity. Those documents which speak in this context of fruitfulness and offspring clearly assume it. This would appear to be the case in those contexts which envision a future on earth centred in Jerusalem and the land. The promise of living for a thousand years might suggest sexual relations have little or no place, but such a conclusion would be based on a narrow understanding of sexual relations as having a place only for the purpose of a procreation, a view not reflected in the material we have considered (cf. *1 Enoch* 15:6-7).

The possibility of human relations, including sexual relations, is present not only where a belief in future bodily resurrection exists, though, like all forms of life, it assumes embodiment of some kind. Conversely, later, in the Jesus tradition where belief in future resurrection without remainder did exist, it was nevertheless possible to assert that there was no place for sexual relations in the age to come, as Mark 12:25 shows. In reworking that statement Luke then explains it on the basis that sexual relations are only for procreation and therefore, redundant, because, like angels, those in the age to come live forever (Luke 20:34-36). Such an issue is never addressed in surviving statements about the future in the sectarian and related documents of Qumran. The impression, on the contrary, is that marriage, family, and sexual relations continue as part of life then, just as in the present belonging in the eternal company of the angels does not entail their denial.[72]

One might imagine a train of thought which might have led to the position enunciated in Mark 12:25 and could have led authors of our documents in that direction. If people thought of future hope as being forever with God and the angels, and thus as living within holy space and time, to which laws of purity applied, then they could easily conclude that all seminal emission (and other impurities) must cease. One would then apply the rules for holy time (e.g., sabbath) and holy space (e.g. the temple, the temple city, the Garden of Eden, the holy assembly) to the future. I have not found evidence of this in the documents and accordingly not found evidence that some opted for celibacy in order to live already now as they would then, such as appears to have been the case in the early

[72] Cf. Fletcher-Louis, *Glory of Adam*, who argues that the Qumran members believed in immortality of angelic life where no procreation would be necessary, pointing to Mark 12:25 in which he claims "Jesus of Nazareth summed up succinctly the prevalent view of (non-Sadducean) Judaism when he said that there is no marriage in heaven (after death) because after the resurrection the righteous live 'as angels in the heavens'" (133). He has not demonstrated that this was the prevalent view in the sectarian and related writings of Qumran despite showing that the community attained angelomorphic life. For evidence of the latter he even cites the "people of the spirit" on *1/4QInstruction* (134), but that document clearly affirms marriage and by implications sexual relations.

Christian movement. What seems most often to be envisaged is replication of the present in the future (and of the future in the present), which thus still includes defined spaces (i.e. a temple, at least, a new one) and apparently defined times, in contrast, for instance, to Revelation, which envisages no temple and by implication a future reality of unlimited holy space described and regulated accordingly. There are signs of development of this line of thinking in *Jubilees* which envisions a future where all will be as infants, but this strand of speculation is not in evidence in the other literature we have considered. Similarly its image of Eden as a temple could have led to seeing a restoration to Eden as implying abstinence, but we find no traces of this. Even the eschatological image of paradise in *1 Enoch* 24 – 25 envisages a separate sanctuary, which those who live their long life on earth may enter, but whose space remains confined.

It is not difficult to find concrete evidence of marriage and family in the present in the documents. At most the question arises to what extent one may generalise from texts. For instance, the *Rule of the Congregation* stipulates that at the age of twenty a man not only enter the community, but also marry, which it expresses in terms of engaging in sexual intercourse. This is portrayed as the norm. It also requires that his wife be prepared to testify against him, presumably on aspects in which she has distinctive knowledge, namely his sexual practices. If we read this in the light of the other documents, the concerns will most probably relate to sexual intercourse in inappropriate periods (during menstruation and after childbirth) or on the sabbath. Only a reading through the lenses of the reports on the Essenes leads to the notion that it might include sexual intercourse for pleasure, a supposed restriction nowhere attested in the documents.

The *Temple Scroll* assumes marriage as a norm throughout, as do *4/1QInstruction*, *4QMMT*, and D. The *Temple Scroll* never indicates any tension between its strict purity provisions and the valuing of marriage, itself, though the provisions would impinge negatively on some, especially women. It assumes the reality of divorce, even accepts taking a foreign captive woman as a wife though with some restrictions, and reserves the requirement of monogyny for the king. *4/1QInstruction*, addressed, apparently to many who are poor, assumes practical monogyny, develops its instruction on marital partnership on the basis of a reading of Genesis 1 – 3 which sees the man in leadership, a woman as inferior but foundational and becoming one with her husband to the extent that it speaks of his womb. It also includes instruction directly addressed to the woman about sustaining intimacy and dealing with what threatens it. Conversely, it urges the man to honour his wife and either to seek information from astrology about his wife's conception or to study the implications of her origins set forth in the Genesis story. It includes warnings against adulterers who effectively trespass on what the husband owns and instruction for him to exercise oversight over her vows. Like D it has instruction about honesty in marrying off one's daughter and concerns itself also with finding a wife for one's son.

D, which has by far the most extensive material in relation to sexuality, including warning and legal judgements, never gives the impression that married life is something to despised or to be deemed second class. It provides for the safeguarding of marriage, oversight in contracting marriage, divorcing and dealing with children involved (CD 13.17b-19a / 4QD[a]/4Q266 9 iii.6-9a). Its warnings about apostates in 19.33b – 20.1a and 20.8b-13, that "neither for them nor their families (למשפחותיהם) shall there be a part in the house of the law (בבית התורה)" (*DSSSE*) (20.13), assume that those who belonged to "the house of the law" include men with families. Different from the *Temple Scroll*, it applies the requirement of monogyny to all, arguing it on the basis of creation and the more dubious rationale that the animals entered the ark two by two, though that, too, would have been understood as reflecting the divine ordering of creation. With the publication of the Qumran fragments of the document we are now able to see that its attack on polygyny did not entail opposition to divorce nor to remarriage.

Our discussion of 4QpapRitMar/4Q502 found the original proposal as still the most likely, namely that it contains a ritual related to marriage. As such it obviously affirms marriage, including the joy of sexual intimacy, the marital partnership together and the prospect of bearing children. It matches the positive stance reflected towards marriage and sexual union reflected in *Jubilees* and may also stand under the influence of the Canticles. *4QVisions of Amram* highlights the special love between Amram and Jochabed as exemplary and an issue in which Amram shows his obedience to the angel of light and refusal to submit to the angel of darkness. It also portrays the seven day wedding festivities of their daughter Miriam to his brother Uzziel in very positive terms. A positive appreciation of the joy of marital intimacy, including sexual intimacy, also enables the author of *4QBarkhi Nafshi*/4Q434-438 to repeat the image of Isa 62:5 of God rejoicing over Israel like a bridegroom over his bride.

A similarly positive stance towards human sexuality is evident in the *Genesis Apocryphon*. The author unabashedly refers to the sexual pleasure enjoyed by Lamech and Bitenosh, when Noah was conceived, reflecting the belief that pleasure in orgasm enhances the prospect of conception, and depicts the fulsome attractiveness of Sarai, the beautiful date palm, from details of her body to the wisdom of her mind. The document reflects the positive approach both to marital intimacy and partnership and to women, characteristic of *Jubilees*.

Like the *Temple Scroll*, D assumes the normalcy of divorce. It appears also therefore to allow the possibility of remarriage of divorced persons, but never marriage to a woman divorced for adultery. The incidental reference in 4QOrd[a]/4Q159 to barring a man who has lodged an invalid complaint against his wife alleging she was not a virgin reflects the assumption that divorce was considered part of normal human life in the community, as was marriage. In this context we have a second reference to women being authorised to testify on particular matters, beside the provision for the new wife in the *Rule of the Congregation*. It appears then that women and men belonged in the community together and that this also included their relating to one another in marriage and sexual intimacy, bearing and bringing up children, foreshadowing what was also promised them in the great future to which they looked forward. Nothing suggests avoidance or embarrassment at things sexual or a will to deny sexual pleasure in the interests of a Stoic-like utilitarian approach to intercourse and instilling strict control of the emotions.

The hymn writers often show themselves fully comfortable with the processes of human procreation, birth and the intimate nurture of infancy. They can speak of their own birth and nurture at the breast (xvii.29b-31) or depict God's love as being like the care of a wet nurse (xv.20b-22; xvii.36). The depiction of conflict using the image of two pregnant women shows an unusually sensitive appreciation of the processes of childbirth. Even when the author alludes to semen under the image of "spit" and, perhaps, water, an issue to which we return below in the discussion of dualisms, the intent does not appear to be to disparage human sexual intercourse itself, any more than its reference to creation from the dust of the ground denigrates God's action.

6. Sexuality, Self-Deprecation, and the Demonic

Within many of the hymns in the *Thanksgiving Scroll*, but also in the hymn with which the *Community Rule* concludes, and in 4QpapRitPur B/4Q512 and 4QprFêtes^{a,b}/4Q507, 508, we find statements in which the writers emphasise human creatureliness. Sometimes the intent appears to be to establish a contrast with God's greatness and goodness and so evoke wonder and thanksgiving. At other times it appears directed towards enhancing awareness of human frailty. Usually it takes the form of highlighting the substances from which human beings were created: dust, dirt, earth, and by derivation, mixed with water: clay. The vocabulary is the same, but the combinations differ, for instance, between the *Thanksgiving Scroll* and the hymn of the *Community Rule*. The same emphasis belongs to the use of flesh (בשר) to describe humanity. In addition, the authors sometimes appear to allude to the processes of procreation when they apparently speak of semen as just spit. None of these substances is portrayed as evil or bad. They are simply very lowly and help account for the lowliness of humanity.

In addition, and as a consequence of the lowly substance which makes up humanity, human beings keep becoming "dirty" in the sense that their bodily processes keep rendering them unclean, making them thus flesh of shame. They are regularly unclean and so unfit to be in God's presence. This is not yet sin, but belongs to their creatureliness and warrants the sense of their inadequacy and God's generosity in making purification possible.

As a third tier of self-deprecation the texts speak also of human sin. Here the authors are not just saying that humans sin, but that they have a propensity or tendency to do so. Many go further and assert that this sinful tendency was there from the beginning – even before birth. But this was already the rhetoric of the psalms. This makes it difficult to identify the extent to which the authors intend to locate human sinfulness in human beings as innate. One of the main expressions used to describe its cause is יצר רע "evil tendency". It means a human being's propensity to sin. While the authors locate this within the reality of being human, they do not treat it as an automatic consequence of human embodiment or identify it with a particular part or aspect of being human such as the genitals or human sexuality. Rather, as the authors attest, God can remove the evil tendency. In the more elaborated discussion in the *Treatise on the Two Spirits* God sets the proportions within each human being.

A similar determinism is assumed in the *Thanksgiving Hymns*, where authors can speak of God both knowing and determining the inclination of every creature. In this deterministic psychological dualism there might have been the potential to link the tendency towards sin with sexuality. The link is certainly there with regard to ritual impurity, evident in the use of מקור הנדה "source/spring of impurity" (1QH[a] ix.22; xx.25). But no such link is made between moral impurity and sexuality. Sexual wrongdoing must be assumed to belong to the sins of which the hymn writers speak, but they never mention it, nor does the hymn in the *Community Rule*, though elsewhere that document clearly identifies sexual wrongdoing among the sins to be eschewed. It does, however, appear in the context of psychological dualism in *4QBarkhi Nafshi*/4Q434-438, but there it belongs to a list of qualities from which God has delivered the author: a "heart of stone", the "evil inclination" (יצר רע), "sexual immorality of the eyes" (זנות עינים), "stiffness of neck", "wrathful anger", "haughtiness of heart and arrogance of eyes", and a "spirit of deceit".

In some other texts the psychological dualism is combined with a demonological perspective. Thus in 4QShir[a,b]/4Q510, 511 we find the vocabulary of creation and procreation used in the *Thanksgiving Scroll,* but, again, as with 1QS/1Q28 11, in different combinations (28+29 2-4). It also speaks, in addition, of sinfulness בחכמי בשרי "in the innards of my flesh", a term attested also in 1QS/1Q28 4.20b-21a; *1QHymnic Composition*/1Q36 14 2 and *4QIncantation*/ 4Q444 1-4 i +5 3. But then in 4QShir[b]/4Q511 48-49+51 ii.2b-4 we find: "by his mouth he frightens [all the spirits] of the bastards to subdue [ ] impurity because in the innards of my flesh is the foundation [and in] my body are battles". The same kind of dualism reappears in *4QIncantation*/4Q444, where we again read of the innards of the flesh as the location of a battle and where the ultimate victory will come with the end of the dominion of the "bastards and the spirit of impurity".

This is different from the psychological dualism which underlies the *Thanksgiving Hymns*, the hymn in 1QS/1Q28 11, and the documents, 4QpapRitPur B/4Q512 and 4QprFêtes[a,b]/4Q507, 508. For in 4QShir[a,b]/4Q510, 511 the human being is a battleground, where to sin is to choose to succumb to the "bastard spirits". The reference to "bastards" reflects the Enoch tradition, in which we read that spirits emerged from the corpses of the slain giants, the offspring of the Watchers (*1 Enoch* 15:8-9; 19:1). There the giants are described as "bastards", the offspring of the liaison between the Watchers and human women, and in our documents their spirits are accordingly designated bastards or bastard spirits.[73] An allusion to the bastard spirits occurs also in 11QapocPs/11Q11 where the demons are addressed as "offspring of] humankind and the seed of the holy ones" (5.6).

The same kind of demonic dualism is assumed in *4QBerakhot*/4Q286-90, although there we lack references to "bastards", but instead read of cursing Belial "in his hateful plans" and "all the spirits of his lot in their wicked plans", described as "plans of defiling impurities", and of cursing "the angel of the pit and spirit of Abaddon" and the plans of their guilty inclination (4QBer[a]/4Q286 7a ii b-d). Similarly, the *Visions of Amram* speaks of two heavenly beings who compete for human allegiance (4Q544 1 9-15), one of whom is named: Malkiresha (4Q544 2 13), and of children of light and children of darkness (4Q548 1 ii-2 9-16). This recalls the language of the *War Scroll* in the context of the eschatological battle, but, in contrast to the *War Scroll*, is related to the individual's struggle.

A similar personal dualism appears in the *Treatise on the Two Spirits* in 1QS/1Q28 3.13 – 4.26, which depicts the human struggle as one between the prince of light and the angel of darkness, but now within the framework of a theological explanation which explains the struggle as divinely planned and determined. Part of that determination includes, according to *4QHoroscope*/4Q186, the allotting of nine parts of light and darkness in a ratio reflecting times of conception and observable in the human body.

The motif of determinism also features in *1/4QInstruction*, though without the framework of demonology. It may allude to God's judgement against the Watchers and associate it with the destruction of "every spirit of flesh", though the latter is never linked to sexual motifs. The fate of all human beings is engraved in a heavenly book, variously described as the mystery that is to come, the book of memorial and the Vision of Hagu. One interpretation of the document sees it using

---

[73] In the *Thanksgiving Scroll* we also read of the "bastards" (xxiv.15; cf. also fr. 2 ii + 6 6), but in the context of the writer's awe at the judgement the Watchers face and not in the context of anthropology.

the two Genesis accounts of creation to refer to the creation of two different kinds of human beings from the very beginning, one designated as the "people of the spirit" and the other as the "spirit of flesh", depending, in particular, on how one reads 4QInstr^{c}/4Q417 1 i.16b-18a. Among subsequent authors who presumably would have known the document, we find, however, no trace of this remarkable claim of two creations, which raises questions about whether it was ever heard or meant this way. An alternative reading does not see that kind of absolute dualism here, but does recognise the language of dualistic determinism implied in people's fate being already engraved and a change for the worse in humanity where now only a few are recipients of revelation and belong to the righteous. The problem with such dualistic language arises from its function which is to reassure the righteous both about their own status and about why others have not joined them. Paradoxically, at the same time, authors who espouse what appears to be a closed system assume that people can indeed swap sides, the righteous can fall and so need exhortation not to do so, and others can repent. This paradox, reflecting the function of the discourse of dualistic determinism, appears to be characteristic of all the texts considered.

1/4QInstruction is thus closest to the *Thanksgiving Hymns* in employing a dualism in relation to human beings without a strongly demonological framework. It differs, however, from the latter in not developing self-deprecatory language. Where it refers to "flesh", however, its focus is mostly not all humanity, but particularly those who are not counted with the righteous. It also lacks the psychological dimensions of the *Treatise on the Two Spirits*, focussing rather on wisdom, understood as following wise instruction such as it presents extensively throughout the document on matters of everyday life, and seems well summarised in its designation of the wise as those who can discern good and evil.

It is beyond the scope of our task to analyse possible developments within these dualisms.[74] We are probably witnessing diverse influences coming from both sapiential and apocalyptic sources. As in the passages reflecting psychological dualism, so also where we have a combination with demonic dualism, the authors

[74] See the major discussion in Frey, "Different Patterns", who argues for "a sapiential type of multi-dimensional, ethically oriented cosmic dualism (as represented by 1QS 3:13 – 4:26)" and "a priestly type of sheer cosmic dualism dominated by the opposition of two angelic powers (as documented by the War Rule, but also in pre-Essene texts such as the Visions of Amram or 11QApPs^{a})" (288). He notes that while some motifs are shared between the two, such as the imagery of light and darkness, the two powers, and the final victory, the differences are major, including the depiction of the opposing angels as of equal rank and "as seemingly independent forces" (312), the different understandings of "the angels of destruction" and to whose side they belong (312), the different names of the contenders, including the absence of "Belial" in the sapiential stream, and the absence of ethical and psychological dualism in the other (312-13).

do not identify human sexuality as problematic. Nowhere do we find in references to the "flesh" or to its basic substances an implication that human sexuality is something negative. In the few instances where we find allusions to the eyes in this context the condemnation is not directed against desire, itself, as the accounts of Josephus and Philo might lead us to expect, but against their misdirection. In any case such sexual wrongdoing does not play a major role in the dualistic discourses. This might have been a possibility, had the Watcher myth been seen as paradigmatic for all sin and the beginning therefore of a plague of sexual sins, but this is not how the Enoch tradition interpreted the myth or depicted the behaviour of the bastards, nor the way the myth is used in the documents considered.

7 Conclusion

Among the vast range of documents we have surveyed there is significant variation in the way attitudes towards sexuality feature. In much of the material, including those documents generally recognised as sectarian, sexual wrongdoing plays only a minor role as one of the sins which one has left behind. The *Thanksgiving Hymns*, which otherwise make creative use of sexual imagery, make no reference to sexual wrongdoing. This is all the more surprising since along with the *Pesharim* and the *Community Rule* its hymns often reflect conflicts which were bound up with the community's identity and origins. The exception is D, which while employing much of the same language of conflict, including the abusive appellations of its opponents, makes it clear that disputes over interpretation of biblical law pertaining to sexual wrongdoing were central to that conflict. Its Admonition not only identifies it as belonging to Belial's nets, but also accuses the opponents of choosing the fair neck and depicts Israel's history as a litany of succumbing to sexual wrongdoing, beginning with the sin of the Watchers.

More polite and less polemical, the author of *4QMMT* also depicts sexual wrongdoing, in particular, intermarriage with Gentiles, as at the heart of many differences over interpretation of the Law which have led him and his follows to withdraw. D and *4QMMT* seem to belong to the earlier stages of a conflict which by the time of the later sectarian documents has ceased to be a dispute over interpretation and has become an *ad hominem* disputing of opponents' integrity. *4QWiles of the Wicked Woman*/4Q184 may also belong at this early stage.

Not all references to issues of sexuality, however, derive from the context of dispute. This is true of the extensive legal material in D. Some of it may well have been contentious, but most of it is not presented that way and probably represents the recording of a tradition of applying biblical law in the wider community over many years. This will also be the case with a number of other legal documents we considered. The *Temple Scroll* is a special case, since it contemplates the building of a huge, new temple, but many of the legal discussions are similar. Concern with ritual impurity is evident. The trend detectable already in the *Temple Scroll* is towards homogenising provisions relating to abnormal male and female discharge and seminal and menstrual impurity and towards enhancing the seriousness of seminal emission. Ritual impurity and moral impurity are not confused, though language of the former, such as נדה, shows evidence of having expanded from a narrow technical sense of "menstrual impurity" to a wider range of categories, but also of being applied to moral impurity.

Concern with sexual wrongdoing in the context of legal exposition covers a wide range of issues, including honesty in offering one's daughter in marriage, finding an appropriate husband or wife, sexual intercourse with another's betrothed, ensuring the virginity of brides, avoiding illicit sexual intercourse in marriage (during menstruation, pregnancy, on the sabbath, in the holy city) and reporting breaches, chastity of widows, accusations of adultery, sexual intercourse with slaves (one's own, another's) and captive women, homosexual acts, and cross-dressing, all to be found in D, but some also discussed elsewhere. The concern with intermarriage with Gentiles whether by priests or people, a theme of *Jubilees* and the *Aramaic Levi Document*, is predictably present in a number of related documents, including the *Genesis Apocryphon*, the *Testament of Qahat* and the *Visions of Amram* and central in *4QMMT*. It is not an issue at all, except for in the royal law, in the *Temple Scroll* and also not clearly evident in D. It then seems to disappear entirely in the later sectarian documents. The *Wiles of the Wicked Woman* addresses sexual wrongdoing and, like D, sees it as leading to some perverse interpretations of the Law. Concern with incest, a major emphasis in *Jubilees*, is attested, though mainly in the concern over marriage to nieces.

Concern with sacred space and time touches at some points on issues of sexuality, for instance, in the prohibition of sexual intercourse on the sabbath and the absence of sexual intercourse in the garden of Eden, which might have had the potential to deny it a place in the future. The future seems, however, to be envisaged as a time of abundance, which includes also the bearing of children and so marriage and sexual relations. Statements concerned to restrict entry into the congregation, which draw on categories of those excluded from the temple, do not appear to exclude women, with the exception of entry into the war camp, where special provisions had always applied. The extent to which women were admitted to all activities of the community is unclear, since some documents exclude them from the Passover and the *Temple Scroll* envisages their exclusion from the court of Jewish men. All documents seem to assume that women belong to the community, that people marry and that they sometimes divorce and remarry.

Given the testimony of Philo, Josephus, Pliny and Hippolytus about celibacy adopted by some Essenes, it is surprising that in these documents, often identified as Essene, we find so little evidence of it. If it was an aspect of the sect, for which only D provides direct evidence, the writers of the scrolls which have survived did not see fit to give it emphasis and certainly did not indicate that its basis was discomfort with, or an aversion in relation to, matters of sexuality. Allusions to marriage and licit sexuality assume it to be a natural part of human life in the present and the future. A number make free use of its imagery, one appears to celebrate the joy of human sexuality in the context of what appears to be a marriage ritual, and like *Jubilees*, the *Visions of Amram* and the *Genesis Apocryphon* emphasise love in marriage, and the latter values the sensual in sexual relations. The extensive advice *1/4QInstruction* both to men and, notably, women, reflects a high valuing of the marital relationship within a patriarchal perspective.

Even the forms of dualism which, either in largely psychological terms or combined with a demonology, bemoan the human condition, its lowly substance illustrated by creation and procreation, its inherent ritual impurities, and its sinful tendencies, never lay the blame at the door of human sexuality. Human sin certainly includes sexual wrongdoing, but human sexuality, though a source of ritual impurity, is not, in itself a source of moral impurity.

It is difficult in considering such a vast array of material, much of it fragmentary, to do more than identify the issues raised or alluded to. It would, for instance, be useful to identify particular trends. Those discerned above must be tentative. They include the observation that concern with intermarriage appears to be confined to material widely recognised as belonging to the older material in the collection, thus, beside *Jubilees*, the *Aramaic Levi Document*, and *4QMMT*, related documents such as the *Testament of Qahat*, the *Visions of Amram*, 4QOrd^{b}/4Q513, all concerned especially with priests, and 4QApocrJer C; *4QHalakhah A*/4Q251; and *4QMiscellaneous Rules*/4Q265. The same appears to be true of those concerned with incest. D shows no indication of concern with intermarriage, but does address incest. Its concern with polygyny may reflect expansion to all of the restrictions which the *Temple Scroll* applied to kings, much as its emphasis on forbidding marriage to nieces reflects what in the *Temple Scroll* appears uncontentious. Along with its third concern, intercourse during menstruation, D would appear to belong to a stage in the conflict where the focus has moved on from intermarriage with Gentiles, but which still depicts that conflict in terms of dispute over interpretation.

What then appear to be the later sectarian documents, including those which retell the community's history of conflict, focus no longer on substance, but on rival claims to authority. As a result, issues of conflict from earlier times, many of which pertained to sexual matters, disappear, or leaves traces only in stereotypical phrases such as lusting eyes, which are now reduced to being listed among behaviours that designate the life which the true member of the sect has left behind. In that sense among the main sectarian writings matters concerning sexuality are not really an issue, not even in its rhetoric of self-deprecation. Even the likelihood that some, perhaps many, chose celibacy, leaves no negative trace of the kind which might disparage sexuality or deem it unfit to have a place in the future glory of Adam promised to the faithful.

The material before us represents a collection of documents belonging to an older tradition and to the re-writing and re-interpreting of that tradition. The legal material is largely expounding biblical law and allows us to see processes of harmonisation and homogenisation. There is a trend towards extending the space and time that is sacred and protecting it with stricter provisions, but not in a way that denigrates non-sacral space and time. This appears also to be the case in relation to eschatology. Thus there remains a time and place for marriage and sexual relations. There will still be sacral and non-sacral places. Furthermore, despite some documents containing extensive reflection on the human condition and its sinfulness, nowhere do they treat human sexuality as problematic. At most it belongs to areas where the faithful need to be attentive to purity and impurity. It is also an arena in which wrongdoing is frequent and disputes over sexual wrongdoing and interpreting the Law in relation to it formed an important component of early conflicts. There is no evidence that then or later people interpreted sexual relations in the right time and place and order as sinful. Some of the stories preserved and retold celebrate sensuality and sexual fulfilment.

In keeping with the traditions they preserve and reinterpret, the documents reflect a social reality in which men are dominant. Where we hear of instruction about marriage, its initiation and maintenance, addressed to males with one notable exception, the assumption is that men rule over women and have the power to determine their place. Women's inferiority is assumed and sometimes explicitly stated. The creation accounts in Genesis 1 – 3 frequently serve as a basis for expanding this order within which love and sexual passion have their secure place. Such power over women extends to claiming the right to sexual relations with slaves, and to making captive women their wives. These rights, enshrined in biblical law, apparently remain, even though at least D goes beyond biblical provisions in insisting on monogyny. The chief concerns, as there, are with controlling women's behaviour and protecting oneself from wicked women. There is very little reference to adultery, perhaps because it had not been controversial. On the other hand, incest looms relatively large as an issue. References to homosexual relations are very few and not such that would suggest it played a major role for the authors and their communities. Nor do issues such as bestiality feature. Attentiveness to ritual impurity was important not only for women, but also for men. The primary concern appears to be right time, right place, and right order – based on a fairly carefully worked out understanding of each. Within these parameters of assumed rightness, however alien to contemporary valuing of human rights and equality, sexuality was seen as unproblematic, and more than that, as belonging to the blessings of creation.

Bibliography

Abegg, Martin G. "4QMMT C 27, 31 and 'Works Righteousness'," *DSD* 6 (1999) 139-47

Abegg, Martin G. "4QMMT, Paul, and 'Works of the Law'," in *The Bible at Qumran: Text, Shape, and Interpretation* (ed. Peter W. Flint; Grand Rapids: Eerdmans, 2001) 203-16

Allegro, John M. "The Wiles of the Wicked Woman: A Sapiential Work from Qumran's Fourth Cave," *PEQ* 96 (1964) 53-55

Anderson, Gary A. "Intentional and Unintentional Sin in the Dead Sea Scrolls," in *Pomegranates and Golden Bells: Studies in Biblical, Jewish, and Near Eastern Ritual, Law, and Literature in Honor of Jacob Milgrom* (ed. David P. Wright et al.; Winona Lake: Eisenbrauns, 1995) 49-64

Anderson, Gary A. "Two Notes on Measuring Character and Sin at Qumran," in *Things Revealed: Studies in Early Jewish and Christian Literature in Honor of Michael E. Stone* (JSJSupp 89; ed. Esther Chazon, David Satran and Ruth Clements; Leiden: Brill, 2004) 141-47

Atkinson, Kenneth. "4QMMT and Psalms of Solomon 8: Two Anti-Sadducean Documents," *Qumran Chronicle* 11 (2003) 57-77

Aubin, Melissa. "'She is the Beginning of all the Ways of Perversity': Femininity and Metaphor in 4Q184," *Women in Judaism: A Multidisciplinary Journal* 2.2 (2001) 1-23

Bachmann, Michael. "4QMMT und der Galaterbrief, מעשי התורה und ΕΡΓΑ ΝΟΜΟΥ," *ZNW* 89 (1998) 91-113

Baillet, Maurice. "Un recueil liturgique de Qumrân Grotte 4: Les Paroles de Luminaires," *RB* 68 (1961) 95-250

Baumgarten, Albert I. "The Perception of the Past in the Damascus Document," in *The Damascus Document: A Centennial of Discovery: Proceedings of the*

Third International Symposium of the Orion Center for the Study of the Dead Sea Scrolls and Associated Literature, 4-8 February 1998 (ed. Joseph M. Baumgarten, Esther G. Chazon, and Avital Pinnick; STDJ 34; Leiden: Brill, 2000) 1-15

Baumgarten, Albert I. "The Temple Scroll, Toilet Practices, and the Essenes," *Jewish History* 10 (1996) 9-20

Baumgarten, Albert I. "Who Cares and Why does it Matter? Qumran and the Essenes, Once Again!" *DSD* 111 (2004) 174-90

Baumgarten, Joseph M. "4Q502, Marriage or Golden Age Ritual?" *JJS* 34 (1983) 125-35

Baumgarten, Joseph M. "A Fragment of Fetal Life and Pregnancy in 4Q270," in *Pomegranates and Golden Bells: Studies in Biblical, Jewish, and Near Eastern Ritual, Law, and Literature in Honor of Jacob Milgrom* (ed. David P. Wright et al.; Winona Lake: Eisenbrauns, 1995) 445-48

Baumgarten, Joseph M. "Celibacy, " *EncDDS*, 122-25

Baumgarten, Joseph M. "Halakic Polemics in New Fragments from Qumran Cave 4," in *Biblical Archaeology Today: Proceedings of the International Congress on Biblical Archaeology, Jerusalem, April 1984* (ed. J. Amitai; Jerusalem: Israel Exoloration Society, 1985) 390-99

Baumgarten, Joseph M. "On the Nature of the Seductress in 4Q184," *RevQ* 15 (1991) 133-43

Baumgarten, Joseph M. "On the Testimony of Women in 1QSa," *JBL* 76 (1957) 266-69

Baumgarten, Joseph M. "Purification after Childbirth and the Sacred Garden in 4Q265 and Jubilees," in *New Qumran Texts and Studies: Proceedings of the First Meeting of the International Organization for Qumran Studies, Paris 1992* (ed. G. J. Brooke; STDJ 15; Leiden: Brill, 1994) 3-10

Baumgarten, Joseph M. "Recent Qumran Discoveries and Halakhah in the Hellenistic-Roman Period," in *Jewish Civilization in the Hellenistic-Roman Period in Jerusalem* (ed. Shemaryahu Talmon; JSPSup 10; Sheffield: JSOT Press, 1991) 147-58

Baumgarten, Joseph M. "Sadducean Elements in Qumran Law," in *The Community of the Renewed Covenant: The Notre Dame Symposium on the Dead Sea Scrolls* (ed. Eugene Ulrich and James VanderKam; Christianity and Judaism in Antiquity Series 10; Notre Dame: University of Notre Dame Press, 1994) 27-36

Baumgarten, Joseph M. "Scripture and Law in 4Q265," in *Biblical Perspectives: Early Use and Interpretation of the Bible in Light of the Dead Sea Scrolls: Proceedings of the First International Symposium of the Orion Center for the Study of the Dead Sea Scrolls and Associated Literature, 12-14 May 1996* (ed. Michael E. Stone and Esther G. Chazon; STDJ 28; Leiden: Brill, 1998) 25-33

Baumgarten, Joseph M. "The 'Halakha' in Miqṣat Ma'aśe Ha-Torah (MMT)," *JAOS* 116/3 (1996) 512-16

Baumgarten, Joseph M. "The Exclusion of *Netinim* and Proselytes in 4QFlorilegium," in *Studies in Qumran Law* (SJLA 24; Leiden: Brill, 1977) 75-87

Baumgarten, Joseph M. "The Law and Spirit of Purity at Qumran," in *The Bible and the Dead Sea Scrolls: The Princeton Symposium on the Dead Sea Scrolls: Volume 2: The Dead Sea Scrolls and the Qumran Community* (ed. James H. Charlesworth; Waco: Baylor University Press, 2006) 93-105

Baumgarten, Joseph M. "The Laws of the Damascus Document – Between Bible and Mishnah," in *The Damascus Document: A Centennial of Discovery: Proceedings of the Third International Symposium of the Orion Center for the Study of the Dead Sea Scrolls and Associated Literature, 4-8 February 1998* (ed. Joseph M. Baumgarten, Esther G. Chazon, and Avital Pinnick; STDJ 34; Leiden: Brill, 2000) 17-26

Baumgarten, Joseph M. "The Laws of the *Damascus Document* in Current Research," in *The Damascus Document Reconsidered* (ed. Magen Broshi; Jerusalem: Israel Exploration Society, The Shrine of the Book, Israel Museum, 1992) 51-62

Baumgarten, Joseph M. "The Purification Rituals in DJD 7," in *The Dead Sea Scrolls: Forty Years of Research* (ed. D. Dimant and U. Rappaport; Jerusalem: Magnes Press, 1992) 199-209

Baumgarten, Joseph M. "The Qumran Sabbath Shirot and Rabbinic Merkabah Traditions," *RevQ* 13 (1988) 199-213

Baumgarten, Joseph M. "The Qumran-Essene Restraints on Marriage," in *Archaeology and History in the Dead Sea Scrolls: The New York University Conference in Memory of Yigael Yadin* (ed. L. H. Schiffman; JSPSup 8; Sheffield: JSOT Press, 1990) 13-24

Baumgarten, Joseph M. "Theological Elements in the Formulation of Qumran Law," in *Emanuel: Studies in Hebrew Bible, Septuagint, and Dead Sea Scrolls in Honor of Emanuel Tov* (ed. Shalom M. Paul, Robert A. Kraft, Lawrence H. Schiffman, and Weston W. Fields; SVT 94; Leiden: Brill, 2003) 33-41

Baumgarten, Joseph M. "Zab Impurity in Qumran and Rabbinic Law," *JJS* 14 (1994) 273-77

Beall, Todd S. *Josephus' Description of the Essenes Illustrated by the Dead Sea Scrolls* (SNTSMon 58; Cambridge: CUP, 1988)

Becker, Jürgen. *Das Heil Gottes: Heils- und Sündenbegriffe in den Qumrantexten und im Neuen Testament* (SUNT 3; Göttingen: Vandenhoeck und Ruprecht, 1964)

Bernstein, Moshe J. "4Q159 Fragment 5 and the 'Desert Theology' of the Qumran Sect," in *Emanuel: Studies in Hebrew Bible, Septuagint, and Dead Sea Scrolls in Honor of Emanuel Tov* (ed. Shalom M. Paul, Robert A. Kraft, Lawrence H. Schiffman, and Weston W. Fields; SVT 94; Leiden: Brill, 2003) 43-56

Bernstein, Moshe J. "4Q252: From Re-Written Bible to Biblical Commentary (4QpGen[a])," *JJS* 45 (1994) 1-27

Bernstein, Moshe J. "4Q252: Method and Context, Genre and Sources: A Response to George J. Brooke," *JQR* 85 (1994) 61-79

Bernstein, Moshe J. "From the Watchers to the Flood: Story and Exegesis in the Early Columns of the *Genesis Apocryphon*," in *Reworking the Bible: Apocryphal and Related Texts at Qumran: Proceedings of a Joint Symposium by the Orion Center for the Study of the Dead Sea Scrolls and Associated Literature and the Hebrew University Institute for Advanced Studies Research Group on Qumran, 15-17 January, 2002* (ed. Esther G. Chazon, Devorah Dimant, and Ruth A. Clements; STDJ 58; Leiden: Brill, 2005) 39-63

Bernstein, Moshe J. "Pentateuchal Interpretation at Qumran," in *The Dead Sea Scrolls after Fifty Years: A Comprehensive Assessment* (ed. Peter W. Flint and James C. VanderKam; Leiden: Brill, 1998) 1.128-59

Bernstein, Moshe J. "The Employment and Interpretation of Scripture in 4QMMT: Preliminary Observation," in *Reading 4QMMT: New Perspectives on Qumran Law and History* (ed. John Kampen and Moshe J. Bernstein; SBLSym 2; Atlanta: Scholars, 1996) 29-51

Bernstein, Moshe J. and Shlomo A. Koyfman, "The Interpretation of Biblical Law in the Dead Sea Scrolls: Forms and Methods," in *Biblical Interpretation at Qumran* (ed. Matthias Henze; Grand Rapids: Eerdmans, 2005) 61-87

Bernstein, Moshe. J. "Women and Children in Legal and Liturgical Texts from Qumran," *DSD* 11 (2004) 191-211

Berrin, Shani. "*Pesher Nahum, Psalms of Solomon* and Pompey," in *Reworking the Bible: Apocryphal and Related Texts at Qumran: Proceedings of a Joint Symposium by the Orion Center for the Study of the Dead Sea Scrolls and Associated Literature and the Hebrew University Institute for Advanced Studies Research Group on Qumran, 15-17 January, 2002* (ed. Esther G. Chazon, Devorah Dimant, and Ruth A. Clements; STDJ 58; Leiden: Brill, 2005) 65-84

Berrin, Shani. "Qumran Pesharim," in *Biblical Interpretation at Qumran* (ed. Matthias Henze; Grand Rapids: Eerdmans, 2005) 110-33

Betz, Otto. *Offenbarung und Schriftforschung in der Qumran Gemeinde* (WUNT 5; Tübingen: Mohr Siebeck, 1960)

Boccaccini, Gabriele. "Qumran and the Enoch Groups: Revisiting the Enochic-Essene Hypothesis," in *The Bible and the Dead Sea Scrolls: The Princeton*

Symposium on the Dead Sea Scrolls: Volume 1: Scripture and the Scrolls (ed. James H. Charlesworth; Waco: Baylor University Press, 2006) 37-66

Boccaccini, Gabriele. *Beyond the Essene Hypothesis: The Parting of the Ways between Qumran and Enochic Judaism* (Grand Rapids: Eerdmans, 1998)

Bokser, B. "Ma'al and Blessings Over Food," *JBL* 100 (1981) 561-62

Borgen, Peder "'At the Age of Twenty' in 1QSa," *RevQ* 10 (1961-62) 267-77

Brady, Monica. "Biblical Interpretation in the 'Pseudo-Ezekiel' Fragments (4Q383-391) from Cave Four," in *Biblical Interpretation at Qumran* (ed. Matthias Henze; Grand Rapids: Eerdmans, 2005) 88-109

Brin, Gershon. "Divorce at Qumran" in *Legal Texts and Legal Issues: Proceedings of the Second Meeting of the International Organization for Qumran Studies, Cambridge, 1995: Published in Honour of Joseph M. Baumgarten* (ed. M. Bernstein, F. García Martínez, and J. Kampen; Leiden: Brill, 1997) 232-44

Brin, Gershon. "Regarding the Connection Between the Temple Scroll and the Book of Jubilees," *JBL* 112 (1993) 108-109

Brin, Gershon. *Studies in Biblical Law: From the Hebrew Bible to the Dead Sea Scrolls* (Sheffield: Sheffield Academic Press, 1994)

Brooke, George J. "4Q252 as Early Jewish Commentary," *RevQ* 17 (1996) 385-401

Brooke, George J. "4Q500 1 and the Use of Scripture in the Parable of the Vineyard," in *The Dead Sea Scrolls and the New Testament* (Minneapolis: Fortress, 2005) 235-60

Brooke, George J. "Biblical Interpretation at Qumran," in *The Bible and the Dead Sea Scrolls: The Princeton Symposium on the Dead Sea Scrolls: Volume 1: Scripture and the Scrolls* (ed. James H. Charlesworth; Waco: Baylor University Press, 2006) 287-319

Brooke, George J. "Biblical Interpretation in the Wisdom Texts from Qumran," in *The Wisdom Texts from Qumran and the Development of Sapiential Thought: Studies in Wisdom at Qumran and its Relationship to Sapiential Thought in the Ancient Near East, the Hebrew Bible, Ancient Judaism, and the New Testament* (ed. Charlotte Hempel, Armin Lange, and Hermann Lichtenberger; BETL 159; Leuven: Peeters-Leuven University Press, 2002) 201-20

Brooke, George J. "From Qumran to Corinth: Embroidered Allusions to Women's Authority," in *The Dead Sea Scrolls and the New Testament* (Minneapolis: Fortress, 2005) 195-213

Brooke, George J. "Miqdash Adam, Eden and the Qumran Community," in *Gemeinde ohne Tempel/Community without Temple: Zur Substituierung und Transformation des Jerusalemer Tempels und seines Kults im Alten Testament, antiken Judentum und frühen Christentum* (ed. Beate Ego, Armin Lange, and Peter Pilhofer; WUNT 118; Tübingen: Mohr Siebeck, 1999) 285-301

Brooke, George J. "The *Commentary on Genesis A* and the New Testament," in *The Dead Sea Scrolls and the New Testament* (Minneapolis: Fortress, 2005) 177-94

Brooke, George J. "The Explicit Presentation of Scripture in 4QMMT," in *Legal Texts and Legal Issues: Proceedings of the Second Meeting of the International Organization for Qumran Studies, Cambridge, 1995: Published in Honour of Joseph M. Baumgarten* (ed. Moshe J. Bernstein, Florentino García Martínez, and John Kampen; STDJ 23; Leiden: Brill, 1997) 67-88

Brooke, George J. "The Genre of 4Q252: From Poetry to Pesher," *DSD* 1 (1994) 160-79

Brooke, George J. "The Structure of $1QH^a$ XII 5 – XIII 4 and the Meaning of Resurrection," in *From 4QMMT to Resurrection: Mélanges qumraniens en homage à Émile Puech* (ed. Florentino García Martínez, Annette Steudel, and Eibert Tigchelaar; STDJ 61; Leiden: Brill, 2006) 15-33

Brooke, George J. "The Temple Scroll: A Law unto Itself?" in *Law and Religion: Essays on the Place of the Law in Israel and Early Christianity* (ed. Barnabas Lindars; Cambridge: James Clarke, 1998) 34-43, 164-66

Brooke, George J. "The Thematic Content of 4Q252," *JQR* 85 (1994) 33-59

Brooke, George J. *Exegesis at Qumran: 4QFlorilegium in its Jewish Context* (JSOTS 29; Sheffield: JSOT Press, 1985)

Broshi, Magen. "Anti-Qumranic Polemic in the Talmud," in *The Madrid Qumran Congress: Proceedings of the International Congress on the Dead Sea Scrolls, Madrid 18-21 March, 1991* (STDJ 11; ed. J. Trebolle Barrera and L. Vegas Montaner; Leiden: Brill, 1991) 2. 589-600

Broshi, Magen. "Beware the Wiles of the Wicked Woman: Dead Sea Scroll Fragment Reflects Essene Fear of, and Contempt for Women," *BAR* 9/4 (1983) 54-56

Broshi, Magen. "Predestination in the Bible and the Dead Sea Scrolls," in *The Bible and the Dead Sea Scrolls: The Princeton Symposium on the Dead Sea Scrolls: Volume 2: The Dead Sea Scrolls and the Qumran Community* (ed. James H. Charlesworth; Waco: Baylor University Press, 2006) 235-46

Broshi, Magen. "The Gigantic Dimensions of the Visionary Temple in the Temple Scroll," in *Understanding the Dead Sea Scrolls: A Reader from the Biblical Archaeology Review* (ed. H. Shanks; New York: Vintage, 1993) 113-15

Burgmann, H. "The Wicked Woman: Der Maccabäer Simon?," *RevQ* 8/31 (1974) 323-59

Campbell, Jonathan G. *The Exegetical Texts* (London: T&T Clark, 2004)

Campbell, Jonathan G. *The Use of Scripture in the Damascus Document 1-8, 19-20* (BZAW 228; Berlin and New York: de Gruyter, 1995)

Carmignac, J. "Poème allegorique sur la secte rivale," *RevQ* 5/19 (1965) 361-74

Castelli, Silvia. "Josephan 'Halakha' and the 'Temple Scroll': Questions of Sources and Exegetic Traditions in the Laws on Purity," *Henoch* 24 (2002) 331-41

Charlesworth, James H. "Prolegomenous Reflections Towards a Taxonomy of Resurrection Texts," in *The Changing Face of Judaism, Christianity, and Other Greco-Roman Religions in Antiquity: Presented to James H. Charlesworth on the Occasion of his 65th Birthday* (ed. Ian H. Henderson and Gerbern S. Oegema with the assistance of Sara Parks Richter; SJSHZ 2; Gütersloh: Gütersloher Verlagshaus, 2006) 237-64

Charlesworth, James H. et al., ed. *The Dead Sea Scrolls: Hebrew, Aramaic, and Greek Texts with English Translations. Vol. 1-* (PTSDDSP; Tübingen: Mohr Siebeck; Louisville: Westminster John Knox Press, 1994-)

Charlesworth, James H. *The Pesharim and Qumran History: Chaos or Consensus* (Grand Rapids: Eerdmans, 2002)

Chazon, Esther G. "The Creation and Fall of Adam in the Dead Sea Scrolls," in *The Book of Genesis in Jewish and Oriental Christian Interpretation: A Collection of Essays* (ed. Judith Frishman and Lucas van Rompay; Traditio Exegetica Graeca 5; Leuven: Peeters, 1997) 13-24

Cherian, Jacob, "The Moses at Qumran: The מורה הצדק as the Nursing-Father of the יחד," in *The Bible and the Dead Sea Scrolls: The Princeton Symposium on the Dead Sea Scrolls: Volume 2: The Dead Sea Scrolls and the Qumran Community* (ed. James H. Charlesworth; Waco: Baylor University Press, 2006) 351-61

Coblentz Bautch, Kelley. *A Study of the Geography of 1 Enoch 17-19: 'No One Has Seen What I have Seen'* (JSJSup 81; Leiden: Brill, 2003)

Cohen, Shaye J. D. "Menstruants and the Sacred in Judaism and Christianity," in *Women's History and Ancient History* (ed. Sarah B. Pomeroy; Chapel Hill: University of North Carolina Press, 1991) 271-99

Collins, John J. "Amazing Grace: The Transformation of the Thanksgiving Hymn at Qumran," in *Psalms in Community: Jewish and Christian Textual, Liturgical, and Artistic Traditions* (ed. Harold W. Attridge and Margot E. Fassler; SBLSymS 25; Atlanta/Leiden: SBL/Brill, 2003) 75-85

Collins, John J. "Forms of Community in the Dead Sea Scrolls," in *Emanuel: Studies in Hebrew Bible, Septuagint, and Dead Sea Scrolls in Honor of Emanuel Tov* (ed. Shalom M. Paul, Robert A. Kraft, Lawrence H. Schiffman, and Weston W. Fields; SVT 94; Leiden: Brill, 2003) 97-111

Collins, John J. "In the Likeness of the Holy Ones: The Creation of Humankind in a Wisdom Text from Qumran," in *The Provo International Conference on the Dead Sea Scrolls: Technological Innovations, New Texts, and Reformulated Issues* (ed. Donald W. Parry and Eugene C. Ulrich; STDJ 30; Leiden: Brill, 1999) 609-18

Collins, John J. "Interpretations of the Creation of Humanity in the Dead Sea Scrolls," in *Biblical Interpretation at Qumran* (ed. Matthias Henze; Studies in the Dead Sea Scrolls and Related Literature; Grand Rapids: Eerdmans, 2005) 29-43

Collins, John J. "Marriage, Divorce and Family in Second Temple Judaism," in *Families in Ancient Israel* (ed. Leo G. Perdue et al.; The Family, Religion, and Culture; Louisville: Westminster John Knox, 1997) 104-62

Collins, John J. "The Eschatologizing of Wisdom in the Dead Sea Scrolls," in *Sapiential Perspectives: Wisdom Literature in Light of the Dead Sea Scrolls: Proceedings of the Sixth International Symposium of the Orion Center for the Study of the Dead Sea Scrolls and Associated Literature, 20-22 May, 2001* (ed. John J. Collins, Gregory E. Sterling, and Ruth A. Clements; STDJ 51; Leiden: Brill, 2004) 49-65

Collins, John J. "The Essenes and the Afterlife," in *From 4QMMT to Resurrection: Mélanges qumraniens en homage à Émile Puech* (ed. Florentino García Martínez, Annette Steudel, and Eibert Tigchelaar; STDJ 61; Leiden: Brill, 2006) 35-53

Collins, John J. "The Mysteries of God: Creation and Eschatology in 4QInstruction and the Wisdom of Solomon," in *Wisdom and Apocalypticism in the Dead Sea Scrolls and in the Biblical Tradition* (ed. Florentino García Martínez; BETL 163; Leuven: Leuven University Press, Peeters, 2003) 287-305

Collins, John J. "The Yahad and 'The Qumran Community'," in *Biblical Traditions in Transmission: Essays in Honour of Michael A. Knibb* (ed. Charlotte Hempel and Judith M. Lieu; Leiden: Brill, 2006) 81-96

Collins, John J. *Jewish Wisdom in the Hellenistic Age* (Louisville: Westminster John Knox, 1997)

Conway, Colleen M. "Toward a Well-Formed Subject: The Function of Purity Language in the Serek ha-Yaḥad," *JSP* 21 (2000) 103-20

Cook, Johann. "The Origin of the Tradition of the יצר הטוב and יצר הרע," *JSJ* 38 (2007) 80-91

Davidson, Maxwell J. *Angels at Qumran: A Comparative Study of 1 Enoch 1-36, 72-109 and Sectarian Writings from Qumran* (JSPSup 11; Sheffield: JSOT Press, 1992)

Davies, Philip R. "Marriage and the Essenes," in *Behind the Essenes: History and Ideology in the Dead Sea Scrolls* (BJS 94; Atlanta: Scholars, 1987) 73-85

Davies, Philip R. "The Ideology of the Temple in the Damascus Document," in *Sects and Scrolls: Essays on Qumran and Related Topics* (South Florida Studies in the History of Judaism 134; Atlanta: Georgia, 1996) 45-60

Davies, Philip R. "The Judaism(s) of the Damascus Document," in *The Damascus Document: A Centennial of Discovery: Proceedings of the Third International*

Symposium of the Orion Center for the Study of the Dead Sea Scrolls and Associated Literature, 4-8 February 1998 (ed. Joseph M. Baumgarten, Esther G. Chazon, and Avital Pinnick; STDJ 34; Leiden: Brill, 2000) 27-43

Davies, Philip R. "The Temple Scroll and the Damascus Document," in *Temple Scroll Studies: Papers Presented at the International Symposium on the Temple Scroll, Manchester, December 1987* (ed. George J. Brooke; JSPSup 7; Sheffield: JSOT Press, 1989) 201-10

Davies, Philip R. and Joan E. Taylor. "On the Testimony of Women in 1QSa," *DSD* 3/3 (1996) 223-35

Davies, Philip R. *The Damascus Covenant: An Interpretation of the "Damascus Document"* (JSOTSup 25; Sheffield: JSOT Press, 1983)

Davila, James R. *Liturgical Works* (Grand Rapids: Eerdmans, 2000)

Davis, Robert. "The History of the Composition of the 'Damascus Document'," (Ph.D. dissertation; Harvard University, 1992)

Dimant, Devorah. "Old Testament Pseudepigrapha at Qumran," in *The Bible and the Dead Sea Scrolls: The Princeton Symposium on the Dead Sea Scrolls: Volume Two: The Dead Sea Scrolls and the Qumran Community* (ed. James H. Charlesworth; Waco: Baylor University Press, 2006) 447-67

Dimant, Devorah. "The 'Pesher on the Periods' (4Q180) and 4Q181," *IOS* 9 (1979) 77-102

Doering, Lutz. "Purity Regulations concerning the Sabbath in the Dead Sea Scrolls and Related Literature," in *The Dead Sea Scrolls: Fifty Years after Their Discovery: Proceedings of the Jerusalem Congress, July 20-25, 1997* (ed. Lawrence H. Schiffman, Emanuel Tov, and James C. VanderKam; Jerusalem: Israel Exploration Society in cooperation with the Shrine of the Book, Israel Museum, 2000) 600-609

Doering, Lutz. "Überlegungen zum Ansatz der Halacha in den Qumrantexten," in *Qumran Kontrovers: Beiträge zu den Textfunden vom Toten Meer* (ed. Jörg Frey and Hartmut Stegemann with the collaboration of Michael Becker and Alexander Maurer; Einblicke 6; Paderborn: Bonifatius, 2003) 89-114

Dombrowski, Bruno W. W. "4QMMT after DJD X, Qumran Cave 4, Part 5," *Qumran Chronicle* 5/2 (1995) 151-70

Drawnel, Henryk. "The Literary Form and Didactic Content of the *Admonitions (Testament) of Qahat*," in *From 4QMMT to Resurrection: Mélanges qumraniens en homage à Émile Puech* (ed. Florentino García Martínez, Annette Steudel, and Eibert Tigchelaar; STDJ 61; Leiden: Brill, 2006) 55-73

Drawnel, Henryk. *An Aramaic Wisdom Text from Qumran: A New Interpretation of the Levi Document* (JSJSup 86; Leiden: Brill, 2004)

Duhaime, Jean. "Cohérence structurelle et tensions interns dans l'Instruction zur des Deux Esprits (1QS III 13 – IV 26)," in *Wisdom and Apocalypticism in the*

Dead Sea Scrolls and in the Biblical Tradition (ed. Florentino García Martínez; BETL163; Leuven: Leuven University Press, Peeters, 2003) 103-32

Duhaime, Jean. *The War Texts: 1QM and Related Manuscripts* (London: T&T Clark, 2004)

Dunn, James D. G. "4QMMT and Galatians," *NTS* 43 (1997) 147-53

Dunn, James D. G. "Noch einmal 'Works of the Law': The Dialogue Continues," in *Fair Play: Diversity and Conflicts in Early Christianity* (ed. Ismo Dunderberg, Christopher Tuckett, and Kari Syreeni; Leiden: Brill, 2002) 273-90

Dunn, James D. G. and James H. Charlesworth, "Qumran's *Some Works of Torah* (4Q394-399 [4QMMT]) and Paul's Galatians," in *The Bible and the Dead Sea Scrolls: The Princeton Symposium on the Dead Sea Scrolls: Volume 3: The Scrolls and Christian Origins* (ed. James H. Charlesworth; Waco: Baylor University Press, 2006) 187-201

Dupont-Sommer, A. "Le Psaume CLI dans 11QPs(a) et le probleme de son origine essenienne," *Sem* 14 (1964) 25-62

Eisenman, Robert H. and Michael Wise, *The Dead Sea Scrolls Uncovered: The First Complete Translation and Interpretation of 50 Key Documents Withheld for Over 35 years* (Shaftesbury: Element, 1992)

Elgvin, Torleif. "An Analysis of 4QInstruction" (diss; Hebrew University of Jerusalem, 1997)

Elgvin, Torleif. "The *Yaḥad* is More Than Qumran," in *Enoch and Qumran Origins: New Light on a Forgotten Connection* (ed. Gabriele Boccaccini; Grand Rapids: Eerdmans, 2005) 273-79

Elgvin, Torleif. "To Master His Own Vessel: 1 Thess 4.4 in Light of New Qumran Evidence," *NTS* 43 (1997) 604-19

Elledge, Casey D. *The Statutes of the King: The* Temple Scroll's *Legislation on Kingship (11Q19 LVI 12 - LIX 21)* (Cahiers de la Revue Biblique 56; Paris: Gabalda, 2004)

Elman, Yaakov. "MMT B 3-5 and Its Ritual Context," *DSD* 6 (1999) 148-56

Erlandsson, S. "זָנָה," *TDOT* 4 (1981) 99-104

Eshel, Esther. "Genres of Magical Texts in the Dead Sea Scrolls," in *Die Dämonen/Demons: The Demonology of Israelite-Jewish and Early Christian Literature in Context of their Environment* (ed. Armin Lange, Hermann Lichtenberger, and K. F. Diethard Romheld; Tübingen: Mohr Siebeck, 2003) 395-415

Eshel, Hanan, Magen Broshi, Richard Freund, and Brian Schultz, "New Data on the Cemetery East of Khirbet Qumran," *DSD* 9 (2002) 135-65

Eshel, Hanan. "4QMMT and the History of the Hasmonean Period," in *Reading 4QMMT: New Perspectives on Qumran Law and History* (ed. John Kampen and Moshe J. Bernstein; SBLSym 2; Atlanta: Scholars, 1996) 53-65

Ewolde, John F. "rwqmh in the Damascus Document and Ps 139:15," in *Diggers at the Well: Proceedings of a Third International Symposium on the Hebrew of the Dead Sea Scrolls and Ben Sira* (ed. T. Muraoka and J. F. Ewolde; Leiden: Brill, 2000) 65-83

Fabry, Heinz-Josef. "Das Buch Levitikus in den Qumrantexten," in *Levitikus als Buch* (ed. Heinz-Josef Fabry and Hans-Winfried Jüngling; BBB 119; Berlin: Philo, 1999) 309-41

Fabry, Heinz-Josef. "Der Begriff 'Torah' in der Tempelrolle," *RevQ* 18/69 (1997) 63-72

Fitzmyer, Joseph A. "A Feature of Qumran Angelology and the Angels of 1 Cor 11:10," in Joseph A. Fitzmyer, *Essays on the Semitic Background of the New Testament* (SBLSBS 5; Missoula: Scholars, 1974) 187-204

Fitzmyer, Joseph A. "Marriage and Divorce," *EncDSS*, 512-15

Fitzmyer, Joseph A. "The Matthean Divorce Texts and Some New Palestinian Evidence," in *To Advance the Gospel: New Testament Studies* (2d ed.; Grand Rapids: Eerdmans, 1988) 79-111

Fitzmyer, Joseph A. *The Genesis Apocryphon of Qumran Cave 1 (1Q20): A Commentary* (3d ed.; Biblica et Orientalia 18/B; Roma: Pontificio Istituto Biblico, 2004)

Fletcher-Louis, Crispin H. T. *All the Glory of Adam: Liturgical Anthropology in the Dead Sea Scrolls* (STDJ 42; Leiden: Brill, 2002)

Flint, Peter W. "Noncanonical Writings in the Dead Sea Scrolls: Apocrypha, other Previously Known Writings, Pseudepigrapha," in *The Bible at Qumran: Text, Shape, and Interpretation* (ed. P. Flint; Grand Rapids: Eerdmans, 2001) 80-126

Fraade, Steven D. "Rhetoric and Hermeneutics in Miqsat Ma'ase Ha-Torah (4QMMT): The Case of the Blessings and Curses," *DSD* 10 (2003) 150-61

Fraade, Steven D. "The 'Torah of the King' (Deut 17:14-20) in the Temple Scroll and Early Rabbinic Law," in *The Dead Sea Scrolls as Background to Postbiblical Judaism and Early Christianity; Papers from an International Conference at St. Andrews in 2001* (ed. James R. Davila; STDJ 46; Leiden: Brill, 2003) 25-60

Fraade, Steven D. "To Whom it May Concern; 4QMMT and its Addressee(s)," *RevQ* 19,4 (2000) 507-26

Frey, Jörg. "Different Patterns of Dualistic Thought in the Qumran Library: Reflections on their Background and History," in *Legal Texts and Legal Issues: Proceedings of the Second Meeting of the International Organization for Qumran Studies, Cambridge, 1995: Published in Honour of Joseph M. Baumgarten* (ed. M. Bernstein, F. García Martíinez, J. Kampen; Leiden: Brill, 1997) 275-336

Frey, Jörg. “Flesh and Spirit in Palestinian Jewish Sapiential Tradition and in the Qumran Texts: An Inquiry into the Background of Paulinian Usage,” in *The Wisdom Texts from Qumran and the Development of Sapiential Thought: Studies in Wisdom at Qumran and its Relationship to Sapiential Thought in the Ancient Near East, the Hebrew Bible, Ancient Judaism, and the New Testament* (ed. Charlotte Hempel, Armin Lange, and Hermann Lichtenberger; BETL 159; Leuven: Peeters-Leuven University Press, 2002) 367-404

Fröhlich, Ida. “‘Mamzer’ in Qumran Texts – The Problem of Mixed Marriages from Ezra’s Time: Law, Literature and Practice,” *Transeuphratène* 29 (2005) 103-15

Fröhlich, Ida. “‘Narrative Exegesis’ in the Dead Sea Scrolls,” in *Biblical Perspectives: Early Use and Interpretation of the Bible in Light of the Dead Sea Scrolls: Proceedings of the First International Symposium of the Orion Center for the Study of the Dead Sea Scrolls and Associated Literature, 12-14 May 1996* (ed. Michael E. Stone and Esther G. Chazon; STDJ 28; Leiden: Brill, 1998) 81-99

Fröhlich, Ida. “Themes, Structure and Genre of Pesher Genesis: A Response to George J. Brooke,” *JQR* 85 (1994) 81-90

Frolov, Serge. “‘King’s Law’ of the Temple Scroll: Mishnaic Aspects,” *JJS* 50 (1999) 298-307

García Martínez, Florentino, and Eibert J. C. Tigchelaar, *The Dead Sea Scrolls Study Edition* (2 vols; Leiden: Brill, 1997, 1998)

García Martínez, Florentino. “4QMMT in a Qumran Context,” in *Reading 4QMMT: New Perspectives on Qumran Law and History* (ed. John Kampen and Moshe J. Bernstein; SBLSym 2; Atlanta: Scholars, 1996) 15-27

García Martínez, Florentino. “Man and Woman: Halakhah Based upon Eden in the Dead Sea Scrolls,” in *Paradise Interpreted: Representations of Biblical Paradise in Judaism and Christianity* (ed. Gerard P. Luttikhuizen; Themes in Biblical Narrative, Jewish and Christian Traditions 2; Leiden: Brill, 1999) 95-115

García Martínez, Florentino. “Marginalia on 4QInstruction,” *DSD* 13 (2006) 24-37.

García Martínez, Florentino. “New Perspectives on the Study of the Dead Sea Scrolls,” in *Perspectives on the Study of the Old Testament and Early Judaism* (ed. F. García Martínez and E. Noort; VTSup 73; Leiden: Brill, 1998) 230-48

García Martínez, Florentino. “Response: The Groningen Hypothesis Revisited,” in *Enoch and Qumran Origins: New Light on a Forgotten Connection* (ed. Gabriele Boccaccini; Grand Rapids: Eerdmans, 2005) 310-16

García Martínez, Florentino. “Temple Scroll,” *EncDSS*, 927-33

García Martínez, Florentino. “The Problem of Purity: The Qumran Solution,” in Florentino García Martínez and Julio Trebolle Barrera, *The People of the*

Dead Sea Scrolls: Their Writings, Beliefs and Practices (tr. W. G. E. Watson; Leiden: Brill, 1995) 139-57

García Martínez, Florentino. "The Temple Scroll and the New Jerusalem," in *The Dead Sea Scrolls after Fifty Years: A Comprehensive Assessment* (ed. Peter W. Flint and James C. VanderKam; Leiden: Brill, 1999) 2.431-60

Gazov-Ginzberg, A. M. "Double-Meaning in a Qumran Work: The Wiles of the Wicked Woman," *RevQ* 6/22 (1967) 279-85

Ginzberg, Louis. *An Unknown Jewish Sect* (New York: Jewish Theological Seminary, 1976)

Goff, Matthew J. "Reading Wisdom at Qumran: 4QInstruction and the Hodayot," *DSD* 11 (2004) 263-88

Goff, Matthew J. *Discerning Wisdom: The Sapiential Literature of the Dead Sea Scrolls* (VTSup 116; Leiden: Brill, 2007)

Goff, Matthew J. *The Worldly and Heavenly Wisdom of 4QInstruction* (STDJ 50; Leiden: Brill, 2003)

Gordis, R. "The Knowledge of Good and Evil in the Old Testament and the Dead Sea Scrolls," *JBL* 76 (1957) 126-38

Grabbe, Lester L. "4QMMT and Second Temple Jewish Society," in *Legal Texts and Legal Issues: Proceedings of the Second Meeting of the International Organization for Qumran Studies, Cambridge, 1995: Published in Honour of Joseph M. Baumgarten* (ed. Moshe J. Bernstein, Florentino García Martínez, and John Kampen; STDJ 23; Leiden: Brill, 1997) 89-108

Green, Dennis. "'Halakhah at Qumran?' The Use of the Root הלך in the Dead Sea Scrolls," *RevQ* 22 (2005) 235-51

Greenfield, Jonas C. "The Meaning of פחז," in *Studies in Bible and the Ancient Near East: Presented to Samuel E. Loewenstamm on his Seventieth Birthday* (ed. Y. Avishur and J. Blau; Jerusalem: E. Rubenstein, 1978) 35-40

Greenfield, Jonas C. "The Root 'GBL' in Mishnaic Hebrew and in the Hymnic Literature from Qumran," *RevQ* 2/6 (1960) 155-62

Grossman, Maxine L. "Reading '4QMMT': Genre and History," *RevQ* 20 (2001) 3-22

Grossman, Maxine L. "Reading for Gender in the Damascus Document," *DSD* 11 (2004) 212-39

Gruber, Mayer I. "Purity and Impurity in Halakic Sources and Qumran Law," in *Wholly Woman, Holy Blood: A Feminist Critique of Purity and Impurity* (ed. Kristin de Troyer, Judith A. Herbert, Judith Ann Johnson and Anne-Marie Korte; Harrisburg: Trinity Press International, 2003) 65-76

Gruber, Mayer Irwin. "Women in the Religious System of Qumran," in *Judaism in Late Antiquity, Part V: Section One: Theory of Israel* (ed. Alan J. Avery-Peck, Jacob Neusner, and Bruce D. Chilton; Leiden: Brill, 2001) 173-96

Hachlili, Rachel. "Cemeteries," *EncDSS*, 125-29

Halpern-Amaru, Betsy. *The Empowerment of Women in the Book of Jubilees* (JSJSup 60; Leiden: Brill, 1999)

Harrington, Daniel J. "Recent Study of 4QInstruction," in *From 4QMMT to Resurrection: Mélanges qumraniens en homage à Émile Puech* (ed. Florentino García Martínez, Annette Steudel, and Eibert Tigchelaar; STDJ 61; Leiden: Brill, 2006) 105-23

Harrington, Daniel J. *Wisdom Texts from Qumran* (London: Routledge, 1996)

Harrington, Hannah K. "Biblical Law at Qumran," in *The Dead Sea Scrolls after Fifty Years: A Comprehensive Assessment* (ed. Peter W. Flint and James C. VanderKam; Leiden: Brill, 1998) 1.160-85

Harrington, Hannah K. "Holiness in the Laws of 4QMMT," in *Legal Texts and Legal Issues: Proceedings of the Second Meeting of the International Organization for Qumran Studies, Cambridge, 1995: Published in Honour of Joseph M. Baumgarten* (ed. Moshe J. Bernstein, Florentino García Martínez, and John Kampen; STDJ 23; Leiden: Brill, 1997) 109-28

Harrington, Hannah K. "Purity in the Dead Sea Scrolls: Current Issues," *Currents in Biblical Research* 4 (2006) 397-428

Harrington, Hannah K. *The Purity Texts* (London: T&T Clark, 2004)

Harter, Stephanie, Françoise Bouchet, Kosta Y. Mumcuoglu, and Joe E. Zias, "Toilet Practices Among Members of the Dead Sea Scrolls Sect at Qumran (100 BCE-68CE)," *RevQ* 21/4 (2004) 579-84

Hayes, Christine E. *Gentile Impurities and Jewish Identities: Intermarriage and Conversion from the Bible to the Talmud* (Oxford: OUP, 2002)

Hempel, Charlotte. "4QOrd[a] (4Q159) and the Laws of the Damascus Document," in *The Dead Sea Scrolls: Fifty Years after Their Discovery: Proceedings of the Jerusalem Congress, July 20-25, 1997* (ed. Lawrence H. Schiffman, Emanuel Tov, and James C. VanderKam; Jerusalem: Israel Exploration Society in cooperation with the Shrine of the Book, Israel Museum, 2000) 372-76

Hempel, Charlotte. "The Earthly Essene Nucleus of 1QSa," *DSD* 3 (1996) 253-69

Hempel, Charlotte. "The Groningen Hypothesis: Strengths and Weaknesses," in *Enoch and Qumran Origins: New Light on a Forgotten Connection* (ed. Gabriele Boccaccini; Grand Rapids: Eerdmans, 2005) 249-55

Hempel, Charlotte. "The Laws of the Damascus Document and 4QMMT," in *The Damascus Document: A Centennial of Discovery: Proceedings of the Third International Symposium of the Orion Center for the Study of the Dead Sea Scrolls and Associated Literature, 4-8 February 1998* (ed. Joseph M. Baumgarten, Esther G. Chazon, and Avital Pinnick; STDJ 34; Leiden: Brill, 2000) 69-84

Hempel, Charlotte. "The Literary Development of the S Tradition – A New Paradigm," *RevQ* 22 (2006) 389-401

Hempel, Charlotte. "The Qumran Sapiential Texts and the Rule Books," in *The Wisdom Texts from Qumran and the Development of Sapiential Thought: Studies in Wisdom at Qumran and its Relationship to Sapiential Thought in the Ancient Near East, the Hebrew Bible, Ancient Judaism, and the New Testament* (ed. Charlotte Hempel, Armin Lange, and Hermann Lichtenberger; BETL 159; Leuven: Peeters-Leuven University Press, 2002) 277-95

Hempel, Charlotte. *The Damascus Texts* (Companion to the Qumran Scrolls 1; Sheffield: Sheffield Academic Press, 2000)

Hempel, Charlotte. *The Laws of the Damascus Document: Sources, Traditions and Redaction* (STDJ 29; Leiden: Brill, 1998)

Himmelfarb, Martha. "Impurity and Sin in 4QD, 1QS, and 4Q512," *DSD* 8 (2001) 9-37

Himmelfarb, Martha. "Levi, Phinehas, and the Problem of Intermarriage at the Time of the Maccabean Revolt," *JSQ* 6 (1999) 1-24

Himmelfarb, Martha. "Sexual Relations and Purity in the Temple Scroll and the Book of Jubilees," *DSD* 6 (1999) 11-36

Himmelfarb, Martha. "The Purity Laws of 4QD: Exegesis and Sectarianism," in *Things Revealed: Studies in Early Jewish and Christian Literature in Honor of Michael E. Stone* (ed. Esther G. Chazon, David Satran, and Ruth A. Clements; JSJSup 89; Leiden: Brill, 2004) 155-69

Høgenhaven, Jesper. "Rhetorical Devices in 4QMMT," *DSD* 10 (2003) 187-204

Holmén, Tom. "Divorce in *CD* 4:20-5:2 and in *11QT* 57:17-18: Some Remarks on the Pertinence of the Question," *RevQ* 18/71 (1998) 397-408

Hultgren, Stephen. "A New Literary Analysis of CD XIX-XX, part 1: CD XIX:1-32a (with CD VII:4b-VIII:18b): The Midrashim and the 'Princes of Judah'," *RevQ* 21/4 (2004) 549-78

Ilan, Tal. *Jewish Women in Greco-Roman Palestine* (Tübingen: Mohr Siebeck, 1995; Peabody: Hendricksen, 1996)

Instone-Brewer, David. "Nomological Exegesis in Qumran 'Divorce' Texts," *RevQ* 18/72 (1998) 561-79

Instone-Brewer, David. *Divorce and Remarriage in the Bible: The Social and Literary Context* (Grand Rapids: Eerdmans, 2002)

Isaksson, Abel. *Marriage and Ministry in the New Temple: A Study with Special References to Mt. 19.13-22 and 1 Cor. 11.3-16* (ASNU 24; Lund: Gleerup, Copenhagen: Munksgaard, 1965)

Japhet, Sara. "The Prohibition of the Habitation of Women: The Temple Scroll's Attitude Toward Sexual Impurity and Its Biblical Precedents," *JANES(CU)* 22 (1993) 69-87

Jeffries, Daryl F. *Wisdom at Qumran: A Form-Critical Analysis of the Admonitions in 4QInstruction* (Gorgias Dissertation Near Eastern Studies 3; Piscataway: Gorgias, 2002)

Jones, Scott C. "Wisdom's Pedagogy: A Comparison of Proverbs VII and 4Q184," *VT* 53 (2003) 65-80

Kampen, John I. "4QMMT and New Testament Studies," in *Reading 4QMMT: New Perspectives on Qumran Law and History* (ed. John Kampen and Moshe J. Bernstein; SBLSymS 2; Atlanta: Scholars, 1996) 129-44

Kampen, John I. "The Matthean Divorce Texts Reexamined," in *New Qumran Texts and Studies: Proceedings of the First Meeting of the International Organisation for Qumran Studies, Paris 1992* (ed. G. J. Brooke; STDJ 15; Leiden: Brill, 1992) 149-67

Kampen, John I. "The Significance of the Temple in the Manuscripts of the Damascus Document," in *The Dead Sea Scrolls at Fifty: Proceedings of the 1997 Society of Biblical Literature Qumran Section Meetings* (ed. Robert A. Kugler and Eileen M. Schuller; SBLEJL 15; Atlanta: Scholars, 1999) 185-97

Kister, Menahem. "A Qumranic Parallel to 1 Thess 4:4? Reading and Interpretation of 4Q416 2 II 21," *DSD* 10 (2003) 365-70

Kister, Menahem. "Notes on Some Texts from Qumran," *JJS* 44 (1993) 280-82

Kister, Menahem. "The Development of the Early Recensions of the Damascus Document," *DSD* 14 (2007) 61-76

Klawans, Jonathan. *Impurity and Sin in Ancient Judaism* (New York: Oxford University Press, 2000)

Knibb, Michael A. *The Qumran Community* (Cambridge Commentaries on Writings of the Jewish and Christian World 200 BC to AD 200 2; Cambridge: Cambridge University Press, 1987)

Koch, Klaus. "History as a Battlefield of Two Antagonistic Powers in the Apocalypse of Weeks and in the Rule of the Community," in *Enoch and Qumran Origins: New Light on a Forgotten Connection* (ed. Gabriele Boccaccini; Grand Rapids: Eerdmans, 2005) 185-99

Kosmala, Hans "The Three Nets of Belial: A Study of the Terminology of Qumran and the New Testament," *ASTI* 4 (1965) 91-113

Kratz, Reinhard G. "Mose und die Propheten: Zur Interpretation von 4QMMT C," in *From 4QMMT to Resurrection: Mélanges qumraniens en homage à Émile Puech* (ed. Florentino García Martínez, Annette Steudel, and Eibert Tigchelaar; STDJ 61; Leiden: Brill, 2006) 151-76

Kugel, James L. "Reuben's Sin with Bilhah," in *The Ladder of Jacob: Ancient Interpretations of the Biblical Story of Jacob and His Children* (Princeton: Princeton University Press, 2006) 81-114

Kugler, Robert A. "Halakic Interpretative Strategies at Qumran: A Case Study," in *Legal Texts and Legal Issues: Proceedings of the Second Meeting of the International Organization for Qumran Studies, Cambridge, 1995: Published in Honour of Joseph M. Baumgarten* (ed. Moshe J. Bernstein, Florentino García Martínez, and John Kampen; STDJ 23; Leiden: Brill, 1997) 131-40

Kugler, Robert, and Esther Chazon, "Women at Qumran: Introducing the Essays," *DSD* 11 (2004) 167-73

Kuhn, Heinz-Wolfgang. *Enderwartung und Gegenwärtiges Heil: Untersuchungen zu den Gemeindeliedern von Qumran mit einem Anhang über Eschatologie und Gegenwart in der Verkündigung Jesu* (SUNT 4; Göttingen: Vandenhoeck und Ruprecht, 1966)

Lange, Armin. "Determination of Fate by the Oracle of the Lot," in *Sapiential, Liturgical and Poetical Texts from Qumran: Proceedings of the Third Meeting of the International Organization for Qumran Studies Oslo 1998: Published in Memory of Maurice Baillet* (ed. D. K. Falk, F. García Martínez, and E. M. Schuller; STDJ 35; Leiden: Brill, 1999) 39-48

Lange, Armin. "Die Weisheitstexte aus Qumran: Eine Einleitung," in *The Wisdom Texts from Qumran and the Development of Sapiential Thought: Studies in Wisdom at Qumran and its Relationship to Sapiential Thought in the Ancient Near East, the Hebrew Bible, Ancient Judaism, and the New Testament* (ed. Charlotte Hempel, Armin Lange, and Hermann Lichtenberger; BETL 159; Leuven: Peeters-Leuven University Press, 2002) 1-30

Lange, Armin. "The Essene Position on Magic and Divination," in *Legal Texts and Legal Issues: Proceedings of the Second Meeting of the International Organization for Qumran Studies, Cambridge, 1995: Published in Honour of Joseph M. Baumgarten* (ed. M. Bernstein, F. García Martínez, J. Kampen; Leiden: Brill, 1997) 377-435

Lange, Armin. "The Qumran Dead Sea Scrolls – Library or Manuscript Corpus," in *From 4QMMT to Resurrection: Mélanges qumraniens en homage à Émile Puech* (ed. Florentino García Martínez, Annette Steudel, and Eibert Tigchelaar; STDJ 61; Leiden: Brill, 2006) 177-93

Lange, Armin. *Weisheit und Prädestination: Weisheitliche Urordnung und Prädestination in den Textfunden von Qumran* (STDJ 18; Leiden: Brill, 1995)

Lawrence, Louise J. "'Men of Perfect Holiness' (1QS 7.20): Social-Scientific Thoughts on Group Identity, Asceticism and Ethical Development in the Rule of the Community," in *New Directions in Qumran Studies: Proceedings from the Bristol Colloquium on the Dead Sea Scrolls, 8-10th September 2003* (ed. Jonathan G. Campbell, William John Lyons, and Lloyd K. Pietersen; Library of Second Temple Studies 52; London: T&T Clark, 2005) 83-100

Leaney, A. R. C. *The Rule of Qumran and its Meaning: Introduction, Translation and Commentary* (London: SCM, 1966)

Levine, Baruch. "The Temple Scroll: Aspects of its Historical Provenance and Literary Character," *BASOR* 232 (1978) 5-23

Levison, John R. "The Two Spirits in Qumran Theology," in *The Bible and the Dead Sea Scrolls: The Princeton Symposium on the Dead Sea Scrolls: Volume*

2: The Dead Sea Scrolls and the Qumran Community (ed. James H. Charlesworth; Waco: Baylor University Press, 2006) 169-94

Licht, J. and J. Baumgarten, "On the Testimony of Women in 1QSa," *JBL* 76 (1957) 266-69

Lichtenberger, Hermann. *Studien zum Menschenbild in Texten der Qumrangemeinde* (SUNT 15; Göttingen: Vandenhoeck und Ruprecht, 1980)

Loader, William. "The Beginnings of Sexuality in Genesis LXX and Jubilees," in *Die Septuaginta – Texte, Kontexte, Lebenswelten* (ed. Martin Karrer and Wolfgang Kraus; WUNT; Tübingen: Mohr Siebeck, 2007)

Loader, William. *Enoch, Levi, and Jubilees on Sexuality: Attitudes Towards Sexuality in the Early Enoch Literature, the Aramaic Levi Document, and the Book of Jubilees* (Grand Rapids: Eerdmans, 2007)

Loader, William. *Sexuality and the Jesus Tradition* (Grand Rapids: Eerdmans, 2005)

Loader, William. *The Septuagint, Sexuality and the New Testament: Case Studies on the Impact of the LXX in Philo and the New Testament* (Grand Rapids: Eerdmans, 2004)

Lövestam, Evald. "Divorce and Remarriage in the New Testament," *Jewish Law Annual* 4 (1981) 47-65

Lyons, William John. "'An Unauthorized Version': The *Temple Scroll* in Narratological Perspective," in *New Directions in Qumran Studies: Proceedings of the Bristol Colloquium on the Dead Sea Scrolls, 8-10 September 2003* (ed. Jonathan G. Campbell, William John Lyons and Lloyd K. Pietersen; London: T&T Clark, 2005) 126-48

Magness, Jodi. "Two Notes on the Archaeology of Qumran," *BASOR* 312 (1998) 37-44

Magness, Jodi. *The Archaeology of Qumran and the Dead Sea Scrolls* (Grand Rapids: Eerdmans, 2002)

Maier, G. *Mensch und freier Wille: Nach den jüdischen Religionsparteien zwischen Ben Sira und Paulus* (WUNT 12; Tübingen: Mohr Siebeck, 1971)

Maier, Johann. "Purity at Qumran: Cultic and Domestic," in *Judaism in Late Antiquity, Part V: Section One: Theory of Israel* (ed. Alan J. Avery-Peck, Jacob Neusner, and Bruce D. Chilton; Leiden: Brill, 2001) 91-124

Maier, Johann. "Ritual of Marriage," *EncDSS*, 783

Maier, Johann. "The Architectural History of the Temple in Jerusalem in the Light of the Temple Scroll," in *Temple Scroll Studies: Papers Presented at the International Symposium on the Temple Scroll, Manchester, December 1987* (ed. George J. Brooke; JSPSup 7; Sheffield: JSOT Press, 1989) 23-62

Maier, Johann. "Wiles of the Wicked Woman," *EncDDS*, 976

Maier, Johann. *The Temple Scroll: An Introduction, Translation and Commentary* (JSOTSup 34; Sheffield: Sheffield Academic Press, 1985)

Mason, Steven. "What Josephus Says About the Essenes in his Judean War," in *Text and Artifact in the Religions of Mediterranean Antiquity: Essays in Honour of Peter Richardson* (ed. S. Wilson and M. Desjardins; Waterloo: Wilfrid Laurier University Press, 2000) 423-55

Meier, John P. "Is there *Halaka* (the Noun) at Qumran?" *JBL* 122 (2003) 150-55

Meinhold, Arndt. "Zur Bedeutung von 4QXII[a] für Mal 2, 10-16." in *Der Freund des Menschen: Festschrift für Georg Christian Macholz* (ed. Arndt Meinhold and Angelika Berlejung; Neukirchen-Vluyn: Neukirchener Verlag, 2004) 93-105

Metso, Sarianna. "Whom does the term YAHAD identify?" in *Biblical Traditions in Transmission: Essays in Honour of Michael A. Knibb* (ed. Charlotte Hempel and Judith M. Lieu; Leiden: Brill, 2006) 213-35

Metso, Sarianna. *The Serekh Texts* (London: T&T Clark, 2007)

Metso, Sarianna. *The Textual Development of the Qumran Community Rule* (STDJ 21; Leiden: Brill, 1997)

Milgrom, Jacob. "4QTohora[a]: An Unpublished Qumran Text on Purities," in *Time to Prepare the Way in the Wilderness: Papers on the Qumran Scrolls by Fellows of the Institute of Advanced Studies in the Hebrew University, Jerusalem, 1989-1990* (ed. Devorah Dimant and Lawrence H. Schiffman; STDJ 16; Leiden: Brill, 1995) 59-68

Milgrom, Jacob. "Deviations from Scripture in the Purity Laws of the Temple Scroll," in *Jewish Civilization in the Hellenistic-Roman Period in Jerusalem* (ed. Shemaryahu Talmon; JSPSup 10; Sheffield: JSOT Press, 1991) 159-67

Milgrom, Jacob. "First Day Ablutions in Qumran," in *The Madrid Qumran Congress: Proceedings of the International Congress on the Dead Sea Scrolls, Madrid 18-21 March, 1991* (ed. J. T Barrera and L. V. Montaner; Leiden: Brill, 1991) 2.561-70

Milgrom, Jacob. "Studies in the Temple Scroll," *JBL* 97 (1978) 501-23

Milgrom, Jacob. "The City of the Temple," *JQR* 83 (1994) 125-28

Milgrom, Jacob. "The Concept of Impurity in *Jubilees* and the *Temple Scroll*," *RevQ* 16 (1993) 277-84

Milik, J. T. "Daniel et Susanne à Qumrân," in *De la Tôrah au Messie: Mélanges Henri Cazelles* (ed. M. Carrez, J. Doré, and P. Grelot; Paris: Desclée, 1981) 337-59

Mink, Hans-Aage. "The Use of Scripture in the Temple Scroll and the Status of the Scrolls as Law," *SJOT* 1 (1987) 20-50

Moore, R. D. "Personification of the Seduction of Evil: 'The Wiles of the Wicked Woman'," *RevQ* 10/40 (1981) 505-19

Morgenstern, Matthew, Elisha Qimron, and Daniel Sivan, "The Hitherto Unpublished Columns of the Genesis Apocryphon," *Abr-Nahrain* 33 (1995) 30-54

Morgenstern, Matthew. "The Meaning of *byt mwldym* in the Qumran Wisdom Texts," *JJS* 51 (2001) 141-44

Muraoka, Takamitsu. "The Community Rule (1QS), Column 4," in *Emanuel: Studies in Hebrew Bible, Septuagint, and Dead Sea Scrolls in Honor of Emanuel Tov* (ed. Shalom M. Paul, Robert A. Kraft, Lawrence H. Schiffman, and Weston W. Fields; VTSup 94; Leiden: Brill, 2003) 335-46

Murphy-O'Connor, Jerome. "A Literary Analysis of *Damascus Document* XIX,33 – XX,34," *RB* 79 (1972) 544-64

Murphy-O'Connor, Jerome. "A Literary Analysis of the *Damascus Document* VI,20 - VIII,3," *RB* 78 (1971) 210-32

Murphy-O'Connor, Jerome. "An Essene Missionary Document? CD II,14-VI,1," *RB* 77 (1970) 201-29

Murphy-O'Connor, Jerome. "The Critique of the Princes of Judah (CD VIII 3-19)," *RB* 79 (1972) 200-16

Murphy-O'Connor, Jerome. "The *Damascus Document* Revisited," *RB* 92 (1985) 223-64

Murphy-O'Connor, Jerome. "The Essenes and their History," *RB* 81 (1974) 215-44

Newsom, Carol A. *The Self as Symbolic Space: Constructing Identity and Community at Qumran* (STDJ 52; Leiden: Brill, 2004)

Nickelsburg, George W. E. "4Q551: A Vorlage to Susanna or a Text Related to Judges 19?" *JJS* 48 (1997) 349-51

Nickelsburg, George W. E. "Patriarchs Who Worry about Their Wives: A Haggadic Tendency in the *Genesis Apocryphon*," in *Biblical Perspectives: Early Use and Interpretation of the Bible in Light of the Dead Sea Scrolls: Proceedings of the First International Symposium of the Orion Center for the Study of the Dead Sea Scrolls and Associated Literature, 12-14 May 1996* (ed. Michael E. Stone and Esther G. Chazon; STDJ 28; Leiden: Brill, 1998) 137-58

Nickelsburg, George W. E. "The Books of Enoch at Qumran: What We Know and What We Need to Think about," in *Antikes Judentum und frühes Christentum: Festschrift für Hartmut Stegemann zum 65. Geburtstag* (ed. Bernd Kollmann, Wolfgang Reinbold, and Annette Steudel; BZNW 97; Berlin and New York: de Gruyter, 1999) 99-113

Nickelsburg, George W. E. *1 Enoch 1: A Commentary on the Book of 1 Enoch Chapters 1-36, 81-108* (Hermeneia; Minneapolis: Fortress, 2001)

Nitzan, Bilhah. "Evil and its Symbols in the Qumran Scrolls," in *Problem of Evil and its Symbols in Jewish and Christian Tradition* (ed. Henning Graf Reventlow and Yair Hoffman; JSOTSup 366; London: T & T Clark, 2004) 83-96

Nitzan, Bilhah. "The Laws of Reproof in *4QBerakhot* (4Q286-290) in Light of the Parallels in the *Damascus Covenant* and Other Texts from Qumran," in *Legal Texts and Legal Issues: Proceedings of the Second Meeting of the International Organization for Qumran Studies, Cambridge, 1995: Published in Honour of Joseph M. Baumgarten* (ed. M. Bernstein, F. García Martínez, J. Kampen; Leiden: Brill, 1997) 149-65

Noam, Vered. "Divorce in Qumran in Light of Early Halakhah," *JJS* 56 (2005) 206-23

Økland, Jorunn. "The Language of Gates and Entering: On Sacred Space in the *Temple Scroll*," in *New Directions in Qumran Studies: Proceedings of the Bristol Colloquium on the Dead Sea Scrolls, 8-10 September 2003* (ed. Jonathan G. Campbell, William John Lyons and Lloyd K. Pietersen; London: T&T Clark, 2005) 149-65

Olyan, Saul M. "The Exegetical Dimensions of Restrictions on the Blind and the Lame in Texts from Qumran," *DSD* 8 (2001) 38-50

Osten-Sacken, Peter von der. *Gott und Belial: Traditionsgeschichtliche Untersuchungen zum Dualismus in den Texten aus Qumran* (SUNT 6; Göttingen: Vandenhoeck und Ruprecht, 1969)

Pérez Fernández, Miguel. "*4QMMT*: Redactional Study," *RevQ* 18/70 (1997) 191-205

Pesthy, Monika. "The Three Nets of Belial from Qumran to the *Opus Imperfectum in Matthaeum*," in *Jerusalem, Alexandria, Rome: Studies in Ancient Cultural Interaction in Honour of A. Hilhorst* (ed. Florentino García Martínez and Gerard P. Luttikhuizen; Leiden: Brill, 2003) 243-53

Pfann, Stephen J. "Historical Implications of the Early Second Century Dating of the 4Q249-250 Cryptic A Corpus," in *Things Revealed: Studies in Early Jewish and Christian Literature in Honor of Michael E. Stone* (ed. Esther G. Chazon, David Satran, and Ruth A. Clements; JSJSup 89; Leiden: Brill, 2004) 171-86

Poznanski S., ed., *A. Geiger's Gesammelte Abhandlungen in hebräischer Sprache* (Warsaw: Tuschijah, 1910)

Puech, Émile. "Resurrection: The Bible and Qumran," in *The Bible and the Dead Sea Scrolls: The Princeton Symposium on the Dead Sea Scrolls: Volume 2: The Dead Sea Scrolls and the Qumran Community* (ed. James H. Charlesworth; Waco, Tex.: Baylor University Press, 2006) 247-81

Puech, Émile. *La croyannce des Esséniens en la vie future: Immortalité, resurrection, vie éternelle?* (EB 21-22; Paris: Gabalda, 1993)

Qimron, Elisha. "Celibacy in the Dead Sea Scrolls and the Two Kinds of Sectarians," in *The Madrid Qumran Congress: Proceedings of the International Congress on the Dead Sea Scrolls, Madrid 18-21 March, 1991*

(STDJ 11; ed. J. Trebolle Barrera and L. Vegas Montaner; Leiden: Brill, 1991) 1.287-94

Qimron, Elisha. "The Halacha of the Damascus Covenant – An Interpretation of 'Al Yitarev'," *Proceedings of the Ninth World Congress of Jewish Studies* D I (1986) 9-15.

Qimron, Elisha. "The Nature of the Reconstructed Composite Text of 4QMMT," in *Reading 4QMMT: New Perspectives on Qumran Law and History* (ed. John Kampen and Moshe J. Bernstein; SBLSym 2; Atlanta: Scholars, 1996) 9-13.

Qimron, Elisha. "The Text of CDC," in *The Damascus Document Reconsidered* (ed. Magen Broshi; Jerusalem: Israel Exploration Society, The Shrine of the Book, Israel Museum, 1992) 9-49

Qimron, Elisha. *The Hebrew of the Dead Sea Scrolls* (Atlanta: Scholars, 1986)

Qimron, Elisha. *The Temple Scroll: A Critical Edition with Extensive Reconstructions* (Beer Sheva: Ben Gurion University of the Negev Press; Jerusalem: Israel Exploration Society, 1996)

Rabin, Chaim. *The Zadokite Documents* (Oxford: Clarendon Press, 1958)

Reed, Annette Yoshiko. *Fallen Angels and the History of Judaism and Christianity: The Reception of Enochic Literature* (New York: Cambridge University Press, 2005)

Regev, Eyal. "Abominated Temple and a Holy Community: The Formation of the Notions of Purity and Impurity in Qumran," *DSD* 10 (2003) 243-78

Regev, Eyal. "Reconstructing Qumranic and Rabbinic Worldviews: Dynamic Holiness vs. Static Holiness," in *Rabbinic Perspectives: Rabbinic Literature and the Dead Sea Scrolls: Proceedings of the Eighth International Symposium of the Orion Center for the Study of the Dead Sea Scrolls and Associated Literature, 7-9 January, 2003* (ed. Steven D. Fraade, Aharon Shemesh, and Ruth A. Clements; STDJ 62; Leiden: Brill, 2006) 87-112

Regev, Eyal. "The 'Yahad'and the 'Damascus Covenant': Structure, Organization, and Relationship," *RevQ* 21 (2003) 233-62

Regev, Eyal. "Were the Priests all the Same? Qumranic Halakhah in Comparison with Sadducean Halakhah," *DSD* 12 (2005) 158-88

Regev, Eyal. "Yose Ben Yoezer and the Qumran Sectarians on Purity Laws: Agreement and Controversy," in *The Damascus Document: A Centennial of Discovery: Proceedings of the Third International Symposium of the Orion Center for the Study of the Dead Sea Scrolls and Associated Literature, 4-8 February 1998* (ed. Joseph M. Baumgarten, Esther G. Chazon, and Avital Pinnick; STDJ 34; Leiden: Brill, 2000) 95-107

Richardson, H. N. "Some Notes on 1QSa," *JBL* 76 (1957) 108-22

Rodgers, Joann Ellison. *Sex: A Natural History* (New York: Times Books, 2002)

Roo, Jacqueline C. R. de. "David's Deeds in the Dead Sea Scrolls," *DSD* 6 (1999) 44-65

Rothstein, David. "Women's Testimony at Qumran: The Biblical and Second Temple Evidence," *RevQ* 21 (2004) 597-614

Sanders, Ed Parish. "The Dead Sea Sect and Other Jews: Commonalities, Overlaps and Differences," in *The Dead Sea Scrolls in Their Historical Context* (ed. Timothy H. Lim et al.; Edinburgh: T&T Clark, 2000) 7-43

Satlow, Michael L. " 'One Who Loves His Wife Like Himself': Love in Rabbinic Marriage," *JJS* 49 (1998) 67-86

Satlow, Michael L. *Jewish Marriage in Antiquity* (Princeton: Princeton University Press, 2001)

Schiffman, Lawrence H. "Contemporizing Halakic Exegesis in the Dead Sea Scrolls," in *Reading the Present in the Qumran Library: The Perception of the Contemporary by Means of Scriptural Interpretations* (ed. Kristin De Troyer and Armin Lange; SBLSymS 30; Atlanta: SBL, 2005) 35-41

Schiffman, Lawrence H. "Exclusion from the Sanctuary and the City of the Sanctuary," *HAR* 9 (1985) 306-18

Schiffman, Lawrence H. "Halakhah and Sectarianism in the Dead Sea Scrolls," in *The Dead Sea Scrolls in Their Historical Context* (ed. Timothy H. Lim et al.; Edinburgh: T&T Clark, 2000) 123-42

Schiffman, Lawrence H. "Halakhic Elements in the Sapiential Texts from Qumran," in *Sapiential Perspectives: Wisdom Literature in Light of the Dead Sea Scrolls: Proceedings of the Sixth International Symposium of the Orion Center for the Study of the Dead Sea Scrolls and Associated Literature, 20-22 May, 2001* (ed. John J. Collins, Gregory E. Sterling, and Ruth A. Clements; STDJ 51; Leiden: Brill, 2004) 89-100

Schiffman, Lawrence H. "Laws Pertaining to Women in the Temple Scroll," in *The Dead Sea Scrolls: Forty Years of Research* (ed. D. Dimant and U. Rappaport; Jerusalem: Magnes Press, 1992) 210-28

Schiffman, Lawrence H. "Miqtsat Ma'asei Ha-Torah," *EncDSS,* 558-60

Schiffman, Lawrence H. "Non-Jews in the Dead Sea Scrolls," in *The Quest for Context and Meaning: Studies in Biblical Intertextuality in Honor of James A. Sanders* (ed. Craig A. Evans and Shemaryahu Talmon; BIS 28; Leiden: Brill, 1997) 153-71

Schiffman, Lawrence H. "Pre-Maccabean Halakhah in the Dead Sea Scrolls and the Biblical Tradition," *DSD* 13 (2006) 348-61

Schiffman, Lawrence H. "Prohibited Marriages in the Dead Sea Scrolls and Rabbinic Literature," in *Rabbinic Perspectives: Rabbinic Literature and the Dead Sea Scrolls: Proceedings of the Eighth International Symposium of the Orion Center for the Study of the Dead Sea Scrolls and Associated Literature, 7-9 January, 2003* (ed. Steven D. Fraade, Aharon Shemesh, and Ruth A. Clements; STDJ 62; Leiden: Brill, 2006) 113-25

Schiffman, Lawrence H. "The Dead Sea Scrolls and Rabbinic 'Halakhah'," in *The Dead Sea Scrolls as Background to Postbiblical Judaism and Early Christianity: Papers from an International Conference at St. Andrews in 2001* (ed. James R. Davila; STDJ 46; Leiden: Brill, 2003) 3-24

Schiffman, Lawrence H. "The Impurity of the Dead in the Temple Scroll," in *Archaeology and History in the Dead Sea Scrolls: The New York University Conference in Memory of Yigael Yadin* (ed. L. H. Schiffman; JSPSup 8; Sheffield: JSOT Press, 1990) 135-56

Schiffman, Lawrence H. "The Law of Vows and Oaths (Num. 30:3-16), in the Zadokite Fragments and the Temple Scroll," *RevQ* 15 (1991) 199-214

Schiffman, Lawrence H. "The Pharisees and their Legal Traditions According to the Dead Sea Scrolls," *DSD* 8 (2001) 262-77

Schiffman, Lawrence H. "The Place of 4QMMT in the Corpus of Qumran Manuscripts," in *Reading 4QMMT: New Perspectives on Qumran Law and History* (ed. John Kampen and Moshe J. Bernstein; SBLSym 2; Atlanta: Scholars, 1996) 81-98

Schiffman, Lawrence H. "The Relationship of the Zadokite Fragments to the Temple Scroll," in *The Damascus Document: A Centennial of Discovery; Proceedings of the Third International Symposium of the Orion Center for the Study of the Dead Sea Scrolls and Associated Literature, 4-8 February 1998* (ed. Joseph M. Baumgarten, Esther G. Chazon, and Avital Pinnick; STDJ 34; Leiden: Brill, 2000) 133-45

Schiffman, Lawrence H. "The Septuagint and the Temple Scroll: Shared Halakic Variants," in *The Septuagint, Scrolls and Cognate Writings: Papers Presented to the International Symposium on the Septuagint and Its Relations to the Dead Sea Scrolls and Other Writings* (ed. George W. Brooke and Barnabas Lindars; Atlanta: Scholars, 1992) 277-97

Schiffman, Lawrence H. "The Temple Scroll and the Systems of Jewish Law of the Second Temple Period," in *Temple Scroll Studies: Papers Presented at the International Symposium on the Temple Scroll, Manchester, December 1987* (ed. George J. Brooke; JSPSup 7; Sheffield: JSOT Press, 1989) 241-55

Schiffman, Lawrence H. "The Theology of the Temple Scroll," *JQR* 85 (1994) 109-23

Schiffman, Lawrence H. *Reclaiming the Dead Sea Scrolls: The History of Judaism, the Background of Christianity, the Lost Library of Qumran* (New York: Doubleday, 1995)

Schiffman, Lawrence H. *The Eschatological Community of the Dead Sea Scrolls: A Study of the Rule of the Congregation* (SBLMS 38; Atlanta: Scholars, 1989)

Schremer, Adiel. "Qumran Polemic on Marital Law and Its Social Background," in *The Damascus Document: A Centennial of Discovery: Proceedings of the Third International Symposium of the Orion Center for the Study of the Dead*

Sea Scrolls and Associated Literature, 4-8 February 1998 (ed. Joseph M. Baumgarten, Esther G. Chazon, and Avital Pinnick; STDJ 34; Leiden: Brill, 2000) 147-60

Schuller, Eileen M. "Response to 'Patriarchs Who Worry about their Wives: A Haggadic Tendency in the *Genesis Apocryphon*," in *George W.E. Nickelsburg in Perspective: An Ongoing Dialogue of Learning* (2 vols; ed. Jacob Neusner and Alan J. Avery-Peck; JSJSup 80; Leiden: Brill, 2003) 1. 200-12

Schuller, Eileen M. "Women in the Dead Sea Scrolls," in *Methods of Investigation of the Dead Sea Scrolls and the Khirbet Qumran Site: Present Realities and Future Prospects* (ed. Michael Wise et al.; Annals of the New York Academy of Sciences 722; New York: New York Academy of Sciences, 1994) 115-31

Schuller, Eileen M. "Women in the Dead Sea Scrolls," in *The Dead Sea Scrolls after Fifty Years: A Comprehensive Assessment* (ed. Peter W. Flint and James C. VanderKam; Leiden: Brill, 1999) 2.117-44

Schwartz, Daniel R. "Law and Truth: On Qumran-Sadducean and Rabbinic Views of Law," in *The Dead Sea Scrolls: Forty Years of Research* (ed. D. Dimant and U. Rappaport; STDJ 10; Leiden: Brill, 1992) 229-40

Schwartz, Daniel R. "MMT, Josephus and the Pharisees," in *Reading 4QMMT: New Perspectives on Qumran Law and History* (ed. John Kampen and Moshe J. Bernstein; SBLSymS 2; Atlanta: Scholars, 1996) 67-80

Sharp, Carolyn J. "Phinehan Zeal and Rhetorical Strategy in *4QMMT*," *RevQ* 18/70 (1997) 207-22

Shemesh, Aharon. "'The Holy Angels are in their Council': The Exclusion of Deformed Persons from Holy Places in Qumranic and Rabbinic Literature," *DSD* 4 (1997) 179-206

Shemesh, Aharon. "4Q251: Midrash Mishpatim," *DSD* 12 (2005) 280-302

Shemesh, Aharon. "4Q271.3: A Key to Sectarian Matrimonial Law," *JJS* 49 (1998) 244-63

Shemesh, Aharon. "Scriptural Interpretations in the Damascus Document and Their Parallels in Rabbinic Midrash," in *The Damascus Document: A Centennial of Discovery: Proceedings of the Third International Symposium of the Orion Center for the Study of the Dead Sea Scrolls and Associated Literature, 4-8 February 1998* (ed. Joseph M. Baumgarten, Esther G. Chazon, and Avital Pinnick; STDJ 34; Leiden: Brill, 2000) 161-75

Shemesh, Aharon. "The Holiness According to the Temple Scroll," *RevQ* 19/75 (2000) 369-82

Sheridan, S. "Scholars, Soldiers, Craftsmen, Elites? Analysis of French Collection of Human Remains from Qumran," *DSD* 9 (2002) 199-242.

Smith, Jay E. "Another Look at 4Q416 2 ii.21, a Critical Parallel to First Thessalonians 4:4," *CBQ* 63 (2001) 499-504

Stegemann, Hartmut. "The Literary Composition of the Temple Scroll and its Status at Qumran," in *Temple Scroll Studies: Papers Presented at the International Symposium on the Temple Scroll, Manchester, December 1987* (ed. George J. Brooke; JSPSup 7; Sheffield: JSOT Press, 1989) 123-48

Stegemann, Hartmut. *Die Essener, Qumran, Johannes der Täufer und Jesus: Ein Sachbuch* (Freiburg: Herder, 1993)

Sterling, Gregory E. "Was there a Common Ethic in Second Temple Judaism?" in *Sapiential Perspectives: Wisdom Literature in Light of the Dead Sea Scrolls: Proceedings of the Sixth International Symposium of the Orion Center for the Study of the Dead Sea Scrolls and Associated Literature, 20-22 May, 2001* (ed. John J. Collins, Gregory E. Sterling, and Ruth A. Clements; STDJ 51; Leiden: Brill, 2004) 171-94

Steudel, Annette, ed. *Die Texte aus Qumran II: Mit Masoretischer Punktation, Übersetzung, Einführung und Anmerkungen* (Darmstadt: Wissenschaftliche Buchgesellschaft, 2001)

Steudel, Annette. "4Q448 – The Lost Beginning of MMT?" in *From 4QMMT to Resurrection: Mélanges qumraniens en homage à Émile Puech* (ed. Florentino García Martínez, Annette Steudel, and Eibert Tigchelaar; STDJ 61; Leiden: Brill, 2006) 247-63

Steudel, Annette. "Ehelosigkeit bei den Essenern," in *Qumran Kontrovers: Beiträge zu den Textfunden vom Toten Meer* (ed. Jörg Frey and Hartmut Stegemann with the collaboration of Michael Becker and Alexander Maurer; Einblicke 6; Paderborn: Bonifatius, 2003) 115-24

Steudel, Annette. "The Houses of Prostration: CD XI,21-XII.1: Duplicates of the Temple (I)," *RevQ* 16 (1993) 49-67

Steudel, Annette. *Der Midrasch zur Eschatologie aus der Qumrangemeinde (4QMidrEschat$^{a.b}$): Materielle Rekonstruktion, Textbestand, Gattung und traditionsgeschichtliche Einordnung des durch 4Q174 ("Florilegium") und 4Q177 ("Catena A") repräsentierten Werke aus den Qumranfunden* (STDJ 13; Leiden: Brill, 1994)

Stone, Michael E. "The Books Attributed to Noah," *DSD* 13 (2006) 4-23

Strugnell, John. "MMT: Second Thoughts on a Forthcoming Edition," in *The Community of the Renewed Covenant: The Notre Dame Symposium on the Dead Sea Scrolls* (ed. Eugene Ulrich and James VanderKam; Christianity and Judaism in Antiquity 10; Notre Dame: University of Notre Dame Press, 1994) 57-73

Strugnell, John. "More on Wives and Marriage in the Dead Sea Scrolls (4Q416 2 ii 21 [Cf. 1 Thess 4:4] and 4QMMT§B)," *RevQ* 17/65-68 (1996) 537-47

Strugnell, John. "Notes en marge du Volume V des 'Discoveries in the Judaean Desert of Jordan,'" *RevQ* 7 (1970) 163-276

Strugnell, John. "The Sapiential Work 4Q415ff and Pre-Qumranic Works from Qumran: Lexical Considerations," in *The Provo International Conference on the Dead Sea Scrolls: Technological Innovations, New Texts, and Reformulated Issues* (ed. Donald W. Parry and Eugene C. Ulrich; STDJ 30; Leiden: Brill, 1999) 595-608

Strugnell, John. "The Smaller Hebrew Wisdom Texts Found at Qumran," in *The Wisdom Texts from Qumran and the Development of Sapiential Thought: Studies in Wisdom at Qumran and its Relationship to Sapiential Thought in the Ancient Near East, the Hebrew Bible, Ancient Judaism, and the New Testament* (ed. Charlotte Hempel, Armin Lange, and Hermann Lichtenberger, BETL 159; Leuven: Peeters-Leuven University Press, 2002) 31-60

Stuckenbruck, Loren T. "4QInstruction and the Possible Influence of Early Enochic Traditions: An Evaluation," in *The Wisdom Texts from Qumran and the Development of Sapiential Thought: Studies in Wisdom at Qumran and its Relationship to Sapiential Thought in the Ancient Near East, the Hebrew Bible, Ancient Judaism, and the New Testament* (ed. Charlotte Hempel, Armin Lange, and Hermann Lichtenberger; BETL 159; Leuven: Peeters, 2002) 245-61

Stuckenbruck, Loren T. "The Origins of Evil in Jewish Apocalyptic Tradition: The Interpretation of Gen 6:1-4 in the Second and Third Centuries B.C.E.," in *The Fall of the Angels* (ed. Christoph Auffarth and Loren T. Stuckenbruck; Themes in Biblical Narrative 6; Leiden: Brill, 2004) 87-118

Stuckenbruck, Loren T. *The Book of Giants from Qumran: Text, Translation, and Commentary* (TSAJ 63; Tübingen: Mohr Siebeck, 1997)

Sulzbach, Carla. "Of Temples on Earth, in Heaven, and In-Between," in *The Changing Face of Judaism, Christianity, and Other Greco-Roman Religions in Antiquity: Presented to James H. Charlesworth on the Occasion of his 65th Birthday* (ed. Ian H. Henderson and Gerbern S. Oegema with the assistance of Sara Parks Richter; SJSHZ 2; Gütersloh: Gütersloher Verlagshaus, 2006) 166-85

Swanson, Dwight D. *The Temple Scroll and the Bible: The Methodology of 11QT* (STDJ 14; Leiden: Brill, 1995)

Talmon, Shemaryahu. "The Community of the Renewed Covenant: Between Judaism and Christianity," in *The Community of the Renewed Covenant: The Notre Dame Symposium on the Dead Sea Scrolls* (ed. Eugene Ulrich and James VanderKam; Christianity and Judaism in Antiquity 10; Notre Dame: University of Notre Dame Press, 1994) 3-24

Taylor, Joan. "The Cemeteries of Khirbet Qumran and Women's Presence at the Site," *DSD* 6 (1999) 285-323

Tiday, Jeffrey. "Examination of the Accused Bride in 4Q159: Forensic Medicine at Qumran," *JANES* 22 (1993) 129-34

Tigchelaar, Eibert J. C. "A Cave 4 Fragment of *Divre Mosheh* (4QDM) and the Text of 1Q22 1:7-10 and *Jubilees* 1:9, 14," *DSD* 12 (2005) 303-12

Tigchelaar, Eibert J. C. "Sabbath Halakha and Worship in *4QWays of Righteousness: 4Q421* 11 and 13 + 2 + 8 par *4Q264a* 1-2," *RevQ* 18 (1998) 359-72

Tigchelaar, Eibert J. C. "Sodom and Gomorrah in the Dead Sea Scrolls," in *Sodom's Sin: Genesis 18-19 and Its Interpretations* (ed. Ed Noort and Eibert J. C. Tigchelaar; Themes in Biblical Narrative 7; Leiden: Brill, 2004) 47-62

Tigchelaar, Eibert J. C. "Your Wisdom and Your Folly: The Case of 1Q-4QMysteries," in *Wisdom and Apocalypticism in the Dead Sea Scrolls and in the Biblical Tradition* (ed. Florentino García Martínez; BETL 163; Leuven: Leuven University Press, Peeters, 2003) 69-88.

Tigchelaar, Eibert J. C. *Prophets of Old and the Day of the End: Zechariah, the Book of Watchers and Apocalyptic* (OTS 35; Leiden: Brill, 1996)

Tigchelaar, Eibert J. C. *To Increase Learning for the Understanding Ones: Reading and Reconstructing the Fragmentary Early Jewish Sapiential Text 4QInstruction* (STDJ 44; Leiden: Brill, 2001)

Toews, Casey. "Moral Purification in 1QS," *BBR* 13 (2003) 71-96

Tosato, Angelo. "Su di una norma matrimoniale 4QD," *Bib* 74 (1993) 401-10

Tov, Emanuel, ed. *The Dead Sea Scrolls Electronic Library* (Revised Edition; Provo: Brigham Young University; Leiden: Brill, 2006)

Van der Woude, A. S. "Wisdom at Qumran," in *Wisdom in Ancient Israel: FS J. A. Emerton* (ed. J. Day, R. P. Gordon and H. G. M. Williamson; Cambridge: Cambridge University Press, 1995) 244-56

VanderKam, James C. "Apocalyptic Tradition in the Dead Sea Scrolls and the Religion of Qumran," in *Religion in the Dead Sea Scrolls* (ed. John J. Collins and Robert A. Kugler; Grand Rapids: Eerdmans, 2000) 113-34

VanderKam, James C. "The Granddaughters and Grandsons of Noah," *RevQ* 16 (1994) 457-61

VanderKam, James C. "The Poetry of 1QApGen XX, 2-8a," *RevQ* 10 (1979-81) 57-66

VanderKam, James C. "The Temple Scroll and the Book of Jubilees," in *Temple Scroll Studies: Papers Presented at the International Symposium on the Temple Scroll, Manchester, December 1987* (ed. George J. Brooke; JSPSup 7; Sheffield: JSOT Press, 1989) 211-36

VanderKam, James C. "Those Who Look for Smooth Things, Pharisees, and Oral Law," in *Emanuel: Studies in Hebrew Bible, Septuagint, and Dead Sea Scrolls in Honor of Emanuel Tov* (ed. Shalom M. Paul, Robert A. Kraft, Lawrence H. Schiffman, and Weston W. Fields; SVT 94; Leiden: Brill, 2003) 465-77

VanderKam, James C. and Peter Flint, *The Meaning of the Dead Sea Scrolls: Their Significance for Understanding the Bible, Judaism, Jesus and Christianity* (London: HarperCollins, 2002)

VanderKam, James C. *Textual and Historical Studies in the Book of Jubilees* (HMS 14; Missoula: Scholars Press, 1977)

Vermes, Geza, and Martin Goodman, ed. *The Essenes according to the Classical Sources* (Sheffield: JSOT Press, 1989)

Vermes, Geza. "Sectarian Matrimonial Halakhah in the Damascus Rule" *JJS* 25 (1974) 197-202

Vermes, Geza. *The Complete Dead Sea Scrolls in English* (London: Penguin, 1997)

Wacholder, Ben Zion, and Martin Abegg, *A Preliminary Edition of the Unpublished Dead Sea Scrolls: The Hebrew and Aramaic Texts from Cave 4* (Fascicle 1; Washington DC: Biblical Archaeology Society, 1991)

Wacholder, Ben Zion. "The Relationship between 11QTorah (The Temple Scroll) and the Book of Jubilees: One Single or Two Independent Compositions," *SBLSP* (1985) 205-16

Wacholder, Ben Zion. *The New Damascus Document: The Midrash on the Eschatological Torah of the Dead Sea Scrolls: Reconstruction, Translation and Commentary* (STDJ 56; Leiden: Brill, 2007)

Wassen, Cecilia. *Women in the Damascus Document* (SBL Academia Biblica 21; Atlanta: SBL, 2005)

Weinert, Francis. "4Q159: Legislation for an Essene Community Outside of Qumran?" *JSJ* 5 (1974) 179-207

Weinfeld, Moshe "The Royal Guard according to the Temple Scroll," *RB* 87 (1980) 394-96

Weissenberg, Hanne von. "4QMMT – Towards an Understanding of the Epilogue," *RevQ* 21 (2003) 29-45

Werman, Cana. "What is the *Book of Hagu?*" in *Sapiential Perspectives: Wisdom Literature in Light of the Dead Sea Scrolls: Proceedings of the Sixth International Symposium of the Orion Center for the Study of the Dead Sea Scrolls and Associated Literature, 20-22 May, 2001* (ed. John J. Collins, Gregory E. Sterling, and Ruth A. Clements; STDJ 51; Leiden: Brill, 2004) 125-40

Wernberg-Møller, P. *The Manual of Discipline* (STDJ 1; Leiden: Brill, 1957)

White Crawford, Sidnie. "Lady Wisdom and Dame Folly at Qumran," *DSD* 5 (1998) 355-66

White Crawford, Sidnie. "Mothers, Sisters, and Elders: Titles for Women in Second Temple Jewish and Early Christian Communities," in *The Dead Sea Scrolls as Background to Postbiblical Judaism and Early Christianity: Papers from an International Conference at St. Andrews in 2001* (ed. James R. Davila; STDJ 46; Leiden: Brill, 2003) 177-91

White Crawford, Sidnie. "Not According to Rule: Women, the Dead Sea Scrolls and Qumran," in *Emanuel: Studies in Hebrew Bible, Septuagint, and Dead Sea Scrolls in Honor of Emanuel Tov* (ed. Shalom M. Paul, Robert A. Kraft, Lawrence H. Schiffman, and Weston W. Fields; SVT 94; Leiden: Brill, 2003) 127-50

White Crawford, Sidnie. "Reading Deuteronomy in the Second Temple Period," in *Reading the Present in the Qumran Library: The Perception of the Contemporary by Means of Scriptural Interpretations* (ed. Kristin de Troyer and Armin Lange; SBLSymS 30; Atlanta: SBL, 2005) 127-40

White Crawford, Sidnie. "The Meaning of the Phrase עיר המקדש in the Temple Scroll," *DSD* 8 (2001) 242-54

White Crawford, Sidnie. "The Rewritten Bible at Qumran," in *The Bible and the Dead Sea Scrolls: Volume 1: Scripture and the Scrolls* (ed. James H. Charlesworth; Waco: Baylor University Press, 2006) 131-47

White Crawford, Sidnie. "Traditions about Miriam in the Qumran Scrolls," in *Women and Judaism* (ed. L. J. Greenspoon, R. Simkins, and J. Cahan; Studies in Jewish Civilization 14; Omaha: Creighton University Press, 2003) 33-44

White Crawford, Sidnie. *The Temple Scroll and Related Texts* (Companion to the Qumran Scrolls 2; Sheffield: Sheffield Academic Press, 2000)

Wilson, A. M., and L. Wills, "Literary Sources of the Temple Scroll," *HTR* 75 (1982) 275-88

Wise, Michael Owen. "That which has been is that which shall be: 4QFlorilegium and the מקדש אדם," in *Thunder at Gemini: And Other Essays on the History, Language and Literature of Second Temple Judaism* (JSPSup 15; Sheffield: JSOT Press, 1994) 152-85

Wise, Michael Owen. *A Critical Study of the Temple Scroll from Qumran Cave 11* (Studies in Ancient Oriental Civilization 49; Chicago: Oriental institute, 1990)

Wise, Michael, Martin Abegg Jr., and Edward Cook, *The Dead Sea Scrolls: A New Translation* (rev. ed.; San Francisco: HarperSanFrancisco, 2005)

Wold, Benjamin. *Women, Men, and Angels: The Qumran Wisdom Document* Musar leMevin *and its Allusions to Genesis Creation Traditions* (WUNT 2.201; Tübingen: Mohr Siebeck, 2005)

Yadin, Yigael. "L'attitude essénien envers la polygamie et le divorce," *RB* 79 (1972) 98-99

Yadin, Yigael. *The Temple Scroll* (3 vols; Jerusalem: Israel Exploration Society, 1977-83)

Zias, Joseph E. "The Cemeteries of Qumran and Celibacy: Confusion Laid to Rest?" *DSD* 7 (2000) 220-53

Index of Modern Authors

Index of Ancient Sources

(reference to individual verses occurring in sequence in major discussions of chapters indicated in bold are not included)

NEW TESTAMENT